SCIENCE AND MATHEMATICS
IN ANCIENT GREEK CULTURE

Science and Mathematics in Ancient Greek Culture

EDITED BY

C. J. TUPLIN
and
T. E. RIHLL

OXFORD
UNIVERSITY PRESS

OXFORD
UNIVERSITY PRESS

Great Clarendon Street, Oxford OX2 6DP

Oxford University Press is a department of the University of Oxford.
It furthers the University's objective of excellence in research, scholarship,
and education by publishing worldwide in

Oxford New York

Auckland Bangkok Buenos Aires Cape Town Chennai
Dar es Salaam Delhi Hong Kong Istanbul Karachi Kolkata
Kuala Lumpur Madrid Melbourne Mexico City Mumbai Nairobi
São Paulo Shanghai Taipei Tokyo Toronto

Oxford is a registered trade mark of Oxford University Press
in the UK and in certain other countries

Published in the United States
by Oxford University Press Inc., New York

British Library Cataloguing in Publication Data

Data available

Library of Congress Cataloging in Publication Data

Data applied for

ISBN 0–19–815248–5

1 3 5 7 9 10 8 6 4 2

Typeset by John Waś, Oxford
Printed in Great Britain
on acid-free paper by
Biddles Ltd., Guildford & King's Lynn

Editors' Preface

THE pages that follow present a selection of the papers read at a conference held in Liverpool in July 1996 under the title 'Science Matters: The Role and Achievement of Science in Greek Antiquity'. A distinctive aim of the gathering was to give an account of some of the achievements and limitations of ancient scientists which might be of value to mainstream classicists and ancient historians, and to insist that Greek scientific endeavour was capable of interacting with the 'ordinary' world and represents a cultural phenomenon which deserves no less attention than traditional objects of respect such as literary or artistic creativity.

That the publication has been so long delayed is entirely due to one of the editors (Tuplin); and that it has none the less happened is entirely due to the other (Rihll). The delinquent editor would like to offer heartfelt thanks to his colleague, both on his own behalf and on behalf of the other contributors, who have shown remarkable forbearance. Thanks are also due to those at the Press who have seen this project through to completion; in particular, to Enid Barker and John Waś, whose help and advice have been invaluable.

The success of the conference as a social and academic event owed much, not only to the enthusiasm of the participants, but also to the efforts of Noreen Fox (co-organizer), the University of Liverpool Conference Office, and the staff of Derby & Rathbone Hall: warmest thanks are due to all of them. Moreover, significant financial assistance was received from the Society for the Promotion of Hellenic Studies, the Classical Association, the Hellenic Foundation, the Wellcome Foundation, and the University of Liverpool Research Development Fund, and for this we were, and are, extremely grateful.

Among those able to attend the conference was Lewis Wolpert—a distinguished practitioner in the biological sciences but also (and most relevantly here) a passionate believer both in the distinctiveness of science as an intellectual activity and in its importance as a component of cultural history—and it is a great pleasure that a brief Foreword from his pen stands at the head of our text.

December 2001   C.J.T.
                                                                     T.E.R.

Contents

Foreword

LEWIS WOLPERT

WOULD we have had science if it had not been for the Greeks?

Science involves a special way of thinking about the nature of the world. Instead of just looking at the obvious relations between cause and effect (for example, the breaking of a stone is due to the force of the hammer), it tries to understand mechanisms at a deeper level, and this leads to serious problems, for the way the world works does not fit with our day-to-day expectations, our common sense. Almost without exception any common-sense view of the world is scientifically false. The most obvious examples are the movement of the sun with respect to the earth, and the proposition that force on a body does not cause movement but acceleration. And how well does Darwin's theory of evolutionary natural selection fit with common sense? With particle physics and quantum mechanics science becomes much more remote from day-to-day experience, and even the number of molecules in a glass of water is beyond anyone's natural expectation. Another feature of science which is rarely used in day-to-day life is mathematical analysis and thus rigorous analysis of events: for example, common-sense estimates of probability can be wildly inaccurate.

Thales of Miletus seems to have been one of the first who tried to explain the world not in terms of myths but in more concrete terms, terms that might be subject to verification. What, he wondered, might the world be made of? His unexpected answer was: water. Water could clearly change its form from solid to liquid to gas and back again; clouds and rivers were in essence water; and water was essential for life. His suggestion was fantastical perhaps—contrary to common sense—and so the essence of science. But more important than his answer was his explicit attempt to find a fundamental unity in nature. It expressed the belief that underlying all the varied forms and substances in the world, a unifying principle could be found. The possibility of objective and critical thinking about nature had begun. Never before, it seems, had someone put forward general ideas about the nature of the world that might be universal explanations, and there was for the first time a conviction that the natural world was controlled by what might loosely be called laws.

Thales' contemporary, Anaximander, did not find Thales' ideas about water persuasive. To Anaximander it seemed that air was a much better candidate for being the primary substance of which all things were made.

And so began the sort of claim and counter-claim for the understanding of nature which eventually gave rise to modern science. There was a crucial ingredient still lacking—experimental method—but the type of discussion was revolutionary: Thales' idea was open for discussion and debate. It was a wonderful leap that was to free thinking from the straitjacket of mythology and the grip of relating everything to man. Here too, for the first time, attention was focused on the nature of the world with no immediate relevance to humankind. Human curiosity had hitherto been entirely devoted to man's relation to nature, and not to nature itself. With the Greeks man and nature were for the first time no longer perceived as inextricably linked, and this made it possible to take a more detached and objective view of the world, without having to worry about the implications for man's image of himself.

While giving the honour of being effectively the first scientist to Thales of Miletus, one recognizes that Thales was himself a philosopher and heir to an intellectual tradition whose origins are obscure. He cannot have been totally unaware of the achievements of the Egyptians and particularly the Babylonians with respect to the use of mathematics. It was nevertheless a radical departure, for one can apparently search earlier Egyptian and Babylonian texts in vain for instances where an individual author explicitly distances himself from and criticises the received tradition . Perhaps this change is a reflection of the nature of Greek society with its traditions in law and literature. The citizens cared about evidence, and it is a major question whether and to what extent philosophical beliefs in other societies prevented them from discovering science. Since science had very few practical applications, it was the love of knowledge that drove them to the philosophy that led to science. And this, as Aristotle made clear, required leisure, for which slaves may have played a key role.

It was also Thales who may have helped to establish mathematics as a science, irrespective of how much he might have learnt from the Babylonians and Egyptians, who had established arithmetical procedures and the elements of geometry for their practical needs. The Babylonians knew elements of geometry as early as 1700 BC, and had tables listing the lengths of the sides of right-angled triangles—so they must have been aware of the key features of Pythagoras' theorem, which states that the square on the hypotenuse is the sum of the squares on the other two sides. Thales turned these tools of measurement into a science. He put forward a number of basic propositions: that a circle is bisected by its diameter; that, if two straight lines cut each other, the opposite angles are equal; and that the angle inscribed in a semicircle is a right angle. Here, for the first time, were general statements about lines and circles—statements of a kind never made before. They were general statements that applied to all circles and lines everywhere, and that is the generality to which science aspires. The Greeks, with Euclid as the exemplar, transformed a varied collection of empirical rules for calculation into an ordered abstract system. Mathematics was no longer merely a tool used for practical problems: it became a science.

Most of Greek science turned out to be wrong—from Aristotle's ideas about motion to his embryology—but some of it was remarkably on target. One of Aristotle's most important contributions was that of setting up postulates and drawing logical conclusions from them, and this was brilliantly exploited by both Euclid and Archimedes. I am not a historian, nor can I read Greek, but my scientific hero is Archimedes. He is for me the first scientist to apply mathematics to physical phenomena correctly and so is probably the first applied mathematician, and his contributions to the mechanics of lever and hydrostatics remain true today: so much for those who claim that scientific ideas are constantly being shown to be wrong and replaced.

Archimedes' analysis of the simple balance and the relationship between weights and their distance from the fulcrum is remarkably ingenious. 'Unequal weights will balance at unequal distances, the greatest weight being at the lesser distance' and 'If two equal weights have not the same centre of gravity, the centre of gravity of both taken together is at the middle point of the line joining their centres of gravity.' This allows him to divide the weights and distribute them along the lever and so prove his key proposition that two weights balance at distances proportional to the magnitudes. Not least, it required the 'invention' of the concept of the centre of gravity—that point through which the weight of any body can be thought to act.

Archimedes' analysis of floating bodies is startlingly original but can be thought of as a continuation or extension of the work on levers, since it is essentially about the analysis of forces at equilibrium. Just consider the achievement of his second postulate: 'Let it be granted that bodies which are forced upwards in a fluid are forced upwards along the perpendicular to the surface which passes through their centre of gravity.' From such postulates he showed that the loss of weight of a body in a fluid is equal to the weight of water displaced and went on to discover the specific gravity of substances. To see just how unnatural even simple science can be, consider the following problem, bearing in mind that Archimedes would have laughed, even sneered, at its simplicity. Imagine that you are in a rubber dinghy floating in a swimming pool. There is a large bag of stones with you in the boat. You throw the bag into the water and it sinks: does the level of the pool go up, go down, or remain the same? It goes down.

The Greeks also provide nice examples of the fundamental difference between science and technology. It is possible to have complex technology without any understanding of the processes involved—indeed, science had little impact on technology in Europe until the late eighteenth century, and all Chinese technology was science-free. The Greek skill in mining and processing silver on a large scale provides another clear example, for there was no understanding of what was going on.

The limited use of experiments of any sort and the failure to develop the experimental method (i.e. to make the design and conduct of experiments a central heuristic feature of investigation of the natural world) are curious features of Greek science. These were advances that evidently required a special mode of thought which only came about in the sixteenth and seventeenth centuries. The fall of a body is a good example. No one really challenged Aristotle's view that the rate of fall of a body is proportional to its weight, even though Philoponus (sixth century AD) did do some experiments which proved it to be wrong. It was not until Galileo's time that the intellectual environment permitted a demonstration that Aristotle's view was both logically inconsistent and experimentally false.

All science as we know it seems to have had its origins in Greece, however much it was later transformed by other cultures. Thus understanding Greek science is essential for all aspects of the history of science and so also our current culture.

List of Illustrations

Illustration Acknowledgements

Acknowledgement is gratefully made to the following for permission to reproduce copyright material:

E. J. Brill: plates from J. Fischer (ed.), *Claudii Ptolemaei Geographiae Codex Urbinas Graecus 82* (Leiden and Leipzig, 1932) (Figs. 3.1, 3.2, 3.5, 3.8).

The British Museum: 1936 3-9 1 (Fig. 7.2).

The Fitzwilliam Museum, Cambridge: GR 100-1906 (Fig. 7.3).

Oxford University Press: C. Singer, E. J. Holmyard, A. R. Hall, and T. I. Williams (eds.), *A History of Technology* (Oxford 1957), iii. 589, fig. 343c (Fig. 7.1).

Staatliche Museen zu Berlin—Preußischer Kulturbesitz. Antikensammlung: Inv. Nr. SK 1606 (Figs. 6.1, 6.2).

List of Tables

Abbreviations

AC	*L'Antiquité classique*
AHES	*Archive for the History of the Exact Sciences*
AJA	*American Journal of Archaeology*
AJP	*American Journal of Philology*
AK	*Antike Kunst*
ANRW	H. Temporini *et al.* (eds.), *Aufstieg und Niedergang der römischen Welt* (Berlin and New York, 1972–)
APF	J. K. Davies, *Athenian Propertied Families* (Oxford, 1972)
BCH	*Bulletin de correspondance hellénique*
BICS	*Bulletin of the Institute of Classical Studies*
CAH	*Cambridge Ancient History*
CCAG	Catalogus Codicum Astrologorum Graecorum
CCSL	Corpus Christianorum, Series Latina
CHI	*Cambridge History of Iran*
CIL	*Corpus Inscriptionum Latinarum*
CMG	Corpus Medicorum Graecorum
CQ	*Classical Quarterly*
CR	*Classical Review*
CSEL	Corpus Scriptorum Ecclesiasticorum Latinorum
CW	*Classical World*
DK	H. Diels and W. Kranz, *Die Fragmente der Vorsokratiker*, 6th edn. (Berlin, 1952)
DSB	C. C. Gillespie (ed.), *Dictionary of Scientific Biography* (New York, 1970–80)
EK	L. Edelstein and I. G. Kidd, *Posidonius: The Fragments* (Cambridge, 1972)
FGrH	F. Jacoby, *Fragmente der griechischen Historiker* (1923–)
FHS&G	W. W. Fortenbaugh, P. M. Huby, R. W. Sharples, and D. Gutas, *Theophrastus: Sources for his Life, Writings, Thought and Influence* (Leiden, 1992)
GRBS	*Greek, Roman and Byzantine Studies*
ID	*Inscriptions de Délos*
IG	*Inscriptiones Graecae*
JDAI	*Jahrbuch des deutschen archäologischen Instituts*
JHA	*Journal for the History of Astronomy*
JHI	*Journal of the History of Ideas*
JHS	*Journal of Hellenic Studies*
JRS	*Journal of Roman Studies*
JWCI	*Journal of the Warburg and Courtauld Institutes*
KA	R. Kassel and C. Austin, *Poetae Comici Graeci* (Berlin and New York 1983–)

KRS	G. Kirk, J. E. Raven, and M. Schofield, *The Presocratic Philosophers*, 2nd edn. (Cambridge, 1983)
Kühn	C. G. Kühn, *Claudii Galeni Opera Omnia* (Leipzig, 1821–33)
L&S	A. A. Long and D. N. Sedley, *The Hellenistic Philosophers* (Cambridge, 1987)
LCM	*Liverpool Classical Monthly*
LSJ	H. G. Liddell and H. Scott, *A Greek–English Lexicon*, rev. by H. S. Jones (Oxford, 1968); rev. supplement by P. G. W. Glare (Oxford, 1996)
MH	*Museum Helveticum*
ML	R. Meiggs and D. M. Lewis, *Selection of Greek Historical Inscriptions* (Oxford, 1968)
Mon. Ant.	*Monumenti antichi pubblicati per cura della Reale Accademia dei Lincei*
OCD	S. Hornblower and A. J. Spawforth (eds.), *Oxford Classical Dictionary*, 3rd edn. (Oxford, 1996)
OSAP	*Oxford Studies in Ancient Philosophy*
PAPhS	*Proceedings of the American Philosophical Society*
PBACAP	*Proceedings of the Boston Area Colloquium on Ancient Philosophy*
PBSR	*Papers of the British School at Rome*
PCPS	*Proceedings of the Cambridge Philological Society*
PG	J. P. Migne, *Patrologiae Cursus Completus: Series Graeca* (Paris, 1857–83)
PLLS	*Papers of the Leeds International Latin Seminar*
PM	*Phusika kai Mustika*, in M. Berthelot (ed.), *Collection des anciens alchimistes grecs* (Paris, 1887–8)
RE	A. Pauly, G. Wissowa, and W. Kroll (eds.), *Real-encyclopädie der classischen Altertumswissenschaft* (Stuttgart, 1893–1978)
SÄK	*Studien zur ägyptischen Kultur*
sch.	scholia
SEG	*Supplementum Epigraphicum Graecum*
SVF	H. von Arnim, *Stoicorum Veterum Fragmenta* (Leipzig, 1903–5)
TAPA	*Transactions of the American Philological Association*
TAPhS	*Transactions of the American Philosophical Society*

I

Introduction:
Greek Science in Context

T. E. RIHLL

THE sixteen papers that make up the bulk of this volume were given at a conference on ancient science held at Liverpool in 1996. This conference was unusual in bringing together scholars who work on completely different areas of Greek science: for example, those working on Euclid and Greek mathematics, those working on Hero and Hellenistic mechanics, and those working on Galen and imperial medicine. The papers provide a rare opportunity for readers to glimpse the state of the art across a wide range of subject specialisms, and more importantly, to consider whether generalizations which have been developed and applied in one area might also apply in other areas. For there are, at present, few generalizations about ancient science that would secure agreement from scholars in all areas. Indeed, careful reading of the papers will show that even within subject specialisms there may be significant differences in the assumptions about both ancient science and ancient society made by the authors. This introductory chapter is intended to put these papers in their intellectual context and to try to draw out common ground between them, better to see where the subject as a whole is going.

1. The Historiography of Greek Science since the 1950s

It is not possible here to give more than a very brief overview of the historiography of Greek science in the last fifty years—the period during which most current practitioners of the art have learnt and contributed to their subject. The reason is not simply a lack of space, nor a lack of well-researched historiographical surveys on which to draw,[1] but more fundamentally the difficulty of dealing with the very recent past and the present—an area in

---

[1] N. Reingold wrote a survey of the history of science and technology in America in the decade 1971–81: 'Clio as Physicist and Machinist', *Reviews in American History*, 10 (1982) 264–80. R. Porter surveyed *The History of Medicine: Past, Present and Future* (Uppsala, 1983). H. Kragh wrote a useful general *Introduction to the Historiography of Science* (Cambridge, 1987), and N. M. Swerdlow has given a valuable historiography of the 'History of the Exact Sciences' in the *Journal of the History of Ideas*, 54 (1993) 299–328, but I know of no recent survey of ancient Greek science other than Vallance's brief article (see n. 4).

which the historian's most valuable tool, hindsight, fails her. What follows is therefore a personal view, and should be read with caution.

For the first time since the Renaissance, the last century saw a great deal of significant work being done on the texts and translations of ancient scientific treatises. For example, the major mathematicians were done by (especially) Heiberg, Heath, and Thomas in the late nineteenth and the first half of the twentieth century. In 1948 Cohen and Drabkin's *Source Book in Greek Science* was published. This brought together a huge number and diverse range of original sources in English translation, and made them available in one volume. This greatly helped to foster a wider appreciation of Greek science, and in particular drew attention to the sort of material that existed but had yet to receive much attention from classical scholars. It also made ancient works more accessible to scientists, who have produced and continue to produce many publications in the history of science as a whole. Work was progressing across the whole range of ancient science; for example, in the 1950s Temkin published his translation of Soranus' *Gynaecology*; Caley and Richards edited, translated, and commented on Theophrastus' *On Stones*; and contributors to the Loeb series of Greek and Latin authors were publishing texts and translations of Aelian and Frontinus, and continuing Aristotle's *œuvre* with the *Parva Naturalia* and *Meteorology*. (The Loeb Aristotle was finally completed in 1991.) Basic work on texts and translations of scientific treatises continued steadily through the 1960s, 1970s, and 1980s (the Loeb edition of Hippocrates, though it began in 1923, had lapsed into what was to become a coma of more than half a century; it is now being completed), and output then jumped with the start of publications in the Ancient Commentators on Aristotle series: works by Alexander, Philoponus, Simplicius, and others have appeared, and more than sixty volumes are planned (of which over forty have been published). Another area where texts and translations are being produced in quantity at the moment is medicine; these developments are surveyed by Nutton. In addition, scholars working independently and separately are producing texts and translations of individual scientists from across the entire spectrum of ancient science. Cohen and Drabkin is no longer the only sourcebook: G. L. Irby-Massie and P. T. Keyser have recently published *Greek Science of the Hellenistic Era: A Sourcebook* (London and New York, 2001), and another, by J. T. Vallance, is forthcoming from CUP. Many authors hitherto effectively inaccessible are now available in whole or in large part (e.g. Posidonius and Herophilus), but there are still gaps. For example, there is no complete edition of the fragments of either Eratosthenes or Hipparchus, and until this gap is filled there can be no adequate monograph on these intellectual giants of antiquity. Major works in e.g. Galen's and Ptolemy's *œuvres* still await translation, and others, e.g. Dioscorides, are in need of new translations to replace those done hundreds of years ago. Meanwhile the widespread adoption of computer technology has revolutionized accessibility to previously existing texts and translations by making them available on CD-ROM and sometimes without charge via the Internet. Many of the scientific treatises and collections of fragments which were missing from earlier issues of the *Thesaurus Linguae Graecae* are now on the E issue (including Archimedes, Ptolemy, and Eratosthenes).[2] Translations are lagging far behind texts in electronic format. For example, the only source known to me for the complete works of Aristotle in English translation is the Past Masters series of philosophers.[3]

Turning from the raw materials to the products made from them, Clagett's *Greek Science* was published in 1955. It has been described as 'the last of the old-style general handbooks'.[4] Since then there have been many changes. Developments in the field of astronomy are indicative of some of them. In a field with so many great contributions to our understanding, it is perhaps invidious to pick out just two; but one stands as a widely recognized monument to its subject, and the other may well be ground-breaking in the historiography of science *per se* and (I venture to predict) could become a model for what can be done in other branches of the discipline. Ancient astronomy has been central to the historiography of ancient science since its inception, probably because it is the field that produced some of the greatest scientific achievements of antiquity, and because those ancient results that relate to the appearance of celestial phenomena can be compared with computed images of the night sky at any place and time in the past. Otto Neugebauer's *History of Ancient Mathematical Astronomy*, which appeared in 1975, twenty years after Clagett's book, has ever since its publication been widely regarded as representing the zenith in technical exposition of its subject. Massively learned, it reconstructs from surviving literary evidence the mathematical astronomy of antiquity: Babylon, Egypt, Greece, and Rome. It is a highly theoretical work, and one which (as Alan Bowen has assured me) was not meant to be read through from p. 1 to p. 1058. This part of the book is written for historians of astronomy. A further 200 pages of appendices make concessions to the astronomically—but not the mathematically—illiterate reader, and it is here that key concepts are explained. In reading the book, one usually needs two of the three volumes open at once, since all the figures are in volume iii, following the appendices.

---

[2] See the website at http://www.tlg.uci.edu/index/html The existing collections of Eratosthenes' fragments on different subjects have thus been brought together, making the job of producing a single critical edition easier. The web version (available by subscription and continually updated) is even more inclusive. For example, it has, in addition, Eudoxus' *Astronomy* and Hipparchus' fragments. Note the slightly different address for the on-line subscriber service: http://ptolemy.tlg.uci.edu/

[3] Details at http://www.nlx.com/pstm/index.htm/ Many (but not all) of Aristotle's works are also available on-line at the Classics Archive: http://classics.mit.edu/

[4] J. T. Vallance, 'Marshall Clagett's *Greek Science in Antiquity*: Thirty-Five Years Later', *Isis*, 81 (1990) 713–21 at 715.

Striking a balance between (*a*) historically accurate scientific content and an interesting and (*b*) readable text is in my opinion one of the greatest challenges facing modern practitioners in the history of science. It is true (as Swerdlow has observed) that 'only history with a serious scientific content has any chance of lasting even a generation',[5] but there is a difference between a history and a reference book, however outstanding.

A further twenty-three years on, James Evans's *History and Practice of Ancient Astronomy* (Oxford, 1998) is an entirely different kind of book, concerned with essentially the same subject, but a lot less comprehensive in its coverage. It carries the fingerprint of a scientist in the 'Exercises' interspersed throughout the text to let readers check whether or not they have understood the serious scientific content which preceded them and whether they can or cannot perform the sort of observations and calculations undertaken by the ancients. It reveals the honed experience of a contemporary teacher in the strenuous efforts it makes 'to minimize the mathematical tedium' (p. viii), to avoid 'subjecting [the reader who dislikes trigonometry] to unnecessary abuse' (p. ix), and in the provision of tables and templates to help the reader complete the exercises. It includes extracts from the primary sources in translation (some the author's own), historiographical discussions on important controversies,[6] and lots of illustrations, especially in the ample margins. It is clearly written, well structured, and very user-friendly. It is written for beginners in the subject, but has something to teach everyone thanks to its concern with the practice, as well as the theory, of astronomy in antiquity.

Obviously not all fields in ancient science lend themselves to this kind of treatment, but many do, and others could sustain a variation on the same theme. In the history of science, the scientific content has to be explained in a manner which can be understood by a historian, while the historical issues have to be explained in a manner which can be understood by a scientist. The scientist exploring the history of his or her science tends to think and write in implicit translations,[7] knowing what came after, and often unconsciously reading back into old sources things which simply are not there. Meanwhile, the historian exploring the science of his or her period tends to think and write in explicit transliterations,[8] fully awake to the text, but often not alert to the scientific significance of some things

---

[5] Swerdlow (n. 1), 326.

[6] e.g. the debate between 'realists' and 'instrumentalists' about what the Greeks meant by 'saving the phenomena', or Ptolemy's debt to Hipparchus for the star catalogue.

[7] i.e. thinking and writing in modern terms and terminology about things discovered or invented by the Greeks, such as presenting Pythagoras' theorem as $a^2 + b^2 = c^2$.

[8] i.e. thinking and writing about things discovered or invented by the Greeks in their own terms; so Pythagoras' theorem would be presented not as in n. 7 but as 'I say that the square on BC is equal to the squares on BA, AC.'

present and some things absent.[9] There is, in my view, no point in calling
for people to be trained in both science and history,[10] since real competence
in each subject presupposes ability and years of study: it cannot be acquired
overnight (as if by fiat) or created simply by training; one needs aptitude,
and most people have an aptitude for one subject and not the other.[11] The
person who has the aptitude for both is born, not made. The same might
be said of comparative studies, which add yet another layer to the difficulty
of mastering the subjects involved. G. E. R. Lloyd has begun to compare
Greek and Chinese science—generating very clear and useful insights in
the process—and the opportunities for future work in this area are clearly
vast. However, few of those with competence in Greek, ancient history, and
one or more sciences are likely to spend the time required to understand a
radically different culture and language while there is so much to be done
with the field of Greek science alone. Likewise, those who have ancient
Chinese, ancient Chinese history, and one or more sciences are not likely to
start learning the language and culture of the ancient Greeks. It becomes
ever more necessary for specialists to speak not just to one another, but also
to the wider community of scholars who may well be interested in their
research but who cannot be expected to know it all.

Astronomy is highly technical and not representative of all branches of
ancient science. For the others I summarize the changes over the last fifty
years, as I see them, in much more general terms. In terms of content, attention has not been focused so directly and brightly as was once the case
on the ancients' answers or results, especially those results which can be
interpreted as forerunners of modern results (such as computations of the
circumference of the earth) or results which were obtained by the use of
methods acceptable today (notably, those involving mathematics). Attention is now also given to the ancients' *questions*, which (it turns out) are
often not the same questions that we moderns might ask. This is a crucially important aspect of another major historiographical difference, that
of taking a less scientifically abstract and more historically sensitive approach to ancient scientific work. The wider philosophical context and the
social and economic context within which such work was generated, discussed or ignored, copied or scraped off (to recycle the papyrus on which

[9] For example, comparing the formulations in nn. 7 and 8, one has algebra and symbols for
the operations, the other does not; one has words, the other does not; one has a visible author,
the other does not.

[10] As e.g. Lakatos did in his remarks on 'history-cum-philosophy of science' in 'History of
Science as an Academic Discipline', in A. C. Crombie (ed.), *Scientific Change* (London, 1963),
784–5, repr. in I. Lakatos, *Mathematics, Science and Epistemology*, ed. J. Worrall and G. Currie
(Cambridge, 1978), 254–5. Philosophy of science ought to be distinguished as a separate, third,
subject; more on this below.

[11] See G. H. Moore, 'Historians and Philosophers of Logic: Are they Compatible? The
Bolzano–Weierstrauss Theorem as a Case Study', *History and Philosophy of Logic*, 20 (2000),
169–80.

it was written)—consideration of these and similar aspects has sometimes proved very fruitful as a way of enhancing our understanding of ancient science. Concern with such issues perhaps stems from debates in modern philosophy of science, but, if so, it is usually implicit rather than explicit. Popper engaged with classicists over the Presocratics;[12] Kuhn developed his famous theory of paradigms through studying Aristotle.[13] But on the whole modern philosophy of science has not been particularly useful for the study of ancient science.[14] Too often it is concerned with the present or the recent, not the distant, past, and this empties it of much of its relevance for students of ancient science. For example, we simply do not know very much about the organization of scientific research in antiquity; such topics are only now beginning to be addressed. In short, there is a good deal of basic research to be done first.

Current research reveals new interests, which can be organized under four broad heads:

(1) the relation between science and philosophy in antiquity;
(2) the relation between the different sciences in antiquity;
(3) the relation between earlier and later practitioners of science in antiquity;
(4) the relation between ancient science and ancient society.

[12] See the discussion by G. E. R. Lloyd, and especially his introductory remarks to the reprint of 'Popper versus Kirk: A Controversy in the Interpretation of Greek Science' as ch. 5 in *Methods and Problems in Greek Science* (Cambridge, 1991), 100–20.

[13] *The Structure of Scientific Revolutions* (Chicago, 1962) had its origins in Kuhn's puzzlement about why so many people could have believed Aristotle's theory of physics for so long when it was patently wrong, and, given that widespread belief in it, why in due course it was completely rejected. See T. S. Kuhn, *The Essential Tension* (Chicago, 1977), preface and ch. 1. To find the answer he had to look at scientific ideas from a much broader perspective than had hitherto been the norm. He realized that to understand a single theory, one had to look not just at the text in which it was advanced, or even at all the texts of the same author, but at the whole constellation of ideas and beliefs within which the theory had been proposed and in which it found adherents and believers. In particular, one had to look at the dominant overarching beliefs of that society at that time (the prevailing paradigm: see his postscript to the second edition of *The Structure of Scientific Revolutions* (Chicago, 1970) on 'paradigm' in the first or sociological sense of the term) and try to read the texts in the light of those beliefs. Single theories will be coherent and sensible within that paradigm, although they may (like Aristotle's dynamics) look like nonsense without it. And that single theory will not fall unless a lot of the strong theories within the paradigm within which it lives fall too. In all paradigms there are anomalies; the anomalies in the old one are cited by the exponents of the new in their arguments to reject the old, while the anomalies in the new one are cited by defenders of the old in their arguments to see off half-baked ideas. A scientific revolution takes place when one paradigm is overturned in favour of a new one, when a whole cluster of theories are set aside in favour of a whole cluster of new ones, which are mutually coherent, make sense with each other, and which together offer greater explanatory power than the pre-existing one. And thereafter it will be more or less difficult to understand what all the fuss was about, and why people ever thought things were otherwise, because with the new paradigm the world is seen through different spectacles.

[14] The debates of the anthropologists and philosophers 'have been, at most, intermittently influential': G. E. R. Lloyd, *Magic, Reason and Experience* (Cambridge, 1979), 4.

Two or more of these different interests are often combined in the same piece of research, and the fourth of them features to some degree in most new work. These interests are not exclusive and in particular do not exclude detailed technical work on specific topics. But they arise in many contexts, implicitly if not explicitly.

2. The Relation between Science and Philosophy in Antiquity

Our starting-point is the fact that, at least from the fifth century BC, anyone in antiquity with any education beyond basic reading, writing, and counting at school studied some or all of mathematics, Greek,[15] and philosophy, which covered a lot of subjects all more or less intertwined[16]—more in the early period and less in the later.[17] Philosophy in the modern sense was not distinct from other subjects. Very few of the people who called themselves philosophers are called philosophers by us (more on this below, pp. 19–20). For the Greeks, a philosopher was a person who loved wisdom, and wisdom comes in many forms.[18] But whatever else they did or believed, they were in broad agreement that reasoned argument and rational debate were the tools by which one could discover or create knowledge. Thus, epistemology and logic (for example) could pop up explicitly in any ancient text on any scientific subject.

What has become clear recently is that these philosophical aspects are not just explicit in some (to us) unlikely places, but that they are implicitly ubiquitous. For example, while there is much debate about the extent, depth,

[15] 'Greek' is meant here in the sense of 'English' in the modern British curriculum, covering a little language and a lot of literature.

[16] Besides rhetoric and logic, which are the main targets of Aristophanes' attack in the *Clouds*, the subjects mentioned as being studied in Socrates' 'Thinking-Shop' include natural history and physical and human geography. Gymnastic exercise (mostly with a view to being fit and trained for military call-up) also featured strongly in classical Greek education, and in the days of independent and democratic poleis, rhetoric was taught explicitly with a view to political and legal application.

[17] 'In Socrates' youth investigating justice would not have been thought a different kind of enterprise from investigating fire': W. Charlton, 'Greek Philosophy and the Concept of an Academic Discipline', in P. Cartledge and F. D. Harvey (eds.), *Crux* (Exeter, 1985), 47–61 at 51. Over the centuries the material studied was disaggregated into what came to be called the 'encyclic' (Greek) or 'liberal' (Roman) arts, which constituted a general education for teenagers until they came of age. This consisted of arithmetic, geometry, music, and astronomy, which were all viewed as aspects of mathematics, and grammar (i.e. the reading and explication of major literary works such as Homer, the tragic poets, and other forms of poetry), rhetoric (the art of persuasion), and logic (or dialectic), which were all viewed as aspects of Greek language. The invention of 'grammar' as we know it was another project on which scholars of the Hellenistic and Roman periods were engaged.

[18] For example, Isocrates, who called himself a philosopher but whom we usually call a sophist, contended that 'that which is of no immediate use either for speech or for action does not deserve the name of philosophy' (15. 118); for him philosophy is not about metaphysics but character formation and management skills.

and rigour involved, there now seems to be widespread agreement that the method Aristotle employed to investigate animals and the way he presented his findings in his biological works were based on the epistemological principles he expressed in his *Posterior Analytics*. Likewise, Galen was a formidable logician as well as a formidable healer, and while (like Aristotle and most of us) he does not always practise what he preaches,[19] his investigations and his treatises were shaped by what he considered to be sound method and argument. See in this volume Hussey on Aristotle, and Nutton and Tieleman on Galen. The importance of sound method as the chief determinant of the acceptability of an argument or piece of evidence has recently been emphasized in astronomy[20] and future detailed studies in different disciplines will probably reveal more cases.[21] Ancient scientists were not working to *our* notion of scientific method—which is why some scholars contend that the use of the word 'science' in the ancient context is wrong. They were following *their* notion of scientific method, which was based on *their* epistemologies, on *their* beliefs about the foundations of knowledge, about what we can know and how we can know it. Those beliefs in turn drove their arguments, and their arguments sometimes drove the theories in one direction rather than another. The question of whether or not what they did is really 'science' is fundamentally an ahistorical question and for the moment it is an unanswerable one. The term is controversial in the modern context,[22] never mind the ancient one, and I think it is a red herring, leading us away from the real quarry and leaving us tangled up in an empty net. There is a long way to go in discovering *what* ancient scientists did through detailed case studies before larger categorical questions of this sort have any chance of being dealt with satisfactorily.

One of the most important points to emerge from recent work on ancient studies of natural phenomena is that the ancients did not all share the same beliefs about what they could know and how they could know it. They (almost) all agreed that epistemology is crucial; but they did not agree about which epistemological assumptions are valid. To take the very basic question of the nature and behaviour of matter itself, for example, there were

[19] For this point in Aristotle see e.g. G. E. R. Lloyd, 'Aristotle's Zoology and Metaphysics', ch. 16 in *Methods and Problems in Greek Science* (Cambridge, 1991), esp. 393–4.

[20] 'It is far from obvious whether Ptolemy and his contemporaries had as clear a notion of the separate Greek and Mesopotamian components in their astronomy as we think we have. At any rate, Ptolemy never speaks in national or linguistic terms, but only of sound or unsound deductive methodology': A. Jones, 'On Babylonian Astronomy and its Greek Metamorphoses', in F. J. Ragep and S. P. Ragep (eds.), *Tradition, Transmission and Transformation* (Leiden, 1996), 139–55 at 154.

[21] The concern with epistemological questions runs through all subjects: in medicine, for example, it runs from the Hippocratic *On Medicine* to Galen's *On the Opinions of Hippocrates and Plato*.

[22] The history of science post-Newton is full of complicated case studies which demand shifts in emphasis, if not meaning, of the term 'science'—and the phenomenon continues.

from the fifth century BC to the end of antiquity two fundamentally op-
posing views: four-elements theory and atomism. Each view was of course
developed and modified over the course of the centuries, largely in response
to the other's arguments, but as a sweeping generalization we may say that
adherents of the four-elements theory believed in a finite cosmos, continua,
and purpose, while atomists believed in infinity, void, and chance. All believed what they did on the basis of arguments and debates to which they
were exposed; both camps believed more or less fervently that the other was
wrong; and despite all the logic and the argument and the rational debate,
neither could persuade the other of the correctness of its own view and
the incorrectness of the other. See Milton's paper in this volume. There
were, in short, *two* prevailing paradigms on the nature and behaviour of
the matter out of which everything is composed.[23] There were also those
who, faced by this debate and others like it, adopted an epistemology which
basically asserted that we cannot know for sure what is right or wrong in any
field, and that the only reasonable attitude to take is a suspension of judgement. These three views are the origin and the central tenets of the three
main 'schools' of ancient natural philosophy—Stoicism, Epicureanism, and
Scepticism—which emerged after the deaths of the giants of the classical
period, Plato and Aristotle, in reaction to the perceived difficulties in some
of their ideas[24] and the apparently irreconcilable differences between them.
But that is not the end of the variation. Within each 'school' there were
divergences and disagreements—so we have, for example, Academic scepticism and Pyrrhonist scepticism—and between each there were areas of
agreement.

3. The Relation between the Different Sciences in Antiquity

Most ancient scientists were polymaths by today's standards. The organization and professionalization of the sciences is a relatively modern phenomenon, having been established only in the nineteenth century, and the
word 'scientist' was not coined until 1834. It then took more than half a
century for many of those practising the subject to prefer this word over
'natural historian', 'natural philosopher', 'man of science', 'savant', and the
other terms previously used to describe enquirers into nature.

As I have already pointed out, education in antiquity presented what we

---

[23] This was first pointed out by D. J. Furley, *The Greek Cosmologists* (Cambridge, 1987).
These basic differences had far-reaching consequences on the believers' ideas about everything
else. For example, on how sense perception works, on what makes us happy or sad, and on
free will, see R. Sharples' discussion, *Stoics, Epicureans and Sceptics* (London, 1996), chs. 2,
4, and 5.

[24] Particularly Plato's theory of Forms and Aristotle's Unmoved Mover. In general the
objections were to incorporeal or immaterial things.

consider to be different subjects in a much more integrated way. Separating out the disciplines was one of the projects on which the ancients were engaged; it was an ongoing process throughout antiquity, and it did not progress very far by modern standards. History and geography as separate topics, for example, presuppose widespread agreement on what subject-matter is proper to history and what to geography, and some clear idea of the difference between them. So-called 'digressions' dealing with non-historical matters in Herodotus or 'digressions' dealing with non-geographical matters in Strabo are testimony to the differences we perceive but they did not.[25] This is not to say that all ancient scientists pursued every topic. Posidonius' own brand of Stoic philosophy inclined him to study a huge range of subjects which he believed were strongly interconnected, from astronomy to psychology and epistemology to ethics and history to prophecy; he is best known today for his work in geography (human and physical).[26] Eratosthenes was renowned as someone who could and did handle a variety of topics, and while his nickname 'Beta' suggests that he was second at everything, it should not be allowed to obscure the fact that many more than two people were involved in each subject and second is better than fifth or fiftieth. Most pursued a more restricted set of subjects, which they did not necessarily perceive as separate. Some subjects seem to have an affinity for each other or to appeal to a certain kind of mind—mathematics and music, for example. In antiquity, music was considered a branch of mathematics, as was mechanics. Physics, as the study of the nature and behaviour of the stuff out of which life, the universe, and everything was made, could crop up anywhere. Mathematics was and is essential to astronomy and certain aspects of physical geography such as cartography (see Berggren's paper), and again could crop up in some to us unlikely places (see Hussey's paper).

The aggregation of subjects, and the particular combinations pursued by different individuals, have implications for each subject individually. It is sometimes necessary to understand what was going on elsewhere in an author's time or in his other works in order to understand why our sources speak in the way they do, and about what they do. Did Archimedes work out the mathematics of spirals in order to understand the water-lifting device he reputedly invented, or did he build the waterscrew because he had already calculated mathematically that it would work, or are the similarities between the machine and the treatise mere coincidence and the differences between

---

[25] There are many modern echoes of ancient practice in these two particular subjects: for example, the *Glamorgan County History* (6 vols.; 1936–88) begins with (vol. i) *Natural History*, covering the geomorphology, geology, climate, meteorology, petrology, botany, and zoology of the county. In France integration of history and geography is one of the core features of the *Annales* school.

[26] See L. Edelstein and I. G. Kidd, *Posidonius: The Fragments* (Cambridge, 1972); I. G. Kidd, *Posidonius: The Commentary* (Cambridge 1989); id., *Posidonius: The Translation* (Cambridge, 1999).

them more significant? Was *On Floating Bodies* 2 inspired by, or the inspiration for, or nothing to do with, Hieron's massive merchant ship? Because of our grossly impoverished knowledge of ancient society and particularly of ancient individuals—most knowledge about them and their times having been lost in the intervening millennia—it is rarely possible for us to do more than speculate about connections between people and ideas. Thus, we can identify possible influences and links, and construct arguments which are more or less plausible that such influences or links did or did not in fact exist. In the papers that follow Coulton suggests that Hero's *Dioptra* was based on an astronomical instrument which Hero modified to apply it to land surveying; Hussey argues that Aristotle's understanding of mathematics influenced his views on the natural world, in particular his aversion to indivisibility and infinitesimals; Rihll and Tucker argue that practical knowledge about the manipulation of natural substances influenced the form and content of scientific method and theories on matter; and Tieleman points out that Galen claimed to be influenced in his methodology by practice in mathematical sciences 'such as architecture' and in the construction of sundials and waterclocks.

4. The Relation between Earlier and Later Practitioners of Science in Antiquity

There has been a significant change of emphasis on this topic recently. Histories of science once traced the development of some idea or theory over time as a more or less explicit progression, with later exponents building on the insights or discoveries of their predecessors, as if all development was movement towards theories which were 'right' according to then-current thinking. 'Wrong' or incomprehensible ancient ideas were ignored, and if they could not be ignored, were excused in one way or another. Today there are few positivists and even fewer teleologists working in the history of science. Instead of jumping across centuries from one intellectual giant to the next in pursuit of the development of the big idea (or method), attention is now being paid to why some subjects stalled, so to speak: obvious examples are zoology after Aristotle and botany after Theophrastus.[27] Again, priority-chasing has never been a particularly strong vice in the historiography of ancient science, probably because we lack so much of the necessary evidence, but the tendency to read into tiny fragments of Presocratic poetry much more, or much less, than is actually there is now being resisted.[28]

This arises from a growing awareness of two things that seem obvious

[27] e.g. J. Lennox, 'The Disappearance of Aristotle's Biology: A Hellenistic Mystery', in T. D. Barnes (ed.), *The Sciences in Greco-Roman Society* (Edmonton, 1994), 7–24.

[28] See C. Osborne, *Rethinking Early Greek Philosophy* (Ithaca, NY, 1987).

once pointed out but are easily forgotten because of the large amount of time that has elapsed since antiquity and the size of our cultural debt to Greece and Rome: first, that 'antiquity' is not one point in time, but spanned more than a thousand years—so that, for example, Aristotle was to Philoponus as Peter Abelard or William the Conqueror is to us;[29] and second, that just because something is written in Greek (or, though only occasionally in the scientific area, in Latin) it does not automatically qualify as a primary source, and it does not come with a guarantee that it is an accurate, honest, clear reflection of what someone thought. It is now recognized that almost all of our sources for the early thinkers are secondary, and the ancients are now allowed to have made mistakes, lied, and even to have been incoherent at times.

Today, apart from a less positivist and a more historical attitude, there is much more recognition that later authors—to whom we are often indebted for our knowledge of earlier theories—*invented* or at least altered the ideas of their predecessors through their own interpretations of them.[30] See Nutton and Tieleman on Galen and Hippocrates, and Wilson on Democritus and Ostanes. Using the past to claim authority for the present is not a new phenomenon, and it is beginning to seem that the modern idea of scientific and technological 'stagnation' after the 'golden' Hellenistic age was based on not recognizing that practice at work in ancient texts. Original contributions by later authors have hitherto been overlooked because we have taken at face value their own assertions about what their predecessors said or thought, and simultaneously the contributions of those earlier authors have been unjustifiably inflated.

There is also now a greater sensitivity to the *restrictive* force of previous ideas and notions of scientific method, to what Tieleman (below, p. 270) calls the 'fixed options' from which a practitioner of science could choose. See the papers of Barker, Milton, and Taisbak.

5. The Relation between Ancient Science and Ancient Society

This area has perhaps seen the biggest change in the last generation and is well exemplified in this volume.[31] Awareness has grown that a better understanding of ancient science follows from some historical knowledge of the

[29] In both cases the former lived *c*.900 years earlier than the latter. 'Antiquity' covers a long, long time.

[30] R. Sorabji is leading a huge research programme to clarify the situation with respect to Aristotle; see in particular his (ed.) *Aristotle Transformed: The Ancient Commentators and their Influence* (London, 1990). In the field of mathematics S. Cuomo, *Pappus of Alexandria and the Mathematics of Late Antiquity* (Cambridge, 2000), has recently investigated the relationship between one late antique author and the mathematical tradition for which he is an important but manipulative source.

[31] 'Whatever science or subject is being studied, history of science is considered by its

society in which that science was created.[32] The past tendency to abstract an ancient scientific idea from the context or even the text in which it appears, and to 'translate' or more commonly to paraphrase it into a modern language, is now supplemented by a much deeper approach. In brief, there is emphasis now on establishing the context of a particular scientific idea, and many different types of context. For example, consideration may be given to the broadly intellectual context of an idea or concept, e.g. Barker on sounds, Bowen on predictive astronomy, Wilson on chemical experiments; or the social context of an author's place and time, e.g. Netz on mathematicians, Nutton on medical practitioners, Rihll and Tucker on the early Lyceum; or the political context of scientific work, e.g. Cuomo on mechanics and *ataraxia*,[33] Hannah on *parapēgmata* (labelled boards) and festival organization, and Taub on scientific instruments and prestige.

We can identify three major factors influencing potential scientists in antiquity, two personal and one historical: inclination, ability, and opportunity.[34] They had first to be curious, keen, and hard-working; they then had to be able to grapple with difficult ideas; and they also had to have some access to previous ideas, and access to a person or persons similarly inclined and able to act as a sounding-board or testing-ground for their own ideas. Inclination and ability varied from individual to individual. Here we need to consider the issue of opportunity. There are two main aspects: education and time.

Access to existing and previous ideas was nothing like what we take for granted in a world of computerized catalogues and search engines, and anachronism is a real danger. The invention and development of catalogues in the few public libraries which existed over a thousand years and a million square miles was another ongoing process. It did not get very far beyond identifying treatises (by breaking up continuous texts or combining isolated ones), dividing treatises into books, attributing treatises to authors, and then listing an author's treatises and saying how many books each contained.[35] Discovering what existed was thus the first hurdle, and was to a

practitioners increasingly as a field of history rather than of science': H. Kragh, *An Introduction to the Historiography of Science* (Cambridge, 1987), 39.

[32] Those who work on ancient science have long argued that the converse is true too—a better understanding of the history of a society follows from some knowledge of the science produced by that society, though this message has only recently begun to be heard.

[33] Freedom from anxiety, or tranquillity.

[34] This point was observed in antiquity. For example, the Hippocratic author of *Laws* 2 identified six necessary factors: ability, precocity (παιδομαθία), love of hard work, teaching, a suitable place, and time. I am subsuming precocity and love of hard work under inclination, and teaching, a suitable place, and time, under opportunity.

[35] For example, Homer's *Iliad* and *Odyssey* were each divided into 24 books by Zenodotus, the first head of the library at Alexandria, in *c.*270 BC, or about 500 years after they were composed. The fifth head of the library, who ran it *c.*180–153 BC, was one Apollonius, who was nicknamed 'the Classifier'. Aesop's fables were not edited until Valerius Babrius did it in the

large degree dependent on what one happened to hear being said by others, and on one's schooling and higher education, if any. See Netz (below, p. 215) on the difficulties of getting an education in mathematics. Ideas and information could be and often were lost, for years, for centuries, or for ever.[36] See Hine on the difficulties of collecting and checking information about sporadic phenomena (below, pp. 63–8) and Berggren on the estimation of distances between places (below, p. 37). Getting access to a papyrus scroll containing the ideas was the second hurdle, and was to a large degree dependent on knowing someone with a good personal library. Someone with such a library was often a teacher of philosophy, and the obvious method of access was to join his 'school'.[37] Furthermore, in a teaching context, the written word was often written to be heard, rather than read.[38] Listening (unlike silent reading) was usually a group activity. Both of these hurdles— hearing about what already existed and then listening to it in its written form—were more easily overcome in places with relatively large populations, i.e. in cities, in their market places and street corners, as well as in their formal educational establishments. Critical mass was needed not just for the getting of wisdom, but also for the development of wisdom, since there was more chance of competitors and catalysts being present. It also improved the odds of being able to make a living out of teaching philosophy to others, should one wish so to do, since it housed many more potential customers. Isolated individuals could overcome these hurdles, particularly if they happened to have been born in a large city (e.g. Archimedes of Syracuse), but they probably struggled harder, and most rural sons with the ability, the inclination, and the opportunity to become a philosopher seem to have moved to cities and stayed in them, e.g. Aristotle from Stagira (on the eastern coast of Chalcidice), Theophrastus from Eresus (Lesbos), and

2nd cent. AD. Meanwhile, although Andronicus had in the 1st cent. BC combined Aristotle's works into the treatises we know today, Diogenes Laertius, writing his list of Aristotle's works at the end of his *Life* in (probably) the 3rd cent. AD, was still using an edition or source which seems to predate Andronicus' efforts. See H. B. Gottschalk, 'The Earliest Aristotelian Commentators', in Sorabji (ed.), *Aristotle Transformed*, 55–81, esp. 55–64.

[36] Important lost works include e.g. Aristarchus' treatise proposing heliocentric theory (we do not even know its title), Crateuas' *Herbal*, Galen's *On Demonstration*, Posidonius' *On the Ocean*, Theophrastus' *On Mines*. Occasionally Roman emperors initiated efforts to try to find works which had been lost by their own times, e.g. Domitian in the 1st. cent. AD (Suet. *Dom.* 20). Unwritten knowledge was even more likely to get lost and be repeatedly rediscovered.

[37] The libraries belonged to the individuals, not the school, and on the owner's death the scrolls were either passed on as part of the estate or sold. For example, Aristotle's and Theophrastus' joint library was left, on Theophrastus' death, to Neleus, and *if* the contents reappeared in the Lyceum shortly afterwards (which they may not have done), it was because Strato, the next head of the school, bought them from Neleus; see H. B. Gottschalk, 'Notes on the Wills of the Peripatetic Scholarchs', *Hermes*, 100 (1972), 314–42, esp. 333. I wish to thank one of the anonymous readers for drawing my attention to this important paper.

[38] On this issue see most recently W. A. Johnson, 'Toward a Sociology of Reading in Classical Antiquity', *AJPh* 121 (2000), 593–627. I wish to thank John Waś and Anthony Spalinger for drawing my attention to this debate.

Posidonius from Apamea (on the River Orontes, south of Antioch). People who became philosophers came from all over the Greek *oikoumenē*, from the northern coast of the Black Sea to the coast of Africa, and from the south of France to Mesopotamia. For example, in the north, Heraclides Ponticus and Bion the Borysthenite;[39] in the south, Eratosthenes and Carneades of Cyrene; in the east, Seleucus of Seleucia and Chrysippus of Soli or Tarsus; and in the west, Pytheas of Massalia and Favorinus of Arelate.[40] Travel was more or less hazardous; natural hazards such as storm and shipwreck were supplemented by human hazards such as pirates and incessant wars.[41] Not surprisingly, then, while many philosophers did travel to get an education or to sell an education, even the most mobile did not make a lot of journeys by modern standards.

One consequence of moving from their home polis to another was that they had to forgo their citizen rights, which they held only in their home towns, and become resident aliens (metics) with more or less circumscribed rights and a duty to pay a head tax in their chosen place of residence. However distinguished they might become, this carried certain risks, as well as the indignities which went with living somewhere other than home. Consider, for example, the case of Xenocrates of Chalcedon, who seems to have spent all of his adult life in Athens, who became head of the Academy in 339 BC, and who even served on two Athenian embassies, one to Philip and another to Antipater. Nevertheless, he was sold into slavery by the Athenians

[39] From Olbia, on the River Bug (ancient Hypanis) but near the estuary of the Dnieper (ancient Borysthenes).

[40] Some even came from neighbouring cultures: for example, from Phoenicia came one Mochus (and Zeno of Citium is sometimes called a Phoenician); from Carthage Herillus (*fl.* 260 BC) and later Hasdrubal (renamed Clitomachus), who was head of the Academy from 129 BC; from Babylon Diogenes (head of the Stoa: *ob.* 152 BC); from Thrace Zamolxis; and from Libya Atlas.

[41] Zeno of Citium was shipwrecked and Hippocrates of Chios was caught by pirates. As a sweeping generalization we could say that in the 5th cent. BC some Greeks fought Persians and Greeks in the east, other Greeks fought Carthaginians and Greeks in the west; in the Greek heartlands Greeks fought Greeks, notably but not only in the generation-long Peloponnesian war; then in the 4th cent. Greeks fought the Macedonians and other Greeks; then some went with Alexander and fought the Persians again, and the Indians; then, in the 3rd cent. under the command of Alexander's successors, they fought each other again, as well as fighting with and against Rome. The Greeks in the west were throughout fighting each other and Carthage, and when the Romans joined in, they fought both with and against them (for example, Archimedes' home town of Syracuse was allied with Rome before being besieged by her). From its foundation Rome was at war with someone somewhere almost without interruption. Augustus claimed that the doors of the Temple of Janus were closed (symbolizing the state at peace) only twice before he was born, and three times during his principate (31 BC, 25 BC, and one other unknown date). I discount the period 714–671 BC, as part of the myth of King Numa; the other pre-Augustan closing was (probably: see below) in 241. W. V. Harris identifies four or five years without war between 327 and 241, then two or possibly four years during the rest of the third century, then four years without war in the second century: *War and Imperialism in Republican Rome*, 2nd corr. edn. (Oxford, 1985), 10 (see also 190–1 for the date of 241 rather than the oft-quoted 235).

when he failed to pay his metic tax.[42] In exceptional circumstances, an individual might be granted *enktēsis* (the right to own land and put a building upon it),[43] or be relieved of the metic tax,[44] or be awarded public honours,[45] or, as the highest honour a city could bestow, granted citizenship in his chosen place of residence: this final accolade was given to Posidonius at Rhodes, and he then went on to be elected to a board of five or six presidents (*prutaneis*) who effectively ran the state for six months.[46]

The already well-educated Hellenistic and Roman person would know or come to hear of the existence of the relatively large libraries which were open to the public at Alexandria, Antioch, Athens, Pergamum, and Rome.[47] Those who consulted written texts from their own or others' collections could then relate the contents to their friends and other interested parties.[48] Obvious channels of communication were conversation at social gatherings or inclusion of a reference in one's own writings (thus producing what scholars now call 'fragments'—quotations from other authors—and 'testimonia'—paraphrases or summaries, often critical, of others' words

[42] Diog. Laert. 4. 8, 9, 14. It is very unusual for a foreigner to be sent on such missions, and it may seem at odds with the second anecdote about Xenocrates. However, in this case the stories are credible, for Xenocrates was well regarded by Philip and Alexander, and was probably one of the latter's tutors. The Athenians, on the other hand, were not so well regarded, thus Xenocrates looks like a good choice for a negotiator between the proud Athenians and the powerful Macedonians. See L. A. Tritle, *Phocion the Good* (London, 1988), 129 and references in n. 44. The story about Xenocrates' enslavement for failing to pay the metic tax concludes with the remark that he was purchased by Demetrius of Phalerum, who controlled Athens' finances for ten years by the will of Cassander, Antipater's son; Xenocrates' treatment is thus explicable as another spat in relations between the Athenians and the Macedonians, if it was not simply the automatic judicial execution of a well-known law: pay the tax or be sold into slavery. For discussion of the latter, see D. Whitehead, *The Ideology of the Athenian Metic* (Cambridge, 1977), 76–7.

[43] It was such a grant to Theophrastus that enabled him to put up the first private buildings of the Lyceum, some time between 317 and 307, while Demetrius was governing Athens on behalf of Cassander.

[44] On which see the discussion by Whitehead (n. 41), 11–13.

[45] For example, Zeno of Citium (Cyprus), the founder of Stoicism, was awarded a golden crown by the Athenians, and copies of the decree recording the honour and the people's fulsome praise were ordered to be set up in the grounds of his main philosophical opponents, the Academy and the Lyceum! See Diog. Laert. 7. 10–12.

[46] See Kidd (n. 26), on T 27.

[47] Libraries open to the public were a Hellenistic invention, and they were usually adornments for the city like baths or gymnasiums. Indeed, the first library at Athens, founded by Ptolemy Philadelphus (mid-3rd cent. BC), was attached to a gymnasium. (I ignore the story in Gell. 7. 17 that Pisistratus founded the first public library in Athens, for there is no other evidence at all to support it.) The famous large library at Athens was that built by the emperor Hadrian, 2nd cent. AD. As in both these cases, even if a library was open to the public, it was privately built, owned, and run as an act of *philanthrōpia* by rich men who wished (for some reason or other) to bestow their favour on a particular community. L. Casson, *Libraries in the Ancient World* (New Haven and London, 2001), 60, is more optimistic about the number and distribution of libraries in Hellenistic times, but even if it is 'not unreasonable' to assume that 'most' gymnasia had a library connected to them—and that is a big if—few are likely to have held scientific treatises, which is our subject here.

[48] As Marcus Aurelius and Fronto do in their correspondence with each other.

or ideas), but less common methods appear as well, such as Diogenes of Oenoanda's decision to give his townspeople access to Epicurus' philosophy by inscribing it on a wall some 80 metres long and over 3 metres high. Notwithstanding the red paint used as a highlighter for the inscribed letters, access to the whole text in this case would have required excellent eyesight or a ladder. In Ptolemaic Alexandria residents were given access not just to a library, but also to astronomical instruments, as Taub discusses in her paper in this volume.

All that I have said thus far concerns learning only about what we might now call scientific or academic ideas, opinions, and theories. But scientists do not live in ivory towers, completely separate from the world in which they live, and that was much more true of ancient scientists. They were influenced by all manner of attitudes, ideas, and beliefs held in the societies in which they grew up, and in which they lived and worked. They knew, for example, the opinions of their next-door neighbours and their distant relatives on life, the universe, and everything; they knew the epics of Homer and the tragedies of Aeschylus; and they knew what were appropriate offerings for Heracles and Aphrodite. A number of papers in this volume draw attention to some of these other influences upon and sources of information used by ancient scientists. Cuomo argues that, at least for Hero, peace of mind is what war machines can offer; Bowen suggests that astronomers were influenced in their choice of phenomena to model by a particular topos or story-line that pops up in historical and biographical literature; Berggren points out that geographers were heavily dependent on sailors and other seafarers for much of their basic data; Hine argues that academic theories on volcanoes and earthquakes were influenced by the opinions of the people who lived near volcanoes and oral traditions about previous eruptions and earthquakes; Rihll and Tucker suggest that physical theories of matter and change were influenced by data gathered from miners and metalworkers; and Barker argues that acoustic theories sometimes have the content they do because of the conceptual baggage and cluster of non-scientific notions wrapped up in key terms, such as ὀξύς and βαρύς.

The second major factor in opportunity was time. The time to listen to others' ideas, to think, to develop one's own ideas, to write or practise. Here again anachronism is a serious danger. In antiquity the movements of sun and moon, not hands on a clock, were the major timekeepers, and hours were seasonal, not equal (see the papers of Hannah and Taub). Nature, not abstract units of time, suggested when jobs should be started and stopped. People did not exhaust themselves in the hope of material advancement or promotion as they do today. Attitudes to work and leisure were quite different. For example, there was no Protestant work ethic, no timesheets, no payslip, and for many people no taxman; there were relatively few material goods to buy with any money one might have, and there was no welfare system. Our word 'school' comes from Greek *scholē*, which means 'leisure'. Schooling was a leisure pursuit: Aristotle even likened education to a rattle for big children. The vast majority of people were self-employed, worked as hard as necessary not to have to worry about surviving through to the next harvest, and spent the rest of their time doing what they enjoyed doing. If they were free, that is.

The whole notion of a job, of working from nine till five on one thing, is inappropriate for the ancient world. Most free men spent some of their time providing for themselves and their families, generally as farmers. Most spent some of their time on management of their slave(s) and the rest of their household. Most spent some of their time on what we would call leisure pursuits, such as chatting with friends in public places and taking physical exercise in public gyms. Most spent some of their time on religious observances, such as performing purification rituals for their dearly departed and going to the theatre (which was more of a holy day than our secularized holiday, but no less entertaining for that—comedy and satire, as well as tragedy, were invented for these religious festivals). Most of those who had a voice in the political system of their place and time spent some of their time on it, formally in meetings and informally talking with friends. In all these cases an ancient might consider what he was doing as 'work': survival meant not just having enough food to eat, but also preserving the community. It was essential to maintain friendships, for family and friends were the only reliable source of succour in hard times (and for Epicureans friends were a key ingredient in their recipe for happiness). Keeping fit was also essential in the ancient world, for general health, as recognized in the number of ancient medical works concerned with 'regimen' (lifestyle, prevention being considered a large part of the doctor's self-appointed task), and for military service, except while and where the *Pax Romana* operated successfully, since a call to arms could come at any time and being fit might make the difference between life or death. Gods were thought to intervene directly in human affairs, to reside temporarily in temples built for them, to accept payment in arrears on deals proposed by worshippers ('I shall sacrifice *n* cows if you [god/dess] do *X*'), to care about the presentation more than the intention, and a host of other things which contrast markedly with modern attitudes to the divine. Most ancients, therefore, strove to keep the gods onside, or at least not knowingly to incur their wrath, in a system dominated by pragmatism and superstition rather than morality. Taking an interest in state affairs was particularly important in the small states of Greece, wherein everybody mattered and everybody was or knew someone who was directly affected by the decisions taken. Pericles apparently drew the Athenians' attention to the fact that they did not say, of the man who took no interest in the affairs of state, that he minded his own business; they said that he had no business there at all (Thuc. 2. 40). Of course, there were people who minded their own business, otherwise Pericles would not have thought to criticize them, but they were a very small minority. Even Socrates, the archetypal philosopher, sometimes portrayed as an economic scrounger on his friends and a pest to people going about their business in the market place, served his country on the battlefield and in the *boulē*, the executive council of the democratic assembly. See Netz (p. 200) on the mathematicians.

It could be argued that the most important institution supporting ancient science was slavery. Greeks and Romans had time for many things because they did not work hard by modern standards and because they had slaves. Slavery was the institution which underwrote science in ancient Greece, in contrast to the redistributive economies of Babylon and Egypt, which enabled kings to employ e.g. astronomer-priests as full-time practitioners of their art. Let us be clear here. I am not suggesting that slavery was a sufficient condition for the emergence and practice of science in antiquity. As Aristotle pointed out, leisure is the necessary condition for all intellectual pursuits. What I am suggesting is that widespread slavery provided such leisure for many people; that it facilitated widespread participation in activities such as science as well as in politics. It is relevant to note here that H. von Staden has recently drawn attention to the fact that 'whether we like it or not, Greek science made some of its greatest discoveries and advances within non-democratic political structures such as those of the Macedonians' Ptolemaic monarchy in Alexandria'.[49] Sicilian Greek tyrants, Hellenistic monarchs, and Roman emperors—all operating in genuine slave societies[50]—had, like their Babylonian and Egyptian predecessors (who were not operating in genuine slave societies), the means to employ intellectuals of various sorts, and a few did. Such 'jobs' offered rare opportunities for the ambitious, but they were often short-term and decidedly risky—they might end in something less pleasant than redundancy: Plato was sold into slavery and Seneca was ordered to commit suicide. With widespread slavery, more or less anyone who wished could spend significant proportions of their time on intellectual pursuits. They needed a farm and a slave rather than a job as an academic.

If they were successful, and they charged for their services (as most did), and they wanted to, then they might attract enough customers to contemplate making a living out of 'philosophy' (which covers many subjects, e.g.

[49] 'The Discovery of the Body: Human Dissection and its Cultural Contexts in Ancient Greece', *Yale Journal of Biology and Medicine*, 65 (1992) 223–41 at 231. While the point is well taken, the phrase '*such as* Ptolemaic Alexandria' is misleading. Ptolemaic Alexandria was wholly atypical of ancient cities; indeed, von Staden's aim in this excellent paper is to try to clarify exactly what exceptions were operating at this time and in this place to enable—for the first and last time in antiquity—systematic dissections on the human body to be performed.

[50] For the difference—and the significance of the difference—between a genuine slave society and a society in which there are slaves, see O. Patterson, *Slavery and Social Death* (Cambridge, Mass., 1982).

medicine and rhetoric). If they lived in or moved to a place where there was, within reasonable walking distance, a market selling food most days of the year (very few places met this requirement), and they wished to break their tie with the land, then they could even leave their farm to be run by a relative or tenant in their absence, and become dependent on the market for their food supplies.[51] One wonders how many actually did this.[52] When Strato was drawing up his will and deciding to whom to leave the Lyceum, he seems to have been presented with Hobson's choice: 'I leave it to Lyco, since of the rest, some are too old and others are too busy' (Diog. Laert. 5. 62). A significant number of ancient scientists about whom we have biographical information—including some of the most eminent—are sons of craftsmen or tradesmen, not farmers.[53] They would have been accustomed to living by the market, to being paid for their work, to the need to have something to sell or to beg—experiences which were held in great disdain by landowning, i.e. most, Greeks. In the harsh ancient world, some became peripatetic not by making such choices but because they were forced, by natural disaster or for judicial, political, or military reasons, to leave their natural or adopted homes.[54] Others, even the most brilliant and successful,

[51] e.g. Strato. No one would give up their farm—their main if not only source of food—unless they were confident (rightly or wrongly) that there would be food for sale or barter in the market on a very regular basis. The stomach, as Diogenes said, is life's Charybdis. If the supply became inadequate in quantity or regularity, they would have moved to better-supplied cities, and if it failed they would have starved to death. There was no possibility of a quick response to food crises in antiquity. Foodstuffs cannot be grown in a hurry, even in perfect conditions, and moving foodstuffs from areas of surplus to areas of dearth was a headache even for Roman emperors—assuming that someone informed them, by travelling over land or sea, that there was a famine somewhere and there was still time to do something about it.

[52] A story about Crates illustrates how much family pressure people might come under in this matter. Crates was apparently a wealthy landowner in his home town of Thebes: converted to a life in philosophy by Diogenes, he let his farm turn into sheep pasture and gave away his money. 'Often some of his relatives would come to visit him and try to divert him from his purpose, and he would drive them away with his stick' (Diog. Laert. 6. 88). The pressure was relieved in due course when his home town (Thebes) was razed to the ground by Alexander the Great, and he was forced into a life of exile, as presumably were those of his relatives not killed or enslaved during the sacking of the city.

[53] For a list of the most famous (including Aristotle) see my *Greek Science* (*Greece and Rome* New Surveys in the Classics, 29; Oxford, 1999), 5–6. In addition, Bion was a slave; Diogenes or his father was a metalworker; Galen's father was an architect (lit. 'leader of builders'); Hippocrates of Chios was a trader; Lacydes (head of the Academy 242–216 BC) is described as 'industrious and poor' (Diog. Laert. 4. 59); Menedemus was a builder and decorator. Many people are described simply as citizens of *X*, with no mention of occupation. For one working in his home town, this might mean either that he was a farmer or that his occupation was not known; for one working outside his home town, being a farmer is highly unlikely for a number of legal, social, and economic reasons, including prohibition on the ownership of land and lack of security to raise a loan or obtain a tenancy.

[54] For example, Xenophanes of Colophon was exiled and perhaps sold into slavery; Anaxagoras of Clazomenae, friend of Pericles (perhaps attacked *because* he was a friend of Pericles), was driven out of Athens by a lawsuit accusing him of impiety; Phaedo was enslaved on the destruction of his city (Elis) and turned up for sale in Athens, where he was bought by friends of Socrates; Diogenes of Sinope (the Cynic/Dog) went or was sent into exile because either

seem to have pursued most if not all of their studies in their own time, and for their own sake, having no pupils and setting up no school, e.g. Archimedes and Galen. Their daily bread or their income was presumably supplied from their farm, their family, or an employer. Archimedes probably worked unasked and unpaid on the defences of Syracuse, trying to preserve his own life and that of his community, and no doubt enjoying the intellectual challenges thrown up by such work too: as he explained in *The Method*, mathematical discoveries may be made by means of mechanics, and thus (he says) he discovered the theorem of the Quadrature of the Parabola.[55]

6. Concluding Remarks

Greek science is an exciting subject at the present time. As I have shown, there is an enormous amount of work being done and still to do, at many different levels, and from many different perspectives. The 'Greek genius' is now not only admired, but also studied, analysed, criticized, and contextualized, so that we can reach a deeper understanding of the motivations of ancient scientists, the circumstances in which they were compelled or chose to work, and the historical and intellectual conditions which inspired, facilitated, hindered, or prevented that work. The extraordinary emergence and development of scientific thinking in ancient Greece is a historical problem of the first order, and not just for ancient historians. Most modern sciences like to trace their origins to ancient Greece; there is some validity in these claims, but to appreciate properly what the Greeks did, and what they did not do, we need much more detailed research into specific topics, such as is provided by the papers in this volume.

he or his father was accused or convicted of adulterating the coinage—in one of the anecdotes attributed to him he claims to have become a philosopher *because* he was an exile (Diog. Laert. 6. 49); Chrysippus likewise is said to have turned to philosophy because his property was confiscated in his home town (Soli or Tarsus), and the confiscation of property is normally an adjunct to the penalty of exile; Aristotle left Athens in 323 after news came through of Alexander's death in Babylon and anti-Macedonian feelings were running high—Aristotle's close connections with the royal family became a liability; Theophrastus was banished from Athens in 306 BC along with all other foreign (i.e. non-Athenian) philosophers.

[55] This is the first work he sent to Dositheus, after hearing of Conon's death, and thus certainly precedes *Sphere and Cylinder*, *Conoids and Spheroids*, and *Spirals*.

2

Words for Sounds

ANDREW BARKER

THIS paper is a very modest contribution to the project of 'placing' ancient science in its relation to the society in which it was embedded. Scientific enquiry, for all its pretensions to objectivity, inevitably has roots in the culture from which it springs, and in its concepts, assumptions, aims, and procedures carries more or less visible traces of its ancestry. These traces and their influence are the subject of the present study; I shall be considering some of the ways in which the pre-scientific assumptions and thought patterns of a culturally inherited tradition can live on in the minds of scientists and significantly colour their work. But that topic is enormous.[1] All I can do is to glance at a very small number of the conceptual stowaways that are concealed in one small cabin aboard one little boat of no pretensions and questionable seaworthiness, bobbing on the fringes of the Greek scientific fleet: that is, the science of physical acoustics.

I shall take two principles as axiomatic without attempting to explore or justify them, though I recognize that the interpretations under which they are true are legitimate matters of debate. The first is that no scientist can be a purely neutral or transparent receiver and reporter of objective data.[2] What we seek to explain, and how, depends on what we take the phenomena to be, what we see them *as*; and that depends in turn on the conceptual resources we bring to bear on them. The casual visitor to a scientific laboratory does not see the images presented through the lens of a microscope *as* a trained scientist sees them; in a loose but acceptable sense they see different things, since the ways in which 'things' are conceived by the microbiologist, for example, are very different from those available to the uninitiated. Nor are

---

[1] In the Greek context the author who has tackled it most vigorously and from the most diverse range of perspectives is G. E. R. Lloyd. See particularly his *Magic, Reason and Experience* (Cambridge, 1979); *The Revolutions of Wisdom* (Berkeley, 1987), whose ch. 4 is especially relevant to the present paper; *Demystifying Mentalities* (Cambridge, 1990), ch. 1; *Methods and Problems in Greek Science* (Cambridge, 1991), 392–4. A stimulating earlier study is N. Goodman, *Ways of Worldmaking* (Hassocks, 1978).

[2] Versions of this principle have been endlessly discussed in the philosophical literature of the last century. For a few examples see P. K. Feyerabend, 'How to be a Good Empiricist', in B. Baumrin (ed.), *Philosophy of Science: The Delaware Seminar*, ii (New York, London, and Sydney, 1963), 3–39; A. F. Chalmers, *What is This Thing Called Science?*, 3rd edn. (Buckingham, 1999), ch. 3; A. Musgrave, *Common Sense, Science and Scepticism* (Cambridge, 1993), ch. 3 (esp. pp. 54–9); D. Gillies, *Philosophy of Science in the Twentieth Century* (Oxford, 1993), ch. 7; E. G. Zahar, 'The Problem of the Empirical Basis', in A. O'Hear (ed.), *Karl Popper: Philosophy and Problems* (Cambridge, 1995) 45–74 (esp. 50–5).

they necessarily even identifying the same things but conceiving them in different ways, since the dividing-lines between 'same thing' and 'different thing' may themselves be differently located in the two conceptual fields.

My second axiom is that something of the character of the conceptual spectacles a scientist is wearing, and of the relations between concepts in his or her repertoire, can be detected through an examination of the idiosyncrasies of the language in which they represent the phenomena. In the modern context we would look first, no doubt, at the behaviour of terms in the technical vocabulary of the scientific tradition in which our scientist was working. But at the point where we shall pick up Greek acoustics, no inherited technical vocabulary existed. The relevant conceptions are those embedded in the language of ordinary educated Greeks, the language that formed, expressed, and transmitted their shared cultural baggage. At the end of the fifth century that meant, inescapably, a language resonating with the usages of poetry, above all those of the Homeric epics. In that case students of this science need to examine rather carefully the behaviour, in the imaginative literature of the preceding period, of the words and word patterns which the scientists subsequently adopted to describe phenomena in their field of operations; and if we neglect that task we may seriously misconstrue the problems they faced and the solutions they offered. If we too casually assume that they conceived their initial data exactly as we would, and that the terms by which they are designated do not matter, we may quite literally fail to grasp what they were talking about, and why their enquiries followed the sometimes curious trajectories that they did.

The two main tasks that Greek acoustics set itself can be stated easily enough. The first focuses on the phenomenon of sound in general. It seeks to explain what sounds are, how they are caused, how they behave, how they are transmitted to the ear and perceived by it. The second concerns itself with what constitutes and what causes the various perceived attributes of sounds, how a sound that is high-pitched or quiet or rough or muffled differs in itself and in its causal antecedents from one that is low-pitched or loud or smooth or clear. Or at least that is how *we* would put the questions: if my preliminary remarks were on the right track, the attributes that the Greeks were investigating may not map altogether directly onto those designated by the English words standardly offered to translate them.

It is on matters to do with the attributes of sounds that I propose to concentrate. I want to suggest that the early scientists' linguistic and conceptual inheritance enmeshed them in difficulties of at least three sorts. The roots of the first problem are in what we might call 'customary syntax'. The poets use adjectives to give colourful descriptions of sounds surprisingly rarely. It is possible to read hundreds of lines of Homer—the whole of the first book of the *Odyssey*, for instance—and large tracts of fifth-century drama without coming across a single example. The point is not that the poets are uninterested in sounds and their qualities: the *Iliad*'s battle-scenes, to take only the most obvious case, are a veritable brouhaha of clangs and thuds and screams and bellows. But most often the colourful work is not done by adjectives, but by nouns—κλαγγή, ὅμαδος, δοῦπος, στοναχή, πάταγος, ἰαχή, ἀλαλητός—or by verbs, as in δούπησεν δὲ πεσών, ἀράβησε δὲ τεύχε᾽ ἐπ᾽ αὐτῷ, or χαμαὶ βόμβησε πεσοῦσα, or λίγξε βιός, νευρὴ δὲ μέγ᾽ ἴαχεν, or ὡς ὅτε κῦμα πολυφλοίσβοιο θαλάσσης | αἰγιαλῷ μεγάλῳ βρέμεται, σμαραγεῖ δέ τε πόντος.[3]

This familiar way of speaking becomes a problem for the scientists simply because it could not be transferred directly into their own analyses. On pain of multiplying classes of entity and classes of activity or process absurdly, they could not treat a δοῦπος and a κλαγγή as distinct and independent types of thing, or treat βρέμειν as an activity different in kind from βομβεῖν. They needed something for which the inherited patterns of discourse made only scanty provision: that is, a way of referring neutrally to a sound of any sort, or to any activity of sounding, together with a rich vocabulary of adjectives to indicate the special attributes associated with each class of instances. The poets' colourful nouns and verbs had to be recast in substance-and-attribute terms, where the subject, sound or sounding, remained constant and relatively neutral, and the various kinds of qualitative colouring were conveyed attributively. The former requirement was quite easily fulfilled. The noun ψόφος could do duty as 'sound' generally, for example, while φωνή, φθόγγος, and ἦχος could be hijacked, relatively harmlessly, for more specialized purposes.[4] The difficulty lay in the adjectives. Because the work of characterization had overwhelmingly been borne by nouns and verbs, the collection of adjectives provided by the tradition was too small to allow room for much picking and choosing by the scientists; and the adjectives it did contain posed additional problems of the two other kinds I want to mention.

The second problem is that when adjectives are applied to sounds by pre-scientific writers, they are rarely being used with merely empirical intent, just to give descriptions of the way sounds sound. A poet who describes a

---

[3] Translations of the 'sound' words here can only be impressionistic, and κλαγγή, the first noun on the list, is an unusually versatile word even by Homer's standards. See LSJ s.v. Rough equivalents for the other nouns, in at least some Homeric contexts, might be 'hubbub', 'thud', 'groan', 'clatter', 'yell', and 'shout' respectively. The sentences containing the relevant verbs mean, approximately, 'he *thudded* as he fell, and his armour *clattered* [not, I think, the time-honoured 'rang'] upon him'; 'it *rang resonantly* [a sort of hollow humming noise] as it fell' [the subject is a helmet]; 'the bow *twanged* and the string *cried out* loudly'; 'as when a wave of the noisy sea *roars* on a great beach, and the ocean *crashes*'.

[4] They are used in various ways. φωνή is often reserved for the human voice, sometimes extended to the 'voices' of instruments, but this is by no means invariable; not infrequently it means simply 'sound'. φθόγγος, in technical writers, is regularly 'musical note'. ἦχος can be used as a vague designator of sound, but has special applications to echo (along with its familiar relative ἠχώ), and to a sound's secondary 'resonance' (e.g. that in a stringed instrument's soundbox or arms, or in the metal or horn 'bell' of a wind instrument; see e.g. [Arist.] *De aud.* 802ᵃ17 ff.).

sound as ὀξύς is not normally *just* characterizing it as high in pitch; such words seem primarily intended to indicate the special kind of psychological or emotional impact that a sound makes on its hearer, not to register the objective sound quality that would be detected by an uninvolved observer. Homer and the archaic lyricists, I believe, do not even have words that just mean 'high-pitched', 'low-pitched', and so on; and one would be hard pressed to find cases where one could confidently claim that as the full sense even in Euripidean drama. Hence the adoption of this terminology into the language of the empirical scientists, who evidently were aspiring to the detached observer's perspective, is unlikely to have been smooth or conceptually unproblematic.[5]

The third difficulty is the most striking. Very few of the adjectives regularly used to designate the attributes of sounds belonged exclusively or even primarily to the acoustic domain. Leaving aside compounds formed with acoustic indicators like -φωνος or -φθογγος as suffixes,[6] there is, I think, only one common exception, the adjective λιγύς;[7] and this plays no significant part in scientific discourse, not even as the name of an attribute whose nature and causal antecedents call for investigation. All the rest, like so many of our own, have important applications elsewhere. Whether it is altogether accurate to label the acoustic uses of ὀξύς, βαρύς, λεῖος, τραχύς, μεγάς, μικρός, σύντονος, ἀνειμένος, and the rest as 'metaphorical' is an issue I shall not

---

[5] ὀξύς always retains in Homer the sense 'piercing', sometimes carrying the idea of psychological or perceptual 'penetration', as in the recurrent phrase ὀξὺ νόησε (e.g. *Il*. 5. 312), usually with the overtones of something hostile, bringing grief or pain. This is obvious in non-acoustic applications (e.g. ὀξὺν Ἄρεα, *Il*. 4. 352; ὀξέϊ χαλκῷ, 5. 132; ὀξεῖαι δ᾽ ὀδύναι, 11. 268), but carries over into acoustic ones, e.g. ὀξέα κεκλήγων of Thersites at *Il*. 2. 222, ὀξέα κεκλήγοντες of the Trojans at 12. 125. Similarly, when βαρύς is applied to sounds, its force seems as much psychological ('heavy' in the sense 'sad' or occasionally 'threatening') as directly descriptive. Not every hero who weeps βαρὺ στενάχων is to be thought of as the possessor of a bass voice; and it is no coincidence that the occurrence of this expression at e.g. *Il*. 9. 16 is immediately followed by Agamemnon's reference to the ἄτη . . . βαρείη sent upon him by Zeus (9. 18). The difficulties that beset any attempt to give the poets' sound-adjectives clearly defined fields of acoustic reference are broadly parallel to the better-known difficulties afflicting adjectives of colour: see e.g. E. Irwin, *Colour Terms in Greek Poetry* (Toronto, 1974).

[6] These suffixes, attached to adjectival stems, form adjectives meaning explicitly 'such-and-such sounded', or 'such-and-such voiced', and so on. Thus μεγαλό-φωνος, for instance, means 'big-voiced', and the suffix serves to establish unambiguously that the intended conception of 'size' is an acoustic one, consisting in sonorous, not spatial 'volume'.

[7] The sense of this term is slippery, but the main element in it seems to be 'clear', 'carrying'. The Peripatetic treatise *De audibilibus* has an interesting paragraph (804ᵃ22–32) on the attribute designated by the related word λιγυρός. It associates being λιγυρός with being slender and compact (λεπτός and πυκνός), with lack of bulk and weight, and with distinctness or precision (ἀκριβεία). It comments that this is an attribute of the sounds of instruments without resonating horns (or 'bells'); the earlier discussion of such horns (802ᵃ17–ᵇ1) indicates that their function is to produce resonances that partially obscure the principal sound of the instrument, and so make it less hard and penetrating. The passage and others related to it are discussed in my paper 'Telestes and the "Five-Rodded Jointing of Strings"', *CQ*, NS 48 (1998), 75–81.

pursue; for most purposes the term will serve.[8] What is perfectly clear is
that the acoustic senses of these terms are not independent of their uses
in other domains. It is from their wider uses that they derive the special,
descriptive meanings they acquire when applied to sounds; and we can reasonably anticipate that the Greeks' conceptions of the sonorous attributes
they name were in some degree affected by the ways they thought about
their non-acoustic counterparts. The specialized conceptual apparatus of
modern science and philosophy has immunized us somewhat to the allure
of the trans-sensual analogies that our language tempts us to make. We can
stand back from our antique metaphors and objectify them instead of thinking with and through them; we are not much inclined, for instance, seriously
to suppose that a 'high' sound is somehow 'up there'. But our ability to do
this depends on our possession of an allegedly neutral scientific vocabulary
through which the phenomena can be designated without apparent detours
into metaphor. There is no good reason to believe that the Greeks of this
period were capable of similar feats of detachment, lacking as they were in
the linguistic resources through which the inherited metaphors could have
been translated into literal terms.

Even if the gist of what I have been saying is true, I have done nothing so far to support my insinuation that any of it made an important
or interesting difference to the character of acoustic science in the fourth
and subsequent centuries; and we are plainly unlikely to uncover persuasive reasons for accepting or abandoning that claim without exploring examples of the scientists' work in some detail. I shall place at centre stage,
as they did, the small group of adjectives that have to do with a sound's
pitch and its volume, leaving more slippery qualitative attributes aside.[9]

[8] These adjectives form pairs: lit. 'sharp/heavy'; 'smooth/rough'; 'big/small'; 'tense/relaxed'.
Of these, both the first pair and the last function as approximate counterparts of our 'high/
low', and the third provides the normal Greek way of referring to volume. The pairing 'rough/
smooth' is applied to sounds in ways not unlike those we use ourselves.

   The modern literature on metaphor is of course vast. Works I have found particularly
useful in the present context include the well-known studies by G. Lakoff and his colleagues,
especially G. Lakoff and M. Johnson, *Metaphors We Live By* (Chicago, 1980), and G. Lakoff
and M. Turner, *More than Cool Reason* (Chicago, 1989); essays in A. Ortony (ed.), *Metaphor
and Thought*, 2nd edn. (Cambridge 1993), especially D. Gentner and M. Jeziorski, 'The Shift
from Metaphor to Analogy in Western Science', 447–80, R. Boyd, 'Metaphor and Theory
Change', 481–532, and T. S. Kuhn, 'Metaphor in Science', 533–42; essays in D. S. Miall (ed.),
Metaphor: Problems and Perspectives (Brighton, 1982), especially F. C. T. Moore, 'On Taking
Metaphor Literally', 1–13, and J. Martin and R. Harré, 'Metaphor in Science', 89–105. For the
study of metaphors in Greek literature, the work of W. B. Stanford, *Greek Metaphor* (Oxford,
1936), though inevitably dated in some respects, is still indispensable. In the present context,
see particularly appendix A to ch. 3 (47–62), on 'Synaesthetic or Intersensual Metaphor'; cf.
Irwin (n. 5), 205–13.

[9] The fullest Greek studies of attributes of this latter sort are in the Peripatetic *De audibilibus*.
For the distinction, and a quantitative scientist's attitude to it, see also Ptol. *Harm.* 1. 3, esp.
pp. 6. 24–7. 21 Düring; a different approach and a wide range of additional sources appear
in the discussion of this chapter by Ptolemy's commentator, Porphyry (*In Harm.* 29. 27–78.
2 Düring).

(The fact that pitch and volume received the bulk of these scientists' attention is due of course to the close historical, theoretical, and practical connections that existed between physical acoustics and the musical sciences, particularly mathematical harmonics;[10] but I shall say nothing of that here.)

My first witness is Aristotle. Aristotle, of course, is quite unusually sensitive to the linguistic forms in which ideas are expressed, and his analyses of τὰ λεγόμενα, 'what people say', regularly provide him with the groundwork for substantial philosophical and scientific constructions.[11] We might expect him to offer some reflections on the peculiar features of terms like ὀξύς and βαρύς, 'sharp' and 'heavy', when they are used in an acoustic context; and so he does. The major passage is at *De an.* 2. 8, 420ᵃ28–ᵇ4, in the course of his general account of the nature of sound, ψόφος. The terms ὀξύς and βαρύς, he says, 'are said by way of transference from tangible things', κατὰ μεταφορὰν ἀπὸ τῶν ἁπτῶν. In his opinion, then, the tactile uses and senses of the words are primary, the acoustic derivative and metaphorical. But he does not for that reason dismiss as illusory the implications about pitch that the metaphors appear to offer. On the contrary. 'For the sharp [τὸ ὀξύ]', he continues,

moves the sense much in a short time, and the heavy [τὸ βαρύ] a little in a long time. It is not that τὸ ὀξύ is swift and τὸ βαρύ slow, but the movement of the one is as it is *because* of swiftness and that of the other *because* of slowness. And it seems to be analogous to the sharp [τὸ ὀξύ] and the blunt [τὸ ἀμβλύ] in the field of touch. For τὸ ὀξύ as it were pierces, while τὸ ἀμβλύ pushes, because one moves things in a short time and one in a long time, so that one of them turns out to be swift and the other slow. (420ᵃ30–ᵇ4)

I want to extract just two main points from this complex passage. First, it is obvious that Aristotle is quite deliberately developing his account of these attributes of sound on the basis of implications 'transferred' with the terms from one domain of reference to another. Despite his explicit recognition of the 'metaphorical' status of these usages, he seems confident that they can guide us to a reliable understanding of the modifications of sound which they designate. His confidence is apparently not diminished by the fact (surely an obvious one) that different metaphors could have been used for this purpose, and indeed sometimes were[12]—though if *their* implications

---

[10] For a sketch of these connections see A. Barker, *Greek Musical Writings*, ii (Cambridge, 1989), 3–11.

[11] See e.g. the classic paper by G. E. L. Owen, '*Tithenai ta Phainomena*', first published in S. Mansion (ed.), *Aristote et les problèmes de méthode* (Louvain, 1961), 83–103, and often reprinted, e.g. in J. Barnes, M. Schofield, and R. Sorabji (eds.), *Articles on Aristotle*, i (London, 1975), 113–26.

[12] The alternative metaphorical axis of tension and relaxation (cf. n. 8) recurs quite frequently in Greek texts from the early 5th cent. onwards. I shall say a little more about it towards the end of this paper (pp. 33–5).

were taken as seriously as Aristotle takes these ones, the conclusions drawn
would necessarily be different.

   The second point I want to make is that, even given this approach, the
story Aristotle tells here is in certain respects embarrassingly unpersuasive.
The expressions are derived from discourse concerned with tangibles, and
what is sharp, τὸ ὀξύ, moves the senses—whether of touch or of hearing—a
lot in a short time. This seems provisionally acceptable, and it helps to
mediate his progression towards a theory of the causation of pitch which
associates it with *speed*. Here he is tapping into a model already developed
to some degree by his predecessors, and this family of theories proved
serviceable, despite some awkwardnesses, for many centuries.[13] But the
companion attribute, τὸ βαρύ, is less amenable to Aristotle's treatment.
What is βαρύ, he says—which as he understands it here means literally
'heavy'—moves the sense a little in a long time. But why on earth should
any reader accept that? No doubt what is heavy is more resistant to *being*
moved; but once a heavy thing is in motion, it is most likely to be thought of
as impinging on our senses with speed and force.[14] The trouble, of course,
is that in their allegedly literal uses ὀξύς and βαρύς are not true opposites.
Aristotle recognizes the fact, implicitly here and explicitly in the *Topics*
(1. 15, 106ᵃ9 ff.; cf. 107ᵃ11 ff.);[15] but it throws into question the status of
his whole analysis, dependent as it is on drawing out the implications of
these words in their 'primary' uses and applying them to cases where they
are used metaphorically.[16] If the words in their primary uses are not strict
opposites, the wholesale transportation of their implications there into the
metaphorical context will bring that lack of strict opposition with it; but
in the new context, of course, they *are* opposites. What Aristotle in fact
appears to do is to take seriously the literal implications of ὀξύς and transfer
them to the acoustic domain, while not doing the same with the literal
implications of βαρύς. But the choice seems arbitrary, and if he had taken
the alternative tack, privileging the implications of βαρύς while suppressing
those of ὀξύς, the resulting analysis would surely have had to be different.
Aristotle is tangled in a confusing and inconsistent web of words. He is, I
suspect, conscious of his predicament, but powerless to extricate himself.
The attributes *are* what the words say they are, but the story they tell is
incoherent.

   [13] Aristotle's main precursors are Archytas fr. 1 (discussed below) and Pl. *Ti.* 67 A–C, 79 E–
80 B. Later examples include [Arist.] *Pr.* 11. 3, 899ᵃ9–14 (and elsewhere; but other theories too
are canvassed in this collection), *De aud.* 803ᵃ6 ff., Adrastus ap. Theon Smyrn. 50. 2 ff., 60.
12 ff. Hiller, Ael. ap. Porph. *In Harm.* 33. 16 ff. Düring, Nicom. *Harm.* 4. For an important
variant see the introductory paragraph to the Euclidean *Sectio canonis*, and for a vigorous
attack on such theories Theophr. fr. 716 FHS&G.
   [14] Compare Arist. *Ph.* 7. 5, 249ᵇ27 ff., with 4. 8, 216ᵇ11 ff.
   [15] It is a pity that he failed to consider the problems raised by this example in the context of
his remarks on 'contraries' in *Cat.* 11, esp. 14ᵃ19 ff.
   [16] Some related difficulties are discussed in *Ph.* 8. 4, particularly at 248ᵇ4 ff.

My second witness is Archytas of Tarentum, perhaps half a century earlier. His first fragment, if it is genuine, as I believe,[17] is the first trace we have of sustained investigation in this field. Archytas stands at the head of the scientific tradition I mentioned above. The fragment identifies the cause of sound as the impact of bodies on one another and on the air, analyses sound itself as a special kind of movement in or of the air, and relates the pitch of a sound to the speed or vigour of this movement. In various versions and at various levels of sophistication, theories of sound recognizably related to this one remained dominant for the rest of antiquity.

The passage that primarily concerns us here comes after Archytas' initial statement that sounds are produced by impacts, and his exploration of some of the conditions under which impacts of the relevant sort occur. It runs as follows:

τὰ μὲν οὖν ποτιπίπτοντα ποτὶ τὰν αἴσθασιν, ἃ μὲν ἀπὸ τᾶν πλαγᾶν ταχὺ παραγίνεται καὶ ⟨ἰσχυρῶς⟩, ὀξέα φαίνεται· τὰ δὲ βραδέως καὶ ἀσθενῶς, βαρέα δοκοῦντι ἦμεν. αἰ γάρ τις ῥάβδον λαβὼν κινοῖ νωθρῶς τε καὶ ἀσθενέως, τᾷ πλαγᾷ βαρὺν ποιήσει τὸν ψόφον· αἰ δέ κα ταχύ τε καὶ ἰσχυρῶς, ὀξύν. οὐ μόνον δὲ κα τούτῳ γνοίημεν, ἀλλὰ καὶ ὅκκα ἄμμες ἢ λέγοντες ἢ ἀείδοντες χρήζομές τι μέγα φθέγξασθαι καὶ ὀξύ, σφοδρῷ τῷ πνεύματι φθεγγόμενοι. ἔτι δὲ καὶ τοῦτο συμβαίνει ὥσπερ ἐπὶ βελῶν· τὰ μὲν ἰσχυρῶς ἀφιέμενα πρόσω φέρεται, τὰ δ' ἀσθενῶς ἐγγύς. τοῖς γὰρ ἰσχυρῶς φερομένοις μᾶλλον ὑπακούει ὁ ἀήρ, τοῖς δ' ἀσθενέως ἧσσον. τωὐτὸ δὲ καὶ ταῖς φωναῖς συμβήσεται· τᾷ μὲν ὑπὸ [τῶ] ἰσχυρῷ τῶ πνεύματος φερομένᾳ μεγάλᾳ τε ἦμεν καὶ ὀξέᾳ, τᾷ δ' ὑπ' ἀσθενέος μικρᾷ τε καὶ βαρέᾳ. ἀλλὰ μὰν καὶ τούτῳ γά κα ἴδοιμες ἰσχυροτάτῳ σαμείῳ, ὅτι τῶ αὐτῶ φθεγξαμένω μέγα μὲν πόρσωθέν κ' ἀκούσαιμες· μικκὸν δ' οὐδ' ἐγγύθεν. (Archytas ap. Porph. *In Harm.* 56. 21–57.14 = 47 B 1. 24–41 DK)

Now when things fall upon our sense, those that arrive swiftly and ⟨strongly⟩ from the impacts appear sharp [ὀξέα], while those that arrive slowly and weakly seem to be heavy [βαρέα]. Thus if someone takes a stick and moves it sluggishly and weakly, he will make a heavy sound with the impact, but a sharp one if he moves it swiftly and strongly. We can grasp the fact not only from this example, but also when we want to utter something big [μέγα, i.e. 'loud'] and sharp, either in speaking or in singing, since we utter with a vigorous breath. The following also happens, as it does with missiles: the ones that are thrown strongly travel to a distance, while those thrown weakly fall nearby. For the air yields more to those travelling strongly, less to those travelling weakly. The same thing will happen to voices too, that a voice travelling under the agency of a strong breath is big and sharp, whereas one travelling under the agency of a weak breath is small [μικρᾷ, 'quiet'] and heavy. We can also see the fact in this most powerful piece of evidence, that when a person utters loudly [lit. 'big'] we can hear them from far away, but when they utter quietly ['small'] we cannot hear them even from nearby.

---

[17] Its authenticity was called in question by W. Burkert, *Lore and Science in Ancient Pythagoreanism* (Cambridge, Mass., 1972), 379 n. 46, but has been defended, with some reservations and qualifications, by A. C. Bowen, 'The Foundations of Early Pythagorean Harmonic Science', *Ancient Philosophy*, 2 (1982), 79–104, and by C. A. Huffman, 'The Authenticity of Archytas fr. 1', *CQ*, NS 35 (1985), 344–8.

It is not surprising, perhaps, that Archytas' pioneering expression of these notions is less than satisfactory as it stands; later writers found in it a number of significant problems which Archytas seems to have overlooked.[18] But the oddest of the passage's apparent shortcomings seems not to arise from an oversight. It is well known that in enunciating his theory of pitch, Archytas fails to disentangle the determinants of pitch from those of volume. He tells us several times that what makes a sound high-pitched is the swiftness, strength, and vigour of the impact causing it and of the movement constituting it; but he also asserts, twice, that a sound whose movements are caused by impacts of that sort is loud as well as high, μεγάλα τε . . . καὶ ὀξεία, whereas one caused by weak or sluggish impacts is quiet as well as low-pitched, μικρᾷ τε καὶ βαρέα. He offers a single recipe for uttering a vocal sound that is simultaneously 'big' and 'sharp'—we do it by uttering with a vigorous breath. The theory seems to imply, then, that a sound which is high is inevitably loud, and one that is low is inevitably quiet; and that seems patently false.

Scholars have been fond of pointing out that this deficiency in Archytas' theory is detected and corrected first by Plato (*Ti.* 67 B–C), and then, more elaborately, by Aristotle (*De an.* 2. 7, 419^{b}4–420^{b}4; *Gen. an.* 5. 7, 786^{b}8–787^{a}23; and elsewhere): the sequence offers a neat example of the way in which science can progress through careful, critical attention paid to problems inherent in an inherited theory. But these scholars seem to have been less inclined to ask why the mistake, if such it is, should have been made in the first place.[19] Archytas was no fool, and this fragment itself (especially in its later parts, not quoted above) shows that he was capable of at least ordinarily acute observation. He cannot possibly have just failed to register the fact that sounds can be both high-pitched and quiet or both low-pitched and loud. Little birds cheeped and thunder roared as much, presumably, in Archytas' Tarentum as in Plato's Athens. What is more, his insistence on coupling the attributes of pitch and volume seems unnecessary as well as perverse. In introducing this passage he claims no more than that he has an explanation of the fact that some sounds present themselves to us as high and others as low, and the rest of the surviving argument is concerned exclusively with high and low pitch, ὀξύτης and βαρύτης. Volume is not introduced as an issue for discussion at all; we merely get these two additional adjectives, 'big' and 'small', attached to 'high' and 'low' in a couple of sentences along the way. In a closing sentence that Porphyry describes as summarizing his whole discussion (συγκεφαλαιοῦται τὸν λόγον, *In Harm.*

[18] See e.g. Arist. *Gen. an.* 5. 7, 786^{b}8–787^{a}23; *Sens.* 7, 448^{a}20 ff.; [Arist.] *Pr.* 11. 3 (899^{a}9–10), 6 (899^{a}22–3), 14 (900^{a}32 ff.), 19–20 (901^{a}20–1), 34 (903^{a}27–8); *De aud.* 803^{a}6–7, where pitch (caused by swiftness) is distinguished from 'hardness' of sound (caused by force).

[19] I have made such observations myself, and been guilty of this omission; see Barker (n. 10), 41 n. 48, 61 n. 68, 81 n. 48. For a more complex account (differing significantly from mine) and further references see Bowen (n. 17), esp. 92–4.

57. 25=47 B 1. 56 DK), Archytas again refers only to ὀξεῖς φθόγγοι and βαρεῖς, 'sharp' and 'heavy' notes, and makes no claims whatever about 'big' and 'small' ones.[20] The offending pair of sentences seem, then, to throw these hostages to fortune needlessly. Archytas is simply not writing about the causation of volume. So why does he insert these adjectives where they could cause nothing but trouble?

We must also give full weight to the fact that the confusion of which he is accused is not extracted from some remote implication of his theoretical position. It is plainly there in the text. Given *that* fact, along with the fact that his explicit association of pitch and volume is evidently not pressed on him willy-nilly by the course of his argument, the reasonable conclusion seems to be that it struck him as altogether natural and harmless. But how could that impression possibly have survived confrontation with the cheeping of chicks and the squeaking of mice?

The answer lies as before, I suggest, in the earlier history of the pivotal words, and especially, once again, in that of ὀξύς. In the fourth-century and later acoustic tradition this word comes to be used of high-pitched sounds regardless of their other features. But I do not think that this is so in earlier literature. A sound that is ὀξύς is not just 'high'. It is *piercing*; it attacks the ear with vigour and force. Though high-pitched sounds can indeed be soft, no writer from Homer to Euripides and his non-technical contemporaries will describe them as ὀξεῖς: that word names an attribute which they simply do not have.[21] The adjective that seems to have struck Greek authors as most appropriate for such sounds, for the voices of children, for instance, is not ὀξύς but λεπτός, 'fine' or 'thin'.[22] Both λεπτός and ὀξύς name attributes which from our perspective are complex. Both imply height of pitch, but λεπτός implies thinness and delicacy in addition, while ὀξύς implies penetration and power.

Now I do not wish to deny that when Archytas wrote this passage he could fairly have been described as setting off to write about pitch, and about nothing else. Musicians had long been able to abstract pitch differences from others; theorists had already gone some distance in their various projects of comparing and quantifying them; and it is likely that the word ὀξύς had already been co-opted as one of the regular terms to designate *simply* high pitch in the context of these researches. But so far as we know these harmonic theorists pursued no investigations into the question that interests Archytas here, the question what pitch *is*, or, more precisely, what exactly the attribute is that the adjective ὀξύς names. When that question *was* asked, the deep resonances of the language inevitably made themselves felt. What pierces our senses cannot be feeble or weak. I suggest, then, that

---

[20] ὅτι μὲν δὴ τοὶ ὀξεῖς φθόγγοι τάχιον κινέονται, οἱ δὲ βαρεῖς βράδιον, φανερὸν ἁμὶν ἐκ πολλῶν γέγονεν.   [21] Cf. n. 5 above.

[22] The attribute is examined at *De aud.* 803[b]18 ff.

this is a case falling squarely under my thesis, that certain oddities in the theories proposed by scientists derive from their sense of the meanings and semantic implications of the inherited terms through which they described, and as it were 'saw', the phenomena.

The two cases I have been discussing are not isolated examples, even if we restrict ourselves to the topic of pitch and the environs of the words ὀξύς and βαρύς. In Peripatetic sources one finds, for example, a number of apparently perverse attempts to replace theories of pitch which referred to speed of movement or frequency of impact with ones representing a sound's pitch in terms of its 'shape'. High-pitched sounds are described as 'pointed', 'acute-angled', or linear and uni-directional, while low-pitched sounds are obtuse-angled, or move on a broad front, or travel all around. Such theories have no apparent scientific advantages comparable to those of the 'speed' hypotheses. They are motivated solely, I think, by an impulse to give a physical interpretation to the implications of the words ὀξύς and βαρύς.[23]

Cases like that provide obvious but rather uninteresting examples of the phenomenon I have been discussing. I want to finish with one that is emphatically neither. Centuries after the period on which we have been focusing, Claudius Ptolemaeus, author of the *Almagest*, wrote his own magnificent work on mathematical harmonics. By way of a preliminary, he sets out to establish that pitch is a quantitative variable, amenable to mathematical treatment, and the long third chapter of book 1 of the *Harmonics* is a highly condensed essay in physical acoustics. Little of the early part of the chapter is original, and as he enters on the passage that deals directly with pitch, any informed reader expects him to offer a version of the 'speed' hypothesis that had served his predecessors so well. The observations from which he starts could easily have been harnessed to that purpose. But the reader is in for a surprise. Ptolemy announces no such theory. We naturally look around for a theory that he *is* offering; and in the past my reading of this chapter has led me to credit him with a new account of his own (though it might be related to ideas current among the Stoics), according to which pitch is correlated with or constituted by the degree of tension imposed on the air by a blow from an agent. That curious but intelligible suggestion I now retract. Though it is not straightforwardly false, it misrepresents what Ptolemy is doing.

He is not primarily concerned, in fact, to offer a physical analysis of what pitch *is* at all, though such an analysis perhaps emerges as a secondary product along the way. His primary concern is simply to establish the credentials of ὀξύτης and βαρύτης as *quantitative* attributes of sounds; and so long as it is agreed that they are indeed quantitative rather than qualitative, other

---

[23] For some examples see [Arist.] *Pr.* 19. 8 (918ᵃ19–21); Theophr. fr. 716. 78–103 FHS&G; cf. *Pr.* 11. 20 (901ᵃ20–9); *De aud.* 800ᵃ2–3; Ptol. *Harm.* 1. 3, p. 7. 10 ff. Düring.

aspects of their nature, in the present context, are of no particular interest to him.

But the route that Ptolemy takes in pursuit of this goal is very curious. He notes first, as a matter of observation, that two attributes of an agent which can cause high pitch, ὀξύτης, in sounds are πυκνότης and λεπτότης, a body's density and its thinness or fineness (*Harm.* 1. 3, p. 7. 23–5 Düring). Evidently we want to know how these attributes are connected with the relevant sort of ὀξύτης; and to explain that, Ptolemy sets off on what looks like a detour. In other domains too, he says—that is, in wholly non-acoustic contexts—λεπτότης and πυκνότης do entail or involve ὀξύτης. What is finer, λεπτότερον, is sharper, ὀξύτερον, because it strikes ἀθρούστερον, more compactly, and so penetrates more quickly; while what is πυκνότερον is ὀξύτερον because it penetrates more, or perhaps 'more vigorously', μᾶλλον; and he offers various concrete examples to convince us that these claims are true (pp. 7. 25–8. 2 Düring).

What Ptolemy seems to have shown so far, then, is that certain features of an agent, its being denser or finer, somehow involve also its being 'sharper', ὀξύτερον, when it goes into action as an agent. Notice that we are still talking about the agent, not the sound caused; nothing has yet been said about ὀξύτης in an acoustic sense. But at this stage Ptolemy seems to feel the need to reduce these two alternative modes of ὀξύτης in the agent to a single, inclusive one. He immediately names it: it is τὸ εὔτονον, 'well-tensedness' or 'high tension' (p. 8. 2–3 Düring). Things are ὀξύτερα, he says, not fundamentally (κυρίως) *qua* denser or thinner but διὰ τὸ εὔτονον, 'because of the well-tensedness'; and he adds an extraordinarily abbreviated, not to say impudent, piece of reasoning to support the claim. It is a fact, he flatly asserts, that things which are denser or finer *are* thereby εὐτονώτερα, more highly tensed; in its impacts what is εὐτονώτερον is σφοδρότερον, more vigorous; and that is ἀθρούστερον, more compact; and that is ὀξύτερον, sharper (p. 8. 3–5 Düring). That is the whole argument.

Ptolemy's commentator, Porphyry, dissects the shortcomings of this bewildering chain of connections with ghoulish enthusiasm (*In Harm.* pp. 50. 13–51. 14 Düring, particularly the final paragraph). But the general strategy is after all clear enough. Ptolemy's remarks are not a summary of the results of scientific experiments designed to establish facts about the constitution of materials, or even reports of a series of observations. They draw attention, rather, to a set of semantic connections between words in the language: when we call an impact 'tense' we thereby implicitly ascribe to it the associated attributes of vigour, compactness, and 'sharpness'. In so far as such distinctions survive the loosely post-Quinean treatment I have been giving them, what Ptolemy has done is to delineate a network of broadly 'conceptual' (rather than 'empirical') linkages between the attribute of εὐτονία, which he takes to be quantitative and in at least some manifestations measurable, and the attribute of ὀξύτης. If something is εὔτονον it thereby *is* ὀξύ in its action—that is, when it goes into action and strikes something else.

But how does an agent's being ὀξύ in this sense establish the thesis— as Ptolemy immediately claims—that the εὐτονία in which this *tangible* (or dynamic) ὀξύτης is implicated is the cause of *acoustic* ὀξύτης in a resulting sound? At one level the answer could hardly be simpler. Ptolemy works more or less consistently in this chapter with a rather naïve theory of causation in general, inherited along with much other material from the Peripatetic treatise *De audibilibus*, according to which the attribute of an effect must be caused by an attribute of exactly the same sort in the agent: rough sounds arise from rough objects, and so on.[24] Hence an agent's εὐτονία can be held responsible for a sound's ὀξύτης only if it can itself be shown somehow to incorporate the attribute of ὀξύτης. That is all well and good, but of course it presupposes that the ὀξύτης of the agent and the ὀξύτης of the sound are indeed the *same* attribute—that whatever it is that constitutes an object's 'sharpness' in its role as an agent also constitutes the 'high pitch' of the sound arising from its action. A good deal of the character of this shared ὀξύτης, as Ptolemy conceives it, can be inferred from the nexus of other concepts in which it is embedded. Being ὀξύς, acoustically as well as tactually, has intimate affinities with being ἀθρόος and σφοδρός and πυκνός and λεπτός, compact and vigorous and dense and fine, and in the last resort is an aspect or mode of being εὔτονος, well-tensioned. It also follows from his position— Ptolemy half-admits this and Porphyry (pp. 51. 4–52. 3 Düring) rubs it in with malicious satisfaction—that any sound caused by a 'highly tensed' agent will derive from it not just one but all of the attributes implicated in being 'tense'; it will not only be ὀξύς but compact and vigorous as well. Plainly the term ὀξύτης is not being used just as a handy label for something perceived independently of linguistic constructions. Ptolemy's conception of it is avowedly dependent on the implications of the *word*, and specifically on its resonances outside the acoustic sphere. As a result, the old poetic associations of acoustic ὀξύτης with piercing penetration are alive and well; and the concept is still as far from behaving as a concept of pure pitch, as we would understand it, as was that of Archytas, five centuries earlier.

The extraordinary manœuvres that Ptolemy goes through in this pas- sage are all the more remarkable for the fact that—like Archytas' alleged mistake—they seem on the face of it quite unnecessary. What Ptolemy wants is a way of representing εὐτονία in the agent as the fundamental cause of high pitch in sound; and he must do so within the constraints of the metathe- ory requiring that cause and effect be identical in character. But locutions involving 'tension' had been used to refer to pitch at least from the time of Pratinas, early in the fifth century. They had been copiously drawn on by Plato in the third and fourth books of the *Republic*, and are exploited by

---

[24] The principle is enunciated at *De aud.* 803ᵇ27 ff; cf. Ptol. *Harm.* 1. 3, p. 7. 5 ff. Düring.

very many writers on music.[25] Describing a high-pitched sound as εὔτονος or σύντονος was never as common as calling it ὀξύς, and calling a low-pitched sound ἀνειμένος, 'relaxed' or 'slack', was never as common as calling it βαρύς, 'heavy', but these alternative metaphors were fully available and comprehensible. Why, then, could Ptolemy not argue, straightforwardly, as follows? The term εὐτονία designates high pitch; so does the term ὀξύτης. Hence in an acoustic setting, regardless of the nuances of the associations transferred with them from their primary contexts, these words are simply alternative labels for the same thing; in effect they are synonyms. Hence we can see at once that there is no obstacle to our treating εὐτονία in the agent as the cause of ὀξύτης in the sound.

But the convolutions of Ptolemy's tortured reasoning make it all too clear that this route was not open to him. He does not and cannot regard εὔτονος and ὀξύς as merely giving differently coded references to the same phenomenon. The attributes the words name are determined by their meanings, and these include everything in the metaphorical penumbra that each carries with it. Since their meanings are different, the attributes they designate are also different, and semantic connections between them have to be laboriously constructed in order to make the causal story admissible. Since so much of the words' significance in acoustic contexts is grounded in metaphor, it is on the specific character and content of these metaphors that the argument that seeks to persuade us of their connections most crucially depends. To rerun a point I used earlier in my discussion of Aristotle, if the Greeks had happened to use a different range of metaphors in their locutions for designating high pitch, an entirely different argument would have been needed; this one would have been merely irrelevant. It is one of the most striking instances I know of argumentation, in a scientific context, which hangs wholly on the assumption that the phenomena *are* what the words of the traditional, pre-scientific language *say* that they are.

[25] See e.g. Pratin. 712(a) Page; Pl. *Resp.* 398 E, 410 D–E, 411 E–412 A; *Leg.* 800 D; Arist. *Pol.* 8. 7. 4 (1341^{b}41), 10–11 (1342^{b}21–3); [Euc.] *Sect. can.* 149. 3 ff.; Aristid. Quint. 6. 28 ff.

3
Ptolemy's Maps as an Introduction to Ancient Science

J. L. BERGGREN

HISTORIANS of mathematics, accustomed to base their studies on the written records of the past, often forget that scientific artefacts other than texts have their stories to tell. Yet such artefacts bear essential witness to the history of science, and, like a text, can be made to tell parts of the history of science that would otherwise have been lost.[1]

Less remarked on is another use of ancient scientific artefacts, namely their pedagogical utility for introducing students to the study of the ancient sciences. This is particularly the case for the ancient exact sciences, even when we have texts that tell the same story, for physical objects incorporating elements of artisanship, or even art, have an attraction for students that geometrical arguments and diagrams of equants and deferents often lack.

I shall illustrate this with a study of the maps associated with the *Geography* of Claudius Ptolemy.[2] I am not concerned here with the much-debated question of whether Ptolemy actually drew maps for his work.[3] Whether he did or not, it cannot be doubted that his work tells how one *should* draw maps. Nor will one doubt, on comparing his instructions in *Geog.* 1. 21–4 on how to draw a map with the maps accompanying the Byzantine and Latin editions of his work, that these maps are, in the main, fair specimens of those that Ptolemy describes.

Of course Ptolemy's *Geography* is also about getting the *data* for map-

---

[1] The value of some supplement to the traditional, textual approach to the history of ancient science is apparent to anyone who considers how many ancient texts have been lost, and books such as D. de Solla Price, *Gears from the Greeks: The Antikythera Mechanism, a Calendar Computer from ca. 80 BC* (*TAPhS*, NS 64. 7; Philadelphia, 1974, and New York, 1975) show what a study of ancient instruments can yield.

[2] This is a common translation of its Greek title, Γεωγραφικὴ ὑφήγησις [*Geographikē huphēgēsis*], which has more accurately been rendered as *The Geographical Guide*. In their translation of the theoretical parts of Ptolemy's work that are not simply tables of localities and their co-ordinates Alexander Jones and the present author suggest that the title may be most accurately rendered as *Guide to Drawing the World Map*: see J. L. Berggren and A. Jones, *Ptolemy's* Geography: *An Annotated Translation of the Theoretical Chapters* (Princeton, 2000; pbk. edn. Princeton, 2001).

[3] For the view that Ptolemy did not publish his work with maps see L. Bagrow, 'The Origins of Ptolemy's Geography', *Geografiska annaler*, 27 (1945), 318–87, and the references contained therein. For the view that he did publish it with maps see O. A. W. Dilke, *Greek and Roman Maps* (Ithaca, NY, 1985), 80.

making, and his text furnishes an important entry-point into the ancient mathematical sciences, for the requirement of gathering accurate data gives him a chance to write about a subject he seldom tires of: the importance of astronomy and mathematical method.

If Ptolemy had had his way, in fact, the treatise would have been much more astronomically based than it is, something he makes abundantly clear. But his astronomical predecessors rather failed him in providing what was necessary to his task, for, as he tells us in *Geog.* 1. 4, only in the work of Hipparchus did he find latitudes of cities, and these few indeed when set against the number he needed. Apart from these few latitudes and some lists of localities situated on the same parallels, his next-best data come from the successors of Hipparchus[4] who listed, on the basis of the winds used in sailing from one place to the next, names of localities that lie on the same meridian.

For the rest, by far the bulk of the places for which he reveals sources, he cites mercantile or military reports, e.g. those of the agents of a Macedonian merchant, Titianus, who travelled the silk routes to China, the account of a certain Diogenes who sailed by the monsoons from the Horn of Africa to India and back, or Julius Maternus' records of marches of Roman legions from Lepcis Magna, near the Mediterranean coast in modern Libya, across the Sahara.[5] As a whole the work exposes the student to the Graeco-Roman world and how a great scientist combined data, often gathered for quite other purposes, with mathematical theory to fashion a work which remained scientifically important for at least 1,400 years.

Now, however, I want to turn to the maps themselves,[6] to show some ways in which they may be used as an introduction to the study of the ancient cosmos. Ptolemy relied on the fact that he and his readers had a common understanding of the cosmos and the place of the *oikoumenē* in it,[7] and as a result an ancient map may be treated as an archaeological site, whose exploration furnishes a student with an entry-point into some of the most common and important scientific ideas of the Greeks and Romans.

[4] Ptolemy does not name them but it is apparent (e.g. from his remarks near the end of *Geog.* 1. 14 on the meridian through the source of the Indus) that they included Marinus of Tyre.

[5] The obscurity of the names cited here is typical of those Ptolemy cites as his sources. Indeed, the only one known to us outside of Ptolemy's work is Hipparchus.

[6] The maps reproduced here are from Codex Urbinas 82 and Codex Vaticanus Latinus 5698 in the edition of J. Fischer, (*Claudii Ptolemaei Geographiae Codex Urbinas Graecus 82 Phototypice Depictus* (Codices e Vaticanis Selecti, 18; Leiden and Leipzig, 1932)). (Unfortunately the colours are not reproduced in Fischer's edition.) However, the points I make in this paper may be equally illustrated by whichever manuscript source one uses for the maps, for they do not differ greatly among themselves. Those wishing to use such maps but who do not have access to Fischer's edition will find satisfactory reproductions in *Claudii Ptolemaei* Cosmographia, *Tabulae* (intr. by Lelio Pagani) (Leicester, 1990), which contains colour reproductions of maps from Cod. Lat. V F. 32 (15th cent.) belonging to the National Library, Naples.

[7] See the remarks near the end of *Geog.* 1. 1 about 'under which parallels of the celestial sphere each of the localities . . . lies'.

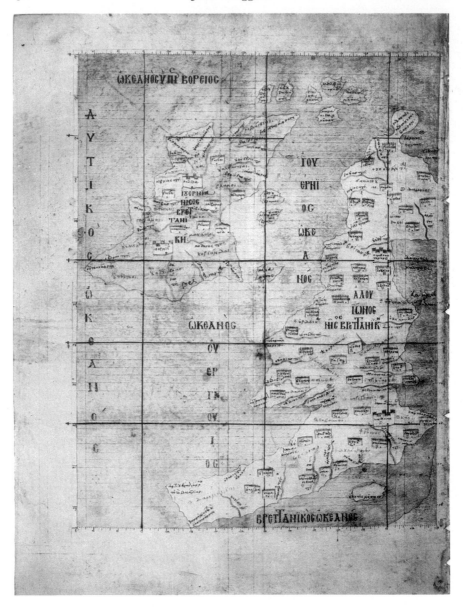

FIG. 3.1. Ptolemy's map of the British Isles (Cod. Urbin. 82)

Figure 3.1 reproduces the western half of the first of Ptolemy's 26 regional maps, that of the British Isles and a bit of the European coast opposite them. One immediately notices the scale of regularly spaced numerals along the western boundary, whose magnitudes correctly suggest that they measure

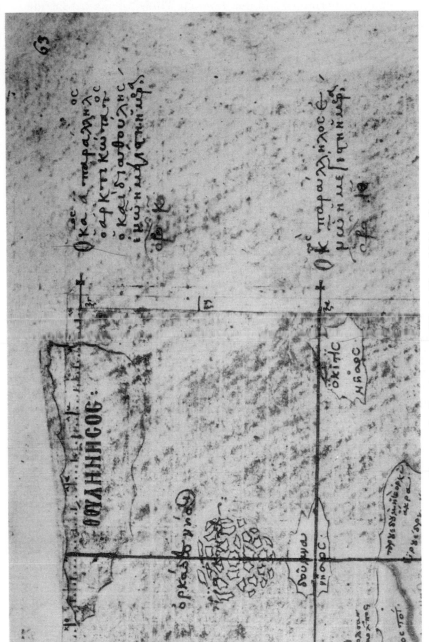

FIG. 3.2. Ptolemy's map of Thule (Cod. Urbin. 82)

latitudes[8]—'the northernmost and that through Thule'[9] being 63° (as the inscription in the north-east corner, shown in Figure 3.2, proclaims). Again, the regular spacing of the scales along the northern and southern edges, and the fact that the numerals assigned to them *increase* from west to east, suggest that they count longitudes *east* of a base meridian. The magnitudes of these numbers (e.g. 7° for the western extremity of Britain) suggest a base meridian somewhere out in the Atlantic, and in fact Ptolemy tells us in *Geog.* 1. 11 that the westernmost limit of his map is the Fortunate Islands, his name for the Canaries. In his earlier work, the *Almagest*, the meridian through Alexandria was 'the meridian for which we establish the times of the positions [of the heavenly bodies]' (*Synt.* 2. 13, p. 188. 14–15 Heiberg) and it was this meridian which he promised to use as reference in a projected geographical work (the *Geography*). When he came to write that work, however, he evidently decided to count longitudes from the western extremity of the *oikoumenē* in order that, as Toomer has suggested, 'all longitudes could be counted in the same direction'.[10]

The organization of a geographic work around latitude (πλάτος) and longitude (μῆκος) is one of Ptolemy's cartographic innovations, as one gathers from his criticism in *Geog.* 1. 18 of the haphazard organization of the map of his immediate predecessor, Marinus, and from his evident need to explain, near the end of *Geog.* 1. 6, why he uses those terms. The concepts of geographic longitude and latitude, as well as the words themselves, are, however, much older, as Aristotle's *Meteorologica* shows (2. 5, 362^{a}32–^{b}30).[11]

A striking feature of these two sets of lines is that the spacing of meridians on the maps of Britain is noticeably less than that of the parallels of latitude spanning the same number of degrees, the reason for the unequal spacing being that Ptolemy, like all Greek writers from the time of Plato on, knew he was representing a spherical earth concentric with a spherical cosmos. In Figure 3.3 one is viewing the slice of the spherical cosmos provided by the meridian circle, ABCD, of one's locality, i.e. the great circle of the celestial sphere that passes through the north and south points (D, B) of one's horizon and is perpendicular to it. The cosmos turns once around the central earth (T) each day, from east to west, on an axis through the celestial poles (N, S) and perpendicular to the plane of the equator (EF).

The curvature of the earth guarantees that representing a portion of its

---

[8] Londonion (London), for example, has latitude 54° on the map (its true latitude being about 51°30').   [9] The Shetland Islands.

[10] G. J. Toomer, *Ptolemy's* Almagest (London, 1984), 130 n. 109. Given that the western half of the *oikoumenē* was much better known than the eastern half, it made sense, if one wanted to count longitudes in one direction, to use the western meridian rather than the eastern one. Toomer (ibid.) also observes that 'a remnant of the original plan survives in *Geography* 7, which includes a summary of time differences from Alexandria to east or west'.

[11] I am indebted to A. Szabó, 'A Battle of Alexander the Great and the "Local Time" in the Ancient Science of the Greek' [sic], in *Ancient Macedonia: Fifth International Symposium* (Thessaloniki, 1993), 1433–8, for this reference.

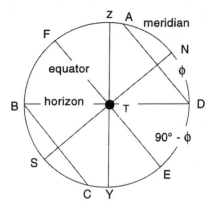

Fig. 3.3. Section of the celestial sphere

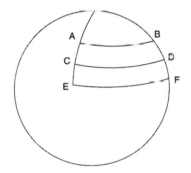

Fig. 3.4. Spacing between meridians

curved surface by a plane does, as Ptolemy puts it, 'require some method',[12] for on the globe the spacing between any two meridians, ACE and BDF in Figure 3.4, decreases as one goes northward from the equator. Hence, for regions some distance north of the equator, using the same spacing between straight lines on a plane for both meridians and parallels would exaggerate distances in the east–west directions, the effect being more pronounced the further north one goes. (For example, even at the latitude of Rhodes, 36°, the distortion would be 25 per cent.) Ptolemy corrects for this in his regional maps by reducing the spacing between the meridians along the whole north–south extent of these maps to what it should be for the parallel in the middle of the region.[13] The main point here, however, is not the mathematics of the stretching of distances in the east–west directions as one proceeds north or

---

[12] *Geog.* 1. 20. All quotations from this work are from Berggren and Jones (n. 2).
[13] Admittedly this solution makes the spacing of the meridians above the central parallel

south of the middle parallel.[14] The point, rather, is that even this relatively superficial excavation has retrieved that fundamental feature of the ancient world-view which Thomas Kuhn[15] called the 'two-sphere theory' of the cosmos, a spherical earth of very small size at the centre of a very much larger spherical cosmos.

With our unearthing of this theory of the cosmos we have opened up a branch of mathematics that is consequent to it and has left its mark on the maps. That theory was known as 'spherics', and its earliest known literary representatives are two works, each bearing the title *Phaenomena*, by Eudoxus of Cnidus and Euclid, and two works (*On the Moving Sphere* and *On Risings and Settings*) by Autolycus.[16] Its purpose was to acquaint the student with geometrically based explanations of the celestial phenomena associated with stars, such as their periods of invisibility and visibility, their risings, settings, and culminations, and the risings and settings of zodiacal signs.

The science of spherics was so much a part of the ancient world-view that, as Taisbak has pointed out,[17] Cleomedes in his work *On the Cyclical Movement of the Heavenly Bodies* 'cites elementary theorems about parallel lines and about similar arcs subtending equal angles—but takes for granted that you know all about items like "great circle", "equator", "horizon", "zodiacal sign", "meridian", and the whole theory of the rotating sphere and the annual movements of the sun'.

It is within the context of the two-sphere theory that geographic latitude becomes an important concept, for one consequence of the sphericity of the earth is that the heavens look different from different latitudes. Indeed, latitude entered early Greek science as the 'elevation of the pole', i.e. the angular distance of the North celestial pole (N in Figure 3.3) from the northern horizon (D), and what Ptolemy literally says in the remark quoted earlier (p. 37) from *Geography* 1 is that Hipparchus found the elevations of the pole for a few localities.

---

rather too great and that below rather too small, but the simplicity of the solution outweighs, for regions of moderate size, the slight distortions.

[14] Distances east–west on a parallel $\Delta\Phi$ degrees north of a mid-parallel, Φ, would be multiplied by the ratio $\cos(\Phi)/\cos(\Phi+\Delta\Phi)$.

[15] T. S. Kuhn, *The Copernican Revolution* (Cambridge, Mass., 1957), *passim*, esp. 25–37.

[16] Eudoxus' work was lost, but survived long enough to form the basis for a poetic version by Aratus. Euclid's *Phaenomena* has been translated and studied in J. L. Berggren and R. S. D. Thomas, *Euclid's* Phaenomena: *A Translation and Study of a Hellenistic Treatise on Spherical Astronomy* (New York and London, 1996). The translation of Autolycus by F. Bruin and A. Vondjidis, *The Books of Autolykos* (Beirut, 1971), is not reliable.

[17] C. M. Taisbak, 'Posidonius Vindicated at all Costs?', *Centaurus*, 18 (1983), 253–69 at 257. For some basic notions of spherics see Berggren and Thomas (n. 16), 19–31, and for the relation of spherics to early Greek astronomy see J. L. Berggren, 'The Relation of Greek Spherics to Early Greek Astronomy', in A. C. Bowen (ed.), *Science and Philosophy in Classical Greece* (Sources and Studies in the History and Philosophy of Classical Science, 2; New York and London, 1991), 227–48.

The connection between local latitude and height of the pole is shown in Figure 3.3, which exhibits the section of the celestial sphere made by an observer's meridian circle, ABCD, where the observer is at T and has Z as the zenith, the point directly overhead. Hence BD is the intersection of the horizon circle and meridian and EF the intersection of the equator and the meridian. TN, the part of the axis of daily rotation of the cosmos that is above the horizon, is perpendicular to EF. Now the latitude, Φ, is the arc of the meridian circle between the observer's zenith and the equator, i.e. arc(FZ). On the other hand, arc(FZ) + arc(ZN) = 90° and arc (ZN) + arc(ND) = 90°. Hence arc(FZ) + arc(ZN) = arc(ZN) + arc(ND), and so arc(FZ) = arc(ND), i.e. Φ = arc(ND), and the latitude is equal to the elevation of the pole.[18]

The celestial circle in Figure 3.3 whose diameter, DA, is parallel to the equator, EF, and which just touches the horizon at its north point, D, was known to the Greeks of Euclid's time as the arctic circle and defined the limit of the always-visible stars, i.e. those stars that, as the cosmos rotated daily, were always above the horizon. The argument of the previous paragraph shows that the angular distance of the circumference of the arctic circle from the pole is Φ, so the size of the arctic circle depends directly on the local latitude. (The greater the latitude the greater the circle until, at the pole, the arctic circle, horizon, and equator coincide and a given star is either always visible or never visible.) Hence the complement of the latitude, 90°−Φ, is exactly the distance from the equator to the arctic circle. So if the angular distance of a northerly star from the equator (its 'declination') exceeds 90°−Φ, the star is always visible at latitude Φ.[19] There are similarly simple criteria determining whether a star is sometimes visible or never visible.

Thus knowledge of the latitude was important because, if one knew it and the distances of stars from the celestial equator, one could determine the appearance of the starry sky at a given locality.

So, the western edge of Ptolemy's regional maps contains one of the principal artefacts of Greek spherics, the latitudes. The western edge of Ptolemy's world map (Figure 3.5) contains another of these artefacts, the characterization of certain parallels of latitude—twenty-one of them are chosen north of the equator—by the maximum length of daylight. At the

---

[18] Since, in Ptolemy's time, there was no star that could function as a pole star this quantity could not be observed directly but had to be calculated either as the mean of the maximum and minimum altitudes of some circumpolar star or (using Ptolemy's table of chords and some trigonometry) from the length of the longest day (as Ptolemy explains in *Synt.* 2. 3, pp. 92. 16–97. 4 Heiberg) or from the ratio of the length of a vertical rod (gnomon) to its shadow on any two of the following three occasions: the summer solstice, the winter solstice, or when the sun is on the equator (the vernal or autumnal equinox).

[19] Hence, to take a non-classical example, since the latitude of Liverpool is 53°25′ and 90−53°25′ = 36°35′, it follows that any star whose declination is greater than 36°35′ is always above the horizon in Liverpool.

FIG. 3.5. Western edge of Ptolemy's world map (Cod. Vat. Lat. 5698)

equator this is twelve hours, and at the northern limit of Ptolemy's *oikoumenē*
it is twenty hours.

The units in which the maximum lengths of daylight are given, the
equinoctial hours, are the equal hours measured by our clocks which we
think of as the 'everyday' hours. However, from long before Ptolemy's time
down to the medieval world, the everyday hours were those which were
one-twelfth of the period of daylight or night and whose length therefore
varied with latitude and the season. For this reason they are called 'seasonal'
hours, and only near the time of the equinoxes did the hours of the day have
the same length as the hours of the night.[20]

Ptolemy could calculate this maximum length of daylight in equinoctial
hours for each latitude on the basis of his table of chords and Menelaus' theorems about the intersection of great-circle arcs on the surface of a sphere.
The calculation is shown in *Almagest* 2. 3, *Synt.* 92. 16–97. 4 Heiberg, but
is hardly suitable for a class of non-mathematicians.

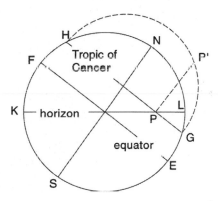

FIG. 3.6. Deriving the maximum length of daylight
from the elevation of the pole: latitude of Liverpool

There is, however, a more direct method of deriving the maximum length
of daylight from the elevation of the pole, according to which (Figures 3.6
and 3.7)[21] one starts with the meridian circle NFSE and draws a line KL
through its centre representing the horizon. One then draws the axis of
daily rotation, NS, at the correct inclination for the local latitude, Φ, so that

[20] As was the case for the maximum length of daylight, the lengths of these seasonal hours
for a given day of the year were calculated, not measured directly. In this case the calculation
(*Synt.* 2. 9, pp. 142. 3–145. 10 Heiberg) was done on the basis of a table of rising times, which
showed how long it takes a given arc of the ecliptic to rise over the local horizon on a given
day. And once this had been done, the calculation of maximum length of daylight would be a
matter of multiplying the length of a seasonal hour on the day of the summer solstice by 12.

[21] In order to show how the result depends on the latitude , I provide the diagram for two
different latitudes, Fig. 3.6 for the latitude of Liverpool and Fig. 3.7 for that of Rome.

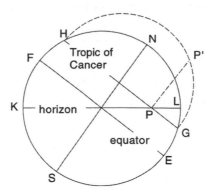

FIG. 3.7. Deriving the maximum length of daylight
from the elevation of the pole: latitude of Rome

arc(NL) = Φ. Then, as Vitruvius explains at 9. 7, one represents the circle
that the sun makes around the heavens on the longest day of the year by a
diameter, namely its intersection with the meridian (GH). The circle is of
course the Tropic of Cancer, which Vitruvius takes as being, nearly enough
for his purposes, 24° above the equator, i.e. one-fifteenth of a full circle. (All
circles referred to so far must be imagined as standing upright on diameters
in the plane of the paper that one is looking at in Figures 3.6 and 3.7, half of
each circle being above the paper and half below.) The tropic intersects the
horizon circle (also standing upright on diameter KL) in a line of which one
sees the end point, the point P, which must be imagined as standing off the
page, between it and the eye. Then one imagines the semicircle of the tropic
above our page rotated around GH, its diameter, down into the plane of the
meridian, to obtain the semicircle GP'H. Since the diameter GH is given,
the rotated semicircle GP'H can easily be constructed. The intersection of
the tropic and horizon rotates onto the meridian plane as the line PP', and
it divides the tropic into a pair of arcs of the same size after rotating as it did
before. PP' is perpendicular to GH, since it arises from the rotation around
GH of a line perpendicular to it, so it is easily constructed. Hence one can
now measure directly arc(HP'), which represents half the visible portion of
the tropic, and the quantity (2 × arc(HP'))/360° multiplied by 24 hours is
equal to the maximum length of daylight.

   In fact, when we look at the western edge of Ptolemy's *world* map in
Figure 3.5, drawn according to the first of the two projections he describes,[22]

---

[22] In modern parlance Ptolemy's first projection is an example of a conical projection, in
which the parallels of latitude are represented by arcs of concentric circles. One imagines a cone
fitted over the globe, its vertex above the north pole, and the surface of the globe is projected
onto the surface of the cone by lines from the centre of the globe. (Ptolemy, however, uses no
such visual image in describing it.) Ptolemy describes the principles of its construction in *Geog.*

we find that the traditional characterization of localities by their maximum
lengths of daylight has entirely superseded Ptolemy's description according
to latitude and longitude evidenced on the regional maps. (Quite apart from
the labels, it is clear from the varying spacing that these cannot be just a
regularly spaced sequence of latitudes.) In the world map, therefore, it is
a net of hours rather than degrees that Ptolemy casts over the *oikoumenē*.
(Even the meridians, though they appear to be based on intervals of 5°,
are in fact described in the text as being spaced at intervals of one-third of
an hour.)

Since, in the Greek view of things, the centre of the earth is the centre
of the cosmos, the Greeks thought of 'down' in the cosmos as 'towards the
centre of the earth' and 'up' as away from the centre. With this understood,
one can imagine each of the circles on the celestial sphere projected onto
a corresponding circle below it on the earth by lines emanating from the
centre. Indeed, Ptolemy refers to localities that we would characterize as
'located on the same parallel' as being 'located *under* the same parallel', and
this mapping of circles of the cosmos onto the earth is an artefact of the
Greek view of the cosmos.

Of special significance among these parallels are the equator ('the circle
of equal days' in Greek) and the two tropics. Because the tropics are astronomically defined as the northern and southern limits of the sun as it travels
along the zodiac each year, those who live between the tropics have signs
of the zodiac passing directly overhead. Consequently, at the times of the
year when the sun is in those signs, it too will be directly overhead. This
gives rise to a rather attractive vignette, located on the eastern edge of the
map shown in Figure 3.8, which shows a detail of the eastern half of the
oikoumenē mapped according to Ptolemy's first projection for a world map.
(Compare Figure 3.5.)

There we see a set of figures representing the signs of the zodiac, paired
according to their distances from the solstices, the sun in each sign and its
rays emanating from it. The northernmost figures lie next to the line for the
parallel of Syene (modern Aswan), which is therefore the Tropic of Cancer.

1. 24, according to which the lengths of the successive meridians, and the angles between them,
are constructed so that these lengths and that of the arc representing the northernmost parallel
are correct relative to the length of the arc representing the equator. In addition, the length
of the parallel through Rhodes is correct relative to the length of the equator. Evidently, the
meridian lines veer towards a common point, the north pole, not shown on the map, and mark
time differences of $\frac{1}{3}$h. The break in direction of these lines at the equator represents Ptolemy's
rough and ready solution to the problem of trying to recreate the effect of the meridians
converging to the south pole. The mathematical analysis, which has been done in fine detail
in H. van Mžik and F. Hopfner, *Theorie und Grundlagen der Darstellenden Erdkunde* (Vienna,
1936), would go rather beyond the interests of most students. An introductory discussion may
be found in O. Neugebauer, *The Exact Sciences in Antiquity*, 2nd edn. (New York, 1969). I
state my own view of Ptolemy's attitude towards the technical problems of cartography in
J. L. Berggren, 'Ptolemy's Maps of Earth and the Heavens: A New Interpretation', *AHES* 43
(1991), 133–44.

FIG. 3.8. Eastern edge of Ptolemy's world map (Cod. Vat. Lat. 5698)

(Notice that the southernmost figure, defining the Tropic of Capricorn, lies south of the southern boundary of the map. Indeed, after a considerable amount of polemic in *Geog.* 1. 7–9 directed at Marinus' use of that tropic as the southern boundary of the *oikoumenē*, Ptolemy concludes that 'it would be best, at this stage of the question' to draw the southern limit not at 23.5° but at approximately 17° south latitude: 1. 10. 1.)

Ptolemy explains the function of these zodiacal figures on the right in *Geog,* 7. 2, where he gives the distance (in degrees) of the sun from the solstice, on the day when the sun passes overhead, for all localities for which the maximum length of daylight lies between 12 hours (the equator) and 13.5 hours (the tropics). A user of the map who wishes to know on which days of the year the sun passes directly overhead in a tropical locality need only consult the right margin to find out which signs the sun is in when it is overhead there. Next to the signs are inscriptions with both the Greek and Egyptian names of the months when the sun is in those signs.[23]

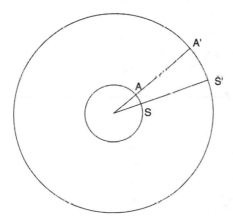

FIG 3 9 Calculating the earth's circumference

If one now looks again at the western half of the world map, in Figure 3.5, one finds written next to the equator the claim that the length of its portion within the *oikoumenē* is 90,000 stades. This implies a value for the circumference of the earth of 180,000 stades, a figure based on what Ptolemy describes in the *Geography* as a hypothesis of Marinus,[24] that a degree of longitude contains 500 stades. If 'stade' refers to the standard Attic stade of 600 Greek feet (606.75 English feet),this gives a circumference of about 20,000 English miles. That the other ancient value, ascribed to Eratosthenes,

---

[23] The Egyptian names are Thot, Phaophi, Hathyr, Choiak, Tybi, Mecheir, Phamenoth, Pharmuthi, Pachon, Payni, Epeiph, and Mesore.

[24] See *Geog.* 1. 7. The figure 180,000 has been ascribed to Posidonius, but Taisbak (n. 17) has argued convincingly that the testimony for this attribution is, at best, inconsistent.

of 250,000 stades is considerably closer to the truth than the first, which is about 20 per cent less than the modern one, is interesting; but, more important for the archaeology of the map is the origin of this artefact in a method which is an elegant example of Greek mathematical sciences and which is sufficiently illustrated by Eratosthenes' simple geometric argument (Figure 3.9), one based on three assumptions about the cities of Alexandria (A) and Syene (B): (a) Alexandria and Syene are, nearly enough, on the same meridian (indeed, Ptolemy's map of Egypt shows the Nile flowing south to north), (b) they are separated by a great-circle arc measuring 5,000 stades, and (c) a great-circle arc in the sky similar to the above measures one-fiftieth of a circle.[25] The circumference of the earth is then 50 × 5,000, namely 250,000, a figure which was later changed to 252,000 so as to be divisible by 60. Eratosthenes' argument, by the way, furnishes a classic example of how one plays off the ability to measure angles in the sky and distances on earth.

Some have suggested that for cartographic purposes the accuracy of Ptolemy's figure is beside the point since in any case the map is simply a scale model of the earth, and whether the scale is one figure or another hardly matters for the purposes of mapping.[26] This would be true had Ptolemy's maps been drawn up by astronomical methods, independent of the size of the earth. However, many of Ptolemy's differences in longitude and latitude are computed by estimating the number of stades between two places and dividing that figure by 500, the number of stades per degree (adjusted, if necessary, for the latitude at which one is working). It follows that a low value for the number of stades per degree will yield a correspondingly high value for the number of degrees of longitude or latitude between two localities, which, in turn, will (among other effects) exaggerate the longitudinal extent of the known world.

In any case, leaving aside the issue of the earth's circumference, we may turn to the other inscriptions along the western edge of the world map (Figure 3.5). We find, as we proceed up the map, that the parallels are numbered but, in contradistinction to the regional maps, not at all equally spaced. In fact, they designate very special parallels, known as *klimata*. They provide a rough grouping of localities by maximum length of daylight, and the very name *klimata* derives from the two-sphere theory, for it refers to the inclination of the polar axis to the horizon, another measure of 'the elevation of the pole'.

As with the equator, so for the parallels. Their lengths too are given. To calculate these from the circumference of 180,000 stades demands the use of Ptolemy's table of chords in a circle as well as some basic arithmetic. Unlike the trigonometric argument needed for computing length of longest

---

[25] This is determined by comparing the shadow cast by a gnomon on the day of the summer solstice at Syene and Alexandria.   [26] See e.g. Taisbak (n. 17).

daylight from latitude and conversely (p. 45), this is not at all complicated and introduces students to the table which, in successive refinements, remained basic to mathematical astronomy from the time of Ptolemy—if not Hipparchus—onwards.

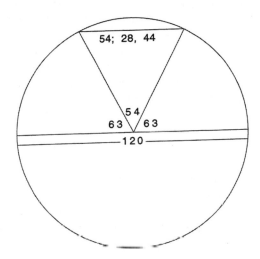

FIG. 3.10. Calculating the circumference of the parallel circle of Thule

For example, the latitude of Thule is 63°, an angle whose complement is 27° (Figure 3.10). The diameter of the parallel circle of Thule[27] therefore subtends a central angle of twice this, 54°, and, in a circle of diameter 120, Crd(54°) = 54;28,44.[28] Since the circumferences of circles are as their diameters this yields the following proportion:

C(Thule)/180,000 = 54;28,44/120.
Thus C(Thule) = 81718.

However, only half of each parallel circle lies within Ptolemy's *oikoumenē*, so he takes half of this figure to obtain 40,859.[29]

This concludes my excavation of the maps, but there remains a basic problem that the maps suggest. How did Ptolemy find out where all those cities, seas, bays, and mountains were? How did he determine their latitudes

[27] The circumference of this circle is denoted below as C(Thule). Also, the notation Crd(54°) refers to the length of the chord subtending a central angle of 54° in a circle of diameter 120 units.

[28] This standard notation for the ancient sexagesimal system is to be read as 54 + 28/60 + 44/3600.

[29] The inscription on the map gives 40,854, a discrepancy for which I can find no obvious explanation. While it is tempting to suppose that it is a simple textual corruption, reading 9 as 4, that would depend on the hand in the source of this map. For example, in the hand of this map one would be more likely to confuse 9 and 5.

and longitudes? For some answers to this question we must turn to the text itself, but before we do we should remark that, whatever Ptolemy's sources, they were literary. There is no evidence that he made any geographical measurements, nor that he had others make them for him. Certainly he makes no claims that he did.

As for the determination of latitudes, the very words of one Greek phrase for the equivalent of latitude, 'the elevation of the pole' (ἔξαρμα τοῦ πόλου), suggest one way it could be measured. However, for the most part Ptolemy could not find such material and was reduced to other measures.

There are, first of all, appeals to astronomical phenomena such as the following, which Ptolemy quotes (as unsuccessful examples) from Marinus in *Geog.* 1. 7:

ἐν γὰρ τῇ διακεκαυμένῃ ζώνῃ ὁ ζῳδιακὸς ὅλος ὑπὲρ αὐτὴν φέρεται· διόπερ ἐν αὐτῇ μετα-βάλλουσιν αἱ σκιαί, καὶ πάντα τὰ ἄστρα δύνει καὶ ἀνατέλλει. μόνη δὲ ἡ μικρὰ ἄρκτος ἄρχεται ὅλη ὑπὲρ γῆν φαίνεσθαι ἐν τοῖς Ὀκήλεως βορειοτέροις σταδίοις [πεντακισχιλίοις] πεντακοσίοις. (1. 7. 4 Nobbe)

. . . in the torrid zone the ecliptic passes overhead so that shadows alternate there,[30] and all the stars set and rise, except for Ursa Minor. The whole of this begins to be always visible when one is 500 stades north of Okelis.

καὶ οἱ μὲν ἀπὸ τῆς Ἰνδικῆς εἰς τὴν Λιμυρικὴν πλέοντες, ὥς φησι Διόδωρος ὁ Σάμιος ἐν τῷ τρίτῳ, ἔχουσι τὸν Ταῦρον μεσουρανοῦντα, καὶ τὴν Πλειάδα κατὰ μέσην τὴν κεραίαν. (1. 7. 6)

The people from India who sail to Limyrike (as Diodorus of Samos says in his third [book]) see Taurus in midheaven and the Pleiades along the middle of the yard.

The extreme of Ptolemy's data for latitudes is indicated by the following passage from 1. 9, where, in discussing the southern limit of the *oikoumenē*, he refers to the evidence that one must often rely on:

αὕτη δέ ἐστιν ἡ κατὰ τὰς ἰδέας καὶ τὰς χρόας τῶν ἐν τοῖς τόποις ζῴων· ἀφ' ἧς—οὐ δὲ μέχρι τοῦ χειμερινοῦ τροπικοῦ—φθάνειν ἀκόλουθόν ἐστι τὸν διὰ τῆς Ἀγίσυμβα χώρας παράλληλον, Αἰθιόπων οὔσης σαφῶς, ἀλλ' ἐγγυτέρω τοῦ ἰσημερινοῦ καταλήγειν. [9] οὐδὲ γὰρ παρ' ἡμῖν ἐν τοῖς ὁμοταγέσι τόποις, τουτέστι τοῖς ὑπὸ τὸν θερινὸν τροπικόν, ἤδη τὰς χρόας ἔχουσιν Αἰθιόπων, οὐδὲ ῥινοκέρωτές εἰσιν ἢ ἐλέφαντες . . . [10] ἐν δὲ τοῖς περὶ Μερόην τόποις ἤδη κατακόρως εἰσὶ μέλανες τὰ χρώματα, καὶ πρώτως Αἰθίοπες ἄκρατοι, καὶ τὸ τῶν ἐλεφάντων καὶ τὸ τῶν παραδοξοτέρων ζῴων γένος ἐπινέμεται. (1. 9. 8–10)

the [evidence] of the forms and colours of the local animals, from which it would follow that the parallel through the country of Agisymba [south of the equator], which clearly belongs to the Aithiopes, is not as far [south] as the winter tropic, but lies nearer the equator. For in the correspondingly situated places on our side [of the

---

[30] By 'alternate' Marinus means 'point sometimes north and sometimes south'. This means that 'the torrid zone' falls within the belt of the globe between the two tropics. In fact, the subsequent statement that only the stars of Ursa Minor are entirely visible within the torrid zone sets the northern limit of this zone at approximately $12\frac{2}{3}°$ degrees north of the equator, i.e. one degree, or 500 stades, north of Okelis.

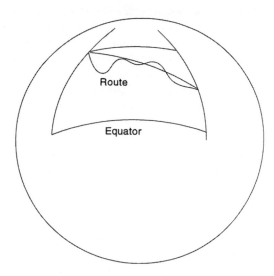

Fig. 3.11. Estimating longitudinal differences

equator], i.e. those on the summer tropic, people do not yet have the colour of the Aithiopes, and there are no rhinoceros and elephants . . . But in places [closer to the equator] around Meroe people are already quite black in colour, and are at last pure Aithiopes, and the habitat of the elephants and more wonderful animals is there.

As for the measurement of longitudes, this was a major problem not only in the ancient world but long afterwards. Ptolemy says that he has, from unnamed sources, lists of cities that lie on the same meridians (i.e. 'are opposite each other'), these based on the direction of sailing-winds. He also mentions a lunar eclipse seen simultaneously at Carthage and Arbela, from which one could calculate the time difference between the two localities.[31] In estimating longitudinal differences—by land or by sea—Ptolemy has a process, which could involve as many as four steps, to which he always adheres (Figure 3.11):

(1) Convert the distance travelled to a straight distance in the same direction by subtracting from it a predetermined, but seemingly arbitrary,
fraction of itself, e.g. one-third.

[31] 1. 4. Arbela, the modern Irbil, in the Kurdish region of Iraq, east of Mosul (36.12° N., 44.01° E.), furnishes an informative test for the quality of data at Ptolemy's disposal for rather well-known places. He lists it in *Geog.* 8. 21. 3 as a famous city of Assyria, perhaps because it was the site of Alexander's victory over Darius III in 331 BC but more likely because it was located on the silk route. In 6. 1. 5 he locates it at 80° E. of the Fortunate Isles. Since Alexandria is given as having longitude 60.5° E., this implies that Arbela is 19.5° E. of Alexandria. Modern values yield about 14.5° for this difference, so Ptolemy places Arbela about 5° too far to the east relative to Alexandria. Clearly not all of Ptolemy's errors in the extent of his known world arise from his notorious overestimate of the length of the Mediterranean.

(2) Correct the distance so obtained for variations in the distances covered daily.

(3) Use an estimate of the direction (in the case of sea voyages one obtained by wind directions)[32] and the trigonometry of a right triangle to convert the distance to an east–west direction.

(4) In converting the above distance to degrees correct for the east–west route's being any significant distance from the equator.

An example of this procedure is the following, from *Geog.* 1. 13. 1–4:

ἀπὸ γὰρ τοῦ μετὰ τὸν Κολχικὸν κόλπον ἀκρωτηρίου, ὃ καλεῖτα Κῶρυ, τὸν Ἀργαρικὸν κόλπον φησὶ διαδέχεσθαι, σταδίων ὄντα μέχρι Κούρουλα πόλεως τρισχιλίων τεσσαράκοντα, καὶ κεῖσθαι τοῦ Κῶρυ τὴν Κούρουλα πόλιν ὡς ἀπὸ βορέου. [2] συνάγοιτ' ἂν οὖν ἡ διαπεραίωσις ὑφαιρουμένου τοῦ τρίτου, κατὰ τὸ ἀκόλουθον τῷ Ἀργαρικῷ κόλπῳ, δισχιλίων τριάκοντα ἔγγιστα σταδίων μετὰ τῆς ἀνωμαλίας τῶν δρόμων. [3] ἐξ ὧν εἰς τὴν συνέχειαν ὑπολογισθέντος ἔτι τοῦ τρίτου καταλειφθήσονται στάδιοι χίλιοι τριακόσιοι πεντήκοντα ἔγγιστα κατὰ τὴν πρὸς βορρᾶν θέσιν. [4] ἧς μεταφορομένης ἐπὶ τὴν τῷ ἰσημερινῷ παράλληλον, καὶ ὡς πρὸς ἀφηλιώτην μειώσει τοῦ ἡμίσεως ἀκολούθως τῇ μεταλαμβανομένῃ γωνίᾳ, ἕξομεν τὴν μεταξὺ τῶν δύο μεσημβρινῶν διάστασιν, τοῦ τε διὰ τοῦ Κῶρυ ἀκρωτηρίου καὶ τοῦ διὰ τῆς Κούρουλα πόλεως, σταδίων μὲν ἑξακοσίων οε, μοίρας δὲ μιᾶς ἔγγιστα καὶ τρίτου, διὰ τὸ τοὺς κατὰ τούτων τῶν τόπων παραλλήλους μηδενὶ ἀξιολόγῳ διαφέρειν τοῦ μεγίστου κύκλου.

Thus [Marinus] says that after the cape marking the end of the Bay of Kolchoi [Gulf of Manar], which is called Kory [the cape at the Pamban Channel], there follows the Bay of Argarou [Palk Strait], which is 3,040 stades, as far as the city of Kouroula; and the city of Kouroula is in the direction of the Boreas [north-north-east] wind from Kory. Hence (1) if a third is subtracted for following the Bay of Argarou, the crossing will amount to approximately 2,030 stades, [apart from] the irregularities of the daily sails. (2) If a third is again subtracted from these [2,030 stades] to get the total distance [corrected for irregularities in sails], approximately 1,350 stades will remain in the direction of the Boreas wind. (3) When this has been transferred to the [circle] parallel to the equator, and to the direction of the Apeliotes [east] wind, by subtracting half in accordance with the subtended angle,[33] we shall get the distance between the two meridians through Cape Kory and the city of Kouroula as 675 stades. (4) Since the parallels through these places do not differ significantly from the great circle [i.e. the equator], this is approximately $1\frac{1}{3}°$.

In summary, I have tried to indicate how an examination of ancient physical artefacts can be combined with the study of ancient texts to introduce important features of ancient science. In particular, I hope to have shown

---

[32] Ptolemy's frequent use of winds as indicators of direction is sufficient evidence that the winds pictured on the medieval maps are not simply quaint vignettes but essential parts of the whole ancient world-view. See e.g. Aristotle's discussion of the names and directions of the winds in *Mete.* 2. 6, 363ᵃ21–365ᵃ15.

[33] The angle between the direction of Boreas and due east is assumed to be 60°.

how a serious examination of ancient maps leads us to the following features of Greek mathematical geography:

- the Greek geometrical model of the cosmos and its companion theory of spherics;
- the measurement of the circumference of the earth;
- the table of chords in a circle and some of its uses;
- the solution of right triangles.

These maps can indeed lead our students to gold.

4

Seismology and Vulcanology in Antiquity?

HARRY M. HINE

1. Introduction

THE modern theory of plate tectonics tells us that the African continental plate has for some millions of years been colliding with the European one in the middle of the Mediterranean. As a result the Graeco-Roman world was well acquainted with widespread seismic activity, and localized volcanic activity. Such activity is regularly mentioned or described in a variety of ancient literature: poetry, history, geography, epistolography, and philosophical and 'scientific' works.[1] The aim of this paper is to begin asking how much coherence these scattered writings have, and whether ancient attempts at rational understanding of these phenomena really qualify as scientific, or indeed as coherent disciplines of any sort. I shall not be attempting a comprehensive answer to what is a large question. After giving some general background, I shall look selectively at four topics: differences between earthquakes and volcanoes in the classical world; the collection of information about earthquakes and volcanoes over long periods of time; the collection of detailed information about individual volcanic and seismic

---

[1] There is a large bibliography, particularly of recent archaeological and scientific works. There are general surveys (not very critical) of ancient scientific ideas on earthquakes and volcanoes in R. J. Forbes, *Studies in Ancient Technology*, vii (Leiden, 1963), 37–60; K. Payne, *Greek Geological Concepts to the Age of Alexander* (diss. Missouri-Columbia, 1990), 131–45, 147–8, 180; and W. Capelle, 'Erdbebenforschung', *RE* suppl. iv (1924), 344–74, is still useful. G. Panessa, *Fonti greche e latine per la storia dell'ambiente e del clima nel mondo greco* (Pubblicazioni della classe di lettere e filosofia, Scuola Normale Superiore, Pisa, 8–9; 1991), i. 155–398, collects descriptions of eruptions and earthquakes in classical authors. M. and R. Higgins, *A Geological Companion to Greece and the Aegean* (London, 1996), describes the volcanoes in the regions that it covers. Other works are mentioned below. I am grateful to participants in the conference, particularly Christopher Tuplin, and to the Press's anonymous reader, for suggesting improvements.

This paper remains substantially as it was written in 1996, although I have made some small changes, thanks to comments from Alwyn Scarth and John Waś. Since 1996 an important study of ancient writing on earthquakes has appeared, G. H. Waldherr, *Erdbeben: Das außergewöhnliche Normale. Zur Rezeption seismischer Aktivitäten in literarischen Quellen vom 4. Jahrhundert v. Chr. bis zum 4. Jahrhundert n. Chr.* (Geographica Historica, 9; Stuttgart, 1997)—see my review in *CR*, NS 49 (1999), 503–5; and ancient ideas on volcanoes are surveyed in H. Sigurdsson, *Melting the Earth: The History of Ideas on Volcanic Eruptions* (New York and Oxford, 1999), esp. pp. 34–70. Both works complement what I have written, though neither asks quite the same questions.

events; and finally, the relationship between theory and observation, and the contribution of the ideas of ordinary people to scientific and philosophical theories.

I have mentioned the wide range of classical literary genres in which earthquakes and volcanoes are discussed. Different writers could have very different motives for writing about these topics. Plainly any earthquake that caused significant damage had personal, social, economic, and political effects, including, for instance, injury, death, anxiety, religious fears, damage to buildings and property, to water supplies, to farmland and communications. Volcanic eruptions might have similar effects. In the aftermath there was scope for, and sometimes expectation of, assistance from rulers and patrons to subjects and clients;[2] religious remedies might be sought from priests,[3] comfort from philosophers;[4] legal issues might arise.[5] Just as societies have their weather lore, so those prone to earthquakes and eruptions have their lore about predicting these events, and the classical world was no exception.[6] Volcanic minerals—including pumice, basalt, tufa—were of economic importance, and quarry men, builders, and traders knew something of their properties, and recognized, in some cases at least, the link with volcanoes.[7] The fertility of the soil formed from volcanic emissions was recognized.[8] Volcanoes then as now were of interest to the tourist trade,[9] and there was a readership for descriptions of these marvels of nature in prose and poetry.

So people in antiquity had many reasons for interest in earthquakes and volcanoes, and the desire of philosophers or students of nature to understand the causes of the phenomena was only one of them.

---

[2] For inscriptional and archaeological evidence of repairs after Italian earthquakes see J.-P. Adam, 'Observations techniques sur les suites du séisme de 62 à Pompeii', and W. Johannowsky, 'Terrae motus: Un' iscrizione nucerina relativa al restauro del teatro', both in C. A. Livadie (ed.), *Tremblements de terre, éruptions volcaniques et vie des hommes dans la Campanie antique* (Naples, 1986), 67–89 and 91–3 respectively. Imperial aid: Strabo 12. 8. 18; Tac. *Ann.* 2. 47, 4. 13. 1.

[3] For example, earthquakes and volcanic eruptions were regularly reported to Rome as prodigies. See below (pp. 64–5) on volcanic eruptions; on earthquakes see A. S. Pease, *Cicero: De Divinatione* (Urbana, Ill., 1920–3), on *Div.* 1. 18 (*se . . . tremefecit*), with bibliography.

[4] For example, both Lucretius (book 6) and Seneca (*Q. Nat.* 6) address the fears caused by these phenomena.

[5] Legal problems arising from earthquake damage are mentioned in *Dig.* 18. 1. 73 pr.; 19. 2. 15. 2; 19. 2. 59; 39. 2. 24. 3–4; 39. 3. 2. 6; 50. 12. 4.

[6] Cf. Cic. *Div.* 1. 112 and Pease (n. 3), ad loc.; Pliny *HN* 2. 196–7 (with J. Beaujeu (ed., trans.), *Pline l'Ancien: Histoire naturelle, livre II* (Paris 1950), ad loc.).

[7] Cf. e.g. Theophr. *Lap.* 19–22; Vitr. 2. 6. 2–3; Pliny *HN* 35. 174–5.

[8] e.g. Strabo 6. 2. 3 =Posidon. fr. 234. References to Posidonius are to L. Edelstein and I. G. Kidd's edition of the fragments (Cambridge, 1972).

[9] Tourists ascending Etna: Strabo 6. 2. 8; Hadrian's ascent of Etna: *SHA Hadr.* 13.3; Seneca suggests that Lucilius might climb Etna: *Ep.* 79. 2 (quoted below, pp. 60–1).

2. Differences between Earthquakes and Volcanoes

Some distinctions need to be made between earthquakes and volcanoes and
their study in antiquity. There was a continuous tradition of writing about
earthquakes in meteorological treatises, in which discussion of earthquakes
was a standard ingredient from at least as early as Aristotle, down to Seneca,
and doubtless in lost meteorological works of Posidonius and others; and the
tradition is reflected in the *Natural History* of the Elder Pliny, and in later
writers.[10] On the other hand, there does not seem to be a continuous tradition of writing about volcanoes, certainly not in surviving works: in Aristotle
there is a brief mention of Hiera, in the Aeolian islands, in the course of
his discussion of earthquakes, but volcanic phenomena are discussed only
incidentally, if at all, in most of the later meteorological tradition. There is
discussion of Etna in Lucretius, of course, and the pseudo-Vergilian *Aetna*
is a substantial poem devoted entirely to description and explanation of the
eruption of Etna, but what sources lay behind it is a matter for conjecture.[11]
There was a lost work of Theophrastus on the lava in Sicily (i.e. on Etna),
but the scope of that work (whether mineralogical or wider) is not known.[12]

An important reason for this disparity in treatment is that, in the classical world, seismic activity was far more widespread geographically than
volcanic activity. Earth tremors and earthquakes were a regular feature of
life in the mainland and islands of Greece and Italy, and in Asia Minor: few
adults in these regions can have been without some experience of at least minor tremors and minor damage. But volcanoes were few and localized, and
activity sometimes apparent only at long intervals. I would argue that the
Greeks had no knowledge of volcanoes until they settled in Magna Graecia.
A simile in Homer has been interpreted in antiquity and in modern times
as a description of a volcano, implying that the knowledge went back much
earlier:

> οἳ δ' ἄρ' ἴσαν ὡς εἴ τε πυρὶ χθὼν πᾶσα νέμοιτο·
> γαῖα δ' ὑπεστενάχιζε Διὶ ὣς τερπικεραύνῳ
> χωομένῳ ὅτε τ' ἀμφὶ Τυφωέϊ γαῖαν ἱμάσσῃ
> εἰν Ἀρίμοις, ὅθι φασὶ Τυφωέος ἔμμεναι εὐνάς·
> ὣς ἄρα τῶν ὑπὸ ποσσὶ μέγα στεναχίζετο γαῖα
> ἐρχομένων· μάλα δ' ὦκα διέπρησσον πεδίοιο.
>
> (*Il.* 2. 780–5)

---

[10] Arist. *Mete.* 2. 7–8, 365ª14–369ª9; Sen. *Q. Nat.* 6; Pliny *HN* 2.191–200; I. G. Kidd,
Posidonius: The Commentary (Cambridge, 1989), on Posidon. frr. 12, 230–3.

[11] Arist. *Mete.* 2. 8, 366ᵇ30–367ª20; Lucr. 6. 639–702. For a judicious discussion of the
sources of *Aetna* see F. R. D. Goodyear, 'The *Aetna*: Thought, Antecedents, and Style',
ANRW II 32. 1 (1984), 344–63.

[12] Listed among Theophrastus' works at Diog. Laert. 5. 49. There are no surviving fragments.

The Achaeans advanced as though the whole earth blazed with fire. And the earth groaned beneath them as beneath the anger of Zeus, who delights in thunder, when he scourges the earth about Typhoeus in Arima, where, they say, is Typhoeus' resting place. So did the earth groan loudly beneath their feet as they went, and very swiftly they advanced across the plain.

Since antiquity many readers have assumed that this passage describes Typhoeus buried under a volcano, and ancient scholars tried to identify Homer's Arima (or Inarime, as it appears in Vergil and later writers) with a specific volcano.[13] However, I think an open-minded reader will see clearly that Typhoeus is not buried beneath a volcano, but is on the surface of the earth being lashed by thunderbolts from above. Similarly, Homer's Hephaestus lives and works on Olympus, not under a volcano, and the Cyclopes are not described as living under volcanoes; nor does Hesiod speak of volcanic activity.[14] The volcanic versions of these myths first emerge in surviving literature in the fifth century, in Pindar on Etna and Ischia (discussed below), and in Thucydides on Hiera in the Lipari islands.[15] Volcanoes remained a western Greek experience until the eruption of Methana on mainland Greece in the third century BC,[16] and the submarine eruptions in the bay of Thera (modern Santorini) in the second century BC and later.[17] So opportunities to witness volcanic activity were rare and localized. Before Vesuvius erupted in AD 79, Etna was the only volcano close enough to major cities to be visible from them.

One ought to ask seriously whether the ancients really had the concept of a volcano at all. There is no word in Greek or Latin corresponding to 'volcano', a name apparently coined by Italian or Portuguese sailors in the fifteenth century.[18] Ancient writers most frequently talk about a specific named volcano—thus Lucretius and the pseudo-Vergilian poem offer explanations of Etna, not of volcanoes in general. Sometimes in prose writers generic terms are used, such as 'outbreathing of fire' or 'burning mountain'.[19] Two things should be noted about such labels. First, they assume that volcanoes involve fire or burning, which is an obvious and, one may say, harmless enough assumption. But in reality it is a potentially misleading one: for it easily leads to the erroneous view that combustion

[13] The form Inarime (based on reading Εἰναρίμοις in Homer as a single word, instead of two, εἰν Ἀρίμοις, 'in Arima') first appears in Verg. *Aen.* 9. 716. For discussion of the location of Arima see Strabo 13. 4. 6; M. L. West, *Hesiod: Theogony* (Oxford 1966), on 304.

[14] See West (n. 13), on 860.

[15] Pind. *Pyth.* 1. 16–28; Thuc. 3. 88. 3. See below, p. 71, on a fragment of Pherecydes that may be earlier than Pindar.

[16] Strabo 1. 3. 18; Ov. *Met.* 15. 296–306; Paus. 2. 34. 1.

[17] Beaujeu (n. 6), on Pliny, *HN* 2. 202; H. M. Hine, *An Edition with Commentary of Seneca Natural Questions Book 2* (New York, 1981; repr. Salem, NH, 1984), on Sen. *Q. Nat.* 2. 26. 4–6.   [18] See the *Oxford English Dictionary* s.v.

[19] See e.g. LSJ s.vv. ἀναφυσάω, ἀναφύσημα, ἀναφυσήσις, ἐκφύσημα; there was a specific word for lava, ῥύαξ. In Latin see e.g. *TLL* ii. 482. 67–81 (*ardeo*), vii/1. 289. 84–290. 8 (*ignis*).

is going on in a volcano, a view reflected in the most prevalent theory of volcanoes, that they are a kind of furnace (see below, p. 69). Second, the range of phenomena that such terms included was wider than our term volcano: thus Pliny the Elder, when he describes the marvels of fire associated with mountains (*HN* 2. 236–8), includes Etna and Hiera, one of the Lipari islands, but between them he sandwiches several locations in Asia Minor and further east where tar or petroleum products came to the earth's surface and burnt spontaneously; and the Aristotelian *Mirabilia* has a similar mix (34–40).[20] Still, the ancients did class together what we call volcanic phenomena, even if they included other things too, and they discussed the causes of truly volcanic phenomena independently of other 'burning' phenomena, so to that extent they had a concept of volcanic activity.

3. Collection of Information over a Period of Time

I start with the beginning of the letter in which Seneca asks Lucilius to investigate Etna:

Expecto epistulas tuas quibus mihi indices circuitus Siciliae totius quid tibi novi ostenderit, et omnia de ipsa Charybdi certiora. Nam Scyllam saxum esse et quidem non terribile navigantibus optime scio: Charybdis an respondeat fabulis perscribi mihi desidero et, si forte observaveris (dignum est autem quod observes), fac nos certiores utrum uno tantum vento agatur in vertices an omnis tempestas aeque mare illud contorqueat, et an verum sit quidquid illo freti turbine abreptum est per multa milia trahi conditum et circa Tauromenitanum litus emergere. [2] Si haec mihi perscripseris, tunc tibi audebo mandare ut in honorem meum Aetnam quoque ascendas, quam consumi et sensim subsidere ex hoc colligunt quidam, quod aliquanto longius navigantibus solebat ostendi. Potest hoc accidere non quia montis altitudo descendit, sed quia ignis evanuit et minus vehemens ac largus effertur, ob eandem causam fumo quoque per diem segniore. Neutrum autem incredibile est, nec montem qui devoretur cotidie minui, nec manere eundem, quia non ipsum ⟨ignis⟩ exest sed in aliqua inferna valle conceptus exaestuat et aliis pascitur, in ipso monte non alimentum habet sed viam. [3] In Lycia regio notissima est (Hephaestion incolae vocant), foratum pluribus locis solum, quod sine ullo nascentium damno ignis innoxius circumit. Laeta itaque regio est et herbida, nihil flammis adurentibus sed tantum vi remissa ac languida refulgentibus. [4] Sed reservemus ista, tunc quaesituri cum tu mihi scripseris quantum ab ipso ore montis nives absint, quas ne aestas quidem solvit; adeo tutae sunt ab igne vicino. Non est autem quod istam curam inputes mihi; morbo enim tuo daturus eras, etiam si nemo mandaret. [5] Quid tibi do ne

[20] Regions that were not volcanically active in the classical period were sometimes thought to have 'fiery' or volcanic origin on the basis of their 'burnt' appearance; for example, Diod. 4. 21 and Strabo 5. 4. 8 present the fiery history of Vesuvius as something to be inferred from its current appearance (contrast the less guarded Vitr. 2. 6. 2); sometimes such inferences were mistaken, as in the case of Strabo 16. 2. 42–4 on the Masada region; for the more complex case of the Katakekaumene region (Strabo 13. 4. 11) see L. Bürchner, 'Katakekaumene (1)', *RE* x (1919), 2462–3.

Aetnam describas in tuo carmine, ne hunc sollemnem omnibus poetis locum adtingas? Quem quominus Ovidius tractaret, nihil obstitit quod iam Vergilius impleverat; ne Severum quidem Cornelium uterque deterruit. Omnibus praeterea feliciter hic locus se dedit, et qui praecesserant non praeripuisse mihi videntur quae dici poterant, sed aperuisse. [6] [Sed] Multum interest utrum ad consumptam materiam an ad subactam accedas: crescit in dies, et inventuris inventa non obstant. Praeterea condicio optima est ultimi: parata verba invenit, quae aliter instructa novam faciem habent. Nec illis manus inicit tamquam alienis; sunt enim publica. [Iurisconsulti negant quicquam publicum usu capi.] [7] Aut ego te non novi aut Aetna tibi salivam movet; iam cupis grande aliquid et par prioribus scribere. Plus enim sperare modestia tibi tua non permittit, quae tanta in te est ut videaris mihi retracturus ingenii tui vires, si vincendi periculum sit: tanta tibi priorum reverentia est. (Sen. *Ep.* 79. 1–7)

I am waiting for letters from you in which you will tell me what new things you have learnt from your round trip of Sicily, and will give a complete and reliable account of Charybdis. For I know perfectly well that Scylla is a rock, and not one that strikes terror into sailors; but I would like a full account of whether Charybdis lives up to the myths, and if you have a chance to examine it (and it is well worth your doing so), let me know whether it is driven into eddies by just one wind, or whether any and every gale turns the sea there into a whirlpool; and whether it is true that everything carried off by that maelstrom is borne along for many miles, out of sight, and surfaces on the beach by Taormina. [2] If you write and tell me that, then I shall be bold enough to instruct you to climb Etna in my honour as well. Some people infer that the mountain is being consumed and gradually subsiding, because it used to be pointed out to people at sea from a rather greater distance than now. The reason could be not that the height of the mountain is diminishing, but that the fire has grown fainter and is emitted with less force and in smaller quantity, that also being the reason why the smoke is less active by day too. Either explanation is credible, both that the mountain is being eaten away and daily getting smaller, and that it stays the same, because the fire does not eat away at the mountain itself, but is produced in some subterranean valley, and wells out from there, the mountain itself providing not its nourishment but its pathway, since it feeds on fuel from elsewhere. [3] In Lycia there is a very famous region (the inhabitants call it Hephaestion); the earth's surface has openings in it at many points, and a harmless fire appears there, without causing any damage to plant life. So the region is fertile and grassy; the flames do not scorch, but just glow with a gentle, feeble force. [4] But let's leave that for further enquiry after you have written to tell me what is the distance between the mountain's mouth and the snows that do not melt even in summer, so safe are they from the nearby fire. But you have no reason to charge me for the trouble of finding out; for you were going to find out for the sake of that weakness of yours, even if nobody instructed you to. [5] What would it take to stop you describing Etna in your poem, and trying your hand at this regular topos of all the poets? Ovid was not the least put off handling it by the fact that Vergil had already exploited it fully; and even the two of them did not deter Cornelius Severus. The topos had a fortunate reception from all of them, and those who came first seem to me not to have pre-empted, but to have revealed, what could be said. [6] It makes a great deal of difference whether you approach a field that has been exhausted or one that has been brought under cultivation: the field expands daily, and past discoveries are no obstacle to those who will make new ones. Besides, the last person is in the best situation: he finds the words all there, and when rearranged they present a new appearance. And he doesn't lay hands on them as though they were somebody else's private property, for they are public. [7] If I know you at all, Etna is making your mouth water; you long to write something grand, a match for your predecessors. Your modesty won't permit you to aim higher; it is so great that it seems to me you would curb the power of your intellect if there were a risk of your surpassing earlier poets, so great is your reverence for them.

This letter is most often discussed with reference to what it says about poetry (5–7), in the vain hope of shedding light on the authorship of *Aetna*.[21] But it is also fascinating for what it says about Etna itself, and it is highly untypical, if not unique, in the surviving literature in this field: normally one gets bald statements of the results of observations after the event, not proposals that an observation should be made in order to help resolve a problem. Here, also, there is implicit recognition that the acquisition of knowledge about Etna is a complex and ongoing process in which numerous people are involved. There is first the report that the mountain is no longer visible from the same distance as it used to be (2). Since the volcano was a tourist marvel and its red glow clearly visible at night, it is plausible that this was a valid observation—but note that Seneca gives no inkling of the timescale involved, whether it is months or years or decades, nor of the exact distances involved (which presumably could be estimated fairly accurately by sailors). Then, second, there are the two rival explanations of the change in visibility (2). Conceivably the second explanation could be Seneca's own speculation, but even if that is the case, there had been discussion about the possibly changing height of Etna, though in what circles, or over what period of time, remains unspecified: Seneca could equally well be referring to Greek treatises (now lost) or dinner conversation among the Roman intelligentsia of Nero's reign. Finally, what of the distance of the snow from the craters? Does Seneca have some data about the distances at earlier periods? He does not say, but without it any information acquired by Lucilius could be of no immediate use, although it might form the starting-point for a future series of measurements. The lack of specific detail might mean that on this occasion[22] Seneca is, as it were, just bluffing, going through the motions of scientific curiosity for literary purposes. Or, more sympathetically, one might suggest that in this highly literary correspondence, written for publication, generic considerations made him disinclined to give precise dates

---

[21] See Goodyear (n. 11).

[22] Elsewhere, in the *Natural Questions*, he discusses such questions in earnest; and there is an established tradition of *problemata* literature (e.g. the Aristotelian *Problemata*), where such questions are often discussed very briefly.

and distances. Be that as it may, we do not know whether anything came of his suggestion to Lucilius, nor indeed how seriously Seneca expected Lucilius or anyone else to take it. In the *Natural Questions*, written around the same time as the letters, Seneca records that Nero had some centurions sent up the Nile to investigate the sources of the river,[23] and presumably Lucilius or Seneca had the resources to send men to investigate Etna if they wanted. But there is no evidence that Seneca ever did such a thing.

Nevertheless, the letter shows a sure sense that the behaviour and appearance of Etna may be changing over time. Collection of information over long periods of time is an important element in the modern study of volcanoes and earthquakes, and it played some part in antiquity. The earliest surviving Presocratic fragment about volcanic activity is an observation by Xenophanes (21 A 48 DK), preserved without broader context, that the fire in Lipara faded for sixteen years but reappeared in the seventeenth. There is no sign of any philosophical writer trying to collect systematic historical data about volcanic activity, but there is mention of a collection of descriptions of earthquakes throughout Greece by Demetrius of Callatis (third century BC), also by Demetrius of Scepsis (third/second century BC), and by others.[24] How comprehensive these lost catalogues were we do not know, but we may expect that the collection and transmission of such data was a rather patchy and haphazard business, because of the familiar difficulties of preserving such information in the ancient world.[25] A simple illustration is provided by surviving ancient discussion of earthquakes on Delos. Pindar is the first witness to a tradition that Delos was, at least initially, free from earthquakes (fr. 33c–d Maehler). Herodotus (6. 98) said that there had been only one earthquake on Delos, in 490 BC; Thucydides (2. 8. 3) agrees there had been only one, but puts it just before the outbreak of the Peloponnesian war in 431. There is certainly a contradiction between Thucydides and Herodotus, though perhaps both earthquakes did take place.[26] According to Callisthenes (124 F 20), there was another in 373. Seneca (*Q. Nat.* 6. 26. 2–3), writing in the early 60s AD, refers to the statements of Pindar, Thucydides, and Callisthenes (but not Herodotus). Pliny (*HN* 4. 66), about a decade later, has a confused account, that Delos had no earthquakes down

---

[23] Sen. *Q. Nat.* 6. 8. 3–4; cf. Pliny *HN* 6. 181, 12. 19.

[24] Demetrius of Callatis, *FGrH* 85 F 6 = Strabo 1. 3. 20; Demetrius of Scepsis ap. Strabo 1. 3. 17. In the latter passage Strabo refers to many writers giving collections of major seismic and volcanic events. It has been conjectured that the former Demetrius was the source of the latter on this topic (E. Schwartz, 'Demetrios (78)', *RE* iv (1901), 2807–13 at 2811).

[25] Cf. J. J. Hall, 'Was Rapid Scientific and Technical Progress Possible in Antiquity?', *Apeiron*, 17 (1983), 1–13.

[26] A. W. Gomme, '"The Greatest War in Greek History"', in id., *Essays in Greek History and Literature* (Oxford, 1937), 116–24 at 122 n. 2, argues that discrepant stories among the inhabitants of Delos lie behind Herodotus and Thucydides. S. Hornblower, *A Commentary on Thucydides*, i (Oxford, 1991), 245–6, thinks there is no factual inconsistency but that Thucydides is 'gently correcting' Herodotus.

to the time of Varro, though Mucianus (Julio-Claudian period) said it had
had two. These passages show the problems for an ancient writer wanting
to discover the seismic history even of so prominent a place as Delos.

There was of course no institutional structure to acquire and preserve
such information in the Greek world—for the efforts of Aristotle's school
did not long outlast Theophrastus, and are not known to have extended to
inventories of earthquakes or eruptions. However, in the Roman world there
was an institution which, by accident, as it were, created a dated list of earthquakes and eruptions over a long period. In Rome prodigies—frightening or
abnormal natural events interpreted as showing divine displeasure—were
reported formally to the Senate, which then decided on the appropriate religious measures to expiate them. Earthquakes and eruptions were counted
as prodigies, and we can see the mechanism by which they were reported in
a passage of Strabo, derived from Posidonius:

Ποσειδώνιος δὲ κατὰ τὴν ἑαυτοῦ μνήμην φησὶ περὶ τροπὰς θερινὰς ἅμα τῇ ἕῳ μεταξὺ
τῆς Ἱερᾶς καὶ τῆς Εὐωνύμου πρὸς ὕψος ἀρθεῖσαν ἐξαίσιον τὴν θάλατταν ὁραθῆναι, καὶ
συμμεῖναί τινα χρόνον ἀναφυσωμένην συνεχῶς, εἶτα παύσασθαι· τοὺς δὲ τολμήσαντας προσ-
πλεῖν, ἰδόντας νεκροὺς ἰχθύας ἐλαυνομένους ὑπὸ τοῦ ῥοῦ καὶ θέρμῃ καὶ δυσωδίᾳ πληγέντας
φυγεῖν, ἓν δὲ τῶν πλοιαρίων τὸ μᾶλλον πλησιάσαν τοὺς μὲν τῶν ἐνόντων ἀποβαλεῖν τοὺς
δ᾽ εἰς Λιπάραν μόλις σῶσαι, τοτὲ μὲν ἔκφρονας γινομένους ὁμοίως τοῖς ἐπιληπτικοῖς τοτὲ
δὲ ἀνατρέχοντας εἰς τοὺς οἰκείους λογισμούς· πολλαῖς δ᾽ ἡμέραις ὕστερον ὁρᾶσθαι πηλὸν
ἐπανθοῦντα τῇ θαλάττῃ, πολλαχοῦ δὲ καὶ φλόγας ἐκπιπτούσας καὶ καπνοὺς καὶ λιγνύας,
ὕστερον δὲ παγῆναι καὶ γενέσθαι τοῖς μυλίαις λίθοις ἐοικότα τὸν πάγον· τὸν δὲ τῆς Σικελίας
στρατηγὸν Τίτον Φλαμίνιον δηλῶσαι τῇ συγκλήτῳ, τὴν δὲ πέμψασαν ἐκθύσασθαι ἔν τε τῷ
νησιδίῳ καὶ ἐν Λιπάραις τοῖς τε καταχθονίοις θεοῖς καὶ τοῖς θαλαττίοις. (Strabo 6. 2. 11 =
Posidon. fr. 227)

Posidonius says that within his own recollection, one morning at daybreak about
the time of the summer solstice, the sea between Hiera and Euonymus was seen
raised to an enormous height, and by a sustained blast remained puffed up for a
considerable time, and then subsided; and when those who were bold enough to
sail up to it saw dead fish driven by the current, and being stricken ill because of
the heat and stench, they took flight; one of the boats, however, approaching more
closely, lost some of its occupants and barely escaped to Lipara with the rest, who
would at times become senseless like epileptics, and then afterwards would recur to
their proper reasoning faculties; and many days later mud was seen forming on the
surface of the sea, and in many places flames, smoke, and murky fire broke forth,
but later the scum hardened and became as hard as mill-stone; and the governor
of Sicily, Titus Flamininus, reported the event to the Senate, and the Senate sent
a deputation to offer propitiatory sacrifices, both in the islet and in Liparae, to the
gods both of the underworld and of the sea. (trans. H. L. Jones (modified))

We see in the final sentence how a report, in this case coming from a
provincial governor, was passed to Rome, from where a delegation was sent
to perform the necessary rituals. It is possible that some or all of the detail
of the eruption given by Strabo goes back to the governor's report, though

this cannot be certain. Such reports, in summary form, are preserved in the annual prodigy lists found in the annalistic historical tradition, represented by Livy, Obsequens, and Orosius. From these historical sources we have records of a number of dated eruptions and earthquakes; and it is noteworthy how these and other Roman writers give us a detailed record of eruptions of Etna and the Lipari islands in the last two centuries BC.[27] However, none of the later scientific works that survive draws systematically on this accumulated information.

4. Descriptions of Specific Earthquakes and Eruptions

One regularly finds mentions and sometimes brief descriptions of specific earthquakes in historical writers, but not so often in the scientific tradition. Aristotle, as we shall see, brings in reference to specific events in the course of his argument, but does not start with any description of earthquakes in general, still less of any specific one. Again Seneca is somewhat unusual: the sixth book of his *Natural Questions* is devoted to earthquakes, and he was writing shortly after a major earthquake in the Pompeii region in AD 62. He starts the book with a brief description, but a selective one: he outlines the different degrees of damage to property in Pompeii, Herculaneum, Nuceria, and Naples; and then adds that a large flock of sheep dropped dead, statues were split, and some people wandered round demented (*Q. Nat.* 6. 1. 1–3). This is all covered very briefly, in less than twenty lines. Right from the start Seneca blends argument with his description, as he remarks that the occurrence of this earthquake in February contradicted the traditional view that earthquakes did not occur in winter (6. 1. 1). Later in the book, in the course of his arguments about causes of earthquakes, he mentions for the first time another feature of the Campanian earthquake, the calm weather that preceded it, something that had been observed in connection with other earthquakes (6. 12. 2); and near the end of the book he returns to the fates of the sheep and statue and offers explanations (6. 27–30).[28] He also adds new details that he has heard at first hand from an old man who was in the bath at the time of the earthquake, and saw the individual pieces of flooring mosaic moving apart

---

[27] On earthquakes see above, n. 3. The following eruptions of Etna and the Lipari islands are recorded between 200 and 50 BC: 183 BC Vulcano (Livy 39. 56. 6; Pliny *HN* 2. 203; Obs. 4; Oros. 4. 20. 30, Cassiod. *Var.* 3. 47); 140 BC Etna (Obs. 23); 135 BC Etna (Obs. 26; Oros. 5. 6. 2); 126 BC Etna (Obs. 29; Oros. 5. 10. 11); 125 BC Vulcano (Posidon. fr. 227 = Strabo 6. 2. 11; Pliny *HN* 2. 203; Obs. 29; Oros. 5. 10. 11); 122–1 BC Etna (Obs. 32; Oros. 5. 13. 3); 91 BC Ischia (Obs. 54). R. B. Stothers and M. R. Rampino, 'Volcanic Eruptions in the Mediterranean before AD 630 from Written and Archaeological Sources', *Journal of Geophysical Research*, 88 (1983), 6357–71, provide a fuller catalogue, including those of the second half of the 1st cent. BC—but these eruptions were not necessarily recorded via the prodigy lists.

[28] Interestingly, the plural statues of 6. 1. 3 have become singular at 6. 30. 1.

and then together again, squeezing out the water from between them (6. 31. 3). Seneca gives no suggestion that he himself was in the worst affected region during the eruption, nor, it seems, did he make any systematic attempt to collect eyewitness accounts, relying instead on information that came his way. He does not seem concerned to give a full and detailed account of the eruption, but merely highlights unusual and sensational features.

Since earthquakes were fairly regular events, it is not altogether surprising that they did not attract detailed first-hand accounts, even when on the scale of the Campanian eruption of AD 62. A major eruption was far less frequent, and might be expected to receive detailed description, and of course there is the long and, in part, eyewitness account of the Vesuvius eruption of AD 79 left by the younger Pliny in two of his letters (6. 16, 6. 20). These letters are justly famous—indeed, I suspect that today they are the most widely disseminated works of classical Latin prose literature, since excerpts feature in virtually any textbook on volcanoes. But in the broader context of what we know of ancient vulcanological writing his letters are an exception, and their very existence a lucky accident. For they were written down some 27 or 28 years after the event,[29] and then at the request of his historian friend Tacitus, not for a description of the eruption, but for an account of the death of his uncle, the elder Pliny. In the first of the two letters the eruption is described as the context for the uncle's last days. At the end of the letter Pliny makes to return to his own experiences with his mother at Misenum, but breaks off saying 'but that has nothing to do with history' (*sed nihil ad historiam*, 6. 16. 21); in the later letter we gather that Tacitus has nevertheless asked to hear about their experiences. Taken together, the two letters give a remarkably detailed account of the eruption, much of which can be confirmed and complemented by recent archaeological and scientific discoveries.[30] Yet it had never occurred to the younger Pliny at the time of the eruption that it would be interesting to give the world a detailed and well-written first-hand account of the event—nor, so far as we know, did it occur to anyone else. There is a short poem by Martial about the damage caused by the eruption and some reference in Statius, and Statius' father composed what was probably a lament for the destruction

---

[29] On the date of composition of book 6 of the letters, AD 106–7, see A. N. Sherwin-White, *The Letters of Pliny: A Historical and Social Commentary* (Oxford, 1966), 36–7. There is a recent discussion of the letters in M. Gigante, *Il fungo sul Vesuvio secondo Plinio il Giovane* (Rome, 1989). There is an excellent treatment of Vesuvius in antiquity in E. Renna, *Vesuvius Mons: Aspetti del Vesuvio nel mondo antico, tra filologia, archeologia, vulcanologia* (Naples, 1992).

[30] See H. Sigurdsson, S. Cashdollar, and S. R. J. Sparks, 'The Eruption of Vesuvius in AD 79: Reconstruction from Historical and Volcanological Evidence', *AJA* 86 (1982), 39–51; H. Sigurdsson, S. Carey, W. Cornell, and T. Pescatore, 'The Eruption of Vesuvius in A.D. 79', *National Geographic Research*, 1/3 (1985), 332–87.

of Pompeii.[31] Cassius Dio's account of the eruption (66. 21–3) certainly contains authentic information that cannot go back to Pliny (for instance, he mentions the initial explosion that threw huge rocks into the air, notes the spread of ash as far as Africa, Syria, and Egypt, and records sensational stories of giants roaming the region, which could go back to contemporary accounts by terrified eyewitnesses), but we do not know what his immediate sources were, nor whether his ultimate sources included first-hand accounts written down by eyewitnesses.

In the modern world eruptions are attended by television crews and photographers and followed up by lavishly illustrated magazine articles and the like, so we have to make an effort to imagine a society which did not do anything comparable. Of course there were practical problems. The eruption of AD 79 was exceptional in scale, fewer people would be close to more modest eruptions, and individual eyewitnesses, who are often confused and frightened, always get a very incomplete impression of what is going on. Significantly, some of the most precise descriptions of individual eruptions are of submarine eruptions in the Lipari or Santorini areas.[32] These, because of their location, stood a good chance of being seen by sailors from the nearby islands, and by their nature they could be observed at close quarters with less risk than terrestrial eruptions. All the same, such considerations do not fully account for the apparent paucity of detailed descriptions of Vesuvius until long after the event; and some of Etna's activity must have been accessible to literate observers.

The paucity of detailed ancient descriptions of earthquakes and eruptions is, I suggest, a literary phenomenon: no one had yet thought of writing such a thing. One should compare the virtual absence from ancient literature of other literary forms that we now take for granted: personal diaries, detailed personal (as opposed to political) autobiography, detailed and sober travel journals—these were non-existent or merely embryonic in the ancient world, for whatever reasons. In the case of earthquakes and volcanoes, the advent of printing and especially of printed illustrations made a vital difference to the practicability, impact, and usefulness of detailed description. To see the difference, one only has to compare Strabo's careful but rather elusive treatment of the shape of Etna's summit as perceived by different visitors with, say, the sketches of the summit of Vesuvius at regular intervals of time published by Sir William Hamilton in the eighteenth century.[33] But that is not the whole story. In the late fifteenth century the future Cardinal Bembo published a classicizing Latin dialogue on Etna, which, besides

---

[31] Mart. 4. 44; Stat. *Silv.* 3. 5. 72–4; 4.4. 78–86; 5. 3. 203–8 (on Statius' father); cf. 2. 6. 61–2; 4. 8. 5; 5. 3. 104–6.

[32] See Strabo 6. 2. 11, quoted above; Sen. *Q. Nat.* 2. 26. 4–6 (with Hine (n. 17), ad loc.).

[33] Strabo 6. 2. 8; Sir William Hamilton, *Campi Phlegraei* (Naples, 1776), and *Supplement to the Campi Phlegraei* (Naples, 1779).

containing speculation about the causes of earthquakes, and literary quotation and allusion, also describes in some detail an ascent of the mountain
recently made by the young Bembo: there are no technical reasons why
such an account could not have been written in antiquity, yet nothing like
it survives or is known to have been written.[34]

That said, it should be added that direct experience or detailed description of earthquakes will never itself help much towards understanding how
they happen: the ground shakes, sometimes cracks and gapes, there is loud
noise, water supplies may be altered—the effects of the damage are visible
enough, but they do not give much of a clue to the causes. The African and
European continental plates meet under the Mediterranean, and there was
no prominent visual evidence of major fault lines on the earth's surface such
as one gets, for example, along the San Andreas fault in California, or in
the aftermath of the Kobe earthquake in Japan. Progress in understanding
earthquakes in recent times accelerated when data about the distribution of
seismic and volcanic activity were collected over an area much larger than
the Mediterranean.

5. The Causes of Earthquakes and Volcanoes

From an early date Greek thinkers sought physical as opposed to religious explanations for earthquakes, and, from a later date, sought them
for volcanoes too. In those writers who offer rational explanation, observations are often described piecemeal and unsystematically in support of
theoretical exposition and argument. Aristotle does not treat the collection
of observational information as an end in itself, but rather brings in particular information at points where it suits his argument. His method in
the *Meteorologica* has recently been investigated by Freeland.[35] In 2. 7–
8, 365ª14–369ª9, he begins characteristically by reviewing the theories of
predecessors, Anaxagoras, Anaximenes, and Democritus. In the course of
rebutting Anaxagoras' theory, Aristotle says that it does not account 'for any
of the peculiar features of earthquakes, which do not occur in any district or
at any time indiscriminately' (2. 7, 365ª34–5). However he does not explain
the nature of the distribution of earthquake occurrence either here or later,
but simply assumes it is known. Later, in support of his own theory that
earthquakes are caused by wind or *pneuma*, he brings in the facts that most
(though not all) occur in calm weather, those which occur in windy weather
are less violent, and the most frequent times of day are during the hours of
darkness or around midday (2. 8, 366ª5–6, 13–18). Here my point is not that

---

[34] *Petri Bembi de Aetna ad Angelum Chabrielem Liber* (Venice, 1495).

[35] C. A. Freeland, 'Scientific Explanation and Empirical Data in Aristotle's *Meteorology*',
OSAP 8 (1990), 67–102.

these alleged facts about earthquakes are untrue, but that Aristotle never collects together all the facts that any adequate theory must explain. This habit is bequeathed to later writers, and their neglect of detailed description of phenomena for its own sake may help to explain the lack of detailed accounts of particular events that was discussed above.

In broad outline the prevalent ancient theories of earthquakes and volcanoes were as follows. Earthquakes, after Aristotle (who was in part anticipated by Archelaus, 60 A 16a DK), were usually explained by the action of wind or *pneuma* underground, though there were various other theories too: Seneca, in *Q. Nat.* 6, for example, systematically reviews theories that they are caused by water, or fire, or earth, or air, or a combination of these.[36] For volcanoes, there were originally two theories, one represented in mythological guise in Plato's *Phaedo* (111 D–E, 113 B), that they come from huge, everlasting underground rivers of fire and mud (this of course invites guarded comparison with the role of magma in modern theory), the other, which dominates later literature, that volcanoes are like great furnaces, where flammable materials are ignited often by the force of wind, and are thus local phenomena, not necessarily linked to a common source.[37]

When trying to identify the authors of the various explanations of earthquakes and volcanoes, one finds a distinction: theories of earthquakes are transmitted to us with tidy doxographic labels attributing them to particular philosophers, but volcanic theories come to us anonymously. This reflects the fact, already noted, that earthquakes were an established topic in meteorological literature from early on, and volcanoes were not—thus earthquakes get two chapters in Aristotle's *Meteorologica* (2. 9, 3. 1), a whole book of Seneca's *Natural Questions* (book 6), and a chapter of Aetius' doxographical work (*Placita* 3. 15), but none of these authors devotes the same attention to volcanoes. Our main sources for theories of volcanoes are not philosophical, but poets, a historian, and late antique scholars (see n. 37). This has naturally inspired a lot of source-hunting in the past, with Posidonius a favourite contender as the source of the ideas of the pseudo-Vergilian *Aetna*.[38]

However, I think we must not simply try to fill the gaps in the history of the philosophical or scientific tradition, but we should also recognize that the information from which the philosophers started already carried with it speculative assumptions. Let us take what is the earliest proper description of an eruption, in a poem of Pindar, writing in the late 470s BC:

. . . Τυφὼς ἑκατοντακάρανος· τόν ποτε
Κιλίκιον θρέψεν πολυώνυμον ἄντρον· νῦν γε μὰν

---

[36] See further Capelle (n. 1), 362–74. Later wind- or *pneuma*-theories simplify Aristotle's view that the *pneuma* in question is formed from *anathumiasis* (exhalation).

[37] e.g. Lucr. 6. 639–702; the *Aetna*; Just. 4. 1; Servius ad *Aen.* 3. 571; Isid. 14. 8. 14.

[38] See e.g. S. Sudhaus's edition of the *Aetna* (Leipzig, 1898); but, for a more cautious recent discussion, Goodyear (n. 11).

ταί θ' ὑπὲρ Κύμας ἁλιερκέες ὄχθαι
Σικελία τ' αὐτοῦ πιέζει
στέρνα λαχνάεντα· κίων δ' οὐρανία συνέχει,
νιφόεσσ' Αἴτνα, πανέτης
χιόνος ὀξείας τιθήνα·

τᾶς ἐρεύγονται μὲν ἀπλάτου πυρὸς ἁγνόταται
ἐκ μυχῶν παγαί· ποταμοὶ δ' ἀμέραισιν
        μὲν προχέοντι ῥόον καπνοῦ
αἴθων'· ἀλλ' ἐν ὄρφναισιν πέτρας
φοίνισσα κυλινδομένα φλὸξ ἐς βαθεῖ-
        αν φέρει πόντου πλάκα σὺν πατάγῳ.
κεῖνο δ' Ἁφαίστοιο κρουνοὺς ἑρπετὸν
δεινοτάτους ἀναπέμπει· τέρας μὲν
        θαυμάσιον προσιδέσθαι,
        θαῦμα δὲ καὶ παρεόντων ἀκοῦσαι,

οἷον Αἴτνας ἐν μελαμφύλλοις δέδεται κορυφαῖς
καὶ πέδῳ, στρωμνὰ δὲ χαράσσοισ' ἅπαν νῶ-
        τον ποτικεκλιμένον κεντεῖ.
                              (Pind. *Pyth.* 1. 16–28)

. . . Typhoeus with his hundred heads, who was nurtured of old by the far-famed Cilician cave; though now the sea-fenced heights off[39] Cyme, and Sicily too, lie heavy on his shaggy breast, and the column that soars to heaven crushes him, even snow-clad Etna, who all the year long nurses her keen snow—Etna, from whose inmost caves burst forth the purest founts of unapproachable fire; in the daytime her rivers roll a lurid stream of smoke, while amid the gloom of night the ruddy flame, as it sweeps along, with crashing din whirls rocks to the deep sea far below. And that monster flings aloft the most fearful founts of fire, a wondrous marvel to behold, a wonder even to hear of from those who were there; such a being is he who lies bound beneath those dark-leaved heights and the plain, while all his out-stretched back is goaded by his craggy couch. (trans. J. E. Sandys (modified))

This, it was argued above, is our earliest non-fragmentary reference to a volcanic eruption. It is cast in mythological terms, the volcanic activity being caused by the struggles of the imprisoned Typhoeus, but at the same time the mythology is blended with physical description. One should observe some of the assumptions inherent in the passage. First, there is an assumption that volcanoes produce fire, something already commented on (above, pp. 59–60). Second, when one contrasts the story of the menacing Typhoeus under Etna with the story of Hephaestus having his forge under Hiera in the Lipari islands (first found in Thuc. 3. 88. 3), one wonders whether the rival myths embody perceptions of different levels of volcanic

---

[39] I take the reference to be to Ischia, with ὑπέρ meaning 'offshore from' (cf. LSJ s.v. A.I.1b, of ships at sea). Some translators take it to mean 'above' or 'behind, inland from', referring to the Phlegraean Plains or even Vesuvius, but ἁλιερκέες, 'sea-fenced', is more appropriate to the rocky island of Ischia than to the Phlegraean Plains or Vesuvius. (Elsewhere Pindar applies it to Aegina (*Ol.* 8. 25) and the Isthmus (*Isthm.* 1. 9).)

activity: is the essentially benign, though awesome, figure of Hephaestus, constantly at work, a picture of the activity characteristic of Hiera—noisy, explosive, but localized and not causing much damage—while the violent Typhoeus, occasionally attempting jailbreaks, is a mirror of the activity of the periodically more destructive Etna? If such a distinction is implied, it was not followed up by later writers, and in fact ancient sources never comment systematically on the diversity of activity in the Mediterranean volcanoes.[40] Third, notice the distinction between daytime and night-time activity, smoke and fire. On the face of it Pindar is saying the volcano does something different by day and by night—but of course this is simply a difference in what is visible, not a substantive difference. This distinction becomes a regular topos in later writers; one may suspect or hope that some of them are aware that this is a distinction of appearance, not of substance, but they never say so; on the other hand, no surviving text attempts to explain the difference between night and day as though it were substantive.[41]

Fourth, and very interestingly, Pindar's Typhoeus is pressed down not just by Etna but by the heights off Cyme. I take this to refer to Ischia (n. 39 above), but even if it refers to the Phlegraean Plains or Vesuvius it does not affect my main point, which is that Pindar, on a literal-minded reading, makes Typhoeus an uncommonly large monster, well over 300 km. in extent. Of course, this is not beyond the reach of the poet's imagination, but Strabo (5. 4. 9), quoting the passage, thinks it refers to the postulate of an underground link between Etna and the Naples region, embracing the Lipari islands too. Is this a correct interpretation of Pindar (except that he does not himself bring in the Lipari islands)? And if so, is the link between Ischia and Etna Pindar's invention, or is he referring to an already existing belief? We must recognize that he has a political motive for including Ischia, because the ode celebrates Hieron, who had founded the new town of Etna, in the Etna region, and had recently won a sea battle near Cumae. The mention of Cumae in this context must allude to the battle—contrast *Ol.* 4. 8–9, where Pindar again refers to Typhoeus under Etna, but there is no mention of the Cumae region. So could Pindar have invented the link between Typhoeus and Ischia for the sake of the political point? The story that Typhon (equivalent to Typhoeus) was buried under Ischia is attributed to Pherecydes, and if this were the sixth-century Pherecydes of Syros rather than the fifth-century Pherecydes of Athens, we should have evidence pre-dating Pindar. But the attribution is disputed, and cannot be decided on available evidence.[42] In any case,

---

[40] Modern textbooks sometimes still use the labels Strombolian, Volcanian, and Vesuvian for different types of eruptions, a classification that was developed in the late 19th cent. and has no ancient precedent. There were, however, classifications of types of earthquake, comet, lightning, and other phenomena in ancient meteorology.

[41] For the daytime/night-time distinction see Hine (n. 17) on Sen. *Q. Nat.* 2. 26. 4.

[42] The fragment is in the scholia on Ap. Rhod. 2. 1210. Jacoby attributed it to Pherecydes

however, it is entirely conceivable that such a tradition already existed, and that Pindar was elegantly combining two different versions: his audience will not perhaps have been much worried by the issue of geographical plausibility.

That hypothesis is possible, but the very brevity of Pindar's allusion to the Cumae region leads me to suspect that he is not coming up with a totally new idea here, but alluding to a current belief that there was a link between Etna and Ischia.[43] Where and when might such a belief have originated? It is tempting to speculate about a Presocratic philosophical source. Xenophanes is a possibility, because we have already seen that he took an interest in the volcanic activity and inactivity of Lipara; and he observed fossils and deduced that there had been changes in the boundaries between sea and land in the past (21 A 33 DK). However, a Presocratic philosopher is not the only possibility: academics have to guard against the occupational hazard of assuming that only fellow professionals can have good ideas. I believe it is possible that local inhabitants or sailors came up with the idea, which is comparable to the popular idea that the river Alpheus disappeared underground in the Peloponnese and reappeared as the spring Arethusa near Syracuse in Sicily, or that the Asopus came from Phrygia. Such beliefs are not normally thought to require a philosophical pedigree.[44]

Another topic where there seems to be interesting but perplexing interplay between the thinking of ordinary people and philosophical theory is the role of wind in earthquakes and eruptions. Aristotle's exposition (*Mete.* 2. 8, $365^b21–369^a9$) derives the theory that *pneuma* is the cause of earthquakes by argument based on a priori principles: wind must be created within the earth by the action of heat on the moisture in it, and since wind is the most violent and penetrating force there is, it must cause earthquakes. He then brings in facts to back up the argument: that the majority of earthquakes occur in calm weather, though they can occur in windy weather too; that they mostly occur at night or around midday, in spring and autumn, etc.

---

of Athens (*FGrH* 3 F 54, with commentary), and Diels–Kranz do not attribute it to Pherecydes of Syros (7 DK), but the earlier Pherecydes was advocated by U. von Wilamowitz, 'Pherekydes', *Sitzungsberichte der preußischen Akademie der Wissenschaften*, phil.-hist. Klasse (1926), 125–46 at 129 = *Kleine Schriften*, v/2 (Berlin, 1937), 127–56 at 133. R. L. Fowler, *Early Greek Mythography*, i (Oxford, 2000), now firmly attributes it to Pherecydes of Athens (fr. 54).

[43] Such a belief is implied later by Plato when he talks of the underworld river of fire emerging at various points on the earth's surface (*Phd.* 113 B). He names no particular volcanoes, but only Etna, the Lipari islands, and Ischia were active in his lifetime.

[44] Alpheus: Ibyc. fr. 323; Pind. *Nem.* 1. 1–4; cf. C. Hülsen, 'Arethusa (11)', *RE* ii (1896), 680; J. Barron, 'Ibycus: Gorgias and Other Paeans', *BICS* 31 (1984), 13–24 at 22. Asopus: Ibyc. fr. 322. More generally: Strabo 6. 2. 4; Paus. 2. 5. 3–4. Some less extravagant claims about Arcadian streams reappearing in or off the shore of the Argolid have been scientifically confirmed: W. K. Pritchett, *Studies in Ancient Greek Topography*, i (Berkeley, 1965), 123, 132–3.

Though not true, such generalizations are widespread in other periods and places, and were doubtless part of popular belief.[45]

To support his argument, Aristotle gives specific detail of an eruption on one of the Lipari islands, Hiera:

σημεῖα δὲ τούτων καὶ πρὸς τὴν ἡμετέραν αἴσθησιν πολλαχῇ γέγονεν· ἤδη γὰρ σεισμὸς ἐν τόποις τισὶν γιγνόμενος οὐ πρότερον ἔληξε πρὶν ἐκρήξας εἰς τὸν ὑπὲρ τῆς γῆς τόπον φανερῶς ὥσπερ ἐκνεφίας ἐξῆλθεν ὁ κινήσας ἄνεμος, οἷον καὶ περὶ Ἡράκλειαν ἐγένετο τὴν ἐν τῷ Πόντῳ νεωστί, καὶ πρότερον περὶ τὴν Ἱερὰν νῆσον (αὕτη δ᾿ ἐστὶν μία τῶν Αἰόλου καλουμένων νήσων)· ἐν ταύτῃ γὰρ ἀνῴδει τι τῆς γῆς, καὶ ἀνῄει οἷον λοφώδης ὄγκος μετὰ ψόφου· τέλος δὲ ῥαγέντος ἐξῆλθεν πνεῦμα πολὺ καὶ τὸν φέψαλον καὶ τὴν τέφραν ἀνῆκεν καὶ τήν τε Λιπαραίων πόλιν οὖσαν οὐ πόρρω πᾶσαν κατετέφρωσε καὶ εἰς ἐνίας τῶν ἐν Ἰταλίᾳ πόλεων ἦλθεν· καὶ νῦν ὅπου τὸ ἀναφύσημα τοῦτο ἐγένετο, δῆλόν ἐστιν. καὶ γὰρ δὴ τοῦ γιγνομένου πυρὸς ἐν τῇ γῇ ταύτην οἰητέον εἶναι τὴν αἰτίαν, ὅταν κοπτόμενον ἐκπρησθῇ πρῶτον εἰς μικρὰ κερματισθέντος τοῦ ἀέρος. (*Mete.* 2. 8, 366^{b}30–367^{a}11)

As evidence [that earthquakes are caused by wind] we may cite occurrences which have been observed in many places. For in some places there has been an earthquake which has not ceased until the wind which was its motive force has broken out like a hurricane and risen into the upper region. This happened recently, for instance, in Heracleia in Pontus, and before that in Hiera, one of the so-called Aeolian islands. For in this island part of the earth swelled up and rose with a noise in a crest-shaped lump; this finally burst and a large quantity of wind broke out, blowing up cinders and ash which smothered the neighbouring city of Lipara, and even reached as far as some of the cities in Italy. The place where this eruption took place can still be seen. (This too must be regarded as the cause of the fire that there is in the earth; for when the air is broken up into small particles, percussion then causes it to catch fire.) (trans. H. D. P. Lee (modified))

Aristotle then proceeds to describe a correlation between atmospheric winds and eruptive activity in the Lipari islands:

τεκμήριον δ᾿ ἐστὶ τοῦ ῥεῖν ὑπὸ γῆν τὰ πνεύματα καὶ τὸ γιγνόμενον περὶ ταύτας τὰς νήσους· ὅταν γὰρ ἄνεμος μέλλῃ πνευσεῖσθαι νότος, προσημαίνει πρότερον· ἠχοῦσι γὰρ οἱ τόποι ἐξ ὧν γίγνεται τὰ ἀναφυσήματα, διὰ τὸ τὴν θάλατταν μὲν προωθεῖσθαι ἤδη πόρρωθεν, ὑπὸ δὲ ταύτης τὸ ἐκ τῆς γῆς ἀναφυσώμενον ἀπωθεῖσθαι πάλιν εἴσω, ᾗπερ ἐπέρχεται ἡ θάλαττα ταύτῃ. ποιεῖ δὲ ψόφον ἄνευ σεισμοῦ διά τε τὴν εὐρυχωρίαν τῶν τόπων (ὑπερχεῖται γὰρ εἰς τὸ ἀχανὲς ἔξω) καὶ δι᾿ ὀλιγότητα τοῦ ἀπωθουμένου ἀέρος. (*Mete.* 2. 8, 367^{a}12–20)

And there is a proof that winds flow beneath the earth in something else that happens in these islands. For when a south wind is going to blow it is heralded by noises from the places from which eruptions occur. This is because the sea, which is being driven forward from far off, thrusts the wind that is erupting out of the earth back again when it meets it. This causes a noise but no earthquake because there is plenty of room for the wind, of which there is only a small quantity and which can overflow into the void outside. (trans. H. D. P. Lee (modified))

---

[45] Cf. R. M. Wood, *Earthquakes and Volcanoes* (London, 1986), 22–3, on attempts, ancient and modern, to link earthquakes to seasons, weather, time of day, and planetary movements.

Aristotle's account is rather brief and enigmatic, but Strabo (6. 2. 10) reports from Polybius (34. 11. 12–20) at greater length on the relation between atmospheric winds and volcanic activity on Hiera and Etna. Strabo first says it has been observed that flames are intensified at the same time as the winds, which he thinks is reasonable because the flames and winds have similar causes. He then gives Polybius' more complicated account of the different effects of north, south, and west winds, and concludes with Polybius' statement that 'certain men of Lipara, when the calm weather made sailing impossible, [from volcanic activity] predicted when winds would blow again, and they were not mistaken'.

The details here are difficult to untangle, and for present purposes it is not necessary to pursue the problem. Aristotle and Strabo are prima facie in conflict, but it may be that their reports are accurate, and that the people of the Lipari islands modified their ideas about the winds over time. What I am concerned with here is a rather elusive relationship between, on the one hand, the people of Lipara (and for that matter of other volcanic regions) and, on the other, the philosophers, geographers, and historians. By the time of Polybius, at any rate, we have travellers who have read writers like Aristotle arriving in places like Lipara. Perhaps such visitors asked leading questions of the local inhabitants and sowed in their minds suggestions of links between winds and eruptions. But it is also entirely plausible that the locals had ideas of their own about the relation between weather and eruptions before any philosophically minded travellers arrived, for there is comparative evidence from other places and times of similar popular ideas (n. 45 above). Of course, it is one thing to see correlations between wind behaviour and volcanic activity, and another to postulate that winds are *causes* of volcanic activity. But I do not think we should rule out the possibility that the step to a causal postulate was taken by local people.

With the Lipari islands there is another dimension, for these were also called the islands of Aeolus or the Aeolian islands, after Homer's Aeolus, who was in charge of the winds. The earliest occurrence of this name is in Thucydides (3. 88. 1), whereas the name 'Liparaean islands' is first used for the whole group in Polybius (1. 25. 4). Strabo, who is convinced of the immense learning of Homer and loses no opportunity to demonstrate it, takes it for granted that the name 'Aeolian islands' pre-dates the poet: in the same passage (6. 2. 10) he goes on to say how the behaviour of the winds around the islands shows how right Homer was to call Aeolus the steward of the winds. We shall not agree with Strabo about the chronology, but we may wonder whether local wind lore led to the adoption of the Homeric name for the islands in the first place, or whether the adoption of the name, and its associations, subsequently encouraged people to observe and speculate about the significance of the winds for the islands and their volcanoes, or whether the two developments were quite independent.

These are a few illustrations of the way in which different groups of people with an interest in earthquakes and volcanoes all contributed to the slowly growing pool of information, misinformation, and speculation about earthquakes and volcanoes that one finds in the ancient world. Of course, the interaction between 'popular' and 'philosophical' views is important in other fields of Greek science, but it has not received much attention in earlier treatments of earthquakes and volcanoes; and in the case of volcanoes particularly, geographical remoteness and infrequency of activity made it harder for popular ideas to be checked by the philosophers. Whether the results achieved deserve to be called scientific is not something that can be decided in this brief, selective discussion, and it is maybe not the most important question; but I hope I have shown that, in studying and assessing the philosophical or scientific accounts, one must never lose sight of the complicated and, for us, often obscure links between the philosophers and students of nature on the one hand and, on the other, the various constituencies of people whose lives were directly affected by the earthquakes and eruptions.

5

The Art of the Commander and the Emergence of Predictive Astronomy

ALAN C. BOWEN

1. Introduction

THE one feature of Graeco-Latin astronomy[1] that has been thought to qualify it as the paradigmatic science is its ability to predict where the heavenly bodies will be at any given time. But what is seldom asked is whether Graeco-Latin astronomy has always been held to possess this marvellous capacity, whether there was ever a time when the idea that astronomers should be able to predict celestial events was a novelty. I presume there was. The earliest extant texts in Greek science date from the fifth and fourth centuries BC, and they typically limit science to explanation, thereby leaving but a small role, if any, for prediction. After all, if it is the duty of science to give the reasons or causes of phenomena conceived universally, then scientific explanations may concern the future only in the sense that the *explananda* may be instantiated at any time. Thus, for instance, Aristotle states his familiar, causal account of eclipses at numerous points in his writings but says nothing about predicting the particular times when they will occur (cf. n. 45). In contrast, however, Ptolemy's *Almagest* supplies its readers with the mathematical tools to compute when eclipses will occur, their magnitude, their duration, and so on. Indeed, this is the first technical

This paper has roots in exchanges over the course of several years with numerous colleagues, among whom I especially thank John P. Britton, Bernard R. Goldstein, Alexander Jones, and David Pingree. I am also grateful to Christopher Tuplin, Noreen Fox, and their Advisory Board for granting me the opportunity to present an earlier version at the conference 'Science Matters: The Role and Achievement of Science in Greek Antiquity' (Liverpool, 1996). The questions, comments, and suggestions I received at that meeting were particularly helpful, as were those I received when I presented a subsequent version of the paper at the annual meeting of the History of Science Society (Atlanta, 1996).

[1] I use 'Greek' and 'Latin' to designate what is found in documents written in the Greek and Latin languages. I reserve 'Hellenic' and 'Roman' for the related social and intellectual cultures.

Note that I also adopt the following convention in representing specific dates: 1 BC is year 0; years prior to 1 BC are written as negative numbers and years AD as positive numbers (see O. Neugebauer, *A History of Ancient Mathematical Astronomy* (Berlin and New York, 1975), 1061–2). All dates are in the Julian calendar unless otherwise noted. Moreover, in writing sexagesimal numbers I use a semicolon to separate the units and the fractions. Thus, for example, 12;23 means 12 and $\frac{23}{60}$.

work in ancient Graeco-Latin astronomy in which the idea of predicting any celestial phenomena is explicit.

So, when, why, and under what circumstances did ancient Graeco-Latin astronomy begin to include making claims about what was actually going to happen in the heavens? To answer this question we should first clarify the sorts of claims about the future we are to consider. Specifically, since the phenomena at issue are periodic, it is important to distinguish a prediction that some celestial event will occur from the mere expectation that such events recur in the natural course of time. Accordingly, let us define an astronomical prediction as an expectation meeting three conditions. First, it has to be an expectation about the future occurrence of a celestial phenomenon that is expressed in a proposition held in the light of, or derived from, what is recognized at the time as an astronomical theory. Second, this proposition must be thought to belong to this theory.[2] And, third, the proposition should at least identify the particular day or date in a calendar on which the celestial event is to take place. The upshot is that an astronomical prediction posits on the basis of theory what I have elsewhere called a dated observation[3]—a report of a celestial event seen at a suitably determined moment in time.

These criteria of astronomical prediction effectively exclude from consideration the assertions correlating star risings and meteorological phenomena throughout a year that are found in numerous Graeco-Latin calendars surviving from antiquity. After all, these assertions are neither suitably dated—they do not give a specific year—nor offered as inferences from some astronomical theory.[4] Granted, they are statements of periodicity that could undoubtedly be used to make predictions (cf. Theophr. *De signis*, 1–2) which might even have been viewed as astronomical. Nevertheless, there is, so far as I am aware, no documentary record of any Greek or Latin writer's explicitly using a calendar to predict that a given phenomenon will occur at a given date.

In any case, let us focus our efforts still more deliberately by limiting our attention to solar and lunar eclipses. Thus, our question now is, When, why, and in what context did Hellenic and Roman astronomers come to think that their proper task included making predictions about eclipses?

---

[2] Thus we undo the distinction between mathematical astronomy and astrology that Ptolemy first introduces.

[3] See B. R. Goldstein and A. C. Bowen, 'The Introduction of Dated Observations and Precise Measurements in Greek Astronomy', *AHES* 43 (1991) 93–132.

[4] The same may be said of predictions like those indicated in Theophr. *Sign.* 23, 43.

2. The Earliest Eclipse Prediction

2.1. *The temporal context*

The *terminus ante quem* is obviously the date of Ptolemy's *Almagest*, i.e. some time in the latter parts of the second century AD, since book 6 of the *Almagest* explains and sets out the tables needed to compute when eclipses will occur as well their characteristic attributes. This is the earliest occurrence in an extant technical work in astronomy of the idea that predicting eclipses is a task for astronomers. Yet, interestingly enough, though this is plainly the underlying purpose of the tables Ptolemy constructs,[5] he does not explicitly talk of predicting eclipses.[6]

The *terminus post quem* is problematic. In the first place, the only technical document written earlier than the *Almagest* which even raises the question of astronomical prediction happens to concern eclipses and it derives from the second century BC. In the course of arguing against the view that the tropic, equinoctial, and zodiacal circles have breadth, a proposition construed to entail that the sun does not move through the middle of the zodiacal signs, Hipparchus remarks that if the sun did move in this way (and thus as the moon does),

ἔδει τὰς τῆς σελήνης ἐκλείψεις πολὺ διαφωνεῖν πρὸς τὰς συντασσομένας ὑπὸ τῶν ἀστρο-
λόγων προρρήσεις, ὑποτιθεμένων γε δὴ αὐτῶν ἐν ταῖς πραγματείαις τὸ μέσον τῆς σκιᾶς
φέρεσθαι ἐπὶ τοῦ διὰ μέσων τῶν ζῳδίων κύκλου· οὐ διαφωνοῦσι δὲ πλέον ἢ δακτύλοις δυσί,
σπανίως δὲ σφόδρα ποτὲ πρὸς τὰς χαριέστατα συντεταγμένας πραγματείας. τό γε μὴν λέγειν
τηλικοῦτον πλάτος ἔχειν καὶ τοὺς κύκλους ἴσον ἐστὶ τῷ ἀπλατεῖς αὐτοὺς ὑποτίθεσθαι, χωρὶς
τοῦ καὶ αὐτὸ ἄδηλον εἶναι, πότερον παρὰ τὴν τοῦ ἡλίου κίνησιν ἢ παρὰ τὴν τῆς σελήνης
τὰ μεγέθη τῶν τῆς σελήνης ἐκλείψεων ἐπὶ τοσοῦτον διαφωνεῖ. (*In Arat.* 1. 9. 3–5)

it would be necessary that eclipses of the moon disagree by much with the predictions compiled by the astronomers, certainly at least by those who posit in their accounts that the middle of the shadow moves on the circle though the middle of the signs. But they [sc. the eclipses] do not disagree by more than two digits, and very very rarely at that, with the accounts that have been compiled most carefully. Nevertheless, saying that the circles do indeed have a breadth of such a size is equivalent to positing

---

[5] Cf. i. 476. 3–11 Heiberg, which characterizes certain computed lunar and solar mean syzygies as signifying eclipses (lit. as 'falling into the class of eclipse signs'); or i. 527. 20–528. 2, which shows how to determine solar eclipses precisely.

[6] I do not follow G. J. Toomer, *Ptolemy's* Almagest (New York and Berlin, 1984), in his rendering of ἐπίσκεψις in this chapter. For example, when Ptolemy writes τούτων δὴ προεκ-τεθειμένων τὴν μὲν τῶν σεληνιακῶν ἐκλείψεων ἐπίσκεψιν ποιησόμεθα τὸν τρόπον τοῦτον (i. 523. 2–4 Heiberg), Toomer has 'Having set out the above as a preliminary, we can predict lunar eclipses in the following manner' (op. cit. 305). But this seems over-interpretative: given that what follows is not an eclipse prediction but an account of how one may use tables to determine the magnitude of the obscuration, its duration, and the like, all the text requires is 'Given these (tables) that have been set out above, we shall make our study of lunar eclipses in this way.' Cf. i. 527. 20–2 Heiberg and Toomer, op cit. 310: again, ἐπίσκεψις need only mean 'study' and διάκρισις may have its customary meaning, 'determination'.

that they are without breadth, apart from the fact that this is itself unclear as well, [namely,] whether the eclipses of the moon disagree to such an extent due to the motion of the sun or due to the motion of the moon.

Now, this is a tantalizing passage in a puzzling argument. Yet so much is certain: it is inadequate as evidence of the sort of prediction we are investigating, and especially so if one imagines with Alexander Jones that the astronomers here mentioned are either Babylonians or others using Babylonian computational procedures.[7] So read, this passage from Hipparchus' commentary would at least be consistent with Diodorus' reports of Babylonian astronomy made less than a century later (see § 2.4 below). In any case, Hipparchus does not here afford good evidence that he, or any other Hellenic astronomer for that matter, regarded making eclipse predictions as part of their discipline or profession—unless, of course, one arbitrarily presumes that Hipparchus and his contemporaries did not see astronomy along ethnic or nationalistic lines and that he is thinking of what we have termed astronomical predictions.

So, let us look beyond the relatively few pre-Ptolemaic astronomical texts to the greater number of pre-Ptolemaic literary documents still available. Surprisingly enough, the earliest source in Greek or Latin to indicate that predicting eclipses is the proper business of the astronomer dates from roughly the mid first century AD. For it is Pliny (23/4–79) in the second book of his monumental *Historia naturalis* who first expresses this idea when he praises Hipparchus, the pre-eminent astronomer in the two centuries just before Ptolemy, for his ability to predict eclipses over a period of 600 years on the basis of astronomical theory (see § 3.2.4 below). Now, Pliny's valorization of Hipparchus comes in the extant literature only less than a century after the very question of an eclipse prediction by a Hellene or Roman was explicitly broached in writing for the first time. That is, it occurs less than a century after Cicero (*De div.* 1. 111–12) states that Thales was the first to predict an eclipse, a claim Cicero does not elaborate beyond adding that Thales was a philosopher (rather than an astronomer) and that his prediction was based on a theory of nature.

I realize, of course, that the weight of learned tradition lies with the view that the first astronomical prediction was reported by Herodotus (fifth century BC) in his celebrated account of Thales (sixth century BC) and events during a battle between the Medes and Lydians:

μετὰ δὲ ταῦτα, οὐ γὰρ δὴ ὁ Ἀλυάττης ἐξεδίδου τοὺς Σκύθας ἐξαιτέοντι Κυαξάρῃ, πόλεμος

---

[7] See A. Jones, 'Evidence for Babylonian Arithmetical Schemes in Greek Astronomy', in H. D. Galter (ed.), *Die Rolle der Astronomie in den Kulturen Mesopotamiens* (Graz, 1993), 77–94 at 86, 88: cf. id., 'On Babylonian Astronomy and its Greek Metamorphoses', in F. J. Ragep and S. P. Ragep (eds.), *Tradition, Transformation, Transmission: Proceedings of Two Conferences on Pre-Modern Science Held at the University of Oklahoma* (Leiden and New York, 1996), 139–55 at 149–51. On Babylonian computational procedures see Neugebauer (n. 1), 664–9.

τοῖσι Λυδοῖσι καὶ τοῖσι Μήδοισι ἐγεγόνεε ἐπ' ἔτεα πέντε, ἐν τοῖσι πολλάκις μὲν οἱ Μῆδοι
τοὺς Λυδοὺς ἐνίκησαν, πολλάκις δὲ οἱ Λυδοὶ τοὺς Μήδους· ἐν δὲ καὶ νυκτομαχίην τινὰ
ἐποιήσαντο· διαφέρουσι δέ σφι ἐπὶ ἴσης τὸν πόλεμον τῷ ἔκτῳ ἔτεϊ συμβολῆς γενομένης
συνήνεικε ὥστε τῆς μάχης συνεστεώσης τὴν ἡμέρην ἐξαπίνης νύκτα γενέσθαι. τὴν δὲ μετ-
αλλαγὴν ταύτην τῆς ἡμέρης Θαλῆς ὁ Μιλήσιος τοῖσι Ἴωσι προηγόρευσε ἔσεσθαι, οὖρον
προθέμενος ἐνιαυτὸν τοῦτον ἐν τῷ δὴ καὶ ἐγένετο ἡ μεταβολή. οἱ δὲ Λυδοί τε καὶ οἱ Μῆδοι
ἐπείτε εἶδον νύκτα ἀντὶ ἡμέρης γενομένην, τῆς μάχης τε ἐπαύσαντο καὶ μᾶλλόν τι ἔσπευσαν
καὶ ἀμφότεροι εἰρήνην ἑωυτοῖσι γενέσθαι. (Hdt. 1. 74)

After this, since Alyattes did not surrender the Scythians to Cyaxares on his demand, there was a war among the Lydians and the Medes for five years. On many occasions the Medes defeated the Lydians and on many other occasions the Lydians defeated the Medes; and they even fought a battle at night. But, as they were carrying out the war with equal success, it happened to them in an engagement in the sixth year that day suddenly became night while the battle was joined. Thales of Miletus had proclaimed to the Ionians that this transformation of day was going to occur, setting as a limit this year in which the change actually occurred. When the Lydians and the Medes saw night coming on in place of day, they ceased from battle and both [sides] were somewhat more eager that there be peace with each other.

But this tradition has little to commend it. The inescapable problem is that Herodotus' account is underdetermined. In the first place, it is hardly certain that the report actually concerns an eclipse: Herodotus says nothing about what caused the sky to go dark and he omits the sort of detail found characteristically throughout the later literary references to eclipses, namely, some description of the fear experienced by the witnesses and of how they allayed it (if they did) or even a remark to the effect that the stars came out (cf. e.g. Thuc. 2. 28. 1). Next, even if the cause was an eclipse, the report is ambiguous. On one hand, it may mean that Thales predicted the eclipse but specified only the year in which it was to occur. And on the other, it may mean that he explained the eclipse and pointed out that such eclipses can occur only at certain moments during the sun's annual course, i.e. when its conjunctions with the moon satisfy certain conditions. (Whether such a causal explanation preceded or followed the eclipse is immaterial: in either case Thales could rightly be said later to have proclaimed that it was going to happen.) Both alternatives are equally problematic and, as we shall see, are found in the ancient literature subsequent to Herodotus (cf. n. 75). Finally, it *need* not have been an eclipse. Suppose instead that the cause was a seasonal storm. Herodotus' report would then mean either that Thales predicted it—perhaps on the basis of a yearly almanac correlating stellar and meteorological phenomena, and of the sort referred to in the literature of Herodotus' time[8]—or that he explained it as an annual event. Moreover, all of this takes for granted a matter of some doubt, namely,

[8] Cf. A. C. Bowen and B. R. Goldstein, 'Meton of Athens and Astronomy in the Late Fifth Century B.C.', in E. Leichty, M. de J. Ellis, and P. Gerardi (eds.), *A Scientific Humanist: Studies in Memory of Abraham Sachs* (Philadelphia, 1988), 39–81 at 74–7.

that the phenomenon observed by the contending armies was the same phenomenon mentioned by Thales to the Ionians.[9] In sum, this passage about Thales in Herodotus' *Historiae* does not even count as good implicit evidence of an astronomical prediction, to say nothing of the view that such predictions are the responsibility of astronomers. So, let us return to Pliny.

Many will find Pliny's testimony sufficient warrant for supposing that the *terminus post quem* is some lost work by Hipparchus. But they will, I fear, be mistaken. There is certainly no independent evidence deriving from Hipparchus or his times to confirm or deny what Pliny writes of Hipparchus. All we have is Hipparchus' remark at *In Arat.* 1. 9. 3–4, and this is regrettably too slight to support any responsible view of the truth of Pliny's report. Granted, it remains possible that Pliny's claim is in fact true. Yet, given the renown of Hipparchus' *In Arati et Eudoxi phaenomena* in the literary genre of *Aratea* and his general stature as a scientific writer, it seems equally possible that a Babylonian procedure for determining the daily progress of the moon over a period of 600 years[10] was wrongly attributed to Hipparchus on the basis of his tantalizing allusion to eclipses and predictions. In the absence of relevant documents dating from the second century BC there is no way to decide the truth or falsity of Pliny' report.

Moreover, in this case, were we to reach a decision now, our conclusion would not only fail to constitute or yield historical knowledge, it might well hinder the acquisition of such knowledge. That is, if we were to decide that Pliny's report is true based on our sense of what is probable, we would in effect thereby locate the question of the introduction of prediction in some technical astronomical documents that are no longer extant. At which point further discussion would either cease for lack of interest or 'advance' only by way of learned but nugatory reconstruction of these documents and their context. In consequence, we would lose the opportunity to move away from the question of the truth of Pliny's report by asking why he writes what he does about Hipparchus, and by noticing that he prefaces his report with a curious story often recounted by ancient writers, that of C.

---

[9] Cf. S. Newcomb, *Researches on the Motion of the Moon Made at the United States Naval Observatory, Washington*, pt. 1. *Reduction and Discussion of Observations of the Moon before 1750* (Washington Observations for 1875, appendix II; Washington, 1878), 28–30.

Herodotus' record as a reporter of eclipses is not good. At 7. 37 he gives a fine description of a solar eclipse in the morning in the early spring of –479; yet no such eclipse was visible at Sardis and points east at that time (cf. W. W. How and J. Wells, *A Commentary on Herodotus* (Oxford, 1928), ii. 144–5). According to my calculations with Planet C 6.2 FPU and Starry Night Deluxe 2.1.3, there was, however, an annular solar eclipse visible at Sardis in the morning of 17 Feb. –477 (cf. H. H. Goldstine, *New and Full Moons from 1001 B.C. to A.D. 1651* (Philadelphia, 1973), 44 no. 6470)—and not on 16 Feb. as is sometimes supposed. But, as Newcomb (op. cit. 31–2) remarks, taking this eclipse to be the one Herodotus has in mind is inconsistent with the received date for the battle of Salamis, –479 (Hdt. 8. 83–95: cf. J. F. Lazenby, *The First Punic War* (Stanford, 1996), 1347).

[10] Cf. B. R. Goldstein and A. C. Bowen, 'Pliny and Hipparchus's 600-Year Cycle', *JHA* 26 (1995), 155–8 at 156–7.

Sulpicius Gallus and events during the battle near Pydna (now Kitros) in
−167. Indeed, according to Pliny, it was on this occasion that Gallus became
the first to make known to the Romans the physical explanation of solar and
lunar eclipses and to predict a lunar eclipse.

Now, this battle is of vital importance historically because it marked the
end of the third Macedonian war. Indeed, with the defeat of Perseus (the elder son of Philip V, an ally of Hannibal) by L. Aemilius Paulus, Macedonia
collapsed as a world power in the face of Roman expansion, and subsequently suffered division by the Romans into four tributary republics. It
is not surprising, therefore, that Greek and Latin writers should view this
battle as a significant moment in the ascendancy of Rome and the decline of
Hellas, and that the events of this battle should undergo elaboration in literary and historical tracts. But, for us, the story of Gallus' role in this battle
as told by Livy (−63 to 11 or −58 to 16) is particularly important because
it contains the earliest extant report in Greek or Latin of any astronomical
prediction whatsoever that meets our criteria, a prediction of a lunar eclipse
no less, and because Livy is one of Pliny's acknowledged sources. So, let
us turn to Livy's account to see what light it sheds on Pliny's report about
Gallus and on Pliny's idea that astronomers should predict eclipses.

2.2. *Livy and the first astronomical prediction of an eclipse*

In his version of events just prior to the battle of Pydna, Livy writes that

[5] Castris permunitis C. Sulpicius Gallus, tribunus militum secundae legionis, qui
praetor superiore anno fuerat, consulis permissu ad contionem militibus vocatis
pronuntiavit, [6] nocte proxima, ne quis id pro portento acciperet, ab hora secunda
ad quartam horam noctis lunam defecturam esse. id quia naturali ordine statis
temporibus fiat, et sciri ante et praedici posse. [7] itaque quem ad modum, quia certi
solis lunaeque ortus et occasus sint, nunc pleno orbe, nunc senescentem exiguo cornu
fulgere lunam non mirarentur, ita ne obscurari quidem cum condatur umbra terrae,
trahere in prodigium debere. [8] nocte quam pridie nonas Septembres insecuta
est dies, edita hora luna cum defecisset, Romanis milit ibus Galli sapientia prope
divina videri; [9] Macedonas ut triste prodigium, occasum regni perniciemque gentis
portendens, movit nec aliter vates. clamor ululatusque in castris Macedonum fuit,
donec luna in suam lucem emersit. (Livy 44. 37. 5–9)

[5] When the camp had been fortified, C. Sulpicius Gallus, a tribune of soldiers
in the second legion, who had been praetor in the preceding year, announced to
the soldiers who had been called to assembly with the permission of the consul,
[6] lest anyone take it as a sign, that there was going to be an eclipse of the moon on
the next night from the second hour of night to the fourth; and that, because this
[phenomenon] occurs at times which are fixed in the order of nature, it can both be
known in advance and predicted. [7] Thus, just as they are not bewildered that the
moon shines now with full orb, now with slender crescent as it wanes, because the
risings and settings of the sun and moon are understood, so [he said] they should

not consider it a portent that [the moon] is eclipsed when it is hidden by the shadow of the earth. [8] On the night before daytime came on the day before the Nones of September [sc. the night of 3/4 September], when the moon was eclipsed at the stated hour, Gallus' wisdom seemed almost divine to the Roman soldiers. [9] But no diviner caused the Macedonians to change their belief that it was a grim portent signifying the downfall of a kingdom and the ruin of a nation. There was shouting and howling in the Macedonians' camp until the moon came forth into its own light.

As Livy would have it, Gallus declared in advance on the basis of astronomical theory that on the following night there would be a lunar eclipse. Now there is, I emphasize, no reason to discount a priori the historical possibility of anyone's making an eclipse prediction of the sort that Livy ascribes to Gallus. For, as the analogy between lunar phases and lunar eclipses suggests, the prediction in question may have been based on a simple cycle. And there were, it happens, eclipse cycles known to Graeco-Latin writers in Livy's era—all are of Babylonian origin—which could certainly have been adapted to the purpose Livy indicates, albeit with varying degrees of difficulty and all with relatively little success in the long term.[11] Of course, this

[11] Scholars have maintained that the ancients knew numerous eclipse cycles. But, in order to keep speculation to a minimum, let us restrict our attention to cycles attested directly in Graeco-Latin literature prior to Ptolemy. Thus, one candidate is the eclipse cycle known today as the Saros, i.e. the cycle of 223 synodic months, which the Babylonians had determined by the 5th cent. BC (cf. J. P. Britton, 'The Structure and Parameters of Column Φ', in J. L. Berggren and B. R. Goldstein (eds.), *From Ancient Omens to Statistical Mechanics: Essays on the Exact Sciences Presented to Asger Aaboe* (Copenhagen, 1987), 23–36; A. Aaboe, J. P. Britton, J. A. Henderson, O. E. Neugebauer, and A. J. Sachs, *Saros Cycle Dates and Related Babylonian Astronomical Texts* (Philadelphia, 1991)) and which is mentioned by Pliny (*HN* 2. 56). The Saros defines *inter alia* the return of the sun and the moon relative to a lunar node, and thus specifies a period after which lunar eclipses of the same character may recur. Accordingly, to use it for making the prediction ascribed to Gallus by Livy, all one would need to know is that there was a lunar eclipse 223 synodic months earlier. (Since lunar eclipses occur only at full moon, i.e. at the middle of the lunar month, the day count does not really matter: it would suffice to keep track only of the number of synodic months.) Any prediction made on this basis, however, would not be particularly reliable. For, as T. von Oppolzer's tables show (*Canon der Finsternisse* (Vienna, 1887)), lunar eclipses do occur frequently at intervals of 223 synodic months, but few such successive eclipses will be observable at a given location. The problem is that the Saros does not define a whole number of days: indeed, Ptolemy (*Alm.* 4. 2) evaluates it as a cycle of $6,585\frac{1}{3}$ days. Thus, a lunar eclipse observed at Pydna at night may recur 6,585 days and 8 hours later during the daytime. It would, of course, be possible to enhance the utility of the Saros somewhat over the short term by tripling it in order to get a whole number of days. Such a cycle of 669 synodic months or 19,756 days, which is called the ἐξελιγμός, is defined by Geminus (*Intro. ast.* 18) in the 1st century BC. On Geminus' date see B. S. Eastwood, 'Heraclides and Heliocentrism: Texts, Diagrams, and Interpretations', *JHA* 23 (1992), 233–60 at 257 n. 11.

Another candidate is the 19-year cycle of 235 synodic months. This cycle was also well established by the Babylonians as early as the beginning of the 5th cent. (cf. Bowen and Goldstein, (n. 8), 42, 50 nn. 54–5; J. P. Britton, 'Scientific Astronomy in Pre-Seleucid Babylon', in Galter (n. 7), 61–76 at 68). The earliest direct evidence for it in Greek texts comes from Aratus (*Phaen.* 752–7), who mentions it in passing, and from Diodorus Siculus (*Bib.* 12. 36. 1–3), who ascribes it to Meton; Geminus (*Intro. ast.* 8. 50–6) ascribes it to Euctemon and adds that it was a cycle of 6,940 days. As for the earliest evidence in Latin texts, Censorinus (*De die nat.* 28. 8), who lived in the 3rd cent. AD, attributes the 19-year cycle of 235 synodic months

does not mean by itself that any Greek or Latin writer living in Livy's time or in the century before actually used such a cycle to predict a lunar eclipse. Nevertheless, even if none had in fact used eclipse cycles in this way, it is still significant that Diodorus Siculus (first century BC) had made widely public the Babylonians' skill in predicting eclipses (see § 2.4 below), that appropriate eclipse cycles were available to Graeco-Latin writers at roughly the same time, and that Livy is right to suppose that they could be applied in this way.

Another remarkable feature of Livy's account is that it is his only eclipse report which mentions seasonal hours of night, i.e. twelfths of the interval from one sunset to the next sunrise: there is no such precision in his report of the solar eclipse observed in −189 at Rome (37. 4. 4), for example. Moreover, Livy's quantitative precision is not only unique in the legend of Sulpicius Gallus, so far as I know, it is also the earliest direct evidence in Greek or Latin of this way of characterizing an eclipse.[12] Evidently, Livy was aware of a model for describing eclipses in a manner considerably more precise than we might have otherwise expected given the evidence of prior or contemporary treatises on astronomy in Greek and Latin which are still extant.[13]

But the real surprise at the heart of Livy's account is that there was in fact no lunar eclipse on the date Livy gives, 3/4 September −167: lunar eclipses occur when the moon is full and in −167 the moon was full on 20 August and 18 September.[14] Yet, there was in −167 a full moon on 21 June[15] and an eclipse of that moon which was theoretically observable at Pydna during the night of 21/2 June. But this eclipse, which was total, did not occur from the second to the fourth nocturnal seasonal hour. Indeed, if one reckons from the moment the moon begins to enter the earth's penumbra to the moment it leaves it, the eclipse began well before the sun even set at Pydna and ended as the sixth seasonal hour of night began. And, if one limits attention to the moon's immersion into the earth's umbra, the eclipse still began long before the second nocturnal seasonal hour but ended during the fourth. As

---

and 6,940 days to Meton. (Again, for present purposes, the day count is not necessary.) This 19-year cycle defines a period in which lunar eclipses of different character may recur. But, if one consults Oppolzer's tables one will discover that the actual recurrence of lunar eclipses after 19 years is infrequent, and that any use of this cycle to predict lunar eclipses on the basis of what happened 19 years earlier will meet with less success than predictions based on the Saros.

[12] On the distinction and use of direct and indirect evidence see A. C. Bowen, 'La scienza del cielo nel periodo pretolemaico', in V. Cappelletti (ed.), *Storia della scienza*, i. *La scienza antica* (Rome, 2001), 806–39 at 806–12.

[13] See also, for example, Pliny, *HN* 2. 180. Note that both eclipse reports come in a military context.

[14] Cf. Goldstine (n. 9), 70 nos. 10310–11.

[15] Cf. ibid. 10308.

for totality itself, this began early in the first seasonal hour of night and ended during the second.[16]

So, what are we to make of this? Perhaps Livy's date, 3/4 September in the Roman calendar, is just 21/2 June in the Julian calendar. It is, after all, well known that the Roman calendar was out of step with the sun before Caesar's reform in −45. Yet the difficulty here is that this passage in Livy's treatise is the *only* basis for the claim that it was 74 days in advance of the sun in −167.[17] Moreover, correlating the Roman and Julian calendars in this way is still problematic, since it does not fit well with other documents dating from the period. Indeed, there is no sure way to correlate the Julian calendar with Roman calendar in the second century BC or, in fact, before −45/−44.[18]

To support the hypothesis that Livy's date of 3/4 September in the Roman calendar is 21/2 June in the Julian calendar, one might adduce inscriptional evidence that the battle was over before the beginning of the archon year at Athens.[19] Thus, if the Athenians began the archon year in −167 when they were supposed to, i.e. with the day beginning at the sunset immediately preceding the first appearance of the lunar crescent after the summer solstice, it would follow that the battle took place some time in early summer before the sunset of 8 July at Pydna.[20] But none of this confirms

---

[16] I am here relying primarily on my computations using Planet C 6.2 FPU, Starry Night Deluxe 2.1.3, and MPj Astro 1.5.1 FPU in part because these computations are in accord with B.-L. Liu and A. D. Fiala, *Canon of Solar Eclipses, 1500 B.C. to A.D. 3000* (Richmond, Va., 1992), no. 3222, and Goldstine (n. 9), 70 no. 10308, which put the occurrence of full moon on 21 June −167 at 18;33 U(niversal) T(ime). I thus discount the eclipse data derived from Voyager II 2.0.2, though it is worth noting that this software application does not yield data consistent with Livy's specification of the eclipse's duration.

[17] The only other astronomical equation seemingly available for understanding the Roman calendar in the 2nd cent. BC likewise comes from Livy. For at 37. 4. 4 he reports that a solar eclipse was seen in Rome on 11 July −189. According to modern computation, however, there was a solar eclipse visible in Rome on 4 Mar.

[18] So E. J. Bickerman, *Chronology of the Ancient World*, 2nd edn. (Ithaca, NY, 1980), 46–7. By contrast, P. S. Derow, 'The Roman Calendar, 190–168', *Phoenix*, 27 (1973) 345–56, and A. Deman and M.-T. Rapsaet-Charlier, 'Notes de chronologie romaine', *Historia*, 23 (1974), 271–96 at 288–9, accept putative Roman–Julian synchronisms in −189 and (the present one in) −167, and calculate tables for the intervening years. (Derow has regular intercalation every other year and an extra intercalation in −168.) See Deman and Rapsaet-Charlier, op. cit. 290 n. 9, for references to those who reject a synchronism of 3/4 Sept. (Roman) and 21/2 June (Julian); and add P. Marchetti, 'La marche du calendrier romain et la chronologie à l'époque de la bataille de Pydna', *BCH* 100 (1976), 401–23 at 401–7, 420–3. The point about the summer solstice (next paragraph) is regularly neglected.

[19] See L. Moretti, *Iscrizioni storiche ellenistiche* (Rome, 1967), no. 35 (=B. D. Meritt, 'Greek Inscriptions', *Hesperia*, 5 (1936), 355–441 at 429–30, no. 17); translated in R. K. Sherk, *Rome and the Greek East to the Death of Augustus* (Cambridge, 1984), no. 23.

[20] The moon was in true conjunction with the sun on 6 July at 22;25 UT (cf. Goldstine (n. 9), 70 no. 10309) and moonset on 7 July took place at 18;15 UT at Athens (38° N., 23;38° E.). This means that, if 1 Hekatombaion, the first day of the archon year, was determined by observation, then co-ordinating the beginning of this day with sunset of 7 July in −167 would require observing the crescent less than 19;50 hours after true conjunction. But, according to Ashbrook,

Livy's account.[21] For the real problem is that Livy (cf. 44. 37. 10–40. 10, 44. 43. 9) also holds that the battle of Pydna was fought in the daytime after the lunar eclipse—that is, it would seem, on 22 June—*and* that the Roman victory occurred after the summer solstice (34. 36. 1). But the sun reached the summer solstitial point on 26 June, some four days later.[22] In short, if 3/4 September in the Roman calendar is to be correlated with 21/2 June in the Julian calendar, 4 September is not the date of the battle; whereas, if 4 September is the date of the battle, 3/4 September should not be correlated with 21/2 June.

This means not only that the detail about the duration of the eclipse at Pydna is in error, but that Livy's chronology for the battle is also at odds with itself. That is, the key elements of the astronomical prediction ascribed to Gallus—the date, the time and duration—are either in error or in doubt because they conflict with Livy's chronology. And there is, so far as I can see, no credible, non-arbitrary way to rectify what Livy tells us. The only independent datum implies that the battle took place before the sunset of 8 July. And even were one disposed to overlook the record of Athenian calendrical practices and to rely on this implication for historical purposes, this datum is still unavailing so far as Livy's story is concerned. Consequently, let us take it for granted no longer that Gallus actually predicted the eclipse, or that the eclipse took place during the night-time before the battle, or that 3/4 September in the Roman calendar is 21/2 June in the Julian calendar.

Those familiar with Livy's manner of historiography will hardly be surprised at this outcome. Livy, like most ancient historians, did not set himself the goal of merely recording what transpired. His monumental history of Rome from its founding to his own day is a work in which, as scholars have long been aware, Livy puts higher value on the literary, i.e. on the didactic

reliable, naked-eye sightings of the new lunar crescent within 20 hours of true conjunction are extraordinary and usually involve knowing where to look and using instruments such as binoculars to locate the crescent first; and reports of seeing the crescent within 24 hours of conjunction are rare (cf. J. Ashbrook, 'Some Very Thin Lunar Crescents', *Sky and Telescope*, 42 (Aug. 1971), 78–9 at 78; 'More about the Visibility of the Lunar Crescent', ibid. (Feb. 1972), 95–6 at 95). So, it seems to me more likely that observers at Athens would have seen the new lunar crescent after sunset of 8 July rather than after sunset of 7 July. The difference in local mean time between Athens and Pydna is less than 15 minutes.

[21] *Pace* F. W. Walbank, *A Historical Commentary on Polybius* (Oxford, 1957–79), iii. 386, who dates the battle to 22 June and regards this as equivalent to Livy's date.

[22] In the Uruk scheme, a Babylonian scheme for solstices and equinoxes named after the location where the cuneiform tablets presenting it were found, the date for the summer solstice in –167 (= Seleucid Era 144) is given as month III day 19: see Neugebauer (n. 1), 361: cf. Bowen and Goldstein (n. 8), 48–50. According to R. A. Parker and W. H. Dubberstein, *Babylonian Chronology 626 B.C.–A.D. 75* (Providence, 1956), 41, month III day 1 began at sunset on 8 June. Thus, in the Uruk scheme, the sun reached the summer solstitial point between sunset of 26 June and sunset of 27 June. But, according to Planet C 6.1 FPU and Voyager II 2.0.2, this happened in the morning of 26 June.

and ethical, merits of his account than he does on its factual accuracy.[23] But this means that Livy's report about Gallus, and hence Pliny's too, should not be read as bald, isolated statements of fact, but as remarks which have a discernible meaning only in respect to a specific literary context. Consequently, if we are to understand not just when but also why and under what circumstances the ancient Hellenes and Romans came to think that predicting eclipses is a duty of astronomers, we need to understand the Livian and Plinian versions of Gallus' contribution at the battle of Pydna. And to do this, we must examine the literary context of these versions to see how each is shaped by and responds to it.

2.3. *Polybius and the art of the commander*

My argument begins with the ancient idea that the antidote to the fear induced in the ignorant at the occurrence of an eclipse is learning that eclipses take place in the regular course of nature and are not omens or signs from the gods. This idea appears early in Graeco-Latin intellectual history and, as we shall see, persists until the second century AD at least (cf. also Sen. *Q. Nat..* 1. 12. 1; 7. 1. 2, 25. 3). Plato (426 to −346) himself would seem to affirm it in his *Timaeus* at 40 C 3–D 3.[24] But, potent as this notion may be, my present interest is in a critical refinement that first appears in Polybius' *Historiae*, a work belonging to the mid-second century BC[25] that defines the *terminus post quem* of our investigation.

The object of Polybius' treatise, as he says at its beginning (1. 1. 5), is to explain how and by what mode of governance the Romans conquered and subjugated the inhabited world in less than fifty-three years. This focus on the Roman ascent to world domination means that military history will be a

---

[23] Livy is often castigated by scholars for neglecting to use historical records presumed available to him, but there is reason to doubt the adequacy of such records even in ancient times: see M. I. Finley, *Ancient History: Evidence and Models* (New York, 1986), 7–18; M. Grant, *Greek and Roman Historians: Information and Misinformation* (London and New York, 1995), 34.

[24] Cf. A. E. Taylor, *A Commentary on Plato's* Timaeus (Oxford, 1928), 241–4. Regarding Aristotle's view of the belief that eclipses are signs from the gods, one should note the numerous instances in which he indicates that eclipses are explained solely by reference to the relative positions of the sun, moon, and earth, i.e. by treating these bodies as material items in space and without mentioning gods or portents: cf. e.g. *An. post.* 90ª15–18; *Cael.* 291ᵇ17–23, 293ᵇ21–5, and 297ᵇ23–30. But it is one thing to know what an eclipse is and another to know whether it is an omen. The argument that, for Aristotle, eclipses are not signs from the gods has to be made on the basis of his account of nature (φύσις) and natural processes: see e.g. D. Gallop, *Aristotle:* On Sleep and Dreams. *A Text, Translation, with Introduction, Notes and Glossary* (Peterborough, 1990), 11, 39–45, for an analysis of Aristotle's view of the belief that dreams are prophetic, and the claim at *Div. somn.* 463ᵇ13–14 that nature is daemon-like but not divine (ἡ γὰρ φύσις δαιμονία, ἀλλ' οὐ θεία).

[25] On Polybius' dates and the composition of this work see F. W. Walbank, *Polybius* (Berkeley, Los Angeles, and London, 1972), 1–31.

very significant part of his didactic account. And, indeed, it is as a military historian that Polybius excels and is renowned even today.[26]

Scattered throughout the *Historiae* itself are many passages stating the particular qualities and skills needed for success as a general. But the fullest account of these is found in a lengthy digression on the art of the commander (ἡ στρατηγία) at 9. 12. 1–20. Here Polybius asserts the value of knowing astronomy and geometry or, at least, as much of these sciences as is relevant to the tasks confronting any general.[27] Though, as Polybius sees it, astronomy is primarily valuable in matters of timekeeping, since timeliness in military ventures is an essential virtue, he proposes as well that, if commanders are to have any hope of success in such ventures, it is also vital for them to understand that eclipses are not ominous events. Polybius makes his point by way of an exemplum—Nicias' defeat in –412 at Syracuse:

[1] καὶ μὴν Νικίας ὁ τῶν Ἀθηναίων στρατηγός, δυνάμενος σῴζειν τὸ περὶ τὰς Συρακούσας στράτευμα, καὶ λαβὼν τῆς νυκτὸς τὸν ἁρμόζοντα καιρὸν εἰς τὸ λαθεῖν τοὺς πολεμίους, ἀποχωρήσας εἰς ἀσφαλές, κἄπειτα τῆς σελήνης ἐκλειπούσης δεισιδαιμονήσας, ὥς τι δεινὸν προσημαινούσης, ἐπέσχε τὴν ἀναζυγήν. [2] καὶ παρὰ τοῦτο συνέβη κατὰ τὴν ἐπιοῦσαν αὐτοῦ νύκτα ποιησαμένου τὴν ἀναζυγήν, προαισθομένων τῶν πολεμίων, καὶ τὸ στρατόπεδον καὶ τοὺς ἡγεμόνας ὑποχειρίους γενέσθαι τοῖς Συρακοσίοις. [3] καίτοι γε παρὰ τῶν ἐμπείρων ἱστορήσας μόνον περὶ τούτων δυνατὸς ἦν οὐχ οἷον παραλιπεῖν διὰ τὰ τοιαῦτα τοὺς ἰδίους καιρούς, ἀλλὰ καὶ συνεργοῖς χρήσασθαι διὰ τὴν τῶν ὑπεναντίων ἄγνοιαν· [4] ἡ γὰρ τῶν πέλας ἀπειρία μέγιστον ἐφόδιον γίνεται τοῖς ἐμπείροις πρὸς κατόρθωσιν. (Polyb. 9. 19. 1–4)

[1] Again, Nicias, the Athenian commander-in-chief, though he was able to save the army at Syracuse and though he had chosen the moment of night that was fitting for escaping the enemy unobserved as he withdrew to safety, nevertheless deferred breaking camp because he was struck by fear of divine interventions when the moon was eclipsed, as if it signified something terrible. [2] And consequently, when he broke camp on the following night, it transpired that both his army and his commanders became prisoners to the Syracusans because the enemy had anticipated him. [3] Yet, if he had only enquired of those with expertise[28] in these matters, he could have been the sort of (leader) to avail himself of the attendant circumstances because of his opponents' ignorance rather than the sort to neglect particular opportunities for such reasons. [4] For, lack of knowledge in those close by proves to be a very great resource for success to those who have expertise.

So far as understanding that eclipses are not omens is concerned, Polybius refers aspiring commanders to experts, i.e. to astronomers, and not, as one might perhaps expect, to commanders that time and experience have proven

---

[26] Cf. ibid. 89.

[27] Polybius (9. 20. 5–10) shows little patience for the view that perfection in the performance of some task entails learning skills and disciplines which do not bear directly on the task at hand, be it leading an army, dancing, or playing a flute. In the digression, he implies that there are parts of astronomy and geometry that are not directly relevant to generalship but does not say what they are.   [28] On ἐμπειρία as expertise cf. Polyb. 9. 14. 1–9.

successful (see 9. 14. 1–5; 9. 19. 5). Polybius does not, however, reveal what these experts say in order to convince the uninformed that eclipses are not omens, or even why he himself dismisses fear of divine interventions (δεισιδαιμονία) and divination (cf. 6. 56. 6–15; 10. 2).[29] Accordingly, I propose that we turn at this point to the *Bibliotheca historica* by Diodorus Siculus in order to get a sense of how celestial science was represented in Graeco-Latin circles during the second half of the first century BC.[30]

2.4. *Diodorus Siculus and astronomy in the first century* BC

As Diodorus explains in the proem to the first book of his treatise,[31] his goal is to write a universal history, i.e. a morally instructive account of the affairs of all peoples from mythological times to his own day (1. 1–5). In the course of this ambitious work, he has occasion to describe the knowledge of the heavens attained by various of these peoples, in particular the Egyptians and Chaldeans. These descriptions merit close attention for numerous reasons, not least of which is that they attest directly to important developments in the Hellenic–Roman reception of Egyptian and Babylonian celestial science, and that the details of Diodorus' accounts are in some measure borne out by earlier and contemporaneous technical documents that have survived independently. Yet we must pass such matters by for now, though they are critical to the modern understanding of the history of Graeco-Latin astronomy, in order to concentrate instead on how Diodorus portrayed astronomy to his contemporaries in the late first century BC.[32] In other words, given that we seek to understand an aspect of how astronomy was conceived in the few centuries before Ptolemy, our primary duty here is to attend to the story about astronomy that influential Graeco-Latin writers such as Diodorus were telling the readers of their own times, and not to assess whether it is a good representation of the Egyptian and Chaldean celestial sciences as we now know them.

According to Diodorus (1. 81. 1–5), Egyptian priests *qua* astronomers (ἀστρολόγοι) had observed and recorded the arrangements and motions of the stars for an incredible number of years. And they had also observed most

---

[29] It is interesting that in his *Strategicus*, a handbook on military leadership, Onasander (1st cent. AD) makes no mention of a commander's need to be able to explain what eclipses are to his troops. Though Onasander does insist that commanders must know sufficient astronomy to tell the time by the stars (39. 1–3), he seems more concerned that they have expertise in reading omens, especially those obtained through extispicy, that they understand their meaning in the present circumstances, and that they be able to convince their troops of this meaning (*Strat.* 10. 25–8: cf. 5. 1). Indeed, it would seem that for Onasander extispicy can yield the same information about the heavens as astronomy: see 10. 28, with C. G. Lowe, *A Byzantine Paraphrase of Onasander* (St Louis, 1927), 5, 38.

[30] For a recent account of Diodorus' life see K. S. Sacks, *Diodorus Siculus and the First Century* (Princeton, 1990), 160–203.

[31] On the question of the sense in which the proems are by Diodorus see ibid. 9–22.

[32] On the history of Graeco-Latin planetary theory before Ptolemy see Bowen (n. 12).

ambitiously the motions of the wandering stars or planets, their periods
and stations, as well as the powers each planet has at the births or nativities
(γενέσεις) of living creatures to produce good or ill. Moreover, he says, these
Egyptians were often successful in making predictions about what would
happen to people in the course of their lives; and they often foretold the
yields of crops as well as the occurrences of pestilences, earthquakes, floods,
and the risings of comets (cf. 1. 73. 4). In essence, Diodorus characterizes the
astronomy practised by Egyptian priests as a mix of horoscopic and judicial
astrology, i.e. as concerned primarily with making predictions about events
in the life of a person or the state that are based on the dispositions of the
celestial bodies at certain moments. He also emphasizes that this is a science
in which arithmetic plays an important role.[33]

One should bear in mind that astrology is a very broad category in the
history of celestial science; and realize that, when Diodorus characterizes
Egyptian astronomy as astrological, he means to include in it what the
Hellenes called astronomy as well.[34] For, as he tells the story, according
to records kept in Egypt which he has putatively seen (1. 69. 7), the key
advances in Greek astronomy made by such traditional luminaries as Democritus, Oenopides of Chios, and Eudoxus derived from their travels to
Egypt and instruction by the priests (1. 96. 2, 98. 3–4). I take this to mean
that, in Diodorus' view, Egyptian astronomy is the source of Hellenic astronomy in regard to its fundamental tenets—for example, in recognizing
the obliquity of the sun's path and its annual motion eastward along this
path[35]—as well as in regard to its general results: note that Diodorus even
goes so far as to attribute Eudoxus' accomplishments in astronomy (or, at
least, whatever was known of them in the first century BC) to the Egyptians.

Diodorus' description (2. 29. 1–3, 30. 1–31. 9) of the Chaldeans is substantially more detailed. As he states, they are the most ancient inhabitants
of Babylonia and have the same duties there as the priests do in Egypt; that
is,

[2] πρὸς γὰρ τῇ θεραπείᾳ τῶν θεῶν τεταγμένοι πάντα τὸν τοῦ ζῆν χρόνον φιλοσοφοῦσι,
μεγίστην δόξαν ἔχοντες ἐν ἀστρολογίᾳ. ἀντέχονται δ' ἐπὶ πολὺ καὶ μαντικῆς, ποιούμενοι

---

[33] It is worth noting that the corpus of extant Greek horoscopes, which begins in the late 1st
cent. BC (cf. O. Neugebauer and H. B. Van Hoesen, *Greek Horoscopes* (Philadelphia, 1987)),
relies on Babylonian arithmetical schemes for computing celestial positions.

[34] Notice that Diodorus does not adjust his terminology in talking of the astronomy of the
Egyptians, Hellenes, and Chaldeans. In all cases, the fundamental verb is ἀστρολογεῖν and the
cognate noun for the activity is ἀστρολογία and for the agent, ἀστρολόγος. The only exceptions
to this are occurrences of ἀστρομαντική and ἀστρομαντεία (both signifying astromancy), which
are found in putative fragments of the *Bib. hist.* located in a collection entitled *Excerpta
Constantiniana* that ultimately derives from the historical anthologies compiled in the 10th
cent. AD for Constantine VII Porphyrogenitus: cf. *Bib. hist.* 36. 5. 1 and 5. 4 respectively.

[35] On Oenopides of Chios see A. C. Bowen, 'Oenopides of Chios', in D. J. Zeyl, D. T.
Devereux, and P. K. Mitsis (eds.), *The Encyclopedia of Classical Philosophy* (Westport, Conn.,
1997), 357.

προρρήσεις περὶ τῶν μελλόντων, καὶ τῶν μὲν καθαρμοῖς, τῶν δὲ θυσίαις, τῶν δ᾽ ἄλλαις τισὶν ἐπῳδαῖς ἀποτροπὰς κακῶν καὶ τελειώσεις ἀγαθῶν πειρῶνται πορίζειν. [3] ἐμπειρίαν δ᾽ ἔχουσι καὶ τῆς διὰ τῶν οἰωνῶν μαντικῆς, ἐνυπνίων τε καὶ τεράτων ἐξηγήσεις ἀποφαίνονται. οὐκ ἀσόφως δὲ ποιοῦνται καὶ τὰ περὶ τὴν ἱεροσκοπίαν ἄκρως ἐπιτυγχάνειν νομίζοντες. (D.S. 2. 29. 2–3)

[2] being assigned to the service of the gods, they pursue wisdom their entire lives, maintaining their greatest reputation in astronomy. But they occupy themselves largely in fact with divination by making predictions about what is going to happen, and they try to contrive the averting of evils and the attainment of goods, in some cases by purifications, in others by sacrifices, and in others by some other charms. [3] They also have expertise in divination though birds, and state interpretations of dreams and portents. And they are not unclever in matters of divining by inspecting sacrificial victims as well, deeming that [in this] they are supremely successful.

After a brief digression in which he compares education in the Hellenic world with that in the Chaldean scribal families, Diodorus turns to Chaldean astronomy.

The details of his account are fascinating and raise questions for the historian of astronomy concerning the nature of Babylonian celestial science as it was transmitted to the Graeco-Latin world. For our purposes, it is important to notice that Diodorus begins by remarking that, for the Chaldeans, the cosmos is ungenerated and eternal and its order is the work of divine providence; and that they regard whatever happens in the heavens as taking place not by chance or spontaneously, but by virtue of some defined and firmly determined decision or decree of the gods (2. 30. 1). Diodorus then explains that, like Egyptian astronomy, Chaldean astronomy is a science of divining the future that includes judicial, horoscopic, and meteorological astrology (cf. 2. 30. 2–5, 31. 1–3). This may seem harmless enough, but it is in fact significant. For the view Diodorus ascribes to the Chaldeans entails as a consequence that the apodoses of their omens are statements of future fact that serve as warnings about what will be the case unless certain magical rituals are performed successfully.[36] And, thus, this Chaldean 'determinism' becomes critically important in those instances when the events predicted on the basis of astral omens are themselves astral.

Indeed, as Diodorus maintains, the Chaldeans foretold the occurrences of eclipses:

[4] τὰ μὲν γὰρ διὰ τῆς ἀνατολῆς, τὰ δὲ διὰ τῆς δύσεως, τινὰ δὲ διὰ τῆς χρόας προσημαίνειν φασὶν αὐτοὺς τοῖς προσέχειν ἀκριβῶς βουληθεῖσι· [5] ποτὲ μὲν γὰρ πνευμάτων μεγέθη δηλοῦν αὐτούς, ποτὲ δὲ ὄμβρων ἢ καυμάτων ὑπερβολάς, ἔστι δὲ ὅτε κομητῶν ἀστέρων ἐπιτολάς, ἔτι δὲ ἡλίου τε καὶ σελήνης ἐκλείψεις, καὶ σεισμούς, καὶ τὸ σύνολον πάσας τὰς

[36] On Mesopotamian divination as it appears in cuneiform documents see A. L. Oppenheim, *Ancient Mesopotamia: Portrait of a Dead Civilization* (Chicago and London, 1964), 206–27, esp. 207–8, 210–12; and F. Rochberg, 'La divinazione mesopotamica e i presagi spontanei', in Cappelletti (n. 12), 249–66.

ἐκ τοῦ περιέχοντος γεννωμένας περιστάσεις ὠφελίμους τε καὶ βλαβερὰς οὐ μόνον ἔθνεσιν
ἢ τόποις, ἀλλὰ καὶ βασιλεῦσι καὶ τοῖς τυχοῦσιν ἰδιώταις. (D.S. 2. 30. 4–5)

[4] For, they say that [the planets] give signs in advance to those who are willing
to pay precise attention to them, in some instances through their rising, in other
instances through their setting, and in some instances through their colour. [5] For
[they say] that sometimes [the planets] disclose the forces of winds, sometimes the
excesses of rains or droughts; and there are times when [they disclose] the risings of
comets and, moreover, eclipses of the sun and of the moon as well as earthquakes,
and, in general, all the conditions that are born of the environment, conditions that
are beneficial and harmful not only to nations and places, but also to kings and to
those who are private citizens.

Unfortunately, Diodorus does not specify what constitutes an eclipse prediction; and he seems untroubled by the idea that one can predict eclipses
on the basis of such planetary phenomena as their risings and settings or
colour, as well as by the implication that eclipses might be averted through
the performance of some ritual act. Still, we should remember in all fairness
that this is not how the Babylonians determined when to look for eclipses,
at least so far as one can tell given the extant documents in cuneiform.[37]

The claim that the Chaldeans predicted eclipses on the basis of astral
phenomena takes on even greater significance when Diodorus adds that they
assigned the moon an orbit closest to the earth, and agreed with the Hellenes
that the moon's light is reflected and that lunar eclipses are caused by the
moon's entering the earth's shadow (2. 31. 5–6). It is, of course, regrettable
that he does not elaborate what the Chaldeans putatively understood in
holding this view of lunar eclipses, and how they supposedly reconciled this
with their view that eclipses are signified by planetary phenomena and are
in theory avertable, or what he means in adding that

περὶ δὲ τῆς κατὰ τὸν ἥλιον ἐκλείψεως ἀσθενεστάτας ἀποδείξεις φέροντες οὐ τολμῶσι
προλέγειν οὐδ' ἀκριβῶς ὑπὲρ ταύτης περιγράφειν τοὺς χρόνους. (D.S. 2. 31. 6)

regarding the eclipse of the sun, they introduce the weakest demonstrations and do
not dare to make a prediction or to circumscribe precisely time intervals for this.

It is not clear whether, for Diodorus, this ability to predict eclipses belongs
to the Chaldeans alone. It certainly does not seem to be a feature of Hellenic
science: all he says about the Hellenes on this score is that Hellenic soldiers
were prone to viewing eclipses as portents of misfortune (cf. e.g. 20. 5. 5).
But, as for the Egyptians—this time the Egyptians at Thebes rather than
the class of Egyptian priests—he writes:

[1] οἱ δὲ Θηβαῖοί φασιν ἑαυτοὺς ἀρχαιοτάτους εἶναι πάντων ἀνθρώπων, καὶ παρ' ἑαυτοῖς
πρώτοις φιλοσοφίαν τε εὑρῆσθαι καὶ τὴν ἐπ' ἀκριβὲς ἀστρολογίαν, ἅμα καὶ τῆς χώρας
αὐτοῖς συνεργούσης πρὸς τὸ τηλαυγέστερον ὁρᾶν τὰς ἐπιτολάς τε καὶ δύσεις τῶν ἄστρων.
[2] ἰδίως δὲ καὶ τὰ περὶ τοὺς μῆνας αὐτοῖς καὶ τοὺς ἐνιαυτοὺς διατετάχθαι. τὰς γὰρ

[37] See Aaboe, Britton, *et al.* (n. 11).

ἡμέρας οὐκ ἄγουσι κατὰ σελήνην, ἀλλὰ κατὰ τὸν ἥλιον, τριακονθημέρους μὲν τιθέμενοι τοὺς μῆνας, πέντε δ' ἡμέρας καὶ τέταρτον τοῖς δώδεκα μησὶν ἐπάγουσι, καὶ τούτῳ τῷ τρόπῳ τὸν ἐνιαύσιον κύκλον ἀναπληροῦσιν. ἐμβολίμους δὲ μῆνας οὐκ ἄγουσιν οὐδ' ἡμέρας ὑφαιροῦσι, καθάπερ οἱ πλεῖστοι τῶν Ἑλλήνων. περὶ δὲ τῶν ἐκλείψεων ἡλίου τε καὶ σελήνης ἀκριβῶς ἐπεσκέφθαι δοκοῦσι, καὶ προρρήσεις περὶ τούτων ποιοῦνται, πάντα τὰ κατὰ μέρος γινόμενα προλέγοντες ἀδιαπτώτως. (D.S. 1. 50. 1–2)

[1] The Thebans say that they are themselves the most ancient of all men and that philosophy and precise astronomy were discovered by them first, since their land in fact works together with them for seeing more clearly the risings and settings of the stars. [2] [They] also [say] that the months and the years are arranged in a way peculiar to them. For they do not keep the days according to the moon but according to the sun; positing months of thirty days, they add five days and a quarter to twelve months and in this way fill up the annual cycle. But they do not introduce intercalary months nor do they subtract days as most Greeks do. *And they seem to have made precise observations concerning the eclipses of the sun and moon, and they make forecasts about them, predicting all the individual things that happen without error.*

So construed, the passage means that the Thebans treated eclipses as signs and had a system of interpreting these signs.[38] But the italicized sentence may also be rendered

And they seem to have made precise observations of the eclipses of the sun and moon, and they make forecasts of them, predicting all the individual things that happen without error.

And so Diodorus' point could equally well be that the Thebans predicted eclipses accurately and in detail. I see no way to decide this matter on the basis of the text itself.[39]

In sum, Polybius first promoted the idea that to be successful a military

---

[38] Cf. E. Murphy, *The Antiquities of Egypt: A Translation with Notes of Book 1 of the* Library of History *of Diodorus Siculus* (New Brunswick and London, 1990), 64: 'Also, they seem to have studied with care the eclipses of the sun and moon and make predictions concerning them, infallibly foretelling every particular.'

[39] There are no judicial predictions or lunar omina in the dream-books, seemingly the only native Egyptian omen literature. So, whatever Diodorus has in mind apparently must ultimately go back to some Babylonian source (cf. R. A. Parker, *A Vienna Demotic Papyrus on Eclipse- and Lunar-Omina* (Providence, 1959), 28 n. 2, 53–4). Indeed, in the Vienna papyrus, a demotic copy made in the late 2nd cent. AD of two separate books, one finds in the copy of the first book or Text A both judicial predictions and assertions about events and conditions that signify eclipses. While there is no doubt that Text A derives from Babylonian sources (with some modifications), it is difficult to say when this text was originally written. All one knows is that Text A makes no mention of the zodiac (which was, I gather, introduced into Egyptian astrological literature in the 3rd cent. BC) and that the identification of Choiak with Nisanu (month I of the Babylonian year) suggests a date roughly between –624 and –481 (cf. Parker, op. cit. 28–30). The problem in assuming that such information is sufficient to date Text A is the existence of Egyptian texts which were created at a relatively late date but written in an ancient style. For a Babylonian-style listing in demotic of lunar eclipses during the 1st cent. BC see O. Neugebauer, R. A. Parker, and K.-T. Zauzich, 'A Demotic Lunar Eclipse Text of the First Century B.C.', *PAPhS* 125 (1981), 312–27.

commander should learn from astronomers that eclipses are not harbingers of disaster. And a century later, while Diodorus was explaining that predicting eclipses was a notable accomplishment of Chaldean (and, perhaps, Egyptian) astronomers, Livy was, it seems, creatively adapting these assertions in elaborating the tale of Gallus' exploits at Pydna.

Let us return now to the accounts written in Greek and Latin before Ptolemy which associate the battle that took place in −167 south of Pydna near present-day Katerini with a lunar eclipse, to set the Livian and Plinian versions more clearly in their literary context.

3. The Story of the Lunar Eclipse and the Battle at Pydna

3.1. *Polybius and the battle of Pydna*

Shortly after the battle of Pydna, Polybius was deported to Rome, where he became a friend of P. Cornelius Scipio Aemilianus Africanus Minor, Paulus' second son and the adoptive son of P. Cornelius Scipio (who was himself the son of P. Cornelius Scipio Africanus Maior). During his years in Rome Polybius, who valued autopsy as a basis for historical writing,[40] had access to official records. Now, he *may* have been one of the earliest historians to recount the battle of Pydna that had so changed his own life. The text ascribed to him in the *Suda*, a tenth-century lexicon, reports what I suspect was a common way of framing such momentous events, namely, by presenting them as foretold in some way:[41]

Πολύβιος· ὅτι τῆς σελήνης ἐκλειπούσης ἐπὶ Περσέως τοῦ Μακεδόνος ἐκράτησεν ἡ φήμη παρὰ τοῖς πολλοῖς ὅτι βασιλέως ἔκλειψιν σημαίνει. καὶ τοῦτο τοὺς μὲν Ῥωμαίους εὐθαρσεστέρους ἐποίησε, τοὺς δὲ Μακεδόνας ἐταπείνωσε ταῖς ψυχαῖς. οὕτως ἀληθές ἐστι τὸ περιφερόμενον ὅτι πολλὰ κενὰ τοῦ πολέμου. (Polyb. 39. 16)

Polybius [writes] that, when the moon was eclipsed during the reign of Perseus of Macedonia, the rumour gained ascendancy among the populace that it signified the eclipse of the king. And, while this made the Romans bolder, it discouraged the Macedonians. So the saying that there are many empty things in war is true.

But there is, I fear, no way to determine if this is in fact what Polybius wrote.

3.2. *The legend of Gallus*

If there is a single criterion by which to distinguish the Greek and Latin accounts of the battle of Pydna and the lunar eclipse in the extant literature pre-dating Ptolemy, it lies in the role assigned to one C. Sulpicius Gallus. On the Greek side, though there are extant a number of fragments thought

---

[40] Cf. Walbank (n. 25), 40–3, 50–2, 71–6, 79–80.
[41] See ibid. 58–65 on Polybius and the idea of the supernatural in history.

by scholars to belong to chapters written by Polybius and Diodorus about the battle, none of them connects Gallus and the eclipse. The same is true of Plutarch's *Aemilius Paulus*, which is complete (see § 3.2.3 below). On the Latin side, however, there are two main strains in the surviving accounts. In one, Gallus predicts and explains the eclipse; whereas in the other, he only explains it. Cicero's *Rep.* 1. 23–4, the earliest source to connect Gallus and a lunar eclipse at Pydna, portrays Gallus as explaining the phenomenon to the anxious Roman troops; whereas Livy's report at 44. 37. 5–9 is the earliest to assert that Gallus actually predicted this eclipse. So, let us begin with Cicero and those later Latin authors that apparently followed his lead.

My thesis is that all the Latin writers who offered versions of the Gallus story were in fact largely indebted to Cicero's account, and that this account is essentially a literary invention guided in part by a reading of Polybius.

3.2.1. *Cicero in praise of Gallus* M. Tullius Cicero (−105 to −42) mentions both Gallus and the battle of Pydna only once, in a fictive philosophical dialogue, the *De re publica*, written in the light of Plato's *Republic* (cf. e.g. *Rep.* 2. 21–2) during the interval from −3 to −50.[42] The central character, Scipio, is a dramatic representation of P. Cornelius Scipio Aemilianus Africanus Minor, who, as already noted, was L. Aemilius Paulus' second son and a close friend of Polybius. In the *De re publica*, though Cicero speaks in his own voice in the prefatory sections and reports the dialogue proper, Scipio is the primary spokesman for his views in this dialogue.[43]

The immediate context of the reference to Gallus and Pydna is the exchange between Scipio and Tubero about the possibility of knowing the causes of such celestial phenomena as the recently reported appearance of two suns, a discussion that quickly turns to the question of the value of understanding the cosmos in general and of astronomy in particular (*Rep.* 1. 15–17, 19). It is during Philus' retelling of an incident concerning Gallus and celestial globes that the issue of eclipses first comes up (*Rep.* 1. 21–2). Unfortunately, immediately after Philus explains Gallus' use of a globe to display the motions of the sun and moon and the occurrences of eclipses, there is a gap in the received text. When it resumes, Scipio is speaking:

[23] . . . quod et ipse hominem diligebam et in primis patri meo Paulo probatum et carum fuisse cognoveram. memini me admodum adulescentulo, cum pater in Macedonia consul esset et essemus in castris, perturbari exercitum nostrum religione et metu, quod serena nocte subito candens et plena luna defecisset. Tum ille, cum legatus noster esset anno fere ante, quam consul est declaratus, haud dubitavit

---

[42] Cf. J. E. G. Zetzel, *M. Tullius Cicero, De re publica: Selections* (Cambridge, 1995), 1–3. On Cicero's philosophical affiliations, especially his 'Platonism', see e.g. J. Glucker, 'Cicero's Philosophical Affiliations', in J. M. Dillon and A. A. Long (eds.), *The Question of 'Eclecticism': Studies in Later Greek Philosophy* (Berkeley, Los Angeles, and London, 1988), 34–69.
[43] Cf. Zetzel (n. 42), 3–4.

postridie palam in castris docere nullum esse prodigium, idque et tum factum esse
et certis temporibus esse semper futurum, cum sol ita locatus fuisset, ut lunam
suo lumine non posset attingere. ain tandem?, inquit Tubero, docere hoc poterat
illos homines paene agrestes et apud imperitores audebat haec dicere? Ille vero et
magna quidem cum . . . [24] . . . ⟨neque in⟩solens ostentatio neque oratio abhorrens
a persona hominis gravissimi; rem enim magnam ⟨erat⟩ adsecutus, quod hominibus
perturbatis inanem religionem timoremque deiecerat. (Cic. *Rep.* 1. 23–4)

[23] ' . . . because I myself loved the man [sc. Gallus] and I was aware that he was
highly esteemed and beloved by my father, Paulus. I recall, as a very young man,
when my father was consul in Macedonia and we were in camp, that our army was
disturbed by superstition and fear because on a clear night a shining full moon was
eclipsed. Then, as he was our legate at the time—it being roughly the year before he
was declared consul—he lost no time the next day in teaching openly in the camp
that it was no omen, and that it had happened at that time and was always going
to happen at fixed times when the sun was so positioned that it could not reach the
moon with its light.'

'Do you really mean', said Tubero, 'that he could teach men who were almost
savages this, and that he dared to say these things before the ignorant?'

'Yes he did, and with great . . .[44] [24] . . .neither immoderate display nor speech
inconsistent with the character of a man of the greatest dignity. Indeed, he secured
a very important result, because he dispelled foolish superstition and fear from men
who were troubled.'

As Cicero would have it, then, Gallus calmed the troops the day after
the lunar eclipse took place by offering a causal explanation mentioning
the relative positions of the sun, moon, and earth, and remarking that such
eclipses occur regularly in the course of celestial events and are not ominous.
This seems simple enough, but it raises a number of questions.

First, in Cicero's view, does this explanation belong to the sort of astronomy that Diodorus ascribes to the Chaldeans and Egyptians? There is
reason, I think, to hold that it does not. To begin, Cicero is plainly aware
of Chaldean and Egyptian astronomical theories: he outlines pretty much
the same account of them at *Div.* 1. 2 as Diodorus offers, albeit, unlike
Diodorus, he registers scepticism about their ability to predict the future.
Indeed, since he takes the issue to be important, Cicero proposes to examine
the arguments for and against divination (cf. *Div.* 1. 7). This he does by way
of a dramatic device, i.e. by 'reporting' a conversation in which his brother,
Quintus, speaks for divination and he speaks against. The upshot of this
conversation is that divination has no proper standing as knowledge, and
this includes the horoscopic astrology associated with the Chaldeans (*Div.*
2. 87–99). So, given this negative assessment of the validity of divination,
I think it fair to suppose that Gallus' purported explanation of the lunar
eclipse in the *De re publica* is of the traditional sort of theory maintained by

---

[44] There is a lacuna here in Ziegler's text: cf. K. Ziegler (ed.), *M. Tullius Cicero:* De re
publica (Leipzig, 1955), 16.

those whom Diodorus calls Hellenes (D.S. 2. 31. 5–6) and is unallied with astrology.

In any case, this theory differs in one significant respect from the sort of account one finds in Aristotle's writings. What is new is the emphasis on the periodicity of the phenomenon. Both the Ciceronian and the Aristotelian theories explain eclipses causally in terms of the relative positions of the sun, moon, and earth; and both reject the view that eclipses are ominous. The Gallus story in Cicero, however, brings to the fore what is only latent in Aristotle's treatises, namely, that eclipses occur periodically in the regular order of nature; and thus it makes periodicity or time *an essential or critical part* of the understanding of what eclipses are.[45] This is a striking innovation with important consequences in the history of Hellenic and Roman astronomy because it opens the way to predicting eclipses and treating them mathematically. There is, however, no way to decide whether this comes from reflection on contemporary Hellenic and Roman astronomy or from the logical requirements of the Gallus story. After all, how effective would Gallus' purported efforts to calm the troops have been if he had neglected to point out that the celestial configurations producing eclipses occur at fixed intervals? Given Tubero's astonishment that Gallus actually dared to address the troops as he did, it seems to me that Cicero would have us believe that they were, because of their lack of education, strongly disposed to treating *any* lunar eclipse as an omen. Thus, if Gallus had neglected to mention the periodicity of the phenomenon and thereby to encompass all such eclipses in his account, his explanation would hardly have been sufficient to counteract their superstitious fear.

Next, was there really a lunar eclipse at the battle of Pydna that Gallus explained to the troops? This is a difficult question that has two parts, the first concerning whether there was a lunar eclipse just before or during the battle and the second, whether Gallus explained it to the assembled Roman troops. By itself, I do not think that *Rep.* 1. 23–4 is good evidence for a verdict on either count. After all, the passage lacks pertinent historical detail and is, moreover, sufficiently explained by literary considerations.

To begin, consider the dramatic setting of the *De re publica* as a whole. Cicero proposes to recount to his brother, Quintus, a conversation that supposedly took place in −128, more than twenty years before Cicero was born. As Cicero indicates, this conversation was reported to him and to young Quintus by P. Rutilius Rufus (cf. *Rep.* 1. 13–14) while they were in Smyrna, and thus nearly fifty years after the event itself and roughly another twenty

---

[45] This is not to say that Aristotle does not recognize that eclipses are regularly recurrent phenomena, only that he does not treat their periodicity as a defining characteristic and so does not emphasize their recurrence in his accounts of what they really are: cf. e.g. *An. post.* 90ᵃ15–18; *Cael.* 291ᵇ17–23, 293ᵇ21–5, and 297ᵇ23–30.

before Cicero recorded it.[46] The detail Cicero supplies in establishing this conversation is impressive: but verisimilitude is no guarantee of historical authenticity. After all, there are many plain signs that this conversation is a fiction or, better, an idealization of past luminaries in Roman political life engaged in a conversation that never took place.[47] Notice, for example, that the opening conversation between Tubero and Scipio (*Rep.* 1. 14–16) takes place *before* Rufus, Cicero's putative source of information about the conversation, enters. Further, as Cicero himself indicates, what he relates is determined by the logical requirements of the subject that he has broached in his preface, namely, the supreme value of public life as he construes it (cf. *Rep.* 1. 1–12). Then, there is the fact that the report about Gallus reaches the reader at third hand. Granted, one might choose to suppose that this is proof of a chain of authority. But the *De re publica* is a philosophical treatise in the form of a dramatic dialogue, and such an interpretation is better suited to historical works—and even then one should not neglect the possibility that it is a rhetorical device. In any case, the reader may recall that a similar sequence of nested recollections is used in the *Parmenides* by Plato, an author Cicero certainly read, where it serves to emphasize the fictive character of the historical setting and thus to focus the reader's attention on the philosophical argument by itself.[48]

Next, there is no doubt that Cicero had read Polybius' *Historiae* and drew on it extensively in writing his *De re publica*.[49] In fact, he explicitly cites Polybius three times, complimenting him for his expertise in political theory (1. 34), acknowledging his authority and his accuracy as a chronologist (2. 27), and noting his criticism of Roman educational institutions (4. 3). At *Off.* 3. 113 Cicero even describes Polybius as among the best, i.e. most reliable, writers.[50] By themselves Cicero's citations of Polybius do not, of course, prove that he read Polybius' digression on the art of the commander. Still, given also that Polybius *may* have reported a story about an eclipse viewed as ominous that was *recalled* at the battle, and that no Greek writer before Plutarch mentions a lunar eclipse on the night prior to the battle itself, it would certainly seem comfortably within the realm of possibility that Cicero has adapted Polybius' account of what the proper commander should know by inventing the episode about Gallus and thereby valorizing him. There are certainly other passages in which Gallus is praised for his knowledge of the heavens (see *Rep.* 1. 21–2: cf. 1. 30; *Off.* 1. 19; *Sen.* 49). But Cicero's praise of Gallus and his conduct at the battle of Pydna serves not only to enhance Gallus' standing as a military and political leader, it

---

[46] Cf. Zetzel (n. 42), 11.   [47] Cf. ibid. 5–8, 12–13.

[48] Cf. R. E. Allen, *Plato's* Parmenides*: Translation and Analysis* (Minneapolis, 1983), 64–6.

[49] Compare book 6 of Polybius (see Walbank (n. 25), 130–56) and Cic. *Rep.* 1. 38–69, on constitutional theory. On Cicero's critical response to Polybius' history of the development of the Roman polity see Zetzel (n. 42), 22–3.

[50] There are two additional references to Polybius, at *Fam.* 5. 12. 2 and *Att.* 13. 30. 2.

also ratifies the superior quality of the Roman command at Pydna, a command which included Paulus' son, Scipio (cf. *Rep.* 1. 1, 18), who apparently distinguished himself at Pydna as well and who is, as the dialogue's leading interlocutor, the main spokesman for Cicero's own views. In sum, the story Cicero retails about Gallus may ultimately be of a piece with Cicero's intention to state his own case on behalf of public life by the device of a 'conversation among men who were the most eminent and wisest of one era of the Republic' (*Rep.* 1. 13). It certainly serves well in its immediate context as a step in Cicero's development of the thesis that astronomy is useful in public affairs (*Rep.* 1. 14–30).

Of course, there is no absolute certainty that Cicero's story of Gallus is a literary invention rather than a historical report. As in any good story, certain elements are demonstrably true: for instance, there really was a C. Sulpicius Gallus who enjoyed an illustrious career in political service; there really was a lunar eclipse observable at Pydna in the early summer of −167; and there really was a battle in the same place which brought the third Macedonian war to a close. Nevertheless, the chance that Cicero's story may still be in essence a literary invention is good enough, I think, to render *Rep.* 1. 23–4 unusable as a basis for historical claims about Gallus' explaining this eclipse to anxiety-ridden Roman troops or even about the chronology of the eclipse and the battle.

There is certainly no hope of settling such matters by recourse to the reports of Gallus and the lunar eclipse at Pydna found in the writings of Valerius Maximus (8. 11. 1) and Quintilian (*Inst.* 1. 10. 46–8), both of whom were active in the first century AD. For, these reports are, it seems, dependent on Cicero's account and his rhetorical theory. Certainly, Valerius Maximus and Quintilian were both familiar with Cicero's writings, especially those concerning rhetoric. And both agree in limiting Gallus to an explanation that convinced his listeners that a lunar eclipse which had already occurred was not an omen, and in treating Gallus' contribution as a valuable service to his fellows. Moreover, they are equally vague about the timing of the eclipse relative to the battle, and about the details of this explanation. The principal difference is that, whereas Cicero presents Gallus' interest in astronomy more as a gentleman's leisure pursuit that just happened to have beneficial use during a particular campaign, they point to the education of such leaders and emphasize that it should involve not only learning the astronomical facts and their explanations but also acquiring the skills needed to convey them. Thus, Valerius and Quintilian seem more 'Polybian' than Cicero because they do not treat astronomy simply as an intellectual adornment befitting a cultivated Roman but affirm a real need for some astronomical learning in non-leisure activities. Nevertheless, such differences do not alter the fact that the burden of proof lies on those who would propose that Valerius and

Quintilian offer independent testimony confirming the dating of the lunar eclipse in relation to the battle of Pydna and Gallus' explanation of it.

In contrast to Cicero, Valerius Maximus, and Quintilian, there were other Latin authors who held that Gallus predicted the lunar eclipse at Pydna in −167. Let us now consider what they have to say.

3.2.2. *Livy* redux   As I have already remarked, the earliest extant source to ascribe a prediction to Gallus was Livy. Now, Livy was roughly contemporary with Diodorus Siculus and a child when Cicero was composing his main philosophical works, which include the *De re publica* and *De divinatione*. Livy's *Ab urbe condita* shows that he was familiar with Polybius' *Historiae*—Polybius is cited favourably several times in books 31–45, which concern the Macedonian and eastern wars down to −166.[51] Yet, as we have seen, Livy did not share Polybius' avowed concern for historical accuracy but put higher value on the literary, i.e. the didactic and ethical, merits of his account.

As for the details of Livy's report of Gallus' prediction of the lunar eclipse, our conclusion thus far is that Livy's dating and chronological arrangement of the four critical events in his story—the prediction of the lunar eclipse, its occurrence, the battle itself, and the summer solstice of that year—is impossible; and that there is no objective way to determine wherein the error lies. Now, my thesis is that the error arises here not because Livy was confused about his sources or because he neglected them. Rather, I see it as an incidental outcome of his efforts to construct a good story.

One of the hallmarks of a good historical anecdote is verisimilitude. And the sort of astronomical knowledge that Livy says Gallus displayed is wholly consistent with the representation of astronomy, especially Chaldean astronomy, found in Diodorus' *Bibliotheca historica*. That is, along with the idea that lunar eclipses are regularly recurrent and thus predictable events is the idea that they are to be explained causally by the moon's entering the earth's shadow. The key difference is that, whereas Diodorus presents such knowledge as the province of expert, albeit foreign, astronomers, Livy seems to acknowledge Polybius in treating it as part of what a successful military commander knows. But such verisimilitude should not deceive us into thinking that what Livy reports of Gallus is indeed true. For there is, I submit, reason to hold that Livy may be indebted primarily to Cicero for the idea that Gallus predicted the eclipse.

To begin, Cicero, in his *Cato Maior de senectute*, a philosophical dialogue completed in −43, adds to what he has indicated elsewhere about Gallus:

Videbamus in studio dimetiendi paene caeli atque terrae Gallum familiarem patris tui, Scipio. Quotiens illum lux noctu aliquid describere ingressum, quotiens nox

---

[51] Cf. Livy 30. 45. 5; 33. 10. 10; 34. 50. 6; 36. 19. 11; 39. 52. 1; 45. 44. 19.

oppressit cum mane coepisset. quam delectabat eum defectiones solis et lunae multo ante nobis praedicere. (*Sen.* 14. 49)

Scipio, we used to see your father's good friend, Gallus, at work all but measuring the heavens and the Earth. How often daylight would catch him drawing something which he had begun at night; how often night would catch him (doing something) when he had begun in the early morning. How it used to delight him to make a prediction for us, much in advance, of an eclipse of the sun and moon.

That is, Cicero credits Gallus not only with understanding the causes of eclipses but also with the ability to predict (*praedicere*) them.[52]

Accordingly, if we take Cicero's stories about Gallus as the background for Livy's own, then one possibility, I suppose, is that Livy, inspired by a reading of Polybius, decided to enhance Cicero's version of the Gallus story in the *De re publica* by combining Cicero's claims about Gallus and the eclipse, by dating the battle to the day after the eclipse, and by adding technical detail about the eclipse itself for heightened literary effect. The aim in this would, perhaps, have been to outdo the account of Gallus and Thales found in Cicero's writings and to supply yet another reason why the Romans surpassed the Greeks at Pydna in −167, thereby giving the Gallus story an interesting polemical spin.

This leaves the question of how Livy settled on the dates in his story and the hours of the eclipse's duration. I suspect that he has adapted a model of reportage otherwise unattested in earlier Graeco-Latin documents.[53] As for the numerical detail itself, it is conceivable that Livy is relying on a real (but garbled) report of the eclipse as observed at a location to the east of Pydna. And it is equally conceivable that this detail is the result of astrological computations made after the fact. After all, if, as Diodorus writes, astrology is predicated on determinism, it would seem to afford an excellent means of demonstrating the inevitability of critical events in the history of great personages and rival nations after the fact. In any case, there is evidence that astrology was used for such purposes in Livy's time.[54] Others will doubtless imagine further possibilities.

But, however the details of Livy's account of Gallus' conduct on the eve of the battle at Pydna were decided and whatever their historical worth, its literary force from a Polybian standpoint is the same as that of the accounts

[52] Note that Cicero attributes the same to Thales: cf. *Rep.* 1. 25 and *Div.* 1. 112. The latter passage is the earliest unambiguous occurrence in Graeco-Latin literature of the claim that Thales predicted the eclipse during a battle between the Lydians and Medes.

[53] There are numerous reports of lunar eclipses in Ptolemy's *Almagest*. Though many state only the (seasonal) hour of night when the eclipse began, two specify its duration in the same way as Livy's report does. See Goldstein and Bowen (n. 3), appendix 1: nos. 30 (22 Sept. −200), 33 (1 May −173), as well as nos. 9 (23 Dec. −382), 10 (18 June −381) with i. 342. 1–2 Heiberg. For an analysis of these eclipses see J. P. Britton, *Models and Precision: The Quality of Ptolemy's Observations and Parameters* (London and New York, 1992), 61–8.

[54] See T. Barton, *Ancient Astrology* (London and New York, 1994), 39–41. I am grateful to Roz Parks for drawing this possibility to my attention.

offered by Cicero, Valerius Maximus, and Quintilian, namely, that Gallus
was indeed a paradigmatic commander. Viewed in this light, Livy's version
is noteworthy because, unlike Cicero and Valerius, who present Gallus as
a legate or commander of a legion, he assigns Gallus the lower rank (in
Republican times, at least) of tribune or senior staff officer in a legion.
Livy's point in making Gallus a tribune is, perhaps, to present the qualities
of the Polybian commander as more widespread among the Roman military
leadership and perhaps even as common among the troops themselves,
given that tribunes were in many instances elected from the ranks.[55] To
a literate reader familiar with Polybius' account of what the successful
military commander needs to know and with Cicero's valorization of Gallus,
Livy's version would thus signify, I expect, that the Roman victory was
morally deserved, at least to the extent that an underlying issue here is the
education of military personnel and their quality.

The only other pre-Ptolemaic Latin author who affirms that Gallus predicted the lunar eclipse at Pydna is S. Iulius Frontinus (*c*.30–104). In his
Strategemata Frontinus recounts incidents in which the fear that sometimes overtakes soldiers when they are confronted by adverse signs is relieved, among which he includes Gallus' achieving this end by predicting
and explaining the eclipse (cf. *Strat.* 1. 12. 1. 8). Since this report may
derive either from Livy or from Cicero's writings, it does not qualify as
independent confirmation of Livy's account.[56]

3.2.3. *Plutarch's response*   The earliest extant text to describe the battle
of Pydna in Greek is the *Aemilius Paulus* of Plutarch (before 50 to after
120). What is interesting here is that Plutarch, who was certainly aware of
Polybius' *Historiae* (cf. *Aem.* 15. 5; 16. 3; 19. 4),[57] follows Livy in placing
the lunar eclipse on the night before the battle.

[7] ἐπεὶ δὲ νὺξ γέγονει καὶ μετὰ δεῖπνον ἐτράποντο πρὸς ὕπνον καὶ ἀνάπαυσιν, αἰφνίδιον
ἡ σελήνη πλήρης οὖσα καὶ μετέωρος ἐμελαίνετο καὶ τοῦ φωτὸς ἀπολίποντος αὐτὴν χρόας
ἀμείψασα παντοδαπὰς ἠφνίσθη. [8] τῶν δὲ Ῥωμαίων, ὥσπερ ἐστὶ νενομισμένον, χαλκοῦ τε
πατάγοις ἀνακαλουμένων τὸ φῶς αὐτῆς καὶ πυρὰ πολλὰ δαλοῖς καὶ δασὶν ἀνεχόντων πρὸς
τὸ οὐρανόν, οὐδὲν ὅμοιον ἔπραττον οἱ Μακεδόνες, ἀλλὰ φρίκη καὶ θάμβος τὸ στρατόπεδον
κατεῖχε καὶ λόγος ἡσυχῇ διὰ πολλῶν ἐχώρει, βασιλέως τὸ φάσμα σημαίνειν ἔκλειψιν. [9] ὁ
δ' Αἰμίλιος οὐκ ἦν μὲν ἀνήκοος οὐδ' ἄπειρος παντάπασι τῶν ἐκλειπτικῶν ἀνωμαλιῶν, αἳ
τὴν σελήνην περιφερομένην εἰς τὸ σκίασμα τῆς γῆς ἐμβάλλουσι τεταγμέναις περιόδοις καὶ
ἀποκρύπτουσιν, ἄχρι οὗ παρελθοῦσα τὴν ἐπισκοτουμένην χώραν πάλιν ἐπιλάμψῃ πρὸς τὸν
ἥλιον· [10] οὐ μὴν ἀλλὰ τῷ θείῳ πολὺ νέμων καὶ φιλοθύτης ὢν καὶ μαντικός, ὡς εἶδε

[55] I thank Vivian Nutton for drawing this to my attention.
[56] The same holds true of whatever presumably Latin source is responsible, via Cassius Dio
and some oversimplification, for the version in Zonaras (*Epit.* 9. 23. 5), where Paulus (not
Gallus) assembles the army and foretells the eclipse.
[57] The consensus among scholars is that Plutarch relied on Polybius in writing *Aemilius
Paulus* (cf. B. Scardigli, *Die Römerbiographien Plutarchs* (Munich, 1979), 57 and n. 280).

πρῶτον τὴν ἀποκαθαιρομένην, ἕνδεκα μόσχους αὐτῇ κατέθυσεν. [11] ἅμα δ᾽ ἡμέρᾳ τῷ
Ἡρακλεῖ βουθυτῶν οὐκ ἐκαλλιέρει μέχρις εἴκοσι· τῷ δὲ πρώτῳ καὶ εἰκοστῷ παρῆν τὰ
σημεῖα καὶ νικὴν ἀμυνομένοις ἔφραζεν. [12] εὐξάμενος οὖν κατὰ βοῶν ἑκατὸν καὶ ἀγῶνος
ἱεροῦ τῷ θεῷ, προσέταξε διακοσμεῖν τοῖς ἡγεμόσι τὸν στρατὸν εἰς μάχην. (Plut. *Aem.* 17.
7–12)

[7] When night had come and after supper when [the soldiers] were taking recourse
to rest and sleep, suddenly the moon, which was full and on high, became dark
and as the light left it turned all sorts of colours in succession and disappeared.
[8] While the Romans, as is their custom, were calling back the moon's light by
the clashing of bronze and holding up many lights to the heavens in the form of
firebrands and torches, the Macedonians did nothing of the sort; but astonishment
and terror seized their camp, and word that the phenomenon signified the eclipse
of a king spread quietly among many. [9] Now, Aemilius [Paulus] was not utterly
without knowledge and experience of the variety[58] of eclipses which cast the moon,
as it goes round, into the shadow of the earth at regular periods of time and conceal
it until it passes beyond the shaded region [of the heavens] and shines forth in
consequence of the sun. [10] Nevertheless, since he was very observant of the divine
and given to sacrifices and like a diviner, Paulus sacrificed eleven heifers to the moon
as soon as he first saw the Moon being purified.[59] [11] And, though he sacrificed
as many as twenty oxen to Heracles at daylight, he did not get favourable signs;
but with the twenty-first the signs were given and indicated victory for them, if
they were on the defensive. [12] So, after he made a vow to the god offering a
hundred oxen and a sacred contest, he ordered his commanders to ready the army
for battle.

Notice in this passage how the different armies respond to the occurrence of
the lunar eclipse. For the Romans, the event was magical: they apparently
feared that the moon was suffering sorcery and attempted to reverse its
effect by making a noise and driving off the sorcerers (cf. Pliny, *HN* 2. 54).
But, for the Macedonians, the event was mantic: the eclipse was construed
as a sign from the gods of impending disaster for a state (cf. Plut. *Pelop.*
31. 2–4). As for Paulus, he was hardly, in Plutarch's account, the Polybian
ideal as a commander, an ideal Plutarch may well have come across in his
extensive reading of Polybius' *Historiae*. All Plutarch allows is that Paulus
was aware by virtue of instruction and experience that eclipses are of different types and magnitudes—Plutarch's remark in 17. 9 that eclipses are
naturally recurrent, causally explicable events only offers reassurance that
he at least knows what they are. Otherwise, Plutarch casts Paulus in the role

---

[58] ἀνωμαλιῶν. B. Perrin, *Plutarch's* Lives: *Dion and Brutus, Timoleon and Aemilius Paulus*
(London, 1918), 400, has 'the irregularities of eclipses'; but the point is surely not that eclipses
are irregular or that they manifest deviations. Given the next lines, it seems better to suppose
that Plutarch is only ascribing to Paulus knowledge that there are eclipses of different sorts
(lunar, solar) and of different degrees (partial, full).

[59] On the significance of the numbers and other details in what follows see C. Liedmeier,
Plutarchus' biographie van Aemilius Paullus: Historische commentaar (Utrecht and Nijmegen,
1935), 295–6, 183–6.

of a diviner who began making the appropriate sacrifices in order to decide what to do next.

So, do we have in Plutarch at last a reliable authority concerning the lunar eclipse and the battle of Pydna? I doubt it. Plutarch's *Aemilius Paulus* belongs to his *Vitae parallelae*, a collection of works describing and then comparing the lives of famous Romans and Hellenes. The basic aim of the collection is to present the moral character of each figure, to illustrate virtue and vice; it is not to record political events faithfully. Obviously, Plutarch had to rely on historical sources in order to construct his own didactic essays. In the case of Paulus and the events just before the battle of Pydna, it would seem that Plutarch's version is more in keeping with the one found in the *Suda* and ascribed to Polybius, at least in omitting any mention of Sulpicius Gallus. The problem here lies in determining the validity of Plutarch's account of what Paulus did. But, that question aside, there are, I think, signs that Plutarch was really addressing Livy's account— certainly scholars have long suspected that he knew this account.[60] As I have already indicated, Plutarch (*Aem.* 17. 2–18. 2) follows Livy in having the battle occur during the daytime after the night in which the lunar eclipse occurred. Then, there is Plutarch's remark (*Aem.* 16. 9) that this battle was fought late in the summer. At first glance this might seem to be new, factual information. But more likely, it seems to me, is that Plutarch has erroneously construed Livy's 3/4 September as a date in the Roman calendar *after* its reform by Caesar in –45[61] and Augustus in –8. Now, I say 'more likely' not only because Livy is, apparently, the only writer prior to Plutarch who dates the battle in relation to the summer solstice, but also because Plutarch's account reads very nicely as a response to Livy's. That is, Plutarch's version of the eclipse with its omission of Gallus and its depiction of how Paulus and the troops of both sides reacted seems an exquisite counter to Livy's chauvinism. In sum, I urge reading Plutarch's account of the eclipse and its effect on the warring camps at Pydna not as factual report but as a literary invention with a pro-Hellenic polemical spin.[62]

This brings us to our final text, a brief account of Gallus' service at Pydna found in the *Historia naturalis* by Pliny (23/4–79). This passage, I

[60] Cf. Scardigli (n. 57), 59 ad *Aem.* 17. 3. Liedmeier (n. 59), 290–1, however, proposes that Plutarch relied on data drawn from Polybius, Scipio Nasica, and Posidonius (the historian). She also contends that, when Livy and Plutarch agree, it is only because they are both adhering to Polybius' version; and that, when they differ, it is because one of them has strayed from the Polybian account.

[61] As Bickerman (n. 18), 47, rightly remarks, the Julian calendar instituted by Caesar is in fact a radical departure from the earlier Roman calendar. Note that by –7, one year after Augustus' intervention, observance of the Julian calendar was properly regularized and that by Plutarch's time this calendar did not diverge appreciably from the course of the sun.

[62] Cf. Grant (n. 23), 73.

shall argue, recasts the tale in a way that illuminates a crucial moment in the history of Hellenic and Roman astronomy.

3.2.4. *Pliny,* HN *2. 53–55*[63] In the course of his remarks (*HN* 2. 41–58) on the sun and the moon, Pliny explains the physical causes of their eclipses and then turns to the question of the history of these explanations:

[53] Et rationem quidem defectus utriusque primus Romani generis in vulgum extulit Sulpicius Gallus, qui consul cum M. Marcello fuit, sed tum tribunus militum, sollicitudine exercitu liberato pridie quam Perses rex superatus a Paulo est in contionem ab imperatore productus ad praedicendam eclipsim, mox et composito volumine. Apud Graecos autem investigavit primus omnium Thales Milesius Olympiados XLVIII anno quarto praedicto solis defectu qui Alyatte rege factus est urbis conditae anno CLXX. Post eos utriusque sideris cursum in sexcentos annos praececinit Hipparchus, menses gentium diesque et horas ac situs locorum et visus populorum complexus, aevo teste haut alio modo quam consiliorum naturae particeps. [54] Viri ingentes supraque mortalia, tantorum numinum lege deprehensa et misera hominum mente iam soluta, in defectibus scelera aut mortem aliquam siderum pavente, quo in metu fuisse Stesichori et Pindari vatum sublimia ora palam est deliquio solis, aut in luna veneficia arguente mortalitate et ob id crepitu dissono auxiliante, quo pavore ignarus causae Nicias Atheniensium imperator veritus classem portu educere opes eorum adflixit: macte ingenio este, caeli interpretes rerumque naturae [55] capaces, argumenti repertores, quo deos hominesque vicistis! Quis enim haec cernens et statos siderum, quoniam ita appellare placuit, labores non suae necessitati mortales genitos ignoscat? (Pliny, *NH* 2. 53–5)

[53] Sulpicius Gallus—who was consul with Marcus Marcellus, but a military tribune at the time—was the first of the Roman people to make public the explanation of the eclipse of each [of the two heavenly bodies] when, on the day before King Perseus was defeated by Paulus, Sulpicius was brought before the assembly of troops by the commander-in-chief in order to predict an eclipse and freed the army from anxiety, and a little later when he wrote a book. Among the Greeks, however, Thales of Miletus, who predicted the eclipse of the Sun which occurred in the fourth year of the 48th Olympiad when Alyattes was king, i.e. in the 170th year from the founding of Rome, was the very first to make enquiry [about eclipses]. After them, the progress[64] of each star for 600 years was proclaimed [*praececinit*] by Hipparchus, who understood the months and days of the nations [of the world], the [seasonal] hours and geographical locations of places, and the appearances of the peoples,[65] and who, as time has shown unequivocally, was partner in the plans of nature.

---

[63] In what follows I take the opportunity to revise and elaborate some claims made in Goldstein and Bowen (n. 10).

[64] *utriusque sideris cursum*: cf. Goldstein and Bowen (n. 10), 156–7.

[65] Rackham—see H. Rackham, W. H. S. Jones, and D. Eichholz, *Pliny*: Natural History (Cambridge, 1942–62), i. 202—renders *menses gentium diesque et horas ac situs locorum et visus populorum complexus* by 'whose work embraced the calendar of the nations and the situations of the places and aspects of the peoples' and adds (i. 202 n. *b*) that *situs* may denote latitude and *visus* longitude. J. Beaujeu, *Pline l'Ancien: Histoire naturelle, livre II* (Paris, 1950), 24, offers 'son œuvre embrasse la détermination des mois dans les diverses régions habitées, la durée des jours et des heures et la situation des lieux à la surface de la terre, les aspects du ciel pour les

[54] O mighty heroes, beyond things mortal, who ascertained the law of such great divinities[66] and freed the wretched mind of man from fear as it shivers in terror of calamities or some death of the stars in eclipses—it is well known that the lofty words of the poets, Stesichorus and Pindar, were [uttered] in this fear of an eclipse of the sun—or as mankind infers sorcery in the case of the moon and on account of this offers assistance with jarring, clashing sound—owing to this terror [of lunar eclipses] Nicias, the commander of the Athenians, who was unaware of their cause, destroyed their resources because he was afraid to bring the fleet out of port—glory to your genius, you interpreters of the heavens [55] able to grasp the nature of things, and discoverers of a theory[67] by which you have vanquished the gods and men! For, who, after discerning these things and the fixed labours—for so

différents peuples'. O. Pedersen, 'Some Astronomical Topics in Pliny', in R. K. French and F. Greenaway (eds.), *Science in the Early Roman Empire: Pliny the Elder, his Sources and Influence* (London and Sydney, 1986), 162–96 at 193, who relies on Rackham and Beaujeu (op. cit. 194), is rightly puzzled by this phrase, though I find implausible his suggestion that its meaning is that Hipparchus included geographical factors in his remarks about eclipses. The problem is that neither Rackham's nor Beaujeu's version is wholly satisfactory.

In the first place, *complexus* modifies *Hipparchus* and means 'who comprehended': there is no warrant here for supposing reference either to a book by Hipparchus or to his work. Next, as Rackham realizes, by pairing *menses gentium diesque*, Pliny conveys that Hipparchus understood the calendars of the various nations, which I take to mean that he knew how to convert dates from one calendar to another. As for *horas ac situs locorum*, Pliny's point is that Hipparchus recognized that the seasonal hours (sc. the twelfth parts of daytime or of nighttime) vary in duration throughout the year at any place in the inhabited world not beneath the celestial equator, and that the duration of the longest daytime at a given place indicates mathematically its κλίμα (sc. the inclination of the North Celestial Pole above its horizon, which is the same as its terrestrial latitude). Finally, *visus populorum* signifies that Hipparchus knew what the various peoples of the world actually looked like, perhaps by way of inference from the characteristics associated with their κλίμα (cf. *HN* 2. 189–90), or perhaps more directly as a collector of travellers' reports: cf. J. S. Romm, *The Edges of the Earth in Ancient Thought: Geography, Exploration, and Fiction* (Princeton, 1992), 94–109, on collectors of wonders and their critics.

In sum, *menses gentium diesque et horas ac situs locorum et visus populorum complexus* singles out Hipparchus for accomplishments as a geographer. It introduces nothing which cannot be extrapolated from Strabo's *Geographia* and its frequent remarks about Hipparchus' treatise attacking the *Geographia* of Eratosthenes.

[66] For *tantorum numinum* Pedersen (n. 65), 168, has 'so many deities (that is, celestial bodies)', thus construing Pliny's claim quite generally. But this seems unlikely: the only celestial bodies at issue are the sun, moon, and earth; and Pliny's encomium makes perfect sense without supposing that he is speaking of laws governing the planets as well. Note that Pliny discusses the five planets later in book 2, and that in his account he does not ascribe any details to any particular person but even presents critical aspects as his own (cf. *HN* 2. 71–8).

[67] *argumenti*: Rackham (n. 65), i. 203, and Pedersen (n. 65), 168, take an *argumentum* to be a principle or law, whereas Beaujeu (n. 65), 24, views it as a theory (cf. M. Beagon, *Roman Nature: The Thought of Pliny the Elder* (Oxford, 1992), 72). I follow Beaujeu. Cf. Pliny, *HN* 18. 210: 'first of all is that a law be sought from the heavens; next, that this (law) should be secured by means of theories'. It appears that, for Pliny, an astronomical law (*lex*) is the detailed statement of a regularity, and that an *argumentum* is its proof or theoretical justification. The idea that *argumentis* designates signs or evidence (Rackham (n. 65), v. 323; Pedersen (n. 65), 169) is not especially compelling. After all, how is one to discern an astronomical law if not in the light of evidence or signs? One might, of course, suppose that the *argumenta* are to confirm the law, but this would be anachronistic.

it has pleased [mankind] to call [them][68]—of the stars does not accept that mortals are born to their own destiny?[69]

Thus, it would appear that Pliny has read the relevant passages in Polybius, Cicero, and Livy, each of whom he cites several times as an authority in book 1 of his *Historia naturalis,* and that he sides with Livy and Frontinus.[70] That is, for Pliny, Gallus made a prediction and gave a causal account of what eclipses are. I presume as well that Pliny follows Livy in supposing that Gallus' speech also included a statement that eclipses are regularly recurrent natural phenomena: only with this addition could Gallus really have freed the troops from their anxiety. The only point requiring explanation to secure this interpretation is Pliny's remark that Gallus 'was brought before the assembly of troops by the commander-in-chief'. Given Livy's claim that the assembly was called with the consul's permission, Pliny need only mean that Gallus had to apply to the consul for permission to hold the meeting and address the troops; and so we may understand that this is the sense in which Gallus was brought forth by the commander-in-chief to make a prediction.[71]

As for *praececinit,* I think Pliny means to ascribe to Hipparchus the ability to specify in advance the (daily) progress of the sun and moon during a cycle of 600 years from a specified date[72] and, thus, to predict all the eclipses that will occur in that period.[73] The verb itself is rare in classical Latin and may have been chosen by Pliny to connote a wondrous accomplishment. the verb *cano* itself is often used to designate the chanting of incantations and the making of prophecies. The difference here is that Hipparchus' putative 'prophecies' are predicated on an arithmetical theory of lunar and solar motion.

On this reading, then, this passage from Pliny advances themes that are fundamental to the *Historia naturalis* as a whole. For, to Pliny, the highest point of human achievement lies in assisting mankind: as he says, 'deus est mortali iuvare mortalem'—'for man to aid man, [that] is god' (2. 18). And one valuable form of this service involves freeing mankind from fear of death and from the desire (*avaritia*) for life after death. Such emotions

[68] Cf. Pliny, *HN* 2. 43; Virgil, *Aen.* 1. 742; *Georg.* 2. 478.
[69] For the text see C. Mayhoff, *C. Plinii secundi naturalis historiae xxxvii* (Leipzig, 1892–1909), i. 143. 4–144. 7.
[70] I owe much of the argument in this paragraph to an anonymous reader for the Press.
[71] Pliny says nothing about how Gallus supposedly made this prediction. From what Pliny indicates about Gallus' knowledge of the heavens—Gallus apparently held that the moon is 126,000 stades (or 78,750,000 paces) from the earth and the sun twice that distance from the moon (*HN* 2. 83: cf. 2. 85)—one can only imagine that Gallus used an eclipse cycle (cf. n. 11) to make his prediction rather than the sort of theory found in Ptolemy's *Almagest.*
[72] Cf. Goldstein and Bowen (n. 10), 157.
[73] There would, of course, be many eclipses of both sorts. But see Lydus, *Ost.* 7, a text written in the 6th cent. AD asserting that Hipparchus ascertained a solar eclipse 600 years in advance.

are the enemy of reason (*ratio*), and chief among them is the fear arising from ignorance that perverts reason by fostering popular religion and the practices of magic and astrology, all of which offend nature and prevent reason from a true relationship with nature.[74] Thus, Thales and Gallus are remarkable for explaining the causes of eclipses to mankind and predicting single solar and lunar eclipses respectively;[75] but Hipparchus is near divine for enabling mankind to foretell eclipses of both kinds for 600 years.[76] Indeed, Pliny later remarks (2. 95) that Hipparchus can never be sufficiently praised, and I suspect that it is for this reason.

At first glance, then, Pliny's innovation lies primarily in supposing that all of this belongs to the Hellenic and Roman intellectual patrimony. This in itself marks a significant departure from the standpoint of Diodorus. For what Diodorus saw as a Chaldean (and, perhaps, an Egyptian) accomplishment is now appropriated by Pliny as part of an imperative for all Hellenes and Romans, an imperative purportedly met superbly by the time of Hipparchus half a century before the publication of the Chaldean (and Egyptian) accomplishments. But there is, I think, still more.

In his encomium of Thales, Hipparchus, and Gallus—they are the mighty heroes (*viri ingentes*) addressed in *HN* 2. 54—Pliny also talks of the law (*lex*) of the sun and moon that sets the minds of men free from fear of eclipses and of the theory (*argumentum*) that enables man to conquer these gods.[77] Moreover, he subsequently elaborates what Hipparchus supposedly knew about the temporal conditions governing the interpositions of the

---

[74] See Beagon (n. 67), 26–106, for a presentation and discussion of these claims that will further illuminate Pliny's encomium at *HN* 2. 54–5.

[75] Not all ancient writers follow Pliny and Cicero in supposing that Thales predicted the eclipse (see n. 52). There is the anonymous commentator (1st or 2nd cent. AD) on book 20 of Homer's *Odyssey* who has Thales stating the configuration of the sun and moon that produces a solar eclipse (P. Oxy. 53. 3710, col. 2. 37–41: cf. A. C. Bowen and B. R. Goldstein, 'Aristarchus, Thales, and Heraclitus on Solar Eclipses: An Astronomical Commentary on P. Oxy. 53. 3710 cols. 2. 33–3. 19', *Physis*, 31 (1994), 689–729). And Theon of Smyrna relates at *Exp.* 3. 40 the report by Dercyllides (early 1st cent. AD: cf. T. H. Martin, *Theonis Smyrnaei liber de astronomia* (Paris, 1849), 69–74) of Eudemus' claim that Thales discovered ($\epsilon\tilde{\upsilon}\rho\epsilon$) the eclipse of the sun, a claim best taken as a reference to the causal explanation of this event.

As for Pliny's date of –583 for Thales' eclipse, by identifying the fourth year of the 48th Olympiad with the 170th year after Rome's founding, Pliny shows that he dates the founding of Rome to –753 (cf. Beaujeu (n. 65), 143 n. 2). Herodotus gives neither the date nor the location of the battle, thus leaving interpreters to infer when the putative eclipse occurred. Scholars have defended –625, –609, –590, and –580 as possibilities (cf. Beaujeu (n. 65), 143). But suppose that the battle took place in Lydia. Calculations made using Planet C 6.2 FPU show that there were only two solar eclipses with an appropriate path of centrality, the first being annular (29 July –587, mag. 11.1) and the second total (28 May –584). Though both eclipses theoretically satisfy Herodotus' report—assuming, for the moment, that it does concern an eclipse—the consensus among scholars today is that Herodotus means the eclipse that occurred on 28 May in –584 (cf. F. R. Stephenson and L. J. Fatoohi, 'Thales' Prediction of a Solar Eclipse', *JHA* 28 (1997), 279–82).

[76] Cf. Pliny, *HN*. 2. 191–2, in which Anaximander and Pherecydes are said to be divine if the stories about their predicting (*praedicere*) earthquakes are true.

[77] On the sense in which they have conquered men, see Beagon (n. 67), 72–4.

sun, moon, and earth that bring about eclipses (cf. *HN* 2. 57), conditions that consequently bear on the question of prediction. Thus he goes beyond Diodorus, who treats astronomy as a disconnected collection of tasks and theories, by suggesting that Thales, Hipparchus, and Gallus relied on a coherent theory.

In sum, Pliny's transformation of the story of Sulpicius Gallus is a masterful piece of cultural appropriation that acknowledges what was by his time a well established literary topos. Less than a century before him, predicting eclipses was presented as a prerogative of the Chaldean or Babylonian astronomers (and perhaps of Egyptian astronomers too); but in his hands it becomes a proper task of Hellenes and Romans, a task incumbent on them as an exalted exercise of reason in the service of humanity. Regardless of whether Pliny's history of astronomy is accurate factually, his appropriation of alien astronomical theory brings to the surface a new question in Hellenic and Roman astronomy: specifically, How is one to integrate the geometrical cosmological models used to explain eclipses with the arithmetical apparatus needed to predict them, i.e. to understand the physical theory of eclipses in such a way that one may compute the date they will occur and even, perhaps, their time and duration? Geminus, Pliny's contemporary, raises a similar question, albeit less explicitly, when he tries to explain the moon's motion in longitude (see *Intro. ast.* 18). In either case, these writers challenged their readers to accommodate Chaldean astronomy in a way that met Hellenic and Roman requirements about what constitutes knowledge. Geminus patently fails on his own terms, as I have argued elsewhere.[78] For his part, Pliny assumes and points to the integrated theory but gives no clue about how he conceives it, though his innovative use of eccentric models in planetary theory (cf. 2. 71) does advance the formulation of the question.

4. Conclusion

Our guiding question was, When, why, and under what circumstances did Hellenic and Roman astronomers come to think that their proper task included stating on the basis of theory the date when eclipses will occur? I have argued that this change in the conception of astronomy occurred in the first century AD and may have been an incidental outcome in the dialectical evolution of a literary topos that has its main roots in comments about military leadership made by Polybius in his *Historiae* some two centuries earlier. This topos appears in diverse contexts. Cicero uses it to show that astronomical knowledge can be useful and beneficial to the Roman people; Pliny follows suit but extends the benefit to all humanity. Livy adapts it in

[78] See A. C. Bowen and B. R. Goldstein, 'Geminus and the Concept of Mean Motion in Greco-Latin Astronomy', *AHES* 50 (1996), 157–85.

his moralizing and even polemical account of the battle at Pydna. Valerius Maximus presents it as an *exemplum* for public speaking. Quintilian offers it as an instance of the beneficial power of oratory and as proof of the value of education in rhetoric. And Frontinus retails it as an instance of sound military leadership.

Now, as I trust I have shown, if one pays attention to the various contexts and ways in which the Gallus story is deployed, one may credibly interpret the topos as essentially a creature of literary imagination. The story does, I admit, have a factual basis, but this basis seems in truth quite slight: there was a battle of Pydna in −167 in which the Romans defeated the Macedonians as well as a lunar eclipse observable there in the same year; and C. Sulpicius Gallus was living at the time. The point is that each of these claims is known to be true on independent grounds. Of course, whether Gallus actually participated in the battle of Pydna is a nice question: under the circumstances perhaps all one should affirm is the disjunctive proposition that either Gallus did or that by the time of Cicero no one knew for certain or cared that he had not. Still, all of this is a far cry from proving that Gallus foretold the eclipse and/or explained it to the troops after its occurrence. For this one has only the sources I have discussed above, and they themselves afford ample reason to doubt that Gallus actually did either. Be this as it may, the upshot is that there is no way to get behind their versions in order to determine the historical *realia* of the Gallus story and some reason to suspect that such a line of enquiry is misguided.

In any case, the documentary evidence extant indicates that the critical step in the transformation of Graeco-Latin astronomy from a qualitative, explanatory science into a quantitative, predictive science was in good measure due to a few literary writers of the first centuries BC and AD, primarily Roman, none of whom was an astronomer. These writers effectively created and publicized the expectation that Hellenic and Roman astronomers be able to predict the positions of the heavenly bodies, thereby pressing on contemporary and subsequent astronomers a new project and goal. Granted, to assess the extent and character of their creativity as well as its consequences we need to examine the assimilation of Babylonian horoscopic astrology into Hellenic and Roman intellectual culture that also began in the first century BC. But this will require considering a much wider range of literary documents in Greek and Latin, documents bearing, for example, on the evolution of the discipline and profession of astronomy during the roughly two centuries before Ptolemy, an evolution seemingly driven in part, for instance, by the effort to understand and appropriate astrology on Hellenic and Roman terms as well as perhaps by competition among practising specialists for remuneration from the devotees of astrology. Thus, for now, the most we should say is that those literary writers who elaborated the story about Gallus and the lunar eclipse apparently created the idea that Hellenic and Roman astronomers should be able to make astronomical predictions about eclipses, and that they may thus have supplemented or ratified an emerging, contemporaneous expectation within Hellenic and Roman astronomy itself that it be both explanatory and predictive in general.[79]

[79] This will seem paradoxical only to those who wrongly take it for granted that ancient astronomical science changed only in response to technical problems within the science itself, or that prediction must have been a feature of Graeco-Latin planetary theory ever since the time of Aristotle and Plato: see Bowen (n. 12).

6

Euctemon's *Parapēgma*

R. HANNAH

1. Introduction

THE smooth functioning of an ordered society still depends today on the possession by that society of a means of regularizing its activities according to a calendar. Different interests—political, economic, religious, agricultural—produce even nowadays different ways of co-ordinating human activities and the natural passage of time and season. The dominance of Western culture in the modern world has meant that its systematization of time—the 'Gregorian' calendar—is accepted worldwide either as the sole means of dating, or as an alternative means which must be acknowledged. That calendar is a simple refinement of the Roman 'Julian' calendar, which, in its turn, is the product of 300 years or so of development by the Greeks of a solar calendar which under the Romans ultimately replaced previous lunar or luni-solar calendars. The purpose of this paper is to re-examine the process by which a solar calendar was formed by the Greeks, by focusing on the role of the Athenian astronomer Euctemon, who worked around 432 BC.

Our earliest record in Greek of the use of the stars as a chronological device occurs in Homer's *Iliad*. At 18. 483–9, for instance, the poet describes the decoration placed by Hephaestus on a new shield for the Greek hero Achilles:

> ἐν μὲν γαῖαν ἔτευξ’, ἐν δ’ οὐρανόν, ἐν δὲ θάλασσαν,
> ἠέλιόν τ’ ἀκάμαντα σελήνην τε πλήθουσαν.
> ἐν δὲ τὰ τείρεα πάντα. τά τ’ οὐρανὸς ἐστεφάνωται,
> Πληϊάδας θ’ Ὑάδας τε τό τε σθένος Ὠρίωνος
> Ἄρκτον θ’, ἣν καὶ Ἄμαξαν ἐπίκλησιν καλέουσιν,
> ἥ τ’ αὐτοῦ στρέφεται καί τ’ Ὠρίωνα δοκεύει.
> οἴη δ’ ἄμμορός ἐστι λοετρῶν Ὠκεανοῖο.

> He made the earth upon it, and the sky, and the sea's water,
> and the tireless sun, and the moon waxing into her fulness,
> and on it all the constellations that festoon the heavens,
> the Pleiades and the Hyades and the strength of Orion
> and the Bear, whom men give also the name of the Wagon,
> who turns about in a fixed place and looks at Orion
> and she alone is never plunged in the wash of the Ocean.

It may be argued that the astronomical content of the decoration of the shield is very season-specific. As the Pleiades, the Hyades, and Orion rose heliacally (i.e. at dawn) in the time of Homer (*c.*750 BC), the circumpolar Bear reached its lower transit across the meridian: this occurred about May–June in our terms, and signalled for Homer's audience the time of summer harvesting. When the Pleiades, the Hyades, and Orion set cosmically (i.e. at dawn), the Bear crossed the meridian at its upper transit: this took place around November, and signalled the time for ploughing and sowing (hence we might see the significance of the Bear's second name, the Plough).[1]

This conjunction between stars and the agricultural seasons is, of course, better known from its more extensive usage by Hesiod, not long afterwards (*c.*700 BC), in his didactic agricultural poem *Works and Days*. The instance from Homer in which I have suggested we are contemplating the time of winter ploughing, with the cosmical setting of the Pleiades, the Hyades, and Orion and the upper transit of the Bear, is in fact recorded explicitly by Hesiod, minus the mention of the Bear (614–17). Elsewhere Hesiod notes the culmination of Orion and Sirius at the time of Arcturus' heliacal rise to indicate the period of the grape harvest in September (609–11). In all, he provides nine observations of the risings or settings of five stars or star groups—Sirius is mentioned once, while the Pleiades, the Hyades, Orion, and Arcturus are all noted twice. Harald Reiche has proposed that these observations are so arranged that the farmer was given a safety-net of successive warnings of the appropriate date for a certain activity on the land by the successive risings or settings of certain stars.[2]

2. Euctemon's *Parapēgma*

After Hesiod's relatively rudimentary star calendar for farmers and sailors, the next stage in the development of this type of timekeeping device is not encountered until the late fifth century BC in Athens. This is in the form of what was called a *parapēgma*, a formal physical means of keeping a record of the times of star rise and star set through the seasonal year. Its invention is connected with the names of two men, Meton and Euctemon, who are

[1] See J. H. Phillips, 'The Constellations on Achilles' Shield (*Iliad* 18. 485–489)', *LCM* 5/8 (1980), 179–80; and, for a response, R. Hannah, 'The Constellations on Achilles' Shield (*Iliad* 18. 485–489)', *Electronic Antiquity*, 2/4 (1994) (http://scholar.lib.vt.edu/ejournals/ElAnt/V2N4/hannah.html). For an explanation of the heliacal rising and cosmical setting of stars see e.g. D. R. Dicks, *Early Greek Astronomy to Aristotle* (London, 1970), 12–13; M. L. West, *Hesiod: Works and Days* (Oxford, 1978), 379–80. The heliacal rising is the star's first visible appearance on the eastern horizon just before sunrise, the cosmical setting its first visible setting just before sunrise. (*Il.* 18. 483–9 is cited above in R. Lattimore's translation.)

[2] H. A. T. Reiche, 'Fail-Safe Stellar Dating: Forgotten Phases', *TAPA* 119 (1989), 37–53 at 44–5; but note how Reiche is forced for the sake of his argument to insert the Hyades into Hesiod's lists at times when the poet does not mention them, e.g. the heliacal risings of the Pleiades and Orion.

otherwise known for their work in what we would recognize today as strict astronomy.[3]

As it has survived archaeologically, the star-based *parapēgma* in its developed form consisted of stone tablets. (Wood may also have been used, but has not survived.) Fragmentary examples have been discovered across the Mediterranean, from Miletus (dated to around 100 BC: Figures 6.1, 6.2) to Athens and Pozzuoli. In these, a peg was moved manually from one day to the next through the year, through a series of holes, alongside some of which were chiselled the stellar observations for the day.[4]

Of Meton's and Euctemon's original *parapēgmata* nothing survives, and evidence for Meton's in later literature is scanty.[5] But for Euctemon's we have a good deal of evidence from literature and inscriptions, for it was one of the most popular calendars used in later periods. Euctemon's *parapēgma* in fact survives in three major forms, each differentiated from the others by its means of arranging the star-sightings.

In the course of a year, the sun appears to pass along a fixed band in the sky, which is called the ecliptic. In this band by the fifth century BC a set of twelve constellations was marked out: Aries the Ram, Taurus the Bull, Gemini the Twins, and so on, as they are known today under the Roman forms of their names. These were called the zodiac, a word which signifies the idea that the constellations were imagined as representing living creatures. These constellations, however, are not equal in size, so for calendrical and astrological purposes the full circuit of the zodiac was divided up into twelve equal divisions of 30° each, which were named after their resident constellation. The collection of *parapēgmata* attached to the *Eisagoge* of Geminus (mid-first century AD) structures the observations for Euctemon's

---

[3] A. C. Bowen and B. R. Goldstein, 'Meton of Athens and Astronomy in the Late Fifth Century B.C.', in E. Leichty, M. de J. Ellis, and P. Gerardi (eds.), *A Scientific Humanist: Studies in Memory of Abraham Sachs* (Philadelphia, 1988), 39–81 at 39–51; B. L. van der Waerden, *Die Astronomie der Griechen: Eine Einführung* (Darmstadt, 1988) 79–86; Dicks (n. 1), 87–8; id., 'Euktemon', *DSB* iv. 459–60.

[4] Figs. 6.1 and 6.2: Berlin SK 1606 (MI and MII). H. Diels and A. Rehm, 'Parapegmenfragmente aus Milet', *Sitzungsberichte der preußischen Akademie der Wissenschaften* (Berlin, 1904), 92–111, pl. II (I am grateful to Dr Liba Taub for facilitating access to this); H. Diels, *Antike Technik* (Leipzig and Berlin, 1914; repr. 1965), pl. I. On *parapēgmata* in general see G. Schiaparelli, *Scritti sulla storia della astronomia antica*, i/2 (Bologna, 1926), 235–85; A. Rehm, *Parapegmastudien* (Munich, 1941); id., 'Parapegma', *RE* xviii (1949), 1295–366; O. Neugebauer, *A History of Ancient Mathematical Astronomy*, ii (Berlin and New York, 1975), 587–9; van der Waerden (n. 3), 76–9. A partial star calendar survives on the geared device discovered on a shipwreck off Antikythera, but its poor state of preservation still prevents a clear understanding of the purpose of the device as a whole and of the calendar on it; see D. de Solla Price, *Gears from the Greeks: The Antikythera Mechanism, a Calendar Computer from ca. 80 BC* (TAPhS, NS 64/7; Philadelphia, 1974, and New York, 1975), esp. 46–9; A. G. Bromley, 'Notes on the Antikythera Mechanism', *Centaurus*, 29 (1986), 5–27 (at p. 23 it is suggested that the calendar might mark 'significant days in the months of some religious or civil lunar calendar').

[5] Rehm, 'Parapegma' (n. 4), 1340–1; van der Waerden (n. 3), 85–6; Bowen and Goldstein (n. 3), 52–3.

FIG. 6.1. Miletus *parapēgma* (SK 1606, MI)

calendar according to these artificial signs of the zodiac.[6] Thus, the calendar tells us that on the *n*th day of the sun's passage through a given zodiacal sign, certain stars rose or set at dawn or dusk, and foreshadowed certain weather conditions. The full entry in Geminus for the 'month' of Leo may serve to illustrate this system:

τὸν δὲ Λέοντα διαπορεύεται ὁ ἥλιος ἐν ἡμέραις λαʹ.

ἐν μὲν οὖν τῇ αῃ ἡμέρᾳ Εὐκτήμονι Κύων μὲν ἐκφανής, πνῖγος δὲ ἐπιγίνεται· ἐπισημαίνει.

ἐν δὲ τῇ εῃ Εὐδόξῳ Ἀετὸς ἑῷος δύνει.

ἐν δὲ τῇ ιῃ ἡμέρᾳ Εὐδόξῳ Στέφανος δύνει.

ἐν δὲ τῇ ιβῃ Καλλίππῳ Λέων μέσος ἀνατέλλων πνίγη μάλιστα ποιεῖ.

ἐν δὲ τῇ ιδῃ Εὐκτήμονι πνίγη μάλιστα γίνεται.

ἐν δὲ τῇ ιϛῃ ἡμέρᾳ Εὐδόξῳ ἐπισημαίνει.

ἐν δὲ τῇ ιζῃ Εὐκτήμονι Λύρα δύεται· καὶ ἔτι ὕει· καὶ ἐτησίαι παύονται· καὶ Ἵππος ἐπιτέλλει.

ἐν δὲ τῇ ιηῃ Εὐδόξῳ Δελφὶς ἑῷος δύνει. Δοσιθέῳ Προτρυγητὴρ ἀκρόνυχος ἐπιτέλλει.

ἐν δὲ τῇ κβῃ Εὐδόξῳ Λύρα ἑῷος δύνει· ἐπισημαίνει.

ἐν δὲ τῇ κθῃ Εὐδόξῳ ἐπισημαίνει. Καλλίππῳ Παρθένος ἐπιτέλλει· ἐπισημαίνει.

---

[6] On the development of the zodiac see below, n. 18. For the full text of the *parapēgmata* in Geminus see G. Aujac, *Geminos* (Paris, 1975), 98–108. The *parapēgmata* represented in Geminus' list date from the 5th to the 3rd centuries BC, so three centuries and more before the time of Geminus himself, and the relationship of the collection to Geminus himself has been debated: Aujac 157–8 favours Geminus' authorship, while Neugebauer (n. 4), 580, opposed it. On the date of Geminus see Neugebauer 578–81.

Fɪɢ. 6.2. Miletus *parapēgma* (SK 1606, MII)

The sun passes through Leo in 31 days.
On the 1st day, according to Euctemon, the Dog [Sirius] is visible, and the stifling heat begins; signs of weather.
On the 5th, according to Eudoxus, the Eagle [Aquila] sets at dawn.
On the 10th, according to Eudoxus, the Crown [Corona] sets.
On the 12th, according to Callippus, the Lion [Leo], half rising, makes a very strong heat.
On the 14th, according to Euctemon, the heat is at its greatest.
On the 16th, according to Eudoxus, signs of weather.
On the 17th, according to Euctemon, the Lyre [Lyra] sets; and it also rains; and the Etesian winds stop; and the Horse [Pegasus] rises.
On the 18th, according to Eudoxus, the Dolphin [Delphinus] sets at dawn. According to Dositheus, Protrygeter [Vindemiatrix?] rises at nightfall.
On the 22nd, according to Eudoxus, the Lyre [Lyra] sets at dawn; signs of weather.
On the 29th, according to Eudoxus, signs of weather. According to Callippus, the Maiden [Virgo] rises; signs of weather.

Overall in the collection, Geminus refers to Euctemon 47 times, second only to Eudoxus, the astronomer of the fourth century BC, who also created a *parapēgma*, and who is mentioned 60 times.

By way of contrast, the *parapēgma* presented in the second century AD by Ptolemy in his *Phaseis* organizes the year according to a quite different scheme.[7] Here the entries for each day are structured around the days of a civil calendar, in the same way as we would expect a calendar to be presented now. In Ptolemy's case, the underlying civil calendar is the Alexandrian one. He presents the appropriate stellar observations for each day, arranged according to different latitudes, and appends the meteorological phenomena associated with any particular day from a variety of authors, including Euctemon. Thus, in the Alexandrian month of Mesori (25 July–23 August) we find the following entry:

ΜΕΣΟΡΙ

γ΄. Εὐκτήμονι καὶ Δοσιθέῳ νοτία καὶ πνίγη.

In the month of Mesori.
. . . On the 3rd day, according to Euctemon and Dositheus, rain and stifling heat.

This entry corresponds to the first day of Leo in Geminus' compilation. It retains Euctemon's weather forecast, but omits the observation of Sirius.

It is clear from these examples that the calendar of Euctemon could be organized according to either system, since his notices either of the stars'

---

[7] For the full text see J. L. Heiberg, *Claudii Ptolemaei Opera Quae Supersunt*, ii (Leipzig, 1907), 1–67. I am grateful to the late Prof. Douglas Kidd for having made a copy of this available to me. While Ptolemy does not subscribe obviously to the zodiacal scheme in his *Phaseis*, but uses instead a civil calendar, nevertheless it was argued by Rehm (*Griechische Kalender*, iii. *Das Parapegma des Euktemon* (Heidelberg, 1913), 7; and *Parapegmastudien* (n. 4), 14–16) that Ptolemy's version of Euctemon's calendar derives from the same model as Geminus', but that Ptolemy reduced it from a zodiacal scheme to the Alexandrian civil calendar.

risings and settings or of meteorological phenomena occur in both. Along with that of Eudoxus, Euctemon's is the most frequently cited *parapēgma* in both Greek and Roman sources, and we find it adapted to either system without much bother, to the extent that it is reduced also to the Julian calendar by the Romans, as entries in Pliny the Elder's farmer's calendar (first century AD) show.[8]

However, Euctemon's *parapēgma* has also come down to us structured in a third way, preserved by the text of a single manuscript in Vienna.[9] Here the structure is neither zodiacal nor civil, but is based on the older system of day-counts between stellar phenomena which is encountered in Hesiod's *Works and Days*. Thus, for example, the period quoted above from Geminus (i.e. the 'month' of Leo) is presented in the following fashion by the Vienna manuscript:

ἀπὸ Ἀετοῦ δύσεως εἰς Κύνα ἡμέραι δ'. ἐτησίαι ἄνεμοι ἄρχονται πνεῖν.
ἀπὸ Κύνος ἐκφανείας εἰς Λύρας δύσιν καὶ Ἵππου ἐπιτολὴν ἡμέραι ιγ'.
ἀπὸ Λύρας δύσεως καὶ Ἵππου ἐπιτολῆς εἰς Προτρυγητοῦ ἐκφάνειαν καὶ Ἀρκτούρου ἐπιτολὴν καὶ †'Οϊστοῦ δύσιν ⟨ἡμέραι . . .

From the setting of the Eagle [Aquila] to (the appearance of) the Dog [Sirius] 4 days. The Etesian winds begin to blow.
From the appearance of the Dog [Sirius] to the setting of the Lyre [Lyra] and the rising of the Horse [Pegasus] 13 days.
From the setting of the Lyre [Lyra] and the rising of the Horse [Pegasus] to the appearance of Protrygeter [Vindemiatrix?] and the rising of Arcturus and the setting of the Arrow [Sagitta] (*x* days).

We miss just one reference to Euctemon from Geminus' report of the same 'month', that to the peak of stifling heat on the 14th day of Leo. But the Vienna manuscript omits many of the meteorological forecasts which we find in Geminus and Ptolemy, its interest being almost entirely in the stellar observations.[10]

Since Rehm published his reconstruction of Euctemon's *parapēgma*, it has been generally accepted that Euctemon structured his calendar from the very start around the zodiacal 'months'. The zodiacal system adopted by Rehm for his reconstruction of Euctemon's *parapēgma* is based, how-ever, not on that presented in Geminus' compilation (which he believed was

---

[8] Pliny, *HN* 18. 201–320 *passim*, esp. 234, 237, 246–8, 255, 269–70, 309–10, 312 (references to Attica being taken to indicate Euctemon's calendar: H. Le Bonniec and A. Le Bœuffle, *Pline l'Ancien: Histoire naturelle, livre XVIII* (Paris, 1972), 263).

[9] Cod. Vind. Gr. philos. 108, fos. 282ᵛ, 283ʳ (published by Rehm, *Griechische Kalender*, iii (n. 7), 14–26). The stars enumerated in it and the vocabulary employed for their phases indicate that the manuscript reflects Euctemon's *parapēgma*.

[10] Of the two *parapēgmata* from Miletus, the earlier acknowledges the sources of its astro-nomical data, and Euctemon is among them. Interestingly, though, it contains no references to climatic conditions: Neugebauer (n. 4), 588–9, suggests that this omission might reflect scepticism about deriving such predictions from stellar phases.

based in fact on Callippus' arrangement from the fourth century BC), but instead on information supplied by the *Papyrus Eudoxeus* (or *Ars Eudoxi*), a document written in the early second century BC but stemming from an original of about 300 BC, and characterized as 'perhaps a student's exercise containing many errors', based on the work of Eudoxus.[11] This work includes the lengths of the four astronomical seasons according to Euctemon, i.e. the four parts of the sun's annual course marked by the solstices and equinoxes.[12] Starting from the summer solstice, he is said by the papyrus to have given these seasons 90, 90, 92, and 93 days respectively. These figures contradict those ascribed to Euctemon in Geminus' compilation, or derivable from there: [92], 89, 89, and [95]. This discrepancy in the figures had led others before Rehm to assume that the *Ars Eudoxi* represented a corrupt version of Euctemon's true data. But Rehm noted that the *Ars Eudoxi* was otherwise able to present accurately the lengths of the seasons according to Eudoxus and Callippus in comparison with the data in Geminus and others; and so he suggested that the papyrus ought to be taken seriously as representing Euctemon's data accurately too. He assumed that Euctemon's astronomical seasons began with the appropriate tropical point (i.e. summer with the summer solstice, and so on), and that he began his calendar at the first day of the sun's entry into the zodiacal sign of Cancer (Cancer 1), the date of the summer solstice. Rehm then proposed that Euctemon's calendar was broken down into twelve zodiacal 'months' of the following numbers of days from Cancer onwards: $30+30+30=90$; $30+30+30-90$; $30+31+31 = 92$; $31+31+31 = 93$ days. In this scheme he saw a 'certain archaic simplicity' assuring 'the stamp of authenticity'.[13] What Rehm seems to have deduced from the lengths of the seasons is that they were probably divided up into a sequence of twelve months, of which the first seven were given 30 days each, and the remaining five 31 days each. Such a scheme is not only very simple, as Rehm noted, but also resembles Greek calendrical practice in other spheres of life, and thereby becomes more plausible.[14]

[11] Rehm, *Griechische Kalender* III (n. 7), 4–11; for the text of the papyrus see F. Blass, *Eudoxi Ars astronomica qualis in charta Aegyptiaca superest denuo edita* (Kiel, 1887), 12–25. The quotation is from Dicks, 'Euktemon' (n. 3), 460. See also Neugebauer (n. 4), 686–9.

[12] For the period under scrutiny here, these astronomical seasons are to be kept distinct from the agricultural seasons, the dates of which were quite different. On this issue see R. Hannah, '*Praevolante nescio qua ingenti humana specie* . . .: A Re-assessment of the Winged Genius on the Base of the Antonine Column', *PBSR* 57 (1989), 90–105 at 96–100.

[13] Rehm, *Griechische Kalender*. iii (n. 7), 8–10; id., *Parapegmastudien* (n. 4), 14–16.

[14] One might compare the distribution of days for the zodiacal months within the Egyptian festival calendar in P. Hibeh 27, as deduced by A. Spalinger, 'Remarks on an Egyptian Feast Calendar of Foreign Origin', *SÄK* 18 (1991), 349–73: (starting from Aries, as the calendar actually does, rather than Cancer) $31+30+30$, $30+30+30$, $30+30+31$, $31+31+31$. This calendar dates to about 300 BC, and reflects some influence from Eudoxus' *parapēgma* (see below, n. 51). Some of the systems for dividing up the political year are similar too: compare the 10-month prytany calendar in Athens, with its sequence of 36- and 35-day months, and variations thereon: A. E. Samuel, *Greek and Roman Chronology* (Munich, 1972), 61–3. Neugebauer

These assumptions regarding the lengths of the Euctemonian seasons and the zodiacal 'months' were accepted without discussion by Pritchett and van der Waerden for their edition of Euctemon's *parapēgma*.[15] Argumentation for this position was provided later by Bowen and Goldstein, who at that time felt that it was 'not improbable' that Euctemon, or his contemporary and colleague Meton, used a zodiacal scheme for their *parapēgmata*.[16] This case involves the assumption that the Babylonian division of the zodiacal belt into twelve segments, each of 30° width, perhaps invented about 500 BC, had become available in Greece by Euctemon's time.[17] The general use of a twelve-part division of the ecliptic in the fourth century, they argue, would suggest this chronology; a Babylonian origin for the Greek zodiac is indicated in any case by the fact that the very names used by the Greeks for the elements of the zodiac were actually just translations of the Babylonian Akkadian names for these sections; and knowledge of the division of the zodiac into twelve equal 'months' could (it is suggested) have come before the discovery of the ecliptic itself as an astronomical element— a discovery which appears to have occurred in Greece in the later fifth century BC.[18]

However, there are good reasons for doubting the use of a zodiacal framework in Euctemon's calendar.[19] First, Bowen and Goldstein themselves have revised their view, arguing more recently that the distinction between actual zodiacal constellations and artificial zodiacal signs of 30° of arc is not attested in extant Greek texts before the third century BC and so post-dates both Euctemon and Eudoxus. This would mean that zodiacal 'months', based on the signs rather than the constellations, could not have been used by Euctemon.[20] Second, Euctemon's and Meton's *parapēgmata* are the first

(n. 4), 628 and fig. 3, noticed a symmetrical distribution of the months on either side of Aries, but this aesthetic principle is unlikely to have been the cause of the placement of the months of different lengths, since it focuses attention on Aries rather than on Cancer and the summer solstice. See further Bowen and Goldstein (n. 3), 58–63.

[15] W. K. Pritchett and B. L. van der Waerden, 'Thucydidean Time-Reckoning and Euctemon's Seasonal Calendar', *BCH* 85 (1961), 17–52; revised in B. L. van der Waerden, 'Greek Astronomical Calendars, I: The Parapegma of Euctemon', *AHES* 29 (1984), 101–14 at 103–6.

[16] Bowen and Goldstein (n. 3), 53–4, esp. n. 75.

[17] Ibid. 53 n. 75. This view conflicts with that of Dicks (n. 1), 172, whose view was based partly on a later date for the Babylonian tablet evidence; but see 254 n. 310, where Dicks points out that 'Sachs' treatment depends on the *assumption* "that the planetary data refer to signs of the zodiac, not constellations" . . .'.

[18] The Greeks appear to have become aware of the ecliptic in the latter half of the 5th cent. BC, probably through the work of Oenopides: Dicks (n. 1), 88–9, 157; KRS 80–2; A. C. Bowen, 'Oenopides', in D. J. Zeyl, D. T. Devereux, and P. K. Mitsis (eds.), *The Encyclopedia of Classical Philosophy* (Westport, Conn., 1997), 357.

[19] Doubts have been expressed in the past by J. K. Fotheringham, 'Cleostratus (III)', *JHS* 45 (1925), 78–83 at 80; Dicks, 'Euktemon' (n. 3), 460; and O. Wenskus, *Astronomische Zeitangaben von Homer bis Theophrast* (Stuttgart, 1990), 29.

[20] A. C. Bowen and B. R. Goldstein, 'Hipparchus' Treatment of Early Greek Astronomy: The Case of Eudoxus and the Length of Daytime', *PAPhS* 135 (1991), 233–54.

that we know of,[21] and are therefore the first literary examples of a calendar since Hesiod's comparatively rudimentary but related farmer's calendar. This had used day-counts, and there is no immediately obvious reason why this system could not have continued in use to the fifth century or beyond. The Vienna manuscript ignores the zodiacal 'months' completely and uses day-counts instead. If the attribution of the calendar in the manuscript to Euctemon is correct (cf n. 9), then it would suggest a continuum of method from the time of Hesiod, and would lead us to suspect that the first major star calendars of the fifth century would at least initially adopt the older method of day-counts.

Finally, Euctemon's list of stars largely ignores the zodiacal constellations, and instead still relies on the core established at least since Hesiod's time. Among stars and constellations along the zodiacal belt only the Scorpion and possibly Vindemiatrix in Virgo[22] are added by Euctemon to the Hyades and Pleiades found in Hesiod's calendar. Otherwise, the vast majority of Euctemon's sightings involve stars or constellations beyond this region of the sky: Sirius, Orion, and Arcturus are there, in common with Hesiod, while new are the Horse (Pegasus), the Eagle (Aquila), the Dolphin (Delphinus), the Kids (Haedi), the Crown (Corona), the Lyre (Lyra), the Goat (Capella), and perhaps the Arrow (Sagitta).[23] The point is perhaps better made by analysing Euctemon's choice of stars. Table 6.1 lists the stars or star groups in Euctemon's *parapēgma*, together with those zodiacal constellations which rise or set at more or less the same time.[24]

In the conventional view, Euctemon organized his whole calendar according to the zodiacal constellations, or rather according to the artificially equal 30° divisions of the zodiac derived from those constellations. Yet it is remarkable that, as the table demonstrates, he largely ignored the zodiacal stars in his list of observations. He inherited five stars or star clusters from traditional star calendars: Orion (no. 1), Sirius (no. 2), Arcturus (no. 7), the Pleiades (no. 11) and the Hyades (no. 13). The Pleiades and the Hyades are already zodiacal, within Taurus, and it made sense to note Sirius (no. 2), the brightest fixed star in the sky, instead of its zodiacal counterpart, the dim stars of the constellation Cancer. Were Euctemon's interests strictly zodiacal, however, it would also have made sense to have observed, either in addition or instead, Gemini (in effect, Castor and Pollux) alongside Orion (no. 1), and Virgo (i.e. Spica as well as Vindemiatrix) and Sagittarius alongside Arcturus (no. 7). Of the new stars included by

---

[21] Cf. Neugebauer (n. 4), 588.

[22] If the identification of Protrygeter as this star is correct.

[23] The very name here depends on a textual correction.

[24] It might be expected that this would be simply a reversal of the lists of stars which rise and set with the zodiacal constellations (the παρανατέλλοντα, in e.g. Arat. 569–732. But the stars from Euctemon's *parapēgma* in Table 6.1 bear little resemblance to those in the later παρανατέλλοντα. His choice of stars is therefore distinctive, and requires explanation.

TABLE 6.1. *Euctemon's stars and*
their accompanying zodiacal stars

Star/group	Rises with	Sets with
1. Orion	Gemini	Taurus
2. Sirius	Cancer	Taurus
3. Aquila	Sagittarius	Capricorn
4. Lyra	Libra, Scorpius	Aquarius
5. Pegasus	Aquarius, Pisces	Pisces
6. Vindemiatrix	Virgo	Virgo
7. Arcturus	Virgo	Sagittarius
8. Sagitta		Aquarius
9. Capella	Pisces	Gemini
10. The Kids	Pisces	
11. The Pleiades	Taurus	Taurus
12. Corona	Virgo	
13. The Hyades	Taurus	Taurus
14. Scorpius	Scorpius	Scorpius
15. Delphinus	Sagittarius	Aquarius

Euctemon, only Vindemiatrix (no. 6) in Virgo and the Scorpion (no. 14) are zodiacal. Again, it makes sense to observe bright stars or star groups beyond the zodiac, like Aquila (no. 3), Lyra (no. 4), and Capella (no. 9), although even in these cases one could argue for an inclusion of the coincident groups of Sagittarius (as Aquila (no. 3) rises), Capricorn (as it sets), Scorpius (as Lyra (no. 4) rises), and again Gemini (as Capella (no. 9) sets). One certainly has cause to wonder why Delphinus (no. 15) is included by the parapegmatist, when its rising coincides with that of the much more easily observed constellation Sagittarius. And if Vindemiatrix (no. 6) is correctly identified with Protrygeter, and so part of Virgo's territory is observed, then it is not immediately obvious why Euctemon chose to include Corona (no. 12) rather than the rest of Virgo, which is more readily seen. Pegasus, as simply the Horse (no. 5), is a reasonably identifiable observation instead of Aquarius or Pisces, in terms of brightness and shape, but in the cases of Sagitta (no. 8, again, if correctly identified) and the Kids (no. 10) it is difficult to see why Euctemon chose such small, barely visible, clusters even in comparison with the stars of Aquarius or Pisces.

Until now it has been assumed that there was no other way for Euctemon to structure his *parapēgma* than by the zodiacal division of the year into twelve almost equal 'months'. Even those who did not believe that Euctemon structured his calendar in this manner offered no alternative means. Yet the use of day-counts in the Vienna manuscript and the avoidance of observations of many of the zodiacal stars themselves suggest strongly that

Euctemon's interests and influences, at least as far as his calendar was concerned, lay elsewhere than in the zodiac. Admittedly, van der Waerden has suggested that Euctemon used both zodiacal 'months' and day-counts together in his calendar, thus combining the evidence of the Geminan text with that presented by the Vienna manuscript.[25] But given the evidence of the stars enumerated by Euctemon, it appears to be more reasonable to argue that Euctemon, at least initially, used only the age-old method of day-counts between his sightings. At some later stage this *parapēgma* was organized according to the zodiacal 'months'. In other words, the Vienna manuscript and the version preserved in Geminus should be treated as chronologically successive.

If Euctemon did use a simple day-count between star observations to organize his calendar, as in the Vienna manuscript, how practical was it as a calendar? Reiche has suggested that any further development of the agricultural calendar beyond that presented by Hesiod would require not only more observations of a greater number of stars, but also the retention of just one or two handfuls of days between each observation to allow the calendar to be usable by farmers.[26] Now, Euctemon does indeed fulfil the first requirement. From Hesiod's nine observations of five stars or star groups (Sirius noted once, and Orion, the Hyades, the Pleiades, and Arcturus all twice),[27] Euctemon advances to about 42 observations of fifteen stars or star groups, preserving Sirius, Orion, and the Hyades (all noted three times), the Pleiades (four times), and Arcturus (four or five times), and adding Aquila, Lyra, Capella (all mentioned four times), Scorpion, Pegasus, Delphinus, Sagitta, Vindemiatrix (?) (all twice), the Kids, and Corona (each once).[28] In addition, Euctemon includes observations certainly of the winter solstice, and also of the summer solstice if we accept Rehm's restoration, as well as of the spring and autumn equinoxes, of some weather changes, and two apparently ornithological observations, independent of any stellar observations.[29] In total, this represents a significant increase in observations, which, potentially, allowed for greater precision in timing of events over certain parts of the year. Only the 'agriculturally dead' part of the year, the month before the summer solstice, is almost bereft of observations.[30]

[25] Van der Waerden (n. 15), 109.
[26] Reiche (n. 2), 41; cf. 45: 'In practice . . . neither Mesopotamian nor Greek farmers were likely to have either the numerical facility or the practical motive to engage in day-counts, except in a few and relatively short time-contexts calling for an advance notice or grace period, and in multiples of five or ten.'
[27] Ibid. 40.
[28] Cf. Rehm, *Parapegmastudien* (n. 4), 12.
[29] For arguments supporting the notion that these ornithological sightings might have been initially stellar observations also, see R. Hannah, 'Is it a Bird? Is it a Star? Ovid's Kite and the First Swallow of Spring', *Latomus*, 56 (1997), 327–42, M. Blomberg, 'The Meaning of χελιδών in Hesiod', *Opuscula Atheniensia*, 19 (1992), 49–57.
[30] R. Osborne, *Classical Landscape with Figures: The Ancient Greek City and its Countryside*

How does this *parapēgma* measure up to Reiche's second desideratum, the retention of just one or two handfuls of days between each observation? The intervals between observations in Euctemon in the Vienna manuscript range from 1 day to 33 days, but there are discernible errors in the figures in this version, as Rehm pointed out, probably due to the textual tradition.[31] According to the version of the *parapēgma* preserved in Geminus, the intervals range from 1 day to 23 days. The gaps between observations do not always keep to Reiche's ideal of a couple of handfuls: in the Vienna manuscript 16 observations have intervals between 1 and 5 days, 5 between 6 and 10, 8 between 11 and 15, 3 between 16 and 20, 1 of at least 21. This suggests that some other means of counting than simply using the fingers of two hands was necessary. So we are probably looking at a formal physical device, the very sort that gave the *parapēgma* its name—a wooden or stone slab with holes in it for a peg to be moved in from day to day.[32] We know that Meton set up stelae in Athens to record in some way his establishment of the solstices.[33] Could these stelae be a reference to his *parapēgma*, set up in the city itself?[34] If this is so, then the users of the *parapēgma* were not primarily farmers or sailors, but others who had a vested interest in timekeeping and the seasons.[35]

Let us return to the question of Euctemon's use of zodiacal 'months' for his *parapēgma*. It was suggested above that this represents a later version of Euctemon's original day-count *parapēgma*. That it was Euctemon himself

(London, 1987), 174, calls July and August 'the agriculturally dead period'. But, after harvest came threshing and the transformation of the earth's goods into consumable food—not a 'dead' period, but one of vital importance from the human perspective.

[31] The 33-day lapse is very unusual. It comes immediately before the summer solstice group, in a month devoted, in the agricultural context, solely to harvesting, so perhaps there was no need for a list of warning signs, until the solstice warned to thresh.

[32] In the Vienna manuscript the use of day-numbers not divisible by 5 (26 sightings) suggests we ought to think in terms of a stone or wooden *parapēgma*, like the preserved fragments of the Milesian *parapēgmata* (Figs. 6.1 and 6.2); certainly the 33-day lapse, and probably all twelve lapses from 11 days upwards, would have to be counted mechanically rather than by fingers on more than two hands.

[33] Ael. *VH* 10. 7.

[34] See Bowen and Goldstein (n. 3), 53 n. 67, for an exposition of modern interpretations of what Aelian meant, and 73–7 for their (convincing) view that Meton was seeking to fix the alignment of the solstices rather than their actual date of occurrence, which, they argue, he knew already from the Babylonians.

[35] Cf. Reiche's comments, (n. 2), 43, on Meton's *parapēgma*: 'when Meton finally inserts stellar phases into the radically improved lunisolar cycle that bears his name, the calendric needs of farmers at last came into their own, albeit in a form inaccessible to all but a literate minority'. It may, however, be worth keeping in mind that the calendar of Euctemon was made in Athens, a state that published its decrees for public viewing, which suggests a fair degree of literacy in the population. Vivian Nutton has pointed out to me that Meton's is the first *written* *parapēgma* and may therefore represent evidence of a shift from orality to literacy in the late 5th cent. BC. See R. Hannah, 'From Orality to Literacy? The Case of the Parapegma', in J. Watson (ed.), *Speaking Volumes: Orality and Literacy in the Greek and Roman World* (Leiden, 2001), 139–59.

rather than a later editor who translated his original *parapēgma* to a zodiacal base cannot be proved, and indeed is unlikely.

As we have seen already, the division of the zodiacal belt into twelve 30° segments was perhaps invented about 500 BC by the Babylonians. By the early fourth century BC all twelve zodiacal constellations were certainly recognized by Eudoxus, to judge from their presence in Aratus' later poetic version of Eudoxus' *Phainomena*.[36] There is a tradition that Eudoxus devised a type of sundial which recorded the passage of the sun into the zodiacal signs, but given the previous testimony, it is unlikely that signs as such are meant, so much as constellations.[37] Either way, this would presuppose an awareness of the zodiac, and that this awareness dates back to the later fifth century is suggested by the further testimony that the Greeks recognized the ecliptic at that time.[38] It is possible, although not necessary, that what they did was to derive from the Babylonian zodiac the underlying geometrical element, the ecliptic, but, whatever the situation in that regard, there is still no evidence at this date of an interest in artificially dividing the ecliptic into twelve equal parts, naming those parts after the resident zodiacal constellations, and applying this structure to a calendar. No doubt from Euctemon's time the area of the sky occupied by the zodiac became a focus of attention for Greek astronomers, but it would be some time before they struck on the idea of using it as a fundamental structural basis for ordering time.

For if Euctemon did engage in such a venture, the result is surprisingly discordant. As we have seen, his *parapēgma* displays little interest in the observation of the zodiacal stars and constellations. But Euctemon is not alone in this. Even Eudoxus, who knew about all twelve zodiacal constellations and purportedly used a sundial to mark the sun's passage through them (or the related signs), made no more use of them for observational purposes in his own *parapēgma* than had Euctemon. All this contrasts markedly with Callippus, later in the fourth century, whose *parapēgma* indicates that it was indeed possible to construct a star calendar based solely on the zodiacal constellations, despite the difficulties mentioned earlier of observation, identification, and organization.[39]

The discordance evident in Euctemon's and Eudoxus' *parapēgmata*, when compared with that of Callippus, gives them an experimental air, as if the

---

[36] Arat. 525–58; Dicks (n. 1), 156–7; Bowen and Goldstein (n. 20), 241–5.

[37] This tradition depends on what is meant by the instrument called an *arachnē* in Vitr. 9. 8. 1: E. Ardaillon, 'Horologium', in C. Daremberg and E. Saglio (eds.), *Dictionnaire des antiquités grecques et romains*, iii (Paris, 1900), 256–64 at 257, gave an optimistic interpretation of the passage, which was accepted by Rehm, 'Horologium', *RE* viii (1913), 2418–19. See also Hultsch, 'Eudoxus', *RE* vi (1909), 944–5; S. L. Gibbs, *Greek and Roman Sundials* (New Haven and London, 1976), 60–1.   [38] See n. 18 above.

[39] For the text of Callippus' *parapēgma* see Aujac (n. 6); and B. L. van der Waerden, 'Greek Astronomical Calendars, II: Callippos and his Calendar', *AHES* 29 (1984), 115–24.

two parapegmatists were groping towards the development of a zodiacal calendar. But this is probably a false impression resulting from hindsight. There is no evidence that either Euctemon or Eudoxus was working consciously towards a *parapēgma* such as Callippus eventually produced. The reason for the discordance probably lies elsewhere, perhaps in the marrying together of a traditional Greek *parapēgma* with a star calendar organized by 'months' which may have come into Greece from the east.

For the organization of a star calendar according to twelve 'months' is not a Greek invention. At least as early as *c*.1000 BC the Babylonians had created such a calendar, which included the risings of certain stars and dates for the solstices and equinoxes, set within an ideal 360-day year, which was itself divided into twelve 30-day months. This type of calendar was still being copied in the Hellenistic period.[40] Perhaps when knowledge of the Babylonian zodiac reached Greece, so too did awareness of idealized Babylonian star calendars of this type, providing a model for astronomers like Euctemon and Meton, who were already working within an old, empirical Greek tradition of star calendars. Euctemon's own work on the lengths of the seasons led to an awareness of four seasons of different lengths (90, 90, 92, and 93 days), and these could easily have been divided up into twelve months in the manner that Rehm proposed (30, 30, 30; 30, 30, 30; 30, 31, 31; 31, 31, 31), perhaps under the influence of cultural conditioning from other religious or political calendars in Athens.

After Euctemon, Eudoxus devised a *parapēgma* which resembles Euctemon's very closely, adding no new stars, even removing a few, but increasing the number of observations of the remaining ones and the number of weather prognostications. From his experiments with the sundial, Eudoxus would have become better aware than Euctemon of the time of the entry of the sun into the zodiacal constellations, relative to the rising and setting of the various stars enumerated in his *parapēgma*. Sundials had already existed in Athens in Euctemon's own time, but there is no indication of their being used then in the fashion that Eudoxus devised,[41] and it may be that Callippus' *parapēgma* in the later fourth century simply represents a formal articulation of the kind of data which could be derived from practical experiments of this sort.

Whoever it was who eventually structured Euctemon's observation into zodiacal 'months' created a version of his *parapēgma* which would represent a significant transition from the older day-count star calendar to a new type of calendar whose focus was more the sun's apparent annual path. A

[40] H. Hunger and D. Pingree, *MUL.APIN: An Astronomical Compendium in Cuneiform* (Horn, 1989), 9, 40–7, 139–41.

[41] Cf. Hdt. 2. 109 (reporting that the Greeks derived sundials from Babylonia); Ar. *Eccl.* 652 (*c*.392 BC), a passage which significantly refers to an evening reading of its shadow, as with a *parapēgma*, and not a midday reading: cf. Bowen and Goldstein (n. 3), 72–3, on this point and on the specific question of the nature of Meton's instrument (the *hēliotropion*).

calendar so tied to the apparent movement of the sun would be better able to keep pace with the seasons through the years and would represent a major step forward in the regulation of those human affairs which were tied to the seasons. It would stand in stark contrast with other types of calendars then in use in Athens and elsewhere in the Greek world, which were easily put out of step with the seasons. At this time Athens possessed a political and a religious calendar. The latter was perhaps lunar-based in origin, but had become corrupted by apparently irregular intercalations and suppressions of days; the former was tied to neither moon nor sun, nor did it coincide with the religious calendar. By the late fifth century BC the religious calendar appears to have been seriously out of tune with lunar phases, even though its days and months were derived from those phases; religious observances, it seems, were no longer carried out at the proper time according to the moon.[42]

The creation of artificial twelfths of the year suggests a desire to establish a regularity in the division of the year, which stands in contrast to the innate mobility and irregularity of a lunar-based calendar. We are talking necessarily of a regularity in the *solar* year, and therefore also of the seasonal year. There is a desire both to calculate the length of the solar year more accurately and to measure the length of the seasons—the explicit notices about the solstices and equinoxes and the tradition about the astronomers' varying measurements of the seasons make this clear. An accurate measure of both the seasons and (their sum) the solar year could not be made until it was possible to identify and mark the equinoxes. If Bowen and Goldstein are correct in their hypothesis that Meton (and Euctemon) set up stelae simply to measure the *alignments* of the solstices, since the dates may already have been a given from Babylonian sources, then the measurement of the equinoxes could have been a much simpler exercise than has been thought hitherto. Rather than requiring a detailed theoretical basis to establish these points accurately, as has been supposed,[43] it may be that all the observer did was to discover by geometric means the midpoint along the horizon between the two indicators of the summer and winter solstices.[44] There would then

[42] Ar. *Nub.* 615–26.

[43] D. R. Dicks, 'Solstices, Equinoxes, and the Presocratics', *JHS* 86 (1966), 26–40 at 32–3.

[44] This is one of the usual methods available to prescientific societies; for a brief discussion, in the context of prehistoric henge monuments in Britain, see D. Trevarthen, 'Illuminating the Monuments: Observation and Speculation on the Structure and Function of the Cairns at Balnuaran of Clava', *Cambridge Archaeological Journal*, 10 (2000), 295–315 at 301–2. Cf. the 'sun observation device' on Easter Island: Ferdon, in T. Heyerdahl and E. N. Ferdon (eds.), *Reports of the Norwegian Archaeological Expedition to Easter Island and the East Pacific*, i. *Archaeology of Easter Island* (London, 1961), 228–9 with fig. 61. Heyerdahl was prepared to believe that some of the larger structures (*ahu*) on Easter Island betrayed an awareness of the equinoctial points: ibid. 94, 159, 214, 218. Similarly, some Mayan structures might have been oriented to allow for equinoctial shadow effects: A. L Slayman, 'Seeing with Maya Eyes', *Archaeology*, 49/4 (1996), 56–60; E. C. Krupp, 'Springing down the Banister', *Sky and Telescope*, 91/3 (Mar. 1996), 59–61; D. Freidel, L. Schele, and J. Parker, *Maya Cosmos: Three*

follow the issue of enumerating the days which elapsed between each tropic, a process which would generate a realization (perhaps against expectations) of the inequality of the seasons and, hence, of the variability of the sun's motion through the year (the solar anomaly).[45] But the main point to note for present purposes is that to pinpoint the equinoxes and the solstices, the observer is driven to watch for the position of the *sun* and indeed to keep an eye on the sun's progress through a whole year. Observing the rising or setting of stars on the sun's path, i.e. specifically zodiacal stars, would then seem to be a natural consequence of the desire to measure the length of the seasons or year via observations of the tropical points. Advance warning of the approach of the sun to any of these tropical points could be provided by prior notices of the rising and setting of stars before them.

The difficulty encountered in actually observing some of the zodiacal constellations emphasizes the fact that there must have been an overriding aim involved in the creation of the belt as a unity of constellations in the sky. They are, of course, bound together by their occurrence on the zone of the sky covered by the sun, the moon, and the planets in their progression through the year, and it must have been the movements of these bodies which drove astronomers to create constellations along the circuit of the sun, even if those constellations were difficult to see.[46] In Babylonia these constellations formed the zodiac, which provided a backdrop to the ominous appearances of the planets. This astrological usage made its way eventually to Greece and beyond. But before then, in classical Greece, in the hands of astronomers like Euctemon and Eudoxus, the zodiac started to become a backcloth on which was marked the sequence of a different series of 'omens', namely the transition from one season to another. The purpose of collating

---

Thousand Years on the Shaman's Path (New York, 1993), 34–6, 155–6. More controversially still, it has been argued that as early as the Neolithic period the Egyptians were aware of the equinoctial points, using the method described in the text here: J. B. Sellers, *The Death of Gods in Ancient Egypt* (Harmondsworth, 1992), 28–32. What is interesting here is that none of these cultures would normally be regarded as having had the theoretical framework which Dicks considered essential for accurate placement of the equinoctial points.

[45] Dicks (n. 43), 34–5; Neugebauer (n. 4), 55–6, 627–9.

[46] Or even if they destroyed earlier asterisms: see Hannah (n. 29). Compare Reiche's assessment of the relative uselessness of the zodiac for farmers ((n. 2), 41), and the relative ease of observing non-zodiacal stars (ibid. 43 n. 11): 'Ginzel . . . surmises that heliacal risings must have been still more difficult to spot, since the ancients were unfamiliar with the horizon-points where first risings would occur. This was no doubt true of the risings of zodiacal stars as watched for by laymen. But farmers used a remarkably small number of calendar-stars . . . Mediterranean farmers may safely be supposed to have used the sort of local backsight–foresight alignments so well attested for their North European counterparts and even American Indians to memorize the horizon-points where Arcturus, Pleiades, Hyades, Orion, and Sirius always effected their annual risings and settings.' The point would appear to be that it is easier to watch for the heliacal risings and settings of stars outside the zodiac, presumably because they are not so caught in the sun's glow as it rises or sets, so long as one has a clear idea of just where to look. After all, one would expect that the sun's own position would make it easier to find a star rising or setting on its path.

such 'omens' would appear to have been the harmonization of certain human activities with seasonal events.[47]

3. Euctemon's Audience

The length of the solar year was important to maintain regularity from one year to the next, so that religious festivals centred on agricultural events, such as sowing and harvesting, could be held at the appropriate, seasonal time. Whereas Hesiod's calendar ties stellar phenomena to agricultural activities, Euctemon's ties them, if to anything, apparently only to meteorological phenomena. Agricultural and maritime activities could be run by it, but they are not explicitly stated, and a *parapēgma* set up in a city is of little immediate use to either farmers or sailors. The absence of an overtly stated practical purpose gives Euctemon's calendar the appearance of a disinterested, 'scientific' construct, created for its own intrinsic interest. This 'scientific' nature of the *parapēgma* of Euctemon, and its presumed solar character, in fact led Pritchett and van der Waerden to argue that it would have attracted Thucydides, who wanted a more reliable system of time measurement than the civil calendars of his time could offer, to use it for his reporting of events in the Peloponnesian war.[48] But was Euctemon's calendar necessarily the piece of disinterested scientific research that some modern scholars would have it be? The very choice of stars in the calendar would seem to argue against this interpretation. The traditional core of observed stars within and outside the zodiacal belt has been extended by far more from outside the belt than from within it. This would suggest that a calendar with the principal purpose of keeping track of the sun's apparent movement in the sky was not Euctemon's intention, since one might expect a list of stars more closely connected with the sun to have been included, as was the case in Callippus' *parapēgma* a century later.

Later stone *parapēgmata* have been found within cities (Athens and Miletus), and there is a suggestion that the local civil/religious calendar could be aligned with the stellar/solar phenomena of the *parapēgma*.[49] But if farmers

---

[47] D. de Solla Price, 'Clockwork before the Clock and Timekeepers before Timekeeping', in J. T. Fraser and N. Lawrence (eds.), *The Study of Time*, ii (Berlin, Heidelberg, and New York, 1975), 367–80, argues strongly that before the 1st cent. BC the Greeks were not interested in measuring time *per se* but in observing the orderly sequences of 'omen events' such as star-rise and star-set, equinoxes and solstices, on which the sequences of agriculture and religion relied.

[48] Pritchett and van der Waerden (n. 15). This view was strongly disputed by B. D. Meritt, 'The Seasons in Thucydides', *Historia*, 11 (1962), 436–46, and more recently by Wenskus (n. 19), 87–9.

[49] Pritchett and van der Waerden (n. 15), 40: 'It is clear that the parapegmata were composed by scientists, but meant for general use in the towns. The parapegma established a correspondence between two kinds of calendars: the seasonal or sidereal calendar and the civil or modified lunar calendar. The seasonal calendar was most important for such persons as peasants and ship-owners, whereas the civil calendar governed the festivals and the town life.'

were not explicitly addressed by this calendar, it may yet be argued that
others further down the agricultural chain, who still relied on the seasonal
cycle but less directly as a basis for their own activities, could have used and
even commissioned the calendar to regulate those activities. These 'others'
would seem to have to be the religious authorities, who wanted to keep the
festivals of the gods in time with the agricultural seasons to which the cults
were attached.

Osborne has noted:

The agricultural year shapes the religious year, both because the farmer's activities
were themselves of vital importance and because they provided a paradigm for the
understanding of other aspects of human life. The annual pattern of sowing, cultivation, and harvest provided a framework for the understanding of events of long
or uncertain periodicity. The life of the farm provided a model of growth, change,
maturity and death; human birth, development, labour and death could be thought
about using that model, and because of the regularity of crop development the uncertain human events could be seen to be part of a larger pattern. Farming directly
provided livelihood and sustenance for the majority of Greeks. It also provided a
way of ordering their lives.[50]

Euctemon's *parapēgma* is still structured around significant, seasonal divisions of the year, even though their agricultural importance is not indicated
at all. This might suggest that the calendar was for the use, not of farmers,
but of people who relied on the seasonal, agricultural cycle also, not as a
livelihood, but as a basis for other activities, i.e. the priests who organized
the festivals of the gods of agriculture. We could go further still, and suggest
that the dramatic increase in the number of observations which Euctemon's
parapēgma provides over the earlier list in Hesiod's poem might be due
to a desire to tie definite agricultural festivals more closely to their proper
time of year. In that case, perhaps some of the observed stars added by
Euctemon have particular significance for certain festivals or the gods associated with those festivals. A preliminary study suggests that this may
well be the case with festivals of Demeter and Persephone, the timing of
which seems to coincide with significant observations (risings, settings, or
culminations) of the Pleiades, the Hyades, Orion, and the Bear. And the
major festival of Athens' patron deity, Athena, might have been intended
to coincide with significant observed positions of the constellation of the
Horse (Pegasus), an appropriate companion to the goddess. While work in
this area is too much in its infancy to warrant detailed discussion here, it is
of interest to note that later periods of history certainly witnessed the use of
star calendars for religious purposes.[51] It has, moreover, been suggested that

---

[50] Osborne (n. 30), 174.
[51] Cf. the later festival calendar (of about 300 BC) preserved in the Hibeh Papyrus (P. Hibeh
27), which depends in some way on the *parapēgma* of Eudoxus while meshing it with an
Egyptian lunar-based calendar, and incorporates indications for the celebration of certain

Euctemon's calendar might have had an even broader, more political, significance. The calendar's ability to offer a more regular progression within the year and from one year to the next might have been extremely attractive to the political leaders of Athens in the later fifth century, as the city tried to increase its control over its allies through centralized cults and festivals.[52] The Eleusinian Mysteries and the Panathenaea are obvious examples of such festivals which were further developed at this time to increase the bond between Athens and her allies.

4. Conclusion

In conclusion, it seems possible that the Vienna manuscript represents a first attempt by Euctemon to construct a useful *parapēgma*, still based on traditional methods of day-counting between observations. It extends dramatically the number of observations beyond the traditional couple of handfuls preserved by Hesiod, and therefore provides a much more carefully constructed 'safety-net' of warnings for activities which were geared to the seasons. The *parapēgma* preserved in the compilation associated with Geminus, on the other hand, may represent a revision in which a zodiacal structure was adopted in the wake of an influx of ideas from the east and of new discoveries by Euctemon, Meton, and others in the later fifth century. The resultant calendar would then be a first step towards the creation of a solar calendar, but would still be something of a hotchpotch, since the stars enumerated in it have little relation with the zodiac. For the fully fledged solar calendar, which utilized the observations of the zodiacal stars, we have to wait until the development of Callippus' *parapēgma* in the later fourth century BC.

Euctemon's *parapēgma* was not explicitly addressed to the agricultural sector, and its intended spectators may not have been farmers themselves, although they would have found it much more secure than the primitive calendar offered by Hesiod. Rather, it was others further down the agricultural

Egyptian religious festivals: B. P. Grenfell and A. S. Hunt (eds.), *The Hibeh Papyri*, i (London, 1906), 138–57; F. Lasserre, *Die Fragmente des Eudoxos von Knidos* (Berlin, 1966), 214–19; Spalinger (n. 14), 349–73. (I am grateful to Vivian Nutton, Alan Bowen, Anthony Spalinger, and David Fowler for references and discussion.) In the early medieval period Gregory of Tours provided stellar observational data (of ultimately classical origin) to enable monks to regulate their timing of night prayer: see S. McCluskey, *Astronomies and Cultures in Early Medieval Europe* (Cambridge, 1998), 97–113.

[52] B. Fehr, 'Zur religionspolitischen Funktion der Athena Parthenos im Rahmen des delisch-athenischen Seebundes—Teil II', *Hephaistos*, 2 (1980), 113–25. There are, of course, also the explicit and frequent references in the *parapēgma* of Euctemon, and other such calendars, to weather prognostications (ἐπισημασίαι). To what extent these were the *raison d'être* of the *parapēgmata*, or a traditional appendage, needs to be studied further: see A. Rehm, 'Episemasiai', *RE* suppl. vii (1940), 175–97; Wenskus (n. 19), 31–2; and Liba Taub's paper in this volume.

chain who may have found the *parapēgma* most useful—the officials charged with the organization of the festivals of Athens. Their purpose is harder to determine, perhaps a desire simply to regulate the annual occurrence of certain festivals so as to keep them in tune with their related seasonal activities, or perhaps, more sinisterly, a wish to centralize the religious observances of her allies in Athens itself and so to increase the city's power.

The principal result of this argument is to suggest that Euctemon's development of the seasonal calendar was not due to disinterested 'scientific' interest, i.e. to the pursuit of knowledge for knowledge's sake, but to the pressure of external socio-political forces and needs.[53] This suggests that a reassessment of Euctemon's scientific work, and perhaps of early Greek astronomy in general, is needed: to what extent were its achievements driven by non-scientific needs? In the history of later Greek astronomy the significant role played by astrology in the development of astronomy is well known. But earlier Greek speculation and advances in astronomy may also have been the result of external interests.

[53] Bowen and Goldstein (n. 3), 73–7, also conjecture extra-scientific motives (to do with public health and town planning) behind Meton's activities.

7

Instruments of Alexandrian Astronomy: The Uses of the Equinoctial Rings

L. TAUB

1. Introduction

UNTIL the early modern period, the writings of the second-century Alexandrian Claudius Ptolemy were widely regarded as the standard works in astronomy. In *The Mathematical Syntaxis* (also known as the *Almagest*) Ptolemy described instruments he had built, and in some cases presumably designed.[1] Just as his astronomical writings provided the foundation for much of later astronomy, so too, in many cases, the instruments described by Ptolemy formed the basis for later observing tools. The instruments of many Islamic observatories and of Tycho Brahe may be mentioned particularly in this context.

While it is clear that many of the instruments described by Ptolemy were specially made for him, he also very briefly alludes to two rather specialized and public instruments which had been in place for some time—a fact evident both from his own account of them and from his citation of a passage in a now lost work by the second-century BC astronomer Hipparchus which indicates that a presumably similar instrument had been in use in Alexandria in his day.[2] These instruments were, it appears, simple bronze rings (Figure 7.1). They may or may not have been graduated,[3] and were of fairly large size; Theon of Alexandria and his daughter Hypatia in their jointly produced commentary on *Syntaxis* book 3 suggested that they were about

My consideration of the equinoctial rings has benefited from discussions with various colleagues, to whom I am grateful. In particular, I wish to thank Dr Sachiko Kusukawa, Professor Sir Geoffrey Lloyd, Professor Vivian Nutton, Professor Ineke Sluiter, and Professor Noel Swerdlow, as well as my anonymous reader and the editors, for their help.

[1] References to the *Syntaxis* throughout are to J. L. Heiberg's edition in *Claudii Ptolemaei Opera Quae Exstant Omnia*, vol. i (2 parts; Leipzig, 1898–1903). Among other instruments mentioned by Ptolemy are the meridian ring (1. 12, pp. 64. 2–66. 4), plinth (ibid., pp. 66. 5–67. 16), parallactic instrument (5. 12, pp. 403. 2–405. 17), armillary astrolabe (5. 1, pp. 350. 13–354. 17), and four-cubit dioptra (5. 14, pp. 417. 1–418. 7). See D. J. Price, 'Precision Instruments to 1500', in C. Singer, E. J. Holmyard, A. R. Hall, and T. I. Williams (eds.), *A History of Technology*, iii (Oxford, 1957), 582–619 at 589–92. See also n. 46.

[2] 3. 1, pp. 195–7 Heiberg. See Fig. 7.1.

[3] Opinions vary. See O. Neugebauer, *A History of Ancient Mathematical Astronomy* (Berlin and New York, 1975), 854, on the divisions of Ptolemy's instruments; N. M. Swerdlow, 'Ptolemy on Trial', *American Scholar*, 48 (1979), 523–31 at 526–7; Price (n. 1), 587.

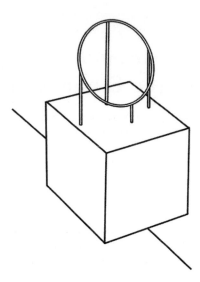

FIG. 7.1. Equinoctial ring (equatorial armillary), based on Price (n. 1), 589

2 cubits, or almost a metre, in diameter.[4] According to all three accounts, the purpose of the rings was to make observations in order to determine the equinoxes. Ptolemy implies that the rings were fairly useless, at least in the state he found them, since they did not give accurate readings and sometimes even indicated two equinoxes during the same day. In the course of his account he notes that he had himself used two other types of instruments to make observations to determine the length of the year, viz. the meridian ring and the plinth.[5]

Given that, in Ptolemy's view, the Alexandrian equinoctial rings were apparently wildly inaccurate, how can we account for their survival? Through a consideration of this question, and some possible answers, I intend to raise broader issues both about the character of astronomical activity in the Hellenistic period and about our writing of the history of ancient astronomy.

[4] A. Rome, 'Le troisième livre des commentaires sur l'Almageste par Théon et Hypatie', *Annales de la Société scientifique de Bruxelles*, 46 (1926), 1–14 at 11, believed Theon was still using the ring in the 4th cent. AD. Theon, *In Ptol. III*, p. 817 Rome, seems to refer to the meridian ring and plinth (mentioned in *Synt.* 1. 12, pp. 64. 12–67. 16 Heiberg). Procl. *Hypotyp.* 3. 5–27, pp. 42. 5–52. 28 Manitius (5th cent. AD), mentioned some of Ptolemy's instruments (the meteoroscopon and meridian ring), but not the equinoctial ring. Pappus (4th cent. AD) describes the ἀστρολάβον ὄργανον at *In Synt V*, pp. 1–16 Rome.

[5] The latter instrument was adapted by Tycho Brahe into the mural quadrant.

2. Problems of Accuracy

First, we would do well to consider Ptolemy's report within the context in which it was presented, in the midst of a discussion about the definition of the year in *Syntaxis* book 3. Here Ptolemy explains that Hipparchus had been 'somewhat disturbed by the suspicion, derived from a series of observations [τηρήσεων] which he made in close succession', that the revolution of the sun does not take the same length of time from one equinox or solstice to the next.[6]

According to Ptolemy, Hipparchus had reported (in a now lost treatise, called *On the Displacement of the Solstitial and Equinoctial Points*) that while he was unable to observe significant discrepancies in the periods between the solstices, 'the irregularity in the length of the year can be accurately perceived from the [equinoxes] observed on the bronze ring situated in the place at Alexandria called the "Square Stoa"'. Hipparchus explained that 'this [ring] is supposed to indicate the equinox on the day when the direction from which its concave surface is illuminated changes from one side to the other'.[7]

Ptolemy listed the times of equinoxes considered by Hipparchus to have been accurately observed and noted that they contain 'no discrepancy worth noticing'.[8] But he also noted that there are potentially serious difficulties in using permanently mounted instruments, owing to problems in correctly positioning the instrument, and to the liability to shift over time. He made it clear that his objections were not merely theoretical, noting that 'one can see

[6] 3. 1, p. 194. 3–6 Heiberg. Unless otherwise noted, all translations of the *Syntaxis* are from G. J. Toomer, *Ptolemy's Almagest* (New York, Berlin, and London, 1984), here p. 132. The sun appears to move around the earth, with a daily motion from east to west. During the course of the year, however, it appears to travel from west to east against the background of the fixed stars. The apparent annual path of the sun's motion is called the ecliptic, and can be imagined as a great circle inclined at $23\frac{1}{2}°$ to the celestial equator, another imaginary circle in the heavens which lies directly above the earth's equator. Astronomically speaking, the equinoxes are the two points during a year—one in spring, the other in autumn—at which the sun, in its motion along the ecliptic, crosses the circle of the celestial equator. When the sun is at the equinoctial points day and night appear to be equal in length. Each point can be thought of as a geometrical point, a point in celestial space, and/or a point (or instant) in time. But in popular usage the equinoxes refer to those two days during which day and night are equal. There are two other important points in the sun's annual path along the ecliptic, namely the tropical (or solstitial) points, one of which occurs in summer, the other in winter, but these are not of so much immediate relevance here.

[7] 3. 1, pp. 194–5 Heiberg. That is, when the sun was north of the equator, the shadow of the upper part of the ring would fall to one side of the bottom of the ring; when the sun was south of the equator, the shadow would fall on the other side. Whether or not the rings were marked with a scale is potentially significant. See A. Rome, 'Les observations d'équinoxes et de solstices dans le chapitre 1 du livre 3 du commentaire sur l'Almageste par Théon d'Alexandrie. I–II', *Annales de la Société scientifique de Bruxelles*, 57 (1937), 213–36 and ibid. 58 (1938), 6–26, at 57: 233–4; id., *Commentaires de Pappus et Théon d'Alexandrie sur l'Almageste*, iii (Vatican City, 1931–43), 817 n. 3.

[8] 3. 1, p. 197. 1 Heiberg—this despite the fact that an error of up to a quarter of a day could occur not only in observation of solstices (cf. p. 195. 1–2) but even in equinox observations.

this in the case of the bronze rings in our palaestra, which are supposed to be fixed in the plane of the equator'. He complained that 'when we observe with them, the distortion in their positioning is apparent, especially that of the larger and older of the two, to such an extent that sometimes the direction of illumination of the concave surface in them shifts from one side to the other twice on the same equinoctial day'. It is clear from his discussion that he believed that this problem had been acquired over time, suggesting that at an earlier date the rings were more accurate and functional.[9]

Some discussion of the bronze equinoctial rings has been very brief; in his 1984 translation of the *Almagest* Gerald Toomer barely commented on them in his footnotes. Otto Neugebauer, author of the *History of Ancient Mathematical Astronomy* (1975), appears not to have discussed them at all. In Anthony Turner's 1994 *Mathematical Instruments in Antiquity and the Middle Ages* the rings do not even merit a full sentence. But other scholars considered the problem of the rings in more detail, attempting to account for the phenomenon reported by Ptolemy of two 'equinoxes' appearing to occur on the same day, as the direction of illumination on the ring shifted twice (3. 1, p. 197. 22–3 Heiberg). I believe it is not only the phenomena of the 'double' equinox which requires explanation, but, in light of Ptolemy's criticism, the existence and use of the rings themselves.

Ptolemy had explained the problem of the double appearance of the equinox as being due to a gradual shifting of the mounts for the rings, causing them to be out of alignment. Karl Manitius explained the problem as due to the effect of refraction, which he claimed would occur even on a correctly aligned ring.[10] (The rays of the sun are refracted, or bent, as they pass through the atmosphere. Different atmospheric conditions affect the degree of refraction.) A. Rome found this view unpersuasive, arguing that the true equinox could still easily have been determined. John Britton, in turn, regarded Rome's view as of doubtful value, since it appeared to be based on a fundamental misunderstanding of Ptolemy's remarks (the whole point of which was that there was something wrong with the rings).[11]

In the 1960s and 1970s Frans and Margaret Bruin constructed an equinoctial ring and made observations at the American University of Beirut. While it is not at all clear that their observing procedure was similar to any followed in antiquity, they did clearly demonstrate that determining the

---

[9] 3. 1, p. 197. 11–23 Heiberg. The date reported for the vernal equinox observation in connection with which Hipparchus mentions the ring at Alexandria is 'the 32nd year of the Third Callippic Cycle, Mechir 27', or 24 Mar. −145 (= 146 BC).

[10] K. Manitius, *Ptolemäus: Handbuch der Astronomie* (Leipzig, 1912–13; repr. 1963), i. 427 n. 21.

[11] Rome (n. 7), 230–5 and 817 n. 3 (818) respectively; J. P. Britton, *Models and Precision: The Quality of Ptolemy's Observations and Parameters* (New York and London, 1992), 16 n. 7: '[Rome] prefers the interpretation that the equinox was merely observed at two different times on two different rings. This interpretation seems somewhat forced, and also unnecessary, since Ptolemy mentions the phenomenon only to indicate the poor alignment of the rings.'

equinox with such a ring is not a straightforward matter.[12] Most recently John Britton has argued, on the basis of calculations, that multiple appearances of the 'equinox' on a properly aligned ring could be expected. Britton points to the significant difficulties associated with using the equinoctial ring, the problem of alignment (mentioned by Ptolemy), and the further problem of refraction, which is 'both significant and highly variable'. He concluded that 'multiple appearances of an equinox on a well-aligned equatorial ring are common rather than exceptional'.[13]

It is of course true that, while the accurate determination of the equinox is not unproblematic, it is a much more straightforward matter than the observational determination of the solstice (something Ptolemy himself knew).[14] Even an imprecise determination of the equinox would not have been without value, since, as Asger Aaboe and Derek de Solla Price pointed out, measurement of the interval from one equinox to another would yield an answer correct to the nearest day.[15] However, it is not clear that all the reported equinox 'observations' were actually observed. Some values must have been calculated, namely those which occur during the night, and Noel Swerdlow has suggested that Ptolemy 'must have interpolated between two observations made a day apart'.[16]

To summarize: observing the equinoxes with the equinoctial rings would have been tricky under the best of circumstances. They would have been difficult to align and would, in any case, be liable to the effects of refraction— a liability apparently unknown to Ptolemy at the time he was writing the

---

[12] F. and M. Bruin, 'The Equator Ring, Equinoxes and Atmospheric Refraction', *Centaurus*, 20 (1976), 89–111. The Bruins' method combined observations and interpolation. They recognized (at 98) that 'it does not follow, of course, that the Ancients were led to a similar method, although it is hard to believe that they would have been satisfied with a single observation'. Their method involves quite an elaborate procedure, and would have required more equipment than just the ring itself. (The Bruins used a 'pack' of 60–80 white filing-cards and sharp lead pencils.)

[13] Britton (n. 11), 25, 28. He states that some of Rome's claims are incorrect and misleading. See also J. Evans, *The History and Practice of Ancient Astronomy* (Oxford, 1998), 206–7.

[14] *Synt.* 3. 1, p. 203 Heiberg. Cf. n. 16.

[15] A. Aaboe and D. J. de Solla Price, 'Qualitative Measurement in Antiquity: The Derivation of Accurate Parameters from Crude but Crucial Observations', in I. B. Cohen and R. Taton (eds.), *Mélanges Alexandre Koyré*, ii. *L'Aventure de l'esprit* (Paris, 1964), 1–20.

[16] Aaboe and Price, ibid. 9, point out that 'at the equinoxes, the declination of the Sun changes by about 24′ per day; we may therefore suppose it possible to fix such a date within about $\frac{1}{4}$ day, corresponding to an uncertainty of 6′ of declination arc'. The observation of the equinox is much easier than determining the solstitial point, for then the 'declination differs 1′ from the extreme value (either maximum or minimum declination)'; not until it is five days away does its declination change by as much as 6′. We must conclude therefore that a solstitial point cannot be located directly to an accuracy better than some three or four days', whereas the equinoxes may be determined observationally with 'reasonable accuracy'. Many historians of astronomy, including Aaboe and Price and Britton, have argued that rounding off must have occurred. It should be noted here that such calculations were not cited as a disparagement of Ptolemy's method by these authors. Of course, the matter of Ptolemy's observations has been the topic of serious debate. See Swerdlow (n. 3).

Syntaxis. At least some equinox times must have been calculated. Furthermore, additional instruments, either sundials or waterclocks, would have
been necessary to establish the time of the observations and would have
added potential complications.

3. The Rings' Purpose and Survival

According to Ptolemy's account (3.1, p. 195. 3–9 Heiberg), Hipparchus was
generally satisfied with the equinox observations which had been made using the ring at Alexandria in his own time, though it is not entirely clear
who had made the observations. But by the second century AD, according to
Ptolemy, the two equinoctial rings in the city—neither of which need have
been the one mentioned by Hipparchus—were no longer reliable. Why were
they there at all, given that they no longer provided a reliable reading? Why
would not one but two inaccurate astronomical instruments survive in what
may have been a very public place over what seems to have been a fairly
long period of time? Were they being used at all, and if so what for?

While various historians have offered explanations, these are difficult
questions to answer because there is so little evidence. Nevertheless, I believe a possible picture of the use of the equinoctial rings can be drawn.

First, let us consider the location of the bronze rings. Two place names
are mentioned by Ptolemy, the Square Stoa, noted by Hipparchus as the
site of the equinoctial ring in his day, and the palaestra (the gymnasium),
given as the location of both rings by Ptolemy. These place names may
refer to the same site, but certainly do not *have* to do so. Unfortunately
the fullest surviving account of Alexandria—that of Strabo, 17. 1. 8–10—
does not mention the Square Stoa, and its description of the gymnasium
is brief and partly affected by textual corruption. The most we can say is
that the rings were displayed in public and that the location(s) may have
been rather prominent[17]—such, at least, has been a widespread assumption
among historians of Greek astronomy and, while the public location may
not be important, I propose that we adopt it as a working hypothesis.

Next, however, there are other—rather more fundamental—assumptions
made by historians of astronomy which need to be considered. Ancient
astronomical instruments have not been much studied—largely because,
for the most part, they do not survive. The study of ancient instruments
requires a peculiar type of archaeology, which relies almost exclusively on
textual evidence. The situation is, oddly, the reverse of what is usually faced

[17] This would be true if Ptolemy's palaestra is the gymnasium which was part of the same
complex as the courts of justice and the groves in the centre of the city (P. M. Fraser, *Ptolemaic
Alexandria* (Oxford, 1972), i. 26, 29) and if the Square Stoa was part of the city agora (ibid. i.
30, ii. 98 nn. 221–3). Toomer (n. 6), 133 n. 7, cites Fraser for information on the two locations
and perhaps assumes the palaestra and Square Stoa to be effectively identical.

by those concerned with the material culture of antiquity; instead of objects in search of documents to illuminate and corroborate dating and usage, the historian is faced with scattered and sketchy references and few physical remains. The necessary focus on texts has also, no doubt, contributed to the emphasis on a particular type of astronomy, namely, that which is mathematical, theoretical, and survives in literary forms. Consequently, issues surrounding instruments have tended to take a back seat to other concerns. But, as we have seen, Ptolemy himself took some care to describe instruments which he both used and, in some cases, designed. While the immediate focus of our enquiry is the equinoctial rings at Alexandria, this can lead to consideration of larger issues related to the character and role of Hellenistic astronomy. In fact, we need to ask: what was astronomy used for in antiquity?[18]

The writing of the history of ancient astronomy has largely been accomplished by a particular group of scholars, who have ties to their intellectual ancestor (and in many cases teacher), Otto Neugebauer (who died in 1990). Neugebauer noted that 'both Babylonian and Greek astronomy are based on a set of relatively few data' and stressed that 'the selection of these data undoubtedly required a great number of observations and much experience to know what to look for'. He argued that 'nevertheless, a mathematical system constructed at the earliest possible stage of the game was generally no longer systematically tested under modified conditions' over a long period of time. In other words, once the parameters had been established, there was no need to go back continually and reobserve the same old phenomena. Neugebauer defended the soundness of this approach, explaining that ancient observers were well aware of the many sources of inaccuracies inherent in instruments and the human eye.[19] Hence 'we notice an outspoken tendency in the development of astronomy to take refuge behind mathematical

---

[18] I have argued at length elsewhere that for some, including Ptolemy, astronomy was useful as an ethical endeavour: L. Taub, *Ptolemy's Universe: The Natural Philosophical and Ethical Foundations of Ptolemy's Astronomy* (Chicago, 1993). See also J. Evans, 'The Material Culture of Greek Astronomy', *JHA* 30 (1999), 237–307, and L. Taub, 'Destini della scienza greca. Eredità e longevità degli strumenti scientifici', in S. Settis (ed.), *I greci: Storia, cultura, arte, società*, iii (Turin, 2001), 889–930.

[19] Neugebauer (n. 3), 14. None the less, the establishment of useful parameters was possible, for period relations 'can be established within a few decades with comparatively high accuracy because the error of individual observations is distributed over the whole interval of time'. This echoes Ptolemy, *Synt.* 3. 1, p. 202 Heiberg: λαμβάνοιτο δ' ἂν ἔγγιστα ἀκριβῶς ἡ τοιαύτη ἀποκατάστασις, ὅσῳ ἂν ὁ μεταξὺ τῶν συγκρινομένων τηρήσεων χρόνος πλείων εὑρίσκηται. καὶ οὐ μόνον ἐπὶ ταύτης τὸ τοιοῦτον συμβέβηκεν, ἀλλὰ καὶ ἐπὶ πασῶν τῶν περιοδικῶν ἀποκαταστάσεων· τὸ γὰρ παρὰ τὴν αὐτῶν τῶν τηρήσεων ἀσθένειαν, κἂν ἀκριβῶς μεθοδεύωνται, γινόμενον διάψευσμα βραχὺ καὶ τὸ αὐτὸ ἔγγιστα ὑπάρχον ὡς πρὸς τὴν παρ' αὐτὰ αἴσθησιν ἐπί τε τῶν διὰ μακροῦ καὶ ἐπὶ τῶν δι' ὀλίγου χρόνου φαινομένων ('the longer the time between the observations compared, the greater the accuracy of the determination of the period of revolution. This rule holds good not only in this case, but for all periodic revolutions. For the error due to the inaccuracy inherent in even carefully performed observations is, to the senses of the observer, small and approximately the same at any [two] observations, whether these are taken at a large or a small interval': trans. Toomer (n. 6), 137).

schemes, rather than to embark on systematic observational programs which are so characteristic for astronomy since the invention of the telescope'.[20]

In addition to the mathematical ability used to construct theories, some observations were, of course, necessary. As Geoffrey Lloyd put it: 'in astronomy it is only with reference to the inevitably more or less imprecise observational data that the elegant and rigorous geometrical theory can be applied to the explananda'.[21] But, following Neugebauer, many have taken the view that observational work did not play a continuing part in ancient Greek astronomical practice. Rather, once sufficient data had been gathered, the focus was on developing mathematical theory. In spite of some evidence to the contrary, e.g. the compilation of star catalogues by both Hipparchus and Ptolemy, the consensus that continuing programmes of observational activity were not undertaken by ancient Greek astronomers has prevailed among many historians.

It will probably not be surprising, then, that there is some agreement that the rings mentioned by Ptolemy were not used for astronomical observations, at least not in the second century AD.[22] Aydin Sayili believed that the instruments were there on exhibition—adding: 'this is, if I remember correctly, Professor O. Neugebauer's opinion'. It is, of course, possible that old, outdated scientific instruments were put on show in a sort of outdoor museum display.[23] Another suggestion has been that the rings were placed there for the arrangement of civic affairs. But what civic affairs might those have been? Unfortunately, the passages from Ptolemy which are cited to support this hypothesis do not offer much help.[24] Price, who described the instrument in some detail, also suggested that 'the public site of the Alexandrian instrument is a reminder of the importance of equinoctial observations for ritualistic and calendrical purposes'.[25] But because the calendar used in Alexandria was not astronomical (but was based on a standard number of days, 365), this latter suggestion may not be as relevant as it might have been

[20] Neugebauer (n. 3), 14. Aaboe and Price (n. 15), 16, contrast the observations of the ancients with those of early modern astronomers: 'In antiquity, we find only the minimum of observations needed to produce the required parameters, while Brahe heralds the modern use of instruments by indiscriminate observation that overdetermines the problem.' G. E. R. Lloyd (discussion) rightly points to star-cataloguing as a sustained observational programme.

[21] G. E. R. Lloyd, 'Observational Error in Later Greek Science', in id., *Methods and Problems in Greek Science: Selected Papers* (Cambridge, 1991), 299–332 at 327 (originally published in J. Barnes, J. Brunschwig, M. Burnyeat, and M. Schofield (eds.), *Science and Speculation: Studies in Hellenistic Theory and Practice* (Cambridge, 1982), 128–64).

[22] If the rings were being used for a continuing observational programme, there are no surviving records of or allusions to such a programme.

[23] *The Observatory in Islam and its Place in the General History of the Observatory* (Ankara, 1960), 350–1, citing Rome (n. 7), 818.

[24] F. Nolte, *Die Armillarsphäre* (Abhandlungen zur Geschichte der Naturwissenschaften und der Medizin, 2; Erlangen, 1922), 10; see also P. Tannery, *Recherches sur l'histoire de l'astronomie ancienne* (Paris, 1893), 76–7.

[25] (n. 1), 587. (Price incidentally mistakenly suggests that Hipparchus used the ring in Alexandria. Cf. Toomer (n. 6), 134 n. 9.)

in other ancient cities.[26] Nevertheless, the determination of the equinoxes was evidently important, to judge from the fact that they were often marked on sundials. Gnomons, the shadow-casters used to tell time, were not unusual in ancient cultures. Originally, simple straight sticks were employed, but eventually an impressive range of sundials was developed. Vitruvius (first century BC) discussed their history and describes them in detail in *De architectura* book 9, and there are well over 200 surviving Graeco-Roman examples, including some from Egypt.[27]

In addition to showing the time of day, by means of the shadow cast by the sun, some sundials were incised or engraved with markings which indicated in general terms the apparent course of the sun during the year. Thus, the dial could serve not only as a device to determine the time of day but also to indicate the time of year. Aaboe and Price note that 'the conical and spherical *skaphe* sundials that were common in the Graeco-Roman world from about 300 BC onwards conventionally contained lines, geometrically constructed on them, showing the path of the Sun's shadow at equinoxes and solstices and quite often at intervals between corresponding to the beginning of the other zodiacal signs'.[28]

Interestingly, the hour numerals are marked on only four of the 250+ known ancient dials, whereas the names of equinoxes and solstices (and

[26] Every four years the first day of Thoth was delayed by one day with respect to the solar year. 'The divergence of the Egyptian year from the course of the sun is almost imperceptible in one lifetime: the difference in forty years amounts only to ten days. . . . The advantages of the Egyptian calendar—its simplicity and regularity—are so obvious that astronomers, from Hellenistic times to Copernicus, used it': E. J. Bickerman, *Chronology of the Ancient World*, rev. edn. (London, 1980), 42–3.

[27] Most of the known ancient dials have been catalogued by S. L. Gibbs, *Greek and Roman Sundials* (New Haven and London, 1976). See also K. Locher, 'Two Greco-Roman Sundials from Alexandria and Dion', *JHA* 24 (1993), 300–2, and M. Catamo, N. Lanciano, K. Locher, M. Lombardero, and M. Valdés, 'Fifteen Further Greco-Roman Sundials from the Mediterranean Area and Sudan', *JHA* 31 (2000), 203–21, for further references. Several are in the British Museum, including one of two dials known from Alexandria (Fig. 7.2), an item found in 1852, which is a unique example of a conical dial with the hours marked in Greek letters, but cannot be reliably dated: the museum describes it as Ptolemaic, but the lettering may be Byzantine (Gibbs 304). Another dial, carved from Egyptian limestone and perhaps from our period (Imperial), is in the Fitzwilliam Museum (Fig. 7.3) and has been described by Derek Price—who found it to be crude and incapable of functioning—in L. Budde and R. Nicholls, *A Catalogue of the Greek and Roman Sculpture in the Fitzwilliam Museum, Cambridge* (Cambridge, 1964), 112–13 (item 185). See also Gibbs 321.

[28] Aaboe and Price (n. 15), 12–13. See also H. Diels, *Antike Technik*, 2nd. edn. (Leipzig and Berlin, 1920; repr. 1965), 169. Aaboe and Price went so far as to suggest that the sundial could have been used to gather observational data useful to astronomical theory: 'with a sundial of this type, and of the conventional size, it would take only half a year of measurement to get with sufficient precision the *crude facts* [my emphasis] . . . One may therefore reasonably conjecture that if in fact Meton, or anyone else in antiquity, did measure the equinoxes and solstices to settle the inequality of the seasons and the solar calendar that is such a necessary preamble to planetary theory, then this is how they set about it.' But even if Aaboe and Price were correct in their suggestion that sundials could be used as astronomical research tools, it seems unlikely that all the sundials which survive should be so regarded.

Fig. 7.2. Sundial (British Museum 1936 3-9 1)

even zodiacal signs) are inscribed on at least 44 of them. As a result of the presence of information of this sort, the sundial was sometimes called a *hēliotropion* ('sun-turning') rather than a *hōrologion* or hour-measurer.[29]

Clearly, sundials were useful in terms of determining the time in the course of the solar year, particularly the equinoxes and solstices, and were not simply used to tell time during the day. And, apparently, the determination of the equinoxes was important enough to warrant the provision of not one but at least two special instruments in Alexandria. What purpose did the determination of the equinox serve?

There was a long-lived tradition among the Greeks of devising calendars (so-called *parapēgmata*) which correlated dates and weather phenomena with the risings and settings of the fixed stars. It has been argued by Bowen and Goldstein that the original motivation behind Greek astronomy (which began as the organization of the fixed stars into constellations) was the construction of such calendars, whose astronomical character is underscored by the fact that in some of them the dates are simply listed in zodiacal 'months'.[30]

[29] e.g. Plut. *Dio* 29.
[30] B. Goldstein and A. C. Bowen, 'A New View of Early Greek Astronomy', *Isis*, 74 (1983), 330–40.

FIG. 7.3. Egyptian limestone sundial (Fitzwilliam Museum GR 100-1906)

Originally the term *parapēgma* described an inscribed stone which was displayed for public use, like a sundial, with holes beside the text, in which a peg could be inserted next to the appropriate day. In the early part of the last century fragments of two *parapēgmata* were excavated in Miletus, one dated to the late second, the other to the early first century BC.[31] Prior to their discovery, only the literary form of *parapēgma* was known, of which the so-called Geminus *parapēgma* is the earliest extant example. Both forms list consecutive fixed-star phases and associated weather prognostications; the literary form simply gives the daily progress of the sun, since no holes are possible.[32]

---

[31] H. Diels and A. Rehm, 'Parapegmenfragmente aus Milet', *Sitzungsberichte der Königlich preußischen Akademie der Wissenschaften* (Berlin, 1904), 92–111. See Figs. 6.1 and 6.2 in the preceding paper.

[32] On the *parapēgma* and its origins in the time of Meton and Euctemon see Hannah's paper in this volume.

Ptolemy, again, is an important source, providing valuable historical information about his predecessors. In his own *parapēgma* calendar (the *Phases of the Fixed Stars*) the (Alexandrian) dates of the equinoxes and solstices are given,[33] and particular mention is made of the significance of certain dates. For example, in the month of Thoth we have: '28. Autumnal equinox. It is significant for the Egyptians and Eudoxus'.[34] Neugebauer explained that such ominous days were normally taken as significant for weather changes.[35]

Weather forecasting has a long history among the Greeks, represented from an early date by Hesiod's *Works and Days* (where, moreover, weather is correlated to astronomical phenomena). As we might expect, much of the focus of the interest seemed to relate to agricultural activity: Virgil's *Georgics* is relevant here, as is Pliny's *Natural History*. But the agricultural authors who wrote on weather were not living in Egypt, where agriculture depended on the cycles of the flood basin. In fact, special instruments, called nilometers, were devised to track the level of the Nile and aid in predicting the time of the annual inundation, and weather prediction seems to have played no particular role.

But for Ptolemy, its contribution to weather prediction was an important reason for studying astronomy, particularly the sort of astronomy which we call astrology and which Ptolemy described in the *Tetrabiblos*, a work later than the *Syntaxis*. (He mentions weather prognostication only in passing in *Syntaxis:* 8. 6, ii. 204. 5 ff. Heiberg.) Astronomy had long been thought useful for weather prediction, but in the Hellenistic period broader predictive capabilities were claimed. That the study of celestial influences on the terrestrial realm was considered a useful part of astronomy during the Hellenistic period is significant, because it points towards a possible explanation of the use of the equinoctial rings at Alexandria. Within the context of astrology the equinoxes are especially important for defining points on the zodiac. In the *Tetrabiblos* Ptolemy explains that the doctrine and efficacy of astrological influence rely on correctly specifying the relations between zodiacal signs and the equinoxes and solstices. (The zodiac is a band around the celestial sphere in which the sun, moon, and planets appear to move; this band overlaps the ecliptic and is divided into twelve equal 30° arcs, or signs.) Ptolemy noted (1. 10, p. 30. 17–22 Boll–Boer) the significance of the spring equinox:

---

[33] As Neugebauer (n. 3), 929, has pointed out, Ptolemy provides only 'round' numbers, taken from theory, rather than observations: 'beginning with the autumnal equinox these dates are I, 28, IV, 26, VII, 26, and XI, 1. For the length of the season, beginning with the vernal equinox at VII, 26 (=March 22), one has the following intervals: 95, 92, 88, 90 days. These are obviously round numbers, taken from the Hipparchian–Ptolemaic solar theory.'

[34] κη΄. μετοπωρινὴ ἰσημερία. Αἰγυπτίοις καὶ Εὐδόξῳ ἐπισημαίνει (Ptol. *Phas.* 17. 9–10 Heiberg).

[35] (n. 3), 929: 'In the prognostications the frequent term "indicative" . . . requires explanation. The Greek term ἐπισημαίνει would normally refer to an object which is 'indicated' by the phase. As a meteorological technical term, however, it means that the weather might change at the phase. One could almost translate "the day is ominous".'

διόπερ καὶ τοῦ ζῳδιακοῦ μηδεμιᾶς οὔσης φύσει ἀρχῆς ὡς κύκλου τὸ ἀπὸ τῆς ἐαρινῆς
ἰσημερίας ἀρχόμενον δωδεκατημόριον τὸ τοῦ Κριοῦ καὶ τῶν ὅλων ἀρχὴν ὑποτίθενται,
καθάπερ ἐμψύχου ζῴου τοῦ ζῳδιακοῦ τὴν ὑγρὰν τοῦ ἔαρος ὑπερβολὴν προκαταρκτικὴν
ποιούμενοι . . .

although there is no natural beginning of the zodiac, since it is a circle, they assume
that the sign which begins with the vernal equinox, that of Aries, is the starting-
point of them all, making the excessive moisture of the spring the first part of the
zodiac as though it were a living creature . . . (trans. Robbins)[36]

In antiquity, astrological knowledge would have been of practical use in
several areas of everyday life. Ptolemy pointed to the usefulness of astrology
for general weather-forecasting, agriculture, and 'astrological geography',
but the application of astrology to medicine should not be overlooked.[37]
Ptolemy noted that 'the Egyptians, those who have most advanced the art
of astrology, have entirely united medicine and astrological prediction',
and Galen also mentioned Egyptian astrologers.[38] Iatromathematics was
one of the most popular uses of astrology. As Tamsyn Barton has noted,
fragmentary evidence suggests that physicians attracted clients by utilizing
astrology.[39]

Earlier, the medical significance of the equinoxes, in particular, had been
mentioned in the Hippocratic *Airs, Waters, and Places*. Here, it was explained that

κατὰ ταῦτά τις ἐννοεύμενος καὶ σκοπεύμενος προειδείη ἂν τὰ πλεῖστα τῶν μελλόντων
ἔσεσθαι ἀπὸ τῶν μεταβολέων. φυλάσσεσθαι δὲ χρὴ μάλιστα τὰς μεταβολὰς τῶν ὡρέων τὰς
μεγίστας . . . μέγισται δέ εἰσιν αἵδε καὶ ἐπικινδυνόταται, ἡλίου τροπαὶ ἀμφότεραι . . . καὶ
ἰσημερίαι νομιζόμεναι εἶναι ἀμφότεραι . . . (*Aer.* 11)

Anyone making observations and drawing deductions can foretell most of the effects
which follow changes in the weather. It is particularly necessary to take precautions
against great changes . . . The most dangerous times are the two solstices . . . and
the equinoxes. (trans. Chadwick and Mann)[40]

Galen, in his commentary on this work (lost in Greek, but extant in Arabic),
concurred with the view that the equinoxes are particularly influential in
their medical effects.[41] Galen's commentary makes clear his view that the

[36] Ptolemy, *Tetrabiblos*, trans. F. E. Robbins (Cambridge, Mass., 1940), 59–61.

[37] Weather-forecasting: Ptol. *Tetr.*, *passim*, esp. 2. 12–14 and book 3. Medicine: cf. Galen's
On Critical Days (*Di. dec.* 3, esp. ix. 901 ff. Kühn), adduced by T. S. Barton, *Power and Knowledge: Astrology, Physiognomics and Medicine under the Roman Empire* (Ann Arbor, 1994), 54.

[38] Ptol. *Tetr.* 1. 3. 18, p. 16. 7–10 Boll–Boer; cf. A. Bouché-Leclercq, *L'Astrologie grecque*
(Paris, 1899), 517–20. Gal. *Di. dec.* 3. 6, ix. 911 ff. Kühn. See Barton (n. 37), 54, and ead.,
Ancient Astrology (London, 1994), 187.   [39] Barton (n. 37), 179.

[40] J. Chadwick and W. N. Mann, in *Hippocratic Writings*, ed. G. E. R. Lloyd (Harmondsworth, 1983), 158–9. See also J. Jouanna, *Hippocrate: Airs, eaux, lieux* (Paris, 1996), 291–3.
The Aristotelian *Problems* (*Pr.* 1. 3–4, 859ᵃ9–28) mentions medical problems which are associated with the change of seasons, and also with the risings of particular stars; it is not certain
that Aristotle was the author of this work.

[41] Translation: G. J. Toomer in 'Galen on the Astronomers and Astrologers', *AHES* 32

heavenly bodies do effect physical changes on earth. Accordingly, he was critical of the lack of astronomical knowledge found among some medical practitioners. But he was also sceptical about the more expansive claims of some, making clear his belief that while astronomical knowledge was useful for medical practice, it was not foolproof.

As has often been noted, the success of certain works tends to eclipse, if not obliterate, others. There is not a lot of evidence regarding the relationship between astronomy and medicine, particularly for the period from the second century BC to the second century AD, the period of greatest interest for the existence of the equinoctial rings. Nevertheless, there is clear testimony from two second-century AD Alexandrians, Ptolemy and Galen, that astrology was an important (and potentially lucrative) practice linked to medicine in Egypt.

Evidence for another type of predictive astronomy is found in astronomical papyri from Egypt and, given a steady increase in the number of horoscopes, this suggests that the period from the end of the first century BC to the second half of the second century AD was one of growth in the practice of astrology.[42] While the equinoctial rings would not have been specifically useful for calculating horoscopes, they could have been used to establish the beginning of the astrological year. It is reasonable to imagine that a second ring might have been installed during this period of increased interest in predictive astronomy, with a view towards obtaining a more accurate reading, or a confirmation of the reading taken with the original instrument.

The equinoctial rings may have been particularly useful for practical and predictive astronomy, and it is important to note that such practices did not require a precise time when the sun crossed the celestial equator but only determination of the day on which this occurred. It is entirely possible that no attempt was made to determine the time of equinox; rather, simply confirming the equinoctial day may have been regarded as sufficient and may well have been all that was possible. In another context (*Syntaxis* 2. 6, p. 101. 4 Heiberg, describing the various latitudes of the earth), Ptolemy noted that 'the moment of the equinoxes is, in itself, somewhat indeterminate', and in book 3 he noted that an error of a quarter-day would not be unusual.[43] Nevertheless, confirmation of the equinoctial day would have been useful for predictive practices. For example, the rings could have been used to 'set' the *parapēgma*, to be used for weather prediction. This hypo-

(1985), 193–206, e.g. at 200. See also G. Strohmaier, 'Hellenistische Wissenschaft im neugefundenen Galenkommentar zur hippokratischen Schrift "Über die Umwelt"', in J. Kollesch and D. Nickel (eds.), *Galen und das hellenistische Erbe* (Verhandlungen des IV. Internationalen Galen-Symposiums, Sudhoffs Archiv, suppl. 32; Stuttgart, 1993), 157–64.

[42] A. Jones, 'The Place of Astronomy in Roman Egypt', in T. D. Barnes (ed.), *The Sciences in Greco-Roman Society* (Apeiron, 27; Edmonton, 1994), 25–52 at 31.

[43] 3. 1, pp. 194–7 Heiberg.

thesis could explain why the rings survived as observational instruments, in spite of their lack of 'precision'.[44]

In this context, the lack of accuracy mentioned by Ptolemy should be reconsidered. Ptolemy must have been an atypical user of such instruments, more mathematically inclined and demanding than most. Furthermore, he had a particular interest in instrumentation. In the *Planetary Hypotheses* Ptolemy indicates that he was, to some extent, addressing his work to instrument-makers, indicating that there was some demand for astronomical instruments.[45] In the *Tetrabiblos* he explains that there were certain instruments used by those engaged in astrology, particularly horoscopic astrolabes, solar instruments, and waterclocks.[46] Such instruments might be employed to determine the exact time of birth and would have served a completely different function from the equinoctial rings.

While he did not go into detail about any of these instruments (and the nature of the horoscopic astrolabe is open to debate), Ptolemy did indicate that the solar instruments were liable to error from the shifting of their positions or of their shadow-casters (gnomons).[47] This warning of the liability to inaccuracies due to the shifting of position is remarkably reminiscent of his description of the equinoctial rings. Nevertheless, Ptolemy's criticism of the accuracy of the rings does suggest that they were being

[44] Ptolemy made it clear in *Synt.* 8. 6, ii. 203. 11–20 Heiberg, that computation of the fixed-star phases is a daunting task—so much so that he declined to undertake it. This complexity is due to οὐ μόνον . . . τὰς διαφορὰς τῶν τε οἰκήσεων καὶ τῶν τοῦ ζῳδιακοῦ ἐγκλίσεων πλείστας οὔσας, ἀλλὰ καὶ . . . αὐτὸ τὸ πλῆθος τῶν ἀστέρων, καὶ ἔτι τὸ κατ' αὐτὰς τὰς τῶν τῶν ἀστέρων φάσεων τηρήσεις ἐργώδές τε εἶναι καὶ οὐκ εὐκατανόητον καὶ τῶν ὁρώντων αὐτῶν καὶ τῶν κατὰ τοὺς ὁρωμένους τόπους ἀέρων ἀνόμοιον καὶ ἀβέβαιον τὸν χρόνον τῆς πρώτης ὑποψίας ποιεῖν δυναμένων, ὡς ἔμοιγε ἀπό τε αὐτῆς τῆς πείρας καὶ τῆς ἐν ταῖς τοιαύταις τηρήσεσι διαφορᾶς γέγονεν εὐκατανόητον ('not only . . . the great number of different terrestrial latitudes and inclinations of the ecliptic involved, but also because of the sheer multitude of the fixed stars; seeing too, that, in respect of the actual observations of the phases it is laborious and uncertain, since the observers themselves and the atmosphere in the regions of observation can produce variation in and doubt about the time of the first suspected occurrence, as has become clear, to me at least, from my own experience and from the disagreements in this kind of observations': trans. Toomer (n. 6), 416–17).

[45] I. I, pp. 71. 11–72. 5 Heiberg. See also B. R. Goldstein, *The Arabic Version of Ptolemy's Planetary Hypotheses* (Transactions of the American Philosophical Society, NS 57.4; Philadelphia, 1967).

[46] *Tetr.* 3. 3. 1–2, pp. 110. 14–111. 2 Boll–Boer: μόνης μὲν ὡς ἐπίπαν τῆς δι' ἀστρολάβων ὡροσκοπείων κατ' αὐτὴν τὴν ἔκτεξιν διοπτεύσεως τοῖς ἐπιστημονικῶς παρατηροῦσι τὸ λεπτὸν τῆς ὥρας ὑποβάλλειν δυναμένης, τῶν δὲ ἄλλων σχεδὸν ἁπάντων ὡροσκοπείων, οἷς οἱ πλεῖστοι τῶν ἐπιμελεστέρων προσέχουσι, πολλαχῇ διαψεύδεσθαι τῆς ἀληθείας δυναμένων, τῶν μὲν ἡλιακῶν παρὰ τὰς τῶν θέσεων καὶ τῶν γνωμόνων ἐπισυμπιπτούσας διαστροφάς, τῶν δὲ ὑδρολογίων παρὰ τὰς τῆς ῥύσεως τοῦ ὕδατος ὑπὸ διαφόρων αἰτιῶν καὶ διὰ τὸ τυχὸν ἐποχάς τε καὶ ἀνωμαλίας ('in general only observation by means of horoscopic astrolabes at the time of birth can for scientific observers give the minute of the hour, while practically all other horoscopic instruments on which the majority of the more careful practitioners rely are frequently capable of error, the solar instruments by the occasional shifting of their positions or of their gnomons, and the waterclocks by stoppages and irregularities in the flow of the water': trans. Robbins (n. 36), 230–1).

[47] *Tetr.* 3. 3, pp. 110. 19–21 Boll–Boer: τῶν μὲν ἡλιακῶν παρὰ τὰς τῶν θέσεων καὶ τῶν γνωμόνων ἐπισυμπιπτούσας διαστροφάς (for translation see previous note). The reference to the gnomon makes it clear that the solar instruments were some sort of sundial.

used to determine equinoxes, just as horoscopic instruments were being used, in spite of their potential shortcomings. The requirements of predictive astronomy may well not have necessitated a precise time of equinox, which, in any case, would have been extremely difficult to provide. While the rings could not have been used for precise determinations, they may nevertheless have provided a reading sufficiently useful for the day-to-day affairs of practical predictive astronomy, weather prognostication, and the astrological applications so widespread in Alexandria. Such practical use of the equinoctial rings would help to explain their longevity.

Furthermore, the difficulty of determining the time of the equinox might even have made the procedure all the more 'expert', requiring special skills to figure out when it really occurred. Indeed, such a specialist sort of ability may have been highly prized. While Ptolemy explicitly pointed to some of the problems and limitations involved in using instruments (cf. n. 47), we can imagine that others might well have demanded the illusion of accuracy which could have been provided by specialist instrumentation. Lloyd has pointed to astrology as an area in which a premium was placed on the elaborate means by which a prediction was made; Tamsyn Barton has recently argued persuasively that elaboration was very much the name of the game for practising astrologers.[48]

Why have previous modern accounts of the equinoctial rings not pointed to their usefulness for predictive astronomy, including weather prognostication and astrological uses? One reason is scholarly hostility to astrology. In 1972 Fraser referred to astrology in the course of only two pages of text as a 'false science', a 'pseudo-science', a 'corrupt science', 'depraved', and a 'bastard' form of astronomy; and a few pages later he added the label 'debased'.[49] He was only prepared to regard scientific instruments as products of a 'legitimate' activity like theoretical astronomy and, although he recognized the enormous impact of astrology in the Hellenistic world, it was inconceivable to him that astrology would 'share' anything with 'legitimate' science. But astrology is now being taken much more seriously by historians: the two books recently published by Tamsyn Barton (see nn. 37, 38) are indicative of the change in attitude.

But perhaps some of the blame should be shifted to Ptolemy himself. After all, his mention of the rings, in a rather dismissive tone, is woven into an account of the fundamental problem of the definition of the year, which he addresses in the *Syntaxis* primarily as a theoretical problem. Yet Ptolemy elsewhere certainly provides abundant evidence that ancient Greek astronomy included a very wide range of activities and interests, by no means exclusively theoretical. Ptolemy's own significant interest in prediction was

[48] G. E. R. Lloyd, *The Revolutions of Wisdom: Studies in the Claims and Practice of Ancient Greek Science* (Berkeley, 1987), 45–6, 280–1; Barton (n. 37), 80, 90–4.

[49] Fraser (n. 17), i. 434–5, 439.

demonstrated in his *Phases*, the *Tetrabiblos*, and the *Handy Tables*. Evidence suggests that Hipparchus also regarded astronomy as a wide-ranging field which encompassed many interests and applications.[50]

4. Conclusion

In the end, we know very little about the bronze rings as physical objects—for example, we do not even know how they were mounted. Nevertheless, our accounts of their possible uses should reflect the range of astronomical interests and practice alive in Alexandria during the period of their existence. Furthermore, we should not rule out the possibility that the rings may have served several functions simultaneously. While they may have only been useful to determine the equinox twice a year, their display throughout the year in a public space would probably have been impressive and added an air of prestige. The public presence of other instruments associated with practical and predictive astronomy, including the sundial, the gnomon, and the *parapēgma*, reinforces the view that our understanding of the equinoctial rings should not be limited to their use and discussion by two heroic astronomers.

The role of astronomy in everyday life during the period was perhaps magnified by the growth of interest in predicting terrestrial events from astronomical phenomena. That mathematical astronomers were involved in this form of astronomy is not doubted. Indeed, astrology was clearly important enough to have justified Ptolemy's composition of a detailed technical account of astrology, the *Tetrabiblos*. Evidence indicates that practising astrologers relied on astronomical tables, such as Ptolemy's own *Handy Tables*. One wonders whether the instrument-makers referred to by him would have found a larger market for their products among the practitioners of the theoretical brand of astronomy or its, apparently, more popular and practical predictive form.

[50] Hipparchus' interests were apparently wide-ranging, encompassing theoretical and observational (e.g. star-catalogue) astronomy, geography, work on the analemma (dialling), as well as astrology. On Hipparchus' interest in astrology cf. Pliny, *HN* 2. 53, 95; A. Rehm, 'Hipparchos (18)', *RE* viii (1913), 1666–81 at 1680–1; D. R. Dicks, *The Geographical Fragments of Hipparchus* (London, 1960), 11 ff., 107, 157–8, 160. But the evidence is not all unequivocal. For example, Pliny, *HN* 2. 95, says that 'no one having done more to prove that man is related to the stars and that our souls are part of heaven, [Hipparchus] detected a new star', but it is not clear that a direct connection with astrology is implied; and not everyone believes that ibid. 2. 53 refers to astrological geography (cf. Bowen's paper in this volume, at § 3.2.4).

8

The Dioptra of Hero of Alexandria

J. J. COULTON

HERO OF ALEXANDRIA flourished in the late first century AD, and a considerable number of works on mechanics and applied mathematics are associated with his name.[1] The *Dioptra*, a relatively brief work describing a rather elaborate sighting-device of that name, illustrates his interest in the meeting of mathematics and the practical world, and apart from a closely derivative late Byzantine text,[2] it stands as the only surviving Greek treatise on land-surveying, in contrast to the substantial body of Latin texts known as the *Corpus Agrimensorum*.[3]

Hero's dioptra is presented in the scholarly literature on ancient surveying as both the most sophisticated instrument of its kind, equivalent to a modern theodolite,[4] and as a clumsy and impractical device, of little use to practising surveyors.[5] Although there have been many brief discussions since H. Schöne's careful reconstructions, first published in 1899,[6] only

[1] For a brief account of his life and works see *OCD* s.v. 'Heron of Alexandria'. Hero's dioptra is now discussed at length by M. J. T. Lewis, *Surveying Instruments of Greece and Rome* (Cambridge, 2001), *passim*, esp. 53–6, 82–9. We reach many of the same conclusions, but to take this important work properly into account would require a major rewriting of the present paper, which is impracticable at such a late stage. I have therefore left the paper unchanged, apart from the addition of references here and in nn. 2 and 8.

[2] Often, without justification, known as 'Hero of Byzantium', but better called Anonymus Byzantinus (Lewis (n. 1), 56–8). See A. J. H. Vincent, 'Extraits des manuscrits relatifs à la géometrie pratique des Grecs', *Notices et extraits de manuscrits de la Bibliothèque impériale et autres bibliothèques*. 19/2 (1862), 348–407, translated by Lewis (n. 1), 289–98; I owe my knowledge of this text to Cyril Mango.

[3] Full edition: F. Blume, K. Lachmann, and A. Rudorff, *Die Schriften der römischen Feldmesser* (Berlin, 1848–52). Partial edition: C. Thulin, *Corpus Agrimensorum Romanorum*, i/1 (Leipzig, 1913). Discussion: O. A. W. Dilke, *The Roman Land Surveyors: An Introduction to the Agrimensores* (Newton Abbot, 1971). See now also J. B. Campbell, *The Writings of the Roman Land-Surveyors* (London, 2000).

[4] e.g. F. T. Hinrichs, *Die Geschichte der gromatischen Institutionen* (Wiesbaden, 1974), 108: 'ein den modernen Theodoliten verwandtes äußerst fortschrittliches Visierinstrument'; J.-P. Adam, *La Construction romaine: Matériaux et techniques* (Paris, 1984), 9: 'véritable théodolite démuni d'optique'; Dilke (n. 3), 40: 'an instrument like a theodolite, capable of measuring vertical angles as well as horizontal'.

[5] Dilke (n. 3), 79: 'presumably regarded as too elaborate, expensive, and unwieldy for regular use'; D. Hill, *A History of Engineering in Classical and Medieval Times* (London, 1984), 120: 'very ingenious but probably not very robust . . . would soon have gone out of adjustment if subjected to the wear and tear of a construction site'.

[6] H. Schöne, 'Die Dioptra des Heron', *JDAI* 14 (1899), 91–103. The reconstruction drawings are repeated without change in his edition of Hero's *Dioptra* (n. 8), and have been often reproduced.

those of A. G. Drachmann have added anything of significance.[7] The aim of the present paper is to look more closely at the form and capabilities of the dioptra, at the methods of surveying proposed by Hero, and at the reasons for the limitations in its design and use.[8]

1. Design

Schöne maintained that there is a lacuna of four manuscript pages in the middle of Hero's description of the dioptra, and that two instruments are involved, a general sighting-instrument and a level.[9] I distinguish these two as the tilting dioptra and the levelling dioptra, but Hero probably regarded them as parts of a single instrument, since they could both be fitted to the same stand.[10] It is worth noting that the four missing pages would hold more text than the surviving description of stand, level, and levelling-staff put together, so that in addition to the obviously missing parts, there is scope for additional features not mentioned later in the surviving text.[11]

The levelling-instrument is unproblematic. It consists of a four-cubit beam holding a long bronze tube whose upturned ends are continued in glass. In front of the glass tubes, sliding plates controlled by screwed rods carry sighting-slits which can be set exactly at the level of water contained in the U-shaped tube, so as to create a well-defined horizontal line of sight.

[7] 'Dioptra', *RE* suppl. vi (1935), 1287–90; id., 'Heron and Ptolemaios', *Centaurus*, 1 (1950–1), 117–31; id., 'Heron's Dioptra and Levelling Instrument', in C. Singer (ed.), *A History of Technology*, iii (Oxford, 1957), 609–12; id., *The Mechanical Technology of Greek and Roman Antiquity: A Study of the Literary Sources* (Copenhagen, 1963), 197–8; id., 'A Physical Experiment in Hero's Dioptra', *Centaurus*, 13 (1968–9), 220–4; id., 'A Detail of Heron's Dioptra', ibid. 241–7.

[8] The text used throughout this paper is that of H. Schöne, *Herons von Alexandria Vermessungslehre und Dioptra* (*Heronis Alexandrini Opera Quae Supersunt Omnia*, 3: Leipzig, 1903), with Greek text and German translation. A full English translation is given in Lewis (n. 1), 256–86; chapters 3–5, 8, 14, 15, and 34 are also translated in M. R. Cohen and I. E. Drabkin, *A Source Book in Greek Science* (Cambridge, Mass., 1966), 336–45.

[9] Schöne (n. 6), 96–7, and (n. 8), xiii–xvii. This had earlier been doubted by Vincent (n. 2), 182–5, followed by F. Hultsch, 'Dioptra', *RE* v (1905), 1073–9, but it has been generally accepted since then.

[10] Dilke (n. 3), 76, regards the general sighting instrument as the 'dioptra proper', but Hero regards both as equally deserving of the name, and Vitr. 8. 5. 1 takes the dioptra as a levelling instrument, although inferior to the chorobates. The term is in fact very general, and Polyb. 10. 45. 6–47. 11 applies it to a pair of parallel sighting-tubes which allowed the observer to distinguish signal torches on the left from those on the right.

[11] For example, fo. 64ʳ of the Paris manuscript shows a plummet and peg fitted to the upper part of the levelling dioptra to ensure that the stand is vertical. Part of the lacuna may also have been occupied by a demonstration that the water in the two legs of a U-shaped tube finds the same level, for as A. G. Drachmann pointed out (*Centaurus*, 13 (1968–9), 220–4), a drawing on fo. 63ᵛ of the Paris manuscript does not relate to the adjoining text, but appears to illustrate such a discussion. The lacuna must also have contained an explanation of the need for horizontal measurement (πρὸς διαβήτην), which is referred to in ch. 8, but lacking from the surviving text.

The level is used with a levelling-staff carrying a circular target which can be slid up and down the staff until the observer signals that the line of sight is exactly bisecting it, when a pointer attached to the disc allows the staff man to read off the level on a graduated scale on the side of the staff.[12] The method of carrying out the levelling to a distant point is virtually the same as is used nowadays, with backsights and foresights booked in separate columns, so that the difference between the sum of the backsights and the sum of the foresights gives the difference in level between the start point and the end point.[13]

A four-cubit sighting-beam may seem clumsy for a level, but the choro-bates, preferred by Vitruvius, has a sighting-beam 20 feet long, and in the absence of a modern telescope, distance between the sights is the only way of defining a precise line of sight.[14] Hero's dioptra was more portable than the chorobates, and, although shorter, its line of sight may well have been more precisely defined and more accurately adjustable to the horizontal. In addition, it could be more conveniently rotated to level points on a line running round a hillside.

Our knowledge of the tilting dioptra is less complete, since the description of its upper part is lost in the lacuna. But much can be reconstructed on the basis of indications later in the text. This upper part could certainly be ro-tated horizontally and tilted in a vertical plane, both movements controlled by a worm-and-gear mechanism. Chapters 17–18 show that there was a disc which could be set in a vertical or a horizontal plane, or at any intervening angle, so that it must have been mounted above the tilting action. Chapter 32 shows that the sighting-arm was mounted on this disc, and since it could be used equally well from either end, the sights must have been identi-cal.[15] For astronomical purposes only, the disc carried a circle calibrated in degrees, with the angular readings indicated by pointers attached to the sighting-arm.[16] Although the calibration was added only for astronomical

[12] It is of a type still in use fifty years ago: see D. Clark, *Plane and Geodetic Surveying for Engineers*, i, 5th edn., rev. J. Clendinning (London, 1958), 122; I take this book, reprinted as late as 1966, to illustrate conventional modern surveying before the advent of electronic instruments.

[13] *Dioptra* 6: cf. Clark (n. 12), 303–11. Dilke (n. 3), 79, says that the difference between each backsight and foresight was recorded.

[14] Vitr. 8. 5. The traditional A-shaped level (διαβήτης), if it is to be used as an accurate sighting-device, must also be over 10 feet long: cf. T. F. Gluck, 'Levels and Levellers: Surveying Irrigation Canals in Medieval Valencia', *Technology and Culture*, 9 (1968), 165–80, esp 169–72 and fig. 1.

[15] The illustration on fo. 64[r] in the Paris manuscript shows cross-shaped sights on the levelling dioptra, which goes against the text. Drachmann, 'Heron's Dioptra and Levelling Instrument' (n. 7), 610, fig. 360, took this to indicate crossed slits for the tilting dioptra, whereas Schöne (n. 6) shows crossed wires (as in Fig. 8.1 here). Anonymus Byzantinus (n. 2), ch. 3 etc., refers to the sights simply as holes. The dioptra is to be used equally from either end, for which no form of sight is ideal, and it is not clear how far Hero's specification would have been based on practical use.

[16] Dilke (n. 3) 78, describes the upper circle as divided into quarters and subdivisions of

use, the text implies that the pointers were already part of the instrument. Since only right angles are required in the surveying applications, the pointers presumably pointed at engraved lines which divided the upper disc into four right angles. Schöne's reconstruction meets all these requirements, but there are three points which deserve further consideration.

First of all, the sighting-arm. Although Schöne does not provide a scale for his reconstruction, it must be drawn at a scale of about 1 : 100 if the sighting-arm is to be at a convenient height,[17] and this makes his sighting-arm about 0.70 m. long. As we have seen, the sighting-arm of the levelling dioptra was four cubits (about 1.80 m.) long, and so too was that of the dioptra of Hipparchus and others, and of the triquetra or Ptolemy's rulers.[18] If a sighting-arm of this length was practicable and desirable to give precision for these purposes, then one of similar size is to be expected for the tilting dioptra. At any rate, Schöne's sighting-arm is probably too slight, for in ch. 32 Hero suggests that when using the dioptra to measure the angle between two stars, the sighting-arm should be removed while the disc is tilted into the plane passing through the observer's position and the two stars concerned. Presumably that was because it would block the observer's view across the disc; a long wooden sighting-arm, necessarily quite thick, would be such an obstacle (Figure 8.1), whereas the thin bronze one shown by Schöne would not. This change would put the dioptra back in the Hellenistic tradition of large sighting-arms, in contrast to the short ones of early modern, but pre-telescopic, surveying instruments.[19]

Second, the stand. Hero calls it a *pageus*, and Drachmann[20] takes this, together with the representation of the dioptra stand by a single line in the manuscript illustrations, as evidence that the stand consisted of an iron-shod pole which could be driven into the ground, like that of the groma.[21] But the

these. Adam (n. 4), fig. 1, illustrates a sighting-device with a circle marked out in degrees, but the instrument, which he calls a dioptra, bears no relation to Hero's text.

[17] A scale of 1 : 100 sets the sighting-beam at c.1.25 m., while a scale of 1 : 125 would set it at c.1.55 m.

[18] For the dioptra of Hipparchus see Ptol. *Synt.* 5. 14, pp. 417. 1–422. 2 Heiberg, esp. 417. 1–418. 7, with Papp. *In Synt.* pp. 90–3 Rome, and Procl. *Hypotyp.* 4. 87–96, pp. 126. 13–130. 8 Manitius. For the triquetrum see Ptol. *Synt.* 5. 12, pp. 403. 1–408. 9 Heiberg; Drachmann, 'Heron and Ptolemaios' (n. 7), 128–30; D. J. de Solla Price, 'Precision Instruments to 1500', in C. Singer (n. 7), 582–619 at 589–90.

[19] J. A. Bennett, *The Divided Circle: A History of Instruments for Astronomy, Navigation and Surveying* (Oxford, 1987).

[20] Drachmann, 'A Detail of Heron's Dioptra' (n. 7). (Drachmann is surely right that the three small elements at the bottom of the dioptra in the Paris manuscript drawing (fo. 64ʳ) are not minuscule tripod legs as Vincent supposed, but the three pins at the bottom of the upper part of the dioptra.)

[21] The best-preserved remains of a groma are from the workshop of the surveyor Verus at Pompeii (M. Della Corte, 'Groma', *Mon. Ant.* 28 (1922), 5–100). The iron-shod staff is also well shown on the grave relief of Nicostratus from Pompeii (Adam (n. 4), 11, fig. 4). The instrument is discussed by Dilke (n. 3), 66–70.

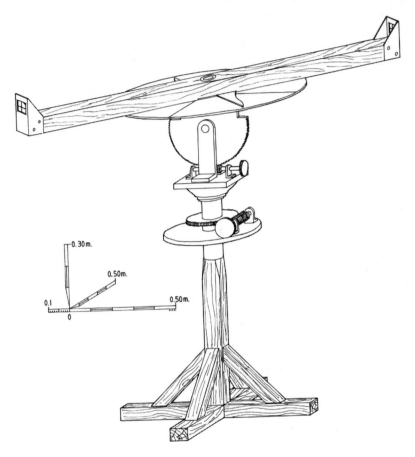

FIG. 8.1. Suggested reconstruction of Hero's dioptra

manuscript illustrations are simplified symbols, and it seems unlikely that
such a stand would be steady enough to justify the dioptra's elaborate worm-
and-gear adjustment. Hero goes on to say that the stand is made as a *styliskos*,
and the rotating upper part is to be like a Doric capital (ch. 2). Schöne
therefore gives it quite a sturdy column shape carried on a simple, low
tripod base. However, the word *styliskos* means an upright, not necessarily
a column of architectural form. Hero uses the same word for the upright
of a catapult stand, which consisted of a wooden post beneath which two
wooden crosspieces met, with sloping struts to brace the upright post,[22]

---

[22] Hero, *Bel.* 88; E. W. Marsden, *Greek and Roman Artillery: Technical Treatises* (Oxford,
1971), 31.

and something like this would form an admirably stable base for a dioptra (Figure 8.1). None of these reconstructions, it should be noted, allows the dioptra to be set up precisely over a peg marking a given point. This is an essential requirement for accurately setting out lines at right angles from a given point, as the dioptra is required to do in several applications. The design of the groma, with the junction of the crossed arms offset to one side of the staff, does allow this, and the Latin surveying texts refer to the need to plumb the centre of the cross over a point.[23] Since Hero never mentions this need, the fault may lie in his conception of the instrument, rather than in the reconstructions of Schöne and others, and it would seriously affect the dioptra's practicality as a surveying instrument.

The third design problem relates to the disc upon which the sighting-arm rotates. It is perhaps worth repeating that for land-surveying this disc was not calibrated in degrees, as many scholars have supposed,[24] but only in quadrants; and there was no facility for measuring vertical angles. It has also not been generally noticed that this disc comes *above* the tilting mechanism, so that the axis about which the sighting-arm pivots is not always vertical. When the disc is tilted, angles laid out on the basis of this sloping plane will usually not correspond to the intended angles on a horizontal plain. In addition, unless the line of sight lies in the same plane as the vertical semicircle, it will not remain in one vertical plane as the sighting-arm is tilted up or down.

Hero is well aware that tilting will affect angular measurements, for in ch. 33 he uses this fact to attack the accuracy of the groma (or *asteriskos*). To explain the problem in more intuitive terms than Hero uses: the arms of the groma form the diagonals of a square, with the plummets hanging from its four corners. If that square is tilted on one edge, the horizontal distance between the upper and lower edges decreases, while the horizontal distance between the other two edges does not. Since the plumb lines hang vertically, they will pass through the corners of a rectangle in the horizontal plane, and the diagonals of a rectangle do not cross each other at right angles. The groma, Hero concludes, is therefore not a reliable way of setting out right angles, its chief function.[25]

---

[23] Although the Pompeii groma had no attachment for a central plummet (Della Corte (n. 21)), Nipsus (*Fl. var.* 17; *Lim. rep.* 15–16) shows that the centre of the cross was plumbed over a fixed point.

[24] e.g. K. Grewe, *Planung und Trassierung römischer Wasserleitungen* (Wiesbaden, 1985), 23; E. Rodriguez Almeida, *Forma urbis marmorea: Aggiornamento generale* (Rome, 1981), 47. I owe this latter reference to Margareta Steinby.

[25] Hero assumes without discussion that the right angles are defined by the diagonals of the square defined by the four plummets, whereas H. Schöne, 'Das Visierinstrument der römischen Feldmesser', *JDAI* 16 (1901), 127–32, proposed that adjacent sides of that square were used. This was hotly disputed by Della Corte (n. 21), 78–82, who interpreted the ironwork discussed by Schöne as the remains of a *modius*. For later views see J. Bouma (ed.), *Marcus Iunius Nypsus: Fluminis Variatio; Limitis Repositio* (Studien zur klassischen Philologie, 77; Frankfurt am Main, 1993), 97–8.

Schöne's reconstruction of the dioptra is open to exactly the same attack, for he shows the perpendicular lines engraved on the disc (which guide the setting out of lines at right angles to each other) placed diagonally with respect to the vertical semicircle. As the disc is tilted to sight on an elevated or depressed point, the square formed by the ends of these lines will be tilted on one edge, just like the square formed by the arms of the groma in Hero's critique. So when projected onto a horizontal plane, this square will become a rectangle, and its diagonals, corresponding to the engraved lines, will no longer be at right angles. Errors less than 1° in levelling have a negligible effect,[26] but a tilt of 10° will produce an error of 1° in the presumed right angle. Ironically enough, this is more likely to occur in the normal use of the dioptra than by accident in setting up the groma.

The whole problem would be removed if the tilting mechanism of the dioptra was mounted on top of the disc instead of below, which would produce an arrangement geometrically similar to a traditional modern theodolite. Unfortunately, Hero's text does not allow this design, but as Drachmann noticed, it does allow one small improvement: one of the engraved lines should be drawn exactly above the toothed semicircle, and the other perpendicular to it (Figure 8.1).[27] With the sighting-arm aligned on the first of these two lines, the line of sight will remain in the same vertical plane as the sighting-arm is elevated or depressed, as the procedures in chs. 8–9 require. Furthermore, the two lines remain at right angles to each other as the disc is tilted. The drawback is that the sighting-arm cannot be elevated or depressed when it is aligned on the second of the two lines, but this effect might have been mitigated by the fact that in many applications the second position is used for setting out lines in the nearground, where sighting on a plumb line could be used in place of tilting. It is uncertain whether Hero appreciated this point, however, and the fact remains that for land-surveying it is a disadvantage to have the disc above the tilting mechanism, whereas for astronomical work it is an advantage, allowing direct measurement of the angle between any two stars, no matter what their position in the sky. This suggests that Hero was perhaps adapting for terrestrial use an instrument originally designed for astronomy[28]—a context in which setting up over a precise point (above, p. 155) is also unnecessary.

---

[26] If the implied square is tilted at an angle of 1°, the error in the right angle is only about 0.5′.

[27] Drachmann stated the need for this three times ('Dioptra', 1288; 'Heron's Dioptra and Levelling Instrument', 610; *Mechanical Technology of Greek and Roman Antiquity*, 198: all cited in n. 7), but never gave the reason.

[28] Cf. Hinrichs (n. 4), 108.

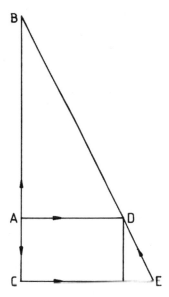

Fig. 8.2. Hero's method of finding the distance to an inaccessible point

2. Applications

The applications described by Hero involve two main methods of surveying. First there is the use of similar triangles. A characteristic example is Hero's method of finding the horizontal distance to an inaccessible point (ch. 8), a procedure which is fundamental to several other applications. The dioptra is set up on a marked point A, and sighted accurately on the distant point B (Figure 8.2). The observer then goes to the other end of the instrument and continues the same line onward to a convenient point C nearby. He then rotates the sighting-arm through a right angle to lay out a line AD. Moving the dioptra to point C, he lays out another line CE, also at right angles to the initial line BAC. With the dioptra at E, he sights once more on the distant point B, tilts the dioptra down, and marks where the line of sight EB crosses the line AD at D. The horizontal distances AD, AC, and CE are carefully measured, and since the triangles BAD and BCE are similar, BA/AD = BC/CE = AC/(CE−AD); the desired distance BA is therefore (AD × AC)/(CE−AD).[29]

Another procedure which is common to several applications involves the repeated setting out of right angles. For instance, to establish the alignment of a tunnel to be cut from both ends (ch. 15), the surveyor starts at one end

[29] The accuracy of this method depends on the scale and accuracy of the nearground work, and on the size of the angle ABD.

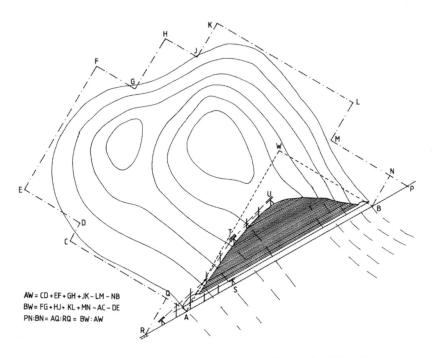

AW = CD + EF + GH + JK − LM − NB
BW = FG + HJ + KL + MN − AC − DE
PN:BN = AQ:RQ = BW:AW

FIG. 8.3. Hero's method of (*a*) finding the required line for a
tunnel and (*b*) laying out a line above an existing straight tunnel

point A of the tunnel, and sets out a convenient line along the side of the
mountain (AC on Figure 8.3). When the mountain begins to turn away from
the line, he marks the point (C), sets up the dioptra, and lays out a second line
CD at right angles to AC. When the mountain begins to rise inconveniently,
he again marks the point (D), and lays out another right angle, so returning
to the original direction. Eventually it is possible to traverse round the
mountain in a series of legs at right angles to each other, until the other end
point of the intended tunnel B is visible; the dioptra is then moved along the
current line (MN) until B appears at right angles to MN. The horizontal
length of each leg of this traverse is measured, and the legs parallel to the
original line and the legs perpendicular to the original line are separately
added up. These two sums can be considered as two sides AW (=CD+
EF+GH+JK−LM−NB) and BW (=FG+HJ+KL+MN−AC−DE) of a
large right-angled triangle AWB, whose hypotenuse AB is formed by the
required line of the tunnel. So using the first and last lines of the traverse
as baselines, triangles QAR and NPB similar to the large one are set out at
A and B, so that each hypotenuse AR and BP extends AB, and if suitably
marked, will guide the tunnellers at each end.

Setting out a traverse like this in mountainous country may well prove difficult in practice, and will need considerable care in measuring each leg horizontally and setting out the right angles precisely. To some extent the inevitable errors will tend to cancel each other out, so that the location of B may not be far out. But the orientation of the final leg MNP, on which the alignment of the tunnel depends, is critical, and being the result of a number of imperfect angle measurements, it is unlikely to be correct. In practice it would be sensible to set out the calculated line straight across the top of the mountain from A to B as a check.[30] The procedure would be the same as that explained by Hero in ch. 16 for locating an access shaft above a pre-existing tunnel (RATU on Figure 8.3), but he nowhere suggests such a line from end to end as a precaution. Whereas modern surveying handbooks deal at length with the problem of inaccuracy, and the need for redundant check measurements and procedures to test for or cancel out errors, they are characteristically ignored in *Dioptra*: what is true in theory is taken to be accurate in practice.[31]

Other problems involve combining right angles and similar triangles with levelling (chs. 12–14), or using the dioptra to extend a straight line (chs. 16 and 27), while chs. 23–4 use the dioptra to measure the area of an irregular piece of land by laying out and measuring offsets at right angles from the sides of a large rectangle inscribed within it (ch. 23), or from a single baseline running through it. These are the same as the methods of land measurement used by the Roman *agrimensores*,[32] and apart from the levelling, most of what Hero describes could be done with a groma. The plummets of a groma were not strictly necessary for accurate sighting of right angles and straight lines in a horizontal plane, but (at least on a calm day) they allowed sights to be taken at a fairly steep upward or downward angle, so taking the place of the tilting mechanism of the sighting dioptra. The chief advantages of the dioptra were that it was little affected by wind, and that it could define and hold (but not measure) a vertical angle, an ability which allowed the surveyor

---

[30] This more direct method was used by Nonius Datus at Saldae (North Africa) in the 2nd cent. AD (*CIL* viii. 2728, 18122; J. G. Landels, *Engineering in the Ancient World* (London, 1978), 52–3). The difference of level between the two end points must also be found in order to calculate the gradient of the tunnel.

[31] By contrast Archim. *Aren.* 11 notes the impossibility of accurate readings because of the imperfection of sight, hand, and instrument, and (ibid. 13–15) describes a way of allowing for the fact that the eye is not a point. Hyginus Gromaticus (Thulin (n. 3), 154. 14–20) notes the special care needed to avoid both instrumental and sighting errors at the origin of a cadastral grid. Ptolemy also comments on instrumental inaccuracy (see Taub's paper in this volume).

[32] Compare *Dioptra* 23–4 with Frontinus (Thulin (n. 3), 15. 6–18. 11), or *Dioptra* 8, 10 with Hyginus Gromaticus (Thulin (n. 3), 192. 17–193. 15). The texts are discussed by Hinrichs (n. 4), 100–4. On their similar mathematics see M. Folkerts, 'Mathematische Probleme im Corpus agrimensorum', in *Die römische Feldmeßkunst: Interdisziplinäre Beiträge zu ihrer Bedeutung für die Zivilisationsgeschichte Roms* (Abh. Akad. Gött., phil.-hist. Kl. 193; Göttingen, 1992), 327–8.

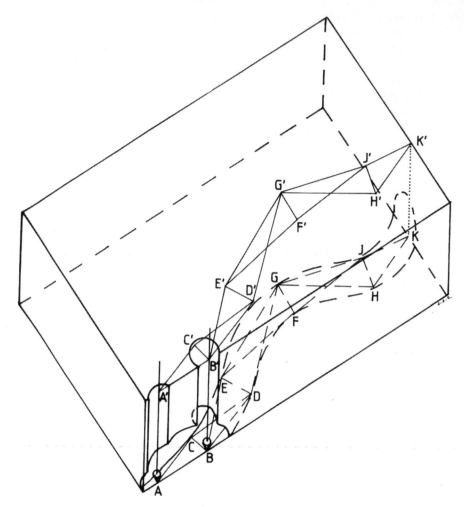

FIG. 8.4. Hero's method for finding the surface
point above a given point in a winding tunnel

to measure the height of an enemy's walls and towers from a safe distance.[33]
The dioptra probably also had a longer interval between sights,[34] but it was
mechanically more complicated, and probably heavier, than the groma, and
it is doubtful whether it could achieve better results in horizontal survey.

[33] Both Hero (*Dioptra* 2) and Anonymus Byzantinus (n. 2) 1 emphasize this ability in
justifying an interest in the dioptra. Compare Hero's justification of his study of artillery,
discussed in Cuomo's paper in this volume.

[34] If the sighting-arm of the tilting dioptra was 4 cubits long, as suggested above (p. 153),
its sights would be twice as far apart as the plumb lines of the Pompeii groma (above, n. 21),
which were 0.90 m. apart.

Two other procedures described by Hero deserve comment. Chapter 16 shows how to find a point on the surface vertically above any desired point in a straight tunnel; ch. 20 shows how to find the equivalent point above a winding tunnel, and without having to start at one end (Figure 8.4). First two plumb lines (A'A and B'B) are set up in neighbouring manholes, and starting from a baseline AB connecting their lower ends, a rigid framework of triangles is set out within the tunnel, and continued until the desired point is reached (ABC . . . HJK). Starting from the upper ends of the plumb lines A'B', and taking care to measure horizontally, an identical series of triangles is laid out on the surface (A'B'C' . . . H'J'K'); the end point K' will be directly above the desired point K in the tunnel. The dioptra plays no part in this method of survey, but it is remarkable for being the only surviving evidence for the use in antiquity of the fundamental principle of modern chain surveying: a rigid framework of carefully measured triangles.[35] This is less subject to angular error than the framework of rectangles used by Hero and the *agrimensores*, and since Hero knew the formula for calculating the area of irregular triangles, it is surprising that he does not recommend this superior system instead. Presumably the more complicated calculations needed, and the widespread use of rectangular land divisions, explain why practical surveyors stuck to the less rigorous but simpler system, but a mathematician might have seen the theoretical advantages in triangles.

The other noteworthy procedure is the use of the tilting disc of the dioptra to establish a horizontal curve at a distance, e.g. a curving harbour mole (ch. 17). In mathematical terms it is true that the curve of the disc, seen from a fixed eyepoint nearby, is similar to a much larger curve at a distance, but the procedure looks distinctly dubious in practice. Although the diameter of the tilting disc is unknown, it is unlikely to have been more than 1.00 m. A 50-m.-long mole whose plan is quarter of the circumference of a circle would have a radius of about 32 m.[36] To set it out from the dioptra disc would therefore involve scaling up the curve by a factor of about 64, so that the horizontal distance from the harbour to the instrument would have to be at least 64 times the diameter of the disc (the minimum distance from the eyepoint to the further edge of the disc), i.e. 64 m.[37] Furthermore, the

---

[35] See e.g. Clark (n. 12), 177–95.

[36] Ancient harbours rarely have a regular geometrical plan. One of the few that does, the hexagonal basin built by Trajan at Portus, had a diameter of 716 m. (R. Meiggs, *Roman Ostia*, 2nd edn. (Oxford, 1973), 162–4), so that the scaling factor would be many times that of the example used here.

[37] Drachmann, 'Heron and Ptolemaios' (n. 7), 126–7, proposes a sighting-arm (and so presumably a disc diameter) of no more than 0.30 m. Such a small disc could certainly be marked out in degrees, but it would much reduce the accuracy of a curve set out in the way proposed here, requiring the curve to be scaled up by a factor of more than 200; the horizontal distance of the dioptra would be unchanged, since for a quadrant of given length L the minimum horizontal distance D is unaffected by the diameter d of the disc: $D = d \times L/(\pi \times d/4) = 4L/\pi$.

viewing-angle across the edge of the disc should not be much less than 30°
if the curvature is to be properly seen. This means that the height of the
eyepoint above the harbour must be about half the horizontal distance, or
32 m. The number of harbour sites with a convenient viewing-point 32 m.
above sea level must be distinctly limited. It would therefore be very rare
for a surveyor to be able to use this method, and a piece of cord attached to a
peg would almost always be a simpler and more effective way of setting out
a circular arc. This is not the only feature to suggest that Hero was more
interested in the theory than in the practicalities of surveying.

3. Conclusion

It may be of interest to end by enquiring why, given the sophisticated system
of rotation and tilting and the calibration of the tilting disc for astronomical
use, the dioptra was not used to measure angles like a theodolite. The
Antikythera calendrical device includes not only complex gearing, but also
a circle about 0.14 m. in diameter divided with reasonable accuracy into 360
degrees,[38] so even though Hero mentions no finer divisions, a larger disc
could have been calibrated in parts of a degree.[39] But what would a surveyor
have done with angular measurements? The simplest way of using them
would be to plot the measured angles and distances onto a suitable surface at
as large a scale as possible, and then scale off the unknown distances or areas
required. But apart from the errors introduced by imprecise calibration and
angle readings, this would introduce additional errors in scaling up from
a relatively small drawing. Hero's method of (in effect) instant plotting on
the ground near the instrument not only avoids the need to read and then
reproduce angular measurements, but it also reduces the scaling errors by
allowing the diagrams to be set out at a much larger scale than is possible
on a drawing board. The practical limitations of this method are obvious,
however: it requires a fairly extensive and reasonably flat area around the
instrument where the working diagrams can be set out, so the dioptra could
not be used for angular observations from a tower or mountain top.

In nineteenth- and twentieth-century surveying, of course, angular measurements are used in conjunction with trigonometrical formulae to calculate distances and locations with far greater precision than scaling off a
drawing board would allow, but this procedure depends on mathematical
and technological advances made long after the time of Hero. Although the-

[38] D. J. de Solla Price, *Gears from the Greeks: The Antikythera Mechanism, a Calendar Computer from ca. 80 BC* (TAPhS, NS 64/7; Philadelphia, 1974, and New York, 1975), 16–20. The maximum cumulative error in calibration is 20 minutes of arc; most individual divisions are within 8% of the mean value.

[39] Anonymus Byzantinus (n. 2), 11, proposes calibrating the tilting disc of his dioptra in degrees and intermediate parts; he records observations in half degrees and thirds of a degree.

orems equivalent to trigonometric ones were developed by mathematicians such as Hipparchus and Menelaus of Alexandria, and a table of chords of angles from 0° to 180° in half-degree steps was calculated by Ptolemy, Greek and Roman mathematicians applied these discoveries almost exclusively to spherical geometry and to problems in astronomy.[40] No doubt Ptolemy could have solved the problems involved in trigonometric land-surveying, but there was no established methodology. A full set of equations for solving plane triangles needed the advances of medieval Islamic mathematicians and their European successors in the fifteenth and sixteenth centuries.[41] The calculation of trigonometrical tables at close intervals at the end of that period, and the development of logarithms in the seventeenth century, allowed surveyors to make practical use of these advances, but their full exploitation required the application of the telescope to survey instruments to allow finer resolution of angles, the invention of the vernier scale and micrometer screw for more accurate readings, and the invention of the dividing-machine for more precisely calibrated circles.[42] Only in the second half of the eighteenth century did these developments come together and allow angle measurement to take over from linear measurement as the basis for the most accurate survey work.

The dioptra is not a figment of Hero's imagination: a sighting-instrument had much earlier been used to establish the height of distant mountains,[43] and Vitruvius knew a levelling-instrument of this name. Possibly a form of dioptra contributed in some way to the production of that masterpiece of ancient surveying, the Severan marble plan of Rome,[44] although nobody has yet shown how.[45] But for the Heronian account three main conclusions emerge. First, Hero's dioptra was not equivalent to a pre-electronic theodolite, and the preconditions for such an instrument did not exist in his time.

[40] T. Heath, *A History of Greek Mathematics* (Oxford, 1921), 253–9, 265–73, 276–83. J Peterson, 'Trigonometry in Roman Cadasters', in J.-Y. Guillaumin (ed.), *Mathématiques dans l'antiquité* (Saint-Étienne, 1992), 185–204, argues that features oblique to a rectangular grid were set out at angles defined by simple integral ratios of distances measured 'across' and 'up' the grid, i.e. angles with a tan(gent) that is a simple integral ratio. This (very plausible) method would require no trigonometrical knowledge (in the modern sense), but corresponds to Hero's preferred method of defining angles by the ratio of two perpendicular measurements, rather than by a number of degrees.
[41] So also Hinrichs (n. 4), 108. For a brief account see the articles 'Trigonometry' in *Encyclopedia Britannica*, 15th edn. (1991), *Macropedia*, xxviii. 884–5, and *Encyclopedia Americana* (1971), xxvii. 109–10.
[42] Bennett (n. 19); A. W. Richeson, *English Land Measuring to 1800: Instruments and Practices* (Cambridge, Mass, 1966). I owe these references to Dr A. S. Bendall.
[43] By Dicaearchus and Eratosthenes in the 4th and 3rd cents. BC: Theon Smyrn. pp. 124. 19–125. 3 Hiller.
[44] G. Carettoni *et al.*, *La pianta marmorea di Roma antica* (Rome 1960); Almeida (n. 24).
[45] Almeida (n. 24), 47, supposes that the dioptra was used to establish a network of primary points to which the detailed surveying was attached. But he supposes wrongly that the dioptra could measure angles, and there is no evidence that Roman surveyors worked from such a primary network, as a modern surveyor would.

Second, the tilting dioptra described by Hero was in some respects more suited to astronomy than to land-surveying, and Hero probably modified an astronomical instrument for this new purpose, following the mainly right-angled methods used with the groma. Third, Hero did not himself have experience of surveying, and so explains it in terms of procedures which are mathematically correct, without any concern for difficulties or inaccuracies in practice. Presumably he was writing for people who shared his interest in mechanical intricacy and the possibilities of applying mathematical principles, but who were not expecting to take up surveying.

9

The Machine and the City:
Hero of Alexandria's *Belopoeica*

S. CUOMO

τῆς ἐν φιλοσοφίᾳ διατριβῆς τὸ μέγιστον καὶ ἀναγκαιότατον μέρος ὑπάρχει τὸ περὶ ἀταραξίας, περὶ ἧς πλεῖσταί τε ὑπῆρξαν ζητήσεις παρὰ τοῖς μεταχειριζομένοις τὴν σοφίαν
καὶ μέχρι νῦν ὑπάρχουσι· καὶ νομίζω μηδὲ τέλος ποτὲ ἕξειν διὰ τῶν λόγων τὴν περὶ
αὐτῆς ζήτησιν. μηχανικὴ δὲ ὑπερβᾶσα τὴν διὰ τῶν λόγων περὶ ταύτης διδασκαλίαν ἐδίδαξε
πάντας ἀνθρώπους ἀταράχως ζῆν ἐπίστασθαι δι' ἑνὸς καὶ ἐλαχίστου μέρους αὐτῆς, λέγω δὴ
τοῦ κατὰ τὴν καλουμένην βελοποιίαν, δι' ἧς οὔτε ἐν εἰρηνικῇ καταστάσει οὔτε ἐνστάντος
πολέμου ταραχθήσονταί ποτε τῇ παραδιδομένῃ ὑπ' αὐτῆς διὰ τῶν ὀργάνων φιλοσοφίᾳ. διὸ
τοῦ μέρους τούτου ἐν παντὶ χρόνῳ καταστῆναι δεῖ καὶ πᾶσαν πρόνοιαν ποεῖσθαι. εἰρήνης
γὰρ πολλῆς ὑπαρχούσης, προσδοκήσαιτο ἄν τις πλείονα ταύτην γένεσθαι, ὅταν ἐν τῷ
περὶ τὴν βελοποιίαν μέρει καταγίνωνται· αὐτοί τε κατὰ συνείδησιν ἀτάραχοι διαμενοῦσι,
καὶ οἱ ἐπιθυμοῦντες ἐπιβουλεύειν, ὁρῶντες τὴν περὶ αὐτὰ γιγνομένην αὐτῶν διατριβήν,
οὐκ ἐπελεύσονται. ἀμελησάντων δέ, πᾶσα ἐπιβουλή, κἂν ἐλαχίστη τυγχάνῃ, ἐπικρατήσει,
ἀπαρασκεύων τῶν ἐν ταῖς πόλεσι περὶ ταῦτα ὑπαρχόντων. ἐπεὶ οὖν οἱ πρὸ ἡμῶν πλείστας
μὲν ἀναγραφὰς περὶ βελοποιικῶν ἐποιήσαντο, μέτρα καὶ διαθέσεις ἀναγραψάμενοι, οὐδὲ
εἷς δὲ αὐτῶν οὔτε τὰς κατασκευὰς τῶν ὀργάνων ἐκτίθεται κατὰ τρόπον οὔτε τὰς τούτων
χρήσεις, ἀλλ' ὥσπερ γινώσκουσι πᾶσι τὴν ἀναγραφὴν ἐποιήσαντο, καλῶς ἔχειν ὑπολαμ-
βάνομεν ἐξ αὐτῶν τε ἀναλαβεῖν καὶ ἐμφανίσαι περὶ τῶν ὀργάνων τῶν ἐν τῇ βελοποιίᾳ,
ὡς μηδὲ ἴσως ὑπαρχόντων, ὅπως πᾶσιν εὐπαρακολούθητος γένηται ἡ παράδοσις. (Hero,
Belopoeica, 71. 1–73. 11)[1]

The largest and most essential part of philosophical study is that which is concerned
with tranquillity [ἀταραξία], about which a great many researches have been made
and are still being made by those who pursue learning; indeed, I think research
on tranquillity will never come to an end through reasoning [λόγοι]. But mechanics
has surpassed teaching of this subject based on reasoning and taught the whole of
mankind how to live a tranquil life [ἀταράχως] by means of a single, very small,
branch of the discipline—I mean, of course, the one dealing with so-called artillery
construction. This ensures that men will never be troubled by the assaults of adversaries and enemies during a state of peace—and when war is upon them they
will never be troubled either, thanks to the philosophy which it provides through
its engines. It is therefore necessary at all times to be calm and to devote thorough
forethought [πρόνοια] to this branch of the discipline. When there has been peace
for a long time, one would expect more of the same to follow, if men have concerned

---

[1] I thank David Sedley for his help with the following translation, which is based on that in
E. W. Marsden, *Greek and Roman Artillery: Technical Treatises* (Oxford, 1971), 18–19. (This
work is cited by author's name only hereafter.) References to the Greek text are to the Teubner
edition of Schmidt, Nix, Schöne, and Heiberg (see n. 4 below).

themselves with this branch of mechanics: they will remain tranquil [ἀτάραχοι] in accordance with their awareness [συνείδησις],[2] while those who wish to plot, observing how they have become engaged in the study of the subject, will not attack. But if they neglect it, any plot, however small, will overwhelm them, since the occupants of the cities will be unprepared in this respect. My predecessors have produced numerous treatises on artillery construction which record measurements and arrangements, but not one of them sets forth the construction of the engines or their uses in due order. Instead they have produced their treatises as though they were writing exclusively for those who are already familiar with the subject. So I consider it a good idea to pick up where they left off, and to explain the engines used in artillery construction, almost as though they were not already in existence, so that everyone may find my report easy to follow.

THIS passage opens the *Belopoeica*, a treatise on the construction of war engines by Hero of Alexandria. We know very little about Hero, but he lived around the second half of the first century AD[3] (probably in Alexandria) and, from the variety of topics covered in his works, he seems to have been a mathematician and designer of machines.[4] Scholarly studies on Hero have been few and far between. They have also, most of them, concentrated on specific parts of his work (e.g. steam-operated machines) in isolation from

[2] This term could also be rendered as 'shared knowledge': cf. Epicur. *Ep. Hdt.* 76 (τινὰ δὲ καὶ οὐ συνορώμενα πράγματα εἰσφέροντας τοὺς συνειδότας παρεγγυῆσαί τινας φθόγγους, 'the men who shared knowledge introduced certain unseen entities, and brought words for them into usage': trans. L&S 19A); Soran. 1. 4 (καὶ οὐ πάντως προτετοκυῖαν . . . ἵνα συνειδήσει τῶν ἀλγημάτων ταῖς τικτούσαις συμπαθῇ, 'it is not absolutely necessary for [a midwife] to have borne children . . . in order that she may sympathize with the mother, because of her experience with pain': trans. O. Temkin, *Soranus'* Gynaecology (Baltimore and London, 1956), 6). On the other hand, its usage with the meaning 'consciousness' is attested in e.g. Chrysippus *SVF* iii. 178 = Diog. Laert. 7. 85; Phld. *Rhet.* 2. 139–40.

[3] His dating remained uncertain until Otto Neugebauer identified the lunar eclipse which Hero describes in *Dioptra* 35, p. 303. 17 ff., as one which occurred in AD 62: O. Neugebauer, 'Über eine Methode zur Distanzbestimmung Alexandria–Rom bei Heron', *Kongelige Danske Videnskabernes Selskabs Meddelelser*, 26 (1938), 21–4. See also A. G. Drachmann, *The Mechanical Technology of Greek and Roman Antiquity: A Study of the Literary Sources* (Copenhagen, 1963), 12, 19; P. Keyser, 'Suetonius *Nero* 41. 2 and the Date of Heron Mechanicus of Alexandria', *CP* 83 (1988), 218–20.

[4] Many of Hero's works are still extant, though sometimes only in Latin (*Catoptrica*) or Arabic (*Mechanica*). There are also some texts of dubious authenticity. (*Definitiones* is tentatively attributed to Diophantus in W. R. Knorr, 'Arithmêtikê stoicheîosis: On Diophantus and Hero of Alexandria', *Historia Mathematica*, 20 (1993), 180–92.) For texts of all of them see W. Schmidt, L. Nix, H. Schöne, and J. L. Heiberg (Leipzig, 1899–1914); but *Belopoeica* and *Cheiroballistra* are best consulted (with translation) in Marsden (whose volume represents not a re-edition of the text, but a critical collation of existing editions and manuscript information). There are English translations of *Mechanica* in Drachmann (n. 3), of *Automatopoetica* in S. Murphy, 'Heron of Alexandria's *On Automaton-Making*', *History of Technology*, 17 (1995), 1–44, and of parts of *Pneumatica* in B. Woodcroft and J. G. Greenwood, *The* Pneumatics *of Hero of Alexandria* (London 1851; repr. London and New York, 1971, with introduction by M. Boas Hall). Cf. also G. Argoud, J.-Y. Guillaumin, and A. Cachard (eds.), *Les Pneumatiques d'Héron d'Alexandrie* (Saint-Étienne, 1997). See most recently K. Tybjerg, *Doing Philosophy with Machines: Hero of Alexandria's Rhetoric of Mechanics in Relation to the Contemporary Philosophy* (diss. Ph.D. Cambridge, 2000), and ead., 'Wonder-Making and Philosophical Wonder in Hero of Alexandria', forthcoming in *Studies in History and Philosophy of Science*.

the role of Hero as an author, from the general structure of the individual treatise which contains, say, the descriptions of steam-operated machines, and from the larger picture of Hero's works taken as a whole.

In this paper I shall concentrate not so much on the war engines themselves, as on the way Hero talks about them and on the way the *Belopoeica* is structured. We are somewhat lucky that, as the passage above abundantly shows, Hero (unlike, say, Euclid) often had something to say about what he was doing and about the way his subject related to other disciplines or to the world at large.

The standard modern edition and English translation of *Belopoeica* was produced by E. W. Marsden, whose commentary on the text was further informed by his experience of reconstructing some of Hero's machines. I shall address some questions which were first raised by Marsden: why did Hero not report the latest developments in the art, but give instead a description of machines that by then were outdated (judging by earlier treatises on the same topic)? Why was Hero talking about threats of war 'in the first century AD when the Mediterranean was enjoying the benefits of the *Pax Romana*'? And why would an ordinary citizen have cared about the construction of war engines? What philosophy was Hero attacking? Is this a criticism of 'the normal Greek attitude towards the practical'?[5]

1. Why Did Hero Not Report the Latest Developments?

Marsden remarked that the most advanced engines described by Hero in his *Belopoeica* 'are slightly earlier, as far as one or two details are concerned, than the standard artillery described by Philon',[6] i.e. Philo of Byzantium, who wrote in the later third century BC. For instance, 'Philon is more precise than Heron in his instructions . . . Philon's method of forming the joint between frame and case . . . seems neater and firmer than Heron's. Whereas Heron describes the earliest *gastraphetes* and early torsion frames, Philon mentions no machinery earlier than the fairly advanced torsion variety'.[7] Hero does refer to 'writers before him' who composed treatises on the construction of war engines, but we do not know exactly who they may be, because we do not have a precise idea of how extensive the literature on artillery construction actually was.[8] Apart from writers on fortifications, who do not deal in detail with artillery engines,[9] before Hero we have two treatises in Greek from the third century BC (those of Philo, which was part of a more general *Mechanical Syntaxis*, and of Biton) and one in Latin from the first

---

[5] Marsden 2, 44 n. 2.   [6] Ibid. 1.   [7] Ibid. 8–9.

[8] Vitruvius quotes Diades, who describes a movable tower, a ram tortoise, and a borer (10. 13. 3–8) and mentions more briefly Hagetor of Byzantium's design for a tortoise (10. 15. 2). It is thought that Vitruvius knew of Diades through the writings of Agesistratus (Marsden 4).

[9] Y. Garlan, *Recherches de poliorcétique grecque* (Paris, 1974).

century BC (Vitr. 10. 10–16) . Another writer, Ctesibius, is mentioned in
the title of Hero's work, was known to Vitruvius,[10] and may have been a
source for Philo.[11] Philo in his turn is mentioned by Hero (*Aut*. 263. 1, 3)
and is arguably one of the sources for his *Pneumatica*.[12] Whether Hero knew
Vitruvius' work is an undecided question.[13]

Whatever Hero's actual dependence on other sources, which is rather
difficult to assess, he marks his difference from them. He claims to be
writing for everyone,[14] just as mechanics has taught all human beings (πάντας
ἀνθρώπους) how to live a tranquil life—the subject may be the same as that
of his predecessors, but its presentation is not. Hero's τρόπος, his 'style', is
geared to the writer's aim and audience. His discourse follows a historical
or developmental order, which starts with the basic need which originated
the discipline, and then describes the various ways human beings have
devised to meet that need.[15] Hero's story is structured as a succession of
difficulties, overcome by technological devices, until a new difficulty arises
and a new technological ruse has to be found. Already with the first machine,
an immediate derivation from the bow, the guiding principles of artillery
construction have become clear: greater power to produce stronger blows,
larger size to throw bigger projectiles or throw them further, and, to a lesser
extent, mobility and cost-effectiveness.[16]

The treatise begins with a definition of 'belopoetics': its object (ὅρος) is
to throw a missile (βέλος) over a distance towards a given target.[17] The first
tool that could perform what required was the bow. This, Hero says, is
the principle (ἀρχή) of these engines, the basic shape and the basic tool.
As human beings were forced (βιαζόμενοι) to project larger missiles at a
greater range, the size of the machines started to increase. Thus, starting
from hand-bows (χειρουργικῶν τόξων: note the stress on 'hand'—τόξον is a
perfectly good word for hand-bow by itself), the first problem was to bend
the arms of the bow in the case of a large weapon. Enter Hero's first machine,

---

[10] 1. 1. 7; 7 pref. 14 ff.; 9. 8. 2 ff.; 10. 7. 1–5.

[11] Marsden 2 dates Ctesibius to the second third of the 3rd cent. BC, and emphasizes Hero's
possible debts to him: the out-of-date character of Hero's account can then be explained by
the fact that he is using an outdated source.

[12] A. G. Drachmann, *Ktesibios, Philon and Heron: A Study in Greek Pneumatics* (Copenhagen, 1948), argues that Hero's *Pneumatica* draws on Philo's book by the same title.

[13] P. Fleury, 'Héron d'Alexandrie et Vitruve. A propos des techniques dites "pneumatiques"', in G. Argoud (ed.), *Science et vie intellectuelle à Alexandrie (Ier–IIIe siècle après J.-C.)*
(Saint-Étienne, 1994), 67–81.

[14] Cf. similar claims in Ael. *Tact*. 1. 3 and Arr. *Tact*. 1. 2, noted in Marsden 44 n. 3.

[15] Cf. a similar progress for geometry in Hero, *Metr*. 2. 3–4. 7; *Geometr*. 176. 1–13 (I owe
this latter reference to Karin Tybjerg).

[16] e.g. *Bel*. 83, 97, 102 (Marsden 24, 30, 34 respectively). Note that, although friction as a
concept does not seem to figure in the treatise, there is a strong awareness of the problems
it causes, so that steps are taken to choose resistant materials, to coat them, and to employ
smooth surfaces at points of great wear and tear.

[17] A similar definition in Philo Mech. *Bel*. 5 (Marsden 108); Papp. *Coll*. 1024. 17–21.

a belly-bow that, instead of relying just on the arms' strength, could lean on the belly of the man operating it and thus allow more pulling power and a more violent blow.[18]

A new difficulty arose when men wanted (βουλόμενοι: note the alternation between various motives men have to improve their weapons—sometimes necessity, sometimes force, sometimes their own decision) to increase the size of the missile and the force of the emission. The solution was a larger machine equipped with a frame (πλίνθιον) and a torsion mechanism to pull the arms back. Hero's second machine was thus a proper catapult with torsion springs—it differed from the belly-bow chiefly in that new elements were added to make the pulling back of the arms more powerful. Twisting the ropes (in the torsion springs) became difficult, so they needed (ἠναγκάσθησαν) to add washers. Because the force (βία) of the arms had become so strong that equal force was needed to pull them back, an axle was added, then a pulley system (πολυσπάστος).[19] The engine was set on a base that enabled the people operating it to turn it in whatever direction they chose. As more and more components were added, human intervention became more and more limited and was in fact reduced to pulling a trigger. Especially if we keep in mind the pseudo-Aristotelian definition of mechanics as the τέχνη which assists human beings when they have to do something against (or beyond) nature (παρὰ φύσιν),[20] Hero's belopoetics can be characterized as the progressive taming of power on the part of men, who start from a basic tool, the bow, itself an extension of the hand, and make it into a more and more composite device, where an increasing number of artificial elements are interposed between the hand and the projectile itself. Human power is increased beyond its natural bounds, thus creating control not only over nature but also over the enemies who are, in more than one sense, at the receiving end of the power itself.

The concluding part of Hero's treatise adds a further touch to the tale. It is again a historical account, this time of how the measurements for the various parts of the engines were obtained. The older mechanicians (οἱ παλαιότεροι), who only considered shape and design (τὸ σχῆμα καὶ τὴν διάθεσιν), did not have very good results in the projection of the missile, because they did not use well-fitting symmetries (ἁρμοστοῖς συμμετρίαις). Their

---

[18] The belly bow (*gastraphetēs*) is sometimes attributed to a Zopyrus of Tarentum (Bito 62 (Marsden 74)), the same city where Archytas, the alleged founder of mechanics (Diog. Laert. 8. 83 = 47 A 1. 36–7 DK), was *stratēgos* seven times running. This Zopyrus is perhaps the mid-4th-cent. Pythagorean of that name mentioned in Iambl. *VP* 267 = 58 A 25 DK (Marsden 98 n. 52).   [19] Hero describes pulley systems at length in *Mech*. 1. 4–6. 22.

[20] *Mech*. pref., 847[a]17–19: ὅταν οὖν δέῃ τι παρὰ φύσιν πρᾶξαι, διὰ τὸ χαλεπὸν ἀπορίαν παρέχει καὶ δεῖται τέχνης. διὸ καὶ καλοῦμεν τῆς τέχνης τὸ πρὸς τὰς τοιαύτας ἀπορίας βοηθοῦν μέρος μηχανήν. Whether Hero knew of this text is still much debated: cf. F. De Gandt, 'Force et science des machines', in J. Barnes, J. Brunschwig, M. Burnyeat, and M. Schofield (eds.), *Science and Speculation: Studies in Hellenistic Theory and Practice* (Cambridge and Paris, 1982), 96–127; G. Micheli, *Le origini del concetto di macchina* (Florence, 1995).

measurements were established on the basis of trial-and-error experience.[21] The ones after them, on the other hand (οἱ μετὰ ταῦτα), made their engines efficient (ἐνεργά) and concordant (σύμφωνα) by addition and subtraction—that is, roughly, by a more sophisticated version of trial and error. Hero can be taken to represent a third phase, where construction has acquired geometric bases—that is, it has been recognized that the spring is, again, the ἀρχή on which the other measurements are based, and the relationship between the various parts of the engine and the projectile to be used has been established mathematically. The difference between lesser and greater efficiency is thus presented as a process taking place over time, a genealogy of the discipline that starts from one ἀρχή and concludes full-circle with another ἀρχή, this time mathematically founded.

Although the final section of Hero's treatise has been considered by some to be so abrupt that the received text must be incomplete, in my opinion it wraps up the whole account rather nicely. He presents a problem (how to build an engine capable of throwing a missile treble the size of a given one, given the diameter of the first engine) and solves it mathematically by means of the duplication of the cube, but (and this is perhaps a nod at his adversaries) in a philosophically justified way—for he corroborates his solution to the problem thus: 'because the spring is the *cause* of the emission of the stone'.[22]

Returning to our initial question, then, Hero is not interested here in an up-to-date report or a new proposal (something which he arguably produces in the *Cheiroballistra*: cf. n. 33). He wants to present the construction of war engines in a certain way: a tale of how better and better solutions have been found to satisfy an original need—throwing a missile (but, if we take on board what we said before, we could also say a need for security)—and of how those solutions themselves have been retrospectively established on solid geometrical foundations.

2. Why Was Hero Talking about War Threats, and Why Would an Ordinary Citizen Have Cared about War Engines?

In commenting on the introduction to the *Belopoeica*, Marsden writes (p. 2): '[Hero's] recommendation is a much more appropriate one . . . to make in the circumstances of the third century BC than . . . in the first century AD when the Mediterranean area was enjoying the benefits of the *Pax Romana*.' The idea that the Mediterranean area was enjoying the benefits of the *Pax*

---

[21] Cf. a similar process in Philo Mech. *Bel*. 50 (Marsden 106–8).

[22] *Bel*. 115 (Marsden 40): ἐπεὶ οὖν αἴτιός ἐστιν ὁ τόνος τοῦ λίθου ἐξαποστολῆς. (The spring is also the ἀρχή.) Hero's solution to the problem of cube duplication is also reproduced in *Mech*. 1. 11, Papp. *Coll*. 62. 14–64. 18, and Eutoc. 58. 15–60. 27 Mugler.

Romana was probably less a description of the actual state of affairs than a Roman propaganda slogan, employed by a new dynastic line of emperors, the Flavians, to assert their claim to power. Hero was a contemporary of the first of the Flavians, Vespasian, who became emperor in AD 70 after his three predecessors had, in rapid succession, been either killed or forced to commit suicide.

Even though Rome had been politically present in the Mediterranean since at least 300 BC,[23] Egypt had only become a Roman province at the end of the first century BC, after the suicide of Cleopatra following Antony's defeat at the hands of Augustus. Alexandria, which already under the Ptolemies had been considered a case by itself, not quite like the rest of Egypt from the point of view of administration,[24] kept some privileged status under the new regime: for instance, Roman citizenship was granted to some of its citizens (essentially the upper-class Greek group) and Roman prefects were usually careful not to impede pre-existing religious and civic rites and customs. However, this did *not* mean that all was well with the world.[25]

If we take the period between Nero's accession to power (AD 54) and Hadrian's death (AD 138) as a good span for Hero's activities, we have a more than substantial number of wars and riots in several parts of the empire. The province of Egypt was affected in particular by wars in Judaea, which first broke out in AD 66 and lasted until 74. In 66 the two Roman legions stationed in Alexandria massacred 50,000 of the local Jewish population after disorders in the city.[26] New wars followed in AD 115–16, when the chief synagogue at Alexandria was destroyed, and again in 132–5, well into the period traditionally known as the age of the *Pax Romana*. The Jewish wars involved sieges (at Jerusalem and, famously, Masada) where catapults and other war machines (rams, siege towers) were extensively employed.[27] Josephus, who participated in the first war, said that it was the greatest war not only of his time, but of all times (*BJ* 1. 1). So, to Hero's audience, talk

---

[23] See A. K. Bowman, *Egypt after the Pharaohs. 332 BC–AD 642, from Alexander to the Arab Conquest* (London, 1986), 31 ff., for a brief overview of the history of Rome's conquest of the eastern Mediterranean.

[24] See A. Measson, 'Alexandrea ad Egyptum', in Argoud (n. 13), 9–52.

[25] Historians have often described the 1st and 2nd cents. AD as a time of acute social tension and instability: R. MacMullen, *Enemies of the Roman Order: Treason, Unrest and Alienation in the Empire* (Cambridge, Mass., 1966); F. G. B. Millar, *The Roman Near East 31 BC–AD 337* (Cambridge, Mass., 1993); A. K. Bowman, 'Egypt', in *CAH*, 2nd edn., x. 676–702. For a study of the concept of *Pax Romana* see G. Woolf, 'Roman Peace', in J. Rich and G. Shipley (eds.), *War and Society in the Roman World* (London and New York, 1993), 171–94.

[26] Joseph. *BJ* 2. 487–98.

[27] Josephus, a direct witness of and participant in the first Jewish war, mentions towers, quick-firers (ὀξυβελῆ: also mentioned by Philo Mech. *Bel.* 54 (Marsden 114)), stone-throwing machines (πετροβόλοι), battering rams, and catapults: *BJ* 5. 263, 269–72; 7. 308–11. cf. also I. A. Richmond, 'The Roman Siege-Works of Masada, Israel', *JRS* 52 (1962), 142–55.

172 S. Cuomo

of war and of the necessity of efficient armaments may have sounded not totally unjustified.

Moreover, wars and riots were not the only disruptions to the fabric of communal life which a citizen of Alexandria in the first century AD may have experienced, directly or indirectly. The enemies Hero talks about in his introduction are both ἐχθροί (adversaries, opponents, 'internal' enemies) and πολέμιοι (enemies of war, 'external' enemies).[28] From the point of view of many Alexandrians, the Roman government counted as either or both. The feelings of the Alexandrian Jews are not hard to guess. Generalized anti-Roman (and anti-Jewish) feelings are also explicitly expressed in some Greek literature of the period: the so-called 'Acts of the Pagan Martyrs' present (mainly fictional) situations with dates ranging from the early first to late second centuries AD in which Roman authorities are accused, among other things, of greed, corruption, and ignorance.[29]

A source slightly earlier than Hero, Philo of Alexandria (c.20 BC–after AD 40), wrote:

ἐστι δέ τις καὶ κατ' εἰρήνην πόλεμος τῶν ἐν τοῖς ὅπλοις οὐκ ἀποδέων, ὃν ἀδοξία καὶ πενία καὶ δεινὴ σπάνις τῶν ἀναγκαίων συγκροτοῦσιν. (*Quod omnis probus liber sit*, 34)

there is a peace-time war no less grave than those fought with arms, a war set on foot by disrepute and poverty and dire lack of the necessaries of life. (trans. Colson)[30]

Another source, this time a contemporary of Hero, Dio Chrysostom (AD 40–120), said in an oration addressed to the Alexandrian people:

τεκμήριον δὲ τὰ τελευταῖα συμβάντα περὶ ὑμᾶς. . . . καὶ νῦν οὕτως ἐπιεικεῖς ἐχόντες ἡγεμόνας εἰς ὑποψίαν αὐτοὺς καθ' ὑμῶν αὐτῶν ἠγάγετε, ὥστε ἐπιμελεστέρας χρῆναι φυλακῆς ᾠήθησαν ἢ πρότερον . . . καὶ οὐ πρότερον ὑμᾶς ἀνῆκαν ἕως ἐγεύσασθε πολέμου καὶ τὸ δεινὸν ἄχρι πείρας προῆλθεν. (Dio Chrys. 32. 70–2)

I cite the most recent chapters in your history. . . . Although you now have such reasonable men as governors [the Romans], you have brought them to a feeling of suspicion toward yourselves, and so they have come to believe that there is need of more careful watchfulness than formerly . . . [After disturbances the Roman troops] did not let you go until you had had a taste of warfare, and what you formerly had dreaded had become a matter of bitter experience. (trans. Crosby)[31]

---

[28] Aeneas Tacticus (4th cent. BC) devotes several parts of his *Poliorcetica* to the problem of internal threats to security, e.g. 10, 11, 17. See D. Whitehead, *Aineias the Tactician* (Oxford, 1990), esp. 25–33.

[29] H. Musurillo (ed.), *Acta Alexandrinorum* (Leipzig, 1961); MacMullen (n. 25), 84–90; H. Idris Bell, *Cults and Creeds in Graeco-Roman Egypt* (Liverpool, 1957), 41 ff.

[30] Philo of Alexandria, *Works*, trans. F. H. Colson, R. Marcus, and G. H. Whitaker (London and Cambridge, Mass., 1929–62). See also D. I. Sly, *Philo's Alexandria* (London and New York, 1996), 90.

[31] Dio Chrystostom, *Orationes*, trans. J. W. Cohoon and H. Lamar Crosby (London and Cambridge, Mass., 1932–51).

Hero's appeal to the security of the city is significant because it is an appeal to *stability* of a social order, of community life, of shared activities.

Correspondingly, war engines produce tranquillity above all not because they actually defeat the enemy, but because they generate a sense of power and security. Hero seems to have captured the essence of psychological or 'cold' warfare, of weapons as a deterrent, when he says that 'those who wish to plot, *observing* . . . will not attack'. Marsden (44 n. 2) comments that 'the theme of the introduction, "si vis pacem, para bellum" . . . became an ancient commonplace' and one cannot but agree. I would like here to try and examine the commonplace more closely.

It is important to note, I think, some of the terms Hero uses. The enemies are described as 'plotting' (ἐπιβουλεύειν). A straightforward 'attack' (ἐπελεύσονται) is contemplated in only one case, and even then it is taken to be a non-possibility. At one point Hero actually remarks: 'very few [engines] are built for urgent use'.[32] The attitude of the people practising the new philosophy of the engines is characterized as powerful, but non-active: terms like 'standing calm' (καταστῆναι) and 'forethought' (πρόνοια) do not suggest active intervention but rather calm awareness of one's power—power that does not need to be exerted in order to affirm its presence.

The picture is thus not one of overt clash in the battlefield, nor of barbarians menacing at the gates. The sources of anxiety are identified as *potentially* threatening, rather than actually enforcing violence, and they are generalized to encompass any kind of opposition—not just enemies in a war situation, but adversaries from every walk of life and social context.

In sum, I think that, although Hero's engines are to be taken seriously as 'real' engines,[33] in *Belopoeica* he is not proposing a solution to an actual war threat, but rather addressing a generalized demand for security. Thus, in the course of the treatise, the machines are not really shown in action and no big claim is made about their destroying power[34]—they represent the community's capacity to oppose threats, to offer shelter and security. It is important that the appeal is indeed to the body politic, not to the individual. *Belopoeica* is not aimed specifically at the town authorities— Hero is addressing everybody, so that his 'communication may be easy to follow for everyone'. The study of the construction of war engines is taken up as a collective enterprise—security or the lack of it, unlike death or disease or old age, which affect the individual *qua* individual, is a problem for the community, so that the solution must also be found on the level of society as a whole.

---

[32] *Bel.* 102 (Marsden 34): οὐ γὰρ κατασκευάζεται πάμπολλα δὴ πρὸς τὰς κατεπειγούσας χρείας.

[33] Another treatise on war engines attributed to Hero (cf. n. 4) describes a sort of small catapult, the *cheiroballistra*. One of the bas-reliefs on Trajan's column, erected not long after AD 106, depicts a machine which corresponds to Hero's description. See Marsden 206–33.

[34] Contrast e.g. Bito *Constr.* 57 (Marsden 72); Philo Mech. *Bel.* 56 (Marsden 116).

3. What Philosophy is Hero Attacking, and is This a Criticism of 'the Normal Greek Attitude towards the Practical'?

The introduction to *Belopoeica* contrasts mechanics and philosophy as different means to reach the same end, tranquillity (ἀταραξία). The difference is both in their method (philosophy operates by means of words or discourses, διὰ τῶν λόγων, mechanics through material, actual products) and in their effectiveness (philosophy is ineffectual; mechanics works). There is no need to say which side Hero is on: in the apparent competition between mechanics and philosophy, mechanics wins because it can subsume the characteristics of the rival form of knowledge, acquiring the right to call itself 'philosophy by means of instruments' (διὰ τῶν ὀργάνων φιλοσοφία).

I do not think we can identify the philosophy to which Hero is referring. Of course, he may be referring to some philosophy in particular, but then again he may be presenting philosophical theories in a general, indefinite fashion, more to construct a straw adversary than to attack a specific one. Hero is clearly not interested in reproducing any philosophical position with accuracy and fairness—the message he wants to convey is about mechanics, and the declaredly broad appeal of his treatise may have recommended the use of general notions and widely used images.

While some other philosophical buzzwords that Hero uses in his introduction (πρόνοια, συνείδησις) are mostly found in Stoic writers, ἀταραξία as a chief concept was at the time fairly unspecific.[35] The first names to spring to mind are Epicureans and Pyrrhonist Sceptics. Both Epicurus and Sextus Empiricus maintain that the aim (τέλος) of philosophical activity is ἀταραξία,[36] and ἀταραξία is specifically associated with fear of war, fear of attack on the part of the enemy, or fear for the security of the city in a passage of Epictetus, which contrasts the great peace allegedly provided by the emperor with the inner state achieved by following the doctrines of the philosophers—a state that comprises peace, freedom from harm, and ἀταραξία.[37]

---

[35] Cf. n. 1 for συνείδησις. πρόνοια is found e.g. in Cic. *ND* 2. 75–6; Diog. Laert. 7. 147; Plut. *Mor.* 1075 E (=L&S 54J, 54A, 54K respectively).

[36] Epicur. *Ep. Pyth.*85. 9–10 (L&S 18c): μὴ ἄλλο τι τέλος ἐκ τῆς περὶ μετεώρων γνώσεως . . . νομίζειν [δεῖ] εἶναι ἥπερ ἀταραξίαν καὶ πίστιν βέβαιον, καθάπερ καὶ ἐπὶ τῶν λοιπῶν, 'we should not think that any other end is served by knowledge of celestial events . . . than freedom from disturbance and firm confidence, just as in other areas of discourse'; id., *Ep. Menoec.* 128. 1–2 (L&S 21B): τούτων γὰρ ἀπλανὴς θεωρία πᾶσαν αἵρεσιν καὶ φυγὴν ἐπανάγειν οἶδεν ἐπὶ τὴν τοῦ σώματος ὑγίειαν καὶ τὴν [τῆς ψυχῆς] ἀταραξίαν, ἐπεὶ τοῦτο τοῦ μακαρίως ζῆν ἐστι τέλος, 'the steady observation of these things makes it possible to refer every choice and avoidance to the health of the body and the soul's freedom from disturbance, since this is the end belonging to the blessed life'; Sext. Emp. *Pyrrhon* 1. 12. *Pyrrhon.* 1. 4 indicates that ἀταραξία is one of the results of the Sceptical δύναμις. It also accompanies the ἐποχή (ibid. 1. 33).

[37] 37. 3. 13. 13: νῦν ἐμοὶ κακὸν οὐδὲν δύναται συμβῆναι, ἐμοὶ λῃστὴς οὐκ ἔστιν, ἐμοὶ σεισμὸς οὐκ ἔστιν, πάντα εἰρήνης μετά, πάντα ἀταραξίας. πᾶσα ὁδός, πᾶσα πόλις, πᾶς σύνοδος, γείτων, κοινωνὸς

The walled city as an image of security is also quite frequent in Hellenistic philosophy. Epicurus is credited with the famous words 'against other things it is possible to obtain security. But when it comes to death we human beings all live in an unwalled city'.[38] A spokesman for Stoic theories in Cicero's *Tusculan Disputations* asserts that the happy man ought to be 'safe, impregnable, fenced, and fortified',[39] while Diogenes of Oenoanda (second century AD) says that one of the characteristics of the life of the gods is that 'everything will be full of justice and mutual friendship, and there will come to be no need of walls or laws and all the things we devise on account of each other'.[40] Walls (which set a boundary between inside and outside but also provide a defence against attack) and laws (which set a boundary between right and wrong but also defend against injustice) are here indicated as two main elements of human society. The third element is also interesting: 'all the things we devise on account of each other' could refer to crafts or trade, or just to the notion of work within a community, where no one can be said to be self-sufficient and all are interdependent.

The city, or the walls of the city, thus provide an image of communal security and express the idea that the need for defence and security is an element of communal life, as essential to it as laws, or as the exchange of goods and labour.[41] The city represents the space where all that constitutes a political and social collectivity takes place, the space where individual identity is determined on the basis of collective identity.[42]

It is thus convenient for Hero to emphasize that mechanics has a strong role to play at the level of the community. A social role for mathematics is vindicated in the *Metrica*: Hero first observes that nature has assigned to greater populations larger portions of land and to smaller populations smaller countries. A similar disparity applies to land distribution in cities, where leaders and people with a potential to govern get larger portions, and

---

ἀβλαβής, [the wise man says] 'now no evil can befall me, for me there is no such thing as a brigand, for me there is no such thing as an earthquake, everything is full of peace, everything full of tranquillity; every road, every city, every fellow-traveller, neighbour, companion, all are harmless' (trans. W. A. Oldfather (London and Cambridge, Mass., 1966)). See also 2. 2, an entire section entitled 'On tranquillity'.

[38] *Sent. Vatic.* 31 (=L&S 24B): πρὸς μὲν τἄλλα δυνατὸν ἀσφάλειαν πορίσασθαι, χάριν δὲ θανάτου πάντες ἄνθρωποι πόλιν ἀτείχιστον οἰκοῦμεν.

[39] *Tusc.* 5. 41 (–L&S 63L): 'volumus enim eum, qui beatus sit, tutum esse, inexpugnabilem, saeptum atque munitum.'

[40] M. F. Smith, *Thirteen New Fragments of Diogenes of Oenoanda* (Vienna, 1974), fr. 21. 1. 4–14 (=L&S 22S: translation slightly modified): δικαιοσύνης γὰρ ἔσται μεστὰ πάντα καὶ φιλαλληλίας, καὶ οὐ γενήσεται τειχῶν ἢ νόμων χρεία καὶ παντῶν ὅσα δι' ἀλλήλους σκευωρούμεθα.

[41] Hero, *Dioptra* 190. 4, 17–26, asserts the importance of his dioptra for building walls and assessing the height of walls when besieging a city. I owe this reference to Karin Tybjerg.

[42] On these themes cf. A. Barigazzi, 'Sul concetto epicureo della sicurezza esterna', in G. Pugliese Carratelli (ed.), Συζήτησις: *Studi sull'epicureismo greco e romano offerti a Marcello Gigante* (Naples, 1983), i. 73–92; B. Inwood, *Ethics and Human Action in Early Stoicism* (Oxford, 1985); M. Schofield, *The Stoic Idea of the City* (Cambridge, 1991).

such divisions are (moreover) carried out in an approximate manner. But, Hero continues:

εἰ δέ τις βούλοιτο κατὰ τὸν δοθέντα λόγον διαιρεῖν τὰ χωρία, ὥστε μηδὲ ὡς εἰπεῖν κέγχρον μίαν τῆς ἀναλογίας ὑπερβάλλειν ἢ ἐλλείπειν τοῦ δοθέντος λόγου, μόνης προσδεήσεται γεωμετρίας· ἐν ᾗ ἐφαρμογῇ μὲν ἴση, τῇ δὲ ἀναλογίᾳ δικαιοσύνη, ἡ δὲ περὶ τούτων ἀπόδειξις ἀναμφισβήτητος, ὅπερ τῶν ἄλλων τεχνῶν ἢ ἐπιστημῶν οὐδεμία ὑπισχνεῖται. (*Metr.* 140. 18–142. 2)

if one wished to divide the places according to a given ratio, so that not even a grain of millet of the proportion, as it were, exceeds or falls short of the given ratio, it takes geometry alone. In this latter, in fact, there is impartial accord, justice by means of the proportion, and the demonstration about these things is indisputable, which none of the other arts or sciences guarantees.[43]

A contrast between mechanics and other forms of knowledge is also found in the introduction to the *Pneumatica*, for instance, where in a discussion of various theories about the existence and nature of the void, Hero says that both philosophers and mechanicians have studied the subject: the former discursively or theoretically (λογικῶς), the latter through the action of sensible objects (διὰ τῆς τῶν αἰσθητῶν ἐνεργείας). Later in the text plausible arguments are contrasted with appeals to sensible phenomena, and Hero says that the former offer no proof of their assertions.[44]

The idea that philosophy as a form of knowledge is different from, and often opposed to, other forms of knowledge is not new to Hero or to the period he lived in, and has been the object of much study. The difference in this case is that, instead of presenting the philosophers' claims to superiority, the roles are reversed. Yet, in my view, with the opposition philosophy/ mechanics or discourses/instruments, Hero is not positing a distinction between a theoretical activity with theoretical aims and a practical activity with practical aims, whatever those may be.

The fact that the two forms of knowledge are set in competition means that they must to some extent speak the same language, share some common ground, have the same objectives. In other words, philosophy *itself* is seen as a way to obtain certain results in practice—where 'in practice' means in a way that 'works' for whatever need motivated the philosophical activity in the first place. Words vs. weapons, which mirrors Lucretius' *dictis, non armis*,[45] is not theory vs. practice—on the contrary, efficacy in practice is assumed as the value and the standard against which both words and weapons are to be assessed.

There does indeed appear to have been a tension, in the philosophy

---

[43] There is another passage about division of land according to proportion (which is the object of geodesy) at *Def.* 102. 1–3. (I owe this latter reference to Karin Tybjerg.)

[44] *Pneum.* 2. 4–28. 15, esp. 2. 5–7. Cf. Tybjerg, *Doing Philosophy with Machines* (n. 4).

[45] 5. 50. On these themes cf. M. Nussbaum, *The Therapy of Desire: Theory and Practice in Hellenistic Ethics* (Princeton, 1994).

of the time, between public and private identities, a contrast that led some observers, now and then, to view philosophy, or rather some philosophers, as insufficiently effective from the point of view of actual, shareable, 'external' results.[46] The rise of rhetoric and law as the most socially valued forms of knowledge in the Roman empire is probably to be related to these demands for a social, public edge to one's education and one's quest for 'wisdom' (σοφία). In its own way Hero's account is also addressing such demands.

[46] e.g. Dio Chr. 32. 8–10, 20; Luc. *Vit. auct.*; Plut. *De Stoicorum repugnantiis* (1033 A–1057 B); *Non posse suaviter vivi secundum Epicurum* (1086 C–1107 C). Cf. also A. A. Long, 'Pleasure and Social Utility: The Virtues of Being Epicurean', in H. Flashar and O. Gigon, *Aspects de la philosophie hellénistique* (Entretiens sur l'antiquité classique, 32; Geneva, 1986), 283–324.

10

The Limitations of Ancient Atomism

J. R. MILTON

THE history of atomism presents a paradox. The atomic theory is a central pillar of modern physics and chemistry, one that could not be removed without causing quite unimaginable chaos in both disciplines. It is also a very old theory, going back in some form to Leucippus and Democritus in the fifth century BC. Atomism can therefore be seen—scientists quite often do see it—as having a unique status among the theories of matter put forward in the ancient world. Other theories—Platonic, Aristotelian, and Stoic—have been abandoned. Atomism alone appears to have survived, or at least to have left a living descendant.

On the other hand, the contribution of atomism to ancient science seems much more meagre. Of course the notion of *science* that we now use is a modern one,[1] and there is always some risk of anachronism whenever it is applied before the nineteenth century. Nevertheless, if one looks at those people in the ancient world for whom the label 'scientist' is at any rate not manifestly inappropriate one sees very little sign of any commitment to atomism. Atoms play no part in such explanations as were advanced, and in so far as philosophical allegiances can be discerned, they are to the atomists' rivals.

What I have said so far is of course very simple, even crude, and cries out for elaboration and qualification. Both of these I shall now attempt to supply.

---

[1] That the Greeks lacked a notion corresponding to our 'science' is not universally agreed. 'We are frequently told that the Greeks had no word for science, as we understand the term. But they did have such a word, *historia*': K. D. White, '"The Base Mechanic Arts"? Some Thoughts on the Contribution of Science (Pure and Applied) to the Culture of the Hellenistic Age', in P. Green (ed.), *Hellenistic History and Culture* (Berkeley, 1993), 211–20 at 211. Others disagree: according to R. K. French, 'to see science in antiquity we need to have a definition of science so broad as to be meaningless' (*Ancient Natural History* (London, 1994), p. xiii). The approach followed here is that of G. E. R. Lloyd, *Demystifying Mentalities* (Cambridge, 1990), 29: 'the qualifications aside, certain investigations that *are* continuous with what is normally included in our term science were initiated in ancient Greece, and by this I mean nothing more sophisticated or more controversial than that *that* is the appropriate rubric to apply to such diverse inquiries as, for example, Greek theoretical astronomy (that is, astronomical model-building), to Archimedes' statics and hydrostatics, to Galen's experimental anatomical and physiological vivisections—and so on. Clearly this is not the *whole* of science as we now understand it . . . and clearly it was not carried out within the institutional framework . . . that now exists. But they are deliberate and systematic investigations of nature that belong, nevertheless, to the same genus.'

I

When presented with an alleged paradox there are several responses that one can make, of which the simplest is a denial that one or other side of the paradox is true at all. One option is therefore to deny that atomism really is a part of modern science. Though this now appears profoundly unpromising, it is worth remarking that its hopelessness is relatively recent. About a century ago serious scientists did maintain exactly this thesis. The opposition of Mach and Ostwald to atomism is well known,[2] but there were many others, including the pioneer historian of Greek alchemy, Marcellin Berthelot.[3]

The other option is to insist that ancient atomism really was scientific. This is a standpoint which has had advocates more recent than Ostwald or Duhem; it had a particular appeal to an older generation of Marxists—those who tried to show that Marxism was a science, as opposed to their less confident successors, who prefer to claim that physics is an ideology: a good example can be found in Benjamin Farrington.[4] Reasons for rejecting this will become apparent shortly, but for the moment we need merely note the importance of distinguishing between *science* and *naturalism*, understood as the doctrine that the physical universe constitutes the whole of reality. While there is no doubt that the latter label applies quite unproblematically to Epicurus and Lucretius, it is much less clear that the former does. This is not the place to pursue all the various problems relating to demarcation criteria, but it can at least be said that any criterion we do offer for status as a scientific theory must be *formal*—that is, it should relate to the intellectual procedures used to evaluate proposed explanations, and not to the content of the explanations, e.g. their recourse to entities of a certain approved type. Maintaining a materialist ontology is neither a necessary nor a sufficient condition for possessing a scientific outlook.

---

[2] H. R. Post, 'Atomism 1900', *Physics Education*, 3 (1968), 1–13.

[3] Berthelot was also a chemist of some distinction, and in his capacity of Inspector General of Higher Education one of the most powerful scientific bureaucrats of the Third Republic. One day in the Senate he indicated to a fellow scientist his unease about the direction in which things seemed to be going: 'I do not want chemistry to degenerate into a religion; I do not want the chemist to believe in the existence of atoms as the Christian believes in the presence of Christ in the communion wafer.' This remark, quoted by A. J. Rocke, *Chemical Atomism in the Nineteenth Century* (Columbus, Oh., 1984), 324, is worth recalling as a reminder both of the existence of ideological issues surrounding the acceptance of atomism and of their complexity: Berthelot did what he could to damage the scientific career of Pierre Duhem, but on atomism itself Duhem's own position was not so very different.

[4] *The Faith of Epicurus* (London, 1967), 93–8.

II

A quite different approach is to accept the paradox—or rather the facts on which it is based—but to deny that there is anything deeply or seriously paradoxical about it. There are again two ways in which this can be done, corresponding to the two halves of the paradox.

In antiquity there were two main traditions of atomist thought, the first initiated by Leucippus but most fully developed by Democritus, the second stemming from Epicurus.[5] None of Democritus' very numerous works has survived, and even the fragments we do possess are for the most part on marginal aspects of his system. For the basic principles and for many of the details we are dependent on his critics, notably Aristotle, and on the doxographical tradition. Though a fairly adequate account of the outlines of Democritus' system can be reconstructed, it is much more difficult to be sure about his motivation—his conception of the reasons why the enquiry into nature was to be pursued.

In the case of Epicureanism such uncertainties do not exist. Epicurus' own summary of his teachings has survived, and reveals his motives with stark clarity:

εἰ μηθὲν ἡμᾶς αἱ τῶν μετεώρων ὑποψίαι ἠνώχλουν καὶ αἱ περὶ θανάτου, μήποτε πρὸς ἡμᾶς ᾖ τι, ἔτι τε τὸ μὴ κατανοεῖν τοὺς ὅρους τῶν ἀλγηδόνων καὶ τῶν ἐπιθυμιῶν, οὐκ ἂν προσεδεόμεθα φυσιολογίας.

οὐκ ἦν τὸ φοβούμενον λύειν ὑπὲρ τῶν κυριωτάτων μὴ κατειδότα τίς ἡ τοῦ σύμπαντος φύσις, ἀλλ᾽ ὑποπτεύοντά τι τῶν κατὰ τοὺς μύθους· ὥστε οὐκ ἦν ἄνευ φυσιολογίας ἀκεραίους τὰς ἡδονὰς ἀπολαμβάνειν. (*Rat. sent.* 11, 12 = L&S 25B)

If we were not troubled by our suspicions of the phenomena of the sky and about death, fearing that it concerns us, and also by our failure to grasp the limits of pains and desires, we should have no need of φυσιολογία.

A man cannot dispel his fear about the most important matters if he does not know what is the nature of the universe, but suspects the truth of some myth. Hence without φυσιολογία it is not possible to attain our pleasures unalloyed. (trans. Bailey, modified)[6]

In the translation I have kept Epicurus' Greek rather than render φυσιολογία

---

[5] English translation and commentary on many of the major texts of Leucippus (67 DK) and Democritus (68 DK) appear in KRS. For Epicurus see G. Arrighetti, *Epicuro: Opere*, rev. edn. (Turin, 1973). An English translation of some major texts, with a good bibliography of recent work, appears in L&S. Both are, of course, quite distinct from Plato's claim (*Ti.* 53 C–68 C) that matter is formed from combinations of four basic geometrical shapes (cf. Wilson's paper in this volume). Although sometimes spoken of as a form of atomism, this is really little more than an arbitrarily mathematized restatement of four-element (fire, water, earth, air) theory. See G. E. R. Lloyd, *Early Greek Science: Thales to Aristotle* (London, 1970), 74 ff.; id., *The Revolutions of Wisdom* (Berkeley, 1987), 227, 280; id., *Methods and Problems in Greek Science* (Cambridge, 1991), 334, 349–50.

[6] C. Bailey, *Epicurus* (Oxford, 1926), 97.

by 'natural science', as Bailey did, because the latter term is liable to mislead. Bailey described φυσιολογία as 'Epicurus' regular technical term for the knowledge of nature and natural laws',[7] but the notion of a natural law in any scientific sense is quite foreign to Epicureanism, as indeed it is to Greek natural philosophy in general.[8] φυσιολογία for Epicurus was not science as we know it, but rather a kind of foundational discipline designed to establish the kind of entities that do and do not exist.[9] He valued it because he thought it essential to establish basic principles, and hence the *kinds* of explanation that are legitimate.[10] Detailed research into particular phenomena (ἱστορία) is much less valuable, and even potentially dangerous: if not grounded on proper principles it can serve to increase wonder, reintroducing fear and the acceptance of myth.[11]

Further evidence of the divergence between Epicurus' method and that of later science can be seen in his employment of multiple explanations. These have been defended by some of Epicurus' interpreters, notably Elizabeth Asmis,[12] as being in accordance with later scientific practice, but Epicurus' own employment of them hardly suggests this.

The basic idea is not difficult to grasp. Epicurus divided objects of enquiry into two groups: those that can be investigated directly (πρόδηλα) and those that cannot (ἄδηλα). In the former case we can at least in principle settle the issue by further investigation, as when we discover the shape of a distant tower by approaching closely and seeing it as it really is.[13] In the case of ἄδηλα such as atoms or the heavenly bodies this is impossible. All we can hope for are accounts which will not be refuted by counter-evidence, and in general there will be a plurality of these.

Something like this situation is of course quite familiar in modern science—one thinks of current disagreements about the extinction of the dinosaurs or the dark-matter problem in cosmology. States of affairs in which rival explanations have proliferated are, however, generally regarded by

---

[7] Bailey (n. 6), 277.

[8] R. M. Grant, *Miracle and Natural Law in Graeco-Roman and Early Christian Thought* (Amsterdam, 1952); H. Koester, 'Νόμος φύσεως: The Concept of Natural Law in Greek Thought', in J. Neusner (ed.), *Religions in Antiquity* (Leiden, 1968), 521–41; J. R. Milton, 'The Origin and Development of the Concept of the "Laws of Nature"', *Archives européennes de sociologie*, 22 (1981), 173–95. In *Ep. Pyth.* 86–7 Epicurus interestingly contrasts φυσιολογία with νομοθεσία—laying down the law to nature. Lucretius uses the phrase *foedera naturai* on a number of occasions (1. 586; 2. 302; 5. 310, 924; 6. 906–7); part of the attraction of this terminology is that it evidently carried no implication of a transcendent lawgiver.

[9] Perhaps a closer analogy would be with materialism as formerly taught in the Soviet Union and its satellites, a discipline occupying the place of religious education in an atheistic society, and (privately) disdained by most scientists.   [10] *Ep. Hdt.* 78.

[11] Ibid. 79.

[12] 'The principle of multiple explanation is, however, in itself a sound scientific one': *Epicurus' Scientific Method* (Ithaca, NY, 1984), 322. Compare Farrington (n. 4), 97–8. There is a more qualified defence in A. A. Long, *Hellenistic Philosophy* (London, 1974), 27.

[13] Diog. Laert 10. 34.

scientists as (mildly) undesirable—a sign that further work needs to be done. Epicurus by contrast seems actually to have *preferred* them:

κένωσίς τε σελήνης καὶ πάλιν πλήρωσις καὶ κατὰ στροφὴν τοῦ σώματος τούτου δύναιτ' ἂν γίνεσθαι καὶ κατὰ σχηματισμοὺς ἀέρος ὁμοίως, ἔτι τε καὶ κατ' ἐπιπροσθήσεις καὶ κατὰ πάντας τρόπους, καθ' οὓς καὶ τὰ παρ' ἡμῖν φαινόμενα ἐκκαλεῖται εἰς τὰς τούτου τοῦ εἴδους ἀποδόσεις, ἐὰν μή τις τὸν μοναχῇ τρόπον κατηγαπηκὼς τοὺς ἄλλους κενῶς ἀποδοκιμάζῃ. (*Ep. Pyth.* 94)

The wanings of the moon and its subsequent waxings might be due to the revolution of its own body, or equally due to successive conformations of the atmosphere, or again to the interposition of other bodies; they may be accounted for in all the ways in which phenomena on earth invite us to such explanations of these phases; provided only that one does not become enamoured of the method of the single cause and groundlessly put others out of court.[14]

It is clear from this that Epicurus was not merely drawing attention to the uncontentious principle that a generic phenomenon such as death usually has quite distinct causes for its different individual occurrences;[15] there is no reason to suppose that he thought that the moon sometimes shone with its own light, but at other times merely reflected light from the sun.[16] The purpose of multiple explanations was not to gain a deeper understanding of nature, but rather to promote peace of mind. The one essential thing was that the divine nature is not brought into any explanation: if this is done the whole enterprise of providing a rational account of the causes of celestial phenomena is in vain.[17]

It is therefore most appropriate to characterize Epicureanism not as a scientific movement, but rather as a secular religion—a doctrine whose *contents* are firmly naturalistic but which elicits from its adherents a type of commitment appropriate to a revelation from a transcendental source. Such commitment has a tendency to raise the founder to a status above that of ordinary humanity; this is observable even in Epicurus' own lifetime,[18] but naturally its fullest efflorescence is to be found among his followers, most conspicuously in Lucretius, where the appropriation of religious language is quite unabashed.[19]

Such attitudes are not wholly unknown in the history of natural science—Newton attracted a rather subservient devotion from some of his followers[20]—but the main modern exemplars have been elsewhere. Indeed, if

[14] Cf. ibid. 92–116; Lucr. 5. 509–33, 614–49.   [15] Lucr. 5. 703–11.

[16] *Ep. Pyth.* 94.   [17] Ibid. 97.

[18] On the assimilation of the Epicurean sage to the gods, see B. Frischer, *The Sculpted Word: Epicureanism and Philosophical Recruitment in Ancient Greece* (Berkeley, 1982), 77–84.

[19] 'deus ille fuit, deus . . . | qui princeps vitae rationem invenit' (5. 8–9). The god who provided the revelation was of course Epicurus: cf. Plut. *Adv. Colotem*, 1117 B–C.

[20] J. E. McGuire and M. Tamny (*Certain Philosophical Questions: Newton's Trinity Notebook* (Cambridge, 1983), 327) reproduce an 18th-cent. engraving that shows the bedroom in which he was born at Woolsthorpe Manor surrounded by a kind of celestial glow.

one wants a parallel one could say that the relation of Epicureanism to Hellenistic natural science is not unlike that of Freudianism to modern psychology.

Anyone who became an Epicurean was therefore joining a sect (in the modern and not merely the ancient sense of that term):[21] a community with its own distinctive identity, beliefs, and even vocabulary. Cleomedes' derisive comparison of Epicurean language with the Greek one could hear near the synagogue is revealing in more ways than one.[22]

III

The institutional ethos and sectarian characteristics of the Epicurean school do appear to go quite a long way towards explaining why no even approximately disinterested enquiry into nature was undertaken within the school, and why Epicureanism apparently had so little appeal for anyone who was minded to engage in such enquiries. Some other questions remain, however, to be answered.

In the first place, why did no other kind of atomism flourish after Epicureanism had become established? Even if the pressures towards conformity within the Epicurean school were insuperable, would this not merely have left more opportunities for rival approaches? Democritean atomism has often been seen as more scientific in temper than its successor, and it certainly had adherents as late as Epicurus' own lifetime—notably his own teacher, Nausiphanes of Teos, a man whom Epicurus is said to have later disowned and vilified.[23] Why was it that no alternative 'scientific' tradition of atomism was able to establish itself, and that Epicurus, so to speak, scooped the pool?

At least part of the answer to this seems to be that in the highly competitive world of Hellenistic philosophy some kind of school organization centred round the study and defence of a set of authoritative texts produced by the school's founder was essential, if not for survival then at least for continued success.[24] The Epicurean school was in many ways more closed

---

[21] On the ancient notion of a sect, see J. Glucker, *Antiochus and the Late Academy* (Göttingen, 1978), 166–206.

[22] Cleom. 2. 1. Cicero comments on the exceptional character of Zeno of Sidon's more elegant style in *ND* 1. 59.

[23] On the problems of Epicurean biography and his relation with other philosophers see D. Sedley, 'Epicurus and his Professional Rivals', in J. Bollack and A. Laks, *Études sur l'Épicurisme antique* (Cahiers de Philologie, 1; Lille, 1976), 121–59.

[24] On the reasons for this see D. Sedley, 'Philosophical Allegiance', in M. Griffin and J. Barnes (eds.), *Philosophia Togata: Essays on Philosophy and Roman Society* (Oxford, 1989), 97–119.

and inflexible than its rivals,[25] but the difference appears to be one of degree rather than of kind.

Such considerations do not, however, go very far in explaining why it was that atomist ideas had such a limited appeal outside the philosophical schools, among the mathematicians, astronomers, physicians, and others whom we can conveniently (if problematically) characterize as scientists. Here one has to be very careful. The state of preservation of Hellenistic science is not good, especially outside mathematics, and arguments from silence are correspondingly precarious. Some use was made of one idea central to atomism—the vacuum—by Hero of Alexandria and other writers on pneumatics. It is not clear, however, that this came from atomism—its antecedents may lie with the deviant Aristotelianism of Strato, though even this is far from certain.[26] Hero himself was not an atomist, and there seems to be no sign of any group of scientists taking atomism as a working philosophy of nature—in spectacular contrast with the situation in the seventeenth century.

One possible reason for this lack of interest in atomism on the part of the scientists of the Hellenistic age lies in disagreements about astronomy. Atomism in both its Democritean and Epicurean forms was associated with a set of astronomical doctrines, including a flat earth and a very small sun, which no one with even a minimal respect for mathematical astronomy could possibly regard with anything other than derision.[27] In the Scientific Revolution this detachment from the main 'two-sphere' cosmological model of antiquity was a real advantage—it is striking how many of the revivers of atomism were also Copernicans[28]—but in the ancient world it formed an all but insuperable barrier.

In response to this it may be said that there is no intrinsic connection between atomism and flat-earth theories. Clearly there is a sense in which this is true—otherwise atomist ideas would never have been revived in the seventeenth century—but the connection between atomism and flat-earth astronomy is by no means purely accidental.[29] The kinds of circular motion employed in Greek mathematical astronomy after the introduction of

[25] Measures taken to ensure conformity included the institution of an oath not to depart from the master's teaching: J. M. Rist, *Epicurus: An Introduction* (Cambridge, 1972), 9, citing Phld. *De lib. dic.* 45. 8–11.

[26] D. Furley, 'Strato's Theory of the Void', in *Cosmic Problems: Essays on Greek and Roman Philosophy of Nature* (Cambridge, 1989), 149–60.

[27] Leucippus 67 A 27 DK; Democritus 68 A 96 DK; Lucr. 1. 1052 ff.; 5. 590–3; Cleom. 2. 1–2.

[28] Notably Harriot, Galileo, and Gassendi. According to Edward Rosen, the autograph of *De Revolutionibus* reveals Copernicus himself to have held some form of atomism: see 'Harriot's Science: The Intellectual Background', in J. W. Shirley (ed.), *Thomas Harriot: Renaissance Scientist* (Oxford, 1974), 5.

[29] In Epicureanism there are epistemological connections between the two: if all perceptions are true, then given that the earth looks flat and the sun looks small, they must really be as they appear.

epicycles and eccentrics are by no means perfectly explained by Aristotelian physics, but this kind of disharmony affected the fine detail, not the general picture. It was by contrast unclear how an atomic theory could explain even such basic phenomena as the uniform diurnal motion of the fixed stars and the passage of the sun along the ecliptic. It is no accident that atomist doctrines return to favour during the Copernican revolution, when both of these motions start to be considered as apparent rather than real.

IV

In order to proceed further we need to look at the content of ancient atomism, as well as at the institutions in which the doctrine was propagated. One can easily imagine a modern scientist listening to the account just given, and saying something like this: 'I am sure an explanation for the failure of ancient atomism in terms of the sectarian character and extra-scientific agenda of the Epicurean school has much to be said for it. Nevertheless, it does not reach to the heart of the matter. The real explanation is that ancient atomism and modern atomism are just too dissimilar for the one to have emerged from the other. This is concealed by an accident of cultural history: the nineteenth century was the great age of the Greek revival, and this had its impact on the sciences, not in their content—they had moved on too far for that—but in terminology. That is why we use words like "cathode", "adiabatic" and "isomerism"—in contrast with the barbarous late twentieth-century vocabulary of gluons and quarks. It is, however, only the *words* that are Greek. Modern atoms have no more in common with the ancient ἄτομοι than energy does with Aristotelian ἐνέργεια. Ancient atomism was scientifically sterile, and would have remained so whatever the organization and ethos of the atomist schools. It is therefore not very surprising that most scientists in the ancient world avoided it, and it is not surprising at all that no results of any scientific value were produced with its help. Atomism came into science during a period that coincides very nearly with the nineteenth century—beginning with Dalton's chemical atomism, subsequently incorporating the kinetic theory of Maxwell and Clausius, and the stereochemistry of Kekulé and van 't Hoff, and culminating with Rutherford and Bohr. The problems addressed by scientists such as these were utterly unlike any that had arisen in the ancient world, and it was inevitable that the atomic theory which finally emerged from their labours was quite different from any of its ancient predecessors.'

One difference between ancient and modern atomism appears reasonably uncontroversial. The allocation of properties to atoms in current physical theory derives ultimately from the interpretation of a great mass of experimental evidence obtained by the use of extremely complex and technologically sophisticated apparatus. In the ancient world nothing like this was available, and casual observation was incapable of supplying data relevant to the issue. The atoms postulated by Democritus and Epicurus were assigned their properties on the quite different ground of analogical extrapolation from macroscopic bodies, regulated by metaphysical debate.

The most obvious and most familiar difference between ancient and modern atoms is that the latter can be split, and indeed have a complex internal structure. Greek atoms were, by definition, uncuttable. This was fundamental—in the absence of any empirical evidence that could be brought to bear, most of the high-level debate for and against atomism concerned this issue. It is very significant that from the seventeenth century onwards this requirement first became marginalized and was then finally rejected altogether.

The problems of divisibility are extremely intricate and intellectually challenging, and as such have quite understandably attracted the attention of philosophers, ancient and modern.[30] Concentration on them can, however, lead one to overlook, or at least pay insufficient attention to, other properties of atoms which from the point of view of natural philosophy are more important.

In its original form, in Leucippus and Democritus, ancient atomism is a physics of the full and the empty, identified with being and not-being respectively; between the two there has necessarily to be a sharp boundary,[31] the extent and configuration of which determines both the identity of the atom and the manner of its interaction with other atoms. The simplicity of these explanatory principles is compensated for by the variety of atomic shapes postulated, the atoms being described as being unlimited in size and in number.[32] This can be taken as implying the existence of atoms of every possible size and shape; whether or not Democritus drew any such conclusion (which is uncertain), there is no doubt that he postulated the existence of a wide variety of atomic shapes.[33] It is also clear that Leucippus' cosmogony, with its description of a membrane forming round each newly arising world,[34] required the existence of atoms capable of becoming entangled with one another, and therefore that atoms with hooks and

[30] M. J. White, *The Continuous and the Discrete: Ancient Physical Theories from a Contemporary Perspective* (Oxford, 1992), contains a good account of earlier contributions. See also Hussey's paper in this volume, § 4.

[31] Strictly speaking, this only follows if one supposes an infinitely divisible space, as in classical Greek geometry. If there are minimal parts of space—indivisible lines—and if the atoms either correspond to such parts or contain subunits that do (as in Epicurus), then the boundary between an atom and the adjacent void would have to be conceived differently, though exactly how is not easy to see.   [32] Diog. Laert. 9. 44 = 68 A 1 DK.

[33] 68 A 37 DK. Theophrastus describes Democritus' use of variously shaped atoms in explaining the tastes of different bodies: *Caus. pl.* 6. 1. 6 = 68 A 129 DK; *Sens.* 66 = 68 A 135 DK.

[34] Diog. Laert. 9. 30–1 = 67 A 1 DK; cf. 67 A 23.

branches were already present in the earliest form of the theory. In Epicureanism the main features of the earlier tradition are retained, though the number of atomic shapes is merely unimaginably great, and the existence of very large atoms is explicitly denied.[35] Atoms retain, however, a great variety of possible shapes.[36]

This entire way of looking at things has now been abandoned. The atoms of modern chemical theory are not differentiated by shape and only rather imprecisely by size, and explanations of how they interact are given in quite different terms.[37] Notions of size and shape are more applicable to molecules, but only because nuclei have a small size and (on the atomic scale) a definite position. Nuclei, however, take no part in chemical reactions, and information about their spatial configurations tells one little about chemical behaviour, especially in simple molecules. If one is told only that a triatomic molecule is linear, with bond lengths of 1.09 and 1.16 ångstrom, no one is going to be able to deduce very much about what it is or what it does.[38]

This characteristic of ancient atomism, in which the identity and hence behaviour of atoms is determined by the configuration of the boundary between the full and the empty, seems to me a far more severe limitation on the scientific potential of the theory than all the problems about infinite divisibility. The latter, like the problem of the ontological status of empty space, could be sidelined—i.e. left to mathematicians and philosophers to worry about.[39] The former could not. It is not just that no one had any grounds (beyond the most childish analogies)[40] for supposing that the atoms had one shape rather than another, and no means whatever for testing any guesses that might be made, though both these things were true. Defects such as these could in principle be rectified, by advances either in theory or in instrumental design. The trouble is much deeper: *no* hypotheses about atomic shapes and sizes could ever be really successful because atoms simply do not have sizes and shapes of the kind supposed.

V

We have therefore two very different (though entirely compatible) explanations for the scientific sterility of ancient atomism, one in terms of the

[35] *Ep. Hdt.* 55–6 = L&S 12A.

[36] Sharp edges, Lucr. 2. 463; other protruding edges, 2. 428; branches, 2. 446; hooks, 2. 395, 405.

[37] At a first semi-pictorial approximation, in terms of electron-shell structure.

[38] The molecule in question is hydrogen cyanide, HCN.

[39] This is not to say that such a sidelining was an obvious—or even a possible—move for ancient philosophers to make, since it presupposes not merely a distinction between mathematics and physics, but an understanding of the latter as an empirical discipline, quite separate from the a priori enquiries proper to mathematics. The point is well made in White (n. 30), 195.

[40] Lucr. 2. 398–425; 4. 658–62.

institutional characteristics of the Epicurean school, the other in terms of the intrinsic limitations of full-and-empty configurational atomism.[41] Both seem to me to contain a great deal of truth, but even when taken together they leave much more to be said.

I propose, therefore, to have a look at atomism during the third of its periods of success: the age of the Scientific Revolution. Rutherford's atoms may not have been at all like Epicurus', but Newton's were,[42] and he was by no means alone in this. On the other hand, the physical system with which Newton's atomism was associated was utterly unlike anything that Epicurus could have imagined or indeed would have welcomed.

The historical significance of seventeenth-century atomism is itself controversial: there is no doubt that Newton and many of his contemporaries were atomists, but it is less clear what role their atomism played in their scientific activity. The 'solid, massy, hard, impenetrable, movable particles' described in Query 31 of the *Opticks* play no part in the rational mechanics of the *Principia* or indeed in the main part of the *Opticks* itself. Galileo's atomism contributed nothing to his work on falling bodies; Huygens's none to his study of double refraction.[43] Does this mean that atomism was irrelevant to the scientific revolution—at best a free-rider, at worst an encumbrance that scientists picked up (because it was fashionable) but did not actually use (because there was no way that they could)? And if it does not, and atomism really did have a more positive role in the science of the seventeenth century, what was it?

There are (at least) two answers that can be given to this. They are not alternatives, and one can accept both, but the second seems to me to go much deeper than the first.

The first is that atomism (or more generally, corpuscularianism)[44] brings along with it the primary/secondary quality distinction—or to be more precise, the particular version of that distinction in which the primary qualities (or at least most of them) are *geometrical*: size, shape, position, and so on. This led to, or at any rate provided auxiliary support for, a

---

[41] By this I mean any theory that accounts for the differences between atoms in terms of the shape and extent of their boundary with the external void.

[42] Newton's atomic theory was actually less close to classical atomism than is often supposed. His atoms exert forces on one another, and it is by means of these, and not through their figured surfaces, that they interact. Newton himself continued to think of atoms having size and shape—though he had no time whatever for hooks and the like—but within his system these qualities are in fact entirely redundant, as Boscovich saw. The world-picture of the 18th-cent. Newtonians was of an almost entirely empty universe populated with extremely small atoms interacting with one another by means of unknown (though by no means unknowable) forces: see A. Thackray, *Atoms and Powers* (Cambridge, Mass., 1970), ch. 1.

[43] As Pierre Duhem was happy to point out, *The Aim and Structure of Physical Theory* (New York, 1954), 35. (Translation by P. P. Wiener of *La Théorie physique: Son object—sa structure* (Paris, 1914).) Duhem's own response was quite clear: atomism is not properly part of physical theory at all.   [44] On the meaning of this term see § VI below.

quantitative style of physics in which only what is measurable is regarded as real.

There is no doubt that this corpuscularian way of thinking did become increasingly widespread during the seventeenth century. Why it did so is a controversial issue, but it certainly was not through supplying detailed, well-corroborated explanations. All it could actually provide were on the one hand explanatory schemata, generic hand-waving sketches of a kind only too familiar to subsequent philosophers, and on the other hand the old Just So stories of sharp-edged acid particles and smooth globules of honey.

There is, however, another connection between atomism and the new science, of a very different kind. With hindsight, the two most serious internal weaknesses of Greek science can be seen as the failure[45] to adopt a heliocentric system of astronomy and the failure to develop any kind of inertial mechanics. There is of course a very important difference between the two. In antiquity heliocentrism was seen as a possibility: an outline at least was proposed by Aristarchus, and the idea was discussed and rejected (on quite cogent grounds) by Ptolemy. Inertial mechanics, as far as we know, was not proposed by anyone,[46] and it does not seem unreasonable to ask why it was not.

It is not hard to understand why the Aristotelian tradition failed to provide fertile soil for inertial mechanics.[47] Aristotle's physics is founded on a distinction between natural and unnatural motion, concepts which are at bottom quite incompatible[48] with any theory of inertia: motion in a void would be impossible because there would at the same time be no mover to cause the motion and no resistance to impede it.[49] Atomism, on the other hand, appears to *need* a concept of inertial motion in order to explain the inter-collisional movements of the atoms.

The central idea of inertial mechanics is that once in motion a body continues to move uniformly in a straight line until it is acted on by a force.

---

[45] The word 'failure' may raise hackles, at least among historians of science terrified by accusations of 'Whiggism', but its use (with due caution) seems to me justifiable. There is a radical difference between the history of science and the history of art, where it really would be absurd to ask why the Greeks failed to develop Gothic architecture.

[46] Richard Sorabji has remarked that the idea of inertia 'was no more than fleetingly glimpsed in antiquity' (*Matter, Space and Motion* (London, 1988), 282), but even this seems to go too far. The glimpses Sorabji mentions are in Epicurus and in Aristotle's attempted refutation of the vacuum in *Physics* 4.

[47] Aristotelian physics did of course give rise to the impetus theory, but even Philoponus' version of this is still quite far removed from true inertial mechanics, notably in his view that the time a body takes to travel from one point to another is the sum of the time needed to travel the distance and an extra delay incurred in overcoming the resistance of the medium: *In Phys.* 681. 30–682. 2 Vitelli (translated in D. Furley and C. Wildberg, *Philoponus:* Corollaries on Place and Void. *Simplicius:* Against Philoponus on the Eternity of the World (London, 1991), 57–8).

[48] This does not preclude intellectually unstable syntheses in which both approaches can be found, e.g. in Galileo.   [49] *Ph.* 4. 8, 215ᵃ1–216ᵃ26.

When—if at all—such motion occurs will depend on the physical system within which the law holds. In Newtonian physics, at least as applied to our world, it never strictly occurs, since no bodies are ever entirely isolated from all gravitational forces; situations in which it very nearly occurs are, however, quite common. In Cartesian physics it never occurs even approximately: bodies are at all times entirely surrounded by other bodies with which they are continuously interacting. In classical body-and-void atomism, on the other hand, inertial motion is the norm: atoms move uniformly through the void except during the infinitesimal intervals of time in which they are in collision with other atoms.[50]

Atomism and inertial mechanics fit neatly together,[51] but the link between them is not one of deductive implication in either direction. One can be an inertialist while being a plenist, as Descartes was, though any attempt to combine the two brings in a large number of extremely intractable problems. One can also be an atomist without being an inertialist.

One reason why there is no concept of inertia in Epicurus emerges if we look at the details of his physics. Unlike Newtonian atoms, which have mass, Epicurean atoms have *weight*—a natural movement downwards through an infinite anisotropic space. This movement is uniform (i.e. unaccelerated), and does not depend on the weight of the atom; were it not for an inherent tendency of the atoms to swerve off line, all that would exist would be a uniform rain of downwardly moving atoms, and no worlds would form.[52]

The effect of each collision is to generate more collisions (rather like a motorway pile-up propagating *ad infinitum*), but this does not cause the atoms to slow down or speed up.[53] Each retains its original speed, which is far

---

[50] Giving a detailed account of the forces involved in collisions between non-deformable bodies is of course not at all straightforward: such bodies must undergo discontinuous changes of velocity, and hence according to Newton's second law be acted on by infinite forces.

[51] The important component of atomism in this connection is of course the doctrine of the void, not the indivisibility of bodies; this goes some way towards explaining why requirements of indivisibility were downplayed in the 17th cent., except among the opponents of atomism. Whatever part Eleatic arguments may have had in the genesis of atomism, they had ceased to concern Newton and his contemporaries, though as Margaret Osler has pointed out to me, they were of concern to Gassendi.

[52] The interpretation of the swerve is a complex issue. The traditional view was that atoms underwent an alteration in their direction of motion, but several modern scholars have suggested that the atoms merely move one spatial minimum to one side and then continue in the same direction as before (W. G. Englert, *Epicurus on the Swerve and Voluntary Action* (Atlanta, 1987), 16–26; P. J. Bicknell, 'Why Atoms had to Swerve: An Exploration in Epicurean Physics', *PBACAP* 4 (1990), 241–76). One problem with this new interpretation is that it makes it very difficult to understand how sustained sideways movement could originate from collisions: if there are no (parts of) atoms in the spatial minima immediately adjacent to the relevant side of the atom that is about to swerve, then the swerving atom will merely move across and the downwards motion continue. If some or all of these minima are occupied then there seem to be two possibilities: either the atom that was to swerve fails to do so because it lacks the power to push its neighbour out of the way, or else the second atom also moves one step to the side; in either case the downward motion then resumes. Nothing capable of generating sustained oblique motion seems to be present in this account.   [53] *Ep. Hdt.* 62 = L&S 11E.

greater than anything we can observe. The aggregates that form perceptible bodies move more slowly because their component atoms are heading in different directions and endlessly rebounding from one another.

Obviously there are parallels between this and a modern kinetic theory of matter, but the differences are at least as significant. There is, for example, nothing resembling the Maxwell–Boltzmann distribution of the velocities of molecules in an ideal gas: all Epicurus' atoms move at the same speed, irrespective of the temperature of the body, and thermal phenomena are explained by distinct atoms of heat and cold.[54]

It is therefore clear why atomism in its Epicurean variety did nothing to encourage any sustained investigation of the mechanics of collisions. All the atoms move at the same speed both before and after impact, and the problem that proved so fruitful in seventeenth-century mechanics from Descartes onwards—given the magnitudes of the bodies and their initial velocities, what are their final velocities?—could not even arise.

There is also another respect in which Epicurean physics resisted quantification. The speed of the atoms is not merely very large; it is in some sense *unthinkably* large. As Epicurus put it, a freely moving atom covers every comprehensible ($\pi\epsilon\rho\iota\lambda\eta\pi\tau\acute{o}\nu$) distance in an inconceivable ($\mathring{a}\pi\epsilon\rho\iota\nu o\acute{\eta}\tau\dot\omega$) time.[55] The precise meaning of this is by no means clear,[56] but it would appear that if unhindered by collisions an atom would cross any distance that we might specify in an inconceivably short time.[57] The same is true of the $\epsilon\ddot{\iota}\delta\omega\lambda a$ which form the immediate objects of sight. Though composite, they are far finer than ordinary bodies, and so experience few collisions as they move through space; moreover, unlike the atoms in such bodies, their atoms all move together. It is because they travel so rapidly that we are able to see distant objects at once: the $\epsilon\ddot{\iota}\delta\omega\lambda a$ move 'as quick as thought',[58] or in Lucretius' scarcely more precise phrase, with the highest kind of speed, *summe celeri ratione*.[59]

VI

There are other more general reasons why ancient atomism failed to encourage any kind of inertial mechanics. In the seventeenth century mechanics achieved the position, which it had quite emphatically not held before but which it has retained ever since, of being the central discipline within physics. The explanation of this is complex, but one important part

---

[54] Epicur. fr. 20. 3 =Plut. *Adv. Colotem* 1110 B.   [55] *Ep. Hdt.* 46 =L&S 11D.

[56] In *Ep. Hdt.* 42 =L&S 12D the number of atomic shapes is described as $\mathring{a}\pi\epsilon\rho\iota\lambda\eta\pi\tau o\acute{\iota}$, rather than simply infinite; the meaning is clearly 'ungraspably large'.

[57] 'Immemorabile per spatium transcurrere posse | temporis in puncto': Lucr. 4. 192–3.

[58] $\ddot{a}\mu a\ \nu o\acute{\eta}\mu a\tau\iota$, *Ep. Hdt.* 61 =L&S 11Ed; cf. 48 =L&S 15A, where the same phrase is used for the speed of the $\epsilon\ddot{\iota}\delta\omega\lambda a$.   [59] 4. 254. cf. *Ep. Hdt.* 47 =L&S 15A.

is a change in world-picture: mechanics became central because natural philosophers were becoming increasingly inclined to picture the world as a *machine*.

In order to understand the connections between atomism and the mechanization of the world-picture, it is useful to make a distinction between *corpuscularianism* and the *mechanical philosophy*. Seventeenth-century writers frequently treated these terms as equivalent—Boyle, for example, often hopped from one to the other in the same sentence[60]—but a distinction needs to be made, and it seems only appropriate to use the available terminology to register it. Corpuscularianism[61] is (very roughly) atomism minus all the problems arising from infinite divisibility. The bodies that we see and touch are aggregates of immense numbers of much smaller bodies (*corpuscula*), and the qualities that we observe arise from the size, shape, and mutual arrangement of these imperceptible parts. This view of the world can be found in a great number of seventeenth-century writers; its most indefatigable advocate was Robert Boyle, though the most familiar source to philosophers is probably Locke's *Essay*. As I have described it, it contains nothing that was not present in Lucretius, though there are important differences of emphasis, notably in the much greater role given to structure in the later period.

Atomists in the seventeenth century were automatically corpuscularians, but the reverse implication does not hold. Descartes was quite vehemently opposed to atomism, on strictly *a priori* grounds, but his physics was entirely corpuscularian in character:[62] the corpuscles move through a sea of subtle matter rather than through a void, but otherwise the pattern of explanation is the same. We meet the usual cast: globules, particles with sharp edges, hooks, branches, and so on; one newcomer is provided by the screw-shaped particles that explain magnetic attraction.[63]

The most original element in Descartes's physics had, however, an origin quite independent of ancient atomism. Mechanism has been defined in a great variety of ways, but about the best short definition I know comes from Michael Ayers: mechanism 'can provisionally and roughly be defined as the view that the perceptible functioning of machinery provides an overt illustration of the intelligible principles which covertly govern nature as a whole'.[64] The great merit of this definition is that it makes the connection

---

[60] *About the Excellency and Grounds of the Mechanical Hypothesis* (1674), in *Works* (London, 1772), iv. 68–78.

[61] The term was deliberately introduced by Boyle as one that could be used by both atomists and Cartesians: *The Origin of Forms and Qualities* (1666), *Works* (n. 60), iii. 5.

[62] One possible explanation for this is that Descartes's approach to physics was formed by his early association (1618–19) with the atomist Isaac Beeckman, long before he formulated the metaphysical doctrines that ruled out the possibility of a vacuum: see D. Garber, *Descartes' Metaphysical Physics* (Chicago, 1992), 121.

[63] Descartes, *Principia Philosophiae*, 4. 146 ff.   [64] *Locke* (London, 1991), ii. 135.

between mechanism and machinery explicit. Mechanism has often been defined in ways that do not do this,[65] and thereby allow it to be projected back onto Democritus or Epicurus, but such definitions conceal rather than bring out the difference between ancient and early modern physics.

If these definitions are accepted, one thing at least becomes clear: corpuscularianism was a classical revival, whereas mechanism was not. Anyone familiar with the natural philosophy of the seventeenth century who looks back at the admittedly much scantier material surviving from the ancient world is likely to be struck by the contrast between the prevalence of mechanical imagery in the later period, and its near total absence in the earlier.[66] Part of the explanation is no doubt that the ancient world was a much less machine-filled place than late medieval or early modern Europe. Another is that the ancient conception of a machine was significantly different from the early modern conception. A machine, according to Vitruvius, is 'a continuous material system having a special fitness for the moving of weights'; as such it differs from a tool or instrument primarily by requiring the effort of many workmen rather than one.[67] Such machines are essentially *mechanical amplifiers* like the pulley and the lever: devices for magnifying forces, not self-regulating automata[68] like the great clocks which had so profound an effect on the seventeenth-century imagination.

Factors such as these are surely important, but I doubt whether they were decisive: world-pictures are never merely reflections of contemporary technology. Both the Epicureans and their opponents had good—though very different—reasons not to think of nature as a machine of any kind. Within the Aristotelian tradition mechanics was seen as being concerned with movements that occur contrary to nature, as the author of the *Mechanica* makes clear;[69] it therefore has no role in explaining the natural motions which constitute the subject-matter of physics. Among both Platonists and Stoics a rather different set of considerations seem to have been most important. Machines lack souls, and were for that reason seen as being inferior to entities that do possess them. The cosmos had therefore to be a ζῷον—a living being endowed with soul and perception. The argument appears in its simplest and least adorned form in Diogenes Laertius' account of Zeno: ζῷον is better than not-ζῷον, nothing is better than the cosmos, therefore the

---

[65] e.g. '*Mechanism* . . . is a thesis about the nature of physical agency: it claims in effect that no body is ever moved except by an external impulse from another, moving body': A. Pyle, *Atomism and its Critics* (Bristol, 1995), p. xi.

[66] Lucretius did use the phrase *machina mundi* once (5. 96), and similar phrases can be found in Lucan, Manilius and Statius: see C. Bailey, *Titi Lucretii Cari De Rerum Natura Libri Sex* (Oxford, 1947), iii. 1335–6.   [67] Vitr. 10. 1. 1, 3.

[68] The devices described as automata by Hero (*Pneum.* 28–30, 49, 79) are not automata in the sense that mechanical clocks are; and the word is indeed used not for the mechanisms as a whole but rather for the parts of them that are constructed so as to resemble birds or other animals.   [69] *Mech.* 1, 847ª16–26.

cosmos is a ζῷον.[70] To think of the world as inanimate seemed to many philosophers not merely erroneous but also unpleasantly arrogant—Pascal's picture of man as a thinking reed, superior by virtue of his awareness to the universe that can so effortlessly crush him,[71] represents a distinctively modern religious sensibility.

The Epicureans had placed themselves outside this consensus, but they had reasons of their own for avoiding mechanism. Machines are most naturally understood as *artefacts*, their existence dependent on and testifying to the existence of an intelligent designer: it is no accident that Paley's physico-theological argument for the existence of God starts with a watch. This was hardly a direction in which the Epicureans wished to go. For Boyle and Newton one of the chief aims of natural philosophy was to provide testimony for the existence of a creator; to Epicurus and Lucretius its main purpose—far more important than predictive accuracy or anything like that—was to provide assurance that no such being exists. This is the very first principle that Lucretius lays down, one more fundamental even than the ontology of atoms and the void: nothing is made from nothing by any divinity whatsoever.[72]

VII

There are two ways in which atomism can have a role in science. One is by being incorporated into science as a scientific theory in the full sense. This has happened in the last two hundred years; it did not happen in the ancient world, and there is no reason to suppose that it was even a possibility. The other possible role of atomism is as a background philosophy of nature, providing a framework in which other scientific advances could be made. This was how it was used in the seventeenth century: atomism, in conjunction with the mechanical philosophy, provided a setting in which inertial mechanics could be developed. Here again there is nothing comparable in the ancient world. Many—though not all—of the components of the corpuscularian/mechanist world-picture were present in Greek thought, but their associations prevented them being combined together.[73] Atomism re-

[70] Diog. Laert. 7. 143.

[71] *Pensées*, 200 (B. Pascal, *Œuvres complètes*, ed. L. Lafuma (Paris, 1963), 528).

[72] 'Nullam rem a nilo gigni divinitus umquam': 1. 150. Cf. *Ep. Hdt.* 38, where the same principle is laid down without any mention of any divinity.

[73] In this connection it is worth mentioning the conclusion of Alexandre Koyré (*Metaphysics and Measurement* (London, 1968), 130) on Epicurus' most devoted 17th-cent. disciple: 'Gassendi tried to establish a system of physics that was still qualitative, basing it on the atomism of antiquity. By renewing, or resurrecting, the atomism of antiquity he was enabled to provide a philosophical basis, an ontological basis, for modern science which has united what he did not know how to unite, namely the atomism of Democritos with the mathematical outlook of Plato, introduced by the Galilean and Cartesian revolution. It was the union of

mained the property of a philosophical sect, isolated from the mainstream, its potential invisible to adherents and opponents alike.

these two streams that produced the Newtonian synthesis of mathematical physics.' In *From the Closed World to the Infinite Universe* (Baltimore, 1957), 278, Koyré saw the main weakness of the Epicurean tradition as lying in its 'extreme sensualism'.

11

Greek Mathematicians: A Group Picture

R. NETZ

As my starting-point for the study of Greek mathematics I take a recent book dealing with modern mathematics. I have in front of me Dauben's fascinating biography of Abraham Robinson,[1] and I turn to pages 142, 331, and 399. The first has a picture with the caption 'Faculty and staff, Royal College of Aeronautics, Cranfield', apparently taken in 1946. Thirty-eight men, mostly middle-aged, sit and stand in three rows; all wearing suits and ties. The second is captioned 'Robinson at the International Congress for Logic, Methodology, and Philosophy of Science, Jerusalem, 1964'. Forty-five men of greatly varying ages (some obviously students) sit and stand in about three or four rows—the arrangement is very informal, and best described as a huddling together rather than a strict arrangement by rows, with the first 'row', in fact, sitting on the floor, Bedouin-style. This does not appear incongruous, since the dress is very informal as well: there are no suits, a single tie, and a variety of shirts, more or less unbuttoned . (Besides the obvious implications for social *mores*, this picture seems to have been taken at the height of an Israeli summer.) The final picture is 'Participants at the UCLA Summer Institute on Axiomatic Set Theory, July 1967'. Eighty-three persons stand in four rows—'persons', for the first time: there are now at least three women in the group. The uniformity is broken ethnically, as well: by contrast with the first two pictures, a considerable minority here do not seem to be of European descent. Dress is as informal and varied as in the second picture (six suits, five ties; and I think I see a clerical collar, and a Scottish kilt—not on the same person—but I admit I might be dreaming both). In short, the three pictures, however unrepresentative and heterogeneous, seem to have a clear moral in terms of the social history of twentieth-century mathematics.

This paper is a close relative—no more—of R. Netz, *The Shaping of Deduction in Greek Mathematics* (Cambridge, 1999), 271–312. I have benefited from the comments of many people but I wish to thank in particular R. Duncan-Jones, R. Sharples, and especially S. Cuomo—none of whom bears any responsibility for the mistakes contained herein or for the views offered.

[1] J. W. Dauben, *Abraham Robinson: The Creation of Nonstandard Analysis. A Personal and Mathematical Odyssey* (Princeton, 1995). Robinson (1918–74) had a rich and variegated mathematical career, and he is chiefly remembered as the author of nonstandard analysis.

If only we could do the same for the Greeks! This is my ambition: to try to think who the Greek mathematicians were—to try to take a group picture. This paper describes and discusses an imaginary picture of this sort, taken at a conference of ancient Greek mathematicians—a conference held in heaven, so that everyone is present, from classical times down to late antiquity. Of course, we shall have to make up our minds who is to receive invitations: the definition of a mathematician is a problem to which I shall return later. To make a start, I shall say that a mathematician is anyone who has written down an original mathematical demonstration, no matter in what context: what he or she may have done besides writing down mathematical demonstrations is a separate issue. Here, then, is the imaginary picture, and I move on to its description.[2]

To begin with, I have used the expression 'he or she' when referring to Greek mathematicians. Do we actually see any female faces in the group? Surprisingly, perhaps, we do. Of course, there is Hypatia, the well-known mathematician and philosopher of the fifth century AD from Alexandria.[3] But, about a century earlier in the same city, we hear from Pappus about another female mathematician,[4] Pandrosion. Pappus is very critical towards her, but then he is just as critical towards Apollonius and indeed towards almost everyone except (to a large extent) Euclid and Archimedes.[5] So there are two well-documented women in our group, which is not a little given the obvious obstacles in the way of women in antiquity. It is probably relevant that both examples are from late Alexandria, a place and a time where many old barriers were brought down,[6] but in general ancient women did not live strictly according to the expectation of either classical society or modern scholarship, and they were not always 'silent': for instance, there are twenty-nine women poets known from antiquity, important qualitatively and not only quantitatively.[7] But there were, of course, many more poets than mathematicians: I shall return to such numbers below.

An issue comparable to that of gender is that of age. How old are the faces

---

[2] For a 'catalogue' of ancient mathematicians see R. Netz, 'Classical Mathematics in the Classical Mediterranean', *Mediterranean Historical Review*, 12 (1997), 1–24. My criteria for identifying mathematicians are quite different from those used by S. Cuomo, *Pappus of Alexandria and the Mathematics of Late Antiquity* (Cambridge, 2000), 9–56, when discussing the place (even 'public profile': 56) of mathematics and mathematicians in late antiquity.

[3] See M. Dzielska, *Hypatia of Alexandria* (diss. Cambridge, Mass., 1995).

[4] Papp. *Coll.* 3. 1, 30. 2.

[5] On Pappus' polemical attitude towards contemporary and earlier mathematicians, see now Cuomo (n. 2), esp. 55, 71, 73–4, 84, 86, 89–90, 108, 128–34, 186–7, 194–9.

[6] P. Brown, *The Body and Society* (New York, 1988), 145 ff.

[7] Quality is important, historically, because it ensures visibility: in the group picture, as it were, it is important to stand in the first row. Sappho—simply one of the greatest poets of all time—could serve as a model for later poets, both female and male. See J. Balmer, *Classical Women Poets* (Newcastle upon Tyne, 1996), for an informal introduction to ancient female poetry, with translations. Among the scholarly studies, I mention J. M. Snyder, *The Woman and the Lyre: Women Writers in Classical Greece and Rome* (Bristol, 1989).

we see? Here, of course, the evidence is even thinner, but some remarks can be made. First of all, to speak in very general terms, Greek culture tended to appreciate old age more, and young age less, than at least some strands of contemporary culture.[8] Against this background, the small evidence there is for mathematical achievement in youth becomes more noteworthy. Theaetetus, of course, is relevant. He appears first in the Platonic dialogue called after him as a mere boy who already proved a certain result (143 E, 147 E–148 A), and in later dialogues he is a vividly characterized figure, the bright youth, a charming contrast to the *gravitas* of the Stranger from Elea in the *Sophist* and the *Statesman*. He becomes the embodiment of young brilliance. A literary topos is thus struck, and in the pseudo-Platonic *Amatores* boys discuss mathematics (132 A–B). This popular image exists independently of Plato. Isocrates associates an interest in mathematics with young age.[9] Aristotle explicitly asserts that the young fare better at mathematics (*Nicomachean Ethics* 6. 8. 5–6, 1142^a3–21).

Popular impressions aside, at what age did mathematicians produce their works? Very little is known for certain, of course. Pythocles, known to us especially from the letter Epicurus sent to him, was known in antiquity for his achievements when not yet 18, and he studied especially mathematics (or astronomy—to the extent that a distinction between the two can be made).[10] The known astronomical observations of the great Hipparchus date from 161 to 126 BC. This makes at least thirty-five years of activity, probably considerably more. So how young was he when he started?[11] Or another example: Diogenes Laertius gives the age of death for many of his subjects. The youngest is Eudoxus, who died aged 52; is this young, given his achievement?[12] On the other hand, we now know that Apollonius must have been quite old when producing the *Conics*; but this is just the tip of his mathematical iceberg.[13] Also, when we look at other sets of dated obser-

---

[8] M. Kleijwegt, *Ancient Youth* (Amsterdam, 1991), argues for the absence of adolescence culture in the ancient world. Less controversially, he points out the value of adulthood in antiquity (e.g. 58 ff., 188 ff.).

[9] 15. 261 ff., where, unfortunately, the issue is complicated by the conjunction of mathematics with philosophy. See also Isoc. 11. 23; 12. 26–7; Plut. *Mor.* 43 A–B, 52 C. The alleged attraction of the young to mathematics has recently been discussed by R. Wallace, 'What was Greek about Greek Mathematics?', *SCI* 15 (1996), 82–9 at 87–8.

[10] Phld. *De morte* (P. Herc. 1050) XII. 30–1; Plut. *Mor.* 1124 C=Epicur. fr. 118. In Epicurus' view 'Pythocles was a sort of Alcibiades' (Alciphr. *Epist.* 2. 3 =Epicur. fr. 162), the model of precocious *jeunesse dorée*. See also Epicur. fr. 81; and D. N. Sedley, 'Epicurus and the Mathematicians of Cyzicus', *Cronache ercolanesi*, 6 (1976), 23–54 at 43–6.

[11] In general for observations known through the *Almagest*, see O. Pedersen, *A Survey of the Almagest* (Odense, 1974), appendix A.

[12] Eudoxus' chronology is, however, very difficult: P. Merlan, *Studies in Epicurus and Aristotle* (Wiesbaden, 1960), 98–104; H. J. Waschkies, *Von Eudoxus zu Aristoteles: Das Fortwirken der Eudoxischen Proportionentheorie in der Aristotelischen Lehre vom Kontinuum* (Amsterdam, 1977), 34–58, esp. 50.

[13] See P. M. Fraser, *Ptolemaic Alexandria* (Oxford, 1972), i. 415–16, or G. Toomer, 'Apollonius of Perga', *DSB* i (1970), 179–93.

vations, they give us much less than the thirty-five years for Hipparchus. The picture is not easy to read, and, it seems, not only because of our limited evidence: apparently there were no simple rules for age, no necessary 'burning out' at a certain age. Such 'burning out' is a modern myth: the ancient myth was different—Archimedes carried away from his diagram by a Roman soldier, at the age of 75.

This confrontation—between the Roman and the Greek—reminds us of another dimension, that of ethnicity. There is in fact a great divide between east and west: almost all our figures come from the eastern Mediterranean.[14] Are they all 'Greek'? The terms themselves are difficult to apply in the ancient world,[15] but it must be stressed immediately that not all ancient mathematicians were Greek—in some senses of the word. Dositheus, to whom Archimedes addressed his works, was probably Jewish.[16] Marinus, a Neoplatonist and a late commentator on Euclid's *Data,* was born a Samaritan.[17] Toomer discusses the possibility that Zenodorus, a mathematician from the early second century BC, may have been of Semitic origin, and notes that Basilides of Tyre, later in the same century, was probably another mathematician from that background.[18] None of these is from the first rank, but Pappus is the most important mathematician from late antiquity—and he may well have been Jewish.[19] The most important thing is not the evidence itself but the fact that the evidence for Marinus is exceptional (as a pagan philosopher, he chose to tell us about his religious progress): for Dositheus, Zenodorus, and Pappus the argument is based purely on their names. From the writings, ethnicity cannot be judged: perhaps this should make mathematics an ideal arena for cross-ethnic achievement? Once again, we see that the distinctions we impose are irrelevant: mathematics would cross the borders of ethnic identities, just as it crossed the borders of gender and age. (I shall go on using the term 'Greek mathematics', meaning 'mathematics written in Greek': just as we would use the term 'Arabic mathematics', later on, to describe mathematics written in Arabic by writers from similarly mixed ethnic backgrounds.)

[14] See Netz (n. 2) for a discussion of the geographical distribution of ancient mathematicians.
[15] F. G. B. Millar, *The Roman Near East, 31 BC–AD 337* (Cambridge, Mass., 1993), for instance, studies the notions of identity in a central period and area, concluding with the absence of clear-cut identities.
[16] R. Netz, 'The First Jewish Scientist?', *Scripta Classica Israelitica,* 17 (1998), 27–33.
[17] See O. Schissel von Fleschenburg, 'Marinos (1)', *RE* xiv (1930), 1759–67 at 1759.
[18] G. J. Toomer, 'The Mathematician Zenodorus', *GRBS* 13 (1972), 177–92. In the end he prefers to identify the mathematician Zenodorus with an Athenian (there is an inscription mentioning an Athenian Zenodorus), but the balance of evidence seems to me in favour of a Semitic Zenodorus.
[19] Jewish inscriptions from Graeco-Roman Egypt can be followed through W. Horbury and D. Noy, *Jewish Inscriptions of Graeco-Roman Egypt* (Cambridge, 1992). There we find several Pappi and related names (with differing spellings): one dedicates a synagogue, another dies at the age of 3 while his brother (sharing the same tomb, dead at the age of 4) was called 'Joseph'. Briefly, we see that among Egyptian Jews Pappus was a common name.

Another border, more difficult to cross, is that of class. Of course, precise definition is again difficult, but the question is clear: what sort of people were the Greek mathematicians? Were they involved in politics, for instance? Naturally, the evidence is skewed. Greek mathematicians would appear to us in fuller personal colours to the extent that they are exceptional, which in itself implies a high status. A few do, which is noteworthy. Archytas was the leading citizen of Tarentum, the most important Italian Greek city of his time.[20] Eudoxus may have been a (if not the) leading citizen at Cnidus.[21] Theaetetus' father was a well-reputed, and especially a very rich, citizen.[22] Meton may have been expected to furnish a trireme: an important citizen, therefore.[23] Hippias was a trusted ambassador of Elis, and also very rich (86 A1 DK). In the Hellenistic world and later, political roles are defined more often in relation to courts, and Eratosthenes, for instance, the Alexandrian librarian, should be thought of as an important courtier.[24] Vitruvius addressed Augustus;[25] Thrasyllus served Tiberius.[26] Philonides' role in the Seleucid court should be compared.[27] Finally, the earliest important Greek mathematician, Hippocrates of Chios, is said on the authority of Aristotle to have been foolish enough to lose a huge sum of money: a sign of some wealth.[28]

What about Archimedes? The greatest mathematician of antiquity merits a brief detour: he may also prove an exception to the evidence above. The literary evidence for Archimedes' social standing is contradictory,[29] and may not represent any specific knowledge on the part of the ancient authors. Neither Cicero (who makes him come from humble origins) nor Plutarch (who makes him a Syracusan aristocrat) is necessarily of any special value as a witness: they had his writings, just as we do. But perhaps both were right? His father may have been called Pheidias,[30] a suggestive name: the *Realencyclopädie* knows of five persons named 'Pheidias': the famous artist, his son, two other artists—and Archimedes' father. The published volumes of Fraser and Matthews' *Lexicon of Greek Personal Names* (i–iiiв) have between them 81 additional individuals, most of whom are too obscure to have anything like their occupation identified. One is a mercenary in Samos, another is a vice-headmaster in Teuthrone, another a *hieraulēs* (sacred flute-player) in Athens, a fourth a chorus-trainer again in Athens; there is also

---

[20] 47 A 1 DK.

[21] Diog. Laert. 8. 88, on the authority of Hermippus (1026 F 9): doubtful, therefore, but not inherently implausible.   [22] Pl. *Tht.* 144 c 5–8.

[23] N. Dunbar, *Aristophanes: Birds* (Oxford, 1995), 551; *APF* 391.

[24] See Fraser (n. 13), 322–3.   [25] See the introduction to book 1.

[26] Tac. *Ann.* 6. 20–1.   [27] See e.g. Fraser (n. 13), i. 416 and n. 322, ii. 602.

[28] The evidence is in 42 A 2 DK.

[29] See E. J. Dijksterhuis, *Archimedes* (Princeton, 1938), 10.

[30] *Aren.* 1. 3, p. 220. 21–2 Heiberg. This Pheidias is mentioned in the context of an astronomical hypothesis, and so he may be assumed to be, at least among other things, an astronomer.

a doctor from Rhodes, living in Athens, and a contractor in Delos:[31] a variety of individuals, but I find it striking that all are artisans. In a famous passage Plutarch noted that, however impressed by him, no aristocrat would wish to become like the banausic Pheidias:[32] and so, to the extent that Plutarch was representative, no such aristocrat would *call* his son 'Pheidias'. The name became marked—Pheidias after all was the most famous artist of antiquity. I know of a young man whose first name is 'Leon Battista Curbosiero' and, surprisingly enough, his father is an architect. (He himself is a mathematician.) A remarkable result, then: I do not know what was Archimedes' social standing, but I guess that his grandfather was an artisan, perhaps an artist. It must have been an extraordinary family: the artist, his son the astronomer, and the grandson Archimedes, the friend of King Gelon—but this becomes fictional biography and the hypothetical social mobility of this family is the exception, not the rule.

The truth is, of course, that ancient society was much more polarized than modern society is or at least used to be. It is doubtful whether the concept of a 'middle class' has much relevance for antiquity. The rich could be more or less rich, the poor could be more or less poor, but the rich were rich and the poor were poor.[33] Thus Greek mathematicians, by and large, should be assumed to have led a privileged life. However, money cannot buy you mathematics, and here is the one negative observation I wish to make on gender, age, ethnicity, and class. Greek mathematicians had many different faces, and there is no need to look far to explain this. Mathematics, perhaps more than other disciplines, calls for specialized cognitive skills. They may be culturally developed, but a residue remains, of highly variable individual capacities. It is such capacities and inclinations, not wealth, status, age, or gender, which determine whether an individual could become a mathematician. Of course upper-class male middle-aged Greeks would have more chance of having their talents developed, or of being exposed to mathematics at all (an important consideration to which I shall return later): but the force of 'mathematical skills' cannot be dismissed altogether—and it is an egalitarian force.

So this is my first observation, which is mainly negative: our picture contains all sorts of people. On the next point I intend to be much more positive. This is what I see as the most important question: not *whom* do we see in the group, but *how many* people we see there. I ask how many Greek mathematicians there were.

I have made a catalogue of known Greek mathematicians (cf. n. 2), which contains 144 individuals. Of course this is to some extent tentative, but I

[31] The references are, respectively, L. Robert, *Études épigraphiques et philologiques* (Paris, 1938), 114; *SEG* xxii. 304. 3; *SEG* xxviii. 170. 46; *SEG* xxvii. 19; *IG* ii². 483. 12–13, 22; *ID* 446 A 3. [32] *Per.* 2. 1.
[33] G. E. M. de Ste Croix, *The Class Struggle in Antiquity* (London, 1981), *passim*.

believe the number is representative. This is roughly the number of individuals about whom we have some scrap of evidence suggesting that they
were mathematicians. Of these, a large number are known through references, often very slight, from late antiquity. Pappus, Proclus, and Eutocius
each refer to about 30 individuals. Another 30 or so are preserved in the
manuscript tradition. These four sources, Pappus, Proclus, Eutocius, and
the manuscript tradition, can be conceived as four selections out of the unknown group of ancient mathematicians. The interesting fact is that these
four selections are quite similar. This offers a first ground for suspicion that
not many mathematicians were known at all, at least in late antiquity.

I pause to explain a methodological point. We are all used to the question
of the transmission of works in manuscripts, and we know that only a small
proportion of works survived from antiquity. But what I am concerned with
now is a very different question: the survival not of a *work*, but of a *name*. To
survive as a name, all you need is that your name will be mentioned in some
surviving manuscript. This is far easier than to have your *work* survive. To
have your *name* survive, all you need to do is to become parasitic, as it were,
upon some other person's work which did survive. And many 'hosts' were
not averse to such 'parasites'—on the contrary, throughout antiquity there
were always authors who were interested in mentioning names from the past.
So the names we hear about from an antiquarian-minded author form a large
proportion of the names *he* heard about and, to a lesser extent, of the names
he *could* hear about. And this can be checked: by comparing the names
mentioned by late commentators, it is possible to extrapolate a probable
number of names the late commentators could be aware of. When Proclus
writes a commentary and mentions some mathematical names, this is not
completely unlike choosing balls out of a box. If four different selections out
of a box are made, it is possible to make a guess at the total number of balls
in the box. This is based on an obvious, crude probabilistic method. And
the number reached in this way is consistently less than 300, even after we
add some natural modifications to the probabilistic model. So I believe the
number of mathematicians whose names were at all known in late antiquity
was not more than 300.[34] Extrapolating from this number, I guess that the
number of mathematicians throughout antiquity was around one thousand.

A. E. Housman estimated that literary critics are rarer than the appearance of Halley's comet.[35] The heavenly body set up to measure the appearances of Greek mathematicians is the sun. Year by year, the sun returned
and a mathematician was born. Of course, nothing as regular as this: but

[34] The data for this calculation are given in R. Netz, *The Shaping of Deduction in Greek
Mathematics* (Cambridge, 1999), 282 ff.

[35] Cambridge Inaugural Lecture (1911), repr. in C. Ricks (ed.), *A. E. Housman: Collected
Poems and Selected Prose* (Harmondsworth, 1988), 302. Orators, poets, sages, saints, and heroes,
by contrast, appear more frequently.

I believe that this is the right order of magnitude, and I now move on to discuss some evidence.

The essence of the probabilistic argument I mentioned above is the close prosopographic repetition between our various sources. No matter from which angle we look at Greek mathematics, we always see the same faces. The trouble with this sort of argument is that we do not actually get to look at Greek mathematics from radically different angles, if what we use is Pappus, Proclus, and Eutocius: the different commentators, to a certain extent, have similar interests, and it may be the similar interests (rather than the limited pool of names they could draw upon) which explain the similar sets of names they mention. It is thus vital to get a completely different hold, to try and view Greek mathematics from as independent a viewpoint as possible. To begin with, the perspective from which the mathematicians themselves viewed mathematics. Both Archimedes and Apollonius carry with them a group of mathematicians for whose existence they alone testify (at least as far as the literary evidence goes): Dositheus, Pheidias, and Zeuxippus in the case of Archimedes, and Attalus, Eudemus, Philonides, Thrasydaeus, and Naucrates in the case of Apollonius. These are contemporaries. As for predecessors, Apollonius refers to Euclid alone, Archimedes to Democritus, Eudoxus, Aristarchus, and (perhaps) Euclid. Furthermore, one of the contemporaries to whom Archimedes writes is Eratosthenes, who is well known as a mathematician from other sources, and another, Conon, is referred to by Apollonius as well. In other words: of the five contemporaries referred to by Archimedes, two are known independently. This is the heyday of Greek mathematics, a period where I am willing to imagine the birth of up to three mathematicians a year, i.e. the total number of active mathematicians might be as large as 100. The brief glance Apollonius and Archimedes afford us is not compatible with anything more than 100— in fact is hardly compatible even with 100 active mathematicians. When Archimedes first approaches Dositheus, following the death of Conon, a note of desperation is detectable—as if he cannot find anyone to whom he can communicate his results;[36] Apollonius, approaching Attalus in the introduction to book 4 of the *Conics*, is in a similar situation. No 'school of mathematics' is ever hinted at by the mathematicians themselves, and the death of a single person seriously affects the network. In the introduction to the *Method* Archimedes hoped that his method would be picked up by 'either present or future' investigators—a meaningful qualification.[37] And in the introduction to *Spiral Lines* he said that 'though many years have

---

[36] *Quadr.* 262. 2–8 Heiberg = 164. 3–9 Mugler: 'Archimedes to Dositheus greeting. When I heard that Conon, who was my friend in his life-time, was dead, but that you were acquainted with Conon and withal versed in geometry, while I grieved for the loss not only of a friend but of an admirable mathematician, I set myself the task of communicating to you, as I had intended to send to Conon' (trans. T. Heath).

[37] *Method* 430. 15–18 Heiberg = 84 Mugler.

elapsed . . . I do not find that any one of the problems has been stirred by a single person'.[38] That is, Archimedes complained that for many years he had not heard about a single person even *attempting* to answer the open problems he had announced to the world through Conon. No wonder he was so desperate following Conon's death.

Another set of evidence—another angle on the mathematical world—is offered by the documentary evidence from antiquity: inscriptions and papyri. This is especially valuable, since this is the closest we come anywhere in classical studies to a random sample. Of course, we no longer deal now with the size of the active community. The data reflect rather the passive audience—an important issue. We get a glimpse of the 'market': and it did not go for mathematics. The papyrological evidence for mathematics is almost non-existent. I ignore here metrology, astrology, cosmological astronomy, and very elementary arithmetic and measurements for schoolchildren. Beyond these, there is almost nothing. The few bits which do exist repeat on the whole material known from Euclid. It is symptomatic of the arbitrary, patchy nature of the mathematical papyri that the most extensive and serious piece of 'papyrus' mathematics is on a series of ostraka.[39] This is while the documentary evidence, both on papyri and on inscriptions, amply testifies to the existence of philosophers, not to mention grammarians, rhetoricians, and, of course, doctors. Very often (relatively speaking), such professions are mentioned in decrees, funerary stelae, and everyday correspondence.[40] On the other hand, the noun μαθηματικός occurs only once in the Duke papyrological collection. Invariably, the use of γεωμετρία and its cognate forms (of which there are over a thousand occurrences in papyri) refers to land measurement for tax purposes. This γεωμετρία is the equivalent of the Latin *agrimensura*, not a reference to the 'geometry' we know from the literary evidence.[41]

A similar comparison can be made through Diogenes Laertius' list, based on Demetrius, of persons having the same name. This list is obviously not a

---

[38] *Spir.* pref. (2. 18–21)=8 Mugler. (I use Heath's translation).

[39] For a full discussion of mathematical papyri see D. H. Fowler, *The Mathematics of Plato's Academy*, 2nd edn. (Oxford, 1999), § 6.2. (Users of the first edition of Fowler's work should note the addition of a new Euclid fragment in W. Brashear, 'Vier neue Texte zum antiken Bildungswesen', *Archiv für Papyrusforschung*, 40 (1994), 29–35.) There are six pieces of literary papyri relating to Euclidean material. Five of these, it should be pointed out, relate to book 1. I do not know of any other Euclidean-style mathematical papyri.

[40] I have made a CD-ROM survey of the following four sequences: ιατρ, φιλοσοφ, ρητωρ, γραμματικ, in the Attica inscriptions and in *P. Oxy.* I have ascertained that the usages are relevant. Attica: ιατρ—103, φιλοσοφ—35, ρητωρ—36, γραμματικ—8. *P. Oxy.*: ιατρ—67, φιλοσοφ—12, ρητωρ—10, γραμματικ—8. We already saw one of those doctors: the Pheidias from Rhodes, mentioned in a decree from 304/3. No decree ever mentions anyone as a mathematician. None of these two sources had any γεωμετρ, αστρονομ, or αστρολογ, and the single μαθημ in *P. Oxy.* (x. 1296. r. 6) is irrelevant.

[41] See Cuomo (n. 2), 16–25, 31, 38–40, on the different ancient meanings of γεωμετρία, and their relations to *agrimensura*.

random sample: it was edited with a view to intellectual pursuits. Of the 188 persons in the list, only three to five at most may be mathematicians, and one of these is known from elsewhere. Or the *Digest*: various exemptions from civic duties are accorded to doctors, rhetors, and grammarians. The numbers allowed for exemption are between 3 and 10, depending on the subject and the size of the city. The *Digest* goes on to explain that 'the number of philosophers has not been laid down, since there are so few philosophers':[42] The numbers in the *Digest* are minima, grudgingly allowed by a tax-hungry empire, and they give little indication of absolute numbers. However, a sense of the relative numbers is made clear, and is consistent with searches on the documentary material. Perhaps as much as half of the professional intellectuals are doctors, the rest being mainly teachers of skills related to language. Mathematicians are so few as to be unquantifiable.

Catalogues have been provided for other areas, similar to the one offered (tentatively) in the article cited in n. 2 (which gives the number of mathematicians as 144). Runia, for instance, reckons that there were 316 pagan writers of philosophy in antiquity.[43] Felix Jacoby's still unfinished *Fragmente der griechischen Historiker* catalogues all ancient Greek historians (again, roughly until the Christianization of the empire): Jacoby himself assembled 856 authors, his successors have already published fragments of a further 81, and the eventual total will be well over a thousand. So more than two philosophers for every mathematician, about ten historians for every mathematician. Add doctors and rhetors—probably the two largest groups—and we can say that no more than about 2 or 3 per cent at most of prose writers were mathematicians. But it must be realized that, where a group is small, the proportion of its membership represented by surviving references may be exaggerated because the few famous individuals form a larger proportion of the whole. So 2–3 per cent may well be an over-estimate and, at any rate, it is clear that it is somewhat misleading to say that 'the ratio of mathematics to philosophy in antiquity was 144:316'. Any acquaintance with the sources shows that the ratio was more heavily towards philosophy: people did not read mathematics that much, as I have already made clear when discussing papyrological evidence. (I shall return to this below.)

But first we must get a sense of the total size of the audience for high culture in antiquity. I am not an expert on demography—and this is an advantage which I shall now try to exploit. Professional demographers have

[42] 27. 1. 6. 7. For the significance of this evidence see R. Duncan-Jones, *Structure and Scale in the Roman Economy* (Cambridge, 1990), 161. I owe the reference to Dr Duncan-Jones. The *Digest* contains a fair amount of evidence about mathematicians in the broad sense (cf. n. 2), which is discussed in Cuomo (n. 2), 30–46.

[43] D. T. Runia, 'Aristotle and Theophrastus Conjoined in the Writings of Cicero', in W. F. Fortenbaugh and P. Steinmetz (eds.), *Cicero's Knowledge of the Peripatos* (New Brunswick, 1989), 23–38. The limitation to pagan writers means that e.g. both Socrates (who did not write) and Augustine (a Christian) are excluded.

a professional reputation to defend, and therefore tend to be cautious in their guesses. But what would be really useful is to have not a prudent guess, but a *precise* guess—a set of numbers. I begin from what still is—remarkably—the starting-point for all such discussions, namely K. J. Beloch, *Die Bevölkerung der griechisch-römischen Welt* (Leipzig, 1886). In that work Beloch estimated the number of inhabitants of the 'Greek east' (i.e. the eastern Mediterranean under Roman rule), at around the death of Augustus, at 28 million (p. 507). Of course not all of these were Greek, and some allowance must be made for this. It is true, as I have argued above, that persons who were ethnically non-Greek could participate in Greek culture, but they had to belong to Greek culture—to begin with, to be literate in Greek: and so the people we are looking for had to belong not only to the Greek geographical sphere, but also to the Greek *cultural* sphere, which must have been more limited. Not everywhere in the 'Greek east' was really Greek. Now I shall soon introduce further constraints, such as 'living in a city', and these to some extent would make the geographical sphere coincide more with the cultural sphere. To live in an eastern city would have been almost the same as being (at least potentially) exposed to Greek culture. But not completely: Greek culture stood in competition with other cultures in the eastern Mediterranean, and highly literate Jews in Palestine, for instance, would not necessarily be primarily literate in *Greek*.[44] Add this to the fact that the death of Augustus is a relatively high point in ancient Greek demography and that we are averaging over the classical, Hellenistic, and Roman eras (a period during which the eastern Mediterranean was *gradually* Hellenized) and I think it is, if anything, optimistic to estimate the population of the Greek cultural sphere at about 20 million persons. I shall use this convenient number.

Of course not everyone in this area was touched by Greek culture. A fair approximation is to assume that only city-dwellers could be touched by high culture: this is the most absolute border in an agrarian society. And the level of urbanization in an agrarian society, again, cannot be high. Fifteen per cent is relatively high, and 3 million city-dwellers in the Greek cultural area is a reasonable number. We know that there were no more than 900 cities in the entire area,[45] so we may assume—just to have a sense of the possibilities—that the five largest cities had between them a million people,[46] that the next hundred had between them another million (with

[44] Jewish Palestine was an extreme case of an inward-looking society (see e.g. M. Goodman, *The Ruling Class of Judaea* (Cambridge, 1987), esp. 97 ff.) but, in general, not all high culture in the eastern Mediterranean became identical with Hellenistic culture.

[45] A. H. M. Jones, *The Cities of the Eastern Roman Provinces* (Oxford, 1937), appendix IV, names 907 cities in a very inclusive list, covering several overlapping administrative surveys from late antiquity.

[46] Alexandria at its most populated was said to have 300,000 free inhabitants (R. Duncan-Jones, *The Economy of the Roman Empire* (Cambridge, 1974), 260–1), which makes its entire population something like half a million, comparable to the megalopoleis of early modern times such as Istanbul and Naples (F. Braudel, *The Mediterranean and the Mediterranean World in*

10,000 inhabitants per city, this would leave room for many respectable-sized cities, by ancient standards), and that the remaining cities, somewhat more than 500 in number, had between them the third million (giving rather fewer than 2,000 inhabitants per city—but the ancients would call a city something we would consider to be a large village).

Of these three million city-dwellers, half were female and nearly half were children: this is an iron certainty (a pre-modern society, with an average life expectancy at birth of 25 or less, can have only about half of its members adults). Again, these borders were not impossible to cross—some young people participated in high culture, and so did some women, but for our immediate statistical purposes this may safely be ignored. In other words, there were at any given point no more than about 850,000 adult males living in Greek cities.

Let us assume that 700,000 of them were free.[47] This then is an important number: it can be said to be the number of 'visible' persons in Greek antiquity. It is a maximum rather than an average: in classical times, for instance, Attica had no more than about 30,000 citizens[48]—and Attica was one of the most populated Greek areas, and certainly one with the highest 'visibility rate'. 'Visible' persons can be defined as the people of whom ancient literature speaks. They are not necessarily yet the people to whom ancient literature spoke. Many of those free urban males were illiterate, or only basically literate: artisans, mercenaries, small-time merchants. Now this is a pure guess, but I suggest that about 300,000 of those 700,000 free urban males were sufficiently literate to be able to read, say, a whole papyrus roll.

Not all of them would do so, at least not on a regular basis. We must still account for sheer philistinism. To be literate is not yet to be interested in written culture; to be able to read a papyrus roll is not yet to have an interest in looking for such rolls and in trying to understand their contents. This then is yet another guess, but again, if anything, an optimistic one: the 'Greek readership' in antiquity comprised no more than about 70,000 people.[49]

---

the *Age of Philip II* (London, 1972), 344 ff.); yet bear in mind that 300,000 is a suspiciously convenient number—and that clearly Alexandria was exceptionally populated (though in a later period it might have been equalled by Antioch and, later still, Constantinopole; while Rome was always a case apart).

[47] A conservative estimate of the number of slaves; see Duncan-Jones (n. 46), 273 (and ibid. 264 for the percentage of adults).

[48] M. H. Hansen, *Demography and Democracy: The Number of Athenian Citizens in the Fourth Century BC* (Herning, 1985), restates the case for the larger number, 30,000; smaller numbers are often preferred in the literature.

[49] Those 70,000 people may be thought of as 'people who did the equivalent of a modern A-level in Classical Greek'. It will be obvious that *England alone* has many more people answering to this description than Greek civilization ever had: we begin to have a sense of how much larger, numerically, modern cultures are.

Not all those readers were also authors (though the ratio of authors to readers must have been much higher than it is now). But it begins to look probable that there were no more than about 5,000 Greek authors active at any one time. Divide them by 20, say, to derive the number of Greek authors born every year, and you get 250. Most wrote poetry, among the dozens of prose writers only a minority were 'scientists'—one of whom, I argued above, was a mathematician.

The point of this somewhat cavalier exercise in numbers is to show that the 'thousand mathematicians in antiquity' hypothesis is compatible with what we know of ancient demography. But this is not just a matter of numbers. The deep historical factor behind the hypothetical numbers above is that traditional, agrarian societies put a double constraint on the size of the population participating in high culture. First, traditional agrarian economies, even in a very large (and fertile) cultural area, can support, at most, some tens of millions of people; second, since such societies are so economically polarized (and large-scale traditional agrarian societies have to be deeply polarized), most of this population is excluded from participation in high culture.[50] I gave the number of inhabitants of the Greek cultural area as 20 million, and the number of non-excluded persons as 300,000: in other words, a participation rate of 1.5 per cent. Modernity breaks both constraints, and contemporary western culture has at least about a billion people in its cultural sphere, of which some 10 per cent can be said to be at least potential participants. It is about *a thousand times* larger than Greek culture.

But I return to my main guess: there were about a thousand mathematicians in antiquity. With some difficulty, we can indeed fit them all in a single picture. I shall return below to the wider historical implications of this guess, but I now return to the picture itself. What more can we say about Greek mathematicians, as a group?

We move, as it were, from the picture to the CV. The question is: what did Greek mathematicians *do*? Were they full-time mathematicians or did they have other areas of interest? One is tempted to answer that surely Greek mathematicians were not full-time mathematicians. We have seen that they were not professional academics, and mathematics did not correspond to any clearly defined career, to a job. We now can see why—there were simply not enough mathematicians. The mathematician was not a member of a mathematical faculty, and hence, there being no faculty barriers, we should expect mathematicians to do much else besides mathematics. And clearly Greek intellectual life in general was not organized in compartmentalized,

---

[50] The high level of cultural exclusion in a traditional agrarian society does not derive from economic polarization alone. It is further exacerbated by the gender exclusion consequent on its traditional patterns of life as well as by its age exclusion: simply, the age distribution of contemporary Western society entails a much higher percentage of *adults*, compared to that of pre-modern societies.

neat faculties. Philosophers, from Empedocles down to Sextus Empiricus, claimed to heal, practised medicine in one way or another; the teaching of rhetoric was always indistinguishable from philosophy, or from grammar. And there is some evidence for similar overlaps with mathematics. Democritus, for instance, was one of the earliest mathematicians; but he did of course much else besides. Eudoxus is well known not only for his mathematics, but also for his views on pleasure and on chronology, to name just two subjects.[51] And other examples can be adduced.

However, this must be qualified. Against the background of the Greek tendency to transgress disciplinary borders, mathematics appears as a relatively well-defined discipline. Most typically, what mathematicians do outside mathematics is cosmology, i.e. astronomy in the non-mathematical sense: people like Oenopides, Hippocrates of Chios, Euctemon, Meton, and so on to Ptolemy and beyond. But this is a development of the interest in astronomy, which is never far from the centre of mathematical attention. And in general there are many people who seem to have been predominantly mathematicians—clearly figures such as Euclid, Archimedes, and Apollonius, and with some qualifications even Ptolemy. It is symptomatic that no good authority ever gives a mathematician as a physician. Mathematicians, on the whole, then, were just mathematicians.

Conversely, very few people who were not active mathematicians ever bothered with mathematics—a fact to which I have already alluded in the demographic discussion above. More than half of the occurrences of γεωμετρία and cognate words in the Greek corpus occur in Aristotle and his commentators, another fifth in Plato and his commentators. Otherwise mentions of geometry tend to occur as random examples, mere flukes. It is remarkable how little educated people in antiquity were aware of what may have been the most enduring intellectual development in their midst. Take, for example, Thucydides. He is unsurpassed in sheer intelligence, he is the Archimedes of history. His description of the plague shows him indebted to Hippocratic medicine. The Melian dialogue is an important text for understanding what is known as the sophistic movement. Yet when he comes to estimate the size of Sicily, he does so by giving an estimate related to its *circumference* (6. 1. 1)—not a silly thing to do, perhaps, but it shows that the author (and the audience) do not approach questions such as 'the size of Sicily' as questions of geometry;[52] and in general, there is no

---

[51] Pleasure: Arist. *Eth. Nic.* 1. 12. 5, 1101^{b}27–32; 10. 2. 1–2, 1172^{b}9–26. Chronology: Pliny, *HN* 30. 3.

[52] Fowler (n. 39), 281, notes a similar phenomenon in Hdt. 1. 170; 5. 106; 6. 2, where Sardinia is evidently treated as the largest island in the world because it has a larger *perimeter* than Sicily (cf. R. J. Rowlands, 'The Biggest Island in the World', *CW* 68 (1975), 438–9). The point at issue (that equal perimeters can enclose unequal areas) was liable to be neglected even in local land measurement: cf. Netz (n. 34), 300, and Dem. 42. 5, where the speaker assesses an estate by assigning it a 40-stade circumference, perhaps hoping to deceive the jury into

real hint in Thucydides' work that anything like mathematics was known
to him.

Polybius' case is much more interesting, and calls for a detailed study.
Look at how *he* approached the geography of Sicily:

τὸ δὲ σχῆμα τῆς Σικελίας ἐστὶ μὲν τρίγωνον, αἱ δὲ κορυφαὶ τῶν γωνιῶν ἑκάστης ἀκρωτη-
ρίων λαμβάνουσαι τάξεις.(1. 42. 3)

Sicily is triangular in shape, the vertices of all its angles being formed by capes.

This language is unmistakably geometrical, and Polybius may be used to
reveal what an educated Greek of his time, who *was* aware of mathematics,
would be aware of: not only because Polybius' writings show an awareness of several sciences, but mainly because he is deeply concerned with
methodological questions: *what makes a good general*, and *what makes a good
historian*? The two are interconnected, and Polybius asserts that generals
should write history and vice versa, idealizing 'historian-generals' on the
explicit model of Plato's 'philosopher-kings' (12. 28. 2–4). Now this is a
useful comparison from our point of view: Plato's philosopher-kings were
given an education with two components, of practical experience and of
theoretical studies, the theoretical studies predominating; and, within those
theoretical studies, mathematics was dominant. Both relations are reversed
by Polybius. The main theme of the methodological discussion in book 12
is the crucial role of personal experience, not just for becoming a general
(more on this later) but even for writing a history: a necessary condition for
a good writer on battles, say, is to have experienced battles (Timaeus, an
earlier historian, is being criticized). As for the role of mathematics within
the theoretical studies, we shall soon see that.

For clearly some theoretical study *is* necessary: book 34, for instance,
was a self-contained geographical survey, and to some extent Polybius'
approach to geography is theoretical (though he keeps mentioning the fact
that he has *personally travelled there*). Most notably, there is a geometrical
argument, where Polybius criticizes a measurement given by Dicaearchus.
(It is typical that these methodological discussions are driven by polemical
concerns.) Dicaearchus gave the distance from the straits of Messina to
the Pillars of Heracles (i.e. the length of the western Mediterranean) as
7,000 stades, which Polybius considers a gross underestimate. His method
is sound:[53]

thinking it bigger than it really was (G. E. M. de Ste Croix, 'The Estate of Phaenippus', in
E. Badian (ed.), *Ancient Society and Institutions* (Oxford, 1966), 109–14). But it seems to have
become a paradigmatic mathematical paradox: see Quint. 1. 10. 39–45 (something an orator
should be aware of); Papp. *Coll.* 5. 1, pp. 304. 1–308. 8 Hultsch (on honeycombs, from a book
aimed at quite a general audience: Cuomo (n. 2), 58); Procl. *In Eucl.* 403. 4–14 Friedlein (in a
context of public utility and ethical propriety: Cuomo (n. 2), 54).

[53] Polyb. 34. 6. 2–8. The passage derives from Strabo 2. 4, but it seems possible to reconstruct
Polybius' original argument as well as, to some extent, his original words. In general, much of

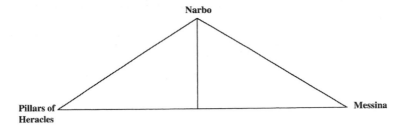

FIG. 11.1. Estimating the distance from Messina to the Pillars of Heracles

- Represent the western Mediterranean as a triangle, with the line from Messina to the Pillars of Heracles as its base and Narbo (at the mouth of the Rhone) its vertex (Figure 11.1).
- Estimate the distances Messina–Narbo and Narbo–Pillars at 11,200 and 8,000 stades respectively, these figures being in all probability based upon journey lengths.
- Drop a perpendicular from Narbo to the base of the triangle, and estimate its length as 3,000 stades (see below).
- Use Pythagoras' theorem to measure the two segments of the base— which turn out, of course, to be much greater than Dicaearchus' account suggests. Significantly, Polybius (who does not seem to have given an explicit calculation) is reported to have referred to this as 'the school-boy's measurement' (ἡ παιδικὴ μέτρησις).

So this is the 'elementary geometry' a historian requires: to be able to extrapolate geographical measurements on the basis of geometrical theorems. But notice the main mistake of Polybius' account. He estimates the length of the perpendicular by the length of travel by sea ('now the longest distance from Europe to Africa across the Tyrrhenian Sea is not more than 3,000 stades; across the Sardinian Sea it is somewhat shorter'),[54] but seems to have failed to understand that there is a theoretical distinction between measuring latitudinal and measuring longitudinal distances, viz. that with latitudinal (north–south) distances—and with them alone—it is possible to use astronomical data to calculate exact ratios between the separate distances. Thus the distance from Narbo to Africa is in principle the most secure piece of data available to Polybius in this measurement, yet he does not even mention astronomy and, in fact, this is the distance he gets most wrong. Bear in mind that in the second half of the second century BC all the foundations of Greek theoretical geography were already available. Polybius after all explicitly criticizes Eratosthenes, in the same book 34—and

Polybius' work survives as (usually long and apparently verbatim) excerpts taken out of context. Fortunately, excerptors were especially interested in Polybius' methodological observations.

[54] Polyb. 34. 6. 6. Here and below I follow the Loeb translation, with minor amendments.

Eratosthenes' estimate of the size of the earth assumes a mastery of the relations between astronomy and geography. Nothing of that is to be seen in Polybius, whose geography might as well have been that of a flat earth. His mathematics does not go beyond the 'schoolboy's measurement', Pythagoras' theorem—and the point of the 'schoolboy' is, of course, polemical: 'even a child knows *that*!'[55]

This impression is confirmed by examination of the second half of Polybius' methodological equation: what theoretical knowledge a *general* ought to have. This is discussed most explicitly in 9. 12–20. The superiority of personal experience over theoretical understanding is stressed once again (9. 14. 1–5), but experience itself requires some theoretical understanding (not too much, Polybius insists), in astronomy and geometry (9. 14. 6). Here are the things one needs to know:

Astronomy: the different length of days, in order (*a*) to estimate correctly the distance one may cover in a single day's march (9. 14. 6–15. 3) and (*b*) to know how to subdivide day and night (e.g. so that one can sound the reveille at the right time: 9. 15. 4–5). This is followed by good practical advice on how to estimate the subdivisions of the night, by observing the stars and the moon, and Polybius then gives several historical exempla of bad timing in warfare and its disastrous consequences.

Geometry: to know what length of ladder is required to scale a given wall (9. 19. 5–9). (More on this remarkable Polybian concern below.)

Geometry: to know how to enlarge camps in proportion to the number of soldiers (9. 20. 2–3). On this subject Polybius merely refers us to his work on tactics, which is unfortunately lost. But we did not lose too much: the discussion closes with Polybius insisting, once again, that he is against too much theoretical study—anything which goes beyond immediate practical application.

Let us instead concentrate on those ladders. A theoretical discussion of ladders was promised by Polybius earlier in the *History*, following a story about the Macedonian king, Philip:

[Philip], pushing on vigorously all night without stopping . . . arrived before Melitea at daybreak, and setting up his scaling-ladders, attempted to storm the town. He terrified the Meliteans so much by the suddenness and unexpectedness of the attack that he could easily have taken the town; but the attempt was foiled by the ladders being far too short for the purpose. (5. 97. 5–6)

Whereupon Polybius explodes, and the following chapter is a remarkable methodological outburst, insisting upon the importance of careful planning

[55] A more extreme claim than even e.g. Strabo 1. 3. 11 (the proposition that the surface of a liquid at rest is spherical, the sphere having the same centre as the earth, is 'known by all who have even touched mathematics').

and understanding on the part of generals. Ladders, in brief, are no trivial matter.

So here is how the length of ladders is to be calculated:

If any of our collaborators can give us the height of the wall the required length of the ladders is evident. For if the height of the wall be, let us say, ten of a given measure, the length of the ladders must be a good twelve. The distance from the wall at which the ladder is planted must be half the length of the ladder, for if they are placed further off they are apt to break when crowded and if set up nearer to the perpendicular are very insecure for the scalers. (9. 19. 6–7)

Polybius goes into some sort of 'theoretical discussion' concerning applied mechanics (anachronistically speaking) rather than mathematics. The mathematical element is the same application of Pythagoras' theorem we saw already, and *it is wrong*. Given the ratio 1:2 between the smaller side and hypotenuse, the ratio of the larger side to the hypotenuse is (in a modern notation) about 10:11.5, not Polybius' 10:'a good twelve'. Clearly what we have here is not a theoretical *derivation* of the right length of ladders, but a clumsy attempt to rationalize an established practice.

So there he is, the Greek intellectual from the second half of the second century BC, writing at the end of three great centuries of Greek mathematical expansion: well-read, universal in the scope of his historical interests—and a major source on Archimedes![56] He claims to have the right grasp of the theoretical knowledge required by a historian; insists that this is limited; and duly exhibits this limitation in his superficial grasp of mathematics, which does not go beyond a few technical terms and a knowledge of Pythagoras' theorem. It seems to me certain that Polybius never set eyes on the works of Archimedes or anything of that sort: perhaps he glanced at Euclid, but that too is doubtful. This then is the mathematical knowledge of the educated Greek of Polybius' time, and once again we see the *isolation* of Greek mathematicians. A function of the small number of mathematicians, to some extent. But in other ways, we can see that mathematics did not appeal to non-mathematicians. We are looking for 'popularized' mathematics—i.e. attempts to bring the contents of Archimedes and his like to the general public—and they are very rare, which is in itself significant. One example of the popularization of technical mathematics appears in a fragment of Eratosthenes preserved in Eutocius' commentary on Archimedes.[57]

This fragment is a letter sent by Eratosthenes to King Ptolemy III. It describes a mean-finding instrument produced by Eratosthenes, and it refers to a dedication Eratosthenes had set up with that instrument, describing the dedication and citing it in full. We thus have access to two

---

[56] 8. 3–7 reports his contribution to the defence of Syracuse against Marcellus' siege engines—on which see also Livy 24. 34. 1–16; Plut. *Marc.* 14–17.

[57] Eutoc. 88. 3–96. 27 Heiberg=64. 5–69. 11 Mugler. I follow W. Knorr, *Textual Studies in Ancient and Mediaeval Geometry* (Boston, 1989), in considering this fragment to be genuine.

acts of popularization of mathematics, one addressed to the king, the other addressed to the Alexandrian public. Both have this in common: that they inscribe the mathematical work into the Greek literary tradition. The letter to the king opens like this:[58]

Eratosthenes to King Ptolemy, greeting.

They say that one of the old tragic authors introduced Minos, building a tomb to Glaucus, and, upon hearing that it was a hundred feet long in every direction, saying:

> *You have mentioned a small precinct of the holy tomb;*
> *Let it be double, and, not losing this beauty,*
> *Quickly double each side of the tomb.*

. . .

And this was investigated by the geometers, too: in what way could one double the given solid, the solid remaining in its own shape, and they called this problem 'duplication of a cube'.

So this is how Eratosthenes introduces the mathematical problem of 'duplicating a cube', a problem which in turn gives rise to the need to find means. As for the public dedication, this consisted mainly of the following epigram:[59]

> If you plan, of a small cube, its double to fashion,
> Or—good sir—any solid to change to another
> In nature: it's yours. You can measure, as well:
> Be it byre, or corn-pit, or the space of a deep,
> Hollow well. As they run to converge, in between
> The two rulers—seize the means by their boundary-ends.
> Do not seek the impractical works of Archytas'
> Cylinders; nor the three conic-cutting Menaechmics;
> And not even that shape which is curved in the lines
> That Divine Eudoxus constructed.
> By these tablets, indeed, you may easily fashion—
> With a small base to start with—even thousands of means.
> O Ptolemy, happy! Father, as youthful as son:
> You have bestowed all that is dear to the Muses
> And to kings. In the future—O Zeus!—may *you* give him,
> From your hand, this, as well: a sceptre.
> May it all come to pass. And may he, who looks, say:
> 'Eratosthenes, of Cyrene, set up this dedication.'

I quote extensively because nothing briefer can convey the certain sense of absurdity in this mode of presentation of mathematics. Reflected in the mirror of the dominant Greek literary tradition, mathematics has a strange

---

[58] Eutoc. 88. 3–16 Heiberg = 64. 5–18 Mugler. This and the following translation are mine—not literal translations, as I find it important to stress the 'literary' character of this text.

[59] Eutoc. 96. 10–27 Heiberg = 68. 17–69. 11 Mugler.

face which we can hardly recognize. Mathematics did not lend itself to popularization, in the Greek context—that of a culture where the literary mode was much more important than the scientific mode.

Briefly, mathematics was not popular—and the main explanation for the unpopularity of mathematics is much more simple than the arguments delineated above. Mathematics is difficult. So is philosophy, no doubt, as so many other ancient disciplines, but mathematics has a major disadvantage peculiar to it, its all-or-nothing nature: the most rugged Roman general can spend time with Greek philosophers, apparently finding some satisfaction in his dim understanding of their utterances on Truth and the Good Life. But what satisfaction is there for him in Euclid? Only the frustration of the feelings of inferiority, so well known to anyone who has passed through our educational system. We invest enormous social and economic capital in forcing children against this obstacle, and still most fail to make it. Lacking these forces, the ancients did not try. Or, to be more precise: we all know the fate of books which suddenly become best-sellers, after being turned into a movie—in the version 'according to the film'. This originated in southern Italy in the late fifth century, but it was Plato who turned this, '*Mathematics: The Movie*', into a compelling vision. This vision remained to haunt Western culture, sending people back again and again to the '*book according to the film*'—the numerology associated with Neoplatonism. But, especially in the Aristotelian tradition, a few people went to the original, until, emerging from the last Platonic revival of the Renaissance, mathematics exploded in the sixteenth century and left Platonism behind it with the rest of philosophy and the humanities. We now take this centrality of mathematics for granted; we should not project it into the past.

I sum up my results. Greek mathematicians formed an inward-looking group. Relatively speaking, they were interested in their mathematics and not in much else beyond. They were few in number, a tiny group at the extreme fringe of the Gauss curve. This is why they were a motley group, why so little can be said to characterize them in general, but also why they must have been rich and influential citizens. If Greek mathematics involved few people, it means that the very access to mathematics was extremely complicated. How many ancient potential Newtons must have passed their lives unnoticed back on their Lincolnshire farm! Under normal conditions, papyrus is not an enduring material. For a work to survive, it must be copied almost every generation. If a city had only a single mathematician, his mathematics would die with him, and would have to be reimported from elsewhere to be born again. Such rebirths must have happened again and again. Continuities were the exception in Greek mathematics. We hear of a few people teaching others: Hippocrates of Chios taught a practically unknown Aeschylus, Theodorus taught Theaetetus (according to the Platonic dialogue of that name), Neoclides taught Leon, and Eudoxus taught

Menaechmus (whose brother was Dinostratus) and Helicon.[60] There are other names, sometimes just names: Oenopides, Andron and Zenodotus, Timocharis and Aristyllus.[61] And of course we know of Archimedes' father (above, p. 200). The lists never get beyond a single generation, and often not even that. For instance, we know that Arcesilaus and Philonides studied mathematics, but we also know that they did not become mathematicians. It should be borne in mind that traditions and transmissions are a literary topos in antiquity. Ancient histories of philosophy, such as that of Diogenes Laertius, are structured by genealogies: 'A taught B who taught C'. There is a great element of legend in this, of course. It is now understood, for instance, that the great schools of philosophy, such as the Academy, did not have the continuity ascribed to them by the ancients.[62] But this only serves to stress the relative absence of similar genealogies for mathematics: mathematicians did not belong to the 'schools', not even in the imagination of later commentators.

The best symbol is the list of astronomical observations mentioned in the *Almagest* (n. 11 above). It is a set composed of intermittent explosions. No site of observation was kept for more than a few consecutive decades. There is only one exception to this—the Babylonian set. Here we begin to see a meaningful pattern. Greek mathematics is not a guild, it is not like the Babylonian family-guild 'Scribes ENUMA ANU ENLIL'.[63] It is an enterprise pursued by *ad hoc* networks of amateurish autodidacts—networks for which the written form is essential; constantly emerging and disappearing, hardly ever obtaining any institutional foothold. So it is not just the accidental absence of ancient cameras which prevents us from having the ancient equivalents of the modern group pictures of faculties and conferences, mentioned at the beginning of this article. The Greek mathematicians did not have faculties and conferences, a fact reflected, as I have argued elsewhere, by their form of presentation and ultimately by the contents of their mathematics.[64]

---

[60] Arist. *Mete.* 1. 6, 343ª1; Pl. *Tht.* 145 C; Procl. *In Eucl.* 66. 18–67. 12 Friedlein, Pl. *Ep.* 360 C.

[61] Procl. *In Eucl.* 66. 2; 80. 15–20 Friedlein; Ptol. *Synt.* 7. 1, p. 3. 3–4 Heiberg; Plut. *Mor.* 402 F.

[62] See especially J. Glucker, *Antiochus and the Late Academy* (Göttingen, 1978).

[63] See O. Neugebauer, *Astronomical Cuneiform Texts* (London, 1955), i. 13 ff.

[64] This argument is pursued in Netz (n. 34).

12
Aristotle and Mathematics

EDWARD HUSSEY

1. How Mathematics Appears in Aristotle

ARISTOTLE's writings often make appeals to mathematics, in various ways and for various purposes.[1] Here is a first, approximate classification.

(1) *Incidental allusions and examples.* There are many passing allusions to axioms, theorems, and procedures of the mathematics of Aristotle's own time, used as analogies and illustrations. (One or two such—the incommensurability of the diagonal of the square with its side, the theorem that the angles of a triangle add up to two right angles—are among his stock examples.) They make it clear that Aristotle was just as interested as Plato was in what the mathematicians of his day were actually doing.

(2) *Mathematics as a paradigm of science.* In the *Analytics*, and particularly in *Posterior Analytics* 1, where Aristotle seeks to determine the explanatory structure of any possible science, mathematics is used systematically as a paradigm case. So we find, not just individual mathematical procedures and methods cited as illustrations, but a concern with, and discussion of, the overall logical and explanatory structure of mathematics.[2]

(3) *Philosophy of mathematics.* Aristotle's own philosophical views on the nature and foundations of mathematics, its objects and its truths, are stated at some points in the *Metaphysics* and *Physics*. So too are his views on how mathematics differs from, and how it is related to, other sciences and especially natural science. Unfortunately, his positive views are mostly given tersely and in passing, though there are extended critiques of rival (mostly Pythagorean and Platonist) views.[3]

(4) *Mathematics in natural science.* Finally, Aristotle *uses* mathematics

An early version of this paper was read to Pierre Pellegrin's seminar in Paris in May 1996. I am indebted to Pierre Pellegrin and Michel Crébullier, and to the other participants in that seminar, as well as to the audience at the Liverpool conference, for their courteous and considered critical comments. Thanks are due also to two anonymous referees for this volume, and to its editors, for their valuable remarks and suggestions.

[1] The pseudo-Aristotelian works *Mechanics*, *On Indivisible Lines*, and *Problems* (presumably later products of Aristotle's school) are not considered here. T. L. Heath, *Mathematics in Aristotle* (Oxford, 1949), gives many of Aristotle's mathematical passages in English translation, with commentary from the point of view of the historian of mathematics.

[2] Cf. Heath (n. 1), 37–75.

[3] Pythagorean and Platonist views of mathematics are discussed at *Metaph.* A 5, 987ᵃ9–21; A 8, 989ᵇ24–990ᵃ32; M 1–3 and 6–9; N 2–6.

in his natural science. Since our theme is *science*, this is the area I shall concentrate on. There are various ways in which, for Aristotle, mathematics enters into natural science, and once again it is useful to start by subdividing the field to be surveyed.

(*a*) In some places Aristotle claims to determine fundamental questions about the structure of the natural world by an appeal to mathematical truths, thereby implying a kind of subordination of physics to mathematics.

(*b*) Aristotle uses particular kinds of mathematicized science, in the study of particular physical phenomena: e.g. geometrical optics in the study of the rainbow. Here too he seemingly insists that, in these areas at least, physics is in some sense, and to some extent, subordinate to mathematics.

(*c*) Aristotle himself carries out mathematical investigations into questions which underlie whole fields of natural science. In particular, he *creates* mathematics (or at least makes an elsewhere unparalleled use of it) in his pioneering study of the structure of continua such as time-stretches, changes, spatial and other quantities. He simultaneously *uses* the results to determine the structure of the natural world.

Finally, (*d*) he formulates in mathematical terms general principles in which mathematical relationships (proportionalities) are said to hold between physical quantities involved in processes and states in the natural world.

It is this area that I shall explore. But something must be said first, as a foundation, about Aristotle's own substantive philosophy of mathematics.

2. Mathematics and the World of Experience

Everything rests on the original connection which Aristotle makes between mathematics and the world of experience. Unlike Plato, he takes mathematics to be, of its very nature, firmly and necessarily rooted in the world of ordinary experience. Mathematical objects and mathematical truths are seen as somehow in correspondence with objects in this world, and with truths about *them*. So the questions are: *how* do they correspond? and, with *which* objects and truths in the ordinary world?

On *how* they correspond, Aristotle says that to pass from the world to mathematics is to go through a process of 'abstraction'. We may sidestep the highly controversial question about the precise meaning of 'abstraction', since for the purposes of this survey it is not essential to decide it.[4]

On the question of *what* ordinary objects and truths mathematics cor-

---

[4] On mathematics as abstracting from the world: *Metaph.* M 3, 1077^{b}17–1078^{a}31; also *Ph.* 2. 2, 193^{b}22–194^{a}12; *De an.* 3. 4, 429^{b}18–22; 3. 7, 431^{b}12–19; *Metaph.* K 3, 1061^{a}28–^{b}7; on sciences generally as always presupposing experience and knowledge of the world, *An. pr.* 1. 30, 46^{a}17–22; *An. post.* 1. 1, 71^{a}1–17; 1. 10, 76^{a}31–6, ^{b}3–11, ^{b}18–19; 1. 18, 81^{a}38–^{b}9. For recent discussion on 'abstraction' and mathematical objects in Aristotle see I. Mueller, 'Aristotle on

responds to, we must distinguish between arithmetic and geometry. Arithmetic is concerned with what can be *counted* (pluralities of discrete objects), and with the properties that things have, in so far as they are countable. Geometry is concerned with what can be *spatially measured*, and with the properties things have in so far as they are measurable. What is primarily countable or measurable is a quantity, and it is the possibility of counting or measuring quantities that in the end makes mathematics possible as a science bearing on the actual world. The differences, and the interdependence, between counting and measuring, which Aristotle investigates with some care, are the grounds for the difference and the interdependence between arithmetic and geometry.[5] (Aristotle does sometimes envisage a more general treatment—like the one in Euclid *Elements* 5, attributed to Eudoxus—which can handle both arithmetical and geometrical quantities.[6] In one place he says that principles of mathematics are the concern of 'first philosophy', i.e. general ontology,[7] but this in no way denies the close connection between mathematics and the actual world of experience.)

Hence, first, arithmetic and geometry are sciences of exceptional generality: they can be applied to all sorts of things, since they are not confined to being true of only one particular kind of substance. Aristotle seems to want to make this generality the explanation for the characteristic 'exactness' *(akribeia)* of mathematics. At any rate, he supposes that mathematics, unlike natural science, *fits* the ordinary world in an exact and wholly exceptionless way.[8]

While mathematics is, in this sense, concerned with the world of experience, it does not follow that it is a branch of natural science, which for Aristotle is confined to the study of the *natural*, i.e. of natural processes and natural substances. Countability and measurability have no *direct*

Geometrical Objects', in J. Barnes, M. Schofield, and R. Sorabji (eds.), *Articles on Aristotle*, iii. *Metaphysics* (London, 1979), 96–107; J. Lear, 'Aristotle's Philosophy of Mathematics', *Philosophical Review*, 91 (1982), 161–92; J. Annas, 'Die Gegenstände der Mathematik bei Aristoteles', in A. Graeser (ed.), *Mathematics and Metaphysics in Aristotle* (Proceedings of the Tenth Symposium Aristotelicum; Bern, 1987), 131–47; E. Hussey, 'Aristotle on Mathematical Objects', in I. Mueller (ed.), Περὶ τῶν μαθημάτων (Apeiron, 24.4; Edmonton, 1991), 105–33; J. J. Cleary, *Aristotle and Mathematics: Aporetic Method in Cosmology and Metaphysics* (Leiden, 1995), chs. 3–5.

[5] On quantities, numbers, and the nature and presuppositions of counting and measuring: *Cat.* 6, 4^{b}20–6^{a}35; *Ph.* 3. 7, 207^{b}7–10; 4. 11, 219^{b}5–9; 4. 12, 220^{b}8–22; 4. 14, 223^{a}21–9, 224^{a}2–15; *Metaph.* Δ 6, 1016^{b}17–24; 13, 1020^{a}7–11; *I* 1; and, on the difference between arithmetic and geometry: *An. post.* 1. 7, 75^{a}38–^{b}20; 1. 27, 87^{a}35–7; *Metaph. I* 3, 1061^{a}20–^{b}3. On Aristotle on numbers and arithmetic, M. Mignucci, 'Aristotle's Arithmetic', in Graeser (n. 4), 175–211, is generally useful.

[6] *An. post.* 1. 5, 74^{a}17–25; 1. 24, 85^{a}28–^{b}15; 2. 17, 99^{a}1–16; *Metaph. E* 1, 1026^{a}23–7; *K* 7, 1064^{b}8–9; *M* 2, 1077^{a}9–10; 3, 1077^{b}17–22.

[7] *Metaph. K* 4, 1061^{b}19–21. cf. *Γ* 3, 1005^{a}19–29.

[8] Mathematics is 'not (said) of any substrate': *An. post* 1. 13, 79^{a}6–10; 1. 27, 87^{a}31–7; mathematics is 'exact' (ἀκριβής): *An. post.* 1. 27, 87^{a}31–7; *Cael.* 3. 7, 306^{a}26–30; *Metaph. A* 2, 982^{a}23–8; *M* 3, 1078^{a}9–17.

connection with the definition of nature as 'a principle of change and of rest'. Hence mathematics and natural science must be distinct, and logically independent of one another.[9] It might seem, then, that any connection or overlap between them will be purely accidental; but it turns out that the situation is more complicated than that.

3. Some Mathematical Branches of Natural Science

In some places Aristotle notes a kind of overlap between mathematical and physical science. In the *Posterior Analytics* he claims that in such cases there are really two sciences in play: one, the subordinate science, is concerned with the *fact*, and is part of natural science; while the higher science is concerned with the *explanation*, and is part of mathematics. The examples given are: optics, mechanics, harmonics, and astronomy.[10] He himself occasionally uses mathematical methods in writing about such areas.[11]

In other works he seems to give a slightly different analysis, according to which there is but one science involved in each case, and one which is a branch of natural science, though mathematics abstracts from it; so that there is still a branch of mathematics that *corresponds* to it, and its explanations are *derived* from mathematics.

He notes that ordinary usage often does not distinguish between the corresponding branches—that, for example, both empirical and mathematical astronomy are called ἀστρολογία—and he himself happily uses ἁρμονική or ἀστρολογία, in different places, to denote a branch of mathematics, or a branch of physics. But he is consistent in always insisting that the branches of natural science in question are somehow subordinate to, or dependent upon, the corresponding branches of mathematics. The claim is that mathematics supplies something indispensable and fundamental in these fields, since it determines the *explanations* of the physical facts. Since the explanations are for Aristotle the essential part of any science, this already amounts to a strong kind of logical subordination.

---

[9] Mathematics distinct from natural science: *Ph.* 2. 2, 193^{b}23–194^{a}12; *Metaph. E* 1, 1026^{a}6–15; *K* 7, 1064^{a}30–3.

[10] This section is based on *An. post.* 1. 7, 75^{b}14–17; 1. 9, 76^{a}9–15, 22–5; 1. 10, 76^{b}3–11; 1. 13, 78^{b}32–79^{a}16; *Ph.* 2. 2, 193^{b}25–35, 194^{a}1–12; *Cael.* 2. 14, 297^{a}2–6; *Metaph. M* 2, 1076^{b}39–1077^{a}9; *M* 3, 1078^{a}14–17.

[11] *Mete.* 3. 5, 375^{b}16–377^{a}29, appeals to geometrical optics to explain rainbows; the details are obscure. *Metaph. Λ* 8, 1073^{b}8–1074^{a}17, uses a modified version of Eudoxus' concentric-spheres model for the motions of sun, moon, and planets. *Sens.* 3–7 invokes arithmetical ratios, in analogy with musical theory, to explain phenomena of simple and mixed colours, flavours, and odours. There are other incidental appeals to elementary mathematics in the physical works; cf. also §§ 6 and 7 below on mathematical analysis and proportionalities in physical explanations.

4. Mathematics Indicates Fundamental
Limitations on the Structure of the Natural World

Further evidence reveals more about this 'subordination' of natural science to mathematics, and makes it clear that Aristotle conceives of the relationship between mathematics and the world of experience in a different way from most modern philosophers.

The most striking example of this 'subordination' is found in Aristotle's rejection of physical atomism, and the grounds he gives for it. Against the possibility that there could be physically indivisible bodies (as asserted by the Atomists), he invokes a fundamental principle of Euclidean geometry: that every line can be divided into two smaller lines, and hence that the division process can proceed *ad infinitum*.[12]

To understand Aristotle's unexpressed reasoning here, we must start from his general view about the truths of mathematics. Since for him they are essentially and basically truths about the world of experience, it follows that the fundamental principles of arithmetic or geometry must have something substantial to say about the world: they must indicate real limitations on what the world can be like.

In what sort of way could it be thought that mathematics 'puts limits' on the nature of the world? Mathematical truths express generalizations from experience. Thus, '2 + 2 = 4' expresses the truth that if you add together two non-overlapping countable collections of two Xs each (where 'X' corresponds to any concept under which things can be counted), you always get a collection of four Xs. Here, the Xs are actual objects in the world (e.g. horses or dogs). The process of adding together the two collections must also correspond to actual processes which might actually occur in the world (e.g. putting all one's horses into the same field), though of course addition may have useful applications to the actual world even when no such merging process actually occurs.

The same is true of geometrical truths. Thus, the truth that every line can be bisected must, if it is really a principle of geometry, correspond to, and be derived from, a fact about the actual world: that every line in the actual world can literally and actually be cut in half. (Aristotle has no room for any distinction between geometry as the science of space, and physics as the science of things that occupy space. As shown by his discussion of *place* in *Ph.* 4. 1–5, there is no such thing for him as a self-subsistent space. Geometry is the science of whatever is spatially extended.)

---

[12] Divisibility *ad infinitum* of magnitudes used against atomism: *Cael.* 1. 5, 271^{b}6–11; 3. 4, 303^{a}20–4; 3. 7, 306^{a}26–30; *Ph.* 6. 1–2, 231^{a}21–233^{b}32; 6. 4, 234^{b}10–235^{b}6. (On Aristotle's rejection of atomism see the works cited in n. 18 below, and D. J. Furley, *Two Studies in the Greek Atomists* (Princeton, 1967), 111–30; on magnitudes as 'divisible everywhere' see n. 27 below.) See also § IV of Milton's paper in this volume.

Given this understanding of mathematical truths, it is not fallacious or irrelevant (as has sometimes been thought) for Aristotle to invoke a geometrical principle to refute physical atomism. It is nevertheless surprising (to a twentieth-century reader) that he shows such unqualified and unexplained confidence in the truth of that particular principle, and in the reliability of 'Euclidean' geometry generally (rather than some other possible geometry, e.g. one allowing indivisible lengths) as a picture of the spatial aspects of the physical world.[13]

What grounded his confidence about this we cannot be sure. But his mention of 'the most *exact* sciences' in this connection suggests that he was invoking the apparently exact fit, in most other respects, between Euclidean geometry and the world. He could point to the elegance, the power, and the empirically confirmed practical usefulness of Euclidean geometry,[14] as giving support to his claim, as well as to the empirical fact that no actually indivisible extended things had ever been discovered. All this would have had to be given up if atomism had been admitted, since, as he notes, the rejection of divisibility *ad infinitum* would amount to a radical revolution in geometry.

If the principle of divisibility *ad infinitum* was, for Aristotle, to be grounded in the ways that have been suggested, that would be in accord with his general theorizing about the discovery and establishment of first principles in the sciences.[15]

This appeal to mathematics in the refutation of atomism is not an isolated instance of the subordination of physics to mathematics, though it is the most striking one. Less obvious, perhaps, but equally far-reaching, is the use of (supposed) mathematical truths in *De caelo* to ground fundamental properties of the cosmos as a whole. Its three-dimensionality is explained by the claim that magnitudes in general cannot be more than three-dimensional. Its sphericity and its division into an upper and a lower region, and the properties and motions of the 'simple bodies', are all ultimately based in part on the analysis of all motions as compounds of two simple types: linear and circular. Sphericity of the cosmos is also grounded on arguments using an analysis of geometrical shapes.[16]

---

[13] It is possible that Democritus had already tried to produce an atomistic alternative to Euclidean geometry, but the evidence is sparse and inconclusive.

[14] Euclidean geometry was in practical use in antiquity in (e.g.) land-surveying, town-planning, map-making, and the construction of tunnels: see O. A. W. Dilke, *Greek and Roman Maps* (Ithaca, NY, and London, 1985); T. E. Rihll and J. V. Tucker, 'Greek Engineering: The Case of Eupalinos' Tunnel', in A. Powell (ed.), *The Greek World* (London, 1995), 403–31. In these applications to the world of experience, it functions as a part of physics (cf. R. Penrose, *The Emperor's New Mind* (Oxford, 1989), 156–62).

[15] On Aristotle's view of how the principles of sciences are arrived at, see M. Burnyeat, 'Aristotle on Understanding Knowledge', in E. Berti (ed.), *Aristotle on Science: The Posterior Analytics* (Padua, 1981), 97–139.

[16] Three-dimensionality of magnitude: *Cael.* 1. 1, 268^{a}7–^{b}5; analysis of motions into circular

Above all, there is the use of the so-called 'Axiom of Archimedes' to show the impossibility of *infinitesimal* quantities in physics, a principle just as fundamental for Aristotle as the impossibility of physical atoms.[17]

The importance to Aristotle of this last principle is worth underlining. The 'Axiom of Archimedes' (presumably formulated by Eudoxus, if not earlier, and therefore sometimes more reasonably called the 'Axiom of Eudoxus') states that, of any two magnitudes of the same sort, either is less than some finite multiple of the other. It is a linchpin of the general theory of magnitudes and ratios formulated in Euclid *Elements* 5, which is thought to be the creation of Eudoxus. For Aristotle, its importance lies in the fact that it ensures that the proportion between any two magnitudes of the same kind will always be a proportion that one finite quantity bears to another finite quantity. So it guarantees, in particular, that proportionalities in physics (see § 7 below) will never require the introduction of infinite or infinitesimal quantities.

5. The Mathematical Structure of Continuity

Mathematics, in this way, indicates limitations on the structure of the world of experience (and thereby indirectly on the shape of natural science as a whole). Yet one might still doubt whether mathematics, for Aristotle, had to be in any way *directly* and *systematically* relevant to any part of his natural science. The decisive evidence that this is indeed so is given by his treatment of *continuity*.

Aristotle takes change itself, as well as time, to be like a geometrical line in being both continuous and one-dimensional. But he goes further: in a decisive step, he notices and explores the consequences of the fact that *all one-dimensional continua share a common abstract structure.* This common structure can therefore be the subject of a corresponding science; and since the structure inheres in the continua by virtue of their measurability, the science must be closely related to geometry. Aristotle spends much time

and linear: 1. 2, 268[b]14–269[a]30; analysis of shapes: 1. 2, 268[b]19–20; 2. 4, 286[b]11–287[a]5, cf. *Ph.* 2. 2, 193[b]30.

In one important respect there is a less close fit than might have been expected between mathematics and the world: the cosmos is spatially finite and of fixed size, although geometry is happy to consider arbitrarily large spatial magnitudes. On Aristotle's modified finitism (expounded in *Ph.* 3. 4–8), akin to intuitionism, in his philosophy of mathematics, and its relation to the world of experience, see e. g. J. Lear, 'Aristotelian Infinity', *Proceedings of the Aristotelian Society*, 80 (1980), 187–210, E. Hussey, *Aristotle:* Physics III and IV (Oxford, 1982), xviii–xxvi and 72–98; M. J. White, *The Continuous and the Discrete: Ancient Physical Theories from a Contemporary Perspective* (Oxford, 1992), 133–87.

[17] 'Axiom of Archimedes': (e.g.) *Ph.* 1. 4, 187[b]25–6; *Cael.* 1. 6, 273[a]27–32; and see H. J. Waschkies, *Von Eudoxus zu Aristoteles: Das Fortwirken der Eudoxischen Proportionentheorie in der Aristotelischen Lehre vom Kontinuum* (Amsterdam, 1977), 308–18; White (n. 16), 62–9.

investigating this structure.[18] He freely uses geometrical axioms, and refers to lettered diagrams and gives general abstract proofs in geometrical style.

Here, then, Aristotle is aware of a mathematical structure which lies at the very heart of all natural process. For him this can hardly be just an accident. He takes the continuity of natural changes as fundamental (in spite of certain partial exceptions),[19] and as something that helps to make possible the overall unity and coherence of the natural world.

In exploring the common structure of one-dimensional continua, Aristotle, it seems, is extending the scope of Greek mathematics, for we know of no previous exploration of this kind. He considers not only spatially extended continua (bodies and their bounding surfaces, lines and points), but temporal ones (time-stretches, changes), and other physical quantities neither spatial nor temporal. In treating time-stretches as wholly analogous to lines, Aristotle is formally 'spatializing' time—an indispensable step on the way to a truly mathematical physics.[20] Just as noteworthy is Aristotle's willingness to draw physical quantities generally within the scope of his analysis. Such quantities as 'power' or 'weight' are 'continuous' and 'one-dimensional' in the extended sense that they can be represented by positive numbers, and admit of continuous increase and decrease; and these quantities too may therefore be represented by lines.

These initial steps towards a truly mathematical physics, and the accom-

[18] (a) Definition of 'continuous': *Ph*. 5. 3, 227^{a}10–17, cf. 226^{b}34–227^{a}6 and 6 1, 231^{a}21–3; (b) role of continua in mathematics: *Ph*. 6. 1, 231^{a}24–^{b}18; *Metaph*. K 4, 1061^{b}21–4; (c) physical magnitudes, changes, time-stretches as continua, as divisible everywhere, divisible *ad infinitum*: *Ph*. 3. 6, 207^{a}21–3; 3. 7, 207^{b}15–17; 4. 11, 219^{a}10–14; 6. 1–2, and 6. 4. Structural correspondence between continua given by the 'following' (ἀκολουθεῖν) relation: *Ph*. 4. 11, 219^{a}10–220^{a}10; 8. 7–8, 261^{a}31–265^{a}12. Part of Aristotle's motivation in all this (but only part) is to answer Zeno's paradoxes.

On Aristotle's theory of the continuum, the best study of the mathematical aspects is Waschkies (n. 17); see also White (n. 16), 133–87; and on some broader related questions W. Knorr, 'Infinity and Continuity: The Interaction of Mathematics and Philosophy in Antiquity', in N. Kretzmann (ed.), *Infinity and Continuity in Ancient and Mediaeval Thought* (Ithaca, NY, and London, 1982), 112–45. Some philosophical aspects are treated in R. Sorabji, 'Aristotle on the Instant of Change', in Barnes, Schofield, and Sorabji (n. 4), 159–77, S. Waterlow, *Nature, Change and Agency in Aristotle's Physics* (Oxford, 1982), 131–58; R. Sorabji, *Time, Creation and the Continuum* (London, 1983), chs. 21, 24, and 26; D. Bostock, 'Time and the Continuum', *OSAP* 6 (1988), 255–70, id., 'Aristotle on Continuity in *Physics* VI', in L. Judson (ed.), *Aristotle's Physics: A Collection of Essays* (Oxford, 1991), 179–212.

[19] But some (non-central) types of change may be *instantaneous*: see *Ph*. 6. 4, 235^{a}13–18, 24–7, 236^{b}1–18; 6. 9, 240^{a}19–^{b}7; 8. 3, 253^{b}23–6; *Sens*. 3–6.

[20] This 'spatialization' of time, for the purposes of mathematical physics, does not imply any philosophical thesis about the nature of time in itself. Aristotle's theory of time (*Ph*. 4. 10–14) in fact insists on the reality of temporal 'flow', and generally on the differences between temporal and spatial continua as well as the analogies. On Aristotle's philosophy of time: G. E. L. Owen, *Logic, Science and Dialectic: Collected Essays in Greek Philosophy* (London, 1986), 295–314; Hussey (n. 16), xxxvi–xlix, 138–75; Sorabji, *Time, Creation, and the Continuum* (n. 18), chs. 1, 4, 6, 7; Bostock, 'Time and the Continuum' (n. 18); White (n. 16), ch. 2.

In studying the systematic correspondence between times, changes, distances travelled, etc., by means of the relation of 'following', Aristotle comes close to formalizing explicitly the notion of *function* in the mathematical sense, which is implicit in his work.

panying mathematical investigation of the continuum, are one of Aristotle's greatest achievements. It must be admitted that Aristotle himself never explains clearly what he is doing. His exposition, in *Ph.* 4 and 6, is often tangled and obscure. Further, Aristotle does not *label* what he is doing as 'mathematics' or 'mathematical physics'. It is obviously not part of arithmetic, nor, quite, of geometry, though it includes geometrical truths within a more general framework. It contains the first beginnings of the mathematical discipline now known as 'topology'.

6. Mathematical Analysis and Synthesis in Natural Science

These steps taken by Aristotle, it may be said, are only *steps in the direction of* a mathematical physics: they do not actually *constitute* a mathematical physics, and Aristotle never constructed any such thing. It is certainly true that natural science, as understood by Aristotle, was not *completely* subordinate to mathematics in the way in which some of its specialized branches were. We have only to think of his biology. But even within the more restricted area of what we would call 'physics' and 'chemistry', Aristotle shows no sign of wishing to make a complete subordination of physics to mathematics. A thoroughly mathematical physics, then, of the modern kind, was never his aim.

So the interesting questions are: (1) how important in Aristotle's natural science were the mathematical, i.e. the countable and measurable, properties and relationships of natural substances and processes? and (2) how far did Aristotle suppose that the scientific study of those properties and relationships had to be subordinated to mathematics?

The evidence shows, I claim, both that countable and measurable properties were (not surprisingly) important in certain branches of Aristotelian natural science, and that Aristotle at least envisaged, though he did not carry through, a wholly mathematical treatment of the relationships holding among those properties in natural processes. In this sense he is (at least in intention) the 'first mathematical physicist'. Not only are his investigations of natural continua (§ 5) difficult to understand as anything other than *preparations* for a thoroughly mathematical treatment. There is more substantial evidence that that is just what they were intended to be.[21]

First, there is good evidence of Aristotle's readiness to use mathematical

---

[21] Aristotle's use of mathematics in physics naturally cannot be separated from his substantive physical theories, and the concepts with which he operates: in particular, the theory of the motions of bodies (as intermittently expounded in *Ph.* 4 and 8 and *Cael.* 3–4) and the concepts of 'power' (δύναμις) and 'impulse' (ῥοπή), and of 'weight (heaviness)' (βάρος) and 'lightness' (κουφότης). Twentieth-century scholarship in this area has mostly followed the lead of Henri Carteron's brilliant book (*La Notion de force dans le système d'Aristote* (Paris, 1923; repr. New York and London, 1979)) in minimizing the mathematical aspects and the analogies and connections with Newtonian concepts. Against Carteron's view, I. E. Drabkin's

operations in the physicist's analysis and synthesis of natural states and processes. In every well-developed physical theory there has to be some systematic recognition of complex physical situations which are 'compounds' or 'superpositions' of simpler situations: for example, two or more forces acting on an object at once, or two or more elemental ingredients in it. The physical theory has to give a description of the resultant thing or process, and it is one of the hallmarks of a mathematical theory that it invokes mathematical relationships in such cases: the analysis and synthesis involved are reduced to mathematical procedures such as addition or multiplications of various quantities.

Aristotle in several places shows that he is thinking mathematically in such cases. One example has already been mentioned (§ 4): in *De caelo* the discussion of simple and complex motions, which shapes his whole treatment of the cosmos, appeals to mathematical analysis to show that there are two kinds of simple motion, into which all others can be analysed. Then there is the extended treatment of 'mixture' of elementary bodies in *De generatione et corruptione*, particularly at 2. 7, 334^b8–30, where properties of compounds are explained as 'mixtures' of properties of their simple components. The analysis of the concepts of *mixture, nourishment*, and *elemental change* is interwoven with a physico-mathematical analysis of what must be actually going on in mixtures: an example of the inseparability, in Aristotle's practice and thinking, of 'science' and 'philosophy'.[22] In one place (*Mete.* 1. 4, 342^a24–6) he appeals to the law of vector addition for speeds and movements. The mathematical addition of the motions of concentric spheres is also the basis of the analyses of planetary motions by Eudoxus and Callippus, which Aristotle draws on and extends in *Metaph.* Λ 8, 1073^b17–1074^a18.[23]

pioneering attempt ('Notes on the Laws of Motion in Aristotle', *AJP* 59 (1938), 60–84) to find 'mathematical laws of physics' in Aristotle is not wholly satisfactory, as shown by Owen (n. 20), 315–33. An attempt to rework Drabkin's interpretation is E. Hussey, 'Aristotle's Mathematical Physics', in Judson (n. 18), 213–42, on which I draw here.

[22] On the problems of Aristotle's theory of mixture see H. H. Joachim, *Aristotle on Coming-To-Be and Passing-Away* (Oxford, 1922), 175–89; R. Sharvy, 'Aristotle on Mixtures', *Journal of Philosophy*, 80 (1983), 439–57; K. Fine, 'The Problem of Mixture', in F. A. Lewis and R. Bolton (eds.), *Form, Matter and Mixture in Aristotle* (Oxford and Malden, 1996), 82–182.

[23] On Eudoxus' model and Aristotle's use of it, some recent publications are: G. E. R. Lloyd, *Aristotelian Explorations* (Cambridge, 1996), ch. 8; 'Heavenly Aberrations: Aristotle the Amateur Astronomer'; id., '*Metaphysics* Λ 8', in M. Frede and D. Charles (eds.), *Aristotle's Metaphysics Lambda* (Oxford, 2000), 245–73; H. Mendell, 'Reflections on Eudoxus, Callippus and their Curves: Hippopedes and Callippopedes', *Centaurus*, 40 (1998), 177–275; I. Yavetz, 'On the Homocentric Sphere of Eudoxus', *Archive for the History of the Exact Sciences*, 51 (1998), 221–78.

7. Proportional Relationships in Natural Science

The final, but again disputable, evidence is provided by those places where Aristotle assumes relationships of proportionality ('as *A* is to *B*, so is *C* to *D*') between physical quantities in natural processes. These are prominent in *Physics* 7 and in some parts of *De caelo*.[24] Many scholars have denied that these statements are meant as anything like 'mathematical laws of physics', and it is true that they often appear with, in the first instance, a negative, dialectical purpose: to reduce an adversary's position to a contradiction.

It need not follow, though, that Aristotle himself put no faith in them. In fact, there are good reasons for thinking that he took them as at least rough guides to the truth of the matter. (1) The dialectical use occurs in so many places that we cannot suppose that his adversaries were the same set of people in all cases. Therefore it is just not plausible to see these assumptions of proportionality as merely *ad hominem*, and the natural conclusion is that Aristotle appealed to them as to something that within his own school, at any rate, would not be questioned. (2) In one case the appeal to a proportionality, though made in a polemical context, is expressly presented as an appeal to a fact of ordinary observation.[25] (3) There are places where the proportionalities occur, outside any argumentative context, ostensibly as part of Aristotle's own thinking. So, above all, at *Ph.* 7, 5, 249^{b}27–250^{a}28, where there is a general statement about the proportionality between the input of 'power' to an object, and the speed and amount of its resulting change.[26]

More work needs to be done on this question. But, if we may assume that Aristotle meant the statements of proportionality seriously, that at least has the merit of giving an intelligible motivation for his investigation of the structure of physical continua. For there are certain things that need to be settled before one can confidently apply proportional relationships to any particular kind of quantity. Above all, one must know that there will always exist a fourth proportional. That is, if we say that as quantity *A* is to quantity *B*, so is quantity *C* to quantity *D*, we must know in advance that, whatever the particular quantities *A*, *B*, and *C* may be in particular cases, there will always exist a possible quantity *D* bearing that relationship to the other three. This is *not* a routine matter; we must know that the types of

---

[24] *Ph.* 7. 5, 249^{b}27–250^{a}28 (on which see Hussey (n. 21), 215–20: the theory of physical change); *Ph.* 4. 8, 215^{a}24–216^{a}11; 8. 10, 266^{b}6–24 (Hussey 227–39: the theory of motion); and e.g. *Cael.* 1. 5–7; 2. 8, 289^{b}15–16; 2. 9, 290^{b}34–291^{a}4; 2. 10, 291^{a}32–^{b}10; 2. 12, 293^{a}10–11; 2. 13, 294^{a}15, ^{b}5–6; 3. 2, 310^{a}26–^{b}16; 3. 5, 304^{a}24–^{b}9, ^{b}15–19; 3. 6, 305^{a}6–7, 11–13; *Mete.* 1. 3, 340^{a}3–19, 341^{a}35–6. For the view that the proportionalities are not stated as general truths of physics, see Carteron (n. 21), 1–32; Owen (n. 20), 329–32.   [25] *Ph.* 4. 8, 215^{a}25–^{b}12.
[26] The context is indeed partly 'dialectical', since it makes a counter (250^{a}19–28) to one of Zeno's arguments; but the counter is founded, not on the proportionality itself, but on a *restriction* to its applicability (250^{a}9–19).

quantity involved are mathematically well-behaved in certain ways. Now, if they have the structure of Aristotelian continua, they are guaranteed to be well-behaved enough for this purpose. For, like the quantities of Eudoxus' general theory as given in Euclid's *Elements* 5, they will obey the 'Axiom of Archimedes' (which bans infinitesimals: above, § 4), and they will also be 'divisible everywhere'. Whatever exactly 'divisible everywhere' means, it must be strong enough to guarantee the existence of the fourth proportional, and should therefore be listed as yet another mathematical principle with a direct bearing on the nature of the world of experience.[27]

All of this suggests that Aristotle put some faith in his proportionalities, but does not tell us why he did so. It is a reasonable guess, though, that he saw in them, as in other principles of mathematics, the product of a dialectical negotiation between experience and generalization, leading to a reflective equilibrium.[28] In one case at least, as pointed out, he deduces them from observation. In many others they can be seen as formalizations of a thought intuitively 'obvious' or 'natural'. Thus the commonplace thought that the more 'power' put in, the greater or the swifter the change that results, is what underlies the formulation of *Ph.* 7. 5.

8. Summary and Conclusion

I have been looking at the way mathematics and the natural world are related, in Aristotle's theory and in his practice. The central points I have underlined are (1) Aristotle's characteristic philosophy of mathematics as derived from the world of experience; (2) his consequent conception of the partial subordination of natural science to mathematics; and, (3) on the detail of that subordination, his general study of the mathematical structure of continua; (4) the 'spatialization' of time and change as one-dimensional continua analogous to lines; and consequently (5) the creation of a mathematical theory of the intrinsic structure of changes of measurable quantities.

I have not tried to tell a chronological story. It may well be that there was a process of development in his thinking on these matters,[29] but the first requirement is to make sense of the texts, so far as possible without making any particular hypothesis about chronology.

[27] 'Divisible everywhere' may possibly indicate something analogous to the modern concept of *order-completeness*; if so, Aristotle (or someone earlier) anticipated Dedekind's construction of the 'real numbers'. On this possibility, see O. Becker, *Das mathematische Denken in der Antike* (Göttingen, 1966), 15, 108; White (n. 16), 133–87.

[28] See above, n.15.

[29] It may be a sign of developmental change that in *Posterior Analytics* 1 Aristotle shows much enthusiasm for mathematics as a paradigm of science, but little interest in the application of mathematics to the natural world, while in other (possibly later) works it is the other way round.

The making of moves (1) to (5) was in itself epoch-making. In the end, it must be admitted, Aristotle did not get much further beyond them towards the construction of a substantive 'mathematical physics'. His steps in that direction look tentative. (It may quite well be that he saw what had to be done, better than he could himself do it—though this is a possibility Aristotelian scholars are always reluctant to consider.) But about the direction in which he was headed, there is no room for doubt.

That Aristotle's achievements and ambitions in this field have gone without full understanding and recognition for so long is something of a reproach to scholarship. Apart from the difficulties presented by the texts themselves, one might identify several factors. One is the exclusivity and 'retrospective imperialism' of different modern traditions. For example: philosophers whose thinking on the nature of mathematics has been formed by Frege's *Foundations of Arithmetic* will assume, rightly, that Frege can help us to grasp the sense and importance of things that Aristotle says about number. Too often they will assume also, and wrongly, that there cannot be any non-Fregean thoughts about number in Aristotle, or that any that there are are unimportant or just mistaken. A second factor is the prevalence of modern assumptions about the nature of mathematics, science, and philosophy and the relations between them. A third is the consequent compartmentalization of scholarly work. Philosophers study Aristotle 'as a philosopher', historians of science (or mathematics) study him 'as a scientist' (or as a source for the history of mathematics). Yet it is evident that, for Aristotle himself, mathematics, natural science, and 'first philosophy', though they are distinct fields of knowledge, are systematically and organically interconnected, and cannot be understood in isolation from one another. To explore and understand those interconnections, it is necessary first of all to take Aristotle seriously as someone who was, equally and simultaneously, all three: philosopher, scientist, and mathematician.

13

Euclid's *Elements* 9. 14 and the Fundamental Theorem of Arithmetic

C. M. TAISBAK

1. THREE propositions in the ninth book of Euclid's *Elements* are famous. The best-known theorem, of course, is 9. 20:

οἱ πρῶτοι ἀριθμοὶ πλείους εἰσὶ παντὸς τοῦ προτεθέντος πλήθους πρώτων ἀριθμῶν.

There are more prime numbers than any assigned multitude of prime numbers.

I shall leave that one alone and mention the very last one of the book: 9. 36, on how to generate perfect numbers:

ἐὰν ἀπὸ μονάδος ὁποσοιοῦν ἀριθμοὶ ἑξῆς ἐκτεθῶσιν ἐν τῇ διπλασίονι ἀναλογίᾳ, ἕως οὗ ὁ σύμπας συντεθεὶς πρῶτος γένηται, καὶ ὁ σύμπας ἐπὶ τὸν ἔσχατον πολλαπλασιασθεὶς ποιῇ τινα, ὁ γενόμενος τέλειος ἔσται.

If as many numbers as we please beginning from a unit be set out continuously in double proportion until the sum of all becomes a prime, and if the sum multiplied into the last make some number, the product will be perfect.

According to definition, a perfect number is one which equals the sum of its proper divisors (or 'parts', to use the Greek term). Well-known perfect numbers are:

$$6 \ (=1+2+3),$$
$$28 \ (=1+2+4+7+14),$$
$$496 \ (=1+2+4+8+16+31+62+124+248).$$

I dealt with that problem in a paper some twenty years ago, suggesting inspiration from the Egyptian method of multiplying.[1] Perfect numbers will also play some role in this paper, whose aim is to clarify some unfamiliar concepts of Euclidean number theory and answer the question: what were (to Euclid) the bricks, the constituents, the formative elements of numbers? What is the stuff that numbers are made of?

The answer is relevant to the third famous theorem, 9. 14, which runs thus, in Thomas Heath's translation:

[1] C. M. Taisbak, 'Perfect Numbers—A Mathematical Pun?', *Centaurus*, 20 (1976), 269–75. An early reference to perfect numbers has now been noted in the scholar-poet Euphorion's *Mopsopia* (*Suppl. Hell.* 417): see J. L. Lightfoot, 'An Early Reference to Perfect Numbers? Some Notes on Euphorion *SH* 417', *CQ*, NS 48 (1998), 187–94.

ἐὰν ἐλάχιστος ἀριθμὸς ὑπὸ πρώτων ἀριθμῶν μετρῆται, ὑπ' οὐδενὸς ἄλλου πρώτου ἀριθμοῦ μετρηθήσεται παρὲξ τῶν ἐξ ἀρχῆς μετρούντων.

If a number is the least that is measured by ⟨some⟩ prime numbers, it will not be measured by any other prime number except those originally measuring it.

Heath's comment on this—'in other words, a number can be resolved into prime factors in only one way'—makes Ian Mueller exclaim: 'it is very difficult to say what he [sc. Heath] has in mind'.[2] Mueller, nevertheless, knows very well what Heath had in mind: *El.* 9. 14 is equivalent to the Fundamental Theorem of Arithmetic (FTA):

Every number is either a prime or a product of primes in one way only.

Mueller is right in pointing out that 9. 14 is considerably weaker than the FTA, if for no other reason than because Euclid does not speak of an arbitrary number, but only of that number which he knows to be the least that is measured by some primes: about the rest of numbers, which are many indeed, he is silent. Mueller is probably also right in his judgement that Euclid's reasons for proving 9. 14 must remain unknown (although I put forward a suggestion in § 8); but I think that we may form a plausible opinion about why he did not state and prove the FTA.

2. Let us look at Euclid's proof, keeping as closely as possible to his text.

ἐλάχιστος ἀριθμὸς ὁ Α ὑπὸ πρώτων ἀριθμῶν τῶν Β, Γ, Δ μετρείσθω· λέγω ὅτι ὁ Α ὑπ' οὐδενὸς ἄλλου πρώτου ἀριθμοῦ μετρηθήσεται παρὲξ τῶν Β, Γ, Δ. εἰ γὰρ δυνατόν, μετρείσθω ὑπὸ πρώτου τοῦ Ε, καὶ ὁ Ε μηδενὶ τῶν Β, Γ, Δ ἔστω ὁ αὐτός. καὶ ἐπεὶ ὁ Ε τὸν Α μετρεῖ, μετρείτω αὐτὸν κατὰ τὸν Ζ· ὁ Ε ἄρα τὸν Ζ πολλαπλασιάσας τὸν Α πεποίηκεν. καὶ μετρεῖται ὁ Α ὑπὸ πρώτων ἀριθμῶν τῶν Β, Γ, Δ. ἐὰν δὲ δύο ἀριθμοὶ πολλαπλασιάσαντες ἀλλήλους ποιῶσι τινα, τὸν δὲ γενόμενον ἐξ αὐτῶν μετρῇ τις πρῶτος ἀριθμός, καὶ ἕνα τῶν ἐξ ἀρχῆς μετρήσει· οἱ Β, Γ, Δ ἄρα ἕνα τῶν Ε, Ζ μετρήσουσιν. τὸν μὲν οὖν Ε οὐ μετρήσουσιν· ὁ γὰρ Ε πρῶτός ἐστι καὶ οὐδενὶ τῶν Β, Γ, Δ ὁ αὐτός. τὸν Ζ ἄρα μετροῦσιν ἐλάσσονα ὄντα τοῦ Α· ὅπερ ἀδύνατον. ὁ γὰρ Α ὑπόκειται ἐλάχιστος ὑπὸ τῶν Β, Γ, Δ μετρούμενος. οὐκ ἄρα τὸν Α μετρήσει πρῶτος ἀριθμὸς παρὲξ τῶν Β, Γ, Δ· ὅπερ ἔδει δεῖξαι.

Let a number A be the least that is measured by the primes B, C, and D. My claim is that A is measured by no other primes than B, C, and D.

If possible, let it be measured by the prime E, which is not the same as any of the numbers B, C, D.

Since E measures A, let it measure it by (the quotient) Z.

Thus E × Z = A.

And A is measured by B, C, and D; but if the product of two numbers is measured by some prime number, that prime will also measure one of the numbers. [*El.* 7. 30]

[2] T. L. Heath, *The Thirteen Books of Euclid's* Elements (Cambridge, 1926), ad loc.; I. Mueller, *Philosophy of Mathematics and Deductive Structure in Euclid's* Elements (Cambridge, Mass., 1981), 99.

Thus B, C, and D will measure one of the numbers E and Z.
They do not measure E, which is a prime and not the same as any of the numbers
    B, C, D.
Therefore they measure Z, which is less than A; but this is impossible, for by
    hypothesis A is the least that is measured by the primes B, C, and D.
Therefore no other primes but B, C, and D will measure A.
Which was to be proved.

3. To appreciate the differences between the FTA and 9. 14 we shall study
the phrasing of the latter somewhat more closely:

(*a*) A certain number has a certain connection with some prime numbers.
(*b*) In fact (we may infer) several numbers have the same connection with
       those primes, but this one is the least of those.
(*c*) The connection is described as *being measured by*.
(*d*) The assertion of the theorem is that the least number which has this
       connection with those primes has no such connection with any other
       prime numbers.

Obviously, the idea of a closed set of primes, into which no alien prime
can intrude, is very reminiscent of the FTA. But in the enunciation of 9. 14
there is no talk of multiplying, only of measuring, and no Greek word for
factor occurs; there are only some prime numbers occupied in measuring.
Even though he knows it, Euclid does not disclose that A is the product of
B, C, and D. The one product which occurs in the proof is of two factors E
and Z which are different from B, C, and D.
    Proposition 9. 14 takes place within a conceptual frame different from
that of the FTA. To acquaint oneself with that frame, it is necessary to be
initiated into some of the idioms of Euclid's theory of number.

4. One important feature of his concept of number is that it is not products and multiplication, but measuring, that is the foundation. The word,
or rather the operation, 'measure' is the fundamental concept in Euclid's
arithmetical books. Any two numbers can be compared by examining how
many times the lesser is contained in the greater, by subtracting the lesser
number from the greater as many times as possible. This may not always
come right, and Euclid uses the verb 'to measure' of this process of subtracting to denote the special situation (or relation) in which the lesser number
can be subtracted from the greater a certain number of times without leaving
any remainder. We may define it thus:

    The number B measures the number C if (and only if) C is a sum of
    numbers equal to B.

Modern readers might prefer the verb 'divides', but I shall follow Euclid
and say 'measures'. Let me quote what Sabetai Unguru has stressed so
vigorously elsewhere: 'Euclid's numbers are definite aggregates of units of
measurement. The presentation is geometric, by means of continuous lines,
precisely because the constitutive units are units of measurement.'[3] Measuring and multiplication are two-handed operations: when you measure a
number C by a number B, with your left hand you subtract (numbers equal
to) B from C, while with your right hand you keep track of the results by
putting down units, one for each B that is subtracted. When the mensura-
tion is done, a number A will have been composed, telling the 'how-many',
the *quotiens* in Latin.

I am sure that this two-hand procedure was present to the mind of the
Greek mathematician whenever he performed multiplication or mensura-
tion. He says: C is measured by B according to (κατά) the units in A.

In *El*, 7, def. 16, Euclid offers the following definition:

ἀριθμὸς ἀριθμὸν πολλαπλασιάζειν λέγεται, ὅταν, ὅσαι εἰσὶν ἐν αὐτῷ μονάδες, τοσαυτάκις
συντεθῇ ὁ πολλαπλασιαζόμενος, καὶ γένηταί τις.

A number is said to multiply a number when the multiplied number is added to
itself as many times as there are units in it [the multiplier], and some [number]
comes-to-be. (trans. Mueller)

When the number C is said to be a multiple of B, it is thought of as being
added up from numbers equal to B; to Euclid, a composite number is an
added number. In Greek, C is said to συγκεῖσθαι from numbers equal to
B, and the definition of a product of integers is always kept in mind: the
product is the sum of numbers equal to the multiplicand.

4.1. Without any difference of meaning we may say either that C is A times
B or that B measures C by the units in A. We can put that into symbols:

$$C = A \times B \text{ means } C = B_1 + B_2 + \ldots + B_A,$$

that is, the total of A numbers equal to B. One may ask: if the several
numbers equal to B are not indexed (as in our notation: B_1, B_2, etc.), what
happens to A? It vanishes into an invisible counter.

When Euclid forms a product of two factors, one of them is lost. The
product C is made up from a sum of Bs; that A is also there, he proves in
7. 15, which deals with a sort of commutativity:

ἐὰν μονὰς ἀριθμόν τινα μετρῇ, ἰσάκις δὲ ἕτερος ἀριθμὸς ἄλλον τινὰ ἀριθμὸν μετρῇ, καὶ
ἐναλλὰξ ἰσάκις ἡ μονὰς τὸν τρίτον ἀριθμὸν μετρήσει καὶ ὁ δεύτερος τὸν τέταρτον.

If a unit measures some number, and another number measures some other number

---

[3] S. Unguru, 'Greek Mathematics and Greek Induction', *Physis*, 28 (1991), 273–89 at
281.

equally many times, then also alternately[4] the unit will measure the third number equally many times as the second measures the fourth.

What about three factors? As nowadays, such products are produced in two steps: first, the product of two of them is produced, and then that number is multiplied by the third number. Two numbers get lost as invisible counters. But those invisible co-operators can be recovered, so to speak, by measuring the product: if they do measure the product, they co-operate all right. Things are not so simple as we might think, however, for quite often a lot of co-operators pop up which we had not thought of. We shall see that in a moment.

5. The operation of measuring may be illustrated by a well-known device: a multiplication table of the familiar sort, set up rectangularly like tables of road distances (see Table 13.1). Each column contains all the numbers measured by the top number; in the leftmost column the quotients can be read off.[5]

If you look for a certain number, say 84, you may of course find it at the edge of the table if the table be big enough. But you will also find it in the field, in the 3-column, the 4-column, the 6-column, the 7-column, the 12-column, etc. Numbers seem to be of two sorts: those which can occur somewhere down the columns, and those which can only be first numbers of their column. If I were to invent a terminology, I might speak of busy numbers and lazy numbers. But I need invent no names, for the Greeks gave them meaningful ones: numbers which can only be first and never go into the field were called by the Greeks first *par excellence*, πρῶτοι ἀριθμοί, which in Latin became *numeri primi*, borrowed by the English as 'prime numbers'. Do not misunderstand me: this is my thesis to explain how the term πρῶτοι ἀριθμοί came into being. There may be other plausible explanations: the ancients gave none.

The other numbers, the busy ones, were called aggregate, in Greek σύνθετοι or 'added up', i.e. produced by successive additions of the top number. (I prefer the word 'aggregate' to the normal 'composite', to avoid wrong connotations. Greeks thought of sums, not products, when speaking of σύνθετοι ἀριθμοί.)

Some columns are secondary to others: they are embedded or merged into

---

[4] This is the traditional rendering of ἐναλλάξ in its special sense: if A:B::C:D, then ἐναλλάξ A:C::B:D. See below, p. 236.

[5] A table of this sort is shown on the 3rd-cent. funerary stela of 'Ptolemaios the geometer', preserved in Geneva and published by J. Chalmay and A. Schärling, 'Représentation d'une table de calculation', *AK* 41 (1998), 52–5. The board hangs (along with a lyre) on the wall of what is presumably Ptolemaios' teaching-room (the scene includes the figure of Ptolemaios and a child). The board is divided into 100 squares, and this is apparently the only known ancient representation of such a thing.

TABLE 13.1. *Multiplication table*

×	1	2	3	4	5	6	7	8	9	10	11	12	13	14	15	16	17	18	19	20	21	22	23	24	25	26	27	28	29	30
1	1	2	3	4	5	6	7	8	9	10	11	12	13	14	15	16	17	18	19	20	21	22	23	24	25	26	27	28	29	30
2	2	4	6	8	10	12	14	16	18	20	22	24	26	28	30	32	34	36	38	40	42	44	46	48	50	52	54	56	58	60
3	3	6	9	12	15	18	21	24	27	30	33	36	39	42	45	48	51	54	57	60	63	66	69	72	75	78	81	84	87	90
4	4	8	12	16	20	24	28	32	36	40	44	48	52	56	60	64	68	72	76	80	84	88	92	96	100	104	108	112	116	120
5	5	10	15	20	25	30	35	40	45	50	55	60	65	70	75	80	85	90	95	100	105	110	115	120	125	130	135	140	145	150
6	6	12	18	24	30	36	42	48	54	60	66	72	78	84	90	96	102	108	114	120	126	132	138	144	150	156	162	168	174	180
7	7	14	21	28	35	42	49	56	63	70	77	84	91	98	105	112	119	126	133	140	147	154	161	168	175	182	189	196	203	210
8	8	16	24	32	40	48	56	64	72	80	88	96	104	112	120	128	136	144	152	160	168	176	184	192	200	208	216	224	232	240
9	9	18	27	36	45	54	63	72	81	90	99	108	117	126	135	144	153	162	171	180	189	198	207	216	225	234	243	252	261	270
10	10	20	30	40	50	60	70	80	90	100	110	120	130	140	150	160	170	180	190	200	210	220	230	240	250	260	270	280	290	300
11	11	22	33	44	55	66	77	88	99	110	121	132	143	154	165	176	187	198	209	220	231	242	253	264	275	286	297	308	319	330
12	12	24	36	48	60	72	84	96	108	120	132	144	156	168	180	192	204	216	228	240	252	264	276	288	300	312	324	336	348	360
13	13	26	39	52	65	78	91	104	117	130	143	156	169	182	195	208	221	234	247	260	273	286	299	312	325	338	351	364	377	390
14	14	28	42	56	70	84	98	112	126	140	154	168	182	196	210	224	238	252	266	280	294	308	322	336	350	364	378	392	406	420
15	15	30	45	60	75	90	105	120	135	150	165	180	195	210	225	240	255	270	285	300	315	330	345	360	375	390	405	420	435	450
16	16	32	48	64	80	96	112	128	144	160	176	192	208	224	240	256	272	288	304	320	336	352	368	384	400	416	432	448	464	480
17	17	34	51	68	85	102	119	136	153	170	187	204	221	238	255	272	289	306	323	340	357	374	391	408	425	442	459	476	493	510
18	18	36	54	72	90	108	126	144	162	180	198	216	234	252	270	288	306	324	342	360	378	396	414	432	450	468	486	504	522	540
19	19	38	57	76	95	114	133	152	171	190	209	228	247	266	285	304	323	342	361	380	399	418	437	456	475	494	513	532	551	570
20	20	40	60	80	100	120	140	160	180	200	220	240	260	280	300	320	340	360	380	400	420	440	460	480	500	520	540	560	580	600
21	21	42	63	84	105	126	147	168	189	210	231	252	273	294	315	336	357	378	399	420	441	462	483	504	525	546	567	588	609	630
22	22	44	66	88	110	132	154	176	198	220	242	264	286	308	330	352	374	396	418	440	462	484	506	528	550	572	594	616	638	660
23	23	46	69	92	115	138	161	184	207	230	253	276	299	322	345	368	391	414	437	460	483	506	529	552	575	598	621	644	667	690
24	24	48	72	96	120	144	168	192	216	240	264	288	312	336	360	384	408	432	456	480	504	528	552	576	600	624	648	672	696	720
25	25	50	75	100	125	150	175	200	225	250	275	300	325	350	375	400	425	450	475	500	525	550	575	600	625	650	675	700	725	750
26	26	52	78	104	130	156	182	208	234	260	286	312	338	364	390	416	442	468	494	520	546	572	598	624	650	676	702	728	754	780
27	27	54	81	108	135	162	189	216	243	270	297	324	351	378	405	432	459	486	513	540	567	594	621	648	675	702	729	756	783	810
28	28	56	84	112	140	168	196	224	252	280	308	336	364	392	420	448	476	504	532	560	588	616	644	672	700	728	756	784	812	840
29	29	58	87	116	145	174	203	232	261	290	319	348	377	406	435	464	493	522	551	580	609	638	667	696	725	754	783	812	841	870
30	30	60	90	120	150	180	210	240	270	300	330	360	390	420	450	480	510	540	570	600	630	660	690	720	750	780	810	840	870	900

those, as e.g. the 12-column is embedded in the 6-, the 4-, the 3-, and the 2-column. The prime-number columns are embedded in no other columns. It looks as if any number is either a prime (i.e. first) or is measured by some prime: we have pronounced an important theorem, proved formally by Euclid in 7. 32.

We may introduce another useful term: common measure. Two numbers in one and the same column have the top number as a common measure. As two primes obviously can be in no common column except the leftmost, which simply lists all the numbers, we infer that prime numbers have no other common measure than 1. Multiplication tables seem to me to be highly informative.

6. Accidentally (but what do we know about ancient accidents?) this table also illustrates another important concept in Euclidean number theory: *logos*, or ratio as we call it by a Latin translation.

Look at two columns at a time. Just as each single column contains all the numbers measured by the top number, so each pair of columns contains all pairs of numbers having the same *logos* or ratio as the top pair: 'the same' meaning what it does, it follows that a pair of numbers in one and the same row of two columns has the same ratio as any other pair of numbers in one and the same row of those columns. (An example: 56 and 84 in the 8- and 12-columns have the same ratio as 8 to 12; but also the same ratio as any other couple of those columns, say 24 to 36.)

Again, do not misunderstand me: Euclid says nothing about multiplication tables in his definition of ratio. The table is nothing more (and nothing less) than a very informative illustration.

Let us look more closely at it. What happens if a wind gets in and over-turns the table by 90 degrees? Now rows are turned into columns and vice versa, and we see that our $56:84::24:36$ becomes $56:24::84:36$. We are observing what Aristotle (*An. post.* 1. 5, 74^{a}18) rightly considered the most effective property of *logos*, the *enallax* or alternate property, proved in *El.* 7. 13 and 15:

If $A:B::C:D$, then $A:C::B:D$.

From that property and one more, to be seen in a moment, most of Euclid's number theory can be deduced.

6.1. Again (cf. § 5) we may speak of embedding: some pairs of columns are secondary to others: they are embedded into them, as e.g. the $8:12$-couple is embedded in the $4:6$-, and the $2:3$-couple. But this last couple is embedded in no other columns. We may compare the situation to that of the prime numbers, which do not occur in the field: the numbers which characterize the non-embedded double columns cannot occur in the field on one and the same level, in one and the same row. They are not necessarily prime numbers, but they can only go together in the top row; they are said to be 'first when together', 'first with each other', πρῶτοι πρὸς ἀλλήλους: we translate that into 'prime to each other'. When *we* say 'prime to each other', we think of numbers having no common divisors but 1, and so did Greeks. The *common measure* of the components in a ratio can be seen in the leftmost column. The common (divisor or) measure of numbers prime to each other is the 1 in the top left corner.

Our pair of numbers in one and the same row, 56:84, are equal multiples of the pair of numbers, 8:12, in the top row, actually 7 times, as expressed by their common measure—no wonder, as this is the way the table works. Particularly, they are equal multiples of the pair of numbers, 2:3, which are top numbers in that pair of columns into which the 8:12 columns can be ultimately embedded; that is, they are equal multiples of the pair of numbers which determine the ratio, namely those which are prime to each other. That property turns out to be the other fundamental property of *logos*, expressed in proposition 7. 20 of the *Elements*:

οἱ ἐλάχιστοι ἀριθμοὶ τῶν τὸν αὐτὸν λόγον ἐχόντων αὐτοῖς μετροῦσι τοὺς τὸν αὐτὸν λόγον ἔχοντας ἰσάκις ὅ τε μείζων τὸν μείζονα καὶ ὁ ἐλάσσων τὸν ἐλάσσονα.

The least numbers of those having the same ratio with them measure those having the same ratio equally many times, the greater the greater and the less the less.

Obviously, it holds for any top couple of numbers, say the 8:12 couple, that it measures the couples of its column the same number of times— for example, 56:84 is measured 7 times by that couple. But, in order to have a complete *logos*, we must isolate the columns that are not embedded; therefore the theorem speaks about the least numbers of those having the same ratio. Such a minimum couple is the 2:3 couple, say; and, for example, the couple 56:84 is measured 28 times by its minimum couple.

How many times the elements of the minimum couple measure their respective partners can be seen in their common measure, which is now their greatest common measure. So now it is clear why Euclid is so keen on finding the greatest common measure of two numbers—so keen that he invented an algorithm for it (*El.* 7. 2).

Note that the top numbers are said to be the 'least numbers' etc. Statements about the least numbers of a ratio and about numbers being 'prime to each other' are equivalent statements, as is proved formally in 7. 21 and 22. We shall need these observations on *logos* to prove the Division Lemma (7. 30), on which theorem 9. 14 hinges, even though the latter says nothing about ratio, but is about prime numbers and measurement only. (See § 8.)

7. 'Number is an aggregate of units, a multitude composed of units', says the second definition in book 7. From our illustration of measurement by a multiplication table we infer, however, that some numbers are composed of numbers, not only of units. The unit 1 is definitely an atom of number, but we might look for bigger atoms (or should I say molecules?) with good candidates in mind: the prime numbers.

Looking for different measures of a given number was, apparently, a programme of research some time before Plato wrote the *Laws*. In book 5 (737 E) he declares the number 5040 to be the optimum number of citizens in a new colony, because that number admits a lot of 'parts' (διανομαί or τομαί), thirds, fourths, .. , sevenths, . . ., tenths—in fact 59 different divisors.

TABLE 13.2. *The divisors of 5040*

$5040 = 2^4 \times 3^2 \times 5 \times 7$
$1 \times 2 \times 3 \times 4 \times 5 \times 6 \times 7$
$10 \times 9 \times 8 \times 7$

Number of divisors $= (4 + 1)(2 + 1)(1 + 1)(1 + 1) = 60$.

Coupled divisors:

5040	1		252	20
2520	2		240	21
1680	3		210	24
1260	4		180	28
1008	5		168	30
840	6		144	35
720	7		140	36
630	8		126	40
560	9		120	42
504	10		112	45
420	12		105	48
360	14		90	56
336	15		84	60
315	16		80	63
280	18		72	70

Plato suggests that 5040 is the best number for its purpose, to admit all parts up to tenths: he does not claim it to be the least number with this property, and it is not. One would expect the least number to be better suited than any chance multiple, and no doubt Greek mathematicians would expect as much. We do not know how the number was generated, but it is. a fair guess that it was found by multiplying 10 by 9, the 90 by 8, the 720 by 7; then it was realized that 5040 is measured by 6, 5, 4, 3, and 2 in the bargain. And a lot more. (See Table 13.2.)[6] Measures (or divisors) come in pairs, according to the definition of measuring, as illustrated in Table 13.2: 140 measures 5040 exactly 36 times, so 140 is a 36th part of 5040, and 36 is a 140th part of 5040. The last two propositions in *El.* 7 deal with the interaction of measurement and aliquot parts of numbers (such as $\frac{1}{3}$, $\frac{1}{7}$, $\frac{1}{15}$, etc). Let me quote 7. 37:

ἐὰν ἀριθμὸς ὑπό τινος ἀριθμοῦ μετρῆται, ὁ μετρούμενος ὁμώνυμον μέρον ἕξει τῷ μετροῦντι.

If a number is measured by some number, the measured number will have a part called by the same name as the measuring number.

For example, if a number is measured by 5, it will have an integer as its fifth part.

Do prime numbers play significant roles in this play of finding measures in numbers? Even big numbers, like 5040, may be measured by very few prime numbers; 2, 3, 5, and 7 are involved, the other divisors are composite or—as I prefer—aggregate numbers. Whoever first made such investigations may have been struck by the impression that prime numbers have a tendency to form exclusive clubs, admitting no strangers. *El.* 9. 14 proves that, but it does not stand alone: 9. 12 and 13 prove of even greater numbers that alien primes cannot intrude in those series of numbers in continuous proportion which begin with a unit. I used to speak of *ab unitate* series; but they are more familiarly known as geometric progressions (e.g. 1, 3, 9, 27, 81, 243). Let 1, A, B, C, D be such a series of numbers. *El.* 9. 12 proves that any prime which measures D will already measure A: no other prime can intrude, even though D, being the 'last' power of A, may be very great. *El.* 9. 13 proves that if A is a prime, D is measured by no other numbers but A, B, and C. That is: powers of a prime are measured by powers of that prime only. It is important to remember that Euclid had no word for power, and even Descartes still spoke of *tres relationes*, three (steps of) ratio, for 'third power'. Consequently Euclid could not easily describe, say, 81 as 'the fourth power of 3'.

8. After these speculations about the investigative processes—observations of what goes on in a multiplication table—that may (I repeat, may) lie behind Euclid's formal proofs in book 7, we are able to understand why neither he nor any other Greek mathematician would formulate, let alone prove, the FTA. Aggregate numbers are made from sums of equal numbers, i.e. from their measures. 5040 can be made from no fewer (Plato says no more) than 59 different sums of equal numbers, as seen above. Could it be made up from sums of unequal parts? Indeed so. Look at this:

5040 = 2520 + 1260 + 630 + 315 + 210 + 105

[6] Cf. B. Vitrac, *Euclide: Éléments*, ii (Paris, 1990), 434 n. 26, on 9. 14.

Any ancient Egyptian, having passed his unit-fractions examination, would be able to produce several decompositions like this, I am sure, as he would know which unit-fractions add up to 1. And now the perfect numbers enter the scene: very few numbers can be generated as the sum of all their measures, with none missing: 6, 28, 496, to mention the least and best known.

When looking for the constituents, the formative elements of number, the ancients were bound to look in the 'wrong' direction—looking for measures, not for factors. Plato knew that 5040 can be produced by multiplying four numbers, 10×9×8×7. But neither he nor anyone else around him would think of this set of numbers as *constituting* 5040.

Why would Euclid prove 9. 14, then? His own reasons for proving it must remain unknown, but I think it quite plausible that he was puzzled by the scarcity of primes among the 59 divisors of Plato's emigrants' number, as he was puzzled by the exclusiveness of primes in the very big numbers of the geometric progressions. So why not prove that different primes, when they get together in numbers measured by them (the least of which Euclid of course knew to be their product), admit of no intruders.

Most numbers escape 9. 14, which is about square-free numbers only. As mentioned in § 1, Euclid does not seem interested in an analysis of the measures of an arbitrary number, but only in the measures of that number which he knows to be the least that is measured by some primes.

What would be his answer to the question: if a number is not the least that is measured by some prime numbers, what is it? How can it be characterized? I am sure that he knew that such a number is measured more than once by the same prime or primes. So that there is still a strong smell of exclusiveness in the club.

The historical significance of 9. 14 is prophetic: when multiplication broke loose from addition and evolved its own algebra—when a new conceptual frame considered multiplication as an operation in its own right—it was fairly easy for Gauss to realize that the FTA must be true, and set about to prove it along the lines that Euclid had drawn.

Until then, numbers that were the least to be measured by a set of primes played a role in mathematical speculation, as we may learn from the stories of Sheherazade in the *Arabian Nights*. Beside being a thrilling number for various non-mathematical reasons, 1001 is the least number that is measured by 7, 11, and 13,—the first primes worth their pay, because the trivial primes 2, 3, and 5 pop up everywhere.

To convince my reader that Euclid had the arguments for proving the Fundamental Theorem of Arithmetic, let me quote the Division Lemma in

Euclid's version as an *envoi*.[7] For some reason he did not want to plead the case for the FTA. My guess is: because he did not see any case.

DIVISION LEMMA (7. 30)

If C = A × B and a prime D measures C, then D measures A or D measures B.

PROOF

Suppose that D does not measure A.

Then D and A are prime to each other, because a prime number is prime to any
    number which it does not measure. (7. 29)

That D measures A × B means there is a number E such that

E × D = A × B   (definition of measure)

D : A :: B : E   (7. 19, equal cross products)

And D : A is the least couple in their ratio, because they are prime to each other.
                                                 (7. 21–2)

Therefore D measures B as many times as A measures E.   (7. 20)

---

[7] The Division Lemma is used in the proof of Euclid 9. 14, just as its modern equivalent (if *p* is prime and *p*|ab, then *p*|*a* or *p*|*b*) is used to prove its corollary, the FTA: see e.g. G. H. Hardy and E. M. Wright, *An Introduction to the Theory of Numbers*, 4th edn. (Oxford, 1960), 3 (**1. 3**), 21 (**2. 10**).

14
Ancient Medicine: Asclepius Transformed

V. NUTTON

FEW areas of classics have seen as great a revival of interest, or so complete a transformation in approach, over the last thirty years as the study of ancient medicine. From being a backwater, visited only occasionally by intrepid Germans and antiquarian doctors, it has become part of the mainstream, with both works of detailed scholarship and general surveys becoming available to attract and inform. Conferences, papers, books, editions, and even two specialist bibliographical journals, *The Society of Ancient Medicine Review* and the *Bulletin du Centre Jean Palerne*, attest to the vitality of a discipline that a generation ago might have appeared moribund. A handful of scholars, the most eminent of them trained in Germany before the Second World War—Karl Deichgräber, Hans Diller, Ludwig Edelstein, and Owsei Temkin—were then coming to the end of their teaching careers; the major publishing centre for ancient medical texts, the Corpus Medicorum at the Berlin Academy of Sciences, was suffering the consequences of the Berlin Wall, and the prospect of a rival in West Berlin; and the general decline in a classical education among potential doctors seemed to presage the demise of interest in the subject among medical historians. Besides, long tradition had canonized what was worth studying: Greek medicine, developing out of or alongside Greek philosophy, had broken away from primitive and irrational superstition to become, with Hippocrates, the foundation of Western medicine. A brief flowering of independent research, stimulated by Aristotle and continued by Herophilus and Erasistratus in Alexandria in the third century BC, was succeeded only by disaster—witness the denunciations of contemporary Greek medicine by the Elder Pliny—and by dogmatism. Galen had never recovered from being dubbed 'the great windbag' by Wilamowitz, or from the accident of birth that had made him too late to be properly Greek and not Latin enough to be truly Roman. The only medical author in the Latin world deemed worthy of note, Cornelius Celsus, was used almost entirely as a quarry for information about the earlier Greek world, and it was universally admitted that he was little more than an elegant compiler of information prepared by others. As for Latin authors, like Scribonius Largus (*fl.* AD 47), or the later Greek encyclopaedists, like Oribasius (*fl.* AD 370), and Latin medical writers, like Vindicianus (*fl.* AD 410), they could safely be left in deserved obscurity.

All this has now changed, and many of the presuppositions that under-pinned earlier work have been swept away. How and why is the theme of this paper, which is not intended to be a bibliographical survey, but rather to expound in broad terms the major developments in ancient medicine since the 1960s, and at the same time to account for this transformation. It is not a detailed account of what has been achieved by this or that scholar—and omissions should not be taken in any way as disapproval or lack of interest by the author—but a highly personal overview, with restricted annotation, of what has been a remarkable outburst of activity, and one whose impact has not yet been fully appreciated by the interested classical amateur.

The cynical observer might argue that this revival of interest owes little to the efforts of historians of ancient medicine themselves, but almost every-thing to the fact that the focus of classicists has shifted away from a concen-tration on classical Greece, from Solon to Alexander, and Rome, from the Gracchi to Juvenal, towards the more exotic worlds of Hellenistic Alexan-dria, the second century AD, and late antiquity. One might admit the for-tunate chance that the first period saw the development of Greek anatomy; that the second includes three of the great names of ancient medicine, Rufus of Ephesus and Soranus of Ephesus (both *fl.* AD 100), and Galen (AD 129–*c.*216); and that the bulk of surviving Latin medical texts were produced after AD 350. But that argument does not explain why one should choose to study the medicine of a certain period any more than its philosophy, or why it should now be found an intellectual challenge.

A more convincing argument might be formed from a theory of supply and demand: the greater the demand for independent work in a thesis or an article, the more unusual the text or topic chosen to be explored. Inevitably then, some have turned to medical texts and themes as a change from Greek tragedy or Cicero, and have discovered that, often, even very basic work needs to be done. It is true that philologists of the calibre of J. J. Scaliger and Wilamowitz had touched on some of the Hippocratic writings, and the general outline of the relationship between the medieval manuscripts had been established since the early years of the twentieth century, but for the Galenic corpus, as indeed for almost all other ancient medical writers save Hippocrates, the study of the text had advanced little since the Renaissance. The most accessible collection of Greek medical authors, that overseen by Karl Gottlob Kühn, professor of medicine at Leipzig from 1785 to 1842, is little more than a reprint of editions at least two centuries older, and the most extensive edition of a Latin author, that of Celsus by Friedrich Marx (1915), is also a monument to that editor's eccentricity. Like the pioneers on the American frontier, then, it might be argued that classicists in their search for something new would inevitably reach the unexplored region of ancient medicine; some might stay, but others would move on, dissatisfied with some of the aridities they found there.

But while the opportunities for successful emendation are undoubtedly higher in Galen than in Thucydides, and there is a greater chance of finding an unknown manuscript of the medical poet Q. Sammonicus than one of Lucretius,[1] and even of publishing an *editio princeps*, the impetus has rarely come from specialists in textual criticism, with the notable exception of France. There, building on the work of the Belgian Robert Joly, Jacques Jouanna has produced since 1983 five volumes of Hippocrates in the Budé series that should be on the desk of anyone interested in Greek language and thought in the fifth and fourth centuries. His pupils, in Strasbourg and more recently at the Sorbonne, have begun to interest themselves in Galen, the complexities of whose tradition, often involving translations into one or more oriental languages, have been more daunting than inviting. There has been a renewal of philological interest in Latin medical texts, but editions have been relatively few compared with studies of style and vocabulary, and, partly because of the very restricted and technical nature of the texts themselves, the results have rarely been put before the wider classical public.[2]

1. Philosophy and Medicine

The history of ancient medicine and science has usually been taught within classics departments by philosophers, a tradition that goes back at least to Hermann Diels in Berlin at the end of the nineteenth century. Early Greek medicine and Greek philosophy can be seen as emerging from the same matrix, to come to full flowering in the later fifth century with Plato and Hippocrates. Treatises like *On Ancient Medicine* with its attack on unjustified philosophical theorizing in medical debates, or *On the Sacred Disease*, with its rejection of a divine cause for a physical illness, can be easily linked with similar developments in Presocratic philosophy. Other Hippocratic texts, such as *Epidemics* 1 and 3, *Airs, Waters, and Places*, and *Prognostic*, show effective powers of clear-sighted observation and thought, by contrast with Egyptian or early Roman primitivism. Rational Hippocratic medicine, like Platonic and Aristotelian philosophy, is thus part of the Greek miracle.[3]

---

[1] Leipzig, Universitätsbibliothek 1127 (olim 1115), fos. 87^r–97^r, contains a text of Sammonicus written out as prose and unknown to Vollmer in his standard edition of 1916 or any other later editor.

[2] To the information contained in the *Bibliographie des textes médicaux latins* (Mémoires du Centre Jean Palerne, 6; Saint-Étienne, 1987), add G. Bendz's Caelius Aurelianus (1990–3), and the first volume of the Budé Celsus (1995). For studies of vocabulary, note J. N. Adams, *The Latin Sexual Vocabulary* (London, 1982); id., *Pelagonius and Latin Veterinary Terminology in the Roman Empire* (Leiden, 1995); and D. R. Langslow, *Medical Latin in the Roman Empire* (Oxford, 2000).

[3] This approach characterizes the two largest general surveys of Greek medicine in English,

A critique of many aspects of this view had been made in the 1930s by Ludwig Edelstein (1902–65), a Berlin scholar who had been forced to flee Germany in 1933 and who spent most of the rest of his life at Johns Hopkins University, Baltimore, where he taught at the leading anglophone institute for the history of medicine. Edelstein saw the history of ancient Greek medicine as a continuum, of which the Hippocratic corpus was only one part, and like his Baltimore colleague Owsei Temkin (1902–), he was interested in the relationship of medical ideas to contemporary thought. In a series of papers from 1931 onwards, Edelstein examined the development of anatomy, medical ethics, dietetics, and magic, trying to identify, as he put it in 1966, the 'distinctive Hellenism of Greek medicine'.[4] In doing so, he challenged many of the standard opinions of his time, gaining in the process the reputation of a *frondeur*. But neither the *Bulletin of the History of Medicine* nor the Leipzig journal in which his earliest articles appeared, *Quellen und Studien zur Geschichte der Naturwissenschaften und der Medizin*, is easily located in a university library, let alone in that of a classics department, and the full impact of Edelstein's work had to wait for the posthumous publication of his selected papers under the title *Ancient Medicine* (cf. n. 6). Edelstein's views, especially on medical ethics, quickly took on the nature of orthodoxy in the USA; his contention that the Hippocratic Oath was the creation of a small and unrepresentative Pythagorean sect contributed in no small part to the landmark decision of the US Supreme Court in *Roe v. Wade* (1973), which established the legality of abortion.

In England at the same time, the 1960s, G. E. R. Lloyd was embarking on a similar quest, looking at the development of Greek 'scientific' ideas, principally in the period from the Presocratics to Aristotle. He made no distinction between medicine and science, but sought to investigate patterns of thought and argument, using the methods of anthropology as well as of traditional ancient philosophy. Whereas Edelstein had ranged widely over the history of ancient medicine, Lloyd has compensated for a more restricted chronological range by a broader conception of what are to be considered scientific ideas.[5] In his most recent books he has taken his investigation of Greek science further by deliberately setting out to compare Greek and Chinese science in order to answer Edelstein's question regarding the unique features of Greek science, although without attributing the same high value

E. D. Phillips, *Greek Medicine* (London, 1973), and J. Longrigg, *Greek Rational Medicine: Philosophy and Medicine from Alcmaeon to the Alexandrians* (London, 1993).

[4] L. Edelstein, 'The Distinctive Hellenism of Greek Medicine', *Bulletin of the History of Medicine*, 40 (1966), 197–255.

[5] G. E. R. Lloyd, *Polarity and Analogy* (Cambridge, 1966), *Magic, Reason and Experience* (Cambridge, 1979), *Science, Folklore and Ideology* (Cambridge, 1983)—the only volume to touch substantially on a later medical author, Soranus—and *The Revolutions of Wisdom* (Berkeley, 1987).

as Edelstein merely to its being Greek.[6] Throughout he has insisted on the relative fluidity of boundaries between disciplines, emphasizing above all the variety, as well as the similarities, within Greek medicine.

Nowhere is this shown more clearly than in his treatment of the Hippocratic corpus, in which far from restricting himself to a few major texts composed by a great name, Lloyd has expressed agnosticism about the possibility of identifying any single text as coming from Hippocrates himself, and has used the disagreements and differences between the putative authors to offer a picture of classical Greek medicine that is both more nuanced than that of Edelstein and more philosophically rigorous. By being incorporated within the wider framework of ideas, Hippocratic medicine is not left to specialists within medicine, or even within science, but is made accessible to all those interested in the Greeks.[7] The Lloyd model, it is fair to say, is now dominant in the anglophone world, and has been widely followed on the Continent, particularly in Italy. In Germany it has faced stronger opposition from an 'old guard' of medically trained historians, like Charles Lichtenthaeler, or from those with a more strictly philological agenda.[8] But it was also anticipated in its use of anthropology by Fridolf Kudlien, whose interest in the medical history of antiquity has a more socially orientated focus.[9]

This move towards a pluralistic view of classical Greek medicine has been strengthened by the demolition of another long-standing construct, the division into Coan and Cnidian medicine, each with its own priorities, theories, and medical methods. Working independently and coming from very different backgrounds, Wesley Smith, Antoine Thivel, and Vincenzo Di Benedetto argued convincingly that such a neat division cannot readily be found within the Hippocratic corpus, where both allegedly Coan and Cnidian elements frequently coexist within the same treatise.[10] The distinction, as a heuristic device, goes back to Galen, if not earlier, but was considerably developed from the seventeenth century onwards by historians of medicine, who sought to justify their own medical theories by relating them to the great Hippocrates. As a consequence, they could safely neglect the Cnidian

---

[6] G. E. R. Lloyd, *Demystifying Mentalities* (Cambridge, 1990), *Adversaries and Authorities: Investigations into Ancient Greek and Chinese Science* (Cambridge, 1996). His selected papers, *Methods and Problems in Greek Science* (Cambridge, 1991), neatly show his intellectual development over thirty years.

[7] G. E. R. Lloyd, Introduction to *Hippocratic Writings* (Harmondsworth, 1978). Edelstein had also anticipated some of his approaches: *Ancient Medicine* (Baltimore, 1967), 401–39.

[8] e.g. C. Lichtenthaeler, *Der Eid des Hippokrates* (Cologne, 1984). The most important result of German philological scholarship is undoubtedly the *Index Hippocraticus* (Göttingen, 1986–9).

[9] F. Kudlien, *Der Beginn des medizinischen Denkens bei den Griechen* (Zurich, 1967).

[10] W. D. Smith, 'Galen on Coans vs. Cnidians', *Bulletin of the History of Medicine*, 47 (1973), 569–85; A. Thivel, *Cnide et Cos?* (Paris, 1981); V. Di Benedetto, *Il medico e la malattia* (Turin, 1986).

treatises as not corresponding to the best ancient medical, i.e. allegedly Hippocratic, practice.[11] The abandonment of the belief that 'proper' Greek medicine must be directly linked with Hippocrates and with Cos has, as a consequence, stimulated fresh interest in the less familiar works of the Hippocratic corpus, many of which have appeared for the first time in English in vols. v–viii of the Loeb Hippocrates, edited by Paul Potter and Wesley Smith (Harvard University Press, 1988–95). The forthcoming appearance of new editions of the Anonymus Londinensis papyrus, by Daniela Manetti and Jackie Pigeaud, should also act as a stimulus to integrate this important, and almost forgotten, testimony to early Greek medicine into the wider picture.

Modern students of ancient philosophy have also been prominent in the revival of interest in Hellenistic and later medicine, principally because Galen is one of the main sources for Stoic and Epicurean epistemology and psychology. As Hellenistic and Roman philosophy became fashionable, from the late 1960s onwards, it was only to be expected that Galen would be rediscovered too. But, if the initial impetus was primarily 'archaeological', to recover fragments and theories of Hellenistic philosophy,[12] it quickly became apparent that with Galen one was dealing with an important philosopher in his own right, whose own theories, prejudices, and interests had played a considerable part in preserving, and at the same time transforming, his source material. Phillip De Lacy's edition of Galen's *De placitis Hippocratis et Platonis* (*On the Opinions of Hippocrates and Plato*), with English translation and commentary (Berlin, 1978–84), made a major philosophical treatise of Galen accessible in English for the first time, and his commentary carefully linked Galen's ideas with those of other ancient philosophers. If this work, as its title indicates, showed Galen as a Platonist bringing the evidence of Hippocratic medicine to bear in order to confute the Stoics, his importance as an Aristotelian was chronicled at length by Paul Moraux in the second volume of his *Der Aristotelismus bei den Griechen* (Berlin, 1984), 687–808. Together these two authors explained and illustrated the main philosophical foundations on which Galen built his own medico-philosophical system.

Galen's independence, however, took a little more time to emerge, in part because his deliberate eclecticism, made up of a refusal to adhere to the tenets of any of the major philosophical schools and an insistence on the importance of proper demonstrative logic, could easily be mistaken for fudge—and has indeed been so termed.[13] It is also unfortunate that the

---

[11] I. M. Lonie, 'Cos versus Cnidus and the Historians', *History of Science*, 15 (1978), 42–75, 77–92.

[12] Notably in L. Edelstein and I. G. Kidd, *Posidonius: The Fragments* (Cambridge, 1972), and I. G. Kidd, *Posidonius: The Commentary* (Cambridge, 1989–99).

[13] By P. Donini, 'Galeno e la filosofia', *ANRW* II 36. 5 (1992), 3484–504. Contrast, for

philosophical treatise of which Galen was most proud, *On Demonstration*, is
almost entirely lost, and the only edition of its fragments is now over a century old, relatively hard to locate, and needs to be supplemented by further
passages taken from Arabic and Hebrew authors.[14] None the less, it became
clear that, not only was Galen a considerable logician—according to some,
the inventor of the fourth figure of the syllogism—but he also employed
this logic consistently throughout his medical life.[15] His views on teleology,
heavily influenced by both Aristotle and Plato, offered a more convincing defence of that principle within nature than was given by either of his
great predecessors.[16] In short, the renewal of interest in post-Aristotelian
philosophy has accorded Galen the respect for his views on logic and epistemology that had been obscured for centuries by a concentration on his
activities and theories as a physician.[17]

2. Galen Fights Back

This rediscovery and re-evaluation of Galen by ancient philosophers is
merely one aspect of a remarkable resurgence of activity around this prolific
writer, chronicled most recently by Jutta Kollesch and Diethard Nickel.[18]
Whereas, thirty years ago, it was hard to find any English translation of a
Galenic text, approximately a quarter of his surviving output is now available, and in 1997 he was granted by Oxford University Press the status of a
World's Classic.[19] Two factors have contributed to this remarkable revival,
the arrival of new texts, and the realization of Galen's crucial information
on many aspects of ancient medicine and society, of which philosophy is
but one.

It may come as a surprise to learn that the Galenic corpus, as represented
in the standard 1821–33 edition of Karl Gottlob Kühn, constitutes approximately 10 per cent of surviving Greek literature from the period before
AD 300, and is more than twice the size of the collected works of his nearest

a much more positive evaluation, R. J. Hankinson, 'Galen's Philosophical Eclecticism', ibid.
3505–22.

[14] I. v. Müller, 'Über Galens Werk vom wissenschaftlichen Beweis', *Abhandlungen der
Akademie der Wissenschaften München*, 20 (1895), 403–78.

[15] J. Barnes, 'Galen on Logic and Therapy', in F. Kudlien and R. J. Durling (eds.), *Galen's
Method of Healing* (Proceedings of the 1982 Galen Symposium; Leiden, 1991), 50–102. See
also the introduction to R. J. Hankinson, *Galen, On the Therapeutic Method, Books I and II*
(Oxford, 1989).

[16] R. J. Hankinson, 'Galen and the Best of All Possible Worlds', *CQ*, NS 39 (1989), 206–27.

[17] Significant is the publication in English translation of three medico-philosophical texts:
R. Walzer and M. Frede, *Galen: Three Treatises on the Nature of Science* (Indianapolis, 1985)
(with an important introduction by Michael Frede).

[18] J. Kollesch and D. Nickel, 'Bibliographia Galeniana', *ANRW* II 37. 2 (1994), 1077–253.

[19] P. N. Singer (trans.), *Galen: Selected Writings* (Oxford, 1997).

rivals, Aristotle and Plutarch. Still more surprising may be the revelation that, since 1960, a previously unknown work of Galen has been published or announced almost every two years. Some are merely fragments, but others are entire treatises, some of them running to several books. Few of them, it must be admitted, are in Galen's original Greek, but recent years have seen the publication of possibly new fragments of Galen's commentary on medicine in the *Timaeus*, by Carlos Larrain (Stuttgart, 1992). The same editor has also recovered Greek fragments of a study of voluntary and involuntary motion, *On Movements Hard to Explain*, which established the authenticity of two versions in medieval Latin that had been neglected since the sixteenth century.[20]

But by far the most significant have been the texts preserved in oriental languages or in medieval Latin (and sometimes in both). A brief list of titles, dates, and editors gives some indication of the amount and scope of these treatises, all of which are available with a translation into a modern Western language:[21]

Anatomical Procedures 9–15: M. Simon (Leipzig, 1906); English version, W. H. L. Duckworth *et al.* (Cambridge, 1962); major revision, I. Garofalo (Turin, 1991).
On Medical Terms: M. Meyerhof and J. Schacht (Berlin, 1931).
Commentary on Epidemics 2: F. Pfaff (Leipzig, 1934).
Commentary on the Timaeus: H. Schröder and P. Kahle (Leipzig, 1934).
On Procatarctic Causes. K. Bardong (Leipzig, 1937).
On the Seven-Month Child: R. Walzer (*Rivista di studi orientali*, 15 (1933), 323–57).
Commentary on Epidemics 6: F. Pfaff (vol. i Leipzig 1940; vol. ii Berlin, 1960).
On Habits: J. Schmutte (Leipzig, 1941).
On Medical Experience: R. Walzer (Oxford, 1944).
Commentary on the Hippocratic Oath: F. Rosenthal (*Bulletin of the History of Medicine*, 30 (1963), 52–87).
On the Parts of Medicine, On Cohesive Causes, On Diet in Acute Diseases, according to Hippocrates: M. C. Lyons (Arabic version), H. Schoene and K. Kalbfleisch, rev. J. Kollesch, D. Nickel, and G. Strohmaier (Latin versions) (Berlin, 1969).
On Homoiomerous Parts: G. Strohmaier (Berlin, 1970).
On Morals: J. N. Mattock (*Festschrift R. Walzer* (Oxford, 1972), 235–60).
Commentary on Airs, Waters, and Places (part): A. Wasserstein (Jerusalem, 1982).
On Examining the Best Doctor: A. Z. Iskandar (Berlin, 1988).
On My Own Opinions: V. Nutton (Berlin, 1999).

Important fragments of Galenic philosophical and medical texts have been published by N. Rescher, *Alexander against Galen on Motion* (Islamabad, 1965), and M. Zonta, *Un interprete ebreo della filosofia di Galeno* (Turin, 1995). In addition, the forthcoming publication has been announced of

[20] C. J. Larrain, 'Galen, *De motibus dubiis*: Die lateinische Übersetzung des Niccolò da Reggio', *Traditio*, 49 (1994), 171–233, with commentary, ibid. 51 (1996), 1–41.
[21] Unless otherwise stated, they are published in the Corpus Medicorum Graecorum series (Leipzig and Berlin).

the whole of the *Commentary on Airs, Waters, and Places*, edited by G. Strohmaier; and possible fragments have been identified of Galen's treatises *On the Eye* and *On the Anatomy of Dead Animals* (which raises interesting questions about the authenticity of another text known in Arabic, *On Vivisection*).[22]

This new material, much of it related to Galen's broad non-medical interests, now allows a much more rounded picture of Galen than that of the traditional dogmatic doctor. He can now be seen wrestling with a variety of problems, and endeavouring to bring all his considerable learning, both intellectual and practical, to bear on them. New areas of his life are also opened up, whether it be his knowledge of earlier meteorology and astronomy, of minor plays by Aristophanes, and of Pergamene antiquities, or his concern, at the very end of his life, with the nature and existence of the human soul. New Galenic cases, not least in psychological medicine, are related along with further details of the impressive series of animal experiments in the 160s that led Galen to his understanding of the gross anatomy of the brain. The accretion of new material has yet to be fully assimilated, even by Galenists, let alone by classical scholars in general, but the constant arrival of new texts and fragments, larger in extent than any papyrus, has acted in its turn as a stimulus to the study of the older Galenic corpus.[23] If the 1979 Cambridge conference on Galen brought together for the first time interested scholars from a wide variety of disciplines to summarize the state of play, its successors, in Kiel, Pavia, Berlin, Madrid, and Lille, were devoted to exploring less familiar areas of Galen's work, such as the *Method of Healing*, the psychological treatises, and pharmacology. One, perhaps unexpected, consequence of this re-evaluation has been the extension of Galen's life from the *Suda*'s canonical three score years and ten to the eighty-seven of his Arabic biographers.[24]

But the very existence of such a body of material of itself cannot explain why scholars might wish to turn to it. One reason was put forward in 1973 by the doyen of studies in ancient medicine, Owsei Temkin. In his *Galenism: Rise and Decline of a Medical Philosophy* (Cornell, 1973) he set out with characteristic modesty and lucidity the development of Galenism (the -ism is important) from the second to the nineteenth century. Far from being an unfortunate anachronism, Galenic ideas often stimulated other physicians

[22] See the articles by G. Strohmaier, I. Ormos, and S. Vardanian, in J. Kollesch and D. Nickel (eds.), *Galen und das hellenistische Erbe* (Stuttgart, 1993), 157–64, 165–72, 193–204.

[23] The last twenty years have seen a major re-evaluation of the manuscript tradition of the Greek corpus, principally by N. G. Wilson, and of the early printed editions, mainly by V. Nutton, with the result that many of the basic guidelines for future editors have now been established.

[24] V. Nutton, 'Galen *ad multos annos*', *Dynamis*, 15 (1995), 25–39; 'Galen on Theriac: Problems of Authenticity', in A. Debru (ed.), *Galen on Pharmacology* (Leiden, 1997), 133–51.

to new thoughts, and Temkin's whole book can be read as a plea for modern doctors to practise medicine as thinking professionals.

If Temkin represents an older type of medical history, stressing the central significance of medical ideas, and if he looks favourably on Galen, the stance taken by the Philadelphia classicist Wesley Smith only six years later was vastly different. In his *The Hippocratic Tradition* (Cornell, 1979) Smith pursued a similar investigation, looking at the way doctors, and occasionally classicists, had over the centuries defined Hippocrates, what he stood for, and what he had written. Smith could show, beyond all doubt, that while respect for Hippocrates had continued unchanged, both the reasons why he was respected and the treatises he was thought to have written had varied considerably. For almost the first time—for Smith had been anticipated by Edelstein—Galen was revealed as the crucial determinant in modern perceptions of Hippocrates, both in setting out the guidelines for judging authenticity and, more subtly, in making Hippocratic medicine appear to be the only true, effective, and scientific way of dealing with health and disease. Galen himself had admitted, on more than one occasion, that in his own day Hippocratism was far from universally accepted, and that both Methodist and Empiricist doctors enjoyed at least equal success. But after Galen, it was taken for granted that Hippocratic medicine—the theory of the four humours, the emphasis on a search for causes, and allopathic therapies—was the only true medicine, and that those ages and regions that did not share in this medicine were benighted or perverse. The formal medical tradition, in Europe and the Near East, became that promulgated by Galen on the basis of his understanding of Hippocrates, and the whole history of medicine could be written in terms of a series of renaissances of this formal medicine—at Baghdad, Salerno, Toledo, Padua, and so on. Galen's prejudices, against the Erasistrateans, the Empiricists, and, above all, the Methodists, became canonized as the truth—and, since most of Galen's opponents could be heard only through the mouth of Galen, they were unable to answer for themselves.

Despite its title, Smith's book is mainly concerned with Galen. Almost half deals directly with Galen, and much of the rest considers either the consequences of Galen's views or material deriving from Galen. The resulting portrait is not always edifying, albeit instructive of Galen's procedures. His formidable learning and intellectual curiosity, so admired by Temkin, are shown to have been accompanied by unscrupulous and arrogant argument that imposed conviction on subsequent generations unable to compete in scholarship, wealth, or genius. By emphasizing how much the formation of the Western medical tradition was owed not to Hippocrates, but to Galen, Smith challenged many of the presuppositions of earlier scholars. Even if it is not the case that in order to study Hippocrates and the Hippocratic corpus one must begin with Galen, a proper understanding of Galen and

Galen's overriding influence is now regarded as crucial to any appreciation of the subsequent development of the history of medicine.[25] As Heinrich von Staden demonstrated in his *Herophilus: The Art of Medicine in Early Alexandria* (Cambridge, 1989), a magisterial study which has opened up afresh the study of medicine in Hellenistic Alexandria, to accept Smith's overall conclusion is not necessarily to denigrate Galen. One can be grateful for the enormous amount of information that Galen provides, for the energy and enthusiasm with which he sought, albeit not entirely with success, to imitate Herophilus and Erasistratus in their anatomizing, but, at the same time, one must be aware how often Galen's priorities have distorted the material that has come down to us. The task of the historian of ancient medicine is not to avoid Galen, but rather to get beyond him.

3. Medicine as Social History

The history of medicine in general has changed considerably over the past twenty years, and the study of ancient medicine cannot help but be affected by such changes. From being a topic left almost entirely to physicians, usually elderly and concerned with the heroic development of their speciality, the history of medicine evolved to become a part of wider social history. If, as has already been stated, the boundaries between ancient medicine, science, and philosophy have been eroded almost to nothing, social historians of medicine have moved still further to consider all varieties of ancient healing practices, whether traditionally medical, religious, magical, or folkloric.[26] At the same time new, or more nuanced, answers have been proposed to the old question about the organization and development of the medical profession—and, indeed, it has been doubted whether the notion of a medical profession is in any way applicable to the more open medical market place of antiquity.[27] Patients, and not only notorious hypochondriacs like Aelius Aristeides and Seneca, now are considered as important negotiators in the healing process, rather than the mere objects of medical ministrations.

This move towards integrating medical history with mainstream ancient history has been more successful with Roman medicine than with Greek, not least because the sheer abundance of literary, papyrological, and epigraphic sources from the Roman imperial period allows a much more varied perspective on medical practice. To put Galen in context as an imperial

[25] Cf. G. E. R. Lloyd, 'Galen on Hellenistics and Hippocrateans', in *Methods and Problems* (n. 5), 398–416.

[26] See the two volumes of P. J. Van der Eijk, H. F. J. Hortsmanshoff, and P. H. Schrijvers (eds.), *Ancient Medicine in its Socio-Cultural Context* (Amsterdam, 1995); and T. S. Barton, *Power and Knowledge: Astrology, Physiognomics and Medicine in the Roman Empire* (Ann Arbor, 1994).

[27] V. Nutton, 'Healers in the Medical Market Place: Towards a Social History of Graeco-Roman Medicine', in A. Wear (ed.), *Medicine in Society* (Cambridge, 1992), 15–58.

doctor requires a considerable acquaintance with Roman social history, and, conversely, the information that Galen provides on all aspects of life in the empire can hardly be neglected by specialists in ancient history. Nutton's commentary on Galen's *On Prognosis* (Berlin, 1979) and a subsequent series of essays provoked scholars such as Darrel Amundsen and Simon Swain to relate ancient medical texts to contemporary ideologies and debates within the Roman world.[28] The three volumes on medicine in the Roman empire in *ANRW* II 37. 1–3 (1993–6) also show how much work has been done around the world, and in a variety of disciplines that, a generation ago, would have scarcely touched on medical history.

Among them, the evidence of archaeology, especially the discovery of surgical instruments, has resulted in two broad surveys that offer useful introductions to ancient medicine in general.[29] How much new developments in ethno- and palaeo-botany, as well as in palaeopathology, have contributed to a new understanding of disease in the ancient world can be easily assessed by comparing the more text-based chapter on ancient diseases in *The Cambridge World History of Human Disease*, which, despite its date of publication, was written in the early 1980s, with the writings of Grmek and Sallares, both of whom have worked with archaeologists and palaeopathologists.[30] Even if many of their conclusions must remain speculative, they have changed considerably historians' appreciation of the background of health and disease against which ancient doctors and ancient patients lived and worked. A similar project, focusing on drugs and plant remedies, has been pursued for many years by John Riddle, whose controversial arguments about the effectiveness of drugs used in antiquity to prevent conception or bring about abortion should not obscure the methodology by which he has tried to relate modern understanding of plant substances to those recorded in ancient pharmacological treatises, especially Dioscorides.[31]

4. Feminism, Fads, and the Future

Riddle's investigations also link with a further major development in ancient medicine that has helped it away from the sidelines. The feminist

[28] V. Nutton, 'The Patient's Choice: A New Treatise by Galen', *CQ*, NS 40 (1990), 235–57; D. W. Amundsen, *Medicine, Society and Faith in the Ancient and Medieval Worlds* (Baltimore, 1996); Simon Swain, *Hellenism and Empire* (Oxford, 1996).

[29] A. Krug, *Heilkunst und Heilkult* (Munich, 1985); R. Jackson, *Doctors and Diseases in the Roman Empire* (London, 1988).

[30] K. D. Kiple (ed.), *The Cambridge World History of Human Disease* (Cambridge, 1993), 262–70; M. D. Grmek, *Diseases in the Ancient Greek World* (Baltimore, 1989); R. Sallares, *The Ecology of the Ancient Greek World* (London, 1991).

[31] J. M. Riddle, *Dioscorides on Pharmacy and Medicine* (Austin, 1983); *Contraception and Abortion from the Ancient World to the Renaissance* (Harvard, 1992). The Belgian scholar Alain Touwaide, who is more philologically sensitive than Riddle, has embarked on a similar project.

movement has made ancient gynaecology one of the most exciting areas of
ancient medicine. From being almost totally neglected a generation ago,
with its major texts in the Hippocratic corpus unavailable in an English
translation, and with the only English versions of any ancient gynaecolog-
ical texts, those by Soranus and Caelius Aurelianus, long out of print and
effectively forgotten, it has become the centre of almost a thriving industry,
in Europe as well as in Britain and the USA. In France Danielle Gourevitch, the author of a popular survey, has also been one of the editors of
the Budé Soranus, which has made accessible a Greek text of the most important medical author on the subject in antiquity.[32] The 1994 overview of
Soranus, the most important writer in the ancient Methodist tradition, by
Ann Hanson and Monica Green, is almost a monograph in its own right,
and Green's Princeton dissertation on women's diseases encompasses a remarkable reconstruction of late antique writings on the subject.[33] Writing
in English, however, has largely concentrated on classical Greece, as in
the book by Lesley Ann Dean-Jones, but the gap in our knowledge of the
Roman imperial period has now been addressed in books by Helen King
and by Rebecca Flemming.[34] No historian of ancient medicine, it is fair to
say, can afford, like Galen, to leave gynaecology almost entirely to others,
for the combination of theoretical sophistication, often deriving from an-
thropological perspectives, and commitment to contemporary issues offers
an important model for historians of more traditional medico-historical
themes, e.g. ethics or surgery.

If feminism has not only helped push medicine into the consciousness
of classicists, but has also brought lasting advances in the understanding of
ancient medicine, the same cannot be said with the same confidence about
some more recent fashions. The 1990s displayed a positively narcissistic
concern with the body and with body image, with perceptions of self and the
ideal of beauty. But while the topic attracted wide audiences to seminar series
and conferences, relatively few contributors to them attempted to investigate
the medical sources, as opposed to finding a medical title under which to
place a (frequently literary) study. But such a complaint about the dilution
of ancient medicine in the course of its move away from traditional concerns
may also be seen in a more positive light: ancient medicine has become an
acceptable part of classics. Nor is an engagement with contemporary issues
necessarily bad if it forces classicists to look at once familiar material in

---

[32] D. Gourevitch, *Le Mal d'être femme* (Paris, 1984); *Soranos d'Ephèse: Maladies des femmes*
(Paris, 1988–94).

[33] A. E. Hanson and M. H. Green, 'Soranus of Ephesus, *Methodicorum Princeps*', in *ANRW*
II 37. 2 (1994), 968–1075; M. H. Green, *The Transmission of Ancient Theories of Female
Physiology and Disease through the Early Middle Ages* (diss. Ph.D., Princeton, 1985).

[34] L. A. Dean-Jones, *Women's Bodies in Classical Greek Science* (Oxford, 1994); H. King,
Hippocrates' Women (London, 1998); R. Flemming, *Medicine and the Making of Roman Women*
(Oxford, 2000).

a new light. Véronique Dasen's work on dwarfism and Robert Garland's more general survey of ancient attitudes towards disability show what can be achieved; both have pointed to medical material long neglected because it was thought to be non-Hippocratic and non-medical, and both, in their turn, have been influenced by modern studies of ancient medicine.[35]

Whether in the next thirty years ancient medicine is going to undergo a re-evaluation and a transformation as radical as those of the last thirty is an open question. The arrival of good surveys, accessible to a wide audience, and incorporating recent discoveries, offers a new starting-point for further research.[36] While the Galen industry may be expected to produce new texts, especially via the Arabic,[37] that require assimilation, and new and better editions are likely to appear of neglected authors like Rufus of Ephesus, much work still requires to be done to understand the role of medicine in Roman society, and not least the changes that occurred during the transition to Christianity and to Galenism. But, while much will remain familiar, the student of Hippocratic and early Greek medicine may have to adopt totally new viewpoints as the material currently being published from Babylonia and Egypt imposes a new consideration of the relationship of Greek medicine to that of the Near East.[38] Even if one still rejects the claims of the 'Black Athena' school for the African origin of Greek medicine, classicists may have to modify some of their sweeping statements about what non-Greek doctors did or did not do. They will also have to integrate more fully than heretofore the social, philosophical, medical, and archaeological evidence for classical Greek medicine, and penetrate behind the veil of prejudice that Galen threw over all that preceded him. If the last generation has shared in the revival of Galen, the next will have to explore further the world both before and after Galen. The consequences of these researches, and the methodologies they will require, are likely to impinge on all areas of classical studies. Far from being a sleepy backwater, the study of ancient medicine may well be—or continue to be—exciting and enlightening.

---

[35] V. Dasen, *Dwarfs in Ancient Egypt and Greece* (Oxford, 1993); R. Garland, *The Eye of the Beholder: Deformity and Disability in the Graeco-Roman World* (London, 1995).

[36] e.g. M. D. Grmek (ed.), *Storia del pensiero medico occidentale*, i. *Antichità e medioevo* (Bari, 1993); L. I. Conrad, M. Neve, V. Nutton, R. Porter, and A. Wear, *The Western Medical Tradition* (Cambridge, 1995). The account in I. Loudon (ed.), *Western Medicine: An Illustrated History* (Oxford, 1997), is less satisfactory as it jumps in a page from early Alexandria to the seventh century.

[37] A reading of the Meshed manuscript of the Arabic translation of Galen's *De libris propriis* by V. Boudon (Paris) has filled a major lacuna in the Greek text of ch. 3, with important consequences for our understanding of Alexandrian anatomy in the years around AD 120: see the paper delivered at a Wellcome Institute/University of London Classical Institute symposium in 1999, to appear in V. Nutton (ed.), *Galen beyond Kühn* (*BICS* supplement).

[38] M. Stol, 'Diagnosis and Therapy in Babylonian Medicine', *Jaarbericht Ex Oriente Lux*, 32 (1991–1992), 42–65; id., *Epilepsy in Babylonia* (Groningen, 1993); J. F. Nunn, *Ancient Egyptian Medicine* (London, 1996).

15

Galen on the Seat of the Intellect: Anatomical Experiment and Philosophical Tradition

TEUN TIELEMAN

1. Introduction

GALEN's vivisection experiments concerned with the nervous system may rank among the most sophisticated known from ancient sources. Galen (AD 129–c.216) appears to inaugurate a new era by systematically working his way along the spinal chord and nerves, making incisions and carefully recording the resultant phenomena of paralysis.[1] None the less, these experiments have on the whole received scant attention from modern historians.[2] My purpose in the present paper is to study the nature and historical significance of this group of experiments as reported in the first three books of Galen's great work *On the Doctrines of Hippocrates and Plato*.[3] These

Research for this article was made possible by a fellowship of the Royal Dutch Academy of Arts and Sciences.

References to *De placitis Hippocratis et Platonis* [*PHP*] are to the edition of P. De Lacy (Corpus Medicorum Graecorum, V. 4; Berlin, 1978–84), with Kühn volume- and page-numbers appended.

[1] See e.g. G. E. R. Lloyd, *Magic, Reason and Experience: Studies in the Origins and Development of Greek Science* (Cambridge, 1979), 167; id., *Methods and Problems in Greek Science: Selected Papers* (Cambridge, 1991), 71; J. Mansfeld, 'The Idea of the Will in Chrysippus, Posidonius and Galen', in J. J. Cleary (ed.), *PBACAP* 7 (1991), 105–43 at 128, 131. On Galen's dates cf. now V. Nutton, 'Galen ad multos annos', *Dynamis*, 15 (1995), 25–39; id., 'Galen on Theriac: Problems of Authenticity', in A. Debru (ed.), *Galen on Pharmacology* (Leiden, 1997), 133–51.

[2] But cf. F. Ullrich, *Die anatomische und vivisektorische Technik des Galens* (diss. Leipzig, 1919), 39–47; R. E. Siegel, *Galen's System of Physiology and Medicine: An Analysis of his Doctrines and Observations on Blood Flow, Respiration, Humors and Internal Diseases* (Basel and New York, 1968), 116–17; id., *Galen on Sense Perception: His Doctrines, Observations and Experiments on Vision, Hearing, Smell, Taste, Touch and Pain, and their Historical Sources* (Basel and New York, 1970), 161–6; id., *Galen on Psychology, Psychopathology and Function and Diseases of the Nervous System: An Analysis of his Doctrines, Observations and Experiments* (Basel and New York, 1973), 39–48, 235–43; Mansfeld (n. 1), 126 ff.; A. Debru, 'L'expérimentation chez Galien', *ANRW* II 37. 2 (1994), 1718–56 at 1731–2.

[3] The same and other related experiments are reported at *AA* 8. 3–9, ii. 661–98 Kühn; 9. 12–14, pp. 21–31 Simon = 17–26 Duckworth; 11. 11, pp. 131–4 Simon = 104–7 Duckworth; 14. 7, pp. 261–9 Simon = 208–14 Duckworth. Being intended for students of anatomy, these reports are more detailed than those in *PHP* from an anatomical point of view but much less informative about the methodological issues which are central to the present paper.

books were the fruit of his tumultuous stay in Rome in the 160s, when he was struggling to establish his reputation as a medical theorist and practitioner. In fact, he first performed the experiments in question publicly, as a means of self-advertisement in an intensely competitive climate. This social and cultural context has been the subject of studies by others and will not be at the forefront of my concerns.[4] Nor shall I concentrate attention on anatomical technicalities—a field in which I have no special competence.[5] My main concern will be with theoretical aspects, that is to say, with the epistemological, or argumentative, status of these experiments as well as with their method. To this end I shall first chart the broader argumentative framework in which the experiments are embedded (§ 2). In an earlier work I have studied this framework in the light of the philosophical and scholastic traditions to which Galen is indebted.[6] One crucial point which emerged was the conjunction of—and resulting tension between—elements from the philosophical and medical traditions. In addition, Galen modelled some of his procedures on the technology of his day. Exactly how, then, have ingredients from different disciplines and traditions been combined? As will be shown, the answer to this question bears directly on the role and status of the experiments, an issue which played only a minor part in my earlier study.

In the next section of this paper (§ 3) I shall deal with the experiments in the light of Galen's overall method. An important aspect here is the polarity between theory and practice. One could assemble such theoretical pronouncements as Galen includes and use these to reconstruct what might be called his methodology. But how does Galen in practice live up to his theoretical claims and standards? I shall conclude (§ 4) by considering Galen's achievement in terms of a second pair of polarities—tradition and innovation. How original was he? And how influential ?

A note on terminology is in order. It is sometimes said to be anachronistic to speak of experimentation with reference to ancient science,[7] and

---

[4] See Lloyd, *Magic, Reason and Experience* (n. 1), 96 ff.; H. Von Staden, 'Anatomy as Rhetoric: Galen on Dissection and Persuasion', *Journal of the History of Medicine and Allied Sciences*, 50 (1995), 47–66; A. Debru, 'Les démonstrations médicales à Rome au temps de Galien', in P. Van der Eijk *et al.* (eds.), *Ancient Medicine in its Socio-Cultural Context* (Clio Medica, 27; Amsterdam and Atlanta, 1995), i. 69–81. Cf. also V. Nutton, 'The Chronology of Galen's Early Career', *CQ*, NS 23 (1973), 158–71.

[5] On Galen's anatomy see M. Simon, *Sieben Bücher Anatomie des Galen*, ii (Leipzig, 1906), v–lii; Ullrich (n. 2); C. Singer, *Galen on Anatomical Procedures* (Cambridge, 1956); W. L. H. Duckworth, M. C. Lyons, and B. Towers, *Galen on Anatomical Procedures: The Later Books* (Cambridge, 1962); Siegel, *Physiology* (n. 2); I. Garofalo, *Procedimenti anatomici* (Milan, 1991); R. J. Hankinson, 'Galen's Anatomical Procedures: A Second Century Debate in Medical Epistemology', *ANRW* II 37. 2 (1994), 1834–55, is concerned with methodology rather than anatomy.

[6] T. L. Tieleman, *Galen and Chrysippus on the Soul: Argument and Refutation in the* De Placitis *Books II–III* (Leiden, 1996).

[7] For views on the question of ancient experimentation see the surveys in G. E. R. Lloyd,

it does indeed make sense to reserve the expression 'experimental *method*' for modern, say post-seventeenth-century, science. But what about experiments, or experimentation, *tout court*? Today no responsible historian would uphold the claim that the ancients performed experiments in a systematic fashion. But neither can we uphold the equally extreme claim that they did not engage in experimentation at all. As Lloyd and others have urged, the performance of different scientists on different subjects and in different periods varied considerably.[8] What we need most at the present stage of research are case-by-case studies, and in concentrating on one particular group of experiments of Galen, I aim to provide just such a case study. In what follows I shall use the term 'experiment' in the rather wide sense of an artificial situation created to test specific claims. That this involves present-day requirements such as repeatability and the control of variables is not something to be taken for granted, though I hope to show that these features are present, albeit in an embryonic form. But let us first take a look at the context in which the experiments are encountered.

2. Dialectic and Science: The Argument of *PHP* 1–3 and 6

Galen projects into the past a unitary tradition of good philosophy-cum-medicine with Hippocrates and Plato as its fountainheads.[9] His main concern in *PHP* is with proving that the greatest doctor and the greatest philosopher are in essential agreement and broadly correct on the main questions of philosophy and medicine. The first issue he addresses is that of the number and seat of the psychic functions, which takes up no fewer than six books out of a total of nine (1–6).[10]

Why did Galen want to defend and (thus) take advantage of Plato's authority? His preference for Plato fits in with the resurgence of Platonism in the second century AD—a phenomenon particularly characteristic of his native Asia Minor. But Platonism (like Hippocratism)[11] also offered certain

'Experiment in Early Greek Philosophy and Medicine', *PCPS*, NS 10 (1964), 50–72 (repr. in Lloyd, *Methods* (n. 1), 70–99); H. Von Staden, 'Experiment and Experience in Hellenistic Medicine', *BICS* 22 (1975), 178–99.

[8] Cf. Lloyd (n. 7).

[9] On the motivation behind *PHP* see further M. Vegetti , 'Tradizione e verità: forme della storiografia filosofico-scientifica nel *De Placitis* del Galeno', in G. Cambiano (ed.), *Storiografia e dossografia nella filosofia antica* (Turin, 1986), 227–43; Tieleman (n. 6), xxviii ff.

[10] Of *PHP* 1 only the final sections are extant. Books 4 and 5 deal with the soul's emotions or passions (πάθη) in relation to the question of the *number* of the psychic powers. In book 6 Galen returns to the question of their location. Books 7–9 discuss further points of agreement between Hippocrates and Plato concerning sense perception, the physical elements, and method of enquiry.

[11] See G. E. R. Lloyd, 'Galen on Hellenistics and Hippocrateans', in J. Kollesch and D. Nickel (eds.), *Galen und das hellenistische Erbe* (Stuttgart, 1993), 125–44 (also printed in Lloyd, *Method* (n. 1), 398–416).

strategic advantages, since it left sufficient room for his own scientific innovations. This can be neatly illustrated by *PHP*. Here Galen defends a
modernized version of the tripartition and trilocation of the soul famously
advanced by Plato in the *Timaeus* and other dialogues: reason resides in the
brain, anger in the heart, and appetite in the liver.[12] This schema—which,
startlingly, he also ascribes to Hippocrates[13]—is backed by his physiological
theory, in which these three organs are the sources of the nervous, arterial,
and veinous systems respectively. Plato himself, of course, did not know
about the nervous system (as Galen himself acknowledges, *In Tim.* 15.
5 ff.), and the physiology of the *Timaeus* had been superseded in other respects as well. So what Galen in effect sets out to do is to bring the Platonic
account up to date in the light of later scientific advances. The nervous
system had been discovered some hundred years after Plato's death by the
great Alexandrian scientists Herophilus and Erasistratus.[14] But Plato had
at least been correct in identifying the head as the principal organ and so
could be presented as anticipating later developments. In the *Timaeus* Plato
is primarily concerned with man's psychic and moral life. Though drawing
on the medical lore of his day, he remains simply vague on the relations
between psychic functions and bodily organs. Obviously, this facilitates
Galen's project of modernization. But even so, he cannot entirely avoid dis-
torting the master's text. To give one salient example, Plato unequivocally
assigns the third part of the soul—appetite—to the belly, not the liver. The
liver plays no part in the physiology of nourishment, which was an insight
of later date. None the less, Galen represents it as genuinely Platonic.[15]

In Galen's day the cardiocentric theory still enjoyed wide support and scientific respectability. The Peripatetics refurbished the arguments advanced
by Aristotle in favour of the heart's primacy in *On the Parts of Animals*
and elsewhere.[16] The Stoics for their part drew on the ingenious defence of
the cardiocentric view mounted by the great scholarch Chrysippus of Soli

---

[12] See *Resp.* 434 E–444 D; *Ti.* 44 D, 65 E, 67 B, 69 D–70 E, 73 C–E; *Phd.* 96 B, *Phdr.* 246 A ff.

[13] On this ascription see Tieleman (n. 6), xxviii ff., where I point to parallels in so-called
doxographic literature. On the nature and motivation of Galen's Hippocratism in general see
now Lloyd (n. 11), with T. L. Tieleman's review, *Mnemosyne*, 48 (1995), 608.

[14] On the discovery of the nervous system see F. Solmsen, 'Greek Philosophy and the
Discovery of the Nerves', *MH* 18 (1961), 150–97, esp. 195–7 (repr. in id., *Kleine Schriften*
(Hildesheim, 1968), i. 536–83); H. Von Staden, *Herophilus: The Art of Medicine in Early
Alexandria* (Cambridge, 1989), 247 ff. On ancient neurology see further A. Souques, *Étapes de
la neurologie dans l'antiquité* (Paris, 1936); W. Creuze, *Die Neurologie des 1. bis 7. Jahrhunderts*
(Leipzig, 1934); D. H. M. Woollam, 'Concepts of the Brain and its Function in Classical
Antiquity', in F. L. N. Poynter (ed.), *The History and Philosophy of Knowledge of the Brain and
its Function* (Springfield and Oxford, 1958), 5–18; E. Clarke and W. Dewhurst, *An Illustrated
History of Brain Function* (Berkeley, Los Angeles, and Oxford,1972); Von Staden 155–6.

[15] See *PHP* 6. 3. 1,v . 519 Kühn, with *Ti.* 70 D 7–E 5, 77 B 3–4, 80 D–81 E. To my knowledge,
the liver's function in digestion is first encountered in Arist. *Part. an.* 3. 7, 670ª27; cf. N. Mani,
Die historischen Grundlagen der Leberforschung (Basel and Stuttgart, 1965), 35 ff.

[16] The central Aristotelian text is *Part. an.* 3. 4, 665ª29–667ᵇ14. On other passages cf.
G. E. R. Lloyd, 'The Empirical Basis of the Physiology of the *Parva Naturalia*', in G. E. R.

(c.280–205 BC) in his *On the Soul*.[17] Citing past masters and stock arguments was typical of the long-standing controversy on the seat of what was called the soul's ἡγεμονικόν, i.e. 'regent part'.[18] This concept—largely equivalent to our 'mind' or 'intellect'—was Hellenistic and in particular Stoic in origin, but it had become common currency in the protracted debate between the schools and was as a consequence readily assimilated to the Platonic concept of the rational part. Galen is contributing to a *traditional* debate with a limited number of *given options*. The main opposition was that between the head—backed up by the authority of Plato and Hippocrates—and the heart—backed up by the authority of Aristotle and the Stoics. The pattern of allegiances and silences emerging from Galen's discussion conforms to what is to be found in the so-called doxographic literature, where we encounter the same schema of options.

Galen was saturated in Aristotelian logic-cum-dialectic.[19] So he starts from a definition of the soul's regent part which is common ground between the participants in the debate.[20]

(D) The regent part is the principle [τὸ κατάρχον] of sensation and volition.[21]

Lloyd and G. E. L. Owen (eds.), *Aristotle on Mind and the Senses* (Cambridge, 1978), 215–39 at 234 ff. (repr. in Lloyd, *Methods* (n. 1), 224–47).

[17] Substantial fragments have been preserved in *PHP* 2 and 3 (=*SVF* ii. 880–911): see Tieleman (n. 6).

[18] On this debate, with special reference to the so-called doxographic literature, see J. Mansfeld, 'Doxography and Dialetic: The *Sitz im Leben* of the *Placita*', *ANRW* II 36. 4 (1990), 3056–229. On clinical aspects see *Meth. med.* 13. 21, x. 929 Kühn; *Loc. aff.* 2. 5, viii. 127 ff.; 3. 7, viii. 166 ff. Kühn.

[19] In common with many Platonists of his day (cf. J. Whitaker, 'Platonic Philosophy in the Early Centuries of the Empire', *ANRW* II 36. 1 (1987), 81–123), Galen viewed Aristotelian logic as a development of what was to be found in the Platonic dialogues. On his knowledge of Aristotle's logical work see P. Moraux, *Der Aristotelismus bei den Griechen*, ii (Berlin and New York, 1984), 687 ff.; Tieleman (n. 6), 106 ff.

[20] *Top.* 8. 3, 158ᵃ37 ff., 158ᵇ24 ff. Cf. Gal. *PHP* 7. 1. 23, v. 593 Kühn; *Meth. med.* 1. 5, x. 41 Kühn.

[21] For this definition and the subsequent demonstration see 2. 3. 4–7, v. 220 Kühn: ἔστι δὲ τὸ ἡγεμονικόν, ὡς καὶ αὐτοὶ βούλονται, τὸ κατάρχον αἰσθήσεώς τε καὶ ὁρμῆς. οὔκουν ἄλλοθεν χρὴ δεικνύναι τὴν καρδίαν ἐν αὐτῇ τὸ ἡγεμονικὸν ἔχουσαν ἢ ἐκ τοῦ πάσης μὲν τῆς καθ' ὁρμὴν κινήσεως ἐξηγεῖσθαι τοῖς ἄλλοις τοῦ ζῴου μορίοις, ἅπασαν δὲ αἴσθησιν εἰς αὐτὴν ἀναφέρεσθαι. πόθεν οὖν τοῦτο δειχθήσεται; πόθεν δὴ ἄλλοθεν ἢ ἐκ τῶν ἀνατομῶν; εἰ γὰρ αὕτη τοῖς κατὰ μέρος ἅπασιν ἐπιπέμπει δύναμιν αἰσθήσεώς τε καὶ κινήσεως, ἀποπεφυκέναι τι πάντως ἀπ' αὐτῆς ἀγγεῖον ἀναγκαῖόν ἐστιν εἰς τὴν αὐτῶν ὑπηρεσίαν. ὥστε ἐκ τῆς ἀποδεικτικῆς μεθόδου πέφηνεν ὅτι τε χρησιμώτερον ἀνατέμνοντας τὰ ζῷα κατασκέπτεσθαι τίνα καὶ πόσα γένη σωμάτων ἐκ τῆς καρδίας ἐκφυόμενα διανέμεται τοῖς ἄλλοις τοῦ ζῴου μορίοις, ὅτι τε τούτων αὐτῶν ὄντων τοιούτων καὶ τοσῶνδε τοῦτο μὲν αἴσθησιν ἢ κίνησιν ἢ ἄμφω παράγει, τοῦτο δ' ἄλλο τι· καὶ οὕτως ἔχειν ἤδη τίνων ἐν τοῖς ζῴοις δυνάμεων ἡ καρδία πηγή. And 8. 1. 2–4, v. 649–50 Kühn: ἐπὶ τὴν ζήτησιν αὐτῶν τραπόμενοι κατὰ τὸν ἀποδεικτικὸν νόμον, ἔννοιαν ὁμολογουμένην ἔφαμεν εἶναι τοῦ τῆς ψυχῆς ἡγεμονικοῦ τὸ κατάρχον αἰσθήσεώς τε καὶ κινήσεως τῆς κατὰ προαίρεσιν, οὐδὲν ὡς πρὸς τὰ παρόντα διαφέροντος, ἢ κατὰ προαίρεσιν, ἢ καθ' ὁρμὴν εἰπεῖν. εὔδηλον δέ, ὅτι ἕτεραι μέν εἰσιν αἱ κινήσεις ἐκτεινόντων τε καὶ συστελλόντων τὰ κῶλα, βαδιζόντων τε καὶ τρεχόντων, ἑστώτων τε καὶ καθημένων, ὅσα τ' ἄλλα τοιαῦτα πραττόντων, ἕτεραι δ' αἱ κατὰ τὴν καρδίαν τε καὶ τὰς ἀρτηρίας, οὐ κατὰ τὴν ἡμετέραν προαίρεσιν

Given this definition, Galen lays down a dialectical πρόβλημα in the Aristotelian sense, that is to say, a question which invites a yes or no answer:[22]

(P₁) Is the heart the seat of the regent part?

Galen first turns to the heart in view of the position of his adversaries—another feature of traditional dialectic. But soon the brain is introduced as an alternative for the heart (2. 5. 2 ff., v. 240–1 Kühn). Thus, there is an analogous problem, which, though left inexplicit, is in force in the subsequent discussion:

(P₂) Is the brain the seat of the regent part?

The proof envisaged by Galen can be summarized as follows. The defining characteristics of the regent part according to (D) presuppose a bodily basis, that is to say, continuous vessels (which we may call 'nerves') which transmit the sensor and motor impulses to and from the centre.[23] This is expressible in terms of an axiom:

(A₁) Where the beginning [ἀρχή] of the nerves is, there is also the regent part.

Anatomical investigation reveals that this centre is none other than the brain. This yields the following deductively valid syllogism:

(S) Where the beginning [ἀρχή] of the nerves is, there is also the regent part.
The brain is the beginning of the nerves.
The regent part is in the brain.[24]

Here 'being the centre of the nerves' constitutes the middle term linking

---

ἀποτελοῦμεναι, καθάπερ καὶ τρίτον ἄλλο γένος κινήσεων, αἱ περὶ τὴν τῆς τροφῆς οἰκονομίαν. ἀλλ' ἀπό γε τῶν προαιρετικῶν ἀρξάμενοι, καθ' ἃς καὶ τὸ καλούμενον ἰδίως ἡγεμονικόν ἐστι τῆς ψυχῆς, ἕνα λόγον ἐδείκνυμεν ἠρωτῆσθαι μόνον ἐπιστημονικῶς, ἀπ' αὐτοῦ τοῦ ζητουμένου τῆς οὐσίας ἔχοντα τὰς προτάσεις, ὄντα τοιοῦτον· ὅπου τῶν νεύρων ἡ ἀρχή, ἐνταῦθα καὶ τὸ τῆς ψυχῆς ἡγεμονικόν. αὕτη μὲν ἡ τοῦ λόγου κυριωτάτη πρότασις ὡμολογημένη πᾶσιν ἰατροῖς τε καὶ φιλοσόφοις. ἡ δ' οἷον πρόληψις αὐτῆς ἀληθὴς μέν, ἡ ἀρχὴ τῶν νεύρων ἐν τῷ ἐγκεφάλῳ, ψευδὴς δέ, ἡ ἀρχὴ τῶν νεύρων ἐν τῇ καρδίᾳ.

[22] 2. 3. 3, v. 219 Kühn: cf. Arist. *Top.* 1. 4, 101ᵇ29 ff.
[23] Cf. P. De Lacy, 'Galen's Concept of Continuity', *GRBS* 20 (1979), 355–69 at 360.
[24] 8. 1. 22–4, v. 655 Kühn: οὕτως γοῦν ὁ ἀληθὴς λόγος ἐστι βραχὺς ὡς ἐγὼ δείξω σοι δι' ὀλίγων συλλαβῶν περαινόμενον αὐτὸν ὄντα τοιοῦτον· "ἔνθα τῶν νεύρων ἡ ἀρχή, ἐνταῦθα τὸ ἡγεμονικόν· ἡ δ' ἀρχὴ τῶν νεύρων ἐν ἐγκεφάλῳ [ἐστίν]· ἐνταῦθα ἄρα τὸ ἡγεμονικόν." εἰς μὲν οὗτος λόγος ἐννέα καὶ τριάκοντα συλλαβῶν, ὅπερ ἐστὶ δυοῖν καὶ ἡμίσεος ἐπῶν ἐξαμέτρων· ἕτερος δ' ἐστὶ πέντε τῶν πάντων ἐπῶν· "ἔνθα τὰ πάθη τῆς ψυχῆς ἐπιφανέστερον κινεῖ τὰ μόρια τοῦ σώματος, ἐνταῦθα τὸ παθητικὸν τῆς ψυχῆς ἐστιν· ἀλλὰ μὴν ἡ καρδία φαίνεται μεγάλην ἐξαλλαγὴν ἴσχουσα τῆς κινήσεως ἐν θυμοῖς καὶ φόβοις· ἐν ταύτῃ ἄρα τὸ παθητικὸν τῆς ψυχῆς ἐστιν." εἰ δὲ συνθείης ὡδὶ τούτους τοὺς δύο λόγους, οὐ πλεῖον ἐπῶν ἐξαμέτρων ὀκτὼ τὸ συγκείμενον ἐξ αὐτῶν πλῆθος ἔσται; cf. 2. 3. 4–7, v. 219–20 Kühn; 8. 1. 4–5, 22, v. 649–50, 655 Kühn. For symbolic representations see J. Barnes, 'Galen on Logic and Therapy', in F. Kudlien and R. J. Durling (eds.), *Galen's Method of Healing* (Proceedings of the 1982 Galen Symposium; Leiden, 1991), 50–102 at 84–5.

the two terms of the dialectical problem (P$_2$) in the conclusion of this syllogism.

With respect to Galen's train of reasoning we would prefer to speak of a hypothesis ('the brain is the seat of the intellect'), an auxiliary hypothesis derived therefrom ('the brain forms the starting-point of the nerves'), and a test implication ('if the nerves involved are intercepted, paralysis will occur below the incisions'). But in fact Galen thinks in terms not of hypotheses in any present-day sense but of self-evident axioms.[25] Even so, empirical testing—in this particular case presupposed by the second premiss of the syllogistic proof—remains crucial for him.

The above proof, though adumbrated at the outset of his argument, is in fact the conclusion of an extensive procedure designed to select an appropriate middle term. Galen starts from a list of perceptible features or attributes (ὑπάρχοντα):

ἀρκτέον οὖν ἀπὸ τῶν ὑπαρχόντων ἁπάντων τῇ καρδίᾳ καὶ λεκτέον ἐφεξῆς ταῦτα πάντα, πρῶτον μὲν ἐν κεφαλαίοις τε καὶ κατὰ γένος, εἶθ᾽ οὕτως καὶ κατὰ μέρος τε καὶ κατ᾽ εἶδος. ὑπάρχει δὴ τῇ καρδίᾳ θέσις καὶ πηλικότης καὶ πλοκὴ καὶ διάπλασις καὶ διάθεσις καὶ κίνησις. (*PHP* 2. 4. 5–6, v. 228 Kühn; cf. 2. 8. 51, v. 284 Kühn)

One should start from the attributes of the heart and list them all, first under main heads and by genera, next according to part and species. The attributes of the heart, then, are position, size, texture, structure, state, and motion.

This list—reminiscent of the Aristotelian *Categories*—presupposes the basic Aristotelian distinction between 'being' or 'essence' on the one hand and its attributes on the other (9. 9. 43, v. 803–4 Kühn). 'Essence' is suppressed here precisely because Galen sets out to discover the essence of the heart. Essence is linked, again in Aristotelian fashion, to the notion of specific function—a point which, as we shall see, is crucial for the role assigned to experimentation.

Galen next reviews a number of attributes which fall under one of the above headings, evaluating each of them in the light of two criteria: first, they must be relevant to the subject under examination, viz. the regent part as defined by reference to the functions of sensation and volition (i.e. definition (D)). Second, they should be a distinctive property (ἴδιον) of the organ under examination (i.e. the brain or the heart) as opposed to other organs. Premisses which satisfy both criteria count as 'appropriate' or 'demonstrative' and hence are acceptable for scientific discourse.[26]

Galen's hard-core version of Aristotle's teleology—encapsulated in his

---

[25] Barnes (n. 24), 76–9.

[26] 2. 3. 9–11, v. 221 Kühn; 2. 4. 3–4, v. 227 Kühn. The concept of appropriateness as used by Galen is a development of such Aristotelian passages as *An. post.* 1. 2, 71^{b}20–3, 72^{a}5 ff., 1. 6, 74^{b}24 ff.; *An. pr.* 1. 30, 46^{a}17 ff. But cf. also *Gen. an.* 2. 8, 747^{a}27 ff., 748^{a}7 ff.; *Gen. corr.* 1. 2, 316^{a}13 ff. On Galen's use of the Aristotelian corpus see Moraux (n. 19), 687–814.

oft-repeated adage 'Nature does nothing without reason'[27]—does much to explain the pivotal role of properties as indications of the essence of the organs under examination.[28] The concept of indication ($\check{\epsilon}\nu\delta\epsilon\iota\xi\iota\varsigma$), however, stems from the medical tradition, in particular from *clinical* contexts, where it refers to those diseased conditions or symptoms which prompt a particular mode of treatment on the part of the physician.[29] Galen has transposed this particular aspect—viz. the intervention prompted by certain symptoms—to the sphere of physiological research.

But how does Galen actually go about using this conceptual apparatus? Aristotle had pointed to the presence of a large quantity of 'nerves' ($\nu\epsilon\hat{v}\rho\alpha$)[30] on the heart—an attribute of the type 'structure' (*Part. an.* 3. 4, 666^{b}14–16). Galen takes him to have correctly recognized the need to determine the source of the nerves, as the vessels necessarily involved in bodily motion. Aristotle, in other words, had effectively subscribed to Galen's axiom (A_1) . But, Galen counters, his ensuing observation was mistaken—there are not many nerves on the heart—and even if it were true, it would not pertain to a *property* of the heart, since other organs have plenty of nerves attached to them as well. Thus it fails to satisfy the second criterion for appropriate premisses (see above). In sum, it is not a significant indication for the heart's function, i.e. for what it essentially is. Galen provides a detailed description of the nervous and arterial systems, with the brain and the heart as their respective centres in the structural sense (1, 7) Whether or not these organs are also the centre in the functional sense can only be established through experimental interventions (cf. 1. 8. 3–6, v. 200–1 Kühn; 2. 8. 27–8, v. 278 Kühn).

Aristotle also appealed to the midmost position of the heart in the body as guaranteeing an even and immediate transmission of the motor and sensor stimuli.[31] Galen's response provides an example of the application of the first criterion—relevance to the subject under investigation (2. 4. 15–16, v. 230 Kühn). Arguments from 'position' presuppose the following axiom:

---

[27] Cf. e.g. Arist. *Cael.* 1. 4, 271^{a}3. On Galen's teleology see R. J. Hankinson, 'Galen explains the elephant', in M. Matthen and B. Linsky (eds.), *Philosophy and Biology* (*Canadian Journal of Philosophy*, suppl. 14; 1988), 135–57; id., 'Galen and the Best of All Possible Worlds', *CQ*, NS 39 (1989), 206–27. Cf. T. L. Tieleman, 'The Hunt for Galen's Shadow: Alexander of Aphrodisias, *De anima* 94. 7–100. 17 Bruns Reconsidered', in K. A. Algra *et al.* (eds.), *Polyhistor: Studies in the History and Historiography of Ancient Philosophy Presented to J. Mansfeld* (Philosophia antiqua, 72; Leiden, 1997), 265–83 at 275.

[28] See *PHP* 6. 3. 2, v. 519 Kühn; 7. 3. 7, v. 602; 2. 8. 23–4, v. 277; 1. 8. 5–6, v. 201; 2. 8. 18, v. 276; *Diff. puls.* 4. 2, viii. 704–6. Cf. also *UP* 10. 6, iii. 787; *Nat. fac.* 3. 8, ii. 175; *Hipp. Epid. VI* 4. 20, xviib. 184.

[29] F. Kudlien, 'Endeixis as a Scientific Term: (A) Galen's Usage of the Word (in Medicine and Logic)', in Kudlien and Durling (n. 24), 103–11.

[30] In Aristotle this term refers primarily to sinews and ligaments: *PHP*, ed. De Lacy, iii. 619.

[31] *Part. an.* 3. 4, 665^{b}18–20, 666^{a}14–15. Cf. S. Byl, 'Note sur la place du cœur et la valorisation de la $\mu\epsilon\sigma\acute{o}\tau\eta\varsigma$ dans la biologie d'Aristote', *AC* 37 (1968), 467–76.

(A₂) All functioning organs have their principle [ἀρχή] nearby.

Galen contests this axiom: there is no obvious connection between functional and positional aspects (2. 5. 3–5, v. 240–1 Kühn). The functioning of organs does not require the proximity of an active principle or cause. For the same reason Galen rejects Platonist arguments which refer to the position of the head as the highest (and so most honourable) organ or the one closest to the sensory organs (2. 4. 17–18, v. 230–1 Kühn).

This should give us some idea of the dialectical procedures which Galen brings to bear. Let us next see how his experiments enter the picture.

Zeno the Stoic had argued that, given the semantic component of spoken language, the source of speech must be identical to that of reason. But since speech enters the windpipe from the heart,[32] it follows that the heart must be the source of reason. This argument, Galen argues, is based on 'position' and hence on (A₂) as well. But he also adduces experimental observations: whenever the windpipe of an animal is cut beneath the larynx, its respiration remains intact whereas its voice is destroyed (2. 4. 20, v. 231 Kühn).[33] This is supported by clinical experience: one may ask a human patient who is injured in the same way to speak up, but however hard he tries, he merely produces a whistling kind of breathing (2. 4. 21–2, v. 231–2 Kühn). Galen next adduces a series of refined vivisection experiments to demonstrate that cutting the recurrent laryngeal nerves (*nervi laryngei recurrentes*) paralyses the functions of respiration and speech. Hence these functions are controlled not by the heart but by the brain. It is the tongue and the larynx which transform breath into speech (2. 4. 25–39, v. 232–7 Kühn).[34]

Galen does then add an observation derived from common experience: sacrificial bulls are sometimes seen to flee in panic while their heart already lies pulsating on the altar. The argument is traditional—other authors, too, tell us about animals which continue living when their heart or their head is

---

[32] This was a scientifically respectable opinion backed by the great Praxagoras of Cos (later 4th cent. BC), who regarded the windpipe (ἀρτηρία τραχεῖα, or 'rough artery') as part of the arterial system: fr. 10. See Chrysippus ap. Gal. *PHP* 3. 1. 11, v. 252 Kühn = *SVF* ii. 885; and cf. Diog. Bab. *SVF* iii. 29, 30.

[33] Galen's anatomy is largely based on animal material. In the ancient world human dissection was prohibited except for a brief period of time in Alexandria in the 3rd cent. BC: see n. 45, and cf. *AA* 3. 5, ii. 384–6 Kühn, where Galen recommends monkeys in view of their likeness to humans, and *Nat. fac.* 3. 2, ii. 146 Kühn. For his vivisections concerned with the nervous system, however, he preferred dogs, pigs, and goats to monkeys because of the disagreeable facial expression shown by the latter, *AA* 9. 11, 13, pp. 18, 27 Simon = 15, 22 Duckworth; *Praec.* 5. 10, xiv. 627 Kühn. Especially with his favourite experiment concerned with the mechanism of speech, pigs and goats, with their loud voices, are guaranteed to yield outspoken results. Galen devoted a (lost) separate tract to vivisection: *AA* 1. 1, ii. 216 Kühn.

[34] Likewise *Praec.* 5. 9–21, xiv. 627–30 Kühn; *UP* 7. 14–15, iii. 567–85 Kühn. Cf. J. Walsh, 'Galen's Discovery and Promulgation of the Function of the Recurrent Laryngeal Nerve', *Annals of Medical History*, 8 (1926), 176–84.

removed[35]—though Galen's version, with its stress on the distinctive motions of either organ (heart, brain), is somewhat more sophisticated than these parallel reports. But it is anatomical experiment which administers the *coup de grâce* to the Stoic speech argument. In the same way Aristotle's observation of 'nerves' on the heart (see above, p. 263) had revealed the need for anatomical experiment as the only means of establishing its essential function. This, then, provides the context of the extensive series of meticulous vivisections in which the spinal column and nerves are successively severed or blocked at certain spots: the paralysis occurring in the parts below these spots indicates the direction followed by the stimuli as well as their source (2. 6. 1–17, v. 262–7 Kühn; 3. 6. 1–8, v. 333–5 Kühn). The demonstration with regard to the heart's function follows an analogous pattern. In 1. 7. 4–55, v. 189–200 Kühn, Galen had also presented a description of the arterial system in which the heart emerged as its structural starting-point.[36] In 2. 6 this is followed by experiments in which the arteries are ligatured in a way that shows the heart to be the source of the pulse.

In fact, the pulse itself—an attribute of the type 'motion'—counts as a property of the heart in its own right. Moreover, since the heart's pulsating motion is independent of the will and its palpitation is associated with mental affections like anger, fear, and sexual arousal (cf. 8. 1. 22–4, v. 655 Kühn),[37] the pulse differs essentially from voluntary movement (? 4. 49, v. 239 Kühn).[38] In line with the Platonic conception of the soul as the principle of movement (*Phdr.* 245 c–d), a distinct and independent type of motion betokens the presence of a distinct soul, or part of the soul. The heart's pulse—and palpitation in a state of emotion—furnishes the middle term of a syllogistic proof analogous to that concerned with the brain and the nervous system (*PHP* 2. 8. 23, v. 277 Kühn, 5. 1. 1–3, v. 428–9; 6. 8. 39, v. 556; 8. 1. 23, v. 655). We need not doubt that the supposed automatism of the heart-beat weighed for a good deal with Galen.[39]

The mutual independence of the brain and the heart had been challenged by Chrysippus, who knew about the discovery of the nerves and was sensitive to the threat it posed to his cardiocentric position (*PHP* 2. 5. 69–70,

[35] Tert. *De an.* 15. 2, 6; Alex. *De an.* 100. 9 ff. Cf. also Chalcid. *In Ti.* 216. Cf. Mansfeld (n. 18), 3110 ff.

[36] Galen also responded to Praxagoras (above, n. 32), who had designated the heart as the ἀρχή, claiming that the arteries end in νεῦρα (fr. 11). Like Aristotle, Praxagoras still used the term νεῦρα in an imprecise sense covering sinews and other kinds of tissues: see n. 30. Chrysippus appealed to Praxagoras: see *PHP* 1. 7. 1, v. 189 Kühn =*SVF* ii. 897.

[37] On the association between the pulse and certain psychic powers see *PHP* 2. 7. 17, v. 270 Kühn; 3. 1. 26, v. 291. Cf. also *Praes. puls.* 4. 12, ix. 421–30 Kühn.

[38] On this (alleged) mistake by Chrysippus see e.g. *PHP* 2. 7. 17–21, v. 270–2 Kühn; 3. 1. 33, v. 293: cf. Tieleman (n. 6), 160 ff., 249 ff.

[39] See R. E. Siegel, 'Galen's Ideas on the Heartbeat', *Proceedings of the Sixth International Congress of the History of Medicine* (1949), 209–312; id., *Physiology* (n. 2), 44–5.; C. R. S. Harris, *The Heart and the Vascular System in Ancient Greek Medicine from Alcmaeon to Galen* (Oxford, 1973), 270 ff.

v. 254–5 Kühn = *SVF* ii. 898): even if it were granted that the brain is the source of the nerves, it is still conceivable that the regent part resides in the heart, with the brain acting as a kind of auxiliary station receiving its commands from the heart and passing them on to the rest of the organism. This is an *ad hoc* hypothesis—not a doctrine Chrysippus ever seriously entertained. But it actually pre-empts the train of reasoning followed by Galen in (S) (see above). Indeed, the kind of inference instantiated by (S) is today known as the fallacy of affirming the consequent. What we have here is an instance of Chrysippus' acuity as a logician.[40] But Galen takes up the challenge. Like Aristotle, Chrysippus had seen the need for anatomical research but failed to follow it up. This task, then, falls to Galen, who presents a sophisticated experiment (2. 6. 3–12, v. 263–5 Kühn), involving the three kinds of vessel linking the heart and the brain—nerves, jugular veins, and carotid arteries.[41] These he blocks separately and successively (a point on which he insists), observing no effects which would permit the conclusion that the brain and the heart are related to one another in the way suggested by Chrysippus. In fact, this experiment is taken to reveal the mutual independence of the two organs.

In sum, function cannot be inferred from perceptible features with absolute certainty. So, ideally, a demonstration of the function of an organ is—as a rule[42]—completed by experiments of the kind we have been discussing. This point is further illustrated by the methodological introduction prefaced to the proof that Plato's appetitive part is situated in the liver (6. 3. 1–6, v. 519–21 Kühn). Here Galen strikes a note of caution (6. 3. 2, v. 519 Kühn):

ὡς οὐκ ἐξ ὁμοίως ἐναργῶν οὐδ' ἐξ αὐτῆς ἄντικρυς τοῦ ζητουμένου τῆς φύσεως ἡ ἀπόδειξις ἔσοιτο, καθάπερ ἐπὶ τῶν ἔμπροσθεν, ἀλλ' ἐκ τῶν τούτῳ συμβεβηκότων ἰδίᾳ.

This proof will not be from equally obvious evidence [as compared with the proof about the brain and the heart in books 1–3] and its premisses, unlike the earlier ones, are not taken from the very nature [i.e. essence] of the thing under investigation but from the properties peculiar to it.

----

[40] In Chrysippean technical terminology Galen's syllogism (S) lacks 'cohesion' (συνάρτησις): see M. Frede, *Die Stoische Logik* (Göttingen, 1974), 90 ff.

[41] Remarkably, Galen takes no account of the vertebral arteries here—in contrast with other works; see in particular his report of an experiment which in all other respects is very similar at *Us. puls.* 2, v. 153–9 Kühn, with D. Furley and J. S. Wilkie, *Galen on Respiration and the Arteries* (Princeton, 1984), 48–51.

[42] Galen holds that there are a few organs whose function can be worked out just by looking at them, e.g. the tongue and the penis-cum-testicles. Here experimental interventions are unnecessary—and in some cases impracticable anyway: *AA* 12. 7, pp. 155–6 Simon = 123 ff. Duckworth, and 10. 3, p. 51 Simon = 41 Duckworth. In *On the Dissection of the Dead*—extant in an Arabic abstract only—Galen stipulated that in view of haemorrhages and other complications dissection of corpses should precede that of living animals: see I. Ormos, 'Bemerkungen zur Galens Schrift "Über die Sektion der Lebewesen"', in Kollesch and Nickel (n. 11), 165–72 at 171. In *PHP* 1. 7. 4–55, v. 189–200 Kühn, he likewise details the structure of the different systems of vessels before presenting experimental reports.

The reason for this difference is very interesting indeed. In the case of the liver, experiments analogous to those concerned with the brain and the heart do not produce unequivocal results. The effects of damaging the liver or intercepting the veins become noticeable only after some time, if at all (6. 3. 5–6, v. 520 Kühn). In consequence, Galen omits interventions of this kind from his demonstration concerned with the liver. It remains confined to the first stage—viz. that of selecting properties which signify its essential function (cf. 6. 8. 1–7, v. 563–5 Kühn). Not surprisingly, Galen appeals here more emphatically to the theme of Nature's design as manifest from the properties of the liver. But his initial caveat evaporates as his argument proceeds. From a full anatomical description he concludes that the liver must be the starting-point of its own system of vessels—the veins—whereby the blood, as the basic foodstuff, is circulated through the body. This warrants the assumption that the liver contains the Platonic desiderative part of the soul (6. 8. 77, v. 582–3 Kühn).

So the caution which in regard to the liver Galen deems necessary on theoretical grounds is not borne out by his attitude in the course of his argument. But even so, the preface to book 6 illustrates the twofold structure of an ideal demonstration—a stage of discovery followed by one of confirmation. These two stages are expressible in terms of the distinction between being and its attributes we have noted (above, p. 262). Galen first takes, so to speak, the upward route from attributes to essence and next goes down again, descending from essence to its observable attributes in the second confirmatory stage. This twofold procedure was taken to be exemplified by geometrical analysis and synthesis respectively.[43] The method of proceeding from observable phenomena to conclusions about unseen causes had been recommended by Aristotle for the natural sciences and later on introduced into the medical tradition by Herophilus.[44] With the work of both Galen was thoroughly acquainted.[45] How far he can be credited with the important, theoretically based, role of the experiments (stage 2) is not easy to say. But there is some evidence pointing to an original contribution on Galen's part. In a passage in *On the Diagnosis of Errors* (4–5) he models his methodology on 'geometrical' sciences such as architecture which are characterized by the twin procedures of analysis and synthesis (54. 7–11, 54. 20–55. 27 de Boer=v. 79, 80–2 Kühn). Galen explains these procedures with reference to technological devices like sundials and waterclocks, whose construction is a matter of putting a particular design to the test. Contrary to accounts

[43] M. Frede, 'On Galen's Epistemology', in V. Nutton (ed.), *Galen: Problems and Prospects* (London, 1981), 65–86 at 74–5 (repr. in M. Frede, *Essays in Ancient Philosophy* (Oxford, 1987), 279–98).

[44] See Arist. *Part. an.* 1. 1, 639^{b}7 ff., 640^{a}14 ff., with Gal. *Nat. fac.* 1. 9–10, ii. 19–24 Kühn; *Subst. nat. fac.* 1, iv. 760 Kühn. Cf. Herophilus T 50–7 with Von Staden (n. 14), 117–18.

[45] For Aristotle see Moraux (n. 19), 687–814; for Herophilus see the *Index locorum* in Von Staden (n. 14), 629 ff.

in other sources, Galen identifies the procedure of testing with synthesis. Indeed, he lays claim to originality on this very point (ibid. 58. 17–59. 8 de Boer = v. 86–7 Kühn). I see no good reason not to trust him here.

3. The Experiments: Analysis

On the whole ancient scientists did not differentiate between ordinary experience as an epistemologically restricted source of knowledge and experimentation as a standard scientific procedure of testing a proposition about the world. They adduced experimental observations either to refute an opponent or to confirm their position, which had often been taken on the basis of philosophical presuppositions. Especially in the latter case over-interpretation of the data is a liability.[46]

How, then, do Galen's experiments concerned with the nervous system fit into this picture? Throughout his demonstration Galen follows a fairly coherent method, of which experiments form an integral part, being the ultimate test as to an organ's function. But does this theoretical foundation of experimentation involve an ideal of unbiased, open-ended research? On a few occasions Galen treats the brain and heart as candidates of equal standing. Thus he discards invalid arguments in favour of the head as well (above, p. 264). We have also seen that he takes account of an alternative interpretation put forward by Chrysippus regarding the functional relation between the two organs at issue (see above, pp. 265–6).

But this important role of experimentation notwithstanding, Galen is also aware of certain limitations. His comments prefacing his demonstration concerned with the liver betray a degree of awareness of the problems involved in certain types of experiment as well as his reflection on the relation between intervention and effect (see above, pp. 266–7). It is also noteworthy that he sometimes stresses that his experiments are repeatable and have in fact often been repeated (7. 3. 13, v. 604 Kühn).[47]

---

[46] See Lloyd (n. 7), 72–3; id., *Magic* (n. 1), 151–2.

[47] See also *Us. puls.* 5, v. 165 Kühn. The requirement of an ample number of identical observations is typical of the Empiricist school, which profoundly influenced Galen: see esp. *Subfig. emp.* 2, pp. 45–6 Deichgräber; *Med. Exp.* 7, p. 94 Walzer; 18, pp. 119–21; cf. *Cris.* 2. 2, p. 128. 18–20 Alexanderson = ix. 644 Kühn. In general K. Deichgräber, *Die griechische Empirikerschule* (Berlin, 1930; repr.1965), 97–118. Here a connotation of the Empiricist key concept of πεῖρα had been fruitful. But already Aristotle had defined the related term experience (ἐμπειρία) by reference to a plurality of observations stored in our memory (*An. post.* 2. 19, 100ᵃ5–9, *Metaph.* A 1, 980ᵇ30–981ᵃ5). The term πεῖρα is often used by Galen and others with reference to what we would call experiments, but in itself it has a wider sense covering more passive kinds of experience such as those preferred by the Empiricists, who had abjured all anatomical experimentation; cf. e.g. *PHP* 9. 6. 20 ff., iv. 766–7 Kühn. See further M. D. Grmek and D. Gourevitch, 'Les expériences pharmacologiques dans l'antiquité', *Archives internationales d'histoire des sciences*, 35 (1985), 3–27; cf. also P. Van der Eijk, 'Galen's Use of the

From a technical point of view, his experiments show an extraordinary degree of sophistication. But his procedures are admirably methodical as well. Arguably, his knowledge of hypothetical logic had stimulated his interest in the design of experiments, that is to say, in the questions to be isolated, the implications involved, and so forth.[48] Particularly striking is his effective use of experimentation as a means of refuting opponents.[49]

But the constructive use of experimentation results more from the need for a functional anatomy in a teleological context than from reflection on the status of experimentation as such. Galen, too, cheerfully aligns experimental observation with common experience, especially where the soul's emotions are concerned, appealing to the supposed experience that mental affections arise in the heart (see above, nn. 37–8 with the text at that point). But then Galen is in need of arguments with respect to mental affections in particular. It is one thing to show experimentally that the heart is the source of the pulse; it is another to prove that the heart is the dwelling-place of emotions like fear and anger. An analogous problem arises in the case of the liver. Here Galen is quick—too quick, we may feel—to take its digestive function to show that it is the seat of desire in the sense required by Plato's appetitive part.[50]

But the alignment of common and expert experience is also made in a theoretical key passage, *PHP* 3. 8. 35, v. 357–8 Kühn. Here Galen specifies the *sources* of appropriate premises: simple perception, what is obvious to thought, technical (or 'expert': κατὰ τὰς τέχνας) experience, and common experience. We need not doubt that 'technical' experience includes what we call experimentation—alongside descriptive anatomy, clinical experience, and other activities typical of the trained professional. It is distinguished from common experience in line with Galen's general insistence on expertise and training. On the other hand, he clearly puts the two kinds on a par as far as epistemic status is concerned.

So, in spite of the high standards achieved by his experiments in other respects, we have to conclude that Galen behaves not so much as an experimental scientist but as an empirical Platonist. This can be seen most clearly from his blind spot with regard to the seat of the emotions. Nowhere does he seriously consider the possibility that the emotions arise in the brain,

Concept of 'Qualified Experience' in his Dietetic and Pharmacological Works', in A. Debru (ed.), *Galen on Pharmacology: Philosophy, History and Medicine* (Leiden, 1997), 35–57.

[48] See in particular *Art. sang.* 1, pp. 144–6 Furley–Wilkie = iv. 703–6 Kühn, where Galen employs formal schemas derived from Stoic syllogistic in describing experimental proofs: cf. Furley and Wilkie (n. 41), 53–4.

[49] Typical of Galen's experimental refutations is the so-called *Modus Tollendo Tollens*: if *p*, then *q*; but not *q*; so not *p*. On this mode of reasoning in Greek science in general cf. Lloyd, *Magic* (n. 1), 25, 71–2.

[50] P. De Lacy, 'The Third Part of the Soul', in P. Manuli and M. Vegeti (eds.), *Le opere psicologiche di Galeno* (Naples, 1988), 43–64.

alongside the cognitive functions. The panicky behaviour of the bull as he himself reports it (above, p. 264) might have forced this interpretation upon his attention.[51] Further, one wonders what exactly is implied by Galen's association of 'certain affections' (or emotions, πάθεσι) with so-called 'forced' inhalation in a passage where he insists on the pivotal role of specific nerves in respiration (2. 4. 33, v. 234–5 Kühn). Why this blind spot ? We should remind ourselves of a point made at the outset (above, p. 260): Galen takes part in a traditional debate with but a few fixed options. The assumption that the emotions as well as cognition are situated in the brain simply fell outside the debate between the Platonists, Stoics, and Aristotelians. In fact, a fully fledged encephalocentric view had been defended by the author of the Hippocratic tract *On the Sacred Disease* in the later fifth century BC (17; cf. 14) and, presumably, by Herophilus and Erasistratus as well.[52] However, their position is never mentioned, let alone considered.

In fact, Galen fails to confront the problem of explaining how the three parts of the soul interact physiologically.[53] Here Galen's lack of a systematic procedure for eliminating alternative interpretations makes itself felt. It is also significant that when he speaks of error he almost invariably means problems of a practical kind.[54] He employs so-called rational methods such as διαίρεσις ('division') to order and so 'upgrade' experience, stripping it of its random character, as when he distinguishes between various types of attributes (above, p. 262). In one striking passage in *PHP* 9 he envisages the possibility that rational method involves trying out (πειραθῆναι) *opposite* hypotheses (6. 19 ff., esp. 25, v. 765–8 Kühn). But to my knowledge he never followed up this insight. In sum, traditional philosophical techniques have furthered his understanding of the function and design of experiments. Yet philosophical considerations also imposed serious limitations. In many ways Galen remained a captive of the traditional debate on the seat of the intellect, especially where the available options at stake were concerned.

4. Epilogue: A Historical Perspective

For quite some time anatomy was not an integral part of medical research but was practised occasionally to settle particular questions such as the seat of the intellect. In the fifth and fourth centuries BC it was still considered adequate to point to any connection between the favoured organ and other

[51] The fact that we are dealing with a non-rational animal does not affect this point. Ironically, Galen takes the Stoics to task for denying emotions to animals, *PHP* 2. 1. 1, v. 211 Kühn.

[52] Solmsen (n. 14), 195 ff.; Von Staden (n. 14), 247–8.   [53] Mansfeld (n. 2), 138 ff.

[54] *PHP* 2. 6. 13ff., v. 265 ff. Kühn; *Art. sang.* 8. 4 ff., pp. 178–82 Furley–Wilkie=v. 732–6 Kühn. Cf. G. E. R. Lloyd, 'Observational Error in Later Greek Science', in J. Barnes, J. Brunschwig, M. Burnyeat, and M. Schofield (eds.), *Science and Speculation: Studies in Hellenistic Theory and Practice* (Cambridge, 1982), 128–64 at 131–2 (repr. in Lloyd *Method* (n. 1), 299–332).

parts.[55] But as the right questions were asked with greater urgency, the time became ripe for the discovery of the nervous system by Herophilus and Erasistratus, who profited from exceptionally favourable conditions, most notably the opportunity of practising human anatomy (as well as vivisection).[56]

Herophilus and Erasistratus pointed to the implications of their discoveries for the question of the seat of the psychic functions. Were their findings based on the same kind of experiments as were conducted by Galen? This assumption is surely encouraged by testimonies on their vivisections as well as the sophistication of their anatomy. However, Galen is our main source and he is not explicit about his dependence on these (or for that matter other) precursors in this respect.[57] We have to rely on a handful of indications. First, there is a quotation from Erasistratus describing the brain as the source of the nerves, and the cerebellum as the seat of intelligence (*PHP* 7. 3. 8–11, v. 602–4 Kühn). This fragment does not rule out experimentation but it does not prove it either. Indeed, Galen claims that Erasistratus had failed to undertake experiments revealing the functions of the different parts of the brain.[58] On the other hand, we do know that Erasistratus conducted experiments to establish the source of the pulse and the functioning of the cardiac valves, e.g. by ligaturing the arteries at certain spots.[59] It is

---

[55] Lloyd, *Magic* (n. 1), 160–1.

[56] See esp. Herophilus T 80, 81 (distinction between motor and sensory nerves), 137, 138 (the cerebellum as the locus of intelligence). Cf. A. Souques, 'Que doivent à Hérophile et à Érasistrate l'anatomie et la physiologie du système nerveux?', *Bulletin de la Société Française d'Histoire de la Médecine*, 28 (1934), 357–65; Solmsen (n. 14), 195 ff.; J. Longrigg, 'Anatomy in Alexandria in the Third Century BC', *British Journal of the History of Science*, 21 (1988), 455–88; id., *Greek Rational Medicine: Philosophy and Medicine from Alcmaeon to the Alexandrians* (London, 1993), 191 n. 77; Von Staden (n. 14), 155 ff., 247–8. It is arbitrary to dismiss as unreliable reports on vivisections having been practised by these scientists on convicted criminals supplied by the Ptolemies from the royal prisons: see esp. Cels. *Med.* 16 with Von Staden (n. 14), 140–1. The fragments of Herophilus have been edited by Von Staden (n. 14). For those of Erasistratus see I. Garofalo, *Erasistrati Fragmenta* (Pisa, 1988).

[57] In view of their *anatomical* doctrines Von Staden (n. 7), 184 ff., ascribes Galen's experiments to Herophilus and in particular Erasistratus. But as it is, there is no direct evidence regarding the *experiments*. Thus, *pace* Von Staden (196 nn. 43, 44), there is no cogent reason to believe that the experiments on the vertebral column at *AA* 8. 6, ii. 683–4 Kühn, go back to Erasistratus. One main problem is Galen's tendency to enhance his own achievement at the expense of his predecessors: cf. V. Nutton, 'Galen and Egypt', in Kollesch and Nickel (n. 11), 11–32, dealing with Galen's curious silence on the time he spent studying in Alexandria. Apart from the problem of his silence, there are instances of inconsistency. Thus Galen at *Trem. pulp.* 5, vii. 605 ff. Kühn, and *Loc. aff.* 3. 14, viii. 212 ff., criticizes Herophilus' anatomy of the nervous system as imprecise. Yet elsewhere he heaps praise on Herophilus for his sophisticated anatomy, *AA* 6. 8, ii. 570–1. Such switches in attitude are largely explicable by reference to contextual differences.

[58] *PHP* 7. 3. 14–18, v. 604–5 Kühn; cf. *AA* 9. 12, pp. 21–4 Simon = 17–20 Duckworth. But note that the quotation had been introduced to show Erasistratus' failure to establish the function of the so-called dura mater (or meninx) only—surely a minor point. Galen often says that he has to provide an experimental proof omitted by one of his predecessors: see above, pp. 263 (Aristotle), 266 (Chrysippus).   [59] Harris (n. 39), 100 ff.

highly likely that this group of experiments provided Galen with a model
for his own procedures designed to establish the heart's function.

As for Herophilus, it is worth noting a passage from *On the Formation
of Embryos*, a tract written some four decades after the first books of *PHP*
but taking up many of the issues raised in it. In this passage (5, iv. 678
Kühn = Herophilus T 57) Galen tells us that Herophilus in one of his writings pointed to the importance of a functional—as opposed to a purely
descriptive—anatomy, adducing as an example the question of the seat of
the psychic functions: theory formation on this subject cannot be based on
the simple perception of certain structures growing out of the heart. Galen
goes on to illustrate the method recommended by Herophilus by reference
to the experiments reported in *PHP* 1–3. This certainly encourages the assumption that Herophilus himself had conducted similar experiments. His
allusion to 'structures growing out of the heart', in fact, refers to the passage from *On the Parts of Animals* where Aristotle claims to have observed
a considerable quantity of 'nerves' on the heart. As we have seen, Galen
discusses this very passage in *PHP* 1, pointing to the need for anatomical
experiment as an indispensable means of establishing the functions at issue
(see above, p. 263). What is more, Galen reports that Herophilus had corrected Aristotle by introducing the expressions 'nerve-like tissues' as a more
proper designation of the structures seen by Aristotle (*PHP* 1. 9. 3, v. 204
Kühn). Obviously, that these tissues are not nerves in the proper sense can
only be established through experimental procedures of the kind followed
by Galen.

Much must remain unclear about Galen's dependence on Erasistratus and
Herophilus. But it seems reasonable to assume that Galen took the basic idea
from Herophilus (with respect to the nervous system) and Erasistratus (with
respect to the arterial system). As we have seen, Galen probably suppresses
the fact that Herophilus and Erasistratus assigned the emotions along with
the intellect to the head. If so, this might be one of the reasons why he was
so coy about the experiments connected with their position.

But it is a fair assumption that Galen refined the method and technique
of the experiments of his predecessors. This was no mean achievement.
Besides, it was important to revive the work of the great Alexandrians in
this particular area.[60] What Galen expounded some four centuries later
was still largely unknown and controversial. Like most of his views, his
advocacy of the Platonic conception of the soul was destined to become
immensely influential. But it would be wrong to suppose that he carried
the day. The Peripatetic Alexander of Aphrodisias delivered a powerful

---

[60] Shortly after their death anatomy and in its wake anatomical experimentation fell into
decay, partly as a result of the emergence of the Empiricist school of medicine: Von Staden
(n. 7) 189 ff.; Longrigg, *Greek Rational Medicine* (n. 56), 218–19. Cf. also n. 47.

response to Galen in the final section of his *On the Soul*.[61] This rejoinder attests to the resilience of the cardiocentric theory; and Galen's own defence of the Platonic tripartition may even have helped to revitalize the assumption that the heart was the seat of at least some psychic functions.

Looking forward in time, we get an impression of Galen's achievement when we note that no proper theory of experimentation took shape before the seventeenth century. Renaissance scientists such as Zabarella (1533–89) or the young Galileo (1564–1642) still engaged in experimentation without a full-blown experimental method.[62] In this respect their work did not appreciably advance beyond the situation we have encountered in Galen's *PHP*. This too is a measure of his achievement.

[61] 94. 7–100. 17 Bruns. See Tieleman (n. 27).
[62] C. B. Schmitt, *Studies in Renaissance Philosophy and Science* (London, 1981), ch. VIII.

16

Practice Makes Perfect: Knowledge of Materials in Classical Athens

T. E. RIHLL AND J. V. TUCKER

It is agreed on all hands that the Greeks were great thinkers. Let nobody suppose that I wish to dispute this fact. But it is widely taught that the Greeks were poor doers as well as great thinkers. I do wish to assert that the best Greek thinking was the companion and helper of vigorous action. Nowadays bookish people have lost the sense for all the intellect that exists outside books. A farm, a factory, an engine, a ship, the back-axle of a motor-car, a wheel-barrow, a fishing-rod, is not seen as an intellectual achievement. No. . . . The mighty minds are all between covers.   B. FARRINGTON[1]

1. Introduction

FROM the fifth century BC complex material-processing technologies were in operation on an industrial scale in classical Athens, in the great enterprises of the Laurium. These productive processes, especially the production of silver, were widely recognized in Athenian society to be important and remarkable. The history of material-processing is of considerable his-

We thank David Gill, Harold Mattingly, David Miller, Christopher Tuplin, and the readers for the Press who have helped us with comments and queries on various points in this paper.

[1] B. Farrington, *Head and Hand in Ancient Greece* (London, 1947), ix. It may be coincidence that Benjamin Farrington, with whose views we have much sympathy, worked at the University of Wales Swansea, as we do. Or perhaps it is the experience of living in an area whose history teems with industrial activity that shapes our outlook on this subject. A point analogous to Farrington's is made in an entirely different context by C. Mattusch, *Classical Bronzes* (Cornell, 1996), 218: 'Today we tend to rank the artist above the technician, giving the latter only secondary importance in the creation of a piece of sculpture and attaching a certain mystique to the artist's creative process. Yet this modern distinction between craft and creativity is not suggested by the word *technē*, which the Greeks used to describe the entire process—the art, the skill, and the craft of production. It is extraordinarily instructive for a layperson to watch the activities in a bronze foundry or in a marble-carving shop. Doing so makes it absolutely clear that the success of the finished sculpture can depend as much on the skill of the bronze founder or the stonecarver as it does on that of the artist making the original model.' See also John Boardman's comments when reviewing Mattusch's book (*JHS* 117 (1997), 260): 'It is interesting to reflect on how most scholars will now accept the importance of near-mechanical processes in the creation of classical realistic/idealistic statuary, bronze or marble, rather than some high-minded faith in the Greek Genius at getting things right. In fact it makes the results both more intelligible and more remarkable in terms of the aims and achievements of the rest of antiquity.'

torical interest, not least because of its influence on the life of classical Athens.[2]

In this paper we are concerned with the intellectual life of the city: more precisely, we attempt to analyse the nature of the practical knowledge on which material-processing was founded, and to relate that practical knowledge to the development of theoretical knowledge about materials in the period.

In ancient Greece, chronologically at least, science follows technology.[3] The starting-point for this investigation is the fact that these technologies and large-scale processes developed and operated successfully *without* knowledge that could be recognized as theoretical in the period. The difficult technical procedures involved could be performed successfully with little or no *understanding* of what was going on. Indeed, what appear on paper to be difficult or sophisticated procedures are not always so in practice: ancient Athenian material-processing offers a cautionary lesson for historians of technology, in the story of the assaying of silver. Nevertheless, the scale, complexity, and success of Laurium establish the existence of a body of advanced practical knowledge and experience. Two questions then arise. What was the precise nature of this knowledge? Did the practical knowledge of materials and the transformation of materials influence early theories about matter and change? To investigate these questions we briefly describe the technologies in operation at Laurium and the relevant ancient written sources, and we propose a characterization of practical knowledge and compare it with a characterization of theoretical knowledge in the period.

The paper is divided into five main sections (§§ 2–6). In § 2 we describe very briefly how the ancient Greeks produced silver. The most complex processes, those for smelting and cupelling, were difficult to effect and were unsupported by theoretical understanding. In § 3 we look at the level of activity in Laurium. Silver was produced on a truly industrial scale in classical times, and it was the *raison d'être* for a large and diverse collection of supporting and supplementary industries in the region. In § 4 we briefly discuss the importance of silver production as recognized in the religious, political, and economic spheres of Athenian society. Against this background of technology, industries, and their so-

[2] A full account of the production of silver and other materials in Laurium, with all technicalities, can be found in T. E. Rihll, 'Making Money in Classical Athens', in D. Mattingly and J. B. Salmon (eds.), *Economies beyond Agriculture* (London, 2000), 115–42. For silver only see also C. Conophagos, *Le Laurium antique* (Athens, 1980).

[3] A more general and sweeping statement of this point is made by L. Wolpert, *The Unnatural Nature of Science* (London, 1992). He and others have noted that, in David Miller's words, 'for most of their histories science and technology proceeded independently of each other, and if there was any influence one way or another it was almost always from technology to science': 'Is Scientific Knowledge an Inexhaustible Economic Resource?', *The Critical Rationalist*, 3. 1: 13 (on line at http://thorung.eeng.dcu.it/~tkpw/ tcr/volume-03/v03no1).

cial importance, in § 5 we consider the theorizing about materials by intellectuals, notably the members of the early Lyceum. Here our aim is to introduce some of the people who lived and thought while Laurium was being exploited, to summarize the intellectual traditions in which they worked and theories that they inherited, and to explore their own ideas about materials. Finally, in § 6 we formulate some working definitions for the concepts of practical knowledge and theoretical knowledge that characterize the knowledge of materials in the period. Here our aim is to clarify and make explicit these ideas as a contribution to the historical quest for 'ancient technology and science'. We do *not* consider the relationship between, on the one hand, the practical and theoretical knowledge of the period and, on the other, modern conceptions of practical knowledge and scientific knowledge. Nor are we suggesting that the existence of technology 'explains' the Greek development of abstract thought, philosophy, or science.

2. How to Produce Silver

Silver has been mined and smelted for millennia,[4] so there was 'knowledge' of what was required for millennia, but this knowledge was practical, not theoretical or scientific.

2.1. *Procedures for silver production*

To produce silver required, in brief:

(1) knowing and finding silver-bearing ore (in this case, cerrusite and galena);
(2) mining that ore;
(3) dressing the ore, to remove as much as possible of the rock matrix in which it occurs, before
(4) smelting it, to separate the metals from the minerals in the ore; and
(5) cupelling the product of the smelting furnace to separate the silver from the lead.

To give some idea of the quantities involved, consider the production of one silver drachma, weighing about 4.3 grammes: about 16 kilogrammes of ore had to be mined and dressed, to select about 5 kilogrammes to smelt, producing about 2 kilogrammes of work-lead to be cupelled, resulting in less than 5 grammes of almost pure silver.

Smelting and cupelling were the most technologically challenging parts of

---

[4] Cupellation has been practised since the early third millennium BC: L. Aitchison, *History of Metals*, i (London, 1960), 46–7.

the operation. Furnaces are designed to melt rock. Thus furnaces are structures which are designed and built by men who are trying to reproduce
what happens naturally inside volcanoes. Small wonder, then, that metallurgy was one of the first crafts to win specialist status: even Odysseus, the
master of DIY in a society of handymen by necessity, makes no claims to
competence in this area.

The output from the smelting furnace was slag and work-lead, which were
directed into separate pits to cool. After cooling, the solidified puddles of
work-lead were broken up, and moved to a cupellation furnace for separating
out the silver.

If a piece of galena is simply dropped in a fire, it will after some time
reduce to lead; if it is left there even longer, the lead oxidizes fully to a
fine white ash, leaving a minuscule bead of pure silver. Cupellation aims to
separate the two metals on a viably large scale, more quickly than on an open
fire and with less loss of silver. It does this by controlling and containing the
heat and having a porous, chemically inert hearth, called a cupel. A cupel
is best thought of in this context as a lined shallow hole in the ground or
in a raised hearth. It is the lining which is the cupel. Suitable materials are
bone ash, wood ash, marl, plaster of Paris, or refractory clay with or without
powdered unglazed pots.

The outputs from the cupellation furnace were silver, litharge, and
hearth-lead.[5] Hearth-lead was resmelted, or ground up to make hydraulic
cement; silver was assayed; and there were several possibilities for the
litharge: either resmelted with ore, or resmelted alone to produce pure
lead, or subjected to other processes to produce pigments or medicaments.

We shall argue below that the knowledge required for the performance
of each of these processes had no theoretical basis. We shall also argue that,
despite the technological difficulties involved in successful smelting and
cupellation, 'knowing' whether the operations had been successful or not
was fairly straightforward, not to say easy.

2.2. *Practical knowledge involved in cupelling silver*

Even now, in some cases, exactly what is going on in a furnace is not
known, and experience and intuition are still a stronger guide than scientific understanding or explanation.[6] Chemical and metallurgical analysis
and the measurement of, for example, temperature are extremely difficult

---

[5] i.e. the lead-soaked part of the cupel. It is called (inconsistently) *molybdaena* by Pliny,
Agricola, etc., for detailed discussion of which see H. C. and L. H. Hoover, *Agricola: De re
metallica* (London, 1912), 475 n. 37. Cupellation debris from Laurium found by Conophagos
consisted of about 75% lead oxide.

[6] 'Even in the most advanced industrial nations, complex metallurgical processes are carried
out by persons having no working knowledge of thermodynamics': R. B. Gordon and D. J.
Killick, 'Adaptation of Technology to Culture and Environment: Bloomery Iron Smelting in
America and Africa', *Technology and Culture*, 34 (1993), 243–70 at 245 n. 4.

in such a physically challenging and complex environment as a working furnace.

Let us consider cupellation. The temperature in an ancient cupellation furnace needed to reach over 800° C: lead melts at the low temperature of 327° C, but if the temperature in the furnace was below 800°, lead oxide would have formed as a crust and solidified, preventing cupellation. Thus it was easy for the ancient cupellers to know if the temperature was too low, without recourse to any instrument or theory. Today we would say that the temperature should not get too high—above *c*.960° C—because then the silver would melt as well as the lead, and some silver would be lost, which is nowadays viewed as a bad thing in general and a very bad thing if it can be avoided. However, this is hardly relevant for ancient cupellation. First, it was not easy with ancient technology and fuel to reach such high temperatures, so the situation was unlikely to arise.[7] Second, even if the temperature rose this high, the cupellation operation would still have 'worked', it just would have done so less skilfully, wasting silver, fuel, and labour time; and it is far from obvious whether, and if so how, anyone in antiquity could have known it to be so.

So a cupellation furnace required a temperature of *c*.810° C or more, and in practice the ancient furnace workers would have judged this by their senses and their experience.

Testing the effectiveness of the cupellation (and smelting) operation needed no measurement or scientific analysis either. It can be assessed by eye, and experienced workmen would have known what to look for, and what were signs of impurities, even if they had no idea what the impurities actually were or why they had that effect.[8] If the silver or the cupel looked wrong, then the silver went back for recupelling, or if it was very bad, resmelting.

When we turn to assaying, the purity and consistency of Athenian coins (from 98.5 per cent to 99.7 per cent silver) might appear to prove the existence of sophisticated assay techniques employed by the cupellers or the mintmen—but appearances are deceptive. Silver has a very peculiar property which enables one easily to assess whether it is more than 98 per cent pure: it spirts.

Spirting is the violent escape of oxygen as silver solidifies. Silver absorbs

---

[7] It was theoretically possible, but if achieved, neither easy nor necessarily desirable, to reach temperatures of 1,600° C in these circumstances. See J. E. Rehder, *The Mastery and Uses of Fire in Antiquity* (Montreal, Kingston, London, and Ithaca, NY, 2000). At pp. 156–7 Rehder corrects grossly inflated modern estimates of the quantity of timber required to produce the amount of charcoal needed to produce silver in Laurium.

[8] In brief, the silver cake should have looked like a slightly flattened elliptical button with an evenly rounded appearance, and the stained portion of the cupel should have been yellow when cold: see H. R. Beringer, *A Text-Book of Assaying for the Use of Those Concerned with Mines*, 15th edn. (London, 1921), 100.

large quantities of oxygen at atmospheric pressure,[9] if heated to around its melting point. When just above its melting point, silver can take into solution about ten times its volume of oxygen (to saturation).[10] This oxygen is dissolved in the molten metal rather as carbon dioxide is dissolved in fizzy drinks, though in the case of fizzy drinks the solution is possible only under pressure. When the bottle is opened and the pressure released, the carbon dioxide comes out of solution, forming bubbles, which rise to the surface and escape, creating the characteristic fizz. An equivalent but more energetic reaction occurs in silver as a result of changing temperature, rather than pressure. As the metal cools, the oxygen is liberated vigorously just before solidification, causing the melt to spirt, the metallurgical equivalent of fizzing. Suddenly the crust of the metal breaks and oxygen and particles of molten metal burst out.[11] Impurities in the melt such as copper or base metals will unite with any oxygen present to form oxides, and thus reduce the spirt to something better described as blistering.[12] Impurities above the level of 2 per cent will prevent spirting altogether. One does not need to know the percentages to use spirting to assay silver. All one needs to know is a rule of thumb: *if it spirts it is pure.* Since Athenian coins consistently reached more than 98 per cent purity, heating the metal to melting point and seeing if it spirted seems the most likely candidate for their method of assay.[13] No great knowledge or observational power was required to assay silver by this foolproof—if somewhat wasteful[14]—method.[15]

---

[9] The only other metal which has this property is palladium.

[10] A. Butts and C. Coxe, *Silver: Economics, Metallurgy and Use* (Princeton, 1967), 126.

[11] [Arist.] *Pr.* 24. 9, 936^{b}26–8, 35, gives a description and physical explanation of spirting, about which one need note only that it involves an analogy with boiling pea soup.

[12] Butts and Coxe (n. 10), 304.

[13] This is presumably what is meant by assay 'by fire', since heat is the only 'tool' used.

[14] As [Arist.] *Pr.* 24. 9, 936^{b}27–8, points out, 'those who clean out the mint make gains by appropriating the remnants, sweeping up the silver which is scattered about' (Forster's translation).

[15] The official assayer (δοκιμαστής) was a public slave responsible for testing the purity of the coins. Assaying was common enough to be used as an analogue in philosophic discussion: Arist. *Rh.* 1. 15. 7, 1375^{b}5–6: justice is like silver, and must be tested by the assayer (i.e. the judge), if the genuine is to be distinguished from the counterfeit. See also Pl. *Leg.* 802 B: musical assayers accept satisfactory songs, reject wholly unsuitable ones, and insist on the revision and correction of defective ones. The purity of silver was tested by various people at various places: Athenian and foreign sceptics, traders, bankers, metalworkers, etc. This suggests that the method used was easy to comprehend and perform, as spirting is. This might also explain why the Greeks chose to make their coins of silver, rather than of any other metal. (The earliest (Lydian) coins were made of electrum—the natural alloy of gold and silver—but most Greek states quickly changed to silver, though there were some significant exceptions, notably Cyzicus, Phocaea, and Mytilene.)

3. The Industries of Laurium

We now turn to the context of silver production in Laurium. We shall look at two aspects of activity there: the scale of production and the processing of other materials. In modern discussions of the ancient economy it is sometimes held that the word 'industry' is inappropriate, as it carries associations of scale and mass production which are wholly misleading, though the term 'cottage industry' is permissible. While generally sympathetic to this view in most cases (including that of ceramic production), we have to state bluntly that what went on in ancient Laurium can only be described as industry, much of it 'heavy'.[16] Moreover, silver production was just one of many productive activities in the region, and these activities have usually been overlooked, even though some of them were interdependent with silver production, and all of them help to fill out the picture of knowledge of materials and material-processing in classical Athens.

3.1. *Scale*

The production of silver is only practicable on a large scale; a one-man mine is at least feasible, but dressing and smelting silver-bearing ore requires significant investment in plant and the employment of a sizeable workforce of varying skills,[17] all of which must be paid for before a grain of silver may be produced. To elaborate, ore-dressing involves preliminary sorting, then breaking, resorting, grinding, washing, resorting, drying, and pelleting of ore. Ore-dressing installations in Laurium were privately owned, and represented considerable capital expenditure by someone: either the farmers on whose land they stood, or specialist ore-dressers, or mine operators whose output justified the investment.

   To give some idea of what is involved, in the case of an average-sized 'workshop', we are talking about a main washery structure with a three-layer hydraulic cement-lined floor area of about 100 m.[2], partially roofed; a similarly-lined cistern of about 300 m.[3], dug out of the bedrock, or built, or a bit of both, sometimes roofed, and in one case corbelled; a number of subsidiary roofed rooms of variable size and function, but usually more than 10 m.[2] floor area; a large yard; and a perimeter wall around the

---

[16] Conophagos estimated that over 10m. t. of gangue and slag were produced over an area of roughly 15 km.[2]: (n. 2), 138–44. This must have had a devastating effect on the region, as was pointed out by H. Mussche, 'Thorikos during the Last Years of the Sixth Century BC', in W. D. E. Coulson *et al*. (eds.), *The Archaeology of Athens and Attica under the Democracy* (Oxford, 1994), 211–15 at 215.

[17] Xen. *Vect.* 4. 5 asserts that in his own time 'everyone' [πάντες] involved in the mining industries said they needed more men and employed as many as they could.

compound with gatehouse.[18] These installations are the ἐργαστήρια of the forensic speeches which deal with mining cases. The valleys of Laurium are littered with such ruins, and in the most heavily industrialized areas, such as the Soureza valley, there are scores of them packed cheek by jowl along the valley floor.[19]

If we turn to the lessees of mining concessions, Xenophon tells us about the three (evidently famous) largest investors, Nicias with a force of 1,000 slaves, Hipponicus with 600, and Philemonides with 300.[20] Folk memory of great achievements rarely records who was second, never mind who was third. Xenophon assumes naturally enough that others held numbers of slaves in proportion to their wealth.

Estimates of the total workforce employed in silver production vary from 11,000 upwards.[21] This is more than the number of citizens in many states in ancient Greece, including Plato's ideal republic, and is probably more than the total population of a good few poleis. An inadequate but illustrative modern comparison may be drawn with companies whose turnover exceeds the GDP of entire countries.

3.2. *Associated products and materials*

Associated with silver production were other materials which were either required by the process or were by-products. In addition, other materials were exploited in Laurium which were not directly related to the silver industry but which also involved mining and processing minerals.[22] We list, first, supplies required by the silver metallurgists:

(1) charcoal;
(2) cupel material (bone ash or other);
(3) furnace stone;
(4) containers.

Each of these categories involves production on a significant scale to supply the silver industry, by charcoal-burners, glue-makers,[23] quarrymen and

---

[18] This may be compared with the so-called 'terracotta factory' in Corinth, which has no kiln and which one of its excavators said 'is best described as a large house'.

[19] Conophagos' map showing mines and metallurgical sites is full but not exhaustive: for example, there are unmarked mines and ἐργαστήρια near the head of the main valley (near the ancient quarry) on Mt. Stephani.

[20] *Vect.* 4. 14–15. These numbers should be compared with the largest known establishments in any and all other sectors, namely 120 in a shield workshop, followed by (at most) 33 in a sword/blade workshop.

[21] 11,000 is Conophagos' conservative estimate in (n. 2), ch. 14.

[22] These are dealt with fully in Rihll (n. 2).

[23] These are the most obvious source of supply of degreased bones in Greek society, which was largely vegetarian (mostly by necessity rather than by choice; but Plutarch, for example, was an evangelical vegetarian). Marl for cupels would presumably have been supplied by potters.

stonemasons, potters, basket-makers, tanners, woodworkers, and of course
hauliers and middlemen. We should also consider here supplies for the
workforce employed in the area, principally foodstuffs. Supplying food for
11,000+ people, even if most of the food was barley,[24] was an impressive
feat in itself. Neglect of this fact underlies the tendency of ancient historians to assume that food imports, especially to Athens, were destined for
consumption by the urban population in the city—an assumption which
clearly requires reconsideration in the light of the number of consumers in
Laurium.

Second, there were the by-products of silver-smelting and cupellation,
principally three different types of lead:

(1) litharge;
(2) hearth-lead;
(3) pure lead oxide.

Litharge and hearth-lead have been mentioned above.[25] Another, but undesirable, by-product was pure lead oxide, a fine white ash which is extremely
toxic if inhaled—bad news for those downwind of the cupellation sites.[26]

Third, other primary production in the area certainly or probably included:

(1) ochre (yellow by nature, and red manufactured from it);
(2) realgar and orpiment (red and yellow arsenic sulphides);
(3) χρυσοκόλλα ('gold-glue'), which may be chalcopyrite;
(4) κύανος, in 'male' and 'female' varieties, which may be malachite and
    azurite;
(5) minium, red lead.[27]

It should be clear even from so brief an outline as this that silver production was just one aspect of life and work at Laurium, and that the region
was a hive of activity for many different people pursuing many different
crafts.

---

[24] Barley was the staple slave food, and for many of the slaves in Laurium barley gruel may
have been the main meal every day.

[25] § 2.1.

[26] Prevailing winds are north-easterlies, so normally blew the toxins out to sea. But there
are a number of comments in the Aristotelian *Problems* on ill health associated with southerly
winds, which presumably refers to those occasions when Laurium air pollution was blown
north towards Athens (26. 17, 942ᵃ16–17; 26. 42, 945ᵃ14–15; 26. 50, 946ᵃ4–5).

[27] The inclusion of minium is probable rather than certain. For discussion of all these
(especially the contentious identifications of χρυσοκόλλα and κύανος) see Rihll (n. 2).

4. The Importance of Laurium's
Productive Processes in Athenian Society

The importance of Laurium and what went on there was widely recognized in Athenian society. Let us consider, for example, its place in the religious, economic, and political life of Athens.

4.1. *Religion*

Greek myth dealt with technology chiefly through four characters: the god Hephaestus,[28] the titan Prometheus, and two humans, Daedalus and his son Icarus. Metallurgy got the god; all-purpose fire[29] got the titan; various clever tricks and inventions[30] got the humans. All these characters have ambivalent status and symbolism: all are exceptionally gifted and the fruits of their labour are admired by all, but the deity has a deformed body, the titan is an outlaw, and the men are hoist with their own petard.

The metal associated with Athens was silver, first and last. Therefore when we consider the Athenians' individual and collective worship of Hephaestus, we should think of silver production as the principal focus of their prayers and gratitude, not bronze-working or iron-smithing. The Athenians built a magnificent temple to their metalworker god—the finest preserved temple in the Greek world—on rising ground overlooking the central city square (the agora), the Hephaesteum.[31] The Hephaesteia was a large and popular festival. It had twenty sacred officers ($\iota\epsilon\rho o\pi o\iota o\iota$)—twice as many as served for what are now considered to be the most famous Athenian festivals, the Eleusinian Mysteries and the Great Panathenaia, each with ten.[32] In general, the number of officials rises with the size and importance of the duties to be carried out, so the assumption should be that Hephaestus' $\iota\epsilon\rho o\pi o\iota o\iota$ have significant work to do—a good deal (if not twice as much) more than their Eleusinian or Panathenaic counterparts. Ten of the twenty for the Hephaesteia were appointed by lot from the Council of 500, which is

---

[28] The Roman equivalent is Vulcan.   [29] See Pliny, *HN* 36. 200–1.

[30] e.g. the lost-wax method of bronze-casting (Daedalus and the honeycomb) and most famously human flight. The Greeks typically remembered or named the inventor or creator of new technologies or applications. For example, Herodotus names the men who bridged the Bosporus, built great temples or tunnels, or invented new tools; Thucydides names the man who invented a new ship design; the screw was remembered as Archimedes' invention, the force pump as Ctesibius'.

[31] That the bronzeworkers' quarter was situated near the temple is neither here nor there: the number of men involved in bronzeworking in Athens in any year could probably be counted on the fingers, while the number of men involved in silver production ran into tens of thousands; the wealth tied up in bronzeworking was peanuts compared with the investments and profits made in the mines; a good number of the wealthiest known Athenians were involved in silver production, while none is known to have had involvement in bronze production or working—the examples of the distinction could be multiplied *ad nauseam*.

[32] Though called $\dot{\alpha}\gamma\omega\nu o\theta\dot{\epsilon}\tau\alpha\iota$ and holding office for four years in the latter case.

not unusual, but the other ten were appointed, in the same way, from among the 6,000 jurors. We have no idea what the jurors have to do with Hephaestus (unless it concerns overseeing an important source of their pay), but their involvement certainly does indicate the importance and relevance of Hephaestus to the ordinary Athenian, for whom 'the juror' is equivalent to the British 'man on the Clapham omnibus'. Similarly, 200 ephebes (young men on the verge of adulthood and full citizenship) participated during the festival in a demonstration of machismo through bull-lifting. Torch races also took place, as for another now little-known celebration of fire and technology, the Prometheia (the festival to honour the technological titan). We also know that, unusually, metics[33] were catered for at the Hephaesteia: three bulls were assigned to them.[34] This is probably to be related to the fact that metics were permitted to work the silver mines on the same terms as citizens.[35]

4.2. *Economics*

4.2.1. *Public income*   The Parthenon and Propylaea building inscriptions record receipts 'from the treasurers of Hephaistikon from Laurium'.[36] We do not know what the *Hephaistikon* was: possibly a treasury of sorts, or a state-run assay office, but whatever it was, its source of income was Laurium, and 20 per cent of its funds were being spent on the most famous public building projects in classical Athens.

Before an Athenian could dig a hole in the ground in search of silver or anything else, he needed a concession from the state: mineral wealth beneath the ground belonged to the Athenian public, and to (try to) exploit it, one had to pay. Fixed-term leases were sold by the Poletai in the presence of the Council of 500. Since most Athenian citizens served on the council once or twice in their adult lifetimes, most would be acquainted with the theory and practice of the state management of the mines, and the value of the leases. The polis made money out of the silver mines through these leases. It probably made money also through a 10 per cent tax on the silver produced. It possibly made money as well through an assay fee, or stampage duty, which was levied on foreign coin at 3 per cent,[37] and may have been the same for domestic silver producers.

4.2.2. *Private income*   The operators kept the lion's share of the silver

---

[33] Resident aliens, of whom we assume quite a number were involved in silver production. This is because they were not allowed to own land, so could not farm and had to make a living through craft, service, or trade occupations. Metics' access to state festivals was more or less circumscribed, and rarely involved participation in the core of the worship, the sacrifice.

[34] See D Whitehead, *The Ideology of the Athenian Metic* (Cambridge, 1977), 86–8. We do not know exactly how many bulls the citizens received, but it was between 130 and 190.

[35] Xen. *Vect.* 4. 12.   [36] *IG* i³ 444. 249–50, and ML 60. 14–15 respectively.

[37] The standards decree (ML 37), § 10.

they produced, probably 90 per cent, less small charges and fees for the lease and perhaps assaying and coining. If this seems a lot to leave in the hands of the operators, one should remember that besides paying rents to the polis, they bore *all* costs, before even a grain of silver was produced, and they had perhaps sustained such investment over many years before finding any silver at all—if indeed they did make a find. The expense is well indicated by an old Spanish proverb which asserts that 'you need a gold mine to run a silver mine', and most of the concessionaires probably needed every obol they made.[38] More than half of the identifiable men mentioned in surviving mine leases and registrations occur only once. A few concessionaires, however, made fortunes.[39]

None, it seems, could sustain their activities as the Peloponnesian war dragged on (431–404), sapping manpower and money and interrupting the import of foodstuffs, and we assume that a considerable number of the 20,000 slaves who fled to the Spartans at Deceleia (Thuc. 7. 27. 5) fled from Laurium. By the end of the war Laurium was practically at a standstill, and it seems to have taken nearly a generation for those who would eventually invest in the mines to accumulate sufficient means and manpower to do so. The mines then enjoyed a resurgence until the 320s, when a combination of food shortage and apparent exhaustion of the silver lode led to near cessation of mining activity until Roman times.

4.3. *Politics*

Knowledge of state revenues was a requirement of any would-be rhetor and statesman, and mastery of the subject was a first priority according to ancient political theorists and pamphleteers.[40] This long-overlooked point has been explored recently in a preliminary study by Kallet-Marx,[41] whose perceptive and persuasive argument emphasizes the link between political leadership and financial acumen. It is often noted that some of the so-called demagogues were associated with manufacturing establishments (tanners, lamp-makers, and the like)[42]—and often overlooked that some of

---

[38] For example, Mantias son of Mantitheus, of Thoricus, στρατηγός in 360/59, seems to have gained nothing (and possibly lost a lot) in spite (or because) of his mining interests. He was a treasurer (so wealthy) in 377/6, and performed at least one trierarchy (the most expensive liturgy) around 365. He had mining concessions in the 360s, and died *c*.358. His sons seem not to have inherited enough to have continued in the liturgical class. See *APF* 9667.

[39] e.g. Nicias in the 5th cent. (Xen. *Vect.* 4. 14; *Mem.* 2. 5. 2; Plut. *Nic.* 4); and in the 4th cent. the metic Callaeschrus, one of the richest men in Athens in the 350s (Dem. 21. 157, with *APF* pp. 590–1 (C12)).

[40] See e.g. Socrates' cross-questioning of a budding young politician in Xen. *Mem.* 3. 6. 1 ff.

[41] 'Money Talks: Rhetor, Demos and the Resources of the Athenian Empire', in R. Osborne and S. Hornblower (eds.), *Ritual, Finance, Politics* (Oxford, 1994), 227–51; 'Preliminary study': 228.

[42] W. R. Connor, *The New Politicians of Fifth Century Athens* (Princeton, 1971), drew attention to this.

their predecessors were associated with mining establishments. To cite the most famous, direct or indirect interests in silver mines are attested for Peisistratus,[43] the sixth-century tyrant; Miltiades, the victor of Marathon; Themistocles, founder of the Athenian fleet and hero of Salamis; Cimon, one of the most important figures in the building of the Delian League; Callias (nicknamed λακκόπλουτος, pit-rich) son of Hipponicus, one of the richest men in Athens and eponym of the most disputed peace treaty in Greek history; Nicias, the famous fifth-century general, who was also a mining entrepreneur *extraordinaire* in terms of the scale, investment, and organization of his operation; Thucydides, general and historian; and the notorious Alcibiades, whose manipulation of people equalled in skill and audacity the Laurium smelters' manipulation of nature.

When the mines of Laurium were slowly being reopened in the 370s and 360s, after the forced cessation of activity during the final stages of the Peloponnesian war and Athens' subsequent defeat, a conservative general and would-be statesmen revived this political tradition too, pretending to knowledge of good management of Laurium's resources: Xenophon, whose treatise *Revenues* suggested that the polis should imitate the practice of (at least some) citizens by buying slaves and renting them out to operators to work in the mines, thereby generating secure state income from the supposedly bottomless (but admittedly variable) pit of riches which was Laurium.

5. Emergence of Theories of Materials

There can be no dispute about the relative chronology of materials technology and materials science: the former precedes the latter. People worked with materials long before they started thinking about what they were doing. And when they did start thinking about what they were doing, they started with what could be called vocational disciplines, which were established before academic disciplines.[44] Thus, the study of subjects for practical use, e.g. rhetoric, music, and medicine, preceded epistemology, logic, ethics, mathematics, natural science, and the rest. Non-vocational or 'use-less' subjects can only be pursued by those who do not need to apply themselves to the business of daily survival: it was obvious even to Aristotle that a society must solve the problem of the production and supply of the necessities of life before it can support 'unproductive' people like natural scientists.[45] We

---

[43] *APF* 11793.

[44] W. Charlton, 'Greek Philosophy and the Concept of an Academic Discipline', in P. Cartledge and D. Harvey (eds.), *Crux* (Exeter, 1985), 47–61 at 58–9.

[45] 'Then when all [the arts concerned with the necessities of life and with recreation] were discovered, the sciences which are concerned neither with enjoyment nor with supplying the

can be relatively precise about the chronology in the case of materials theory in ancient Athens.

5.1. *Writers on materials*

That some intellectuals in classical Athens were interested in technology and practical skills is illustrated, for example, by the fact that Crito of Athens (a contemporary and friend of Socrates, and eponym of a Platonic dialogue), Simmias of Thebes (another contemporary of Socrates),[46] and Xenocrates of Chalcedon (a pupil of Plato, friend of Aristotle,[47] and head of the Academy in 339–314 BC) all wrote books entitled either *On Craft/Art* or *On Crafts/Arts* (Περὶ τέχνης or Περὶ τεχνῶν), as, a little later, did Aristotle.[48]

The revival of Laurium in the 370s and 360s coincided with Aristotle's arrival in Athens in 367. Following the death of his father, he came from Stagira as a teenager to join Plato's Academy, where he remained for twenty years. After an absence of about eleven years,[49] he returned to Athens, and established his own school, the Lyceum, offering an alternative education to the Platonic Academy, at this time under Xenocrates' leadership. In 323, following the death of Alexander the Great, Aristotle left Athens again, now to live in Chalcis in Euboea, his mother's ancestral home, where he died the following year in his sixties.

Interest in innovation and technical development in this generation is indicated in the persons of Heraclides of Heraclea on the Pontus (a pupil of Plato,[50] active *c*.360–340 BC), Theophrastus of Eresus (370–286, contemporary and friend of Aristotle, heir to his library and the headship of the Lyceum), and Straton of Lampsacus (head of the Lyceum after Theophrastus), who all wrote works *On Inventions* or *On Discoveries* (Περὶ εὑρημάτων),[51]

---

necessities of life were invented . . . Philosophy originated at a time when almost all the basic necessities of life were available and was taken up as a leisure time and recreational activity' (Arist. *Metaph.* 1. 1. 16, 981ᵇ21–3; 1. 2. 11, 982ᵇ24–7).

[46] See *Der Kleine Pauly* s.v.

[47] After Plato's death in 347 they went together to Atarneus, whose tyrant Hermias set them up in Assos: J. Barnes, *Companion to Aristotle* (Oxford, 1995), 5.

[48] Diog. Laert. 2. 121 (Crito), 2. 124 (Simmias), 4. 13 (Xenocrates). The meanings of τέχνη are several, and the meaning can be different within, as well as between, ancient authors: they are well discussed by C. Janaway, *Images of Excellence* (Oxford, 1995), ch. 2.

[49] On Plato's death in 347 he left Athens, travelled, married, and continued his philosophical investigations. According to widely believed but far from secure evidence, in 343 or thereabouts he accepted the post of tutor to a precocious 13-year-old: Alexander, son of Philip II of Macedon, later known as the Great. For discussion see A.-H. Chroust, *Aristotle* (London, 1973), 125–32.

[50] H. B. Gottschalk, *Herakleides of Pontus* (Oxford, 1980).

[51] Diog. Laert. 5. 47, 60, 88; Theophr. fr. 727 (11), 728 FHS&G. The relevant verb (εὑρίσκω) can mean both: we would use the term 'invention' with respect to e.g. the potter's wheel, which the scholiast on Pind. *Ol.* 13. 27 said Theophrastus attributed to Hyperbius of Corinth; we would use the term 'discovery' with respect to e.g. stone quarries, which Pliny, *HN* 7. 195–6, said Theophrastus attributed to the Phoenicians.

as well as more specifically technological works (see below). Theophrastus
states in his *Metaphysics* that we can learn about nature from studying τέχνη:

ἐπιποθεῖ δέ τινα καὶ τὰ τοιάδε λόγον, πῶς ποτε τῶν ὄντων ὁ μερισμὸς εἰς ὕλην καὶ μορφήν,
πότερον ὡς τὸ μὲν ὄν, τὸ δὲ μὴ ὄν, δυνάμει δ' ὂν καὶ ἀγόμενον εἰς ἐνέργειαν· ἢ ὂν μέν,
ἀόριστον δὲ καθά περ ἐν ταῖς τέχναις, ᾗ δὲ γένεσις, ἡ οὐσία γ' αὐτῶν τῷ μορφοῦσθαι κατὰ
τοὺς λόγους . . . ὅλως δὲ κατ' ἀναλογίαν ληπτέον ἐπὶ τὰς τέχνας καὶ εἴ τις ὁμοιότης ἄλλη.
(*Metaph.* 17, 8ª8–20)

the following problems also want some discussion—how the division of things into
matter and form is to be understood; are we to take the one as being and the other as
not-being, but as being potentially and being drawn towards actuality; or to say that
it is being, but indeterminate, as is the material used in the arts, and that where there
is generation, the essence of the things generated depends on their being shaped in
accordance with their definitions? . . . And in general we must understand matter
by virtue of an analogy with the arts, or any other similarity that may exist. (trans.
W. D. Ross)

Theorizing does not take place in a vacuum; theorists generate their ideas
in the physical, as well as the intellectual, world they occupy. The Greek
theorists were no exception; and at this particular time those living in Athens
knew that Laurium had produced great riches within living memory, and
now did not.[52]

So far as the practice and theory of material-processing are concerned,
Aristotle ends *Mete.* 3 with a promise of a treatise on metals and minerals.[53] This does not appear to be *Mete.* 4 (despite the significant amount of
material in that book concerned with smelting) and is certainly not extant
in any other form. Even more unfortunate for our enquiry is the fact that,
although Theophrastus' *On Stones* has survived, his two-book work *On
Metals* has not.[54] Theophrastus' successor as head of the Lyceum, Straton

---

[52] Cf. Xen. *Mem.* 3. 6. 12 (perhaps composed in the 360s): εἴς γε μήν, ἔφη, τἀργύρεια οἶδ' ὅτι
οὐκ ἀφῖξαι, ὥστ' ἔχειν εἰπεῖν δι' ὅ τι νῦν ἐλάττω ἢ πρόσθεν προσέρχεται αὐτόθεν. οὐ γὰρ οὖν ἐλήλυθα,
ἔφη. καὶ γὰρ νὴ Δί', ἔφη ὁ Σωκράτης, λέγεται βαρὺ τὸ χωρίον εἶναι, ὥστε, ὅταν περὶ τούτου δέῃ
συμβουλεύειν, αὕτη σοι ἡ πρόφασις ἀρκέσει. σκώπτομαι, ἔφη ὁ Γλαύκων. ('SOCRATES. Now for the
silver mines. I am sure you (a would-be politician) have not visited them, and so cannot tell
why the amount derived from them has fallen.   GLAUCON. No indeed, I have not been
there.   SOCRATES. To be sure: the district is considered unhealthy, and so when you have
to offer advice on the problem, this excuse will serve.   GLAUCON. You are mocking me':
trans. E. C. Marchant, with slight modifications).   [53] 3.6, 378ª15–378ᵇ6.
[54] Diog. Laert. 5. 44, Theophr. frr. 197–205 FHS&G. (Note that fr. 197 =Olympiod. *In
Arist.Mete.* 1. 1, 338ª20, describes it as a single-book work and appears to attribute it to
Aristotle.) It is also mentioned in the opening paragraph of *On Stones* (1. 1), and what seems
to be a stray paragraph (fr. 200) is transmitted at the end of *On Odours*. Fragments which
survive as quotations in other authors indicate the level of detail: Pollux 10. 149 (=fr. 198):
'the implements of the miner are bags, crucible, riddle. The comic poets say that miners are
bag-carriers, and the crucible and riddle [are mentioned] by Theophrastus in *On Metals*, the
crucible being the vessel in which they mix the iron, the riddle the miner's sieve'. Harpocrat. s.v.
κεγχρεών (=fr. 201): 'Demosthenes, in the plea against Pantaenetus: "and then he persuaded
my slaves to sit in the grindery" (place of granulation), instead of the washery (place of
purification), where they cleaned the grains of silver from the mines, as Theophrastus indicates

of Lampsacus, wrote a book on *Mine Machinery*—which likewise is lost.[55]
Evidently mining and metallurgy were a serious topic of research in the
early Lyceum.[56]

5.2. *Traditions and problems*

One element of the mental space in which the theorists worked was the
intellectual inheritance—the earlier speculative ideas about the nature of
matter. These were principally the four-elements theory from Empedocles and atomism from Leucippus and Democritus. Atomism and Plato's
Forms were vigorously rejected by Aristotle, and more or less vigorously
by his followers. The theoretical writings also included explicit discussions about the nature of the enquiry as part of the process of developing
them. 'It is abundantly clear that he [*sc.* Aristotle] conceived the business
of philosophy to lie as much in the defining of problems, the debating of
alternative views, and the exploring of difficulties, as in the propounding of
solutions.'[57] Theophrastus also thought long and hard about the different
kinds of knowledge that exist.[58] In these respects, then, the philosophical tradition influenced the new theories, and this is well documented and
discussed in the modern literature.[59]

But the philosophical tradition was not the only element in an ancient
Greek thinker's mind. Even the intellectual inheritance included all sorts
of other wisdom and knowledge, which was not then and is not now classed
as philosophical, and which has received very little attention to date. Yet
Archimedes, like Aristotle,[60] surely knew his Aesop, and Aesop's crow could
have cawed 'eureka' centuries before Archimedes took his famous bath.[61]

in *On Metals*' (trans. modified from FHS&G). Hesych. s.v. σκαρφών (=fr. 202): 'a type of
furnace, in *On Metals*'; and id., s.v. σύζωσμα (=fr. 203): 'in *On Metals*, the bronze that flows
out'.

[55] Diog. Laert 5. 59. See H. B. Gottschalk, 'Strato of Lampsacus', *Proc. Leeds Phil. and Lit.
Society*, 11 (1965), 95–182.

[56] In the 2nd cent. this interest was maintained by at least some members of the Stoa.
Posidonius studied the mines in Spain: test. 22 EK=Strabo 3. 2. 5; fr. 237 EK=Strabo 13. 1.
67; see also e.g. fr. 243 EK=Strabo 3.4.15 for his familiarity with copper-smelting on Cyprus.

[57] G. E. R. Lloyd, *Methods and Problems in Greek Science: Selected Papers* (Cambridge,
1991), 129–30.

[58] e.g. *Metaph.* 23–4, 9ª23–6: πόσοι δ' οὖν τρόποι καὶ ποσαχῶς τὸ εἰδέναι, πειρατέον διελεῖν. ἡ
δ' ἀρχὴ πρὸς αὐτὰ ταῦτα καὶ πρῶτον τὸ ἀφορίσαι τί τὸ ἐπίστασθαι ('at all events, we must try to
distinguish how many methods [of enquiry] there are, and how many kinds of knowledge there
are. The starting point for these problems, and the first thing to be done, is to determine what
knowledge is': trans. W. D. Ross).

[59] See e.g. R. K. French, *Ancient Natural History* (London, 1994), D. Scott, *Recollection
and Experience* (Cambridge, 1995), for theories of learning and discovery; and G. Freudenthal,
Aristotle's Theory of Material Substance (Oxford, 1995), for theories on innate heat and πνεῦμα.

[60] *Mete.* 2. 3, 356ᵇ10–18, and *Rh.* 2. 20. 5–8, 1393ᵇ12–1394ª12, make explicit reference to
the fables of Stesichorus and Aesop.

[61] 390 Perry: Κορώνη καὶ ὑδρία. κορώνη διψῶσα προσῆλθεν ἐπὶ ὑδρίαν καὶ ταύτην ἐβιάζετο

This wider intellectual inheritance is another, as yet untold, story, and is not our subject here.

We wish to add and emphasize another element in the picture: practical knowledge. When people first started thinking hard about materials, about their nature, and how they are changed from one thing into another, the knowledge base upon which they built was practical and technological knowledge of materials. And the concepts they had to think with were practical and technological. (This practical foundation to theoretical investigation is not confined to materials, of course.[62])

As data for e.g. zoological works came in from farmers, fishermen, huntsmen, herders, and others who worked with animals,[63] and data for Theophrastus' On Odours and On Fire came from perfumers (Od. 38) or fire-eaters (below), so data for materials came in from miners, quarriers, craftsmen, and others who worked with materials.[64] Intellectuals did not do

ἀνατρέψαι. ἀλλ᾽ ὅτι ἰσχυρῶς ἑστήκει οὐκ ἠδύνατο αὐτὴν καταβαλεῖν, ἀλλὰ μεθόδῳ ἐπέτυχεν ὃ ἠθέλησεν· ἔπεμπε γὰρ ψήφους εἰς τὴν ὑδρίαν καὶ τούτων τὸ πλῆθος ἀπὸ κάτωθεν τὸ ὕδωρ ἄνω ὑπερέχεεν. καὶ οὕτως ἡ κορώνη τὴν ἰδίαν δίψαν κατέπαυσεν ('The crow and the pitcher. A thirsty crow found a pitcher with some water in it, but so little was there that, try as she might, she could not reach it with her beak, and it seemed as though she would die of thirst within sight of the remedy. At last she hit upon a clever plan. She began dropping pebbles into the pitcher, and with each pebble the water rose a little higher until at last it reached the brim, and the knowing bird was enabled to quench her thirst': trans. V. S. Vernon-Jones). The crow discovered the displacement of water, Archimedes measured it and discovered specific gravity.

[62] A similar point is made by Lloyd (n. 57), 139, in a different context: 'logic and ethics may, without too much exaggeration, be said to derive ultimately from the debates of the market places, law courts, and assemblies of the city-state'. J. Ritter's point ('Measure for Measure? Mathematics in Egypt and Mesopotamia', in M. Serres (ed.), A History of Scientific Thought (London, 1995), 44–72), talking of Egyptian and Babylonian mathematical tables, is more developed: 'But the mere existence of tables for certain domains provides a privileged space for reflection on the nature of the results thus tabulated. Regularities, patterns, relationships become clearer; they seem to impose themselves on the eye of the user. Techniques cease to be merely tools for treating problems coming from the "outside", those posed by the productive needs of society. Instead, new problems, arising from a study of the tables underlying the implementation of these techniques, start to become the origin of further problems. That is, new problems, arising from the "inside" of mathematical practice, mark a new level of autonomy and abstraction in mathematics' (pp. 68–9); 'Nor does there appear to be a "straight line" leading from "practical problems" to "abstract" ones. Different [mathematical] techniques may suggest different directions of exploration and these, in turn, may well present different levels and kinds of problems and approaches further removed from the immediate productive needs of society' (p. 72). See Taisbak's paper in this volume on Greek multiplication tables and prime numbers.

[63] See M. Boylan, Method and Practice in Aristotle's Biology (London, 1983), esp. 41–3, and ch. 4.

[64] There is an excellent essay on Theophrastus' small works which, while focusing on the biological ones, has much of relevance to the other short treatises mentioned here: P. Huby, 'Theophrastus in the Aristotelian Corpus, with Particular Reference to Biological Problems', in A. Gotthelf (ed.), Aristotle on Nature and Living Things: Philosophical and Historical Studies Presented to David M. Balme on his Seventieth Birthday (Bristol, 1985), 313–25. For Aristotle, note e.g. J. Ferguson's remark, 'Teleology in Aristotle's Politics', ibid. 259–73 at 272, about it being Aristotle's 'particular genius to combine a solid base in observed fact with the capacity to fit this into a theoretical framework which arises out of those very observations'. Or I.

much in the way of systematic collection of data; and they worked largely with the data supplied by others. This is said to be one of their greatest weaknesses, but we would argue that it demonstrates unequivocally their dependence on utilitarian knowledge—knowledge about the world which was of utility to man: man the farmer, man the hunter, man the maker. Theorizing did not take place in an intellectual vacuum; it took place in a mental space furnished with existing knowledge, which was utilitarian knowledge, by and large. Sponge-divers were using diving bells when philosophers thought that the purpose of respiration was heat exchange between the internal fire of the body and the external cold of the air.[65]

Theories were tested against all sorts of everyday observations. The Aristotelian *Problems*, some of which are surely by Theophrastus and many of which are directly relevant to his known treatises, are essentially catalogues of questions based on ordinary life experiences, which are answered more or less satisfactorily by the application of general principles. Most of them give the impression of being puzzles to be solved, or even test questions for students in the school or philosophical opponents. With this kind of text, we appear to have one-directional traffic: clean, crisp, everyday phenomena in need of an explanation, with one or two theoretical principles being used to provide one. By contrast, there are no predictions, no problems of the form 'hypothesis H implies what?' (which could equally well serve as test questions), nothing, in short, to suggest that these problems are theory-led, still less theory-driven. These questions range from the ordinary, such as 'why is it that [all perfumes] appear to be sweetest when the scent comes from the wrist?',[66] to the unexpected, such as 'why are people who hold red-hot spits more tightly less burnt or not burnt at all (those who walk through

---

Tolstoy's remark (*The Knowledge and the Power* (Edinburgh, 1990), 35) that '[Aristotle] was an empiricist: he saw science as going from observation to general principles and back to observation', going on to quote *An. post.* 2. 19, 100ᵃ4–9. Or S. M. Cohen's conclusion to *Aristotle on Nature and Incomplete Substance* (Cambridge, 1996), 176, that Aristotle's metaphysics 'is both (1) more driven by the conclusions he draws from natural processes (the behaviour of submerged bladders, wine's turning into vinegar, the structure of an embryo in various stages of development) and (2) more Platonic than is generally thought . . . some will think (1) and (2) conflicting, [but I want] to suggest that a nuts-and-bolts interest in how nature operates is compatible with (2)'.

[65] For the diving bell see [Arist.] *Pr.* 32. 5, 960ᵇ21–34, which may well have been written by Theophrastus in preparation for *On the Senses*. The divers may have had no notion of what goes on when they breathe (and no interest in it either), but they knew that they could hold their breath for only so long, that the quality of sponges increases with the depth of the water, that the upside-down cauldron would not fill with water if it was not tilted during submersion, and that breathing the air within it would allow them to stay under water longer. Another technology used by divers was some kind of breathing tube, with which Aristotle compared the elephant's trunk (*Part. an.* 2. 16, 659ᵃ8–15).

[66] Theophr. *Od.* 53.

hot embers say they do this as well as their other exercises)?'[67] Even more extraordinary is the following:

διὰ τίνα αἰτίαν οἱ νάνοι γίνονται; ἔτι δὲ μᾶλλον καθόλου, διὰ τί τὰ μὲν ὅλως μεγάλα, τὰ δὲ μικρά; εἶτα οὕτω σκεπτέον. δύο δὴ τὰ αἴτια· ἢ γὰρ ὁ τόπος ἢ ἡ τροφή. ὁ μὲν οὖν τόπος, ἐὰν ᾖ στενός, ἡ δὲ τροφή, ἐὰν ὀλίγη, ὥσπερ καὶ ἤδη γεγενημένων πειρῶνται μικροποιεῖν, οἷον οἱ τὰ κυνίδια τρέφοντες ἐν τοῖς ὀρτυγοτροφείοις. ὅσοις μὲν οὖν ὁ τόπος αἴτιος, οὗτοι πυγμαῖοι γίνονται. τὰ μὲν γὰρ πλάτη καὶ [τὰ] μήκη ἔχοντες γίνονται κατὰ τὸ τῶν τεκόντων μέγεθος, μικροὶ δὲ ὅλως. τούτου δὲ αἴτιον, ὅτι διὰ τὴν στενότητα τοῦ τόπου συγκλώμεναι αἱ εὐθεῖαι καμπύλαι γίνονται. ὥσπερ οὖν οἱ ἐπὶ τῶν καπηλείων γραφόμενοι μικροὶ μέν εἰσι, φαίνονται δ' ἔχοντες πλάτη καὶ βάθη, ὁμοίως συμβαίνει καὶ τοῖς πυγμαίοις. ὅσοι δὲ διὰ τροφῆς ἔνδειαν ἀτελεῖς γίνονται, οὗτοι καὶ παιδαριώδη τὰ μέλη ἔχοντες φαίνονται. καὶ ἐνίους ἰδεῖν ἔστι μικροὺς μὲν σφόδρα, συμμέτρους δέ, ὥσπερ τὰ Μελιταῖα κυνίδια. αἴτιον δὲ ὅτι οὐχ ὡς ὁ τόπος ἡ φύσις ποιεῖ. ([Arist.] *Pr.* 10. 12, 892ᵃ6–23)

For what reason are there dwarfs? Or, to put the question more generally, why are some creatures quite large, others small? Let us examine the latter question. The causes of smallness are two, either space or nourishment—space if it be narrow, and nourishment if it be scanty, as happens when attempts are made to make animals small after their birth, for example by keeping puppies in quail cages. Those who suffer from lack of space become pygmies, for they have width and depth corresponding to the dimensions of their parents, but they are quite small in stature. The reason for this is that owing to the narrowness of the space in which they are confined the straight lines become crushed and bent. So pygmies are like figures painted on shops which are short in stature but are seen to be of ordinary width and depth. Those who fail to come to perfection from lack of nourishment clearly have the limbs of children, and one sometimes sees persons who are very small and yet perfectly proportioned, like Maltese lap-dogs. The reason is that the process of growth has a different effect from that of space. (trans. E. S. Forster)

Clearly here the general explanation for variation in size within a species is based first and foremost on the direct observation of dogs which had been deformed by human manipulation, the observation of pictures of dwarfs who appeared to be deformed in a similar way, and a deduction that what caused the deformation in the dog, lack of space, must also be the cause of the person's deformity.[68]

---

[67] Theophr. *Ign.* 57. The method of working is quite explicit here, in that the question quoted is preceded by the comment 'the differences in kinds of fire are numerous, and we must try to deal with each of them in turn, in the form of the following questions'.

[68] It is perhaps significant that of the handful of concrete examples given in the discussion of growth in *On Generation and Corruption*, Aristotle chooses the strikingly odd idea of a man's shin: ἀπορήσειε δ' ἄν τις καὶ τί ἐστι τὸ αὐξανόμενον, πότερον ᾧ προστίθεταί τι, οἷον εἰ τὴν κνήμην αὐξάνει, αὕτη μείζων, ᾧ δὲ αὐξάνει, ἡ τροφή, οὔ ('What is that which grows? Is it that to which something is added? If, for example, a man grows in his shin, is it the shin which is greater—but not that whereby he grows, viz. not the food?': 1. 5, 321ᵃ30 ff., trans. H. H. Joachim).

5.3. *Explanations*

When philosophizing about change, in particular about how things come into (actual or potential) existence and pass out of existence, Aristotle (who adheres to the four-elements theory of physics) uses terms normally employed to signify human manipulation or transformation of natural materials, drawing frequently on terms for cooking food. He explains—or excuses—this terminology by pointing out that

ὄπτησις μὲν οὖν καὶ ἕψησις γίγνονται μὲν τέχνῃ, ἔστιν δ᾽, ὥσπερ λέγομεν, τὰ εἴδη καθόλου ταὐτὰ καὶ φύσει· ὅμοια γὰρ τὰ γιγνόμενα πάθη, ἀλλ᾽ ἀνώνυμα. (Arist. *Mete.* 4. 3, 381^{b}4–6)

roasting and boiling are, of course, artificial processes, but as we have said, in nature too there are processes specifically the same, for the phenomena are similar though we have no terms for them. (trans. H. D. P. Lee)[69]

He adds that human manipulations and transformations imitate natural ones,[70] and Theophrastus makes the same point. For example, when explaining how matter acquires properties, Theophrastus attributes colour to the action of heat, as when yellow ochre turns to red when heated:

τιθέασι δ᾽ εἰς τὰς καμίνους χύτρας καινὰς περιπλάσαντες πηλῷ· ὀπτῶσι γὰρ διάπυροι γινόμεναι· ὅσῳ δ᾽ ἂν μᾶλλον πυρωθῶσι, τοσούτῳ μᾶλλον μελαντέραν καὶ ἀνθρακωδεστέραν ποιοῦσι. μαρτυρεῖ δ᾽ ἡ γένεσις αὐτή· δόξειε γὰρ ἂν ὑπὸ πυρὸς ἅπαντα ταῦτα μεταβάλλειν, εἴπερ ὁμοίαν ἢ παραπλησίαν δεῖ τὴν ἐνταῦθα τῇ φυσικῇ νομίζειν. (*Lap.* 54)

New pots luted with 'earth' [Attic yellow ochre, also mined in Laurium] are placed in a furnace. When the pots are thoroughly exposed to the fire [in the kiln], they cause the ochre to be baked, and the more they are burnt, the darker and more glowing the ochre becomes. The process of generation testifies to the truth of this. For fire would appear to be the agent responsible for all these transformations if we are to suppose the process employed here to be similar to, or comparable with, the natural process of generation. (trans. D. E. Eichholz, modified)

Like Aristotle, Theophrastus assumes that art imitates nature, and uses then current theories of natural processes as evidence to support his hypothesis about how artificial processes work. But we would argue that it is knowledge of the artificial processes which led to the formation of the hypothesis about natural processes in the first place; in other words, irrespective of the direction in which Aristotle and Theophrastus *thought* or (usually)[71] *said*

---

[69] For a general discussion of technological imagery in early Greek thinking (especially Plato's Demiurge or Craftsman-Creator) see G. E. R. Lloyd, *Polarity and Analogy* (Cambridge 1966), 272–94.

[70] *Mete.* 4. 3, 381^{b}6–7. This is commonplace in Aristotle: see e.g. *Ph.* 2. 2, esp. 194^{a}33–^{b}15.

[71] For an example where the train of thought is explicitly from man-made to natural and back again, see especially Arist. *Ph.* 2. 8–9, 198^{b}10–200^{b}11, talking of final causes (purpose in nature): 'now, unless something intervenes, how an action is done corresponds to how things are in nature, and vice versa. But actions have a purpose, and so therefore do things in nature. For example, a naturally occurring house—supposing that such a thing were possible—would happen (be made) in exactly the same way that a skilfully made house does . . . and in general

that the analogy went, their theories on natural processes were built upon knowledge based on practical manipulation of matter. For their language reveals that the imitation and analogy go from art to nature: Greeks and the Greek language conceptualize and signify the natural world in (characteristically) human terms, though instead of the anthropomorphism of natural forces and processes which gave rise to the pantheon of gods, what we find here is human activity and technology providing the model/explanation for speculation and theorizing about natural matter and substance.

Aristotle's language of material substances is the language of the technologist, and we mean not just concepts but modes of thought. For example, consider his enumeration of the intrinsic properties of homoeomerous substances. Homoeomers are uniform substances composed of the four elements, and they constitute the basic materials of everything—animal, vegetable and mineral—in the natural world, e.g. blood, bone, wood, sap, gold, salt.[72] The following properties are the analytical features by which the great majority of homoeomerous substances may be distinguished from each other, says Aristotle. In keeping with the Greek tendency for polarity, they are all pairs of contraries. Things are apt to be: solidifiable/not solidifiable; soluble/insoluble; softenable by heat/not softenable by heat; softenable by water/not softenable by water; flexible/inflexible; breakable/unbreakable; fragmentable/not fragmentable; impressionable/unimpressionable; plastic/non-plastic; squeezable/unsqueezable; ductile/non-ductile; fissile/non-fissile; cuttable/uncuttable; viscous/friable; compressible/incompressible; combustible/incombustible; vaporizable/non-vaporizable.[73] These analytical features are *operationally* expressed: some of them involve deliberate attempts at manipulation, some of them

---

human skill either completes what nature is incapable of completing or imitates nature. If artificial products have some purpose, then, natural things obviously do too . . . Even the province of human skill is not free from error: scribes can write incorrectly, doctors can prescribe the wrong medicine. Evidently, then, mistakes can happen in the province of nature too. Now, if it is possible for there to be products of human skill which correctly serve some purpose, and mistakes in this province constitute failed attempts at some purpose, then the same should go for natural things too, and monstrosities would constitute failures to achieve that natural purpose . . . It is ridiculous for people to deny that there is purpose if they cannot see the agent of change doing any planning. After all, skill does not make plans [he seems to be saying that a skilled person dispenses with the conscious planning stage, and does it on auto-pilot, so to speak]. If shipbuilding were intrinsic to wood, then wood would naturally produce the same results that ship-building does [i.e. naturally occurring ships, cf. houses]. If skill is purposive, then, so is nature' (trans. Waterfield). Also [Arist.] *Pr.* 10. 45, 895[b]32–8: 'so we find the same state of affairs in the products of nature as in those of the arts. For among the latter there are always badly-made objects, and the bad are more numerous than the good, beds for instance and garments and the like; and, where a good object is produced, it is always possible to find also a bad one, but, where a bad object is produced, it is not always possible to find a good one . . . So likewise nature always produces inferior specimens and in greater number, and superior specimens in a smaller number or not at all' (trans. E. S. Forster).

[72] See e.g. *Mete.* 4. 12, 389[b]27–8.   [73] *Mete.* 4. 8, 385[a]1–21.

are clearly not based on natural processes (e.g. cuttable/uncuttable),[74] some of them are wholly irrelevant to cultivation of the earth or other primary exploitation of natural resources, but all of them are relevant to man the maker.[75]

Likewise, when discussing physical ideas on body, interpenetration in the same place, and the notion of void, in particular the atomists' arguments against the notion of a plenum and their arguments for the notion of void (*Phys.* 4. 6, 213ᵃ12–213ᵇ30), Aristotle includes two pieces of observational evidence: (1) the contraction of wineskins under pressure; and (2) 'what happens to ash: ash in a vessel can hold as much water as the empty vessel can'.[76] The former seems a natural example in a society where wine is as common as water (as a drink, an indispensable ingredient in social and religious rituals, and a medicament), and much male culture revolves around its production and consumption, but where did the latter example arise? Adding water to ash is the essence of making a cupel; it also occurs in laundering and in making various pigments and medicaments, i.e. in a variety of technological processes. And since Aristotle condemned the use of obscure examples and illustrations,[77] we can assume that he expected his audience to be familiar with these processes. So, could observation and experience specifically in mining have been the basis of some theories concerning minerals and metals?

In *On Stones* Theophrastus explains the formation of homoeomerous stones and earths by three processes: conflux, which is the deposition of sediment in a watery medium, and which is what happens to the gangue when washing ore, though he does not give that example; filtering, which is the deposition of water-borne mineral particles in cracks and fissures

---

[74] Here his following discussion (4. 9, 387ᵃ4–11) really emphasizes the point: τμητὰ δ᾽ ἐστὶν τῶν συνεστώτων σκληρῶν ἢ μαλακῶν ὅσα δύναται μήτ᾽ ἐξ ἀνάγκης προηγεῖσθαι τῆς διαιρέσεως μήτε θραύεσθαι διαιρούμενα· ὅσα δὲ μὴ ὑγρὰ ᾖ, τὰ τοιαῦτα ἄτμητα ('hard or soft solid bodies are apt to be cut if they do not entirely split *at the blow in advance of being cut* or break into fragments when divided. Liquids and those that do so cannot be cut': trans. I. Düring, *Aristotle's Chemical Treatise* (Göteborg, 1944)).

[75] The same sort of operationally expressed distinction is apparent in his basic differentiation of earthy materials into τὰ ὀρυκτά and τὰ μεταλλευόμενα, things dug and things mined, usually translated as 'fossils' and 'metals'. 'Things mined' are also distinguished by the fact that they are fusible or malleable, unlike 'things dug', and it follows naturally from this that the fusible 'things mined' are theorized to be water-based (on the four-elements theory), while 'things dug', which will not melt in fire, are earth-based. Although written fifty years ago, D. E. Eichholz, 'Aristotle's Theory of the Formation of Metals and Minerals', *CQ*, 43 (1949), 141–6, has not yet been superseded.

[76] *Phys.* 213ᵇ14–23 (trans. R. Waterfield). This is developed at greater length in *Pr.* 25. 8, 938ᵇ14–939ᵃ9.

[77] e.g. *Gen. an.* 2. 8, 747ᵃ34 ff., which concerns Empedocles' reference to mixing tin and copper (another metallurgical analogy) to explain why the mule, offspring of horse and donkey, is sterile. What exactly Aristotle thought was obscure here is quite open to speculation; tin's rarity suggests that *it* is an obvious candidate. (Many ancient Greek 'bronzes' are not true tin bronze, but arsenical copper.)

in rock to form veins, and which accounts nicely for the appearance of stereotypical metal-ore deposits; and some other process which he does not explain or elaborate but by which Theophrastus allows for the creation of those types of stone (e.g. pumice) which he thinks could not have been formed by conflux or filtering. Once laid down, the material is 'cooked' or hardened by heat or cold, whichever is opposite to the process by which it could be 'dissolved' or disintegrated again. So, for example, if an earth can be 'dissolved' by water, then it was hardened by fire. 'Dissolving' earths went on at Laurium, in the production of ochre.

More specific to mining is the idea that some 'stones', notably but not exclusively metal ores, could regenerate or replenish themselves if left alone for a time.[78] This idea could be based on the fact that many ores, when exposed to the elements, erode to the same mineral as was originally ex-tracted;[79] it may also have been stimulated by the observation of crystals

---

[78] Aristotle's idea that metals formed from vaporous exhalations cooled in contact with rock (e.g. *Mete.* 3. 6, 378^{a}30–1) is not an explicit statement that ore replenishes itself, but it seems to be implied by the continuing presence of such vapours, and more generally by his principle of development, that all material things (in the earthly sphere) naturally change and develop from an immature to a mature form, unless hindered or stopped by external force or circumstance. Theophrastus follows his master on this point: 'a stone was once found on Cyprus half of which was a smaragdus and the other half an iaspis, as though the transformation of the stone from water was not yet complete' (*Lap.* 27). It seems to us that Aristophanes' aside to the judges about Laurium owls breeding to hatch little coinlings (*Av.* 1104–10) is more likely to be based on an idea that (all) matter grows than on any economic notion, and if so, it is the earliest evidence we know for the idea (the joke would be akin to the modern 'moths flying out of a wallet'; generation takes place only if the material is left untouched for a long time, implying extreme miserliness). Theophrastus, commenting on the various properties of stones says 'the greatest and most remarkable power, if this is true, is that possessed by the stones which breed other stones' (*Lap.* 5: trans. D. E. Eichholz), and refers to 'stones which are found inside other stones when these are split' (8), giving as examples the Lipara stone and pumice from Melos (14), and rock crystal, amethyst, and sard (30), but we do not think this is the sort of 'breeding' Aristophanes had in mind, for in each case the inner stone and encasing stone are of quite different types. For specific statements about generation/replenishment of ore or stone see e.g. [Arist.] *Mir.* 42–3, 833^{a}28–36; 47–8, 833^{b}18–31; 93, 837^{b}26–32—the title of this treatise, *On Marvellous Reports*, indicates either ignorance or disbelief of the idea; Strabo 5. 2. 6; Pliny, *HN* 34. 142, 164–5 (where he confines this property to lead mines, and cites examples); 36. 125 (marble said by 'Papirius Fabianus, an outstanding natural scientist' to grow in quarries, which Pliny thinks marvellous). Dioscorides simply assumes that stones grow, e.g. 5. 84, 106, 120, 144. The idea of self-replenishment got a boost in the wake of the alchemists, and lasted a long time: mining texts of the 18th cent. AD commonly advise abandonment of a mine for thirty years.

[79] Mining exposes unweathered minerals to the elements; upon such exposure, some miner-als change, over time, from a less familiar unweathered version (e.g. chalcopyrite) into a more familiar weathered version (e.g. malachite). We call such change decomposition; the Greeks and Romans thought of it as composition. Pliny seems to be referring to this exposure in *HN* 34. 165, explaining replenishment by 'infusion of air through the open orifices', and he cites two mines in Baetica where this was observed to have happened during a period of abandon-ment; the mines were subsequently let out at higher rents (one doubling in price) than were paid before abandonment. See also J. Healey, *Mining and Metallurgy in the Greek and Roman World* (London, 1978), 19; id., *Pliny the Elder on Science and Technology* (Oxford, 1999), 178, with modern examples of similar beliefs; and J. N. Friend, *Man and the Chemical Elements* (London, 1951), 18–19.

growing in a mineral solution.[80] That this idea was current among practising miners (if not among intellectuals) in the middle of the fourth century may be indicated by the fact that by far the most expensive lease yet found was for a mine classified as παλαιὸν ἀνασάξιμον,[81] which sold for a phenomenal sum of at least 17,550 drachmas.[82] (The auction 'reserve price' for a working mine was less than 1 per cent of this, at 150 drachmas.)

6. Characterizations of Greek Practical and Theoretical Knowledge of Materials

Our examination and interpretation of Greek knowledge of materials have focused on the relationship between practical knowledge and theoretical understanding of material-processing in classical Athens. To sharpen the picture we need some working definitions for 'practical knowledge' and 'theoretical knowledge'. These definitions must be historically sensitive. First, in § 6.1, we propose seven characteristics of practical knowledge, and consider their relation to productive processes of the period. Then, in § 6.2, we use these characteristics to develop an analysis of theoretical knowledge of materials, and compare it with practical knowledge.

6.1. *Practical knowledge of materials*

Here are seven aspects of practical knowledge that we believe characterize ancient material-processing. Practical knowledge has the following characteristics:

   1. *Content*. The knowledge is about the manipulation or transformation of natural materials with the definite goal of producing something.
   2. *Use*. The knowledge is directed at making things of use. Applications are the exclusive motivation for the knowledge.
   In the case of practical knowledge of material-processing these two features are easily satisfied. Theophrastus, *Od.* 7, for example, asserts matter-of-factly that 'in the case of those odours and tastes which are artificially and deliberately produced, it is clear that improvement [on nature] is always

---

[80] See e.g. Pliny, *HN* 35. 184, on alum.

[81] Literally (though ἀνασάξιμον does not occur elsewhere and its meaning is derived from etymology, which is not always a reliable guide) an 'old full-up' mine, generally interpreted as a 'long-abandoned' mine. This lease was published by M. Crosby, 'More Fragments of Mining Leases from the Athenian Agora', *Hesperia*, 26 (1957), 1–23 at 13, supplementary stele 5.

[82] This is the figure remaining, but we do not have the start of the number or the symbol to signify that the number starts where it does (numbers were signified by letters, which were distinguished from the text either side by a colon), so it could have been 2, 3, or even 4 talents plus 5,550 drachmas. The lowest possibility, at nearly 3 talents, is almost twice as much as the next-highest known price of 9,000 drachmas (Dem. 37. 22), and three times as much as the next below that (6,100).

what we have in view; for that is the aim of every artificial process'. Of course, the knowledge is not confined to what is useful produce for modern tastes.

3. *Form*. The knowledge is systematic in that it is designed to achieve definite goals through a series of procedures. It need not possess a conceptual framework or explanations in terms of fundamentals. The knowledge is not normally written down.

Its form is determined by the needs of the productive process. Practitioners need to know what to do and when to do it; they do not need to know why something happens. This kind of knowledge might be called 'know what'. It is often not written down because it simply is not communicable by the written word; it is knowledge which can be passed on only by 'being there' and being tutored by one who already possesses the knowledge:[83] observing, listening, smelling, tasting,[84] and feeling (with the hand either directly or via some implement) phenomena associated with different materials and their transformation. An apprentice may watch a process many times before participating in it, and may participate in it many times before being considered competent to go it alone.

4. *Experience*. The knowledge is based on procedures which consist of actions, observations, and tests, all with intentional and recognizable effects. The procedures are controlled by rules and experiences of materials and their properties. The knowledge includes criteria to distinguish between pass and failure in any product resulting from application of the procedures. The knowledge is required to be repeatable.

This kind of knowledge might be called 'know how': the practitioner knows what effects are desired and how to achieve them, without necessarily having any idea why those effects are produced by those actions. If a procedure is not repeatable, then it is not known how the result was achieved, and the achievement is considered a one-off or fluke—for example, the Lycurgus cup, a Roman glass cage-cup which looks pea-green when illuminated from outside, and red-violet when illuminated from inside, made by somehow including tiny fragments of gold and silver in the melt.[85]

[83] For example, Theophr. *Od.* 52 refers to but does not bother to spell out blends of wines, perfumes, and colours 'mentioned by and known to experts'.

[84] This sense was much more used in antiquity than now; notice how often Aristotle, for example, refers to the flavour of different types of earth, e.g. Arist. *Mete.* 2. 3, 359^b8–22. Later, Dioscorides frequently recommends tasting and attempting to chew minerals (the latter seems to be a way of establishing their softness—a sort of dental Mohr scale; see e.g. 5. 84) as a reliable indicator in identifying them.

[85] For illustrations see D. Harden, *Glass of the Caesars* (Milan, 1987), no. 139. Harden notes (247) that 'five other fragments of glass of about the same period are known to have the same properties and similar chemistry', and two of these are certainly from a different melt, as their colour is buff when illuminated from outside, and clear brown when light is transmitted through the glass from the inside. Nevertheless, neither the person(s) who made these pieces nor we know how this glass was made, as is clear from the rarity of such pieces, and modern science and technology's continuing inability to explain their production.

5. *Changes and progress.* The knowledge changes through changes of goals, skills, materials, and procedures. Change is effected mostly by changes in the workforce and in the materials.

6. *Experimentation.* This is likely to be based on processing in similar ways different primary materials with characteristics of e.g. appearance or location similar to those of the previously known material. Experimentation is also based on observations of the results of variation of the procedures.

Sticking closely to our subject (for these points could be elaborated at great length),[86] a passage in Theophrastus (*Lap.* 58–9) indicates clearly that practising miners were not slow to experiment with and exploit any interesting-looking rocks they found: he says that Callias, whom he describes as 'an Athenian from the silver mines', invented a process for manufacturing synthetic cinnabar from the red sands of Ephesus, which he collected and experimented upon, 'thinking that it contained gold owing to its glowing appearance', but finding cinnabar instead. Theophrastus dates this invention to *c*.405 BC,[87] about thirty-five years before he was born.

7. *Communality and Transfer.* The knowledge is the result of experience of working with the process and is learnt by involvement in the process. It is transmitted within a select circle of people who participate in the process and is likely to be owned by individuals. At times it is likely to be secret, scarce, valuable, and for sale by hiring or buying the person who owns the knowledge.

The knowledge exists in experienced people's heads, and they, as in Laurium, were often slaves. To cite the most famous example, Nicias paid a massive 6,000 drachmas—equivalent to 12,000 jurors' day wages for service in the law courts—for a Thracian slave mine manager called Sosias,

[86] For example, Gal. *Subfig. emp.* 10 relates the chance discovery of a cure for elephantiasis, which involved a snake drowning in wine; he heard about two separate instances of this chance cure, and then (with agreement from the patient) 'imitated these chance experiences' to good effect. He was then approached by another man suffering the same condition, and the snakes were prepared in a different manner. Then another man, attending a religious healing shrine and on orders from the god, took a snake drug externally and was cured. 'Encouraged by all these experiences, I confidently began to use the snake drug copiously, in the manner prescribed by the god. They call it "theriac antidote". Moreover, I also used theriac salt, which by now many prepare by burning live snakes with certain drugs in a new earthenware vessel, to which they also add snake food. I myself remove the heads and tails of the snakes, just as in the preparation of theriac rolls' (trans. M. Frede). And so the introduction of a new medicine, developing from chance observation, involves changes in the extra-essential (i.e. everything but the snake) ingredients, in the manner of preparation (soaked, cooked), in the mode and method of application (ingested, anointed), and in adjunctive treatment (Galen first purges the patient and, if he is young and strong, bleeds him before giving the snake remedy).

[87] 'About ninety years before the archonship of Praxibulus'. This is an odd way of dating an event. Without too much effort, Theophrastus could have found out who was archon ninety years before Praxibulus. Why did he not do so? Perhaps the quality of the information he was using (possibly one of the lost *On Inventions* texts (cf. § 5.1), or a source for such a work, which would have given an approximate date for the invention, in terms of generations prior to the time of composition of the text or telling of the tale) did not justify such an exact figure. On metalworkers experimenting in other ways, see Wilson's paper in this volume.

who then undertook the day-to-day management of Nicias' mining concessions, with a workforce of 1,000 slaves. No one would pay anything for a
layman's knowledge.[88] In such circumstances secrecy can be important, and
nowhere is secrecy a more obvious feature than in metal-processing—in the
form of activity known later as alchemy (on which see Wilson's paper in this
volume).

6.2. *Theoretical knowledge of materials*

As with practical knowledge, there are several ways to analyse and classify
theoretical knowledge. Our specific task is to analyse the nature of the
ancient forms of both practical and theoretical knowledge of materials.
Therefore, we shall now consider in turn the seven aspects of knowledge
we used to characterize practical knowledge of material-processing in § 6.1,
and compare the characteristics of theoretical knowledge:

   1. *Content*. The knowledge is about the nature of things in the natural
world and their behaviour. The goal is to ask questions and to answer them
without recourse to supernatural ideas. The knowledge need not contain
procedures and actions.
   2. *Use*. Curiosity raises certain questions. The knowledge is directed at
understanding specific aspects of nature.
   Atomism perhaps represents a fine example of this sort of knowledge.
Developed early (about a century before the Lyceum came into existence),
this theory of the material world involved no deities, unobservably small
basic units of matter, and (at the time) undemonstrable void. Procedures
and actions were developed in due course both by its proponents and by its
opponents in order to try to prove or disprove the notion of void, but all
anyone could do to dispute the unobservable indivisible atoms was to argue,
like Aristotle, that it raised all kinds of problematic implications.[89]
   The inapplicability of theories about the natural world, as opposed to the
usefulness of the study of human nature, was recognized. For example, in

[88] Plato gives a good idea of a layman's knowledge in *Plt.* 303 E (where he uses an analogy
with gold-refining to establish how far his discussants have got in their efforts to differentiate
types of politician). 'The workers first remove earth and stones and all that sort of thing, and
after that there remain the precious materials which are mixed with the gold and are akin to
it and can be removed only by fire—copper and silver and sometimes adamant. These are
removed by the difficult processes of boiling and testing on the touchstone, leaving before our
eyes what is called unalloyed gold in all its purity' (trans. H. N. Fowler, modified). 'Adamant'
designates something exceptionally hard or unbreakable (not the same thing), e.g. steel (e.g.
Hes. *Theog.* 161, 239; *Op.* 147), corundum (e.g. Theophr. *Lap.* 19; E. R. Caley and F. C.
Richards, *Theophrastus: On Stones* (Columbus, Oh., 1956), 91–2, 148), or—in Roman times—
diamond (Manil. 4. 926; Pliny, *HN* 37. 56–8): J. F. Healey, 'Pliny on Mineralogy and Metals',
in R. K. French and F. Greenaway (eds.), *Science in the Early Roman Empire: Pliny the Elder,
his Sources and Influence* (London and Sydney, 1986), 111–46 at 134–8. Its meaning here, if
indeed the speaker has any inkling of what gold ores may or may not contain, is anyone's guess.
[89] See *Phys.* books 3–6, *passim*. On ancient atomism see the paper of Milton in this volume.

his reminiscences of Socrates' conversations and opinions, Xenophon puts the following speech into Socrates' mouth:

ἆρ', ὥσπερ οἱ τἀνθρώπεια μανθάνοντες ἡγοῦνται τοῦθ' ὅ τι ἂν μάθωσιν ἑαυτοῖς τε καὶ τῶν ἄλλων ὅτῳ ἂν βούλωνται ποιήσειν, οὕτω καὶ οἱ τὰ θεῖα ζητοῦντες νομίζουσιν, ἐπειδὰν γνῶσιν αἷς ἀνάγκαις ἕκαστα γίγνεται, ποιήσειν, ὅταν βούλωνται, καὶ ἀνέμους καὶ ὕδατα καὶ ὥρας καὶ ὅτου ἂν ἄλλου δέωνται τῶν τοιούτων, ἢ τοιοῦτον μὲν οὐδὲν οὐδ' ἐλπίζουσιν, ἀρκεῖ δ' αὐτοῖς γνῶναι μόνον ᾗ τῶν τοιούτων ἕκαστα γίγνεται; περὶ μὲν οὖν τῶν ταῦτα πραγματευομένων τοιαῦτα ἔλεγεν. (*Mem.* I. I. 15)

Students of human nature think that they will apply their knowledge in due course for the good of themselves and any others they choose. But do those who pry into heavenly phenomena imagine that, once they have discovered the laws by which these are produced, they will create at their will winds, waters, seasons and such things to their need? Or have they no such expectation, and are they satisfied with knowing the causes of these various phenomena? Such then, was his criticism of those who meddle with these matters. (trans. E. C. Marchant)[90]

3. *Form.* The knowledge is broad, though some depth is achieved in some topics. The knowledge is systematic in that it is created by reasoning: that is, it has assumptions and observations that are used to make arguments and explanations. Easily appreciated illustrations and examples are commonplace. The knowledge is written down.

Most ancient thinkers were polymaths by today's standards. The whole of the material world came under natural history, rather than being subdivided into clearly demarcated disciplines, even transcending what we would call pure and applied disciplines:[91] for example, Aristotle frequently uses housebuilding as an illustration in the *Physics*.[92] (Most ancients built their own houses.) But the theoretical works are not merely collections of empirical data, since particulars are organized according to general guiding hypotheses. (The difference is akin to that between a chronicle and a history.)

The knowledge is written down, possibly because it is abstracted from the world and thus less easy to comprehend and remember. Students take notes to help them learn, while teachers make notes to help them remember. Each lecture was unique, in at least the same sort of way as a bard's recital of the Homeric epics was unique: even on a well-thought-through topic the

[90] This is the last of many criticisms of 'natural history' as a discipline. Another criticism is that the theorists not only disagree among themselves, but hold contrary opinions (one vs. many, reality vs. illusion, steady state vs. constant flux, etc.). In essence, the complaints are that (1) nobody knows what nature is or how it works, and (2) even if they did, their knowledge would yield no practical benefit.

[91] This is in part true even of mathematics, as is (implicitly at least) clear in several papers in this volume (Berggren, Coulton, Cuomo, Hussey, Netz, Taisbak), though some of the applications are of a rather special sort.

[92] e.g. 1. 4, 188ᵃ15–16; 1. 8, 191ᵇ5, which is worth quoting in support of the next sentence: οἰκοδομεῖ μὲν οὖν ὁ ἰατρὸς οὐχ ᾗ ἰατρὸς ἀλλ' ᾗ οἰκοδόμος ('a doctor builds a house not *qua* doctor but *qua* housebuilder'—and this is written by the son of a doctor!); 2.3, 195ᵇ4–6; 3. 1, 201ᵇ7–15.

teacher would not reproduce exactly his last lecture on it—or his published treatment, if such a thing existed. Most of Aristotle's surviving written works, of course, appear to represent lecture notes, in striking contrast to, say, a Platonic dialogue or an Archimedean 'letter'.

4. *Experience*. The knowledge is not necessarily based on experience. It can involve very detailed observations as befits specialization. Knowledge of materials is based sometimes on technological and household processes.

Aristotle's objection to atomism was chiefly the presumption of too-small-to-be-seen quantities as the basic units of matter. He was an empiricist; others were not. He argued that physics must confine itself to the visible. But visible is not the same as verifiable. His hypotheses about the superluminary cosmos, for example, were unverifiable; and his natural processes are often based more or less clearly on cooking, metalworking, or other processes and procedures developed in crafts, as argued above in § 5.3.

5. *Changes and progress*. The knowledge changes through discussion and debate. Change is effected mostly by new examples, concepts, and arguments that arise through reasoning.

6. *Experimentation*. Knowledge is subject only to the test of critical review and debate; indeed, it need not be physically verifiable.

This is clearly demonstrated in numerous authors who in the course of advancing an argument refer implicitly or explicitly to predecessors' and contemporaries' views. All who came after Parmenides had to deal with the logical problem of being, not-being, and change, which Aristotle, for example, solved (to his own satisfaction) by advancing the concepts of potential being and actual being. Theophrastus is one of the finest examples of the ancient debater: he provides summaries of others' views which are concise and amazingly impartial,[93] followed by a critique and, usually, a reasoned statement of his own opinion. The Aristotelian *Problems* appear to be case studies which test theories about assorted physical and mechanical phenomena. Multiple theories and positions existed simultaneously because few could be refuted to everyone's satisfaction by evidence or argument.

7. *Communality and transfer*. The knowledge is learnt by involvement in a process of education. It is transmitted within a circle of people who participate in preserving and developing the knowledge. It may be owned and sold. It can be competitive but it is commonly open.

The level of education provided in schools was low; basic reading, writing, and numeracy constituted just one part of a general programme which was also concerned with physical education (essential in a world where all free adult males were called to arms, and where war was monotonously regular) and music (chiefly poetry recitations, singing, and playing instruments). Formal schooling was neither free nor required by law, so some had no formal education at all. Further improvement of the mind—and that is

[93] See e.g. *Sens.* 1–91.

how it was viewed: the aim was to deepen one's understanding of nature (including human nature), and no formal educational qualifications were required for any occupation in ancient Greece—was available through study of philosophy, covering all the academic disciplines recognized at the time, which was offered freely by some (like Socrates, who tried to get people thinking whether they wanted to or not) loitering around public spaces, and charged for by others, who usually had no dedicated place to go to either.

Theoretical knowledge of the kind we have been discussing was obtained apparently by regular attendance at the lectures of a master of that knowledge. Such masters were often autodidacts, and they were few and far between in time and space, but the Greeks liked to create continuities for sages as well as for gods and lawgivers, so that a famous sage acquires a 'genealogy' as pupil of a famous predecessor and master to an intellectual successor. However, in the fourth century BC really well-organized groups of like-minded intellectuals, with views defined largely through contrast with other groups, set up 'high schools', notably Plato's Academy,[94] Aristotle's Lyceum (otherwise known as the Peripatos),[95] and Epicurus' Garden. (The second was set up in rivalry to the first, and the third in rivalry to both the others.) While most students at these schools were perhaps relatively well-heeled young men,[96] occasionally slaves owned by one or more of the individuals within the group were educated alongside them, and might even achieve fame as philosophers in their own right, as in the case of Phaedo.[97]

Most full-time intellectuals made their living by teaching, from the fees

[94] A publicly owned wooded area outside the city walls, dedicated to the hero Akademos, with a gymnasium. Although this is usually called the first such school, Aristophanes' *Clouds* is set in a fictional philosophical school, in which students are studying natural history as well as rhetoric, and the production date of this play precedes Plato's opening of the Academy by decades.

[95] Another public wood, next to a temple of Apollo Lykeios (the wolf), also with a gymnasium. The 'school' did not have a dedicated space from which the general public could be excluded until Theophrastus took over the headship and successfully applied for a special grant, which allowed him to build. (Neither Aristotle nor Theophrastus had Athenian citizenship, so they were prohibited from owning land or houses in Attica unless granted ἔγκτησις.) The term Peripatos derives from the footpath running through or round the wood, along which the teachers were wont to stroll.

[96] This at least is what is always assumed. However, it is worth noting that Socrates' father was a stonemason, Aristotle's a doctor (not regarded as a top job: see e.g. Aesop's 'The cobbler turned doctor' (Perry 475), Plato's—admittedly philosophically motivated—critique of the profession in *Resp.* 405 D–410 A; *OCD* s.v. *medicine*, § 1; V. Nutton, 'Murders and Miracles: Lay Attitudes to Medicine in Classical Antiquity', in R. Porter (ed.), *Patients and Practitioners* (Cambridge, 1985), 23–53), Theophrastus' a fuller (i.e. textile miller and/or clothes-washer), and there are many more examples of full-time philosophers emerging from modest family backgrounds. Note also Xen. *Mem.* 4. 1. 5, which runs contrary to the modern assumption that one should identify the 'educated' with the 'élite': Socrates chided those who prided themselves on riches and thought that they had no need of education, supposing that their wealth would suffice them for gaining the objects of their desire and winning honour among men. Furthermore, at least two of Plato's students were women. Compare Netz's discussion in this volume of the backgrounds of mathematicians.

[97] Diog. Laert. 2. 105; Gell. 2. 18. E. I. McQueen and C. J. Rowe, 'Phaedo, Socrates and

paid by their pupils, like Gorgias, or received gifts or food in kind, like Socrates, or lived like a dog, like Diogenes. In a few cases the teacher went to the student. Plato's decision to go to Syracuse to teach the new ruler, Dionysius, may have been motivated by a desire to experiment with his idea of philosopher-kings and put his theory into practice, but it allegedly resulted in his being sold into slavery by his disaffected and powerful pupil, and encouraged the Academicians to forget practice and focus on theory alone.[98] Aristotle may or may not have been one of Alexander's teachers (cf. n. 49), but he too travelled to find employment in his early years. Given this, it would be a mistake to assume that the intellectual giants of Greek history were motivated solely by pure abstract thought and were not ever influenced in their choice of subject or place of work by their paymasters, especially since most of them were not in any sense 'employed' in 'schools'.

Moreover, while most were keen to recruit followers either from the competition or from intellectual debutants, secrecy seems sometimes to have had a place in the intellectual sphere as well as in the practical. For example, the impression given by Aristophanes' portrayal of the 'Thinking-Shop' in *Clouds* is that of a closed shop, while Archimedes claims in the introduction to *On Spirals* to have deliberately published erroneous theorems in order to expose those who claimed his ideas as their own.

7. Concluding Remarks

The aim of this paper is to understand better ancient Greek knowledge of materials in its historical context. This requires taking seriously the idea that the history of a technology should be fully integrated into the history of the society which produced and used it. Specifically, in this paper, we have

- pointed out that there was a range of large-scale material-processing activities going on in Laurium, not merely silver (§ 3)
- pointed out that these complex processes could be undertaken by following relatively simple procedures involving easy empirical tests (§ 3)
- emphasized the social awareness in Athens of the importance of these activities (§ 4)
- discussed a range of theoretical writings by contemporaries, emphasizing their interest in materials and their transformation (§ 5)
- tried to characterize practical and theoretical knowledge of materials in the period (§ 6).

the Chronology of the Spartan War with Elis', *Methexis*, 2 (1989), 1–18, defend a story whose historicity has often been questioned (we owe this reference to Christopher Tuplin).

[98] See Gottschalk (n. 50), 31.

The objective of § 6 was to clarify the meaning of the key terms 'practical' and 'theoretical' knowledge in the case of materials. It has not been our objective here to undertake a theoretical investigation of the contemporary conceptions of technological vs. scientific knowledge nor to compare our views with the philosophical or historiographical literature on technology and science which sometimes makes use of the ancient world.[99] However, the investigation of our historical problem is relevant to the history and philosophy of science, engineering, and practical know-how in other periods and in general. In the case of materials in classical Athens, we have argued that practical knowledge does not depend on theoretical knowledge, but that practical knowledge may influence the formulation of theoretical knowledge. We believe that these propositions are not confined to material-processing in classical Athens.

[99] Cf. e.g. the popular analysis of science by Wolpert (n. 3), and the Kirk–Popper–Lloyd exchanges discussed in G. E. R. Lloyd, 'Popper versus Kirk: A Controversy in the Interpretation of Greek Science', in (n. 57), 100–20.

17

Distilling, Sublimation, and the Four Elements: The Aims and Achievements of the Earliest Greek Chemists

C. ANNE WILSON

A LARGE collection of chemical recipe texts has come down to us through the tenth-century manuscript Marcianus 299 and a number of later manuscripts now distributed through several European libraries.[1] The original texts date from the end of the first century BC to the Byzantine period. They are notable because they appear to describe actual chemical experiments and reactions carried out with the object of transforming the outward appearance of copper first to silver, then to gold. But the gold is not a realistic imitation designed to deceive the unwary, like the adulterated or imitation gold and silver of the recipes in the Egyptian goldsmiths' notebooks of the third century AD.[2] To determine what the experimenters were really trying to do, I shall first examine the theoretical background to the experiments; then I shall consider the role of distilling (the evaporating of liquids and collection of the recondensed vapour) and sublimation (the heating of minerals within a sealed vessel to release gases which can react with other substances placed in the vessel). Finally I shall suggest that metalworkers already skilled in those technologies were among the founders of the chemical art, and shall discuss the significance to them of Democritus.

1. The Φυσικὰ καὶ μυστικά: Physical Matters and Mystical Matters

Phusika kai Mustika (hereafter *PM*), the earliest chemical text, belongs to the late first century BC or early first century AD, but it is believed to have been recompiled from a text originally composed in Egypt about 200 BC or not much later.[3] Its supposed author was Democritus, often named simply 'the philosopher', and still regarded as founder of the chemical art by

[1] M. Berthelot, *Collection des anciens alchimistes grecs* (Paris, 1887–8; repr. London, 1963). The 1963 edition contains separately paginated sections entitled 'Introduction', 'Textes', and 'Traduction', distributed across three volumes ('livraisons'). Hereafter cited by author's name.

[2] R. Halleux, *Les Alchimistes grecs*, i (Paris, 1981), 84–109 and 110–51 for texts.

[3] Berthelot, text II.1, texte grec 41–53, traduction 43–57. Possible earlier version: Halleux (n. 2), 68; M. Wellmann, *Die Phusika des Bolos Demokritos* (Abhandlungen der preußischen Akademie der Wissenschaften, phil.-hist. Kl. 7; Berlin, 1928), 9 etc. The *terminus ante quem* is

Zosimus, who gathered a large number of existing chemical recipe texts into an encyclopaedia about AD 300.

But in the first century AD that art had become known to other groups, possibly because Anaxilaus of Thessaly had given a wider circulation to recipes hitherto kept secret. Recipe texts were produced which claimed other founders, including Hermes and Isis; and the chemical art also passed to the Sethian Gnostics,[4] and to various Christian Gnostic sects. Basilides the Gnostic in the second century AD combined Zoroastrian and Christian teachings, and his followers first claimed Ostanes as founder of the chemical art, backing up their claim with forged texts bearing Ostanes' name.[5]

Our version of *PM* comprises recipes for the gold-tinting and silver-tinting of metals, originally followed by two more sections for artificial gemstones and purple-dyeing,[6] but now simply preceded by a few purple-dyeing recipes. Most of the many later texts are devoted to metal treatments, but a few describe the production of θεῖον ὕδωρ (*theion hudōr*: sulphur water), often used in gold-tinting recipes. The latest of all are commentaries rather than instructions for practical metal-tinting.

In practice the experiments began with a thin tablet of copper or an amalgam of four base metals including copper (called the τετρασώματα: *tetrasōmata*). It was treated by contact with various earths, crystals, liquids, compound pastes, or volatile metals such as mercury or arsenic, applied by cooking, steeping, or simply prolonged juxtaposition. The base metal was silvered, and then tinted, often with sulphur-rich compounds, to change its appearance to gold. But realism was not the primary objective. The work was carried out, as explained in *PM* 15, as a 'healing and release from all pain for the soul' (τὸ τῆς ψυχῆς ἴαμα καὶ παντὸς μόχθου λύτρον). The chemical art thus emerges as one of the new mystery cults of the Hellenistic age.

In *PM* 3 Democritus, the supposed author, tells how through contact with a recently dead teacher and his living pupil (both unnamed: see below, p. 311) he learnt how to harmonize the natures, and how the entire *logos* could be summed up in three phrases: one nature delights in another nature, one nature conquers another nature, one nature overrules another nature.[7] The gold-tinting and silver-tinting recipes follow, and after each recipe appears one of the three phrases, literally as 'the nature overrules the nature' etc., but usually translated as 'one nature overrules another nature' etc.

the use of the phrase 'one nature is conquered by another' in the astrological book *The Revelation of Nechepso and Petosiris* (E. Riess, *Nechepsonis et Petosiridis Fragmenta Magica* (*Philologus*, suppl. 6; Göttingen, 1891–3), p. 37, fr. 28 = Firm. Mat. *Math.* 4. 16), dated about the mid-2nd cent. BC by A. J. Festugière, *La Révélation d'Hermès Trismégiste* (Paris, 1944–54), i. 76–7, 232.

[4] See Hippol. *Ref.* 5. 21 for the Sethians and their 'art of separation'.
[5] C. A. Wilson, *Philosophers, Iosis and Water of Life* (Proc. Leeds Phil. and Lit. Soc., Lit. and Hist. Section, 19.5; Leeds, 1984), 54–5 = 160–1. On Ostanes see also below, p. 312.
[6] Still present in the 4th cent. AD and referred to by Synesius: see Berthelot, text II. 3. 1.
[7] ἡ φύσις τῇ φύσει τέρπεται καὶ ἡ φύσις τὴν φύσιν νικᾷ καὶ ἡ φύσις τὴν φύσιν κρατεῖ.

So much for the mystical side. In chemical terms the silver and gold colorations were achieved, as Joseph Needham explained, 'by altering the composition of the surface layers (of the base metal), or by depositing microscopically-thin films'.[8] Recipes in *PM* indicate by their result that sublimation methods were utilized in some cases to silver-coat copper with arsenic. Elemental arsenic, called 'mercury from orpiment or realgar' (20–1), could not have been obtained from those two sulphides by any other means, and *PM* 21 refers to the addition of vegetable oil, a necessary ingredient in the final sublimation process.[9] Distillation is not described in *PM*, though sulphur water is named as an ingredient (10); and a recipe for producing it is in a later text.[10] Both techniques are mentioned in *PM* 29, where the author refers the reader to his other writings, now lost, for accounts of sublimation (ἄρσις τῆς νεφέλης) and distilling (ἄρσις τοῦ ὕδατος).

But what were the real aims of the experimenters, and what was the theoretical basis for their practical chemistry? Their chemical art was established in Egypt before the mid-second century BC when the phrase about one nature conquering another nature was reused in the astrological treatise on *The Revelation of Nechepso and Petosiris* (cf. n. 3 above). Bolus of Mendes was involved somehow in its earliest phase; and Columella later claimed that Bolus wrote a book called *Cheirokmeta* 'under the false name of Democritus'. Bolus also wrote a book on sympathies and antipathies; and some modern scholars have believed him to be the true author of *PM*.[11] The Bolus question is too complicated to go into here, but the enigma is apparent from entries in the *Suda*, where he appears twice, first as Bolus Democritus and then as the Pythagorean, Bolus of Mendes.[12]

Pythagorean ideas certainly emerge in *PM*. In 15 the νεοί (newcomers) are attacked for their failure to appreciate the significance of the chemical changes because 'they do not understand the natures, how one form overturns ten'. The 'ten' must refer to the Pythagorean tetraktys, the fundamental formula of $1+2+3+4=10$, brought by Pythagoras himself to his followers, and honoured thereafter in their most sacred oath. The other system of ideas linked unquestionably with Pythagoras is metempsychosis or the transmigration of souls.

Theon of Smyrna listed eleven tetraktyes, beginning with that of the Pythagorean oath. The second is that of odd and even numbers, and the

---

[8] *Science and Civilization in China*, v/2 (Cambridge, 1974), 253.

[9] Realgar sublimed with sulphur yields orpiment. This, or mineral orpiment, must be fused with natron (soda) or mercury to yield arsenious oxide; and the oxide must then be combined with vegetable gum and resublimed to yield elemental arsenic. By a further sublimation the arsenic can be applied as a silver coating to copper. See R. P. Multhauf, *The Origins of Chemistry* (London, 1966), 107–8.   [10] Berthelot, text III. 8. 1–3.

[11] Colum. 7. 5. 11. Bolus as author of *PM*: Halleux (n. 2), 62–74; Wellmann (n. 3), 1–69.

[12] See P. Kingsley, 'From Pythagoras to the *Turba Philosophorum*: Egypt and Pythagorean Tradition', *JWCI* 57 (1994), 1–13 at 5–9, for recent discussion of Bolus as a Pythagorean.

third that of the progression from point to solid body. The fourth, that of the elements (1 = fire; 2 = air; 3 = water; 4 = earth), is the earliest one to be linked to physical matter.[13] The tetraktys introduced by Pythagoras to his followers in Italy was, however, too early for the concept of the four elements; and I would suggest that it derived its power originally from the belief that it represented the four realms.

The sources and limits of the four realms were already defined as heaven, earth, sea, and misty Tartarus in Hesiod's *Theogony* (807–10); and Homer's gods themselves swore solemn oaths by three of the four realms (heaven, earth, and the waters of the River Styx), giving a divine precedent for the underlying idea in the tetraktys oath.[14] For Pythagoreans the 1 would have been the number of the heavenly realm filled with light and fire, which was also a place of stillness where the soul could find rest after having been buffeted through its lives in the other three realms of air (symbolized by 2), water (symbolized by 3), and earth (symbolized by 4).[15] A very old concept, going back to Mycenaean times, made the 1 and the 3 male numbers, and the 2 and the 4 female ones.[16]

The Pythagoreans believed that their souls, having fulfilled their spans in the bodies of plants, animals, children, and women, were finally reborn into men who would become Pythagoreans, live ascetic lives, and carry out the required rituals, so ensuring that, after the body's death, they (the souls) would pass to their rest in the heavenly light and their release from all pain. The tetraktys was laid out on the ground as a triangular pebble figure, with one pebble at the apex and four at the base.[17] In this form it may have had a role in initiation ceremonies, since it has the interesting characteristic that the relationship between the 1 and the 4 depends on the position of the

[13] Theon Smyrn. *Math.* 97–8. Cf. Diog. Laert. 8. 25; Sext. Emp. *Adv. Math.* 10. 283. Arist. *Metaph. A* 5. 3, 986ª9–10, refers to the decad of the Pythagoreans, but not to the tetraktys, which may have been in his lost work about them.   [14] *Il.* 15. 36–8; *Od.* 5. 185–7.

[15] For fire rushing upwards and spreading through *aithēr* to form heavenly bodies, see P. Kingsley, *Ancient Philosophy, Mystery and Magic* (Oxford, 1995), 49–53, and cf. the Pythagorean *akousma*: 'What are the Islands of the Blest? Sun and Moon' (Iamb. *VP* 82). *Aēr* was already the 'lower air' in *Il* 14. 288, though its other meaning, 'mist', survived through the 5th cent.: see C. H. Kahn, *Anaximander and the Origins of Greek Cosmology* (New York, 1966), 146–52. The verbal link with Hesiod's 'misty Tartarus' could have helped the shift from that realm to the airy realm to fit the Pythagoreans' beliefs: cf. also Emp. 31 B 6 DK and the ancient interpretation of Aidoneus as 'air'. P. Kingsley, 'Empedocles and his Interpreters: The Four-Element Doxography', *Phronesis*, 39 (1994), 239–47, argued convincingly for this interpretation as Theophrastean, probably going back to Xenophanes and to Pythagoreans of the late 5th cent..

[16] J. Chadwick, *The Decipherment of Linear B*, 2nd edn. (Cambridge, 1967), 45: a male horse or pig is depicted as an animal head above a single stroke, and a mare or sow a head above either two strokes or one stroke with two crossbars. Aristotle's table of the Pythagorean pairs of opposites (*Metaph. A* 5. 6, 986ª22–7) assigns male to the same column as odd (of number), light, etc., and female to the other column, with even, darkness, etc.

[17] W. Burkert, *Lore and Science in Ancient Pythagoreanism*, trans. E. L. Minar (Cambridge, Mass., 1972), 72.

viewer: the pebble at either end of the line of four representing earth could become the apex if seen from one of the other two sides. The tetraktys could thus have symbolized a bridge from earth to the fiery heaven.

After Empedocles had defined the elements as four, moving together and apart through love and strife,[18] a second line was added to the Pythagorean oath which described the tetraktys as 'holding the fountain and roots of ever-flowing nature'.[19] It links the tetraktys with the four 'roots', Empedocles' term for the elements, thus suggesting that the Pythagoreans soon identified each of the four with the number of the corresponding realm—not difficult, since the names of the three lower realms were the same as those of three of the elements, and fire could parallel the fiery heavenly realm. The identification would have taken place well before Plato developed, or adapted Pythagorean ideas for, the chemistry of the *Timaeus*.[20]

In *PM* 15 the phrase 'one nature overturns ten' ($\ddot{\epsilon}\nu$ $\epsilon\ddot{\iota}\delta os$ $\delta\acute{\epsilon}\kappa a$ $\dot{a}\nu a\tau\rho\acute{\epsilon}\pi\epsilon\iota$) is a covert reference to the four elements contained in the tetraktys. But the chemistry of the recipes does not derive directly from that source, but from Plato's reworking of it in the *Timaeus*. There he assigns three-dimensional shapes to the basic particles of the elements: the four-sided pyramid to fire; the eight-sided octahedron to air; the twenty-sided icosahedron to water; and the six-sided cube to earth.[21] In the particles of fire, of air, and of water the surfaces were made up in each case from triangles identical in shape, i.e. the halves of an equilateral triangle. The cube, the most stable of the solids, was assigned to earth, but the surfaces of the cube were formed from isosceles triangles, incompatible with the triangles of the other three elements (*Ti.* 53 A–56 C). Plato argued that the upper three elements could break up and change into one another because of their identical triangles, but the particles of earth, although they could be united temporarily with the others, would eventually dissolve out of their compounds and become earth again.

The changes of the elements begin, in *Ti.* 56 D–E, with the upward cycle, with one particle of water broken up to form two of air plus one of fire, and one particle of air forming two of fire. The downward cycle begins when a small quantity of fire is enclosed by a large quantity of air and water and

[18] Aet. 1. 3. 20; Arist. *Metaph. A* 4. 8, 985ª31–3; Simpl. *In Phys.* 158. 15–20=KRS 346–7, 349.

[19] οὐ μὰ τὸν ἀμετέρᾳ γενεᾷ παραδόντα τετρακτύν | παγὰν ἀενάου φύσεως ῥίζωμά τ' ἔχουσαν. Burkert (n. 17), 186, recognized that the second line could not have predated Empedocles. But Empedocles himself hinted at the link between the 'exchange' of the element and the tetraktys oath thus: 'the time of exchange . . . has been defined by a broad oath' (Arist. *Metaph. B* 4. 19, 1000ᵇ9–16).

[20] For Pythagoreans' readiness to extend application of their number theory see Arist. *Metaph. N* 6. 10, 1093ᵇ14–16.

[21] See Iambl. *Th. ar.* 82 for Speusippus' view that the five shapes given by Plato to the elemental particles were Pythagorean. The fifth was the dodecahedron assigned at *Ti.* 55 C to τὸ πᾶν (the All). τὸ πᾶν appears in the protochemical texts in the phrase ἓν τὸ πᾶν: 'all is one'.

is conquered (νικηθέν), so that two particles of fire unite to make one of air. And when air is overruled (κρατηθέν), then two and half particles of air form one of water. The author of *PM* took these two verbs, νικᾶν and κρατεῖν, and applied them to the changes of the upper elements: 'the nature conquers the nature', 'the nature overrules the nature'. The 'ever-flowing nature' of the revised tetraktys oath could have inspired the adoption of the word 'nature' into the three significant phrases, one of which concludes each recipe in *PM*.

Plato's *Timaeus* (59 B) accounts for the choice of copper or the amalgam of four base metals including copper (four was the tetraktys number for earth) as the starting-point for the protochemical experiments. Copper is there described as having particles resembling those of gold but containing also small and fine portions of earth, so it is partially earth. But it is also a metal, and metals are defined by Plato (*Ti.* 58 D) as 'fusible water'; so copper represented earth already on its way to becoming water. Transformed to silver by mercury or arsenic, it represented water on its way to becoming air because both those metals were obtained from their sulphides by a vaporization process which seemed to demonstrate the gaseous or airy nature concealed within them. Gold coloration of the silvered metal was achieved by combination of ingredients, among which were sulphur, sulphur water, and various yellow earths and plant dyes. At this stage it could have represented air on its way to becoming fire, because it carried the gold colour of fire or light. The final stage was brought about either by further cooking with appropriate ingredients or by a lapse of time sufficient to prove that the colour was truly fixed. At that point the metal became ἰός (*ios*), or achieved ἴωσις (*iōsis*). ἰός was an archaic word meaning 'one' in use among Pythagorcans,[22] so could have signified the tetraktys number for fire. But it may also have carried the idea of 'fiery verdigris', the counterpart to the 'earthy' ἰός (true verdigris) which Plato said would eventually separate out from copper. A few texts, including *PM*, contain recipes where ἰός appears to be the stage in which treated metal becomes reactive, i.e. can be used to tint gold another untreated tablet of copper.[23]

In Hellenistic times Pythagoreans regarded Plato as the transmitter of true Pythagorean lore[24]—hence the adoption of the theory of matter in the *Timaeus* to underpin chemical experiments aimed at changing the elemental nature of metals. The unnamed teacher in *PM* 3, said there to be guided by his daemon and to have died after taking a drug to separate his soul from his body, is Socrates; and his unnamed pupil is Plato.

[22] Recorded as Pythagorean in the feminine form ἴα by Lyd. *Mens.* 4. 1. Some prefer to derive ἴωσις from ἰός = rust, e.g. J. Dillon, 'Greek Alchemy', *CR*, NS 36 (1986), 35–8 at 37.

[23] *PM* 5, 11, 13. Only one recipe (3) names the final stage as ἰός. For later examples of a reactive product see e.g. Berthelot, texts III. 8. 3, 11. 4, 16. 6.

[24] See Burkert (n. 17), 28–96, esp. 83–96, for a full survey of the evidence; and id., 'Hellenistica Pseudopythagorica', *Philologus*, 105 (1961), 16–43 and 226–46 at 236, for 3rd-cent. and later pseudo-Pythagorean literature identified as stemming from 'underground Platonism'.

Democritus' quest for knowledge in *PM* 3 takes him to the temple; and in this section Herman Diels inserted the name of Ostanes as an emendation of the Greek οὐτ᾽ ἄν τις ('no one'), an emendation which has been accepted by some modern editors.[25] A closer examination of the role of Ostanes in the history of the chemical texts shows why it should be discarded. The Περὶ συμπαθειῶν καὶ ἀντιπαθειῶν, the book on sympathies and antipathies, variously ascribed to Democritus (by Columella and Tatian), Bolus the Democritean (by Stephanus of Byzantium and the scholiast on Nicander's *Theriaca*), and the Pythagorean Bolus of Mendes (by the *Suda*), was about the sympathies between various plants, animals, and stones;[26] and it drew on lore from the pseudo-Zoroastrian texts in the library at Alexandria. When Pliny referred to Democritus and Pythagoras as eager followers of the Magi, he supplied in each case details of strange properties of certain plants taken from the Περὶ συμπαθειῶν.[27] Even when Tatian wrote in c.AD 150 that Democritus 'having boasted of the Magus Ostanes will be delivered on the day of consummation as fuel for the eternal fire' (*Ad Graec.* 17), he was abusing the supposed author of the Περὶ συμπαθειῶν, upon which he delivered a sharp attack. The link between Ostanes and the Democritus of the chemical texts came later, after the followers of Basilides the Gnostic forged chemical texts under the name of Ostanes;[28] and by the fourth century Synesius could claim that Ostanes initiated Democritus into the chemical art.[29]

With Plato's *Timaeus* underpinning *PM* we can appreciate why Bolus was called a Pythagorean. Democritus' link with the chemical art is less obvious, but his role may become clearer when we have examined the two technologies named at the end of *PM*, sublimation and distilling.

2. Distillation and Sublimation

Distilling is almost certainly the older of the two. It was the means whereby θεῖον ὕδωρ, the divine sulphur water, and other 'waters' were produced for use in the metal treatments. The distillates were always called 'waters', a usage which survives to this day: rose-water, eau de Cologne, Kirschwasser. Certain protochemical treatises include not only descriptions but also drawings of the stills themselves. In the tenth-century MS Marcianus 299 earlier

[25] 68 B 300. 18 DK (ii. 219 n.).
[26] Colum. 11. 3. 64; Tat. *Ad Graec.* 17; Steph. Byz. s.v. Ἀψύνθιον; sch. Nic. 764. *Suda* B 482 reads 'sympathies and antipathies of stones', but Halleux (n. 2), 64, believed the title originally included 'animals' and 'plants'. Ancient authors who drew on this work wrote of peculiarities of animals and plants, mainly plants.
[27] *HN* 24. 156, 160; 25. 13–14; 26. 19.
[28] Isidore was the son of Basilides, and part of a forged text may survive in Berthelot, text IV. 2, which is addressed by 'Ostanes the philosopher to Petasios' (the Egyptian form of Isidore): see M. Berthelot, *Origines d'alchimie* (Paris, 1885), 158.
[29] Berthelot, text II. 4. 1.

drawings referred to in the text have been copied on the versos of the relevant pages. The stills of the first century AD, the δίβικος (*dibikos*) in the
drawing entitled 'The Goldmaking of Cleopatra', and the τρίβικος (*tribikos*)
invented, supposedly, by Maria the Jewess, have almost globular stillheads
with two or three outlet tubes. The βῖκος (*bikos*) was the receiving vessel,
hence the names δίβικος and τρίβικος. The stillheads were called either φιάλη
or 'the bronze' or sometimes just βῖκος.[30] φιάλη (*phiale*=cup) suggests that
these sophisticated stills had simpler predecessors with cup-shaped stillheads.

Closer to the cup shape was the μαστάριον (*mastarion*) or breast-shaped
stillhead, employed in prolonged and repeated distillations of eggs to produce sulphur water. The μαστάριον had a single outlet tube and was made of
glass after the invention of glass-blowing; but bronze would have been the
material of any predecessor, as it often was of the later τρίβικος stillhead.[31]

In use each stillhead was sealed firmly to a wide cylindrical tube, which
in turn was sealed to the base vessel, while the outlet tubes were sealed to
the receiving vessels. Usually the base vessel stood over a furnace, but for
the eggs distilled with the μαστάριον the sealed apparatus was warmed via a
very low heat source such as a dung-heap or a pastry-cook's oven. Another
type of still was the σωλήν (*sōlēn*), the tube-still, shaped like an inverted L
and joined at the lower end to its base vessel and at the upper to its receiver.
Here the vapour was cooled and recondensed not in a stillhead but within
the long tube; and the upper part of the tube was itself cooled with cold
water and a sponge.[32] The terms used in the texts to indicate distilling were
'to boil' (ἕψειν) or 'to raise the water' (ὕδωρ αἴρειν).

Applications of the distilling technique were few outside the enclosed
world of the chemical art. Although Aristotle (*Mete.* 2. 3, 358^{b}16–18) knew
'by experience' that drinkable water could be evaporated from sea water,
the practical usage probably came later. Sailors on long voyages, reported
Alexander of Aphrodisias, made fires on deck and heated cauldrons of sea
water with covers over them; the steam condensing on the covers turned
into drinkable water. Another application, described by Dioscorides, was
the boiling of pitch-pine wood with a clean fleece stretched above to catch
the vapour; afterwards liquid pitch oil was wrung from the fleece.[33]

Wine was distilled, but wine-distilling was practised in secret as a cultic
activity in both Gnostic Christian and pre-Christian contexts, which explains why it has not been more widely recognized. The method appears

---

[30] φιάλη in 'The Goldmaking of Cleopatra' (Berthelot, Introduction 132, fig. 11); 'the bronze'
(id., texts III. 47. 2, 50. 1); βῆκος=βῖκος (id., Introduction 138, fig. 14).
[31] Berthelot, texts III. 8. 1–2; for use of the μαστάριον to produce a different θεῖον ὕδωρ cf.
text II. 3. 6. Invention of glass-blowing in the 1st cent. BC: D. B. Harden, 'Ancient Glass',
Archaeological Journal, 126 (1969), 46–8.
[32] Berthelot, Introduction 140, fig. 16; texts III. 47. 2, 50. 2.
[33] Alex. *In Mete.* 136 Smet; Dsc. 1. 72. 3.

in a Greek recipe of about AD 200 in Hippolytus, *Ref.* 4. 31. It is one of several for creating magic lights described there as 'tricks of the Gnostics and Magi'—at that date the followers of Basilides had already implicated Ostanes in the chemical art[34]—and Diels first identified it as instructions for wine-distilling.[35] The wine, with added sea salt, was 'boiled', i.e. distilled, in an earthenware jar. Thereafter the distillate was reheated and set alight with a lamp, and then 'if poured on the head it does not burn it at all'. This implies that the operation had concentrated the alcohol in the wine to a strength at or near 35 per cent, something which could only have been achieved via a distilling technique. The recipe in Hippolytus continues by recommending the addition of manna, a scented resinous sap, and ends with the words: 'it does better still if you put to it some sulphur'.

The distillate, or 'water', was applied to the head, and we know from Tertullian and other Christian writers that the Gnostic heretics baptized initiates on the head.[36] Tertullian also claimed that it was possible for the Gnostics 'by human ingenuity to summon a spirit into the water and animate their incorporated nature through hands held above with another spirit of such brightness [*tantae claritatis*]'.[37] He finished this curious statement with a reference to God being able to modulate upon the water-organ the music of spiritual sublimity, and there may be an implicit contrast between the fire-organ (ὄργανον was the word for a still in the protochemical texts) and the water-organ, used as a metaphor for the contrast between fire- and water-baptism.

The followers of Marcus the Gnostic were said by Saint Irenaeus to baptize initiates upon the head with oil and 'water', or sometimes with balsam and water, and here again 'water' may have meant distillate. The balsam corresponds to the scented manna of the recipe in Hippolytus' *Refutationes*, and could have symbolized the fragrance of the Holy Spirit. Elsewhere Irenaeus claimed that Marcus combined the tricks of Anaxilaus with the skulduggery of the Magi.[38]

Anaxilaus of Thessaly was named in an earlier context by pseudo-Cyprian, when writing about the followers of Simon Magus, who had in-

---

[34] See above, p. 307; also nn. 5 and 28.

[35] *Die Entdeckung des Alkohols* (Abhandlungen der preußischen Akademie der Wissenschaften, phil.-hist. Klasse, 3; Berlin, 1913), 21–5, 35. The stillhead is not mentioned in the recipe in Hippolytus, which could indicate that his source was a secret recipe of practical use only to somebody already possessing the necessary technical knowledge and expertise.

[36] Tert. *De praescr. her.* 40; Iren. *Adv. haer.* 1. 21. 4.

[37] Tert. *De bapt.* 8: 'Sane humano ingenio licebit spiritum in aquam arcessere et concorporationem eorum accommodatis desuper manibus alio spiritu tantae claritatis animare, Deo autem in suo organo non licebit per manus sanctas sublimitatem modulari spiritalem?.'

[38] *Adv. haer.* 1. 21. 5 (oil and water); 1. 21. 3 (balsam and water); 1. 13. 1 (Anaxilaus). Hipp. *Ref.* 5. 21 records an Art of Separation practised by the Sethians whereby they could 'separate out' the gold in bronze, 'and already someone separates the water mixed with wine'. He thus indicates that in his day the non-Christian Gnostic Sethians knew how to distil wine.

stituted a cultic baptism in which, as soon as the initiand stepped into the water (as for baptism by immersion), 'fire appears straight away upon the water'. The last-mentioned water could have been the distillate of wine, for the text continues: 'whether this is done by some trick which, as many of them affirm, is a trick of Anaxilaus . . . or whether it is the work of a malign being and the magic *virus* that can express fire from the water'.[39]

The most striking examples of Gnostic baptism are those in *The Books of Jeu*, the English title for a Coptic manuscript brought to Britain from Egypt in the eighteenth century: Schmidt's edition was republished with a new English translation in 1978.[40] Here three baptisms are recorded in due order: that of the Water of Life, of Fire, and of the Holy Spirit. They show the concept of the upper three elements still attached to wine-distilling rituals, but the order now Christianized and changed from (*a*) water, air or πνεῦμα (*pneuma*), and fire at the apex to (*b*) water, fire, and πνεῦμα in the ultimate position as Ἅγιον Πνεῦμα (*Hagion Pneuma*), the Holy Spirit. For each baptism the disciples bring fire and the vine-wood, and the Gnostic Jesus-figure places one wine pitcher on the right and one on the left, with incense offerings above. He recites long prayers including many magic words, and calls on Zorokothora to bring forth the water of the baptism of life in one of the pitchers. 'And at that moment,' says the text, 'the wine which was on the right of the offering became water.'[41]

The critical piece of apparatus is the vine-wood,[42] known later in the West as *vitis*. It was a long undulating cooling tube through which the distillate passed, and it gave its name to *aqua vitis*, an alternative term for *aqua vitae*.[43] For the disciples in *The Books of Jeu* (116, § 48) the three baptisms guaranteed immortality. Later Gnostic sects also used fire rituals; the Messalians, for example, had a rite at which, according to Saint Augustine, 'there enters into the initiate in visible form a fire which does not consume'.[44]

Strong alcohol is highly inflammable, so how was it made safe? The clue lies in a short statement which concludes a few of the earliest medieval Latin recipes for wine-distilling:

---

[39] [Cypr.] *De rebapt.* 16. *Virus* (poison) is one of the meanings of the Greek ἰός, the term which in the protochemical texts meant that the metal had achieved the stage of fixed gold, representing fire.

[40] *The Books of Jeu*, ed. C. Schmidt, trans. V. McDermot (Nag Hammadi Studies, 13; Leiden, 1978). [41] Ibid. 108, § 45.

[42] Ibid. 106 n. 3 for Coptic *peloole* meaning literally 'vine-wood', though translated in the text as 'vine branches'.

[43] M. Savonarola, *Libellus . . . de Aqua Ardenti*, in Joannes de Rupescissa [= Joan de Peratallada, 14th cent.], *De Consideratione Quintae Essentiae* (ed. Basel, 1561), 250–1, 253. The 'serpentine tube' replaced *vitis* as the usual term for the cooling tube; hence the 'worm' and 'wormtub' of the English distillers.

[44] August. *Haer.* 57. Psell. *De op. daemon.* 7 reported on the authority of 'a Thracian' that the Euchites, the later Messalians under their Greek name, were still engaged in producing visible manifestations of δαίμονες with bodies 'either of air or of fire, or a mixture of those two elements'.

Hanc aquam si experiri volueris, sulphuris tres p. igitur in ea extingues.[45]

If you wish to test this 'water', you should extinguish three parts of sulphur in it.

Hermann Degering arranged for alcoholic spirits to be tested thus, and published the results in 1917. Lighted sulphur plunged into spirits of wine continued to burn until the alcohol content reached 35 per cent, when it was extinguished. If the liquid at a strength of 35 per cent alcohol was then ignited upon cloth or hair, it burnt away safely and completely leaving no mark.[46] This discovery may first have been made by people who plunged lighted sulphur into distillate of wine with a view to increasing its fire content. Accidental spillage of the liquid on hair or clothing in the vicinity of a naked flame would have revealed the safe-burning fire. An oblique reference to the sulphur test may be concealed in the final words of the wine-distilling recipe in Hippolytus' *Refutationes* (cf. p. 314 above): 'it does better still if you put to it some sulphur'. But the test could go back to a much earlier period.

Evidence for pre-Hellenistic wine-distilling is tenuous, but hints at its practice in the Dionysus cult. It could have originated when someone heated wine in a vessel with a bronze cup over its mouth in an attempt to capture the fiery principle which escaped when wine was boiled in an open pot. If the operation was carried out slowly and carefully, very small amounts of alcohol-rich spirits would have condensed on the inside of the cup and run to the bottom if it was quickly turned upright again. By using a series of cups it would have been possible to collect more of the distillate. Later, perhaps much later, came the evolution of the stillhead equipped with a spout to carry off the distillate.

There are hints to suggest that real-life maenads once carried bronze cups. Nonnus says that Mystis, when teaching Dionysus the usage of the mystic objects, 'first thought of fitting bronze φιάλαι over her breasts' (*Dionysiaca* 9. 125–6)—a practice of which there is no record elsewhere in art or literature. Perhaps his source actually reported that real-life maenads carried (φέρειν = 'carry' or 'wear') bronze φιάλαι, adding that the φιάλη was a type of μαστάριον, and Nonnus, knowing nothing of stillheads, took μαστάριον to mean a breast covering.[47] Much earlier Euphorion and Callimachus told how the titans put the dismembered limbs of Dionysus in a cauldron (λέβης) and gave it to his brother Apollo. Euphorion added:

[45] H. Degering, 'Ein Alkoholrezepte aus dem 8. Jahrhundert', *Sitzungsberichte der preußischen Akademie der Wissenschaften*, phil.-hist. Klasse (1917), 506 (Weissenau recipe); I. Puccinotti, *Storia della medicina* (Livorno 1850–66), ii, doc. 6, p. lxiv, from which the version quoted here is taken.

[46] Degering (n. 45), 513.

[47] In Nonnus' day Gnostics had been banished beyond the imperial frontiers and pagan cults had almost ceased to exist. See C. A. Wilson, 'Dionysian Ritual Objects in Euphorion and Nonnus', *PLLS* 7 (1993), 216–17.

ἐν πυρὶ βάκχαν δῖον ὑπὲρ φιάλην ἐβάλοντο.
On the fire godly Bacchus over a φιάλη they threw.[48]

This makes little sense, but it is susceptible to a different interpretation if ὑπέρ ('over') is read as *following* the noun it governs. The literal translation then becomes '. . . godly Bacchus over they threw a φιάλη'.[49] If Bacchus' limbs in the cauldron represent wine, we may have here another reference to a distilling ritual. There was a tomb of Dionysus at Delphi,[50] and a possible scenario would be the distilling of wine in the spring when Dionysus departed on Apollo's return, the storing of the distillate in the tomb, and the flaming of the alcohol at the beginning of winter as an epiphany to mark the reawakening of trieteric Dionysus.

Various earlier authors referred to 'boiling' in connection with rebirth. Demos in Aristophanes' *Knights* (1321) is boiled to make him young. Plato, *Euthydemus* 285 c, used the simile of being destroyed and even boiled, as though being boiled by Medea, so as to be reborn as a good man with true knowledge. Most strikingly, the hypothesis to Euripides' *Medea* records that in Aeschylus' lost play *The Nurses* (fr. 246a Radt) Medea boiled the nurses of Dionysus, i.e. the maenads, and made them young again. A. B. Cook and F. M. Cornford both saw this as an allusion to a Dionysiac 'rite of regeneration or resurrection'.[51] It may, in fact, hint at rituals of real-life maenads in Macedonia and Thrace, where 'boiling', i.e. wine-distilling, took place. Athenian soldiers on the Eion campaign in 476/5 could have brought back rumours about local initiation rituals which involved 'boiling'.[52]

Euripides wrote the *Bacchae* in Macedonia, and at lines 755–8 the maenads carry unnamed objects of bronze and iron balanced on their shoulders, while fire burns harmlessly upon their hair.[53] They are not in a ritual situation, for they have rushed down the mountainside in fury after being spied upon by local herdsmen. My view is that the models for Euripides'

[48] Callim. fr. 643, Euphor. fr. 13. The translation of this line has caused difficulties. Lobeck, Meinecke, Scheidweiler, and Powell emended φιάλην to φιάλης, which yields the reading 'On the fire they threw godly Bacchus over a φιάλη.' It makes little sense; a φιάλη (drinking-cup) is not put onto a fire, and the god's limbs had already been thrown into a cauldron (λέβης), a vessel which is suitable for setting on the fire.

[49] Some words are corrupt in some texts, but ὑπὲρ φιάλην is present in all manuscripts: Wilson (n. 47), 217.

[50] Philoch. 328 F 7 and [Clem.] *Recog.* 10. 24 report tombs of Dionysus at (respectively) Delphi and Thebes; *Orph. Hym.* 53. 1–4 has a trieteric Dionysus sleeping in the halls of Persephone and returning as Chthonius in the alternate years. Further discussion: C. A. Wilson, 'Wine Rituals, Maenads and Dionysian Fire', *PLLS* 10 (1998), 157–68.

[51] F. M. Cornford, *The Origin of Attic Comedy* (London, 1914), 88–9; A. B. Cook, *Zeus* (Cambridge, 1914), i. 627. Unaware of possible ritual wine-distilling, they both linked the 'boiling' with the Orphic phrase 'a kid I have fallen into the milk'.

[52] M. L. West, *Studies in Aeschylus* (Stuttgart, 1990), 49, notes the possibility that Aeschylus took part in the Eion campaign.

[53] ὁπόσα δ' ἐπ' ὤμοις ἔθεσαν, οὐ δεσμῶν ὕπο | προσείχετ' οὐδ' ἔπιπτεν ἐς μέλαν πέδον | οὐ χαλκός, οὐ σίδηρος, ἐπὶ δὲ βοστρύχοις | πῦρ ἔφερον, οὐδ' ἔκαιεν.

herdsmen were Macedonian men who really had spied upon the nocturnal mountain rituals of the local maenads, and passed on to other men the secret that the safe-burning fire was somehow associated with the bronze φιάλαι.[54] In the *Bacchae* passage the maenads are no longer engaged in secret rituals, but the fire on their hair is a powerful indicator of the presence of Dionysus. It also suggests that wine-distilling and the associated ritual use of the distillate were already practised in fifth-century Macedonia.

A somewhat later date is likely for the invention of the technique of sublimation, developed initially to ease the task of extracting mercury from its red sulphide, cinnabar. Cinnabar (alias vermilion) was in use as a pigment in the Greek world from the sixth century onwards; and small amounts of free mercury occurred—and still occur—in the deposit near Ephesus which Theophrastus regarded as the main source of cinnabar in his day.[55] But the Greeks apparently paid little attention to mercury before the fourth century, for our earliest reference to it comes from the comic poet Philippus, who wrote that Daedalus made a hollow wooden statue of Aphrodite and poured mercury into it to make it move.[56] Aristotle told this tale, saying it came from Democritus, who was among those who believe that the soul moves the body.

Near Ephesus the cinnabar was sandy, and Theophrastus said that mercury was extracted by mixing the red earth with vinegar and grinding it in a copper bowl with a copper pestle. Modern experiments have shown this to be a very slow method of obtaining mercury.[57] Theophrastus also knew of cinnabar in two other places, Colchis and Iberia, and in both it was 'hard and stony'. The uplands behind Colchis, at the eastern end of the Black Sea and adjoining Iberia, were in the foothills of the Caucasian mountains, in Scythian territory.[58] The hard crystalline cinnabar could have stimulated metalworkers in the neighbouring regions to find an easier mode of extraction,[59] and this was achieved by the invention of sublimation.

Dioscorides described the method: 'For putting an iron saucer containing

---

[54] 'The bronze' was one name for the stillhead (n. 30). 'The iron' could have been the short sword carried by Macedonian maenads to enable them to sacrifice a goat or hare to Dionysus at the beginning of secret rituals held in a mountain glen or cave. Vase paintings show the sword-bearing maenads in association with Lycurgus or Pentheus, and Macedonian maenads carried short swords in the grand procession of Ptolemy II (Callixen. 627 F 2 = Ath. 198 E). See Wilson (n. 50).

[55] Theophr. *Lap.* 60. E. R. Caley and F. C. Richards, *Theophrastus: On Stones* (Columbus, 1956), 194, note the use of cinnabar as pigment on 6th-cent. statues in the Acropolis Museum and on 5th-cent. lekythoi.   [56] Fr. 1 KA, reported in Arist. *De an.* 1. 3, 406^{b}15–20.

[57] Theophr. *Lap.* 60; Caley and Richards (n. 55), 204–5.

[58] Theophr. *Lap.* 58. I follow Caley and Richards (n. 55), 195–6, in locating Iberia in the Caucasus, and accept their interpretation of Vitr. 7. 8. 1, 7. 9. 4. D. E. Eichholz, *Theophrastus: De Lapidibus* (Oxford, 1965), 125–6, takes a different view; but there is no evidence that Spanish cinnabar was either worked or exported before Roman imperial times.

[59] For cross-influences between Thracians, Greek colonies, and the Caucasus in classical times see R. F. Hoddinott, *The Thracians* (London, 1981), 97.

cinnabar upon an earthenware dish, they fit onto the latter an ἄμβιξ (*ambix*), luting it around with clay. Then they heat it over charcoal. For the vapour adhering to the ἄμβιξ, when scraped off and cooled, becomes mercury' (5. 95). The ἄμβιξ was a deep earthenware cup tapering towards its brim, and, as with the φιάλη-stillhead of the wine-distillers, it was inverted over the base vessel and sealed to it to exclude the air.

Because the method has affinities with wine-distilling, i.e. both rely on the reaction of vapour or gas recondensing in the upper part of a sealed vessel, it is tempting to believe that this sublimation process was devised by people who already knew something about the use of the φιάλη in wine-distilling. Although maenads may have carried out distilling rituals, the cups themselves must have been made by metalworkers; and the goldsmiths who created delicate gold foliage wreaths for initiates and other precious objects for the Dionysus cult could have produced the bronze φιάλαι and understood their usage.

If cinnabar was heated in a pottery base-vessel fitted with a bronze cup (a combination often used in wine-distilling), then some part of the mercury displaced from its sulphide by the copper would have adhered to the upper walls of the pottery base. Further experiment would have produced the optimum combination of earthenware base, earthenware cup or ἄμβιξ, and a copper saucer (later replaced by cheaper iron which yielded the same reaction) to hold the cinnabar.

A further pointer to a north-eastern provenance for the invention of the sublimation process is the secret name for mercury in a much later word-list compiled by the experimenters in Egypt, viz. Scythian water.[60] Egypt lacked cinnabar deposits, and interest in its sublimation is unlikely to have arisen there prior to the arrival of the Ptolemies. They introduced the cult of Dionysus, already greatly honoured in their Macedonian homeland, and encouraged newer cults such as that of Serapis, and some of the skilled metalworkers from Macedonia and Thrace almost certainly migrated to Egypt in their wake to help provide artefacts of precious metal for temples and for the many adherents of the new cults.

Either in Macedonia or later in Egypt, the metalworkers began to exercise their skills in distillation and sublimation on new materials: the distillation of eggs and the sublimation of the arsenical sulphides.[61] They already recognized that their extraction methods could reveal hidden aspects of the materials under treatment: the fire in the water distilled from wine, the

[60] Berthelot, text I. 2 s.v. ὕδωρ Σκυθικόν. The name remained a cultic secret, but could have been coined by metalworkers in the Thracian/Macedonian region when they first used the sublimation method to extract mercury from Caucasian cinnabar. Later, when the experimenters in Egypt practised their chemical art, their cinnabar could have come from near Ephesus or (in imperial times) Spain.

[61] The latter (see n. 9) is more likely to have been developed in Egypt, where deposits of natron in dry lake beds were already being exploited for various purposes.

mobile shining mercury within the red-earth cinnabar. Interest in those hidden properties is clear from the terms used in *PM* and other protochemical texts, where mercury is sometimes called 'cinnabar turned outwards', and arsenic is called either 'the mercury of orpiment' or 'the mercury of realgar' or 'orpiment turned outwards'.

The experimenters may even have regarded the hidden nature as a form of soul—certainly in the case of the fire in the 'water' distilled from wine. Democritus said that both fire and soul were formed from the most mobile atoms, those that were spherical in shape.[62] Mercury was endowed with soul-like properties by the story about mercury being poured into a statue to make it move as the human soul moves the body (cf. n. 56). For Democritus, as for Socrates, the soul was a physical entity, but made from finer material than other physical things, except perhaps fire.

If the techniques of distilling and sublimation, along with some of Democritus' ideas on the nature of matter, reached Egypt from the northern Greek world in the manner here suggested, then it was not long before a further theme was added. The adoption of Bolus' doctrine of sympathies could well have been a milestone in the evolution of the metal-tinting and other experiments of the incomers into one of the new mystery cults of Hellenistic Egypt, for it provided authority for the belief that bringing forth the fire in wine or the gold nature representing fire hidden 'within' base metal could by sympathy draw forth the fieriest part of the soul of the operator and release it from future toil and pain. Bolus' reputation for writing books under the name of Democritus may have arisen at that stage.

The Pythagorean input could have been a later development, leading to the adoption of the mysterious phrases about the 'natures' which we now realize were derived from terms used about changes of the three upper elements in Plato's *Timaeus*. With them came the newly invented myth that Democritus, by now accepted as a founder figure for the cult, had learnt the chemistry of the natures from Socrates and Plato. Later still, breakaway groups claimed different founders, and some practised different techniques, using a little gold to act as a ferment for base metal and transform it all into gold.[63] But the discoveries made through chemical experiments on metals and minerals remained throughout Roman imperial times as secret knowledge within the cultic groups, who attached to them meanings far beyond simple recognition of the chemical reactions which took place.

The one exception was mercury, less rare once Spanish cinnabar became available.[64] Mercury was employed in gilding, and in silver-coating copper with tin; and its ability to amalgamate with fine particles of gold led to its

[62] Arist. *De an.* 1. 2, 405[a]3–13.

[63] Berthelot, texts III. 10. 3 (gold as a leaven or ferment) and I. 13. 7 (Isis: gold engendering gold).

[64] It was sent under seal to Rome for processing: Pliny *HN* 33. 118.

use for gold ink and for removing gold from embroideries in old discarded clothing.[65]

3. Later Developments

Chemical experimentation in the Hellenistic and Roman periods did not lead to great advances in knowledge outside the cultic groups. Even within them the achievement is difficult to evaluate. Some results are verifiable: elemental arsenic could only have been extracted from its sulphides and used to coat copper through sublimation. But many experiments in the texts are impossible to repeat because of uncertainty about ingredients. In the Greek world different names were often given to the same mineral when found in different places, and the same name to different minerals of similar appearance. Gold colour in any ingredient was thought to indicate fire content. Some recipes offer many alternative ingredients and methods are often unclear, with instructions such as οἰκονόμει ὡς ἔθος ('operate as usual') or ὡς ἐπινοεῖς ('as you know how'). In so far as the work was noticed outside the cults, it met with disapproval from state and early Church alike, as a form of magic, and the heretical 'baptism' using distilled wine was particularly abhorrent to the Church. The further expansion of experimental chemistry was thus destined to take place beyond the frontiers of the Graeco-Roman world.

The activities of the gold-makers had already come under suspicion in the time of Diocletian, who commanded their books on gold- and silver-making to be burnt in 296 'lest the opulence of the Egyptians should inspire them with confidence to rebel against the empire'.[66] Some gold-makers crossed into Persian territory at that stage, and more followed them a century later to avoid converting to orthodox Christianity. All experimental work of the type described in the protochemical recipes ceased within the Byzantine empire, though at a later date some of the ancient recipe texts reached Constantinople and were studied by Christian commentators, who regarded the progress from base metal to gold as an allegory for the journey of the Christian soul.

The Persians, however, welcomed a chance to learn new technology from Egyptian gold-makers, Gnostic Messalians, and other migrants from the Roman empire. The preparation of medicinal herbal waters was a new application of the distilling technique, perhaps first fully developed using the plants of the medical botanical garden established by Khusro I Anoshirvan

[65] Ibid. 33. 65. Gilding: Leiden Papyrus X (Halleux (n. 2), 84–109), nos. 55, 73, 79; silver-coating: ibid., no. 26; gold ink: ibid., nos. 33, 69; embroideries: Vitr. 7. 8. 4.

[66] Io. Ant. fr. 165; *Suda* s.v. Διοκλητιανός: μηδὲ χρημάτων αὐτοὺς θαρροῦντας περιουσίᾳ τοῦ λοιποῦ ῾Ρωμαίοις ἀνταίρειν. Translation: E. Gibbon, *Decline and Fall of the Roman Empire*, i. 13.

(531–79) around his famous hospital at Jundishapur in Khuzistan.[67] Later, under the Arabs, rose-water was distilled on a vast scale with multiple stills evolved from Greek φιάλη prototypes. Early in the Arab period some ancient Greek protochemical texts were translated into Syriac and Arabic, and their content studied, reinterpreted, and transformed into alchemy.[68]

The last and most striking achievement of Greek chemical distilling was probably due to experimental work by Gnostics settled in the Persian–Syrian borderlands. The importance they attached to elemental fire or light meant that they continued the practice of wine-distilling and fire-baptism. Thus they already possessed the technological ability to distil 'Median oil' (crude petroleum); but they also discovered and added a suitable 'filler' to the distillate, which vaporizes very rapidly at ordinary temperatures, and invented a method of propelling it through 'siphons' (force-pumps).[69] The secret was given, or sold, to the Byzantine emperor when Arab naval forces threatened Constantinople. Their wooden ships were defenceless against the flaming 'moist fire' or 'sea fire' (later known as 'Greek fire') projected at them through siphons, and so the city was saved.[70]

[67] H. M. Leicester, *The Historical Background of Chemistry* (New York, 1956), 50–1; R. N. Frye, *The Golden Age of Persia* (London, 1975), 22, 163–4; *CHI* iii/1. 161, 486, 573; D. Gutas, *Greek Thought, Arabic Culture* (London 1998), 14, 118, 133, 135–6. M. Levey, *Early Arab Pharmacology* (Leiden 1973), 30, calls it 'the world's greatest center of scholarship at the time'. In the protochemical texts the πνεῦμα of plants was their colour, removed by the distilling process (Berthelot, texts III. 47. 7). The Persians and Arabs took πνεῦμα more literally to be the aroma of essential oils in herbs and flowers, which they extracted by distillation.

[68] Rose-water stills: R. J. Forbes, *Short History of the Art of Distillation* (Leiden, 1948), 29–54 and figs. 16–20. Possible Persian original of an Arab text in the Greek protochemical tradition: H. E. Stapleton *et al.*, 'The Sayings of Hermes', *Ambix*, 3 (1949), 88.

[69] One of the two recipes for 'Greek fire' in the 13th-cent. Latin *Liber Ignium* of Marcus Graecus (J. R. Partington, *A History of Greek Fire and Gunpowder* (Cambridge, 1960), 50, no. 26) appears to derive from a Greek text composed when the earliest vocabulary of distilling was still current, since it contains the verb 'to boil' (ἕψειν) with the meaning 'distil'.

[70] Moist fire (πῦρ ὑγρόν): Const. P. *Adm.* 48; sea fire (θαλάσσιον πῦρ): Theophan. 295. The first critical sea battle took place in the 670s, the second in 715. Later the Arabs and Franks learnt the process: see Partington (n. 69), 47–8, no. 10, for a Latin recipe using the Arab cucurbit. For the coming of wine-distilling to the west as a secret Cathar practice, and the later adoption of distilled wine as a wonderful new medicine, see Wilson (n. 5), 192–7.

Notes on Contributors

ANDREW BARKER is Professor of Classics at the University of Birmingham and a British Academy Research Professor in Humanities (2000–3). The most recent of his many publications on Greek music, musical theory, and philosophy is *Scientific Method in Ptolemy's* Harmonics (2000). A collection of 'musical explorations', in Italian, will appear shortly. He is currently writing a book on Greek musical criticism, while simultaneously pursuing research for an extensive history of the ancient musical sciences.

LENNART BERGGREN teaches mathematics and its history at Simon Fraser University. His recent books include *Ptolemy's* Geography: *An Annotated Translation of the Theoretical Chapters* (jointly with Alexander Jones), *Euclid's* Phaenomena: *A Translation and Study of a Hellenistic Treatise on Spherical Astronomy* (jointly with Robert Thomas), and *Pi: A Source Book* (jointly with Jonathan and Peter Borwein). He has written on the history of a number of topics in the mathematical sciences in ancient Greece and medieval Islam, and he is currently editing and translating the collected works of Abū Sahl al-Kūhī.

ALAN C. BOWEN is Director of the Institute for Research in Classical Philosophy and Science (Princeton). He has edited *Selected Papers of F. M. Cornford* (1987) and *Science and Philosophy in Classical Greece* (1991), and is the author of many articles on the history of Graeco-Latin astronomy and harmonic science. He has just completed *Physics and Astronomy in Later Stoic Philosophy: Cleomedes,* Meteora ('*The Heavens*') with Robert B. Todd for the University of California Press, and is currently writing a book on Hellenistic astronomy.

J. J. COULTON is Reader in Classical Archaeology at the University of Oxford. He is author of *Ancient Greek Architects at Work* and numerous other publications on ancient Greek architecture, particularly on its technical aspects. He has also worked extensively on settlement history and water supply in south-western Asia Minor.

SERAFINA CUOMO is a lecturer at the Centre for the History of Science, Technology and Medicine, Imperial College, London. She is the author of *Pappus of Alexandria and the Mathematics of Late Antiquity* (2000) and *Ancient Mathematics* (2001). She is now working on technical knowledge in Graeco-Roman antiquity.

ROBERT HANNAH is Associate Professor in the Department of Classics at the University of Otago in Dunedin, New Zealand. His current research areas are Greek and Roman archaeoastronomy, the use of Virtual Reality in museums, early imperial Roman art, classical Greek art, and the classical tradition. He has written widely on the use of astronomy in Greek and Roman cultures, and is currently working on the star calendars of ancient Greece.

HARRY M. HINE is Scotstarvit Professor of Humanity at the University of St Andrews. He has written extensively on the younger Seneca, and has produced editions of the *Naturales Quaestiones* (1996), and the *Medea* (2000). He is currently collaborating with Professor Charles Burnett of the Warburg Institute on an edition and translation of medieval cosmological texts.

EDWARD HUSSEY is a Fellow of All Souls College, Oxford, and Lecturer at the University of Oxford. His research interests include Greek science, mathematics, and philosophy, particularly in the sixth to fourth centuries BC, and the interactions between them. He has published *The Presocratics* (1972), *Aristotle:* Physics *III and IV* (1983), and other writings chiefly on the Presocratic philosophers and Aristotle.

J. R. MILTON is a Senior Lecturer in the Department of Philosophy, King's College, London. He has published widely on the philosophy and science of the early modern period and on its roots in ancient and medieval thought. He is currently working on an edition of Locke's early writings on toleration.

REVIEL NETZ is an Assistant Professor in the Department of Classics at Stanford University. He has published extensively in his main field of research, Greek mathematics. His books include *The Shaping of Deduction in Greek Mathematics: A Study in Cognitive History* (1999), as well as a translation (with commentary) of the complete works of Archimedes, whose first volume (*The Two Books on The Sphere and The Cylinder, with Eutocius' Commentaries*) is now in the press.

VIVIAN NUTTON is Professor of the History of Medicine at the Wellcome Trust Centre for the History of Medicine at University College, London. He has written extensively on the history of medicine from antiquity to the seventeenth century. His publications include the *editio princeps* of Galen's *On My Own Opinions* (1999). He is engaged in writing a history of ancient medicine from Homer to Paul of Aegina.

T. E. RIHLL is Lecturer in the Department of Classics and Ancient History at the University of Wales, Swansea. She is the author of *Greek Science* (1999) and of many articles both on Greek history and on ancient science and technology. She is currently working on the ancient theory and practice of colour, and on larger questions about the interplay between science and society in ancient Greece.

CHRISTIAN MARINUS TAISBAK was formerly Reader in Mathematical Sciences in Antiquity at Copenhagen University. He is the author of *Division and Logos: A Theory of Equivalent Couples and Sets of Integers Propounded by Euclid in the Arithmetical Books of the* Elements (1971), *Coloured Quadrangles: A Guide to the Tenth Book of Euclid's* Elements (1982), and many articles on ancient Greek mathematics, astronomy and geography. He is currently preparing a translation (with commentary) of Euclid's *Data*.

LIBA TAUB is Curator and Director of the Whipple Museum of the History of Science, part of the Department of History and Philosophy of Science at the University of Cambridge, and a Fellow of Newnham College. She is the author of *Ptolemy's Universe: The Natural Philosophical and Ethical Foundations of Ptolemy's Astronomy* (1993) and numerous articles on ancient science. She is currently working on a book on ancient Greek and Roman meteorology.

TEUN TIELEMAN is a lecturer in Ancient Philosophy at Utrecht University. He has published *Galen and Chrysippus on the Soul: Argument and Refutation in the* De

Placitis *II–III* (1996) and a number of articles on Galen and on ancient Stoicism. Forthcoming is a sequel to his first monograph: *Galen and Chrysippus on the Emotions: Argument and Refutation in the* De Placitis *IV–V*.

J. V. TUCKER is Professor of Computer Science at the University of Wales, Swansea. His main fields of research are the theory of computation and mathematical logic. He is also deeply interested in the historical interplay between science and technology, and has collaborated with T. E. Rihll on other topics in ancient Greek science and technology.

CHRISTOPHER TUPLIN is Reader in Ancient History at the University of Liverpool. Despite occasional forays into Roman history, Latin literature, and medieval hagiography, his research has mostly revolved around the Achaemenid empire and the writings of Xenophon. He is the author of a large number of papers on these topics as well as of *The Failings of Empire: A Reading of Xenophon* Hellenica *2. 3. 11–7. 5. 27* (1993) and *Achaemenid Studies* (1996). He has also edited two forthcoming conference volumes on *Pontus and the Outside World* and *The World of Xenophon*.

C. ANNE WILSON was formerly Assistant Librarian at the Brotherton Library (University of Leeds). The author or editor of several books on the history of food in Britain, she has also published *Philosophers, Iosis and Water of Life* (1984) and articles on Pythagorean numbers and the four elements, ancient and medieval distilling and sublimation, and the evidence for stills in Dionysiac cult, and is currently preparing a book on the history of distilling, 500 BC–AD 2000.

LEWIS WOLPERT is Professor of Biology as Applied to Medicine in the Department of Anatomy and Developmental Biology at University College, London. His research is on pattern formation in the development of the embryo. His books include *The Unnatural Nature of Science* (1992) and *Malignant Sadness: The Anatomy of Depression* (1999). He has a passion for Archimedes, but is currently working on the biology of belief.

Bibliography

AABOE, A., and PRICE, D. J. DE SOLLA, 'Qualitative Measurement in Antiquity: The Derivation of Accurate Parameters from Crude but Crucial Observations', in I. B. Cohen and R. Taton (eds.), *Mélanges Alexandre Koyré*, i. *L'Aventure de la science* (Paris, 1964), 1–20.

—— BRITTON, J. P., HENDERSON, J. A., NEUGEBAUER, O. E., and SACKS, A. J., *Saros Cycle Dates and Related Babylonian Astronomical Texts* (Transactions of the American Philosophical Society, 81.6; Philadelphia, 1991).

ADAM, J.-P., *La Construction romaine: Matériaux et techniques* (Paris, 1984).

—— 'Observations techniques sur les suites du séisme de 62 à Pompéi', in Livadie, *Tremblements de terre*, 67–89.

ADAMS, J. N., *The Latin Sexual Vocabulary* (London, 1982).

—— *Pelagonius and Latin Veterinary Terminology in the Roman Empire* (Leiden, 1995).

AITCHISON, L., *History of Metals*, i (London, 1960).

ALLAN, D. J. (ed.), *Aristotelis de caelo* (Oxford, 1955).

ALLEN, R. E., *Plato's* Parmenides: *Translation and Analysis* (Minneapolis, 1983).

ALMEIDA, E. R., *Forma urbis marmorea: Aggiornamento generale* (Rome, 1981).

AMUNDSEN, D. W., *Medicine, Society and Faith in the Ancient and Medieval Worlds* (Baltimore, 1996).

ANNAS, J., 'Die Gegenstände der Mathematik bei Aristoteles', in Graeser, *Mathematics and Metaphysics in Aristotle*, 131–47.

ARDAILLON, E., 'Horologium', in C. Daremberg and E. Saglio (eds.), *Dictionnaire des antiquités grecques et romains*, iii (Paris, 1900), 256–64.

ARGOUD, G. (ed.), *Science et vie intellectuelle à Alexandrie (Ier–IIIe siècle après J.-C.)* (Saint-Étienne, 1994).

—— GUILLAUMIN, J.-Y., and CACHARD, A. (eds.), *Les Pneumatiques d'Héron d'Alexandrie* (Saint-Étienne, 1997).

ARRIGHETTI, G., *Epicuro: Opere*, rev. edn. (Turin, 1973).

ASHBROOK, J., 'More about the Visibility of the Lunar Crescent', *Sky and Telescope*, 43 (Feb. 1972), 95–6.

—— 'Some Very Thin Lunar Crescents', *Sky and Telescope*, 42 (Aug. 1971), 78–9.

ASMIS, E., *Epicurus' Scientific Method* (Ithaca, NY, 1984).

AUJAC, G., *Geminos: Introduction aux phénomènes* (Paris, 1975).

AYERS, M., *Locke* (London, 1991).

BAGROW, L., 'The Origins of Ptolemy's Geography', *Geografiska annaler*, 27 (1945), 318–87.

BAILEY, C., *Epicurus* (Oxford, 1926).

—— *Titi Lucretti Cari De Rerum Natura Libri Sex* (Oxford, 1947).

BALMER, J., *Classical Women Poets* (Newcastle upon Tyne, 1996).

BARDONG, K., *De Causis Procatarcticis* (CMG suppl. 2; Leipzig, 1937).

BARIGAZZI, A., 'Sul concetto epicureo della sicurezza esterna', in G. Pugliese Carratelli (ed.), Συζήτσις: *Studi sull'epicureismo greco e romano offerti a Marcello Gigante* (Naples, 1983), i. 73–92.

BARKER, A., *Greek Musical Writings*, ii (Cambridge, 1989).

—— 'Telestes and the "Five-Rodded Jointing of Strings"', *CQ*, NS 48 (1998), 75–81.

BARNES, J., *Companion to Aristotle* (Oxford, 1995).

—— 'Galen on Logic and Therapy', in F. Kudlien and R. J .Durling (eds.), *Galen's Method of Healing* (Proceedings of the 1982 Galen Symposium; Leiden, 1991), 50–102.

—— BRUNSCHWIG, J., BURNYEAT, M., and SCHOFIELD, M. (eds.), *Science and Speculation: Studies in Hellenistic Theory and Practice* (Cambridge and Paris, 1982).

—— SCHOFIELD, M., and SORABJI, R. (eds.), *Articles on Aristotle*, i. *Science*; ii. *Ethics and Politics*; iii. *Metaphysics*; iv. *Psychology* (London, 1975, 1977, 1979, 1979).

BARNES, T. D. (ed.), *The Sciences in Greco-Roman Society* (Apeiron, 27; Edmonton, 1994).

BARRON, J., 'Ibycus: Gorgias and Other Paeans', *BICS* 31 (1984), 13–24.

BARTON, T. S., *Ancient Astrology* (London and New York, 1994).

—— *Power and Knowledge: Astrology, Physiognomics and Medicine in the Roman Empire* (Ann Arbor, 1994).

BEAGON, M., *Roman Nature: The Thought of Pliny the Elder* (Oxford, 1992).

BEAUJEU, J. (ed. and trans.), *Pline l'Ancien: Histoire naturelle, livre II* (Paris, 1950).

BECKER, O., *Das mathematische Denken in der Antike* (Göttingen, 1966).

BELL, H. I., *Cults and Creeds in Graeco-Roman Egypt* (Liverpool, 1957).

BELOCH, K. J., *Die Bevölkerung der griechisch-römischen Welt* (Leipzig, 1886).

BEMBO, CARDINAL, *Petri Bembi de Aetna ad Angelum Chabrielem Liber* (Venice, 1495).

BENEDETTO, V. DI, *Il medico e la malattia* (Turin, 1986).

BENNETT, J. A., *The Divided Circle: A History of Instruments for Astronomy, Navigation and Surveying* (Oxford, 1987),

BERGGREN, J. L., 'Ptolemy's Maps of Earth and the Heavens: A New Interpretation', *AHES* 43 (1991), 133–44.

—— 'The Relation of Greek Spherics to Early Greek Astronomy', in A. C. Bowen (ed.), *Science and Philosophy in Classical Greece* (Sources and Studies in the History and Philosophy of Classical Science, 2; New York and London, 1991), 227–48.

—— and GOLDSTEIN, B. R. (eds.), *From Ancient Omens to Statistical Mechanics: Essays on the Exact Sciences Presented to Asger Aaboe* (Acta Historica Scientiarum Naturalium et Medicinalium, 39; Copenhagen, 1987).

—— and JONES, A., *Ptolemy's Geography: An Annotated Translation of the Theoretical Chapters* (Princeton, 2000; pbk. edn. Princeton, 2001).

—— and THOMAS, R. S. D., *Euclid's Phaenomena: A Translation and Study of a Hellenistic Treatise on Spherical Astronomy* (New York and London, 1996).

BERINGER, H. R., *A Text-Book of Assaying for the Use of Those Concerned with Mines*, 15th edn. (London, 1921).

BERTHELOT, M., *Collection des anciens alchimistes grecs* (Paris, 1887–8; repr. London, 1963).

—— *Origines d'alchimie* (Paris, 1885).

BICKERMAN, E. J., *Chronology of the Ancient World*, 2nd edn. (London and Ithaca, NY, 1980).

BICKNELL, P. J., 'Why Atoms Had to Swerve: An Exploration in Epicurean Physics', *PBACAP* 4 (1990), 241–76.

BLASS, F., *Eudoxi Ars astronomica qualis in charta Aegyptiaca superest denuo edita* (Kiel, 1887).

BLOMBERG, M., 'The Meaning of χελιδών in Hesiod', *Opuscula Atheniensia*, 19 (1992), 49–57.

BLUME, F., LACHMANN, K., and RUDORFF, A., *Die Schriften der römischen Feldmesser* (Berlin, 1848–52).

BOARDMAN, J., review of Mattusch, *Classical Bronzes*, in *JHS* 117 (1997), 260.

BONNIEC, H. LE, and BŒUFFLE, A. LE, *Pline l'Ancien: Histoire naturelle, livre XVIII* (Paris, 1972).

BOSTOCK, D., 'Aristotle on Continuity in *Physics* VI', in Judson, *Aristotle's Physics*, 179–212.

—— 'Time and the Continuum', *OSAP* 6 (1988), 255–70.

BOUCHÉ-LECLERCQ, A., *L'Astrologie grecque* (Paris, 1899).

BOUDON, V., 'Galen's *On My Own Books*: New Material from Meshed, Rida, Tibb. 5223', in V. Nutton (ed.), *Galen beyond Kühn* (*BICS* suppl., forthcoming).

BOUMA, J. (ed.), *Marcus Iunius Nypsus: Fluminis Variatio; Limitis Repositio* (Studien zur klassischen Philologie, 77; Frankfurt am Main, 1993).

BOWEN, A. C., 'The Foundations of Early Pythagorean Harmonic Science', *Ancient Philosophy*, 2 (1982), 79–104.

—— 'Oenopides of Chios', in D. J. Zeyl, D. T. Devereux, and P. K. Mitsis (eds.), *The Encyclopedia of Classical Philosophy* (Westport, Conn., 1997), 357.

—— 'La scienza del cielo nel periodo pretolemaico', in Cappelletti, *Storia della scienza*, i. 806–39.

—— and GOLDSTEIN, B. R., 'Aristarchus, Thales, and Heraclitus on Solar Eclipses: An Astronomical Commentary on P. Oxy. 53. 3710 cols. 2. 33–3. 19', *Physis*, 31 (1994), 689–729.

—— —— 'Geminus and the Concept of Mean Motion in Greco-Latin Astronomy', *AHES* 50 (1996), 157–85.

—— —— 'Hipparchus' Treatment of Early Greek Astronomy: The Case of Eudoxus and the Length of Daytime', *PAPhS* 135 (1991), 233–54.

—— —— 'Meton of Athens and Astronomy in the Late Fifth Century B.C.', in E. Leichty, M. de J. Ellis, and P. Gerardi (eds.), *A Scientific Humanist: Studies in Memory of Abraham Sachs* (Philadelphia, 1988), 39–81.

BOWMAN, A. K., 'Egypt', in *CAH*, 2nd edn. x. 676–702.

—— *Egypt after the Pharaohs. 332 BC–AD 642, from Alexander to the Arab Conquest* (London, 1986).

BOYD, R., 'Metaphor and Theory Change', in Ortony (ed), *Metaphor and Thought*, 481–532.

BOYLAN, M., *Method and Practice in Aristotle's Biology* (London, 1983).

BOYLE, R., *The Works of the Honourable Robert Boyle* (London, 1772).

BRASHEAR, W., 'Vier neue Texte zum antiken Bildungswesen', *Archiv für Papyrusforschung*, 40 (1994), 29–35.

BRAUDEL, F., *The Mediterranean and the Mediterranean World in the Age of Philip II* (London, 1972).

BRITTON, J. P., *Models and Precision: The Quality of Ptolemy's Observations and Parameters* (New York and London, 1992).

—— 'Scientific Astronomy in Pre-Seleucid Babylonia', in Galter, *Die Rolle der Astronomie in den Kulturen Mesopotamiens*, 61–76.

—— 'The Structure and Parameters of Column Φ', in Berggren and Goldstein, *From Ancient Omens to Statistical Mechanics*, 23–36.

BROMLEY, A. G., 'Notes on the Antikythera Mechanism', *Centaurus*, 29 (1986), 5–27.

BROWN, P., *The Body and Society* (New York, 1988).

BRUIN, F., and BRUIN, M., 'The Equator Ring, Equinoxes and Atmospheric Refraction', *Centaurus*, 20 (1976), 89–111.

—— and VONDJIDIS, A., *The Books of Autolykos* (Beirut, 1971).

BUDDE, L., and NICHOLLS, R., *A Catalogue of the Greek and Roman Sculpture in the Fitzwilliam Museum, Cambridge* (Cambridge, 1964).

BÜRCHNER, L., 'Katakekaumene (1)', *RE* x (1919), 2462–3.

BURKERT, W., 'Hellenistica Pseudopythagorica', *Philologus*, 105 (1961), 16–43, 226–46.

—— *Lore and Science in Ancient Pythagoreanism*, trans. E. L. Minar (Cambridge, Mass., 1972).

BURNYEAT, M., 'Aristotle on Understanding Knowledge', in E. Berti (ed.), *Aristotle on Science: The Posterior Analytics* (Padua, 1981), 97–139.

BUTTS, A., and COXE, C., *Silver: Economics, Metallurgy and Use* (Princeton, 1967).

BYL, S., 'Note sur la place du cœur et la valorisation de la μεσότης dans la biologie d'Aristote', *AC* 37 (1968), 467–76.

CALEY, E. R., and RICHARDS, F. C., *Theophrastus: On Stones* (Columbus, 1956).

CAMPBELL, J. B., *The Writings of the Roman Land-Surveyors* (London, 2000).

CAPELLE, W., 'Erdbebenforschung' *RE* suppl. iv (1924), 344–74.

CAPPELLETTI, V. (ed.), *Storia della scienza*, i. *La scienza antica* (Rome, 2001).

CARETTONI, G., et al., *La pianta marmorea di Roma antica* (Rome, 1960).

CARTERON, H., *La Notion de force dans le système d'Aristote* (Paris, 1923; repr. New York and London, 1979).

CASSON, L., *Libraries in the Ancient World* (New Haven and London, 2001).

CATAMO, M., LANCIANO, N., LOCHER, K., LOMBARDERO, M., and VALDÉS, M., 'Fifteen Further Greco-Roman Sundials from the Mediterranean Area and Sudan', *JHA* 31 (2000), 203–21.

CHADWICK, J., *The Decipherment of Linear B*, 2nd edn. (Cambridge, 1967).

—— and MANN., W. N., in G. E. R. Lloyd, *Hippocratic Writings* (q.v.).

CHALMAY, J., and SCHÄRLING, A., 'Représentation d'une table de calculation', *AK* 41 (1998), 52–5.

CHALMERS, A. F., *What is this Thing Called Science?*, 3rd edn. (Buckingham, 1999).

CHARLTON, W., 'Greek Philosophy and the Concept of an Academic Discipline', in P. Cartledge and F. D. Harvey (eds.), *Crux* (Exeter, 1985), 47–61.

CHROUST, A.-H., *Aristotle* (London, 1973).

CLAGETT, M., *Greek Science in Antiquity* (New York, 1955).

CLARK, D., *Plane and Geodetic Surveying for Engineers*, i, 5th edn., rev. J. Clendinning (London, 1958).

CLARKE, E., and DEWHURST, W., *An Illustrated History of Brain Function* (Berkeley, Los Angeles, and Oxford, 1972).

CLEARY, J. J., *Aristotle and Mathematics: Aporetic Method in Cosmology and Metaphysics* (Leiden, 1995).

COHEN, I. B., and TATON, R. (eds.), *Mélanges Alexandre Koyré* (Paris, 1964).

COHEN, M. R., and DRABKIN, I. E., *A Source Book in Greek Science* (Cambridge, Mass., 1966).

COHEN, S. M., *Aristotle on Nature and Incomplete Substance* (Cambridge, 1996).

CONNOR, W. R., *The New Politicians of Fifth Century Athens* (Princeton, 1971).

CONOPHAGOS, C., *Le Laurium antique* (Athens, 1980).

CONRAD, L. I., NEVE M., NUTTON, V., PORTER, R., and WEAR, A., *The Western Medical Tradition* (Cambridge, 1995).

COOK, A. B., *Zeus* (Cambridge, 1914).

CORNFORD, F. M., *The Origin of Attic Comedy* (London, 1914).

CORTE, M. DELLA, 'Groma', *Mon. Ant.* 28 (1922), 5–100.

CREUZE, W., *Die Neurologie des 1. bis 7. Jahrhunderts* (Leipzig, 1934).

CROIX, G. E. M. DE STE, *The Class Struggle in Antiquity* (London, 1981).

—— 'The Estate of Phaenippus', in E. Badian (ed.), *Ancient Society and Institutions* (Oxford, 1966), 109–14.

CROMBIE, A. C. (ed.), *Scientific Change* (London, 1963).

CROSBY, M., 'More Fragments of Mining Leases from the Athenian Agora', *Hesperia*, 26 (1957) 1–23.

CUOMO, S., *Pappus of Alexandria and the Mathematics of Late Antiquity* (Cambridge, 2000).

DASEN, V., *Dwarfs in Ancient Egypt and Greece* (Oxford, 1993).

DAUBEN, J. W., *Abraham Robinson: The Creation of Nonstandard Analysis. A Personal and Mathematical Odyssey* (Princeton, 1995).

DAVIES, J. K., *Athenian Propertied Families* (Oxford, 1971).

DEAN-JONES, L. A., *Women's Bodies in Classical Greek Science* (Oxford, 1994).

DEBRU, A., 'Les démonstrations médicales à Rome au temps de Galien', in P. Van der Eijk *et al.* (eds.), *Ancient Medicine in its Socio-Cultural Context* (Clio Medica, 27; Amsterdam and Atlanta, 1995), i. 69–81.

—— 'L'expérimentation chez Galien', *ANRW* II 37. 2 (1994), 1718–56.

—— (ed.), *Galen on Pharmacology: Philosophy, History and Medicine* (Leiden, 1997).

DEGERING, H., 'Ein Alkoholrezepte aus dem 8. Jahrhundert', *Sitzungsberichte der preußischen Akademie der Wissenschaften*, phil.-hist. Klasse (1917), 503–15.

DEICHGRÄBER, K., *Die griechische Empirikerschule* (Berlin, 1930; repr. 1965).

DEMAN, A., and RAPSAET-CHARLIER, M.-T., 'Notes de chronologie romaine', *Historia*, 23 (1974), 271–96.

DEROW, P. S., 'The Roman Calendar, 190–168', *Phoenix*, 27 (1973), 345–56.

DESCARTES, R., *Œuvres de Descartes*, ed. C. Adam and P. Tannery, new edn. (Paris, 1964–76).

DICKS, D. R., *Early Greek Astronomy to Aristotle* (London, 1970).

—— 'Euktemon', *DSB* iv (1981), 459–60.

—— *The Geographical Fragments of Hipparchus* (London, 1960).

—— 'Solstices, Equinoxes, and the Presocratics', *JHS* 86 (1966), 26–40.

DIELS, H., *Antike Technik*, 2nd edn. (Leipzig and Berlin, 1920; repr. 1965).

—— *Die Entdeckung des Alkohols* (Abhandlungen der preußischen Akademie der Wissenschaften, phil.-hist. Klasse, 3; Berlin, 1913).

—— and KRANZ, W., *Die Fragmente der Vorsokratiker*, 6th edn. (Berlin, 1960).

—— and REHM, A., 'Parapegmenfragmente aus Milet', *Sitzungsberichte der Königlich preußischen Akademie der Wissenschaften*, phil.-hist. Klasse (Berlin, 1904), 92–111.

DIJKSTERHUIS, E. J., *Archimedes* (Princeton, 1938).

DILKE, O. A. W., *Greek and Roman Maps* (London and Ithaca, NY, 1985).

—— *The Roman Land Surveyors: An Introduction to the Agrimensores* (Newton Abbot, 1971).

DILLON, J., 'Greek Alchemy', *CR*, NS 36 (1986), 35–8.

DONINI, P., 'Galeno e la filosofia', *ANRW* II 36. 5 (1992), 3484–504.

DRABKIN, I. E., 'Notes on the Laws of Motion in Aristotle', *AJP* 59 (1938), 60–84.

DRACHMANN, A. G., 'A Detail of Heron's Dioptra', *Centaurus*, 13 (1968–9), 241–7.

—— 'Dioptra', *RE* suppl. vi (1935), 1287–90.

—— 'Heron and Ptolemaios', *Centaurus*, 1 (1950–1), 117–31.

—— 'Heron's Dioptra and Levelling Instrument', in C. Singer (ed.), *A History of Technology*, iii (Oxford, 1957), 609–12.

—— *Ktesibios, Philon and Heron: A Study in Greek Pneumatics* (Copenhagen, 1948).

—— *The Mechanical Technology of Greek and Roman Antiquity: A Study of the Literary Sources* (Copenhagen, 1963).

—— 'A Physical Experiment in Heron's Dioptra', *Centaurus*, 13 (1968–9), 000 4.

DUCKWORTH, W. L. H., LYONS, M. C., and TOWERS, B., *Galen on Anatomical Procedures: The Later Books* (Cambridge, 1962).

DUHEM, P., *The Aim and Structure of Physical Theory*, trans. P. P. Wiener (New York, 1954); original French edn. *La Théorie physique: Son object — sa structure* (Paris, 1914).

DUNBAR, N., *Aristophanes: Birds* (Oxford, 1995).

DUNCAN-JONES, R., *The Economy of the Roman Empire* (Cambridge, 1974).

—— *Structure and Scale in the Roman Economy* (Cambridge, 1990).

DÜRING, I., *Aristotle's Chemical Treatise* (Göteborg, 1944).

DZIELSKA, M., 'Hypatia of Alexandria' (diss. Cambridge, Mass., 1995).

EASTWOOD, B. S., 'Heraclides and Heliocentrism: Texts, Diagrams, and Interpretations', *JHA* 23 (1992), 233–60.

EDELSTEIN, L., *Ancient Medicine* (Baltimore, 1967).

—— 'The Distinctive Hellenism of Greek Medicine', *Bulletin of the History of Medicine*, 40 (1966), 197–255.

—— and KIDD, I. G., *Posidonius: The Fragments* (Cambridge, 1972).

EICHHOLZ, D. E., 'Aristotle's Theory of the Formation of Metals and Minerals', *CQ*, 43 (1949), 141–6.

—— *Theophrastus: De Lapidibus* (Oxford, 1965).

EIJK, P. J. VAN DER, 'Galen's Use of the Concept of "Qualified Experience" in his Dietetic and Pharmacological Works', in Debru, *Galen on Pharmacology*, 35–57.

—— HORTSMANSHOFF, H. F. J., and SCHRIJVERS, P. H. (eds.), *Ancient Medicine in its Socio-Cultural Context* (Amsterdam, 1995).

ENGLERT, W. G., *Epicurus on the Swerve and Voluntary Action* (Atlanta, 1987).

EVANS, J., *History and Practice of Ancient Astronomy* (Oxford, 1998).

—— 'The Material Culture of Greek Astronomy', *JHA* 30 (1999), 237–307.

FARRINGTON, B., *The Faith of Epicurus* (London, 1967).

—— *Head and Hand in Ancient Greece* (London, 1947).

FEHR, B., 'Zur religionspolitischen Funktion der Athena Parthenos im Rahmen des delisch-athenischen Seebundes—Teil II', *Hephaistos*, 2 (1980), 113–25.

FERGUSON, J., 'Teleology in Aristotle's Politics', in Gotthelf, *Aristotle on Nature and Living Things*, 259–73.

FESTUGIÈRE, A. J., *La Révélation d'Hermès Trismégiste* (Paris, 1944–54).

FEYERABEND, P. K., 'How to be a Good Empiricist', in B. Baumrin (ed.), *Philosophy of Science: The Delaware Seminar*, ii (New York, London, and Sydney, 1963), 3–39.

FINE, K., 'The Problem of Mixture', in F. A. Lewis and R. Bolton (eds.), *Form, Matter and Mixture in Aristotle* (Oxford and Malden, 1996), 82–182.

FINLEY, M. I., *Ancient History: Evidence and Models* (New York, 1986).

FISCHER, J. (ed.), *Claudii Ptolemaei Geographiae Codex Urbinas Graecus 82 Phototypice Depictus* (Codices e Vaticanis Selecti, 18; Leiden and Leipzig, 1932).

FLEMMING, R., *Medicine and the Making of Roman Women* (Oxford, 2000).

FLEURY, P., 'Héron d'Alexandrie et Vitruve: A propos des techniques dites "pneumatiques"', in Argoud, *Science et vie intellectuelle à Alexandrie*, 67–81.

FOLKERTS, M., 'Mathematische Probleme im Corpus agrimensorum', in *Die römische Feldmeßkunst: Interdidiziplinäre Beiträge zu ihrer Bedeutung für die Zivilisationsgeschichte Roms* (Abh. Akad. Gött., phil.-hist. Klasse, 193; Göttingen, 1992), 327–8.

FORBES, R. J., *Short History of the Art of Distillation* (Leiden, 1948).

—— *Studies in Ancient Technology*, vii (Leiden, 1963).

FORTENBAUGH, W. W., HUBY, P. M., SHARPLES, R. W., and GUTAS, D., together with BARKER, A. D., KEANEY, J. J., MIRHADY, D. C., SEDLEY, D. N., and SOLLENBERGER, M. G. (ed. and trans.), *Theophrastus: Sources for his Life, Writings, Thought and Influence* (Leiden, 1992).

FOTHERINGHAM, J. K., 'Cleostratus (III)', *JHS* 45 (1925), 78–83.

FOWLER, D. H., *The Mathematics of Plato's Academy*, 2nd edn. (Oxford, 1999).

FOWLER, R. L., *Early Greek Mythography*, i (Oxford, 2000).

FRASER, P. M., *Ptolemaic Alexandria* (Oxford, 1972).

FREDE, M., 'On Galen's Epistemology', in V. Nutton (ed.), *Galen: Problems and Prospects* (London, 1981), 65–86; repr. in Frede, *Essays in Ancient Philosophy* (Oxford, 1987), 279–98.

—— *Die Stoische Logik* (Göttingen, 1974).

FREELAND, C. A., 'Scientific Explanation and Empirical Data in Aristotle's Meteorology', *OSAP* 8 (1990), 67–102.

FREIDEL, D., SCHELE, L., and PARKER, J., *Maya Cosmos: Three Thousand Years on the Shaman's Path* (New York, 1993).

FRENCH, R. K., *Ancient Natural History* (London, 1994).

—— and GREENAWAY, F. (eds.), *Science in the Early Roman Empire: Pliny the Elder, his Sources and Influence* (London and Sydney, 1986).

FREUDENTHAL, G., *Aristotle's Theory of Material Substance* (Oxford, 1995).

FRIEND, J. N., *Man and the Chemical Elements* (London, 1951).

FRISCHER, B., *The Sculpted Word: Epicureanism and Philosophical Recruitment in Ancient Greece* (Berkeley, 1982).

FRYE, R. N., *The Golden Age of Persia* (London, 1975).

FURLEY, D. J., *Cosmic Problems: Essays on Greek and Roman Philosophy of Nature* (Cambridge, 1989).

—— *The Greek Cosmologists* (Cambridge, 1987).

—— 'Strato's Theory of the Void', in id., *Cosmic Problems*, 146–60.

—— *Two Studies in the Greek Atomists* (Princeton, 1967).

—— and WILDBERG, C., *Philoponus:* Corollaries on Place and Void. *Simplicius:* Against Philoponus on the Eternity of the World (London, 1991).

—— and WILKIE, J. S., *Galen on Respiration and the Arteries* (Princeton, 1984).

GALLOP, D., *Aristotle*: On Sleep and Dreams. *Text, Translation, with Introduction, Notes, and Glossary* (Peterborough, 1990).

GALTER, H. D. (ed.), *Die Rolle der Astronomie in den Kulturen Mesopotamiens* (Grazer morgenländische Studien, 3; Graz, 1993).

GANDT, F. DE, 'Force et science des machines', in Barnes *et al.*, *Science and Speculation*, 96–127.

GARBER, D., *Descartes' Metaphysical Physics* (Chicago, 1992).

GARLAN, Y., *Recherches de poliorcétique grecque* (Paris, 1974).

GARLAND, R., *The Eye of the Beholder: Deformity and Disability in the Graeco-Roman World* (London, 1995).

GAROFALO, I., *Erasistrati Fragmenta* (Pisa, 1988).

—— *Galeni Anatomicarum Administrationum Libri* (Naples, 1986–2000).

—— *Procedimenti anatomici* (Milan, 1991).

GENTNER, D., and JEZIORSKI, M., 'The Shift from Metaphor to Analogy in Western Science', in Ortony, *Metaphor and Thought*, 447–80.

GIBBS, S. L., *Greek and Roman Sundials* (New Haven and London, 1976).

GIGANTE, M., *Il fungo sul Vesuvio secondo Plinio il Giovane* (Rome, 1989).

GILLIES, D., *Philosophy of Science in the Twentieth Century* (Oxford, 1993).

GLUCK, T. F., 'Levels and Levellers: Surveying Irrigation Canals in Medieval Valencia', *Technology and Culture*, 9 (1968), 165–80.

GLUCKER, J., *Antiochus and the Late Academy* (Göttingen, 1978).

—— 'Cicero's Philosophical Affiliations', in J. M. Dillon and A. A. Long (eds.), *The Question of 'Eclecticism': Studies in Later Greek Philosophy* (Berkeley, Los Angeles, and London, 1988), 34–69.

GOLDSTEIN, B. R., *The Arabic Version of Ptolemy's* Planetary Hypotheses (Transactions of the American Philosophical Society, NS 57.4; Philadelphia, 1967).

—— and BOWEN, A. C., 'The Introduction of Dated Observations and Precise Measurements in Greek Astronomy', *AHES* 43 (1991), 93–132.

—— —— 'A New View of Early Greek Astronomy', *Isis*, 74 (1983), 330–40.

—— —— 'Pliny and Hipparchus' 600-Year Cycle', *JHA* 26 (1995), 155–8.

GOLDSTINE, H. H., *New and Full Moons from 1001 B.C. to A.D. 1651* (Memoirs of the American Philosophical Society, 94; Philadelphia, 1973).

GOMME, A. W., '"The Greatest War in Greek History"', in id., *Essays in Greek History and Literature* (Oxford, 1937), 116–24.

GOODMAN, M., *The Ruling Class of Judaea* (Cambridge, 1987).

GOODMAN, N., *Ways of Worldmaking* (Hassocks, 1978).

GOODYEAR, F. R. D., 'The *Aetna*: Thought, Antecedents, and Style', *ANRW*, II 32. 1 (1984), 344–63.

GORDON R. B., and KILLICK, D. J., 'Adaptation of Technology to Culture and Environment: Bloomery Iron Smelting in America and Africa', *Technology and Culture*, 34 (1993), 243–70.

GOTTHELF, A. (ed.), *Aristotle on Nature and Living Things: Philosophical and Historical Studies Presented to David M. Balme on his Seventieth Birthday* (Bristol, 1985).

GOTTSCHALK, H. B., 'Strato of Lampsacus', *Proc. Leeds Phil. and Lit. Society*, 11 (1965), 95–182.

—— 'Notes on the Wills of the Peripatetic Scholarchs', *Hermes*, 100 (1972), 314–42.

—— *Herakleides of Pontus* (Oxford, 1980).

—— 'The Earliest Aristotelian Commentators', in Sorabji, *Aristotle Transformed*, 55–81.

GOUREVITCH, D., *Le Mal d'être femme* (Paris, 1984).

—— *Soranos d'Ephèse: Maladies des femmes* (Paris, 1988–94).

GRAESER, A. (ed.), *Mathematics and Metaphysics in Aristotle* (Proceedings of the Tenth Symposium Aristotelicum; Bern, 1987).

GRANT, M., *Greek and Roman Historians: Information and Misinformation* (London and New York, 1995).

GRANT, R. M., *Miracle and Natural Law in Graeco-Roman and Early Christian Thought* (Amsterdam, 1952).

GREEN, M. H., 'The Transmission of Ancient Theories of Female Physiology and Disease through the Early Middle Ages' (diss. Ph.D., Princeton, 1985).

GRENFELL, P., and HUNT, A. S. (eds.), *The Hibeh Papyri*, i (London, 1906).

GREWE, K., *Planung und Trassierung römischer Wasserleitungen* (Wiesbaden, 1985).

GRMEK, M. D., *Diseases in the Ancient Greek World* (Baltimore, 1989).

—— (ed.), *Storia del pensiero medico occidentale*, i. *Antichità e medioevo* (Bari, 1993).

—— and GOUREVITCH, D., 'Les expériences pharmacologiques dans l'antiquité', *Archives internationales d'histoire des sciences*, 35 (1985), 3–27.

GUTAS, D., *Greek Thought, Arabic Culture* (London, 1998).

HALL, J. J., 'Was Rapid Scientific and Technical Progress Possible in Antiquity?', *Apeiron*, 17 (1983), 1–13.

HALLEUX, R., *Les Alchimistes grecs*, i (Paris, 1981).

HAMILTON, SIR W., *Campi Phlegraei* (Naples, 1776).

—— *Supplement to the Campi Phlegraei* (Naples, 1779).

HANKINSON, R. J., *Galen: On the Therapeutic Method, Books I and II* (Oxford, 1989).

—— 'Galen's Anatomical Procedures: A Second Century Debate in Medical Epistemology', *ANRW* II 37. 2 (1994), 1834–55.

—— 'Galen and the Best of All Possible Worlds', *CQ*, NS 39 (1989), 206–27.

—— 'Galen Explains the Elephant', in M. Matthen and B. Linsky (eds.), *Philosophy and Biology* (*Canadian Journal of Philosophy*, suppl.14; 1988), 135–57.

—— 'Galen's Philosophical Eclecticism', *ANRW* II 36. 5 (1992), 3505–22.

HANNAH, R., 'The Constellations on Achilles' Shield (*Iliad* 18. 485–489)', *Electronic*

Antiquity, 2/4 (1994) (an electronic journal, http://scholar.lib.vt.edu/ejournals/ ElAnt/V2N4/hannah.html).

—— 'Is it a Bird? Is it a Star? Ovid's Kite and the First Swallow of Spring', *Latomus*, 56 (1997), 327–42.

—— 'From Orality to Literacy? The Case of the Parapegma', in J. Watson (ed.), *Speaking Volumes: Orality and Literacy in the Greek and Roman World* (Leiden, 2001), 139–59.

—— '*Praevolante nescio qua ingenti humana specie . . .*: A Re-assessment of the Winged Genius on the Base of the Antonine Column', *PBSR* 57 (1989), 90–105.

HANSEN, M. H., *Demography and Democracy: The Number of Athenian Citizens in the Fourth Century BC* (Herning, 1985).

HANSON, A. E., and GREEN, M. H., 'Soranus of Ephesus, *Methodicorum Princeps*', *ANRW* II 37. 2 (1994), 968–1075.

HARDEN, D. B., 'Ancient Glass', *Archaeological Journal*, 126 (1969), 46–8.

—— *Glass of the Caesars* (Milan, 1987).

HARDY, G. H., and WRIGHT, E. M., *An Introduction to the Theory of Numbers*, 4th edn. (Oxford, 1960).

HARRIS, C. R. S., *The Heart and the Vascular System in Ancient Greek Medicine from Alcmaeon to Galen* (Oxford, 1973).

HARRIS, W. V., *War and Imperialism in Republican Rome*, 2nd corr. edn. (Oxford, 1985).

HAUPT, H., 'Lunar Eclipses', in G. D. Roth (ed.), *Compendium of Practical Astronomy* (Berlin, Heidelberg, and New York, 1994), ii. 131–58.

HEALY, J. F., *Mining and Metallurgy in the Greek and Roman World* (London, 1978).

—— *Pliny the Elder on Science and Technology* (Oxford, 1999).

—— 'Pliny on Mineralogy and Metals', in French and Greenaway, *Science in the Early Roman Empire*, 111–46.

HEATH, T. L., *A History of Greek Mathematics* (Oxford, 1921).

—— *Mathematics in Aristotle* (Oxford, 1949).

—— *The Thirteen Books of Euclid's* Elements (Cambridge, 1926).

HEIBERG, J. L., *Claudii Ptolemaei Opera Quae Exstant Omnia* (Leipzig, 1898–1907).

HEYERDAHL, T., and FERDON, E. N. (eds.), *Reports of the Norwegian Archaeological Expedition to Easter Island and the East Pacific*, i. *Archaeology of Easter Island* (London, 1961).

HIGGINS, M., and HIGGINS, R., *A Geological Companion to Greece and the Aegean* (London, 1996).

HILL, D., *A History of Engineering in Classical and Medieval Times* (London, 1984).

HINE, H. M., *An Edition with Commentary of Seneca* Natural Questions *Book 2* (New York, 1981; repr. Salem, NH, 1984).

—— review of Waldherr, *Erdbeben*, in *CR*, NS 49 (1999), 503–5.

HINRICHS, F. T., *Die Geschichte der gromatischen Institutionen* (Wiesbaden, 1974).

HODDINOTT, R. F., *The Thracians* (London, 1981).

HOOVER, H. C., and HOOVER, L. H., *Agricola:* De re metallica (London, 1912).

HORBURY, W., and NOY, D., *Jewish Inscriptions of Graeco-Roman Egypt* (Cambridge, 1992).

HORNBLOWER, S., *A Commentary on Thucydides*, i (Oxford, 1991).

HOUSMAN, A. E., *The Confines of Criticism: The Cambridge Inaugural 1911*, complete text with notes by John Carter (Cambridge, 1969).

HOW, W. W., and WELLS, J., *A Commentary on Herodotus* (Oxford, 1928).

HUBY, P., 'Theophrastus in the Aristotelian Corpus, with Particular Reference to Biological Problems', in Gotthelf, *Aristotle on Nature and Living Things*, 313–25.

HUFFMAN, C. A., 'The Authenticity of Archytas fr. 1', *CQ*, NS 35 (1985), 344–8.

HÜLSEN, C., 'Arethusa (11)', *RE* ii (1896), 680.

HULTSCH, F., 'Dioptra', *RE* v (1905), 1073–9.

—— 'Eudoxus (19)', *RE* vi (1909), 944–5.

HUNGER, H., and PINGREE, D., *MUL.APIN: An Astronomical Compendium in Cuneiform* (Horn, 1989).

HUSSEY, E. L., *Aristotle:* Physics *III and IV* (Oxford, 1982).

—— 'Aristotle on Mathematical Objects', in I. Mueller (ed.), Περὶ τῶν μαθημάτων (Apeiron, 24.4; Edmonton, 1991), 105–33.

—— 'Aristotle's Mathematical Physics', in Judson, *Aristotle's Physics*, 213–42.

INWOOD, B., *Ethics and Human Action in Early Stoicism* (Oxford, 1985).

IRBY-MASSIE, G. L., and KEYSER, P., *Greek Science of the Hellenistic Era: A Sourcebook* (London and New York, 2001).

IRWIN, E., *Colour Terms in Greek Poetry* (Toronto, 1974).

ISKANDAR, A. Z., *De Optimo Medico Cognoscendo* (CMG suppl. orientale, 4; Berlin, 1988).

JACKSON, R., *Doctors and Diseases in the Roman Empire* (London, 1988).

JACOBY, F., *Die Fragmente der griechischen Historiker* (Berlin, 1923–58; 1999).

JANAWAY, C., *Images of Excellence* (Oxford, 1995).

JOACHIM, H. H., *Aristotle on Coming-To-Be and Passing-Away* (Oxford, 1922).

JOHANNES [Johanesse] DE RUPESCISSA [Joan de Peratallada], *De Consideratione Quintae Essentiae* (14th cent.) (ed. Basel, 1561).

JOHANNOWSKY, W., 'Terrae motus: Un'iscrizione nucerina relativa al restauro del teatro', in Livadie, *Tremblements de terre*, 91–3.

JOHNSON, W. A., 'Toward a Sociology of Reading in Classical Antiquity', *AJPh* 121 (2000), 593–627.

JONES, A., 'On Babylonian Astronomy and its Greek Metamorphoses', in F. J. Ragep and S. P. Ragep (eds.), *Tradition, Transmission and Transformation* (Leiden, 1996) 139–55.

—— 'Evidence for Babylonian Arithmetical Schemes in Greek Astronomy', in Galter, *Die Rolle der Astronomie in den Kulturen Mesopotamiens*, 77–94.

—— 'The Place of Astronomy in Roman Egypt', in Barnes, *The Sciences in Greco-Roman Society*, 25–52.

—— and BERGGREN J. L., *Ptolemy's Geography* (Princeton and Oxford, 2000).

JONES, A. H. M., *The Cities of the Eastern Roman Provinces* (Oxford, 1937).

JOUANNA, J., *Hippocrate: Airs, eaux, lieux* (Paris, 1996).

JUDSON, L. (ed.), *Aristotle's Physics: A Collection of Essays* (Oxford, 1991).

KAHN, C. H., *Anaximander and the Origins of Greek Cosmology* (New York, 1966).

KALLET-MARX, L., 'Money Talks: Rhetor, Demos and the Resources of the Athenian Empire', in R. Osborne and S. Hornblower (eds.), *Ritual, Finance, Politics* (Oxford, 1994), 227–51.

KEYSER, P., 'Suetonius *Nero* 41. 2 and the Date of Heron Mechanicus of Alexandria', *CP* 83 (1988), 218–20.

KIDD, I. G., *Posidonius: The Commentary* (Cambridge, 1989).

—— *Posidonius: The Translation* (Cambridge, 1999).

KING, H., *Hippocrates' Women* (London, 1998).

KINGSLEY, P., *Ancient Philosophy, Mystery and Magic* (Oxford, 1995).

—— 'Empedocles and his Interpreters: The Four-Element Doxography', *Phronesis*, 39 (1994), 239–47.

—— 'From Pythagoras to the *Turba Philosophorum*: Egypt and Pythagorean Tradition', *JWCI* 57 (1994), 1–13.

KIPLE, K. D., (ed.), *The Cambridge World History of Human Disease* (Cambridge, 1993).

KLEIJWEGT, M., *Ancient Youth* (Amsterdam, 1991).

KNORR, W. R., 'Arithmêtikê Stoicheîosis: On Diophantus and Hero of Alexandria', *Historia Mathematica*, 20 (1993), 180–92.

—— 'Infinity and Continuity: The Interaction of Mathematics and Philosophy in Antiquity', in N. Kretzmann (ed.), *Infinity and Continuity in Ancient and Mediaeval Thought* (Ithaca, NY, and London, 1982), 112–45.

—— *Textual Studies in Ancient and Mediaeval Geometry* (Boston, 1989).

KOESTER, H., 'Νόμος φύσεως: The Concept of Natural Law in Greek Thought', in J. Neusner (ed.), *Religions in Antiquity* (Leiden, 1968), 521–41.

KOLLESCH, J., and NICKEL, D., 'Bibliographia Galeniana', *ANRW* II 37. 2 (1994), 1077–253.

—— —— (eds.), *Galen und das hellenistische Erbe* (Verhandlungen des IV. Internationalen Galen-Symposiums, Sudhoffs Archiv, suppl. 32; Stuttgart, 1993).

KOYRÉ, A., *From the Closed World to the Infinite Universe* (Baltimore, 1957).

—— *Metaphysics and Measurement* (London, 1968).

KRAGH, H., *An Introduction to the Historiography of Science* (Cambridge, 1987).

KRUG, A., *Heilkunst und Heilkult* (Munich, 1985).

KRUPP, E. C., 'Springing down the Banister', *Sky and Telescope*, 91/3 (Mar. 1996), 59–61.

KUDLIEN, F., *Der Beginn des medizinischen Denkens bei den Griechen* (Zurich, 1967).

—— 'Endeixis as a Scientific Term: (A) Galen's Usage of the Word (in Medicine and Logic)', in Kudlien and Durling, Galen's Method of Healing, 103–11.

—— and DURLING R. J. (eds.), *Galen's Method of Healing* (Proceedings of the 1982 Galen Symposium; Leiden, 1991).

KÜHN, J-H., and FLEISCHER, U., *Index Hippocraticus* (Göttingen, 1986–9).

KUHN, T. S., *The Copernican Revolution* (Cambridge, Mass., 1957).

—— *The Essential Tension* (Chicago, 1977).

—— 'Metaphor in Science', in Ortony, *Metaphor and Thought*, 533–42.

—— *The Structure of Scientific Revolutions* (Chicago, 1962; 2nd edn. Chicago, 1970).

LACY, P. DE, *Galeni De placitis Hippocratis et Platonis* (Berlin, 1978–84).

—— 'Galen's Concept of Continuity', *GRBS* 20 (1979), 355–69.

—— 'The Third Part of the Soul', in P. Manuli and M. Vegeti (eds.), *Le opere psicologiche di Galeno* (Naples, 1988), 43–64.

LAKATOS, I., *Mathematics, Science and Epistemology*, ed. J. Worrall and G. Gurrie (Cambridge, 1978).

LAKOFF, G., and JOHNSON, M., *Metaphors We Live By* (Chicago, 1980).

—— and TURNER, M., *More than Cool Reason* (Chicago, 1989).

LANDELS, J. G., *Engineering in the Ancient World* (London, 1978).

LANGSLOW, D. R., *Medical Latin in the Roman Empire* (Oxford, 2000).

LARRAIN, C. J., 'Galen, *De motibus dubiis*: Die lateinische Übersetzung des Niccolò da Reggio', *Traditio*, 49 (1994), 171–233; commentary in *Traditio*, 51 (1996), 1–41.

—— *Galens Kommentar zu Platons Timaios* (Stuttgart, 1992).

LASSERRE, F., *Die Fragmente des Eudoxos von Knidos* (Berlin, 1966).

LAZENBY, J. F., *The Defence of Greece* (Warminster, 1993).

—— *The First Punic War* (Stanford, 1996).

LEAR, J., 'Aristotelian Infinity', *Proceedings of the Aristotelian Society*, 80 (1980), 187–210.

—— 'Aristotle's Philosophy of Mathematics', *Philosophical Review*, 91 (1982), 161–92.

LEICESTER, H. M., *The Historical Background of Chemistry* (New York, 1956).

LENNOX, J., 'The Disappearance of Aristotle's Biology: A Hellenistic Mystery', in Barnes, *The Sciences in Greco-Roman Society*, 7–24.

LEVEY, M., *Early Arab Pharmacology* (Leiden 1973).

LEWIS, M. J. T., *Surveying Instruments of Greece and Rome* (Cambridge, 2001).

LICHTENTHAELER, C., *Der Eid des Hippokrates* (Cologne, 1984).

LIEDMEIER, C., *Plutarchus' biographie van Aemilius Paullus: Historische commentaar* (Utrecht and Nijmegen, 1935).

LIGHTFOOT, J. L., 'An Early Reference to Perfect Numbers? Some Notes on Euphorion *SH* 417' *CQ*, NS 48 (1998), 187–94.

LIU, B.-L., and FIALA, A. D., *Canon of Solar Eclipses, 1500 BC to AD 3000* (Richmond, Va., 1992).

LIVADIE, C. A. (ed.), *Tremblements de terre, éruptions volcaniques et vie des hommes dans la Campanie antique* (Naples, 1986).

LLOYD, G. E. R., *Adversaries and Authorities: Investigations into Ancient Greek and Chinese Science* (Cambridge, 1996).

—— *Aristotelian Explorations* (Cambridge, 1996).

—— *Demystifying Mentalities* (Cambridge, 1990).

—— *Early Greek Science: Thales to Aristotle* (London, 1970).

—— 'The Empirical Basis of the Physiology of the *Parva Naturalia*', in G. E. R. Lloyd and G. E. L. Owen (eds.), *Aristotle on Mind and the Senses* (Cambridge, 1978), 215–39; repr. in id., *Methods and Problems in Greek Science*, 224–47.

—— 'Experiment in Early Greek Philosophy and Medicine', *PCPS*, NS 10 (1964), 50–72; repr. in id., *Methods and Problems in Greek Science*, 70–99.

—— 'Galen on Hellenistics and Hippocrateans', in Kollesch and Nickel, *Galen und das hellenistische Erbe*, 125–44; also in Lloyd, *Methods and Problems in Greek Science*, 398–418.

—— (ed. and intro.), *Hippocratic Writings*, trans. J. Chadwick *et al.*, 2nd edn. (Harmondsworth etc., 1983).

—— *Magic, Reason and Experience: Studies in the Origins and Development of Greek Science* (Cambridge, 1979).

—— '*Metaphysics Λ* 8', in M. Frede and D. Charles (eds.), *Aristotle's* Metaphysics *Lambda* (Oxford, 2000), 245–73.

—— *Methods and Problems in Greek Science: Selected Papers* (Cambridge, 1991).

—— 'Observational Error in Later Greek Science', in Barnes *et al.*, *Science and Speculation*, 128–64; repr. in Lloyd, *Methods and Problems in Greek Science*, 299–332.

—— *Polarity and Analogy* (Cambridge, 1966).

—— 'Popper versus Kirk: A Controversy in the Interpretation of Greek Science', in id., *Methods and Problems in Greek Science*, 100–20.

—— *The Revolutions of Wisdom: Studies in the Claims and Practice of Ancient Greek Science* (Berkeley, 1987).

—— *Science, Folklore and Ideology* (Cambridge, 1983).

LOCHER, K., 'Two Greco-Roman Sundials from Alexandria and Dion', *JHA* 24 (1993), 300–2.

LONG, A. A., *Hellenistic Philosophy* (London, 1974).

—— 'Pleasure and Social Utility: The Virtues of Being Epicurean', in H. Flashar and O. Gigon (eds.), *Aspects de la philosophie hellénistique* (Entretiens sur l'antiquité classique, 32; Geneva, 1986), 283–324.

—— and SEDLEY, D. N., *The Hellenistic Philosophers* (Cambridge, 1987).

LONGRIGG, J., 'Anatomy in Alexandria in the Third Century BC', *British Journal of the History of Science*, 21 (1988), 455–88.

—— *Greek Rational Medicine: Philosophy and Medicine from Alcmaeon to the Alexandrians* (London, 1993).

LONIE, I. M., 'Cos versus Cnidus and the Historians', *History of Science*, 13 (1978), 42–75 and 77–92.

LOUDON, I., (ed.), *Western Medicine: An Illustrated History* (Oxford, 1997).

LOWE, C. G., *A Byzantine Paraphrase of Onasander* (Washington University Studies, New Series: Language and Literature, 1; St Louis, 1927).

LYONS, M. C., *De Partibus Artis Medicae, De Causis Contentivis, De Diaeta in Morbis Acutis secundum Hippocratem* (Berlin, 1969).

McCLUSKEY, S., *Astronomies and Cultures in Early Medieval Europe* (Cambridge, 1998).

McGUIRE, J. E., and TAMNY, M., *Certain Philosophical Questions: Newton's Trinity Notebook* (Cambridge, 1983).

MACMULLEN, R., *Enemies of the Roman Order: Treason, Unrest and Alienation in the Empire* (Cambridge, Mass., 1966).

McQUEEN, E. I., and ROWE, C. J., 'Phaedo, Socrates and the Chronology of the Spartan War with Elis', *Methexis*, 2 (1989), 1–18.

MANI, N., *Die historischen Grundlagen der Leberforschung* (Basel and Stuttgart, 1965).

MANITIUS, K., *Ptolemäus: Handbuch der Astronomie* (Leipzig, 1912–13; repr. 1963).

MANSFELD, J., 'Doxography and Dialectic: The *Sitz im Leben* of the *Placita*', *ANRW* II 36. 4 (1990), 3056–229.

—— 'The Idea of the Will in Chrysippus, Posidonius and Galen', in J. J. Cleary (ed.), *PBACAP* 7 (1991), 105–43.

MARCHETTI, P., 'La marche du calendrier romain et la chronologie à l'époque de la bataille de Pydna', *BCH* 100 (1976), 401–23.

MARSDEN, E. W., *Greek and Roman Artillery: Technical Treatises* (Oxford, 1971).

MARTIN, J., and HARRÉ, R., 'Metaphor in Science', in Miall, *Metaphor*, 89–105.

MARTIN, T. H., *Theonis Smyrnaei Liber de Astronomia* (Paris, 1849).

MATTOCK, J. N., 'De Moribus', in S. M. Stern, A. Hourani, and V. Brown (eds.), *Islamic Philosophy and the Classical Tradition: Essays Presented by his Friends and Pupils to Richard Walzer on his Seventieth Birthday* (Oxford, 1972), 235–60.

MATTUSCH, C. C., *Classical Bronzes* (Cornell, 1996).

MAYHOFF, C., *C. Plinii Secundi Naturalis Historiae Libri xxxvii* (Leipzig, 1892–1909).

MEASSON, A., 'Alexandrea ad Egyptum', in Argoud, *Science et vie intellectuelle à Alexandrie*, 9–52.

MEIGGS, R., *Roman Ostia*, 2nd edn. (Oxford, 1973).

MENDELL, H., 'Reflections on Eudoxus, Callippus and their Curves: Hippopedes and Callippopedes', *Centaurus*, 40 (1998), 177–275.

MERITT, B. D., 'Greek Inscriptions' *Hesperia*, 5 (1936), 355–441.

—— 'The Seasons in Thucydides', *Historia*, 11 (1962), 436–46.

MERLAN, P., *Studies in Epicurus and Aristotle* (Wiesbaden, 1960).

MEYERHOF, M., and SCHACHT, J., *Galen, Über die medizinischen Namen* (Abh. Berlin Akad., phil.-hist. Klasse, 3; Berlin, 1931).

MIALL, D. S. (ed.), *Metaphor: Problems and Perspectives* (Brighton, 1982).

MICHELI, G., *Le origini del concetto di macchina* (Florence, 1995).

MIGNUCCI, M., 'Aristotle's Arithmetic', in Graeser, *Mathematics and Metaphysics in Aristotle*, 175–211.

MILLAR, F. G. B., *The Roman Near East, 31 BC–AD 337* (Cambridge, Mass., 1993).

MILLER, D., 'Is Scientific Knowledge an Inexhaustible Economic Resource?', *The Critical Rationalist*, 3.1: 13 (http://thorung.eeng.dcu.it/~tkpw/tcr/volume-03/vo3no1).

MILTON, J. R., 'The Origin and Development of the Concept of the "Laws of Nature"', *Archives européennes de sociologie*, 22 (1981), 173–95.

MOORE, F. C. T., 'On Taking Metaphor Literally', in Miall, *Metaphor*, 1–13.

MOORE, G. H., 'Historians and Philosophers of Logic: Are they Compatible? The Bolzano–Weierstrauss Theorem as a Case Study', *History and Philosophy of Logic*, 20 (2000), 169–80.

MORAUX, P., *Der Aristotelismus bei den Griechen*, ii (Berlin and New York, 1984).

MORETTI, L., *Iscrizioni storiche ellenistiche* (Rome, 1967).

MUELLER, I., 'Aristotle on Geometrical Objects', in Barnes, Schofield, and Sorabji, *Articles on Aristotle*, iii. 96–107.

—— *Philosophy of Mathematics and Deductive Structure in Euclid's* Elements (Cambridge, Mass., 1981).

MÜLLER, I. VON, 'Über Galens Werk vom wissenschaftlichen Beweis', *Abhandlungen der Akademie der Wissenschaften München*, 20 (1895), 403–78.

MULTHAUF, R. P., *The Origins of Chemistry* (London, 1966).

MURPHY, E., *The Antiquities of Egypt: A Translation with Notes of Book I of the Library of History of Diodorus Siculus* (New Brunswick and London, 1990).

MURPHY, S., 'Heron of Alexandria's *On Automaton-Making*', *History of Technology*, 17 (1995), 1–44.

MUSGRAVE, A., *Common Sense, Science and Scepticism* (Cambridge, 1993).

Mussche, H., 'Thorikos during the Last Years of the Sixth Century BC', in W. D. E. Coulson *et al.* (eds.), *The Archaeology of Athens and Attica under the Democracy* (Oxford, 1994), 211–15.

Musurillo, H. (ed.), *Acta Alexandrinorum* (Leipzig, 1961).

Mžik, H. van, and Hopfner, F., *Theorie und Grundlagen der Darstellenden Erdkunde* (Vienna, 1936).

Needham, J., *Science and Civilization in China*, v/2 (Cambridge, 1974).

Netz, R., 'Classical Mathematics in the Classical Mediterranean', *Mediterranean Historical Review*, 12 (1997), 1–24.

—— 'The First Jewish Scientist?', *Scripta Classica Israelitica*, 17 (1998), 27–33.

—— *The Shaping of Deduction in Greek Mathematics* (Cambridge, 1999).

Neugebauer, O., *Astronomical Cuneiform Texts* (London, 1955).

—— *The Exact Sciences in Antiquity*, 2nd edn. (New York, 1969).

—— *A History of Ancient Mathematical Astronomy* (Berlin, Heidelberg, and New York, 1975).

—— 'Über eine Methode zur Distanzbestimmung Alexandria–Rom bei Heron', *Kongelige Danske Videnskabernes Selskabs Meddelelser*, 26 (1938), 21–4.

—— and Van Hoesen, H., *Greek Horoscopes* (Philadelphia, 1987).

—— Parker, R. A., and Zauzich, K.-T., 'A Demotic Lunar Eclipse Text of the First Century B.C.', *PAPhS* 125 (1981), 312–27.

Newcomb, S., *Researches on the Motion of the Moon Made at the United States Naval Observatory, Washington*, pt. 1. *Reduction and Discussion of Observations of the Moon before 1750* (Washington Observations for 1875, appendix II; Washington, 1878).

Nobbe, C. F. A. (ed.), *Claudii Ptolemaei Geographia* (3 vols.; Leipzig, 1843–5).

Nolte, F., *Die Armillarsphäre* (Abhandlungen zur Geschichte der Naturwissenschaften und der Medizin, 2; Erlangen, 1922).

Nunn, J. F., *Ancient Egyptian Medicine* (London, 1996).

Nussbaum, M., *The Therapy of Desire: Theory and Practice in Hellenistic Ethics* (Princeton, 1994).

Nutton, V., 'The Chronology of Galen's Early Career', *CQ*, NS 23 (1973), 158–71.

—— *Galen: De Propriis Placitis* (CMG V. 3. 2; Berlin, 1999).

—— *Galen:* On Prognosis (Berlin, 1979).

—— 'Galen and Egypt', in Kollesch and Nickel, *Galen und das hellenistische Erbe*, 11–32.

—— 'Galen *ad multos annos*', *Dynamis*, 15 (1995), 25–39.

—— 'Galen on Theriac: Problems of Authenticity', in Debru, *Galen on Pharmacology*, 133–51.

—— 'Healers in the Medical Market Place: Towards a Social History of Graeco-Roman Medicine', in A. Wear (ed.), *Medicine in Society* (Cambridge, 1992), 15–58.

—— 'Murders and Miracles: Lay Attitudes to Medicine in Classical Antiquity', in R. Porter (ed.), *Patients and Practitioners* (Cambridge, 1985), 23–53.

—— 'The Patient's Choice: A New Treatise by Galen', *CQ*, NS 40 (1990), 235–57.

Oppenheim, A. L., *Ancient Mesopotamia: Portrait of a Dead Civilization*, rev. edn. completed by E. Riener (Chicago and London, 1964).

OPPOLZER, T. VON, *Canon der Finsternisse* (Akademie der Wissenschaften, Wien, Denkschriften, 52; Vienna, 1887).

ORMOS, I., 'Bemerkungen zur editorischen Bearbeitung der Galenschrift "Uber die Sektion toter Lebewesen"' in Kollesch and Nickel, *Galen und das hellenistische Erbe*, 165–72.

ORTONY, A. (ed.), *Metaphor and Thought*, 2nd edn. (Cambridge, 1993).

OSBORNE, C., *Rethinking Early Greek Philosophy* (Ithaca, NY, 1987).

OSBORNE, R., *Classical Landscape with Figures: The Ancient Greek City and its Countryside* (London, 1987).

OWEN, G. E. L., *Logic, Science and Dialectic: Collected Essays in Greek Philosophy* (London, 1986).

—— 'Tithenai ta Phainomena', first published in S. Mansion (ed.), *Aristote et les problèmes de méthode* (Louvain, 1961), 83–103, and often reprinted, e.g. in Barnes, Schofield, and Sorabji, *Articles on Aristotle*, i. 113–26.

PANESSA, G., *Fonti greche e latine per la storia dell'ambiente e del clima nel mondo greco* (Pubblicazioni della classe di lettere e filosofia, Scuola Normale Superiore, Pisa, 8–9; 1991).

PARKER R. A., *A Vienna Demotic Papyrus on Eclipse- and Lunar-Omina* (Providence, 1959).

—— and DUBBERSTEIN, W. T., *Babylonian Chronology 626 B.C.–A.D. 75* (Providence, 1956).

PARTINGTON, J. R., *A History of Greek Fire and Gunpowder* (Cambridge, 1960).

PASCAL, B., *Œuvres complètes*, ed. L Lafuma (Paris, 1963).

PATTERSON, O., *Slavery and Social Death* (Cambridge, Mass., 1982).

PAYNE, K., 'Greek Geological Concepts to the Age of Alexander' (diss. Missouri-Columbia, 1990).

PEASE, A. S., *Cicero: De Divinatione* (Urbana, Ill., 1920–3).

PEDERSEN, O., 'Some Astronomical Topics in Pliny', in French and Greenaway, *Science in the Early Roman Empire*, 162–96.

—— *A Survey of the* Almagest (Odense, 1974).

PENROSE, R., *The Emperor's New Mind* (Oxford, 1989).

PERRIN, B., *Plutarch's* Lives: *Dion and Brutus, Timoleon and Aemilius Paulus* (Oxford, 1918).

PETERSON, J., 'Trigonometry in Roman Cadasters', in J.-Y. Guillaumin (ed.), *Mathématiques dans l'antiquité* (Saint-Étienne, 1992), 185–204.

PFAFF, F., *In Hippocratis Epidemiarum Librum II Commentarii* (CMG V. 10. 1; Leipzig, 1934).

—— *In Hippocratis Epidemiarum Librum VI Commentarii* (CMG V. 10. 2. 2; Leipzig and Berlin, 1940–60).

PHILLIPS, E. D., *Greek Medicine* (London, 1973).

PHILLIPS, J. H., 'The Constellations on Achilles' Shield (*Iliad* 18. 485–489)', *LCM* 5/8 (1980), 179–80.

PORTER, R., *The History of Medicine: Past, Present and Future* (Uppsala, 1983).

POST, H. R., 'Atomism 1900', *Physics Education*, 3 (1968), 1–13.

PRICE, D. J DE SOLLA, 'Clockwork before the Clock and Timekeepers before Timekeeping', in J. T. Fraser and N. Lawrence (eds.), *The Study of Time*, ii (Berlin, Heidelberg, and New York, 1975), 367–80.

—— *Gears from the Greeks: The Antikythera Mechanism, a Calendar Computer from ca. 80 BC* (TAPhS, NS 64/7; Philadelphia, 1974, and New York, 1975).

—— 'Precision Instruments to 1500', in C. Singer, E. J. Holmyard, A. R. Hall, and T. I. Williams (eds.), *A History of Technology*, iii (Oxford, 1957), 582–619.

PRITCHETT, W. K., *Studies in Ancient Greek Topography*, i (Berkeley, 1965).

—— and WAERDEN, B. L. VAN DER, 'Thucydidean Time-Reckoning and Euctemon's Seasonal Calendar', *BCH* 85 (1961), 17–52.

PUCCINOTTI, I., *Storia della medicina* (Livorno, 1850–66).

PYLE, A., *Atomism and its Critics* (Bristol, 1995).

RACKHAM, H., JONES, W. H. S., and EICHHOLZ, D., *Pliny*: Natural History (Cambridge, 1942–62).

REHDER, J. E., *The Mastery and Uses of Fire in Antiquity* (Montreal, Kingston, London, and Ithaca, NY, 2000).

REHM, A., 'Episemasiai', *RE* suppl. vii (1940), 175–97.

—— 'Horologium', *RE* viii (1913), 2418–19.

—— *Griechische Kalender* iii. *Das Parapegma des Euktemon* (Heidelberg, 1913).

—— 'Hipparchos (18)', *RE* viii (1913), 1666–81.

—— 'Parapegma', *RE* xviii (1949), 1295–366.

—— *Parapegmastudien* (Munich, 1941).

REICHE, H. A. T., 'Fail-Safe Stellar Dating: Forgotten Phases', *TAPA* 119 (1989), 37–53.

REINGOLD, N., 'Clio as Physicist and Machinist', *Reviews in American History*, 10 (1982), 264–80.

RENNA, E., *Vesuvius Mons: Aspetti del Vesuvio nel mondo antico, tra filologia, archeologia, vulcanologia* (Naples, 1992).

RESCHER, N., *Alexander against Galen on Motion* (Islamabad, 1965).

RICHESON, A. W., *English Land Measuring to 1800: Instruments and Practices* (Cambridge, Mass., 1966).

RICHMOND, I. A., 'The Roman Siege-Works of Masada, Israel', *JRS* 52 (1962), 142–55.

RICKS, C. (ed.), *A. E. Housman: Collected Poems and Selected Prose* (Harmondsworth, 1988).

RIDDLE, J. M., *Dioscorides on Pharmacy and Medicine* (Austin, Tex., 1983).

—— *Contraception and Abortion from the Ancient World to the Renaissance* (Harvard, 1992).

RIESS, E. (ed.), *Nechepsonis et Petosiridis Fragmenta Magica* (*Philologus*, suppl. 6; Göttingen, 1891 3).

RIHLL, T. E., *Greek Science* (*Greece and Rome* New Surveys in the Classics, 29; Oxford, 1999).

—— 'Making Money in Classical Athens', in D. Mattingly and J. B. Salmon (eds.), *Economies beyond Agriculture* (London, 2000), 115–42.

—— and TUCKER, J. V., 'Greek Engineering: The Case of Eupalinos' Tunnel', in A. Powell (ed.), *The Greek World* (London, 1995), 403–31.

RIST, J. M., *Epicurus: An Introduction* (Cambridge, 1972).

RITTER, J., 'Measure for Measure: Mathematics in Egypt and Mesopotamia', in M. Serres (ed.), *A History of Scientific Thought* (London, 1995), 44–72.

ROBERT, L., *Études épigraphiques et philologiques* (Paris, 1938).

ROBBINS, F. E. (trans.), *Ptolemy:* Tetrabiblos (Cambridge, Mass., 1940).

ROCHBERG, F., 'La divinazione mesopotamica e i presagi spontanei', in Cappelletti, *Storia della scienza*, i. 249–66.

ROCKE, A. J., *Chemical Atomism in the Nineteenth Century* (Columbus, Oh., 1984).

ROME, A., *Commentaires de Pappus et Théon d'Alexandrie sur l'Almageste* (Vatican City, 1931–43).

—— 'Les observations d'équinoxes et de solstices dans le chapitre 1 du livre 3 du commentaire sur l'Almageste par Théon d'Alexandrie, I', *Annales de la Société scientifique de Bruxelles*, 57 (1937), 213–36.

—— 'Les observations d'équinoxes et de solstices dans le chapitre 1 du livre 3 du commentaire sur l'Almageste par Théon d'Alexandrie, II', *Annales de la Société scientifique de Bruxelles*, 58 (1938), 6–26.

—— 'Le troisième livre des commentaires sur l'Almageste par Théon et Hypatie', *Annales de la Société scientifique de Bruxelles*, 46 (1926), 1–14.

ROMM, J. S., *The Edges of the Earth in Ancient Thought: Geography, Explanation, and Fiction* (Princeton, 1992).

ROSEN, E., 'Harriot's Science: The Intellectual Background', in J. W. Shirley (ed.), *Thomas Harriot: Renaissance Scientist* (Oxford, 1974), 1–15.

ROSENTHAL, F., 'An Ancient Commentary on the Hippocratic Oath', *Bulletin of the History of Medicine*, 30 (1963), 52–87.

ROWLANDS, R. J., 'The Biggest Island in the World', *CW* 68 (1975), 438–9.

RUNIA, D. T., 'Aristotle and Theophrastus Conjoined in the Writings of Cicero', in W. F. Fortenbaugh and P. Steinmetz (eds.), *Cicero's Knowledge of the Peripatos* (New Brunswick, 1989), 23–38.

SABBAH, G., CORSETTI, P-P., and FISCHER, K-D., *Bibliographie des textes médicaux latins* (Saint-Étienne, 1987).

SACKS, K. S., *Diodorus Siculus and the First Century* (Princeton, 1990).

SALLARES, R., *The Ecology of the Ancient Greek World* (London, 1991).

SAMUEL, A. E., *Greek and Roman Chronology* (Munich, 1972).

SAVONAROLA, M., *Libellus . . . de Aqua Ardenti* (Pisa, 1484); repr. in Joannes [Johanesse] de Rupescissa [=Joan de Peratallada, 14th cent.], *De Consideratione Quintae Essentiae* (ed. Basel, 1561).

SAYILI, A., *The Observatory in Islam and its Place in the General History of the Observatory* (Ankara, 1960).

SCARDIGLI, B., *Die Römerbiographien Plutarchs* (Munich, 1979).

SCHIAPARELLI, G., *Scritti sulla storia della astronomia antica*, i/2 (Bologna, 1926).

SCHISSEL VON FLESCHENBURG, O., 'Marinos (1)', *RE* xiv (1930), 1759–67.

SCHMIDT, C., *The Books of Jeu*, trans. V. McDermot (Nag Hammadi Studies, 13; Leiden, 1978).

SCHMITT, C. B., *Studies in Renaissance Philosophy and Science* (London, 1981).

SCHMUTTE, J., *De Consuetudinibus* (CMG suppl. 3; Leipzig, 1941).

SCHOFIELD, M., *The Stoic Idea of the City* (Cambridge, 1991).

SCHÖNE, H., 'Die Dioptra des Heron', *JDAI* 14 (1899), 91–103.

—— *Herons von Alexandria Vermessungslehre und Dioptra* (Heronis Alexandrini Opera Quae Supersunt Omnia, 3; Leipzig, 1903).

—— 'Das Visierinstrument der römischen Feldmesser', *JDAI* 16 (1901), 127–32.

SCHRÖDER, H., and KAHLE, P., *In Platonis Timaeum Commentarius* (CMG suppl. 1; Leipzig, 1934).

SCHWARTZ, E., 'Demetrios (78)', *RE* iv (1901), 2807–13.

SCOTT, D., *Recollection and Experience* (Cambridge, 1995).

SEDLEY, D. N., 'Epicurus and the Mathematicians of Cyzicus', *Cronache ercolanesi*, 6 (1976), 23–54.

—— 'Epicurus and his Professional Rivals', in J. Bollack and A. Laks (eds.), *Études sur l'Épicurisme antique* (Cahiers de Philologie, 1; Lille, 1976), 121–59.

—— 'Philosophical Allegiance', in M. Griffin and J. Barnes (eds.), *Philosophia Togata: Essays on Philosophy and Roman Society* (Oxford, 1989), 97–119.

SELLERS, J. B., *The Death of Gods in Ancient Egypt* (Harmondsworth, 1992).

SHARPLES, R., *Stoics, Epicureans and Sceptics* (London, 1996).

SHARVY, R., 'Aristotle on Mixtures', *Journal of Philosophy*, 80 (1983), 439–57.

SHERK, R. K., *Rome and the Greek East to the Death of Augustus* (Cambridge, 1984).

SHERWIN-WHITE, A. N., *The Letters of Pliny: A Historical and Social Commentary* (Oxford, 1966).

SIEGEL, R. E., *Galen on Psychology, Psychopathology and Function and Diseases of the Nervous System: An Analysis of his Doctrines, Observations and Experiments* (Basel and New York, 1973).

—— *Galen on Sense Perception: His Doctrines, Observations and Experiments on Vision, Hearing, Smell, Taste, Touch and Pain, and their Historical Sources* (Basel and New York, 1970).

—— 'Galen's Ideas on the Heartbeat', in *Proceedings of the Sixth International Congress of the History of Medicine* (Paris, 1949), 209–312.

—— *Galen's System of Physiology and Medicine: An Analysis of his Doctrines and Observations on Blood Flow, Respiration, Humors and Internal Diseases* (Basel and New York, 1968).

SIGURDSSON, H., *Melting the Earth: The History of Ideas on Volcanic Eruptions* (New York and Oxford, 1999).

—— CAREY, S., CORNELL, W., and PESCATORE, T., 'The Eruption of Vesuvius in A.D. 79', *National Geographic Research*, 1/3 (1985), 332–87.

—— CASHDOLLAR, S., and SPARKS, S. R. J., 'The Eruption of Vesuvius in AD 79: Reconstruction from Historical and Volcanological Evidence', *AJA* 86 (1982), 39–51.

SIMON, M., *Sieben Bücher Anatomie des Galen*, ii (Leipzig, 1906).

SINGER, C., *Galen on Anatomical Procedures* (Oxford, 1956).

SINGER, P. N. (trans.), *Galen: Selected Writings* (Oxford, 1997).

SLAYMAN, A. L., 'Seeing with Maya Eyes', *Archaeology*, 49/4 (1996), 56–60.

SLY, D. I., *Philo's Alexandria* (London and New York, 1996).

SMITH, M. F., *Thirteen New Fragments of Diogenes of Oenoanda* (Vienna, 1974).

SMITH, W. D., 'Galen on Coans vs. Cnidians', *Bulletin of the History of Medicine*, 47 (1973), 569–85.

—— *The Hippocratic Tradition* (Cornell, 1979).

SNYDER, J. M., *The Woman and the Lyre: Women Writers in Classical Greece and Rome* (Bristol, 1989).

SOLMSEN, F., 'Greek Philosophy and the Discovery of the Nerves', *MH* 18 (1961), 150–97; repr. in id., *Kleine Schriften*, i (Hildesheim, 1968), 536–83.

SORABJI, R., 'Aristotle on the Instant of Change', in Barnes, Schofield, and Sorabji, *Articles on Aristotle*, iii. 159–77.
—— (ed.), *Aristotle Transformed: The Ancient Commentators and their Influence* (London, 1990).
—— *Matter, Space and Motion* (London, 1988).
—— *Time, Creation and the Continuum* (London, 1983).
SOUQUES, A., *Étapes de la neurologie dans l'antiquité* (Paris, 1936).
—— 'Que doivent à Hérophile et à Érasistrate l'anatomie et la physiologie du système nerveux?', *Bulletin de la Société Française d'Histoire de la Médecine*, 28 (1934), 357–65.
SPALINGER, A., 'Remarks on an Egyptian Feast Calendar of Foreign Origin', *SÄK* 18 (1991), 349–73.
STADEN, H. VON, 'Anatomy as Rhetoric: Galen on Dissection and Persuasion', *Journal of the History of Medicine and Allied Sciences*, 50 (1995), 47–66.
—— 'The Discovery of the Body: Human Dissection and its Cultural Contexts in Ancient Greece', *Yale Journal of Biology and Medicine*, 65 (1992), 223–41.
—— 'Experiment and Experience in Hellenistic Medicine', *BICS* 22 (1975), 178–99.
—— *Herophilus: The Art of Medicine in Early Alexandria* (Cambridge, 1989).
STANFORD, W. B., *Greek Metaphor* (Oxford, 1936).
STAPLETON, H. E., *et al.*, 'The Sayings of Hermes', *Ambix*, 3 (1949), 88.
STEPHENSON, F. R., and FATOOHI, L. J., 'Thales' Prediction of a Solar Eclipse', *JHA* 28 (1997), 279–82.
STOL, M., 'Diagnosis and Therapy in Babylonian Medicine', *Jaarbericht Ex Oriente Lux*, 32 (1991–2), 42–65.
—— *Epilepsy in Babylonia* (Groningen, 1993).
STOTHERS, R. B., and RAMPINO, M. R., 'Volcanic Eruptions in the Mediterranean before AD 630 from Written and Archaeological Sources', *Journal of Geophysical Research*, 88 (1983), 6357–71.
STROHMAIER, G., *De Partium Homoeomerium Differentia* (CMG suppl. orientale, 3; Berlin, 1970).
—— 'Hellenistische Wissenschaft im neugefundenen Galen-kommentar zur hippokratischen Schrift "Über die Umwelt"', in Kollesch and Nickel, *Galen und das hellenistische Erbe*, 157–64.
SWAIN, S., *Hellenism and Empire* (Oxford, 1996).
SWERDLOW, N. M., 'Montucla's Legacy: History of the Exact Sciences', *Journal of the History of Ideas*, 54 (1993), 299–328.
—— 'Ptolemy on Trial', *American Scholar*, 48 (1979), 523–31.
SZABÓ, A., 'A Battle of Alexander the Great and the "Local Time" in the Ancient Science of the Greek [sic]', in *Ancient Macedonia: Fifth International Symposium* (Thessaloniki, 1993), 1433–8.
TAISBAK, C. M., 'Perfect Numbers: A Mathematical Pun?', *Centaurus*, 20 (1976), 269–75.
—— 'Posidonius Vindicated at all Costs?', *Centaurus*, 18 (1973–4), 253–69.
TANNERY, P., *Recherches sur l'histoire de l'astronomie ancienne* (Paris, 1893).
TAUB, L., 'Destini della scienza greca: Eredità e longevità degli strumenti scientifici', in S. Settis (ed.), *I greci: Storia, cultura, arte, società*, iii (Turin, 2001), 889–930.

—— *Ptolemy's Universe: The Natural Philosophical and Ethical Foundations of Ptolemy's Astronomy* (Chicago, 1993).

TAYLOR, A. E., *A Commentary on Plato's* Timaeus (Oxford, 1928).

TEMKIN, O., *Galenism: Rise and Decline of a Medical Philosophy* (Cornell, 1973).

—— *Soranus' Gynaecology* (Baltimore and London, 1956).

THACKRAY, A., *Atoms and Powers* (Cambridge, Mass., 1970).

THIVEL, A., *Cnide et Cos?* (Paris, 1981).

THULIN, C., *Corpus Agrimensorum Romanorum*, i/1 (Leipzig, 1913).

TIELEMAN, T. L., *Galen and Chrysippus on the Soul: Argument and Refutation in the* De Placitis *Books II–III* (Leiden, 1996).

—— 'The Hunt for Galen's Shadow: Alexander of Aphrodisias, *De anima* 94. 7–100. 17 Bruns Reconsidered', in K. A. Algra *et al.* (eds.), *Polyhistor: Studies in the History and Historiography of Ancient Philosophy Presented to J. Mansfeld* (Philosophia Antiqua, 72; Leiden, 1997), 265–83.

—— review of Kollesch and Nickel, *Galen und das hellenistische Erbe*, in *Mnemosyne*, 48 (1995), 600–7.

TOLSTOY, I., *The Knowledge and the Power* (Edinburgh, 1990).

TOOMER, G., 'Apollonius of Perga', *DSB* i (1970), 179–93.

—— 'Galen on the Astronomers and Astrologers', *AHES* 32 (1985), 193–206.

—— 'The Mathematician Zenodorus', *GRBS* 13 (1972), 177–92.

—— *Ptolemy's* Almagest (New York, Berlin, and London, 1984).

TREVARTHEN, D., 'Illuminating the Monuments: Observation and Speculation on the Structure and Function of the Cairns at Balnuaran of Clava', *Cambridge Archaeological Journal*, 10 (2000), 295–315.

TRITLE, L. A., *Phocion the Good* (London, 1988).

TURNER, A. J., *Mathematical Instruments in Antiquity and the Middle Ages: An Introduction* (London, 1994).

TYBJERG, K., 'Doing Philosophy with Machines: Hero of Alexandria's Rhetoric of Mechanics in Relation to the Contemporary Philosophy' (diss. Ph.D. Cambridge, 2000).

—— 'Hero of Alexandria's Pneumatics: Mechanical Philosophy and Ethical Machines' (M.Phil. essay in History and Philosophy of Science, University of Cambridge, 1996).

—— 'Wonder-Making and Philosophical Wonder in Hero of Alexandria', forthcoming in *Studies in History and Philosophy of Science*.

ULLRICH, F., 'Die anatomische und vivisektorische Technik des Galens' (diss. Leipzig, 1919).

UNGURU, S., 'Greek Mathematics and Greek Induction', *Physis*, 28 (1991), 273–89.

VALLANCE, J. T., 'Marshall Clagett's *Greek Science in Antiquity*: Thirty-Five Years Later', *Isis*, 81 (1990), 713–21.

VARDANJAN, S., 'Galen und die mittelalterliche armenische Medizin', in Kollesch and Nickel, *Galen und das hellenistiche Erbe*, 193–204.

VEGETTI, M., 'Tradizione e verità: Forme della storiografia filosofico-scientifica nel *De Placitis* del Galeno', in G. Cambiano (ed.), *Storiografia e dossografia nella filosofia antica* (Turin, 1986), 227–43.

VINCENT, A. J. H., 'Extraits des manuscrits relatifs à la géometrie pratique des

Grecs', *Notices et extraits de manuscrits de la Bibliothèque impériale et autres bibliothèques*, 19/2 (1862), 348–407.

VITRAC, B., *Euclide: Éléments*, ii (Paris, 1990).

WAERDEN, B. L. VAN DER, *Die Astronomie der Griechen: Eine Einführung* (Darmstadt, 1988).

—— 'Greek Astronomical Calendars, I: The Parapegma of Euctemon', *AHES* 29 (1984), 101–14.

—— 'Greek Astronomical Calendars, II: Callippos and his Calendar', *AHES* 29 (1984), 115–24.

WALBANK, F. W., *Historical Commentary on Polybius*, iii (Oxford, 1979).

—— *Polybius* (Berkeley, Los Angeles, and London, 1972).

WALDHERR, G. H., *Erdbeben: Das außergewöhnliche Normale. Zur Rezeption seismischer Aktivitäten in literarischen Quellen vom 4. Jahrhundert v. Chr. bis zum 4. Jahrhundert n. Chr.* (Geographica Historica, 9; Stuttgart, 1997).

WALLACE, R., 'What was Greek about Greek Mathematics?' *SCI* 15 (1996), 82–9.

WALSH, J., 'Galen's Discovery and Promulgation of the Function of the Recurrent Laryngeal Nerve', *Annals of Medical History*, 8 (1926), 176–84.

WALZER, R., 'Galen's Schrift über die Siebenmonatskinder', *Rivista di studi orientali*, 15 (1933), 323–57.

—— *On Medical Experience* (Oxford, 1944).

—— and FREDE, M., *Galen: Three Treatises on the Nature of Science* (Indianapolis, 1985).

WASCHKIES, H. J., *Von Eudoxus zu Aristoteles: Das Fortwirken der Eudoxischen Proportionentheorie in der Aristotelischen Lehre vom Kontinuum* (Amsterdam, 1977).

WASSERSTEIN, A., *Galen's Commentary on the Hippocratic Treatise* Airs, Waters, Places (Jerusalem, 1982).

WATERLOW, S., *Nature, Change and Agency in Aristotle's Physics* (Oxford, 1982).

WELLMANN, M., *Die Phusika des Bolos Demokritos* (Abhandlungen der preußischen Akademie der Wissenschaften, phil.-hist. Klasse, 7; Berlin, 1928).

WENSKUS, O., *Astronomische Zeitangaben von Homer bis Theophrast* (Stuttgart, 1990).

WEST, M. L., *Hesiod:* Theogony (Oxford 1966).

—— *Hesiod:* Works and Days (Oxford, 1978).

—— *Studies in Aeschylus* (Stuttgart, 1990).

WHITAKER, J., 'Platonic Philosophy in the Early Centuries of the Empire', *ANRW* II 36. 1 (1987), 81–123.

WHITE, K. D., '"The Base Mechanic Arts"? Some Thoughts on the Contribution of Science (Pure and Applied) to the Culture of the Hellenistic Age', in P. Green (ed.), *Hellenistic History and Culture* (Berkeley, 1993), 211–20.

WHITE, M. J., *The Continuous and the Discrete: Ancient Physical Theories from a Contemporary Perspective* (Oxford, 1992).

WHITEHEAD, D., *Aineias the Tactician* (Oxford, 1990).

—— *The Ideology of the Athenian Metic* (Cambridge, 1977).

WILAMOWITZ, U. VON, 'Pherekydes', in *Sitzungsberichte der preußischen Akademie der Wissenschaften*, phil.-hist. Klasse (1926), 125–46; repr. in *Kleine Schriften*, v/2 (Berlin, 1937), 127–56.

WILSON, C. A., 'Dionysian Ritual Objects in Euphorion and Nonnus', *PLLS* 7 (1993), 213–19.

—— *Philosophers, Iosis and Water of Life* (Proc. Leeds Phil. and Lit. Soc., Lit. and Hist. Section, 19.5; Leeds, 1984).

—— 'Wine Rituals, Maenads and Dionysian Fire', *PLLS* 10 (1998), 157–68.

WOLPERT, L., *The Unnatural Nature of Science* (London, 1992).

WOOD, R. M., *Earthquakes and Volcanoes* (London, 1986).

WOODCROFT, B., and GREENWOOD, J. G., *The* Pneumatics *of Hero of Alexandria* (London, 1851; repr. London and New York, 1971, with introduction by M. Boas Hall).

WOOLF, G., 'Roman Peace', in J. Rich and G. Shipley (eds.), *War and Society in the Roman World* (London and New York, 1993), 171–94.

WOOLLAM, D. H. M., 'Concepts of the Brain and its Function in Classical Antiquity', in F. N. L. Poynter (ed.), *The History and Philosophy of Knowledge of the Brain and its Function* (Springfield and Oxford, 1958), 5–18.

YAVETZ, I., 'On the Homocentric Sphere of Eudoxus', *Archive for the History of the Exact Sciences*, 51 (1998), 221–78.

ZAHAR, E. G., 'The Problem of the Empirical Basis', in A. O'Hear (ed.), *Karl Popper: Philosophy and Problems* (Cambridge, 1995), 45–74.

ZETZEL, J. E. G., *M. Tullius Cicero:* De re publica. *Selections* (Cambridge, 1995).

ZIEGLER, K. (ed.), *M. Tullius Cicero:* De re publica (Leipzig, 1955).

ZONTA, M., *Un interprete ebreo della filosofia di Galeno* (Turin, 1995).

Index Locorum

Precise references to passages discussed in the text are usually given in the footnotes, and so the majority of page-references in this index specify the note in which the reference occurs, to enable the reader to locate the passage quickly. Edition-specific references are generally given in parentheses.

Index Locorum

1. 11: 40
1. 13. 1–4: 54
1. 18: 40
1. 20: 41
1. 21–4: 36
1. 24: 46 n. 22
6. 1. 5: 53 n. 31
7: 40 n. 10
7. 2: 49
8. 21. 3: 53 n. 31
Harmonics (ed. I. Düring, Göteborg, 1930; repr. New York, 1980)
  1. 3 (6. 24–7. 21): 26 n. 9, 32–3
Phases of the Fixed Stars (Phaseis) (ed. J. L. Heiberg, *Claudii Ptolemaei Opera Quae Exstant Omnia* vol. ii, Leipzig, 1907): 117
  17. 9–10: 144
Planetary Hypotheses (ed. J. L. Heiberg, *Claudii Ptolemaei Opera Quae Exstant Omnia* vol. ii, Leipzig, 1907)
  1. 1 (71. 11–72. 5): 147
Tetrabiblos (ed. F. Boll and Æ. Boer, *Claudii Ptolemaei Opera Quae Exstant Omnia*, vol. iii, Leipzig, 1957)
  1. 3. 18 (16. 7–8): 145 n. 38
  1. 10 (30. 17–21): 144–5
  2. 12–14 (95. 9–104): 145 n. 37
  3. 3. 1–2 (110. 14–111. 1): 147 nn. 46, 47

Quintilian
Institutes
  1. 10. 39–45: 209 n. 52
  1. 10. 46–8: 99

Scholia
on Ap. Rhod. 2. 1210: 71 n. 42
on Nicander, *Theriaca* 764: 312
on Pindar, *Ol.* 13. 27: 287 n. 51

Scriptores Historiae Augustae
Life of Hadrian, 13. 3: 57 n. 9

Seneca
Letters (Epistulae)
  79. 1–7: 60–2
  79. 2: 57 n. 9
Natural Questions (Quaestiones Naturales)
  1. 12. 1: 87
  2. 26. 4–6: 59 n. 19, 67, 71 n. 41
  bk. 6: 57 n. 4, 58, 69
  6. 1. 1–3: 65
  6. 8. 3–4: 63
  6. 12. 2: 65

6. 13: 65 n. 28
6. 26. 2–3: 63
6. 27–30: 65
6. 31: 66
7. 1. 2: 87

Servius Grammaticus
on *Aeneid* 3. 571: 69 n. 37

Sextus Empiricus
Against the Professors (Adversus mathematicos)
  10. 283: 309 n. 13

Simplicius
Commentary on Aristotle's Physics (In Aristotelis Physica commentaria) (ed. H. Diels, Berlin, 1882–95)
  158. 15–20: 310 n. 18

Soranus
Gynaecology
  1. 4: 166 n. 2

Statius
Silvae
  2. 6. 61–2: 66 n. 31
  3. 5. 72–4: 66 n. 31
  4. 4. 78–86: 66 n. 31
  4. 8. 5, 66 n. 31
  5. 3. 104–6: 66 n. 31
  5. 3. 203–8: 66 n. 31

Stoicorum Veterum Fragmenta
  (ed. I. von Arnim, Leipzig, 1921–4)
  ii. 885: 264 n. 32
  ii. 897: 265 n. 36
  ii. 898: 265–6
  iii. 178: 166 n. 2

Strabo
Geography
  1. 3. 11: 212 n. 55
  1. 3. 17: 63 n. 24
  1. 3. 18: 59 n. 16
  1. 3. 20: 63 n. 24
  3. 2. 5: 289 n. 56
  3. 4. 15: 289 n. 56
  5. 2. 6: 296 n. 78
  5. 4. 8: 60 n. 20
  5. 4. 9: 71
  6. 2. 3: 57 n. 8
  6. 2. 4: 72 n. 44
  6. 2. 8: 57 n. 9, 67 n. 33
  6. 2. 10: 74
  6. 2. 11: 64
  12. 8. 18: 57 n. 2
  13. 1. 67: 289 n. 56

General Index

49
Moore, G. H. 5 n. 11
Moraux, P. 247, 260 n. 19
Moretti, L. 85 n. 19
motion 226, 249
movement 29–30, 226
Mueller, I. 218 n. 4, 231
Müller, I. von, 248 n. 14
Multhauf, R. P. 308 n. 9
multiplication table/board 234–6, table
    13.1
Murphy, E. 93 n. 38
Murphy, S. 166 n. 4
Musgrave, A. 22 n. 2
music 10, 27, 35
Mussche, H. 280 n. 16
Musurillo, H. 172 n. 29
Mžik, H. van, 46 n. 22

naturalism 179, 182
nature 263
Naucrates 203
Nausiphanes of Teos 183
Needham, J. 308
Neoclides 215
nerves 261, 265
Netz, R. 13, 19
Neugebauer, O. 3, 46 n. 22, 76 n. 1,
    83 n. 11, 90 n. 33, 93 n. 39, 114
    n. 4, 133 n. 3, 136, 166 n. 3, 216
    n. 63
Newcomb, S. 81 n. 9
Newton, Sir Isaac, 182, 188, 190, 194
Nicias 281, 286, 299
    defeat at Syracuse 413 BC 88
Nickel, D. 248, 249
Nicostratus, surveyor at Pompeii 153
Nipsus 155 n. 23
nouns 24
nourishment 259
Noy, D. 199 n. 19
numbers 238, 308–9
    aggregate 234, 239
    busy 234
    composite 233
    lazy 234
    odd and even 308–9
    perfect 230, 240
    prime 234, 236–7, 240
    tetraktys 308–10
numeri primi: *see* numbers: prime
Nunn, J. F. 255 n. 38
Nussbaum, M. 176 n. 45
Nutton, V. 8, 12, 13, 102 n. 55, 124 n.
    35, 256 n. 1, 257 n. 4, 271 n. 57,
    303 n. 96

objectivity 22
Obsequens 65
observation:
    in acoustics 33
    in anatomy 263, 265, 267
    in assaying 279
    in astronomy 43 n. 18, 135–40, 153,
        156, 216
    in general 268, 292
    in mathematics 227–8, 236–9
    in medicine 299 n. 86
    in metallurgy 278
    in physics 295–7
    in surveying 157–8
    of volcanoes 67
    see also measurement
ochre 282
Odysseus 277
Oenopides of Chios 90, 120, 216
oikoumenē 37, 49, 52
Okelis 52
ὀξύς (*oxus*) 25, 27, 34
ὀξύτης (*oxutēs*) 33
Oppenheim, A. L. 91 n. 36
opposites 28
optics 220
Oribasius 242–3
Ormos, I. 250 n. 22, 266 n. 42
Orosius 65
orpiment (an arsenic sulphide) 282,
        308, 320
Osborne, C. 11 n. 28
Osborne, R. 123 n. 30, 130
Ostanes 307, 312, 314
Ostwald, W. 179
Ovid 61
Owen, G. E. L. 27 n. 11, 224 n. 20,
        259 n. 16

palaeopathology 253
Paley, W. 194
Panathenaia (festival) 283
Pandrosion 197
Panessa, G. 56 n. 1
Pappus 197, 199, 202
parallels of latitude 40–1
parapēgma 112, 124, 142–4, 146
Parker, R. A. 86 n. 22, 93 n. 39
Parmenides 302
Parthenon 284
Partington, J. R. 322 n. 69
Pascal, Blaise 194
patronage 16–17
Paulus, L. Aemilius 82, 95, 102–3,
        105
Pederson, O. 105 n. 65, 198 n. 11
Peisistratus 286